T0289856

Blockchain, Crypto and DeFi

Blockchain, Crypto and DeFi

Bridging Finance and Technology

Marco Di Maggio

WILEY

Library of Congress Cataloging-in-Publication Data is Available

ISBN 9781394275892 (Cloth)
ISBN 9781394275915 (ePDF)
ISBN 9781394275908 (ePub)

Cover Design: Wiley
Cover Image: © monsitj/Getty Images
Author Photo: Courtesy of the Author

SKY10082007_081424

Contents

Preface

Welcome to "Blockchain, Crypto, and DeFi," the only guide you'll need in the rapidly evolving frontier of blockchain technology. This isn't just another textbook or professional book; it's your secret weapon to mastering the chaos of cryptocurrencies and the magic of decentralized finance (DeFi) and Web3.

Anyone who's ever attended one of my lectures or talks knows I strive to make the experience interactive and entertaining. I believe learning should be enjoyable, not a chore. This book carries the same philosophy. Each chapter is crafted with a touch of whimsy—a witty preface here, a sprinkle of humor there—all designed to engage you, the reader, in a dialogue rather than a monologue. So, as you turn these pages, expect to participate, laugh, and perhaps even question as you would in one of my live sessions. Let's make this journey through blockchain as lively and spirited as a room full of curious minds!

What's Inside? More Than Just Your Average Geek Speak: Dive into the core of blockchain technology with a structure that's as layered as your favorite lasagna! We start with the basics, then crank up the heat with in-depth case studies and spicy code examples that are sure to keep you on your toes.

But it's not all algorithms and geek speak. Prepare for tales of crypto calamities and triumphs, deep dives into the digital dough of NFTs, and real-world revolutions in everything from gaming to governance. This isn't just about making you blockchain-savvy; it's about preparing you to partake, and perhaps even pivot, this technological tumult.

Whether you're a student flirting with finance, an academic hunting for cutting-edge analysis, or a professional itching to decode the cryptic world of crypto, this book has a little something for everyone.

From Zero to Crypto Hero in Three Parts:

- **Foundations of Blockchain Technology**: Ground yourself with the building blocks of blockchain technology. It's like the ABCs, but for future tech moguls.
- **The Crypto Universe**: Blast off into the cosmos of cryptocurrencies. Learn about Ethereum's crafty contracts, unravel the mysteries of stablecoins, without overlooking the emerging world of Central Bank Digital Currencies (CBDCs), where traditional finance meets the frontier of blockchain innovation, promising to redefine money as we know it.
- **Decentralized Finance (DeFi)/Web3**: Strap in for a tour through the revolutionary world of DeFi, from lending schemes to yield farming, and discover why your bank is scared. And what the heck an AMM is anyway!

But Wait, There's More! Real-World Heroics and Code Wizards: Each chapter unfolds like the plot of a thriller, beginning with an appetizer of introductions, moving on to a main course of rigorous analysis with code snippets, and ending with a dessert of real-world Harvard Business School case studies that reveal the business brains behind the brawn.

Already a blockchain buff? Feel free to leapfrog the introductory chapters and dive straight into the deeper waters of The Crypto Universe and Decentralized Finance (DeFi). This book is designed to cater to both newcomers and seasoned enthusiasts, so pick up from where you find the most value and let the advanced topics challenge and expand your understanding.

Frequently Asked Questions

1. **Did I hear blockchain? I was looking at cooking books. . .**
   Well, imagine if blockchain could help you monetize Grandma's secret recipe or even the views on your latest YouTube channel. This technology isn't just about crafting a perfect soufflé; it's about adding value to your digital creations and transactions. By the end of this book, you might find the concept of blockchain as tantalizing as mastering the art of making the perfect risotto or turning your passion for homemade tiramisu into a profitable venture. Dive into the world of digital transactions and discover how blockchain can be the key ingredient to enriching your favorite Italian culinary creations and beyond!
   You might enjoy Chapters 9, 10 and 14.
2. **I heard my son-in-law bought these cryptocurrencies and he believes he is going to be rich, is he an idiot?**
   Like all sons in law, he probably is (as a father of two daughters I speak from experience). However, this book will help you understand why this time he might be onto something. . . or just onto his next wild goose chase. Furthermore, you will be able to show off at the next "meet the parents" dinner!

3. As a Wall Street whiz, should I be brushing up on blockchain or just stick to trusty spreadsheets?

While your spreadsheet magic is undeniable, dabbling in blockchain won't make you a relic of the finance world—just yet. Consider it like learning a new financial spell; blockchain could add some serious sparkle to your portfolio. Dive into the blockchain waters now and you might just surf your way into the future, as the Wolf of Blockchain Street, leading the pack rather than playing catch-up. Who knows, you might even revolutionize those old-school financial practices and give those young crypto-warlocks a run for their money!

You might enjoy Chapters 7, 8, 9 and 12 the most! You might want to skip Chapter 13.

4. I don't run a drug cartel—do I really need to know about crypto?

If your idea of cryptocurrency comes from sensational headlines, you might think it's all covert operations and shady transactions. But think again! Crypto is swiftly becoming as normal as your morning coffee run. This book will peel back the curtain on how everyday activities—buying coffee, booking vacations, and yes, even grandma padding her nest egg—are increasingly powered by crypto. Let's move past the tabloid tales and dive into the legitimate, surprisingly mundane, and perfectly legal uses of cryptocurrency. It's time to see beyond the headlines and discover how integrated crypto is becoming in our everyday financial lives!

While it's true that the juiciest stories about cryptocurrency often involve wild price swings or the occasional scandal (which make headlines for the same reason car chases do!), this book digs deeper. We explore the solid, less sensational side of blockchain and crypto that the New York Times might not cover in their daily drama. So, no need to brace for a rollercoaster of scams and volatility here—just steady, informative insights on how blockchain really works and why it's more than just headline fodder.

5. I just mastered turning on a computer; should I even be considering crypto?

From zero to hero—why not? Leaping straight from powering up a PC to decrypting the blockchain might sound like trying to fly a rocket before you can ride a bike, but this book is your rocket fuel!

If you're eager to dive into the technical depths and maybe even dabble in some coding, we start from the basics and guide you to tech wizardry. There are even additional tutorials on the book webpage.

But hey, if you're more the laid-back learner, looking to grasp concepts without tangling up in code, that's cool too. You can easily glide over the tech-heavy bits; we'll keep your secret. Either way, this journey has a route for everyone.

6. As a computer scientist who devours algorithms for breakfast, will this blockchain book keep me engaged or put me to sleep?

Ah, the perennial fear of the gifted coder—will this be another book becoming a shelf warmer while you nod off from simplicity? Not this time! While we cover the essentials, we quickly dive into the cryptographic abyss that's as complex and challenging as any problem set you've faced. You'll encounter advanced consensus algorithms, delve into the nitty-gritty of smart contract security, and tackle network scalability issues that are the bread and butter of blockchain innovation. Fear not, we promise no shallow dives here—only deep, technical explorations that will keep even the most avid code wizard wide awake and wired.

Chapters 6, 7 and 8 will be fun for you.

7. **By adopting blockchain, do I become the Tony Stark of my industry, or do I still have to pretend to be an adult at board meetings?**

Adopting blockchain might not equip you with an Iron Man suit, but it could definitely give you Stark-level swagger in your industry's tech scene. However, even Tony Stark had to suit up for those pesky board meetings, right? Don't worry, though—this isn't just about adding flash; it's about adding cash flow. With plenty of real Harvard Business School case studies woven through the chapters, you'll learn from the top dogs who've turned blockchain blips into booming business models. So yes, you'll still need to act the adult part now and then, but you'll be doing it with a secret weapon up your sleeve. Let's turn those boardroom snoozefests into your personal revenue stream brainstorm sessions!

8. **My friend says blockchain is the future, but he still has a flip phone. Should I trust him?**

Maybe take his tech advice with a grain of salt—or better yet, give him this book! After both of you have read it, you can decide together whether to join the future or just keep flipping phones.

9. **Why should I trust a book to teach me about blockchain? Aren't all authors just failed tech entrepreneurs?**

Ouch, that hurts! But maybe—just maybe—you might find that some authors can explain complex tech in ways even failed tech entrepreneurs understand.

10. **Is this going to be another book collecting dust on my shelves?**

Only if you put it there! Give it a read, and it might just end up as that one book you constantly refer back to—like that one cookbook with the best lasagna recipe.

11. **Will reading this book on blockchain make me a millionaire or just make me feel like I'm missing out?**

Ah, the million-dollar question—quite literally! While devouring this book won't magically fill your wallet with Bitcoins, it'll definitely arm you with the golden nuggets of blockchain wisdom. You'll journey through the thrilling highs and the agonizing lows of cryptocurrency markets. Yes, you might kick yourself for not mining Bitcoin when it was just a hobby for computer geeks but remember: hindsight is 20/20 and the next big opportunity might just be a chapter away. So, while I can't promise you'll make your first million directly from reading this book, you'll be well-equipped to spot the next wave of opportunities in the digital currency world. And who knows? With this newfound knowledge, you might just become the savviest crypto investor on the block!

12. I've got a killer blockchain idea but I'm no tech whiz. Is this book my blueprint or just bedtime reading?

You don't need to be a coding virtuoso to bring your blockchain brainchild to life—this book is your secret weapon. Packed with everything from the ABCs of blockchain basics to the XYZs of executing smart contracts, it's designed to turn dreamers into doers. We'll guide you through the techie talk with real-world examples, practical advice, and maybe even a few laughs. By the end, you won't just be ready for bedtime; you'll be ready to build, pitch, and launch your blockchain project. Who knows, if your idea is as killer as you believe, I might even invest in your project!

13. Does it mean you are a crypto bro?

Not necessarily, but if understanding blockchain makes one a crypto bro, then get ready to join the club! We promise, though, no hoodies or obscure tech jargon required.

In fact, while we dive deep into the significant aspects of blockchain, I've consciously decided to leave out some of the more fleeting trends, like memecoins. Why? Because while they capture headlines and stir up social media buzz, they often lack the underlying fundamentals that give enduring value to more established cryptocurrencies. This book focuses on substantial topics that provide real insight and utility rather than fleeting amusement. It's about equipping you with knowledge that stands the test of time—not just what's trending on Twitter this week.

14. Is this book going to be obsolete by the time I finish it?

Given how fast the tech world moves, it's possible. But don't worry, we came up with a tome so timely that it practically updates itself. (Okay, not really, but it's as current as you can get without live-streaming the authors.) While the specific technologies and tools may evolve, the foundational principles, strategies, and philosophical underpinnings of blockchain and cryptocurrency we delve into will equip you with a durable understanding. Moreover, I've included a section on emerging trends and how to stay updated, ensuring that you remain on the cutting edge even after turning the last page. This book aims to not only educate you about the current landscape but also to develop your ability to adapt as the technology grows.

15. As a professor, can I seriously consider using this book for a course on blockchain, or is it too cool for school?

Absolutely, Professor! You can use this as a textbook, though it's not your typical snooze-inducing tome filled with drab theories and forgettable facts. Imagine a textbook that doesn't just sit on your desk collecting cobwebs but actually gets you and your students excited about learning.

This book is crafted to bridge the gap between high-level academia and practical, real-world application, making it a perfect candidate for your blockchain course. It's designed to engage students not just with the technical mechanics of blockchain but also through lively discussions, relevant case studies, and even some humor to lighten the mood during those intense learning sessions. Each chapter is peppered with insights and frameworks that are classroom-ready, complete with slide decks to facilitate lectures (available online). It's ideal for sparking curiosity and fostering a deep understanding of blockchain technology among students who are used to dynamic and interactive content.

It can be used in courses in Computer Science, Technology, Finance, Economics and Business. Depending on your focus and discipline, you can focus on some areas and some parts of the chapters rather than others.

So, rest assured, it's scholarly enough for your syllabus, yet cool enough to keep everyone awake—no caffeine needed!

16. As a small business owner, how can blockchain technology benefit my operations?
Wondering if blockchain is just for the big players? Think again! For the small business owner, blockchain can streamline operations, reduce costs through smarter contracts, and ensure the authenticity of your supply chain Imagine giving your transactions and customer data a Fort Knox-style security makeover. This book isn't just about the whys; it's crammed with the hows. Dive in to discover a treasure trove of practical ways blockchain can turbocharge your business efficiency and fortify your data defenses, all without needing a Silicon Valley budget!

17. As an artist peering into the wild world of blockchain, wondering what magic it holds for my canvas?
Buckle up, Picasso!

Blockchain isn't just flipping finance on its head; it's sending shockwaves through the art galleries too! Ever dreamt of turning your art into a digital goldmine? Welcome to the era of NFTs (Non-Fungible Tokens), where your creations don't just hang on walls—they vault into the virtual world, giving you power to mint money directly from your masterpieces. This book is your backstage pass to the blockchain revolution in art. This book will dive into real-world examples of artists who are embracing blockchain to bypass traditional marketplaces, connect with audiences, and secure their artistic creations like a digital Fort Knox. Get ready to paint your portfolio with a splash of blockchain brilliance!

You might enjoy Chapters 9, 10 and 13.

18. As a lawyer knee-deep in legal briefs, why should I dive into the crypto craze when my clients are bombarding me with blockchain bafflements?
Is your inbox overflowing with clients buzzing about Bitcoin and babbling about blockchain?

This book is your legal lexicon to the labyrinthine world of cryptocurrencies and blockchain. From deciphering the ins and outs of smart contracts to navigating the murky waters of cryptocurrency regulation, you'll find yourself equipped to not just answer your clients' frantic phone calls but to guide them through the blockchain jungle with the confidence of a seasoned safari leader. Get ready to transform those puzzling questions into billable hours as you become the go-to legal whiz on all things crypto!

You will definitely enjoy Chapter 11!

19. **As an environmental activist, I'm really keyed up about the energy munching habits of blockchain technologies. Will this book calm my green heart?**

    Your concern for our planet is bang on—blockchain does gobble up quite a bit of energy. But don't fret, this book isn't just about singing praises; it tackles the gritty questions head-on. Leap into sections that break down blockchain's appetite for electricity, the innovative strides being made to trim down that consumption, and even how blockchain is turning into a tool for environmental goodness. From tracking carbon footprints to enforcing green policies, you'll see how this tech is not just a challenge but part of the solution. By leveraging its inherent transparency and security, blockchain can track the lifecycle of carbon credits with impeccable accuracy, ensuring every credit is accounted for and not double-counted. So, gear up to turn those worries into action plans with a deep dive into eco-friendly blockchain endeavors!

20. **With so many buzzword-stuffed tomes on the shelves, why should I pick yours? What makes you the expert here?**

    Great question! In a sea of jargon-heavy reads, why should my book be the one to navigate you through the blockchain universe? Here's why: I have a PhD at MIT, but I'm not just another armchair theorist. Over the past several years, I've been at the coalface, teaching blockchain intricacies to sharp minds at Harvard Business School. This isn't regurgitated content; it's a course that's been honed and refined through rigorous academic scrutiny and real-world applications. I also co-founded the Fintech, Crypto and Web3 Lab at Harvard University.

    My work extends beyond academia into palpable industry collaborations that shape how blockchain technology is implemented in real businesses, big and small. I have been an advisor for Coinbase Institute, a board member for Mina Foundation just to cite a few of the collaborations with top projects in this space. I routinely speak to both traditional institutions and investors gatherings to help them innovate in this space. Add to this my portfolio of influential research papers that have moved the needle on digital assets discussions globally.

    So, while the bookstore shelves might be groaning under the weight of blockchain guides, mine stands out because it's built on a foundation of actual teaching, innovating, and collaborating with the best in the business. With this book, you're not just reading another manual; you're gaining a mentor who has walked the walk and can guide you step-by-step through the often mystifying world of blockchain.

Acknowledgments

I would like to begin by expressing my deepest gratitude to my long-time collaborators. Wenyao Sha, your insights and contributions to our joint cases and articles about crypto have been invaluable. Nicolas, our stimulating conversations over the years have greatly enriched this book and my understanding of the blockchain space.

I would also like to extend my heartfelt gratitude to Andrew Wu for his invaluable notes, comments, and feedback. Your insights have significantly shaped the content of this book. A big thank-you to Sila Ordu for her support in tailoring the book to students' needs and for making the coding examples and figures as precise as humanly possible. Your contributions have been essential to this book.

A thank-you to the team at Wiley, especially Bill and Stacey, for deciding with me to take on the Herculean task of speeding things up and setting deadlines so tight that we could have written a thank-you card, but instead, we wrote a whole book. Your confidence in my abilities (and your knack for suspense) ensured I was always on the edge of my seat, turning this endeavor into a thrilling adventure.

Now, to my dear colleagues at Harvard Business School: your unyielding devotion to traditional finance and your allergic reaction to new technologies have been a constant source of amusement and motivation for me. Who knew that your insistence on clinging to the past would make writing this book so much fun?

On a more personal note, I want to thank my daughters, Adriana (murzillo) and Andrea (bubu). You made working from home a joy, especially when you were at school. You turned our home into a vibrant playground of creativity, joy, and chaos.

To my wife, the most important person in my life: I am incredibly lucky to have convinced you to marry me. You're so amazing that I often feel like I'm suffering from impostor syndrome whenever I remember you're my wife. Your belief in me, your willingness to dance in the rain, and your ability to keep us smiling through every storm have meant the world to me. Thank you for being my partner in every sense. This book is as much yours as it is mine.

To my father, you have been the sweetest rock, and your unwavering support has always been felt, even from the other side of the world. You've shown me what loving someone for more than 50 years looks like and supported me wholeheartedly, even when you didn't fully understand what was going on. Thank you for being my constant source of strength and love.

And to my late mother, your belief in my abilities has always been a source of inspiration. Thank you for always believing in me, even when I doubted myself. I inherited my passion for teaching from you and can only hope to have made an impact on my students a fraction of the impact you made. I still feel your voice guiding me when I need it most.

Finally, to everyone who's been part of this journey, if you enjoyed the book, I'm glad I could make you think and smile. If not, consider it a perfect gift for someone you want to confuse about blockchain.

Chapter 1

Chain Reactions

From Basement Miners to Blockchain Revolutionaries

Preface

Greetings, dear reader! Before you dive headfirst into the cryptographic brilliance and digital daring of this book, let's take a moment to set the stage—or, in our case, prepare the blockchain. You're about to enter a world where "mining" doesn't require a pickaxe, but rather a formidable electricity bill, and "hash" isn't something you had for breakfast.

Imagine the blockchain as the bass guitarist in a rock band: immensely powerful, slightly misunderstood, and deserving of a stunning solo. This chapter (and this book) will give it that spotlight, showing how a blend of mathematics, cryptography, and sheer human stubbornness can create a system that's both secure and as transparent as Grandma's living room curtains.

Enter Bitcoin, the Mick Jagger of cryptocurrencies. It's flashy, it's backed by a mysterious creator (cheers, Satoshi!), and it's weathered storms to remain at the forefront of digital currency. Introduced in 2008, Bitcoin swung onto the scene with a rebel yell of "Who needs central banks?"—a sentiment that had traditional financial institutions raising an eyebrow in alarm.

Let's shift gears to the underground heroes of the cryptocurrency world—miners. These modern-day prospectors are armed with graphical processing units (GPUs) and a relentless pursuit for digital treasure. Mining in the Bitcoin realm isn't about blasting rock but about racing to solve cryptographic puzzles that would leave even the sharpest minds scratching their heads. It's a digital gold rush where the tools of the trade are silicon and software, not steel. These miners aren't digging through dirt; they're crunching numbers at breakneck speeds, hunting for the next block like fortune seekers panning for gold in a river of data. And yes, occasionally, the quest for crypto riches might just barbecue a graphics card or two.

In the realm of blockchain, consensus isn't just a fancy word tossed around at boring meetings. Imagine trying to get your entire extended family to agree on a pizza topping and you'll have a slight inkling of what blockchain goes through with every transaction. You see, every node (a fancy term for a computer connected to the blockchain) has to agree on the legitimacy of the information before it can be etched into the digital ledger. It's an epic saga of agreement that makes the United Nations look like a casual debate club.

And then there's proof of work, the Herculean task that keeps the blockchain ticking. Imagine a Sudoku puzzle that, if solved, helps maintain the digital world's balance. Every 10 minutes, a new block is mined and added, and the grand ledger of Bitcoin marches on. Then there's proof of stake, which is like the VIP lounge of consensus mechanisms—only the high rollers with the most coins get a say. It's like saying, "The richer you are, the more trustworthy you become," which as any scandalous billionaire will tell you, is obviously true.

From the basics of what a block really is (spoiler: it's not the kind you stacked as a kid) to tackling the Byzantine generals problem that might have given Alexander the Great a headache, this chapter covers everything you need to know to sound like the smartest person in the room—or at least at your next cryptocurrency meetup.

Initially conceived as a simple ledger for Bitcoin transactions, blockchain technology quickly outgrew its cocoon, bursting onto the tech scene with a proposition that said, "Hey, why just reinvent money when we can revamp everything else too?"

So buckle up, charge your laptops, and prepare for your mind to be expanded, your wallet to be intrigued, and your worldview to be irrevocably changed. Blockchain isn't just a technology; it's a revolution. And as with any revolution, it promises to be one heck of a ride. Let's get started, shall we?

The blockchain revolution

1. Introduction

The quest for secure and efficient means of digital exchange dates back several decades.

In fact, the roots of blockchain technology can be traced back to the early 1990s, where key cryptographic concepts and digital timestamping methods laid the groundwork for decentralized systems. In 1991, Stuart Haber and W. Scott Stornetta published pioneering research on secure digital timestamping, introducing cryptographic techniques to create tamper-evident timestamps for digital documents. This seminal work formed the basis for secure data authentication and verification.

Ralph Merkle introduced Merkle trees, a data structure that efficiently verifies the integrity of large datasets. Merkle trees became a fundamental component of blockchain technology, enabling secure and scalable data authentication.

Adam Back proposed Hashcash, a proof-of-work system designed to combat email spam and denial-of-service (DoS) attacks. Hashcash required senders to perform computationally expensive calculations to include proof-of-work tokens in email headers, thereby deterring spamming activities.

In 1998, Wei Dai introduced B-Money, a cryptographic currency system that envisioned decentralized consensus and digital signatures as the basis for a peer-to-peer electronic cash system. Around the same time, Nick Szabo proposed Bit Gold, a precursor to Bitcoin, which emphasized cryptographic puzzles and proof of work for decentralized currency creation.

Furthermore, the cypherpunk movement of the late 20th century advocated for the use of cryptography and decentralized systems to safeguard individual privacy and autonomy. Figures like David Chaum, with his invention of cryptographic digital cash, and Wei Dai, with his proposal for "b-money," explored ideas that foreshadowed the decentralized currency systems enabled by blockchain.

Several digital currency projects, including DigiCash and E-Gold, attempted to create centralized digital cash systems. These projects faced regulatory challenges and ultimately failed to achieve widespread adoption due to concerns over centralization, regulation, and scalability.

While the term *blockchain* was not widely used until the emergence of Bitcoin, the foundational concepts of cryptographic hashing, decentralized consensus, and digital timestamping formed the basis for blockchain technology's development.

The historical evolution before Bitcoin highlights the gradual progression of cryptographic techniques, digital currencies, and decentralized systems that laid the groundwork for the invention of Bitcoin and the subsequent proliferation of blockchain technology.

One thing is crucial, though: the difference between blockchain and Bitcoin. While these terms are often used interchangeably, they represent distinct concepts with divergent implications. Understanding this dichotomy is essential for discerning skeptics and enthusiasts alike.

Blockchain technology is the underlying innovation that powers cryptocurrencies like Bitcoin. At its core, blockchain is a decentralized ledger system that records transactions in a secure, transparent, and immutable manner. As we are going to see, this technology holds immense promise for transforming various industries, including finance, supply chain management, healthcare, and more.

While blockchain serves as the foundational technology behind Bitcoin, the cryptocurrency represents just one application of this innovation. Bitcoin was the first decentralized digital currency, introduced in 2008 by the pseudonymous Satoshi Nakamoto. It aims to enable peer-to-peer transactions without the need for intermediaries like banks or governments. Just as email is one application of internet technology, Bitcoin is one application of blockchain technology. Electricity powers various devices and appliances, including light bulbs. Similarly, blockchain technology powers various applications, including cryptocurrencies like Bitcoin.

In conclusion, it's essential to recognize that blockchain is not synonymous with Bitcoin. While skepticism toward Bitcoin may be warranted due to its volatility and regulatory uncertainties, the underlying technology of blockchain continues to drive innovation and reshape industries worldwide. By understanding this distinction, we can appreciate the broader implications of blockchain technology beyond the realm of cryptocurrencies.

To really explain what blockchain is and how it works, let's start with the basic definition and then we can unpack its components.

At its core, a blockchain is a digital ledger—a decentralized and transparent record-keeping system that stores information across a network of computers. Imagine it as a shared, tamper-proof database where transactions and data are securely recorded in a series of blocks, forming a chain.

Here's how it works: when a transaction occurs, such as transferring money or recording ownership of a digital asset, it's grouped with other transactions into a block. Each block contains a unique cryptographic identifier, known as a *hash*, computed using a hashing algorithm, a timestamp, and a reference to the previous block, creating an unbreakable chain of blocks. Once added to the blockchain, transactions are irreversible and transparent, visible to all participants in the network.

But what makes blockchain truly groundbreaking is its decentralized nature. Unlike traditional databases controlled by a central authority, blockchain operates on a peer-to-peer network, where every participant (or node) has a copy of the entire ledger. This decentralization ensures that no single entity has control over the data, making it resistant to censorship, fraud, and tampering.

Blockchain technology is powered by *consensus mechanisms*, algorithms that validate and confirm transactions. Popular consensus mechanisms include proof of work (PoW) and proof of stake (PoS), which ensure that transactions are legitimate and secure before they're added to the blockchain.

If you got half of that, good for you. To really understand how it works, let's proceed with a few questions about this definition that should clarify things.

2. Blockchain in 16 Questions

1. Isn't blockchain just a database like an Excel file?

This is one of the most common questions I get asked all the time.

While both blockchain and traditional databases like Excel files are used for storing and managing data, there are significant differences between the two.

1. **Structure:**
   - **Blockchain:** A blockchain is a distributed, append-only ledger that stores transactions in a series of blocks linked together in a chronological order. Each block contains a cryptographic hash of the previous block, creating a tamper-evident chain of blocks.
   - **Excel File (Traditional Database):** An Excel file is a centralized database that typically organizes data into rows and columns within sheets. It does not inherently provide a built-in mechanism for tamper-evident data storage or decentralized consensus.

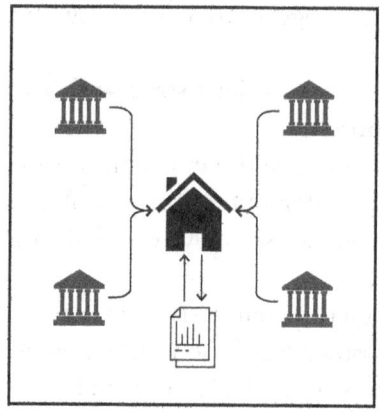 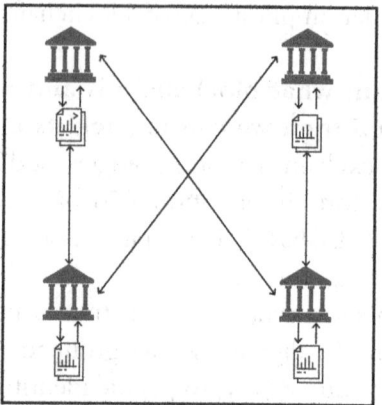

Traditional Centralized Ledger   **Distributed Ledger**

Figure 1   Traditional ledger versus distributed ledger

2. Decentralization:

- **Blockchain:** Blockchain operates on a decentralized network of nodes, as depicted in **Figure 1**, where each participant maintains a copy of the entire ledger. Transactions are validated and confirmed through a consensus mechanism, such as PoW or PoS, eliminating the need for a central authority.
- **Excel File (Traditional Database):** Excel files are typically stored on a single device or server and managed by a centralized authority. Access to the data is controlled by permissions set by the administrator.

3. Immutability:

- **Blockchain:** Once data is recorded on the blockchain, it becomes immutable and tamper-resistant. Altering or deleting previously recorded transactions is extremely difficult due to the cryptographic hashing and consensus mechanisms.
- **Excel File (Traditional Database):** Data in Excel files can be easily edited, modified, or deleted by users with appropriate permissions. There is no built-in mechanism to ensure the immutability of data.

4. Trust and Transparency:

- **Blockchain:** Blockchain provides transparency and trust by allowing all participants to view and verify transactions recorded on the ledger. The decentralized nature of blockchain ensures that no single entity controls the data, reducing the risk of manipulation or fraud.
- **Excel File (Traditional Database):** Trust in traditional databases relies on the integrity of the centralized authority managing the data. Users must trust that the administrator accurately records and maintains the data without manipulation.

In summary, while both blockchain and traditional databases serve the purpose of storing and managing data, blockchain offers unique features such as decentralization, immutability, and transparency that differentiate it from traditional database systems like

Excel files. These features make blockchain particularly well-suited for applications requiring tamper-resistant and trustless data storage, such as cryptocurrencies, supply chain management, and smart contracts.

2. What Is a Hash?

Hashing is a fundamental concept in computer science and cryptography. It involves taking an input (or *message*) and producing a fixed-size string of characters, which is typically a hexadecimal number. The output, known as a *hash value* or *hash digest*, is generated by a hash function.

Let's use the SHA-256 hashing algorithm to hash the "This book is fun" message.

Here's the hash value of the message "This book is fun" computed using the SHA-256 algorithm:

8f5d2b51c115a418b5bf1de20b3926a6c58f0c0250ad5a42280d1f4b9185a9d8

Each character in the string represents a hexadecimal digit, and the entire string represents the unique cryptographic fingerprint or hash of the input message.

It's important to note that even a small change in the input message would result in a drastically different hash value. For example, changing the message to "This book is fun!" would result in a completely different resulting hash.

9ae5d60b7d76a5394b6e660a07a181e22ac5b9bfcab3d8d87d0b7f7bb7c770e0

This property of hash functions—producing vastly different outputs for even minor changes in input—is what makes them useful for ensuring data integrity and security in various applications, including blockchain.

These are the things to remember about how hashing works and why it's important:

- **One-Way Function:** A hash function is a one-way function, meaning it's easy to compute the hash value of an input, but it's computationally infeasible to reverse the process and determine the original input given only the hash value. This property ensures that hash functions are secure for storing sensitive information like passwords.
- **Deterministic:** For a given input, a hash function always produces the same output. This deterministic nature is crucial for ensuring consistency and reliability in applications where hashing is used.
- **Fixed Output Size:** Regardless of the input size, a hash function always produces a hash value of fixed size. For example, the SHA-256 hash function, which is commonly used in blockchain and other cryptographic applications, produces a 256-bit (64-character hexadecimal) hash value.
- **Collision Resistance:** A good hash function should minimize the likelihood of two different inputs producing the same hash value, a scenario known as a *collision*. While collisions are theoretically possible due to the fixed output size, modern hash functions are designed to have extremely low collision probabilities.[1]

---

[1] SHA-256 produces a 256-bit output, which means there are 2^{256} possible hash values. This astronomical number makes finding a collision computationally infeasible.

Overall, hashing is a powerful tool in computer science and cryptography, providing a secure and efficient way to represent data in a condensed and tamper-resistant format. Its properties make it essential for ensuring data integrity, security, and privacy in a wide range of applications.

3. What Is a Block?

A *block* is a fundamental component of blockchain technology, serving as a container for a set of transactions and other important data. It represents a single unit of information within the blockchain network and plays a crucial role in maintaining the integrity, security, and transparency of the ledger. See **Figure 2** for a representation of a block.

Each block typically consists of the following key elements:

- **Block Header:** In blockchain technology, a block header serves as a crucial component of each block. It contains essential metadata about the block, such as its version number, timestamp (indicating when the block was created), and a reference to the previous block in the chain, known as the *previous block hash*. Now, we saw that a hash is a cryptographic function that takes an input (in this case, the block header's data) and produces a fixed-size output, which is a unique alphanumeric string representing the input data. Additionally, the block header includes a nonce—a random value used in the mining process. Miners manipulate this nonce along with other block header data to generate a hash value that meets the network's difficulty target. The difficulty target is a parameter set by the network protocol that determines the level of difficulty required to find a valid hash for a new block. By adjusting the nonce and other parameters, miners attempt to find a valid hash value that satisfies the difficulty target.

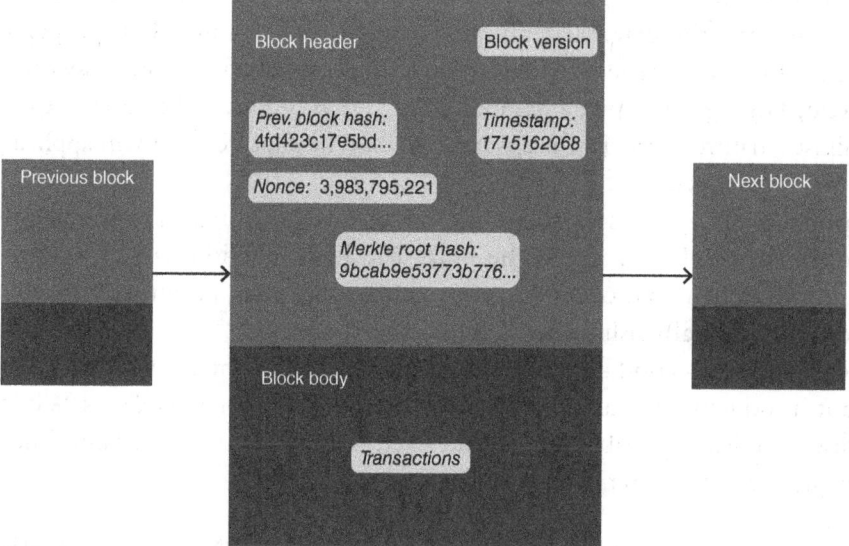

Figure 2   A representation of a block

- **Transactions:** The block contains a set of transactions, which represent various actions or exchanges of value recorded on the blockchain. These transactions can include transfers of digital assets (e.g. cryptocurrencies), smart contract executions, or any other data stored on the blockchain. Each transaction is cryptographically signed by the sender and includes inputs (references to previous transaction outputs) and outputs (destination addresses and amounts).
- **Merkle Tree Root:** The Merkle tree root, also known as the *Merkle root*, is a cryptographic hash of all transactions contained within the block. It serves as a condensed summary or fingerprint of the transactions, allowing network participants to efficiently verify the integrity of the block's data without needing to process every transaction individually.
- **Block Hash:** The block hash is a unique identifier generated by hashing the block header's contents, including the Merkle root. It serves as the block's unique identifier within the blockchain network and is crucial for maintaining the chain's integrity. Any alteration to the block's data would result in a completely different hash value, making it easy to detect tampering or manipulation.

Together, these elements form a block—a self-contained unit of data that is added to the blockchain in a sequential and immutable fashion. As new transactions are initiated and validated by network participants, they are grouped into blocks and added to the blockchain through a process known as *mining* (in PoW-based systems) or validation (in PoS-based systems). This continuous addition of blocks forms a chain of interconnected data, creating a secure and transparent ledger that powers blockchain technology. **Figure 3** provides an example of an actual block in the Bitcoin chain.

4. What Is a Merkle Tree? How Is the Merkle Root Calculated?

The Merkle tree is a fundamental data structure used in blockchain technology and other systems that require secure and efficient verification of large datasets. **Figure 4** provides a representation capturing its structure. Here's an overview of its structure:

- **Leaf Nodes:** The bottom layer of the Merkle tree consists of leaf nodes. These are the hashed values of the data blocks (e.g. transactions in a blockchain). Each piece of data is individually hashed using a cryptographic hash function, such as SHA-256, to produce the leaf nodes.
- **Intermediate Nodes:** Above the leaf nodes, the intermediate nodes are formed by pairing and hashing the child node hashes. For instance, if there are four transactions, their hashes will be paired and hashed, reducing them to two hashes. This process is repeated, combining and hashing pairs of hashes to form the next level of the tree.
- **Root Node:** The process of pairing and hashing continues upward through the tree until a single hash remains. This top hash is the Merkle root. It represents a summary of all the underlying data in the leaf nodes.

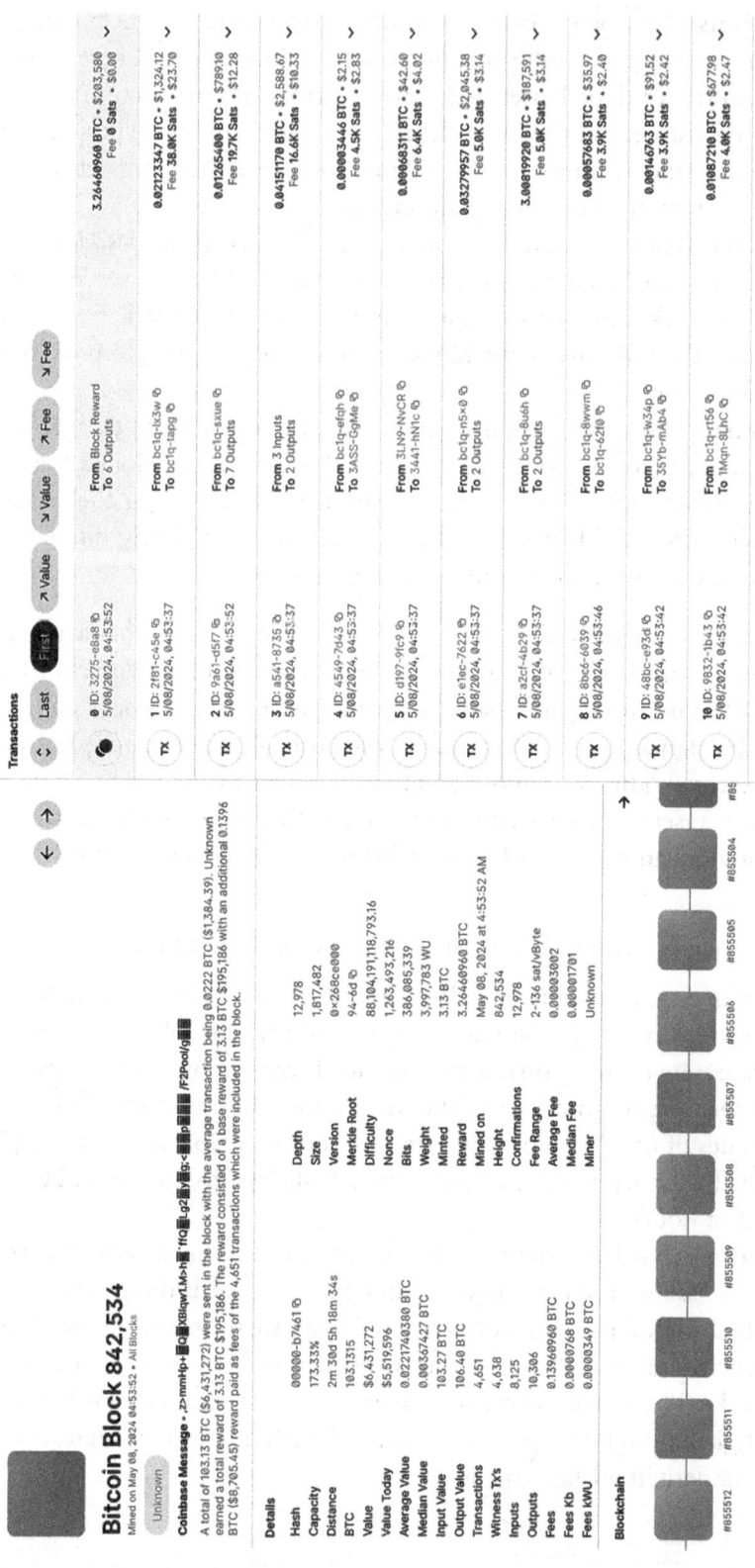

Figure 3 An actual block on Bitcoin blockchain; the header (left) and the body with the transactions (right) (BLOCKCHAIN .COM/https://www.blockchain.com/explorer/last accessed May 22, 2024)

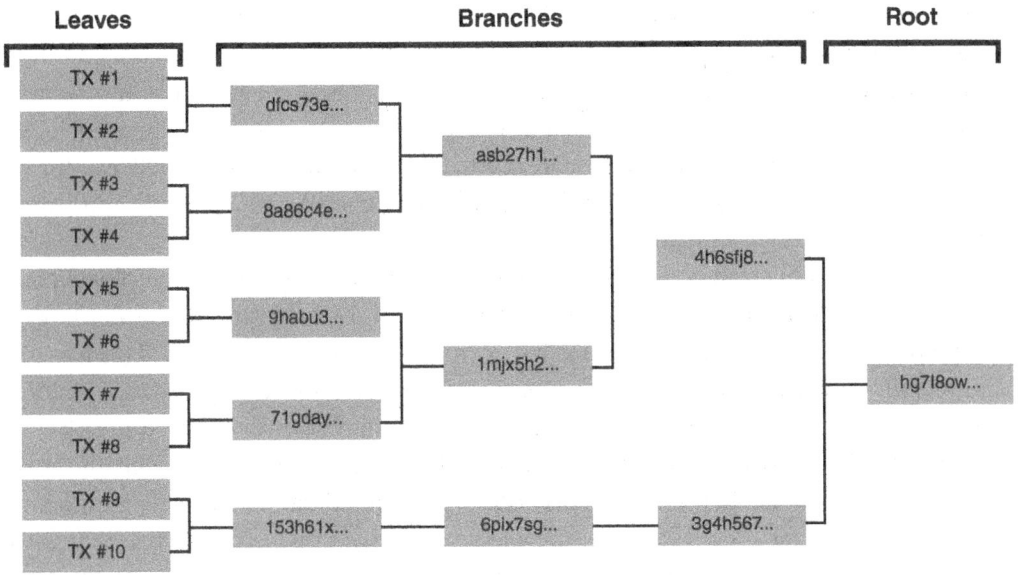

Figure 4   Structure of a Merkle tree

All transactions could have been just hashed into a singular list; however, if this was the case, to find out which specific transaction ID was used to create the hash, we would need to know all the other transaction IDs.

The advantage of Merkle tree is we need to know only some of the branches along the tree to check which specific transaction ID was included to create the root hash.

The calculation of the Merkle root begins by listing all transactions in the block. If there is an odd number of transactions, the last transaction is duplicated to even out the count. Each transaction is then hashed using a cryptographic function like SHA-256, generating a series of hash values that form the leaves of the Merkle tree. These hashes are paired sequentially, with each pair's hashes concatenated and then hashed together, effectively reducing every two transactions to a single hash. This pairing and hashing process is repeated, continually halving the number of hashes, until only one hash remains. If the number of hashes at any step is odd, the last hash is duplicated to ensure even pairing. The final remaining hash is the Merkle root, a compact and secure representation of all transactions in the block, crucial for verifying data integrity within blockchain technology.

5. Why Are Transactions in Blocks?

Transactions are organized into blocks in blockchain technology for several important reasons.

- **Efficiency:** By grouping transactions into blocks, blockchain networks can process multiple transactions simultaneously, improving efficiency and scalability. Instead of handling transactions one by one, blocks allow for batch processing, reducing latency and optimizing network performance.

- **Data Structure:** Blocks serve as a structured way to organize and store transaction data within the blockchain. We saw that each block contains a header, which includes metadata such as a timestamp and reference to the previous block, as well as a list of transactions. This organized structure facilitates easy retrieval and verification of transactions by network participants.

- **Security:** Bundling transactions into blocks enhances the security of the blockchain by creating a chain of interconnected blocks. Each block is cryptographically linked to the previous one through its hash value, forming an immutable ledger. This linkage ensures the integrity and immutability of transactions, as any attempt to alter a block would require changing all subsequent blocks—a computationally infeasible task.

- **Consensus Mechanisms:** Blocks play a crucial role in the consensus mechanisms of blockchain networks, such as PoW and PoS. Miners or validators compete to validate transactions and add new blocks to the blockchain. By organizing transactions into blocks, consensus mechanisms incentivize network participants to collectively agree on the validity of transactions and maintain the integrity of the ledger.

- **Incentive Structure:** In many blockchain networks, miners or validators are rewarded with transaction fees and newly minted coins for successfully adding a new block to the blockchain. By grouping transactions into blocks, blockchain networks create a predictable reward structure for participants, incentivizing them to contribute to the security and stability of the network.

Overall, organizing transactions into blocks is a foundational aspect of blockchain technology, enabling efficient processing, secure storage, and consensus-driven validation of transactions within decentralized networks.

6. What Is a Node and a P2P Network?

In the context of a peer-to-peer (P2P) network, a node refers to any device or computer that participates in the network by running network software and maintaining a copy of the network's shared data. Nodes play a crucial role in facilitating communication, validating transactions, and maintaining the integrity of the network. Here's how nodes operate in a P2P network:

1. **Network Participation:** Nodes join the network voluntarily by running compatible software that allows them to communicate with other nodes. Each node has its own unique identifier, typically in the form of an address or public key, which distinguishes it from other nodes in the network.

2. **Data Storage:** Nodes maintain a copy of the network's shared data, which may include transaction records, smart contracts, or other information relevant to the network's purpose. In a blockchain network, for example, nodes store a copy of the blockchain ledger, allowing them to verify transactions and participate in the consensus process.

3. **Communication:** Nodes in a P2P network communicate with each other through a protocol, which defines the rules and procedures for exchanging data and maintaining network integrity. By sharing information with other nodes, such as transactions or new blocks in a blockchain, nodes ensure that the network remains synchronized and up-to-date.

4. **Validation:** Depending on the network's design, nodes may be responsible for validating transactions and ensuring their integrity before they are accepted and added to the network's shared data. In a blockchain network, for example, nodes participate in the consensus process by verifying transactions, solving cryptographic puzzles (in PoW systems), or staking cryptocurrency (in PoS systems) to validate transactions.

5. **Relaying Transactions:** Nodes relay transactions and blocks to other nodes in the network, helping to propagate information efficiently across the network. This ensures that all nodes have access to the latest data and can participate in the network's operation.

6. **Resilience and Redundancy:** P2P networks are inherently decentralized, meaning that no single node or entity controls the network. This decentralization provides resilience against attacks or failures, as the network can continue to operate even if some nodes are compromised or go offline. Additionally, the redundancy of having multiple copies of the network's data stored on different nodes helps prevent data loss and ensures the network's integrity.

Overall, nodes are the building blocks of P2P networks, enabling decentralized communication, data storage, and consensus among network participants. By working together, nodes help create a robust and resilient network infrastructure that powers a wide range of decentralized applications and services.

7. What Is a Consensus Mechanism?

A consensus mechanism is a set of rules or protocols used by decentralized networks to achieve agreement among participants on the validity of transactions and the state of the network. Consensus mechanisms are essential for ensuring that all nodes in the network reach a common understanding of the shared data and can collectively agree on the next steps in the network's operation. Consensus mechanisms are necessary for several reasons.

- **Decentralization:** Decentralized networks, such as blockchain networks, lack a central authority to dictate the validity of transactions or resolve disputes. Instead, decisions about the network's operation must be made collectively by network participants. Consensus mechanisms provide a way for nodes to reach agreement on the state of the network without relying on a central authority.
- **Security:** Consensus mechanisms help protect the network against malicious actors or attacks by ensuring that transactions are validated and added to the network's shared data only if they meet certain criteria. By requiring a majority of nodes to agree on the validity of transactions, consensus mechanisms help prevent double-spending, fraud, and other security vulnerabilities.

- **Immutability:** Consensus mechanisms contribute to the immutability of decentralized networks by ensuring that once a transaction is confirmed and added to the network's shared data, it cannot be altered or removed without consensus from the majority of network participants. This immutability is crucial for maintaining the integrity and trustworthiness of the network's data over time.
- **Scalability:** As decentralized networks grow and handle increasing transaction volumes, consensus mechanisms must be scalable to accommodate the network's needs. Efficient consensus mechanisms enable networks to process transactions quickly and securely, even as the network expands in size and complexity.
- **Incentives:** Many consensus mechanisms incorporate economic incentives to encourage network participants to act honestly and contribute to the network's operation. For example, in PoW systems like Bitcoin, miners are rewarded with newly minted coins and transaction fees for successfully adding new blocks to the blockchain. These incentives align the interests of network participants and help maintain the network's security and integrity.

Overall, consensus mechanisms are a foundational component of decentralized networks, enabling secure, transparent, and trustless transactions without the need for a central authority. By establishing rules for decision-making and incentivizing honest behavior, consensus mechanisms ensure the smooth operation and resilience of decentralized networks in a wide range of applications and industries.

8. How Does Bitcoin Fit into This?

Bitcoin is a specific application of blockchain technology, and it plays a central role in the broader ecosystem of blockchain-based systems.

Bitcoin introduced the concept of blockchain technology to the world through its white paper published by Satoshi Nakamoto in 2008. The Bitcoin blockchain serves as a decentralized ledger for recording transactions of the digital currency, Bitcoin. Bitcoin demonstrated the viability of using blockchain technology to create a decentralized, peer-to-peer electronic cash system. It proved that transactions could be securely recorded and verified without the need for a central authority.

Bitcoin operates on a decentralized network of nodes, where transactions are verified and added to the blockchain through a consensus mechanism known as *proof of work*. This decentralized nature ensures that no single entity controls the Bitcoin network.

Bitcoin transactions involve the transfer of value (Bitcoins) between addresses on the blockchain. Each transaction is recorded in a block and secured through cryptographic hashing, making it tamper-resistant and immutable.

In summary, Bitcoin serves as a pioneering example of how blockchain technology can be applied to create decentralized digital currencies and payment systems. Its innovative design and decentralized architecture have influenced the development of numerous blockchain-based applications and platforms across various industries.

9. Who Are Miners? And What Do They Do?

Miners play a crucial role in blockchain networks, particularly those that use PoW as their consensus mechanism, such as Bitcoin. Miners are individuals or entities (often specialized computer systems known as *mining rigs*) that participate in the process of validating and confirming transactions on a blockchain network. In decentralized blockchain networks, anyone can become a miner by dedicating computational resources to solve cryptographic puzzles and add new blocks to the blockchain.

Miners collect and validate pending transactions from the network's *mempool* (pool of unconfirmed transactions). They verify that each transaction adheres to the network's rules and has sufficient fees attached to incentivize miners to include them in the next block.

Miners group validate transactions into a new block and create a block header, which includes information such as a timestamp, a reference to the previous block, and a nonce (a random number).

Miners compete to solve a computationally intensive mathematical puzzle based on the block header and the content of the block. This process, known as *proof of work*, requires miners to find a hash value that meets a predetermined difficulty target.

The first miner to solve the puzzle broadcasts their solution to the network. Other miners verify the solution and then add the new block to their copy of the blockchain if it is valid.

10. Why Are They Doing All of This Work?

Miners are rewarded for their efforts with newly minted cryptocurrency (in the case of Bitcoin, miners receive newly minted Bitcoins) and transaction fees included in the block they mined. This reward serves as an incentive to secure the network and validate transactions.

In the case of Bitcoin, initially, the block reward was 50 Bitcoins per block, but this reward undergoes a halving approximately every four years (or every 210,000 blocks). This halving mechanism is designed to gradually reduce the rate at which new Bitcoins are created, mimicking the extraction of physical gold, which becomes harder to mine over time.

Halving events are critical junctures in Bitcoin's monetary policy. These events ensure a decreasing rate of Bitcoin issuance, creating a deflationary pressure on the cryptocurrency. There have been four halving events to date:

- **First Halving (2012):** Reduced the block reward from 50 to 25 Bitcoins
- **Second Halving (2016):** Reduced the block reward from 25 to 12.5 Bitcoins
- **Third Halving (2020):** Reduced the block reward from 12.5 to 6.25 Bitcoins
- **Fourth Halving (2024):** Reduced the block reward to 3.125 Bitcoins

Is the blockchain going to stop working if the rewards are too low or non-existent? No.

In addition to the block reward, miners also collect transaction fees attached to each transaction they include in the block. These fees serve as an additional incentive for miners to prioritize transactions with higher fees attached.

In summary, miners play a critical role in the operation of blockchain networks by validating transactions, creating new blocks, and securing the network through the PoW consensus mechanism. Their efforts help maintain the integrity, security, and decentralization of the blockchain network.

11. Putting All of These Elements Together, How Does PoW Work?

To understand why PoW works the way it does, let's introduce the problem it tries to solve. It is usually described as the Byzantine generals problem, a thought experiment that illustrates the difficulties of achieving consensus in a distributed network where participants might fail or act maliciously. The scenario involves several generals, each commanding a portion of the Byzantine army, who need to agree on a battle plan. However, they can communicate only via messengers, and some of the generals or messengers might be traitors trying to prevent consensus. In the context of blockchain, nodes in the network can be thought of as generals who need to agree on the current state of the ledger (the battle plan). The "traitors" in this scenario could be nodes that attempt to disrupt the network by not following protocol rules, submitting false transactions, or colluding to rewrite parts of the blockchain.

Byzantine fault tolerance is a property of a system that allows it to continue functioning correctly even if some of the participants (nodes) fail or act maliciously. A system is considered Byzantine fault tolerant if it can handle up to a certain number (usually less than one-third) of faulty or malicious nodes.

PoW makes Bitcoin Byzantine fault tolerance. In a PoW system, network participants called *miners* compete to solve complex mathematical puzzles. These puzzles require significant computational power to solve but are easy to verify once a solution is found. Miners aim to find a special number, called a *nonce*, that, when combined with the block's data and hashed, produces a hash value below a certain target threshold. See **Figure 5** for a process chart of a PoW chain.

For example, imagine a miner is trying to solve a puzzle by finding a nonce that, when combined with a block's data (which includes transaction information, a timestamp, and a nonce), produces a hash value starting with a certain number of zeros. The miner iterates through different nonce values until they find one that meets the target difficulty level.

Miners use a cryptographic hash function, such as Secure Hash Algorithm 256-bit (SHA-256), to hash the block's data and nonce. A hash function takes an input (in this case, the block's data and nonce) and produces a fixed-size output (the hash value). It's essential that the hash function is cryptographically secure and produces unpredictable outputs.

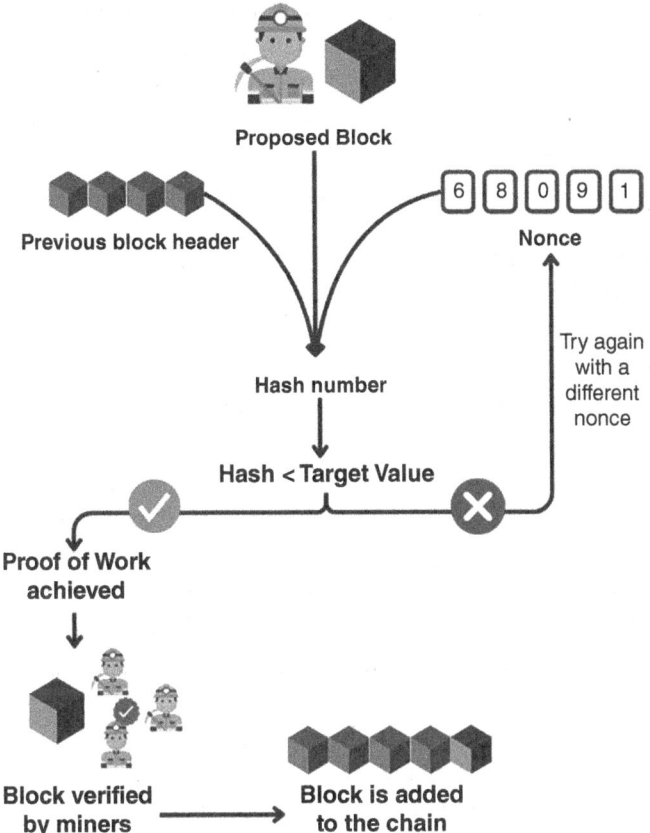

Figure 5   Proof of work simplified process chart

For example, when a miner hashes a block's data and nonce using SHA-256, they get a unique hash value. We saw that changing any part of the input, even a single bit like a small change to a transaction (e.g. Marco receiving 10 BTC rather than 1 BTC), will produce a completely different hash value.

The difficulty target is a parameter set by the network protocol that determines the level of difficulty required to find a valid hash for a new block. The target is adjusted periodically to ensure that new blocks are mined at a consistent rate, typically every 10 minutes in the case of Bitcoin. For example, if the difficulty target is set so that a valid hash must start with four leading zeros, miners must find a nonce that, when hashed with the block's data, produces a hash value with at least four zeros at the beginning.

Once a miner discovers a valid hash value that meets the difficulty target, they broadcast the solution to the rest of the network as proof of work. Other nodes in the network can quickly verify the validity of the solution by hashing the block's data with the provided nonce (they all observe the same inputs so can verify the output of the SHA-256 function) and confirming that the resulting hash value meets the difficulty target.

Once a valid solution is verified by the network, the new block is added to the blockchain, and the miner who found the solution is rewarded with a predetermined amount of cryptocurrency (e.g. Bitcoin) and any transaction fees included in the block. This process incentivizes miners to invest computational resources and contribute to the security and operation of the network.

In other words, Bitcoin achieves Byzantine fault tolerance for the following reasons:

- **Network Agreement through Computational Work:** PoW requires nodes (miners) to solve complex mathematical puzzles that consume significant computational resources. The solution to these puzzles, known as *proof of work*, is easy to verify by other nodes but hard to produce. This mechanism ensures that any participant who wants to add new blocks to the blockchain must demonstrate a substantial investment of computational effort and, by extension, energy.
- **Economic Incentives and Costs:** The design of PoW incorporates economic incentives to follow the rules. Miners invest significant resources in the form of hardware and electricity to solve the computational puzzles. Once they find a solution, they are rewarded with transaction fees and, in the case of Bitcoin, a block reward. The high cost of participating in the mining process disincentivizes malicious behavior because it would nullify the investment made by the miners if they were to attack the network or act dishonestly.
- **Majority Control for Consensus:** PoW ensures that as long as the majority of the computational power in the network is controlled by honest nodes, the network can maintain a truthful and accurate ledger. This is central to PoW's BFT property. In Bitcoin, for example, it is assumed that if at least 51% of the computational power (hashrate) is controlled by honest participants, the network can resist attempts by a minority to alter past transactions or double-spend coins.
- **Increasing Difficulty of Attacks:** To alter any information on the blockchain, an attacker must redo the PoW for the target block and all subsequent blocks (because these subsequent blocks are all linked through the hashes to this target block), which becomes exponentially difficult as more blocks are added. This requirement not only secures past transactions but also ensures that a majority of honest nodes will always have the longest valid chain, a principle that nodes use to determine the canonical history of transactions.

Overall, PoW ensures the security and integrity of decentralized networks by requiring participants to expend computational resources to validate transactions and add new blocks to the blockchain. The decentralized nature of PoW ensures that no single entity can control the network, making it resistant to attacks and censorship. However, PoW is energy-intensive and has scalability limitations, leading to the development of alternative consensus mechanisms such as PoS and delegated proof of stake (dPoS).

12. What Happens If Two Blocks Are Mined at the Same Time?

When two blocks are mined at approximately the same time, it creates a temporary situation known as a *fork* in the blockchain.

Here's what happens in this scenario. Miners in a blockchain network work independently to validate transactions and create new blocks. Occasionally, multiple miners solve the cryptographic puzzle and successfully mine a new block at nearly the same time. As a result of this simultaneous mining, there are now two valid blocks competing to be added to the blockchain at the same block height. This creates a temporary fork in the blockchain, with two competing branches.

Both valid blocks are broadcast to the network, and different nodes in the network may receive one block before the other. As a result, some nodes may initially perceive one block as the valid continuation of the blockchain, while others may perceive the other block as valid.

The blockchain network relies on consensus mechanisms, such as PoW, to resolve forks and determine which block becomes part of the longest, most valid chain. Miners continue to mine on top of the block they received first, extending their chosen branch of the fork. As more blocks are added to one branch of the fork, it becomes the longest chain.

In most blockchain networks, including Bitcoin, the longest valid chain is considered the "true" blockchain. Nodes automatically switch to the longest chain, abandoning the shorter branch of the fork. The blocks on the shorter branch of the fork are considered "orphaned" and are not included in the main blockchain. Why the longest chain? Because it is the most secure as the larger the number of blocks, the more computational power it would take to alter it.

Once consensus is reached and one branch of the fork becomes the longest chain, the blockchain is reorganized to reflect this decision. Transactions that were included in the orphaned blocks are returned to the mempool, where they await confirmation in future blocks.

In summary, when two blocks are mined at the same time, it creates a temporary fork in the blockchain. Through the consensus mechanism and the principle of the longest chain, the network resolves the fork by selecting one branch as the valid continuation of the blockchain, while the other branch is discarded. This process ensures the integrity and stability of the blockchain network.

13. What Prevents People from Double Spending Their Digital Currency?

This is essentially the key problem that a decentralized system needs to solve. When there is a central authority like a bank, this has the power and the ability to determine which transactions are valid if multiple transactions are submitted and there is not enough money in the account. But how to do it in a system where nobody has such a power?

Let's consider a scenario where an individual, Alice, attempts to double spend her digital currency, such as Bitcoin, by initiating two conflicting transactions.

- **Attempted Double Spend:**
  1. Alice owns 1 BTC and decides to spend it twice, once to purchase goods from Merchant A and again to purchase goods from Merchant B.
  2. She creates two separate transactions: Transaction 1, sending 1 BTC to Merchant A, and Transaction 2, sending 1 BTC to Merchant B.
  3. Both transactions are broadcast to the Bitcoin network simultaneously.
- **Network Propagation:**
  1. Nodes in the Bitcoin network receive both Transaction 1 and Transaction 2 and propagate them across the network.
  2. Miners, who validate and confirm transactions, receive these conflicting transactions and must decide which one to include in the next block.
- **Consensus Mechanism:**
  1. Miners begin the process of validating transactions and adding them to a new block through the consensus mechanism, such as PoW.
  2. Miners select transactions from the mempool (pool of unconfirmed transactions) to include in the next block and compete to solve a cryptographic puzzle to append the block to the blockchain.
- **Mining Process:**
  1. Some miners may receive Transaction 1 first and begin mining a block that includes this transaction.
  2. Other miners may receive Transaction 2 first and start mining a block that includes this transaction instead.
- **Blockchain Confirmation:**
  1. Eventually, one of the miners successfully mines a block containing either Transaction 1 or Transaction 2.
  2. This block is added to the blockchain, making the transaction irreversible and confirming the transfer of funds to either Merchant A or Merchant B.
  3. The winning transaction is considered valid and recognized by the network, while the conflicting transaction is rejected and considered invalid.
- **Prevention of Double Spend:**
  1. By design, the decentralized nature of the blockchain network ensures that conflicting transactions are resolved through the consensus mechanism.
  2. Miners collectively agree on the validity of transactions and select a single transaction to include in the blockchain, preventing double spending attempts from succeeding.
  3. Additionally, the transparency and immutability of the blockchain ledger make it easy to detect and reject fraudulent transactions.

In summary, while double spending attempts may occur, the consensus mechanism and decentralized nature of the blockchain network effectively prevent such attempts from being successful. Miners collectively validate and confirm transactions, ensuring that only one valid transaction is included in the blockchain, while conflicting transactions are rejected. This process maintains the integrity and security of the blockchain ledger, making it resistant to fraudulent activities like double spending.

The prevention of double spending in digital currency systems, particularly in decentralized systems like blockchain, is primarily ensured through consensus mechanisms and cryptographic techniques. Here's how:

1. **Consensus Mechanisms:** In blockchain networks, transactions are validated and added to the distributed ledger through consensus mechanisms such as PoW and PoS. These mechanisms require network participants (miners or validators) to invest resources (computational power or cryptocurrency stakes) to verify transactions. By reaching a consensus on the validity of transactions, the network ensures that double spending attempts are detected and rejected.

2. **Transaction Validation:** Before a transaction is considered valid and added to the blockchain, it must be verified by a majority of network participants. Each transaction includes digital signatures and references to previous transactions (inputs) that prove the ownership and authenticity of the digital currency being spent. Validators check these signatures and ensure that the spender has sufficient funds and hasn't already spent the same funds in a previous transaction.

3. **Blockchain Immutability:** Once a transaction is confirmed and added to the blockchain, it becomes part of an immutable and sequentially ordered ledger. Any attempt to tamper with or modify a transaction would require altering all subsequent blocks in the chain, which is computationally infeasible due to the decentralized nature of the network and the cryptographic hash functions used to link blocks.

4. **Confirmation Process:** In blockchain networks, transactions typically undergo a confirmation process, during which they are included in a block and added to the blockchain. Depending on the network protocol and consensus mechanism, transactions may require multiple confirmations to be considered final and irreversible. This process adds another layer of security against double spending attempts.

5. **Network Integrity:** Decentralized networks rely on the integrity and honesty of network participants to maintain the security of the system. Any attempt to double spend digital currency would require control of a majority of the network's computing power or stake, making it economically impractical and highly unlikely in well-established blockchain networks.

Overall, the combination of consensus mechanisms, transaction validation, blockchain immutability, confirmation processes, and network integrity ensures that double spending is effectively prevented in digital currency systems, particularly in decentralized blockchain networks.

14. What Would It Take to Tamper with a PoW Blockchain?

In a PoW blockchain setting, tampering with the blockchain would require significant computational power and resources due to the security measures inherent in the PoW consensus mechanism.

First, tampering with the blockchain would involve recalculating the hashes of blocks and potentially rewriting transaction histories. This requires an immense amount of computational power to outpace the honest nodes in the network.

To successfully tamper with the blockchain, an attacker would also need to control a majority of the network's computational power, known as a *51% attack*. This allows the attacker to create a longer, alternative chain that overtakes the honest chain, enabling them to rewrite transaction history and potentially double-spend coins.

PoW blockchains rely on network-wide consensus to determine the valid chain. Honest nodes in the network will accept only the longest valid chain with the most accumulated computational work (PoW). Therefore, an attacker would need to maintain majority control of the network for an extended period to execute a successful tampering attack.

Performing a 51% attack on a PoW blockchain requires a significant investment in computational hardware and electricity costs. Additionally, the longer the blockchain, the more difficult and costly it becomes to manipulate. Therefore, the cost of launching such an attack may outweigh any potential gains. "Would quantum computing break the blockchain?" is another common related question I get asked. The answer? Maybe it will.

However, more importantly than computing power, in my opinion, is the inherent economic incentives that would make such an attack unprofitable. Remember that miners are rewarded with newly minted coins and transaction fees. Any attempt to tamper with the blockchain would undermine the trust and value of the cryptocurrency, potentially resulting in financial losses for the attacker. In other words, the moment somebody is able to breach the security of a blockchain to steal the underlying digital currency, such as Bitcoin, the value of Bitcoin would collapse, which would make the attack. . .worthless!

15. How Are Transactions Selected to Be Included in a Block?

The *mempool* is a temporary storage area where unconfirmed transactions wait to be included in a block by miners. When a user initiates a transaction, it is broadcasted to the network and enters the mempool. Miners monitor the mempool and select transactions to include in their blocks based on the factors mentioned earlier. Transactions that offer higher fees or have shorter waiting times in the mempool are more likely to be included in the next block. However, if the mempool becomes congested, some transactions may experience delays or even be dropped from the mempool if they remain unconfirmed for an extended period.

Miners select transactions to be added to a block based on several factors, including the following:

- **Transaction Fees:**
  - Miners prioritize transactions with higher fees because they receive these fees as rewards for adding transactions to the block. Transactions offering higher fees are more attractive to miners as they increase their potential earnings.
- **Transaction Size:**
  - Miners aim to maximize the block size without exceeding the network's capacity limits. They may prioritize smaller transactions to fit more transactions into a block, thereby maximizing their potential fee earnings.
- **Transaction Confirmation Time:**
  - Miners generally prefer transactions that have been waiting in the mempool (the queue of unconfirmed transactions) for a shorter duration. This helps minimize the time taken to confirm transactions and improves the overall efficiency of the blockchain network.
- **Transaction Priority:**
  - Some miners may prioritize transactions from certain users or applications based on predefined criteria. For example, they may give priority to transactions from reputable entities, exchanges, or decentralized finance (DeFi) platforms.
- **Network Congestion:**
  - During periods of high network congestion, miners may prioritize transactions with higher fees to optimize their earnings. Conversely, during periods of low activity, miners may include a broader range of transactions to fill blocks more efficiently.
- **Transaction Validity:**
  - Miners verify the validity of transactions by ensuring that they meet all protocol rules and have sufficient funds to cover the transaction amount. They exclude invalid or malformed transactions from being added to blocks.

Suppose a miner is constructing a block and has the following transactions available in the mempool:

Transaction A:	**Transaction B:**	**Transaction C:**
• Transaction Fee: 0.002 BTC	• Transaction Fee: 0.003 BTC	• Transaction Fee: 0.001 BTC
• Size: 250 bytes	• Size: 350 bytes	• Size: 200 bytes
• Waiting Time: 10 minutes	• Waiting Time: 5 minutes	• Waiting Time: 20 minutes
Transaction D:	**Transaction E:**	**Transaction F:**
• Transaction Fee: 0.004 BTC	• Transaction Fee: 0.0025 BTC	• Transaction Fee: 0.005 BTC
• Size: 400 bytes	• Size: 300 bytes	• Size: 100 bytes
• Waiting Time: 3 minutes	• Waiting Time: 15 minutes	• Waiting Time: 10 minutes

The miner needs to decide which transactions to include in their block. Here's how the factors might influence their decision:

1. **Transaction Fees:**
   - Transaction F offers the highest fee (0.005 BTC), making it the most lucrative option for the miner.
2. **Transaction Size:**
   - Transaction D is the largest in size (400 bytes), followed by Transaction B (350 bytes). If the miner is aiming to maximize block space efficiency, they might prioritize smaller transactions to fit more into the block.
3. **Transaction Confirmation Time:**
   - Transactions B and D have shorter waiting times (five and three minutes, respectively), indicating higher priority. The miner may choose these transactions to minimize confirmation time for users.
4. **Network Congestion:**
   - If the network is experiencing high congestion, the miner might prioritize transactions with higher fees (such as Transaction F) to maximize their earnings during peak periods.

Taking these factors into account, the miner might choose to include transactions D, B, and E in their block, as they offer the highest fees, shorter waiting times, and relatively smaller sizes compared to the other transactions. However, the specific criteria and priorities may vary depending on the miner's strategy, network conditions, and individual preferences.

16. What Happens If the Wrong Transaction Is Submitted?

It depends.

If the transaction contains invalid data or fails to meet the protocol's rules, it will be rejected by the nodes in the network. Invalid transactions are not included in blocks and therefore do not become part of the blockchain ledger. In some cases, the wrong transaction may be initially accepted by a node but subsequently rejected as it propagates through the network. Nodes in the network perform validation checks on incoming transactions, and if they identify any discrepancies or invalidities, they will reject the transaction and not forward it to other nodes.

If a wrong transaction is included in a block and added to the blockchain, it can potentially be reversed through a process known as a *blockchain reorganization*. This typically occurs in situations where the wrong transaction is identified promptly, and the network reaches a consensus to roll back the blockchain to a point before the incorrect transaction occurred. However, blockchain reorganizations are rare and typically occur only in extreme circumstances, such as security breaches or protocol errors.

The most likely outcome? Once a transaction is confirmed and added to the blockchain, it becomes part of the immutable ledger and is considered irreversible. In this case, if the wrong transaction is included in a block and added to the blockchain, it cannot be directly reversed or modified. Participants may need to rely on other mechanisms, such as refund transactions or off-chain resolutions, to address the consequences of the incorrect transaction.

While blockchain technology provides security and immutability, it also necessitates careful attention to transaction accuracy and validation to prevent errors and mitigate their potential consequences. Remember that in most cases there is no 800 number to call in case you submit the wrong transaction!

Figure 6 puts all of these questions and short answers together.

Question	Answer
Isn't blockchain just a database like an excel file?	No, blockchain is decentralized, immutable, and transparent, unlike a centralized and easily modifiable Excel file.
What is a hash?	A hash is a fixed-size alphanumeric string produced by a hash function from an input, which is crucial for data integrity and security in various applications, including blockchain.
What is a block?	A block is a unit of data in the blockchain, containing transactions and secured by cryptographic hashes.
What is a Merkle tree and how is it calculated?	A Merkle tree begins with hashing individual transactions to form leaf nodes. These nodes are then paired and the hashes of each pair are concatenated and hashed again, this process repeats up the tree until a single hash, the Merkle root, remains at the top.
Why are transactions in blocks?	Grouping transactions in blocks improves efficiency, security, and structure, supporting batch processing and consensus mechanisms in blockchain networks. Grouping transactions in blocks improves efficiency, security, and structure, supporting batch processing and consensus mechanisms in blockchain networks.
What is a node and a P2P network?	A node is a device in a P2P network that helps maintain the network's data, facilitates communication, and ensures the integrity and resilience of the network.
What is a consensus mechanism?	A consensus mechanism is a protocol in decentralized networks for all participants to agree on data validity, ensuring security and preventing fraud.
How does Bitcoin fits into this?	Bitcoin uses blockchain to operate a decentralized digital currency system, demonstrating blockchain's utility in enabling secure, peer-to-peer transactions without a central authority.
Who are Miners? And what do they do?	Miners validate and record transactions into blocks using computational power to maintain secure blockchain networks.
Why are they doing all of this work?	Miners are incentivized through rewards (new coins and transaction fees) to contribute network security operation.
How does PoW work?	In PoW, miners solve complex puzzles to validate transactions and add blocks the blockchain, securing network ensuring decentralized consensus.

Figure 6   Blockchain Q&A

Question	Answer
What happens if two blocks are mined at the same time?	This creates a temporary fork; the network resolves it by choosing branch with longest chain, which becomes accepted history.
What prevents people from double spending their digital currency?	Consensus mechanisms, transaction validation, and blockchain immutability prevent double spending by ensuring a transaction is only accepted once into the blockchain.
What would it take to tamper with a PoW blockchain?	Tampering would require immense computational power to override the network, making it practically and economically unfeasible due high costs low gains from fraud.
How are transactions selected to be included in a block?	Transactions are chosen based on fees, size, waiting time, and network conditions, with miners prioritizing transactions that maximize their rewards efficiency.
What happens if the wrong transaction is submitted?	If detected before confirmation, it gets rejected; if wrongly included and confirmed, becomes irreversible but might be remedied through additional transactions or agreement

Figure 6   (Continued)

3. Where It All Started: Bitcoin

Bitcoin is a cornerstone in the evolution of blockchain technology, being the first successful deployment of blockchain and proving that financial transactions could be securely managed without central authorities. This pioneering application not only highlighted blockchain's potential in securing digital transactions but also ignited interest across various sectors, paving the way for innovative uses beyond cryptocurrency.

History of Bitcoin: Early Concepts

The early concepts leading to Bitcoin's development were influenced by several digital cash technologies. David Chaum and Stefan Brands introduced issuer-based ecash protocols, setting foundational ideas for digital currency systems. The significant concept of using computational work to assign value, essential for Bitcoin's PoW, was initially proposed by Cynthia Dwork and Moni Naor in 1992 and was later developed into a practical application by Adam Back with his hashcash system in 1997. Parallel to this, Wei Dai's b-money and Nick Szabo's bit gold introduced ideas of distributed digital scarcity and the embedding of PoW into a decentralized currency system. Hal Finney built upon these concepts by creating reusable PoW (RPOW), leveraging hashcash's algorithm, which further evolved the practicality and security aspects of digital currencies.

Who Is Satoshi Nakamoto?

Satoshi Nakamoto is the pseudonym for the mysterious person or group responsible for the creation of Bitcoin (**Figure 7**). Nakamoto introduced Bitcoin in 2008 with the release of a white paper titled "Bitcoin: A Peer-to-Peer Electronic Cash System." This document laid the foundation for a decentralized digital currency, independent of centralized authorities, facilitating peer-to-peer transactions without the need for intermediaries.

Although Nakamoto's true identity remains unknown, their involvement in the development of Bitcoin was active and crucial during the initial years, from 2008 until around mid-2010. During this period, Nakamoto was involved in coding the first block-chain database, collaborating with other developers, and contributing to forum discussions about the digital currency. By 2011, Nakamoto claimed to have moved on to other projects and ceased to participate visibly in the Bitcoin community.

The mystery surrounding Nakamoto's identity has led to numerous investigations and speculation. Various individuals and groups within the cryptography and computer science communities have been suspected, but none has been conclusively identified as Nakamoto. Notable investigations by media outlets proposed several potential candidates, including cryptographers and computer scientists linked through academic, professional, or circumstantial evidence to the creation of Bitcoin. Each proposed candidate has denied being Nakamoto.

Figure 7   Satoshi Nakamoto bust in Budapest (Fekist/Wikimedia Commons/CC BY-SA 4.0)

Even if we don't know who Nakamoto is, it might still be worthwhile reading what they had to write as they were working on the Bitcoin whitepaper. Here are a few posts and private emails that have recently surfaced.

FORUM POST OF SATOSHI NAKAMATO ON P2P FOUNDATION (BITCOIN.COM/SATOSHI-ARCHIVE)

Bitcoin open source implementation of P2P currency
Posted by Satoshi Nakamoto on February 11, 2009 at 22:27

I've developed a new open source P2P e-cash system called Bitcoin. It's completely decentralized, with no central server or trusted parties, because everything is based on crypto proof instead of trust. Give it a try, or take a look at the screenshots and design paper:

Download Bitcoin v0.1 at http://www.bitcoin.org

The root problem with conventional currency is all the trust that's required to make it work. The central bank must be trusted not to debase the currency, but the history of fiat currencies is full of breaches of that trust. Banks must be trusted to hold our money and transfer it electronically, but they lend it out in waves of credit bubbles with barely a fraction in reserve. We have to trust them with our privacy, trust them not to let identity thieves drain our accounts. Their massive overhead costs make micropayments impossible.

A generation ago, multi-user time-sharing computer systems had a similar problem. Before strong encryption, users had to rely on password protection to secure their files, placing trust in the system administrator to keep their information private. Privacy could always be overridden by the admin based on his judgment call weighing the principle of privacy against other concerns, or at the behest of his superiors. Then strong encryption became available to the masses, and trust was no longer required. Data could be secured in a way that was physically impossible for others to access, no matter for what reason, no matter how good the excuse, no matter what.

It's time we had the same thing for money. With e-currency based on cryptographic proof, without the need to trust a third party middleman, money can be secure and transactions effortless.

One of the fundamental building blocks for such a system is digital signatures. A digital coin contains the public key of its owner. To transfer it, the owner signs the coin together with the public key of the next owner. Anyone can check the signatures to verify the chain of ownership. It works well to secure ownership, but leaves one big problem unsolved: double-spending.

Any owner could try to re-spend an already spent coin by signing it again to another owner. The usual solution is for a trusted company with a central database to check for double-spending, but that just gets back to the trust model. In its central position, the company can override the users, and the fees needed to support the company make micropayments impractical.

Bitcoin's solution is to use a peer-to-peer network to check for double-spending. In a nutshell, the network works like a distributed timestamp server, stamping the first transaction to spend a coin. It takes advantage of the nature of information being easy to spread but hard to stifle. For details on how it works, see the design paper at http://www.bitcoin.org/bitcoin.pdf

The result is a distributed system with no single point of failure. Users hold the crypto keys to their own money and transact directly with each other, with the help of the P2P network to check for double-spending.

Satoshi Nakamoto
http://www.bitcoin.org

In addition to technical discussions, Nakamoto's writings and the timing of their forum posts suggested personal details such as linguistic tendencies and possible geographic location, indicating that the individual might be of British origin. This speculation arises from the use of British English in their writings and the embedded headline from a UK newspaper in Bitcoin's genesis block. From the inception of Bitcoin until his disappearance in 2011, Nakamoto used emails as a primary mode of communication with other early adopters and developers. His emails were often detailed, discussing technical aspects of Bitcoin's architecture, potential vulnerabilities, and philosophical implications of a decentralized digital currency. These communications were pivotal for guiding the early community of developers, who were instrumental in refining the protocol and expanding its functionalities. I emphasized a few points myself.

EMAIL TO MIKE HEARN (BITCOIN.COM/SATOSHI-ARCHIVE):

From: Satoshi Nakamoto <satoshin@gmx.com>
Date: Sun, Apr 12, 2009 at 10:44 PM
To: Mike Hearn <mike@plan99.net>
Subject: Re: Questions about BitCoin

Hi Mike,

I'm glad to answer any questions you have. If I get time, I ought to write a FAQ to supplement the paper.

There is only one global chain.

The existing Visa credit card network processes about 15 million Internet purchases per day worldwide. Bitcoin can already scale much larger than that with existing hardware for a fraction of the cost. It never really hits a scale ceiling. If you're interested, I can go over the ways it would cope with extreme size.

By Moore's Law, we can expect hardware speed to be 10 times faster in 5 years and 100 times faster in 10. Even if Bitcoin grows at crazy adoption rates, I think computer speeds will stay ahead of the number of transactions.

I don't anticipate that fees will be needed anytime soon, but if it becomes too burdensome to run a node, it is possible to run a node that only processes transactions that include a transaction fee. The owner of the node would decide the minimum fee they'll accept. Right now, such a node would get nothing, because nobody includes a fee, but if enough nodes did that, then users would get faster acceptance if they include a fee, or slower if they don't. The fee the market would settle on should be minimal. If a node requires a higher fee, that node would be passing up all transactions with lower fees. It could do more volume and probably make more money by processing as many paying transactions as it can. The transition is not controlled by some human in charge of the system though, just individuals reacting on their own to market forces.

Eventually, most nodes may be run by specialists with multiple GPU cards. For now, it's nice that anyone with a PC can play without worrying about what video card they have, and hopefully it'll stay that way for a while. More computers are shipping with fairly decent GPUs these days, so maybe later we'll transition to that.

A key aspect of Bitcoin is that the security of the network grows as the size of the network and the amount of value that needs to be protected grows. The down side is that it's vulnerable at the beginning when it's small, although the value that could be stolen should always be smaller than the amount of effort required to steal it. If someone has other motives to prove a point, they'll just be proving a point I already concede.

My choice for the number of coins and distribution schedule was an educated guess. It was a difficult choice, because once the network is going it's locked in and we're stuck with it. I wanted to pick something that would make prices similar to existing currencies, but without knowing the future, that's very hard. I ended up picking something in the middle. If Bitcoin remains a small niche, it'll be worth less per unit than existing currencies. If you imagine it being used for some fraction of world commerce, then there's only going to be 21 million coins for the whole world, so it would be worth much more per unit. Values are 64-bit integers with 8 decimal places, so 1 coin is represented internally as 100000000. There's plenty of granularity if typical prices become small. For example, if 0.001 is worth 1 Euro, then it might be easier to change where the decimal point is displayed, so if you had 1 Bitcoin it's now displayed as 1000, and 0.001 is displayed as 1.

Ripple is interesting in that it's the only other system that does something with trust besides concentrate it into a central server.

Satoshi

Nakamoto's emails to individuals such as Mike Hearn and Gavin Andresen, key figures in the development of Bitcoin, show a methodical and cautious approach to the cryptocurrency's growth. He expressed concerns about scalability and the importance of keeping nodes small enough to be operated by individuals to maintain decentralization. His correspondence also revealed a strategic thinker, aware of the potential regulatory and security challenges that Bitcoin might face.

EMAIL TO WEI DAI (BITCOIN.COM/SATOSHI-ARCHIVE):
From: Satoshi Nakamoto <satoshi@anonymousspeech.com>
Sent: Friday, August 22, 2008 4:38 PM
To: Wei Dai <weidai@ibiblio.org>
Cc: Satoshi Nakamoto <satoshi@anonymousspeech.com>
Subject: Citation of your b-money page

I was very interested to read your b-money page. I'm getting ready to release a paper that expands on your ideas into a complete working system.

Adam Back (hashcash.org) noticed the similarities and pointed me to your site.

I need to find out the year of publication of your b-money page for the citation in my paper. It'll look like:

[1] W. Dai, "b-money," http://www.weidai.com/bmoney.txt, (2006?).

You can download a pre-release draft at

http://www.upload.ae/file/6157/ecash-pdf.html Feel free to forward it to anyone else you think would be interested.

Title: Electronic Cash Without a Trusted Third Party

Abstract: A purely peer-to-peer version of electronic cash would allow online payments to be sent directly from one party to another without the burdens of going through a financial institution. Digital signatures offer part of the solution, but the main benefits are lost if a trusted party is still required to prevent double-spending. We propose a solution to the double-spending problem using a peer-to-peer network. The network timestamps transactions by hashing them into an ongoing chain of hash-based proof-of-work, forming a record that cannot be changed without redoing the proof-of-work. **The longest chain not only serves as proof of the sequence of events witnessed, but proof that it came from the largest pool of CPU power. As long as honest nodes control the most CPU power on the network, they can generate the longest chain and outpace any attackers.** The network itself requires minimal structure. Messages are broadcasted on a best effort basis, and nodes can leave and rejoin the network at will, accepting the longest proof-of-work chain as proof of what happened while they were gone.

Satoshi

One of the most significant batches of Nakamoto's emails was his exchanges with Wei Dai, the creator of b-money, an early proposal for a digital currency system. In these emails, Nakamoto cites Dai's work as an inspiration for Bitcoin, highlighting the collaborative and cumulative nature of technological innovation in the cryptographic community.

Despite the technical focus, Nakamoto's emails occasionally provided glimpses into his motivations and personality. He appeared motivated by a distrust of central banking and governmental control over money, aligning with the ethos of many early cryptocurrency advocates. However, he remained meticulous about concealing his identity, using anonymous email services and never revealing personal details.

From: Satoshi Nakamoto <satoshin@gmx.com>
Date: Sat, Apr 23, 2011 at 3:40 PM
To: Mike Hearn <mike@plan99.net>
Subject: Re: Holding coins in an unspendable state for a rolling time window

>I had a few other things on my mind (as always). One is, are you planning on rejoining the community at some point (eg for code reviews), or is your plan to permanently step back from the limelight?

I've moved on to other things. It's in good hands with Gavin and everyone.

I do hope your BitcoinJ continues to be developed into an alternative client. It gives Java devs something to work on, and it's easier with a simpler foundation that doesn't have to do everything. It'll get critical mass when impatient new users can get started using it while the other one is still downloading the block chain.

After Nakamoto's last email in April 2011, in which he stated that he had "moved on to other things," his direct communication ceased, leaving the stewardship of Bitcoin to others. This mysterious departure only added to the legend of Nakamoto and led to increased speculation about his identity and whereabouts.

Despite the ongoing curiosity and significant impact of their work, Nakamoto's anonymity has persisted, adding to the enigma of Bitcoin's origins. This mystery has not detracted from the cryptocurrency's growth; instead, it has fueled an enduring intrigue and discussion within both the crypto community and the broader public. The identity of Satoshi Nakamoto has become one of the great mysteries of the internet age, underscoring the transformative and yet contentious nature of cryptocurrency.

Timeline of Bitcoin

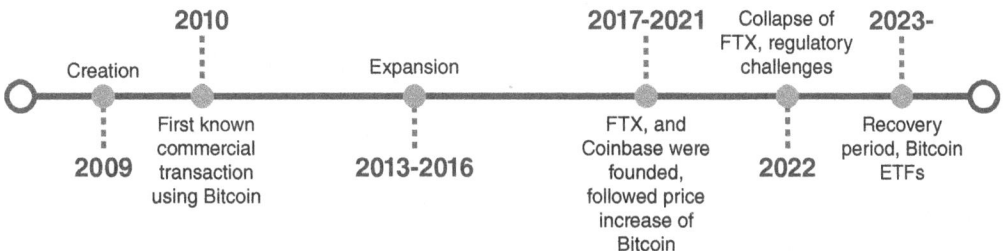

Figure 8   Timeline of Bitcoin

2009: Creation

Figure 8 provides a timeline of the evolution of Bitcoin. The domain name bitcoin.org was registered on August 18, 2008, marking the formal start to what would become the Bitcoin project. Later in the year, on October 31, Nakamoto shared a link to a paper titled "Bitcoin: A Peer-to-Peer Electronic Cash System" on a cryptography mailing list, outlining a method for conducting electronic transactions via a peer-to-peer network without the need for trust. The Bitcoin network itself went live on January 3, 2009, when Nakamoto mined the first block, known as the *genesis block*, which included a reward of 50 Bitcoins and a hidden message referencing a contemporary news headline about bank bailouts, which underscored the motive behind Bitcoin's creation. Shortly thereafter, on January 9, the first open-source Bitcoin client was released on SourceForge. The network's first transaction took place on January 12, 2009, when Nakamoto sent 10 Bitcoins to programmer Hal Finney. Early contributors also included figures like Wei Dai and Nick Szabo, who had developed the concepts of b-money and bit gold, respectively. Nakamoto is estimated to have mined about 1 million Bitcoins before stepping back from direct involvement and handing leadership to developer Gavin Andresen, who became a leading figure at the Bitcoin Foundation, guiding the burgeoning Bitcoin community.

2010–2012: Early Days of Bitcoin

During these years, Bitcoin began to gain public awareness and utility. The notable events started with the famous Bitcoin Pizza Day on May 22, 2010, where Laszlo Hanyecz exchanged 10,000 Bitcoins for two pizzas, marking the first known commercial transaction using Bitcoin. In 2011, Bitcoin's open-source nature led to the emergence of other cryptocurrencies. The Electronic Frontier Foundation, among others, started accepting Bitcoin but temporarily halted due to legal uncertainties, only to resume in 2013. BitPay was founded in 2011, enhancing Bitcoin's commercial viability. By late 2012, companies like WordPress had also begun accepting Bitcoin, signaling growing mainstream acceptance.

2013–2016: Bitcoin's Expansion and Turbulence

This period was marked by significant growth and several major setbacks. In 2013, Bitcoin's price saw unprecedented spikes, at one point reaching more than $1,000, driven by increased investor interest and media coverage. However, it also faced serious challenges, such as the 2014 collapse of Mt. Gox, one of the largest Bitcoin exchanges, which filed for bankruptcy following a massive hack. This event shook the confidence in Bitcoin's security and stability. Despite these setbacks, technological and regulatory developments continued to advance. The network's underlying technology, the blockchain, attracted interest from both financial institutions and governments, seeing it as a potential tool for various applications beyond currency. The years also saw the introduction of regulatory measures and increased oversight, as authorities worldwide began to understand and integrate Bitcoin into existing financial systems.

2017–2021: Mainstream Adoption and Market Volatility

During these years, Bitcoin experienced both explosive growth and significant volatility, highlighting its emergence into mainstream financial awareness. In 2017, Bitcoin's price surged to nearly $20,000 in December, driven by retail and speculative investor interest, before experiencing a sharp decline in the following year. The cryptocurrency market saw increased institutional interest; major financial players and corporations began to acknowledge Bitcoin's potential as an investment and a hedge against inflation. In 2020, the COVID-19 pandemic accelerated digital transformation and interest in digital currencies, with Bitcoin again reaching new highs and surpassing $60,000 in 2021.

In this period, Bitcoin not only saw substantial price increases and corrections but also witnessed significant developments in cryptocurrency exchanges and platforms. Coinbase, one of the largest cryptocurrency exchanges, went public in April 2021 through a direct stock listing, which was seen as a landmark event for the crypto industry, underscoring its acceptance into mainstream finance. The listing boosted confidence in digital currencies, with Coinbase being viewed as a gateway for retail and institutional investors into the crypto world.

Meanwhile, FTX, founded in 2019, rapidly grew to become one of the top cryptocurrency exchanges under the leadership of Sam Bankman-Fried. It was known for introducing innovative trading products and services and played a significant role in integrating cryptocurrencies into traditional finance. However, the landscape was not without challenges. The rise of such platforms also brought regulatory attention and the need for (more) robust legal frameworks to manage the burgeoning crypto market effectively.

2022: Regulatory Challenges and Market Corrections

This year marked significant turbulence for cryptocurrency markets, not least because of the collapse of FTX in late 2022. The downfall of FTX, due to liquidity crises and alleged financial mismanagement, sent shockwaves through the crypto markets, affecting Bitcoin's price and the broader perception of the crypto industry. The event highlighted the critical need for regulatory clarity and better oversight of cryptocurrency operations. Regulatory bodies around the world increased their scrutiny of crypto exchanges, pushing for more stringent compliance with financial regulations to protect investors.

2023: Resilience and Institutional Integration

Despite the setbacks from the previous year, 2023 has shown Bitcoin's and the broader crypto market's resilience. See **Figure 9** for the BTC price dynamics and key market events. The fallout from FTX's collapse has led to calls for improved regulatory frameworks and has increased efforts to establish better standards and protections for cryptocurrency investors.

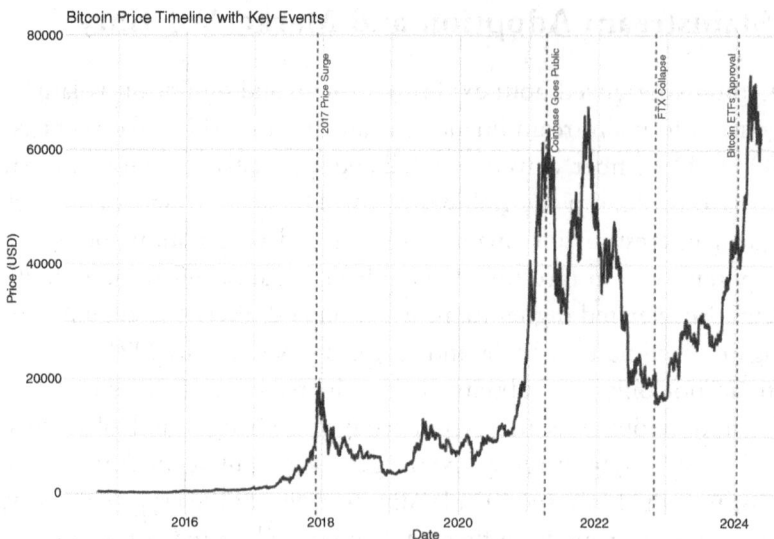

Figure 9   Bitcoin price over time

Institutions continue to cautiously engage with Bitcoin, looking at it as a potential asset class for diversification. The biggest step forward in this direction has been the approval of several BTC exchange-traded funds (ETFs). The U.S. Securities and Exchange Commission (SEC) approved the first Bitcoin ETFs on January 10, 2024. This long-awaited decision marked a significant milestone in the cryptocurrency industry, as it allowed, for the first time, Bitcoin ETFs to be listed and traded on regulated exchanges. It heralds a new era of institutional acceptance and potential widespread adoption.

Why does it matter? For several reasons   Bitcoin ETFs bring substantial *liquidity* to the cryptocurrency market. By offering a structured and regulated investment avenue, these ETFs make it easier for institutional investors and the general public to invest in Bitcoin without the complexities of direct cryptocurrency handling (e.g. wallet management, private keys). This accessibility can lead to increased buying activity and potentially more stable market conditions.

The approval of Bitcoin ETFs by regulatory bodies, like the U.S. SEC, adds a layer of *credibility* to Bitcoin as a legitimate asset class. This regulatory endorsement can alleviate some concerns about the risks associated with cryptocurrency investments, encouraging more conservative investors to consider Bitcoin as part of their investment portfolio.

With the introduction of Bitcoin ETFs, more investors are likely to view Bitcoin as a viable investment, similar to traditional stocks. This could lead to broader *adoption* of Bitcoin and, by extension, other cryptocurrencies as part of diversified investment strategies.

The anticipation and launch of Bitcoin ETFs have historically triggered positive movements in Bitcoin's price. The increased *demand* from new institutional and retail investors entering the market through ETFs can drive up prices. However, there is also a potential for increased volatility, especially if large amounts of Bitcoin are frequently traded through these ETFs.

Overall, the introduction of ETFs is seen as a step toward the *maturation* of the cryptocurrency market. They provide a bridge between traditional financial markets and the cryptocurrency ecosystem, enhancing price discovery and market efficiency. This maturation can help reduce the speculative aspect of cryptocurrency investments, making them more appealing for long-term investment strategies.

Despite the positives, Bitcoin ETFs also face criticism, particularly concerning the potential for market manipulation and the detachment from the original decentralized ethos of cryptocurrencies. Some purists argue that ETFs, by centralizing the ownership of Bitcoin, could undermine the decentralized nature of cryptocurrencies and give disproportionate influence to large institutional players.

Is Bitcoin the digital gold?

This is another very common question when readers start diving into this space.

Bitcoin is often referred to as "digital gold" due to its potential to act as a store of value, similar to gold. This comparison is rooted in several key similarities and differences that make Bitcoin an intriguing alternative to traditional stores of value like gold.

- **Scarcity:** Both Bitcoin and gold are scarce resources. Bitcoin's supply is capped at 21 million coins, which creates a sense of rarity akin to gold's finite availability in the earth's crust, and which contrasts sharply with fiat currencies that can be printed at will by central banks. This limited supply is crucial for their value retention. Gold has been mined for millennia and continues to be extracted, but its annual supply increase is relatively stable and low.
- **Decentralization:** Neither Bitcoin nor gold is controlled by a central authority. Gold's value has been recognized across different cultures and economies for thousands of years without the need for a central regulatory body. Similarly, Bitcoin operates on a decentralized network where no single entity can control it, enhancing its appeal as a global store of value.
- **Store of Value:** Both assets are viewed as a hedge against inflation and economic uncertainty.[2] Investors often turn to gold during times of economic turmoil due to its historical stability. Bitcoin, although more volatile, is increasingly seen as a digital hedge against currency devaluation and inflation, particularly due to its predictable and decreasing supply growth rate.

---

[2] See a recent paper I co-wrote showing that investors do act as if BTC was digital gold by investing more in crypto when inflation increases. Aiello, Darren and R. Baker, Scott and Balyuk, Tetyana and Di Maggio, Marco and Johnson, Mark J. and Kotter, Jason D., Who Invests in Crypto? Wealth, Financial Constraints, and Risk Attitudes (November 18, 2022). Available at SSRN: https://ssrn.com/abstract=4281330.

As Bitcoin matures, its role as a store of value is becoming more pronounced. The 2024 halving event, which reduced the rate at which new Bitcoins are created, lowered Bitcoin's inflation rate to 0.83%, below that of gold. This reduction in supply growth could enhance Bitcoin's appeal as a stable store of value.

However, the narrative that Bitcoin is a "safe haven" asset like gold remains debated. While Bitcoin has shown potential to act as a hedge during economic stress, its high volatility and shorter history compared to gold mean it has not consistently behaved as a traditional safe haven. Empirical data indicates that the correlation between Bitcoin and gold is generally weak, though they may react similarly to certain macroeconomic events.

Ownership and Identity

To complete our discussion of blockchain technology, we need to dive deeper into how it addresses the critical issue of establishing and recording ownership and the identities of participants. Without these elements, trust between parties deteriorates, as there is no assurance that individuals will act as agreed. Moreover, the security of transactions becomes highly compromised. If ownership cannot be accurately verified, the very essence of engaging in transactions becomes futile because there is no reliable way to confirm who is exchanging what with whom. Additionally, without maintaining the integrity of the system, it opens the door to fraudulent activities and data manipulation, undermining the entire system's functionality and purpose. In fact, I would go as far as to say that it would be meaningless to have transactions if ownership cannot be verified and the integrity of the system cannot be maintained.

For example, imagine a scenario where a digital marketplace operates without a secure way to verify ownership or participant identity. A buyer might attempt to purchase a digital artwork, but without a system to prove that the seller legitimately owns the artwork or even confirm the seller's identity, the transaction becomes risky and susceptible to fraud. The buyer has no guarantee that the seller is the rightful owner or that the artwork isn't simultaneously being sold to multiple buyers. In such an environment, the lack of trust and security could lead to widespread disputes and reluctance among users to engage, ultimately causing the marketplace to fail. This scenario underscores why blockchain's ability to provide a secure, transparent record of ownership and identity is so vital.

Think about how traditional finance solves these issues.

Trust and security are managed through a combination of institutional oversight, legal frameworks, and various verification processes. For instance, traditional financial systems rely heavily on identity verification processes known as *know your customer* (KYC). This involves collecting and verifying information about a customer's identity when opening an account or conducting financial transactions. This process ensures that the identity of each party in a transaction is known and verified by the financial institution. Similarly, to ensure the integrity of transaction data, traditional financial institutions utilize centralized databases that are protected by layers of security, including physical security measures, secure communication protocols, and internal access controls. The integrity of data is maintained through control mechanisms and audits. Finally, when disputes arise over whether a party initiated a transaction, institutions refer to signed documents, recorded verbal agreements (e.g. phone recordings), and the trail of transaction paperwork. Legal agreements and contracts provide the binding terms that each party agrees to, and failure to comply can result in legal actions.

In the realm of blockchain technology, public key and private key cryptography, collectively known as *asymmetric cryptography*, plays a crucial role in blockchain technology by addressing several fundamental problems related to digital trust and security.

Digital Identity Verification: In the context of blockchain, each participant, or *node*, is identified by a public key, which acts somewhat like a digital identity. This public key is derived from a private key, which is a secret and unique alphanumeric code known only to the owner. The public key can be shared with anyone, while the private key remains confidential. This setup ensures that any message or transaction signed with a private key can be verified by others using the corresponding public key. This helps in authenticating that a transaction was indeed authorized by the holder of the private key without revealing the private key itself.

Data Integrity: Blockchain transactions need to maintain integrity, meaning that once a transaction is recorded, it should not be alterable by anyone. Public and private keys contribute to this by allowing data (or transactions) to be signed digitally. When a transaction is created, it is signed using the sender's private key. This digital signature is verified by other nodes in the blockchain network using the sender's public key. If the transaction data were altered in any way after it was signed, the digital signature would fail to verify, thus ensuring data integrity.

Non-repudiation: Non-repudiation is a way to guarantee that the sender of a message or transaction cannot deny having sent the message. In blockchain, when a transaction is signed with a sender's private key, it provides a mathematical proof that the transaction was indeed created by the owner of the private key. This feature is crucial for trustless environments like blockchain, where interactions occur without intermediaries.

Secure Communications: The use of public and private keys allows for secure, encrypted communications over the blockchain network. Although blockchain itself is a public ledger, the contents of a transaction, or parts of it, can be encrypted using the recipient's public key. Only the recipient's private key can decrypt such information, ensuring that sensitive data remains confidential between the involved parties.

Authorization and Access Control: In more complex blockchain systems, such as those involving smart contracts or decentralized applications, public and private keys can be used to control access to certain functionalities. For example, a private key can be required to execute specific functions within a smart contract, ensuring that only authorized users can perform those actions.

Let's delve deeper into one key component that makes Bitcoin (and blockchain networks) work as they do: digital signatures.

When a participant initiates a transaction or generates a message on the blockchain, they employ their private key to create a *digital signature*—a cryptographically unique representation of the transaction or message content. This process involves applying a mathematical algorithm to the transaction data, yielding a fixed-size hash value that is then encrypted with the private key.

Upon receipt of a digitally signed message or transaction, other participants in the blockchain network utilize the sender's public key to verify the authenticity and integrity of the data. This verification process involves decrypting the digital signature with the sender's public key to obtain the original hash value. Subsequently, the same hashing algorithm is applied to the transaction data, generating a new hash value. If the two hash values match, it provides cryptographic proof that the data originated from the purported sender and remains unchanged.

One of the primary benefits of digital signatures lies in their ability to confer non-repudiation, rendering it infeasible for the sender to deny authorship of the message or transaction. Furthermore, digital signatures ensure the integrity of the data by detecting any unauthorized modifications or tampering attempts during transmission. Even minor alterations to the data would result in a completely different hash value, thereby thwarting any fraudulent activity.

Let's use an example to really understand how this works beyond the curtains.

Alice's Message: "Send 1 BTC to Bob."

Hashing the Message: Alice calculates a hash of the message (using SHA-256), which outputs a hash code. Suppose the SHA-256 hash of this input is a8f5f167f44f4964e6c998dee827110c.

Signing the Hash: Alice uses her private key to sign this hash. Technically, this involves using the private key to transform the hash into a signature through a cryptographic algorithm (like RSA or ECDSA).[3] This transformation is unique to the private key. Suppose the signature generated is 5a686d7da8b555b602c3cbe9e84c3023.

The Signature: This result, the digital signature, travels with the message. It is unique to both the message and the private key.

When Bob (or any other participant in the blockchain) receives the message and the signature, the following happens:

Hash the Message Again: Bob hashes the received message to get a hash value. Since the transaction content hasn't changed (i.e. "Send 1 BTC to Bob."), hashing it again will yield the same hash: a8f5f167f44f4964e6c998dee827110c.

---

[3] RSA (Rivest–Shamir–Adleman) is one of the first public-key cryptosystems and is widely used for secure data transmission. Named after its inventors Ron Rivest, Adi Shamir, and Leonard Adleman, it was publicly described in 1977. Elliptic Curve Digital Signature Algorithm (ECDSA) is a variant of the Digital Signature Algorithm (DSA) which uses elliptic curve cryptography. As a newer approach, ECDSA offers similar levels of security to RSA but can achieve this with much shorter keys. This makes ECDSA more efficient in terms of processing speed and power consumption.

Verify the Signature: Bob uses Alice's public key to check the signature. The signature received is 5a686d7da8b555b602c3cbe9e84c3023. Bob uses Alice's public key to verify the signature against the hash. If Alice's public key confirms that this signature corresponds to the hash a8f5f167f44f4964e6c998dee827110c, the verification is successful.

This verifies that the message hasn't been changed after Alice signed it and that Alice, who holds the private key associated with the public key, is indeed the sender.

Digital signatures might seem like just another element of modern cryptography, but they are truly revolutionary in enabling something many might have thought impossible: creating a system where transactions and communications are secure without any central authority and without needing to trust your counterparty directly. This cryptographic innovation underpins the foundational technology of blockchain, allowing it to function as a transparent, decentralized network where trust is built into the system rather than relying on traditional institutions. The profound impact of digital signatures extends beyond securing information; they enable a new paradigm of digital trust and collaborative exchange that once might have seemed merely visionary.

4. Isn't It Too Slow and Clunky to Be Used for Payments? Enter the Lighting Network

As Bitcoin's popularity grew, it became apparent that its original blockchain infrastructure faced significant scalability challenges, particularly in terms of transaction throughput. Originally, the Bitcoin network could handle only about seven transactions per second (TPS). In comparison, traditional payment systems like Visa can process more than 24,000 TPS. This stark difference poses a substantial barrier to Bitcoin's potential as a daily transactional currency.

The limitations stem primarily from the size and frequency of blocks in Bitcoin's blockchain. Each block is 1MB in size and is added approximately every 10 minutes. This constraint not only limits the number of transactions that can be processed per block but also leads to increased transaction fees and longer confirmation times during periods of high demand. For instance, during the 2017 Bitcoin boom, users experienced delays that lasted hours and even days, along with transaction fees that surged to $50 for a single transaction.

These issues highlight a critical need for solutions that can scale Bitcoin's infrastructure. The Lightning Network emerges as a promising layer-2 protocol designed to address these throughput challenges by enabling off-chain transactions that are both fast and cost-effective. By allowing users to transact multiple times without committing all transactions to the Bitcoin blockchain immediately, the Lightning Network aims to drastically increase transaction capacity, reduce costs, and achieve near-instantaneous payments.

The Lightning Network acts as a supplementary protocol layer to Bitcoin, aiming to enhance its scalability and transaction efficiency. It achieves this by facilitating transactions that do not directly engage the main Bitcoin blockchain, a concept known as *off-chain* transactions. These transactions occur away from the primary blockchain, which reduces congestion and results in quicker, less costly transactions. **Figure 10** provides a representation of the Lightning Network and the payment channels.

At the heart of the Lightning Network is the concept of *payment channels*. These channels are established between two parties who want to conduct multiple transactions. To initiate a payment channel, both parties deposit a specified amount of Bitcoin into a joint account on the blockchain, a setup known as a *multisig* (multi-signature) wallet. This initial transaction is recorded on the Bitcoin blockchain.

Once this payment channel is open, the two parties can execute unlimited transactions among themselves. These transactions are instantaneous and generally free because they occur off the main blockchain. Instead of recording each transaction on the blockchain, the parties simply update a private balance sheet that reflects how much Bitcoin each party holds after each transaction. This balance sheet functions as a digital ledger, and it is secured by the signatures of both parties, ensuring that only they can authorize changes.

The channel remains open until the parties decide to close it. Closing the channel involves updating the Bitcoin blockchain with the final state of their transactions. Therefore, only two transactions are recorded on the blockchain for any number of transfers between the parties—the opening and the closing of the channel.

Beyond facilitating transactions between two parties, the Lightning Network supports a broader network of such payment channels. If you need to transact with someone

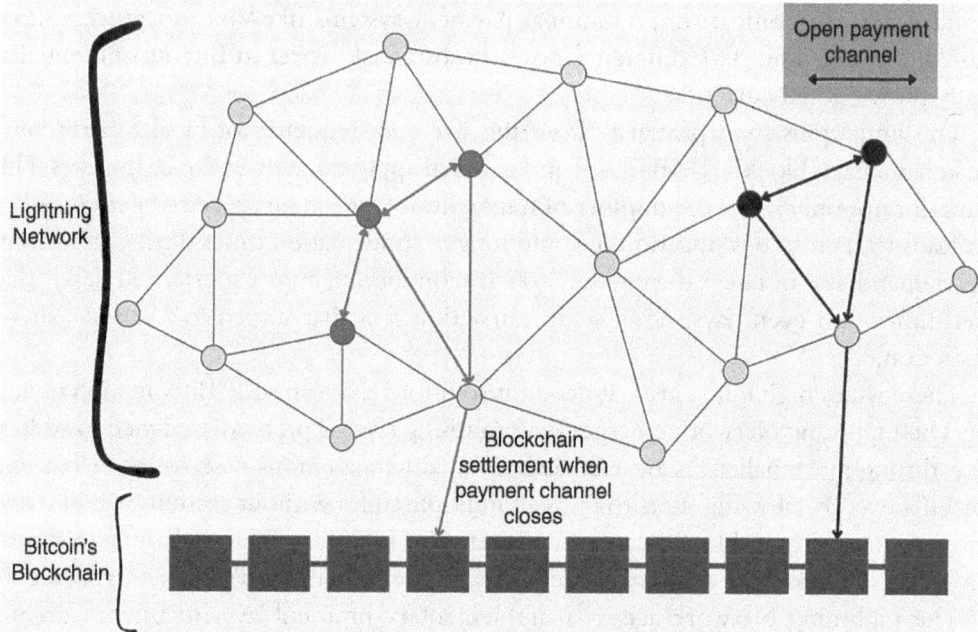

Figure 10 Lightning Network

but do not have a direct payment channel with them, the network identifies the shortest path through this mesh of channels. This process might involve "routing nodes," which help connect various channels across the network. These nodes can relay transactions across different channels to reach the intended recipient. Routing nodes might charge a nominal fee for this service, helping to sustain the network's infrastructure.

Thus, the Lightning Network provides a scalable, efficient layer on top of the Bitcoin blockchain, enabling faster transactions and reducing the workload on the main blockchain by confining most transaction details to off-chain channels.

Let me give you an example of how this works.

Imagine that Carol and Dave frequently transact with each other and want to avoid the delays and fees associated with recording every single transaction on the Bitcoin blockchain. To achieve this, they open a payment channel by each depositing 2 BTC, making a total of 4 BTC available in the channel. This initial transaction is recorded on the blockchain to establish the channel.

Whenever Carol wants to send 1 BTC to Dave, they don't broadcast this transaction to the blockchain. Instead, they update the balance of the payment channel: Carol's balance decreases to 1 BTC, and Dave's balance increases to 3 BTC. Both parties sign this updated balance to acknowledge the transaction.

This process can be repeated for multiple transactions. Suppose Carol sends another 0.5 BTC to Dave. They update the balance again: Carol now has 0.5 BTC, and Dave has 3.5 BTC. These transactions occur instantly and with negligible fees since they don't involve the blockchain each time.

The real benefit of the Lightning Network emerges with its ability to connect multiple channels. Imagine Carol also wants to pay Ellen, but they don't have a direct channel. However, Dave has a channel open with Ellen. Carol can route the payment through Dave: she sends 1 BTC to Dave, who then sends 1 BTC to Ellen using his channel. This way, Carol successfully pays Ellen without needing a direct channel.

These interconnected payment channels form a network that enables rapid, low-fee transactions across many users. Each transaction is secure and trustless because it uses cryptographic techniques to ensure that funds can only be transferred as intended by the users.

At any time, Carol or Dave can close their payment channel. The final balances (e.g. Carol with 0.5 BTC and Dave with 3.5 BTC) are recorded on the Bitcoin blockchain, ensuring that the net result of all off-chain transactions is securely settled.

This method drastically reduces the number of transactions that need to be recorded on the main blockchain, speeding up the transaction process and reducing costs, while still maintaining the security and integrity of the Bitcoin network.[4]

In summary, the Lightning Network represents a significant advancement in enabling faster, cheaper, and more frequent transactions for Bitcoin. **Figure 11** captures its key advantages and limitations. By handling transactions off the main blockchain and settling them later, it offers a practical solution to some of Bitcoin's scalability challenges.

---

[4] Additional details are available at https://www.lightspark.com/developers/primer.

Advantages	Limitations
Microtransactions The Lightning Network makes microtransactions viable due to low or non-existent fees, something not practical on the main Bitcoin blockchain due to higher transaction costs.	**Limited Capacity** Each channel has a limited capacity, determined by the amount of Bitcoin initially committed to the channel.
Speed Transactions are almost instantaneous, which is a significant improvement over the often slower transaction times on the Bitcoin blockchain.	**Online Requirement** Participants need to be online to conduct transactions, which can be a limitation compared to the main Bitcoin blockchain.
Scalability It significantly increases Bitcoin's transaction capacity, helping to alleviate the scalability issues faced by the Bitcoin network.	**Still Developing** While promising, the Lightning Network is still a work in progress, and its adoption and infrastructure are still developing.

Figure 11   Advantages and key limitations of the Lightning Network

Every chapter will showcase a business case study about a real protocol or company as a real example of the topics discussed in the chapter. I have picked this case about Lemonade, because in an era where blockchain technology is often synonymous with cryptocurrencies and financial speculation, the Lemonade Crypto Climate Coalition (LCCC) stands out as a shining example of how this technology can be harnessed for profound societal impact. From now on, when you hear that blockchain is a solution looking for a problem, you should cite this as one of the many problems it solves!

Real Case Study: "Lemonade Crypto Climate Coalition: Navigating Innovation and Sustainability in Agricultural Insurance"[5]

LCCC's initiative moves beyond the realm of digital currencies to address a pressing global challenge: the vulnerability of smallholder farmers to the caprices of climate change. This pioneering project illustrates the potential of blockchain to

---

[5] For more details about this case and additional teaching materials, see the Harvard Business School case I wrote available at https://hbsp.harvard.edu/product/224058-PDF-ENG?Ntt=marco%20di%20maggio&itemFinding Method=search.

create significant, tangible benefits in sectors traditionally disconnected from the high-tech world of digital assets.

At the heart of LCCC's mission is the utilization of blockchain to reimagine agricultural insurance. By employing blockchain to provide decentralized, efficient, and transparent insurance solutions, LCCC is demonstrating how the technology can be applied to critical real-world problems—offering stability and support to some of the world's most at-risk populations. This approach not only challenges the prevailing narrative around blockchain but also illuminates its capacity to foster sustainability and resilience in global food systems.

As we delve into the workings and achievements of the Lemonade Crypto Climate Coalition, it becomes clear that blockchain's true value lies in its ability to effect meaningful change, far beyond the confines of financial markets. This discussion aims to explore how LCCC leverages blockchain to protect livelihoods, enhance agricultural practices, and secure economic stability for smallholder farmers, setting a precedent for future tech-driven humanitarian efforts.

In an era increasingly defined by the challenges of climate change, agriculture faces unprecedented threats that jeopardize global food security. Against this backdrop, the LCCC emerges as a potentially transformative force, harnessing blockchain technology to provide innovative insurance solutions for smallholder farmers, who are among the most vulnerable to climate unpredictability. Led by visionary leader Roy Confino, LCCC is pioneering an approach that integrates the resilience of blockchain with the pressing needs of agriculture.

The global agricultural landscape, especially in developing regions, is under significant stress due to erratic weather patterns and limited access to modern farming techniques and financial resources. These challenges are exacerbated for smallholder farmers who manage minimal plots but are responsible for a substantial portion of the world's agricultural output. Traditional insurance models, with their high costs and complex claims processes, have largely failed these farmers, leaving them disastrously unprotected against crop failures caused by climate irregularities.

Enter blockchain technology. With its capacity for transparency, security, and immutability, blockchain is ideally suited to address the inefficiencies of traditional insurance models. Through smart contracts, blockchain can automate insurance payouts based on specific triggers, such as certain weather conditions, thereby reducing administrative costs and ensuring timely support for farmers. Moreover, blockchain's decentralized nature facilitates direct engagement between farmers and insurers, enhancing trust and ensuring that solutions are finely tuned to farmers' unique needs.

Roy Confino's leadership is pivotal in steering LCCC toward a sustainable business model that is not solely dependent on donations but is self-sufficient, continuing to serve smallholder farmers effectively. His approach is not merely about implementing advanced technology but also about re-envisioning how social enterprises can operate sustainably while generating profound social impact. Confino's strategy involves creating a balance between innovation and practicality, ensuring the technological solutions are accessible and directly beneficial to the farmers.

Confino envisions LCCC not just as a provider of temporary relief but as a beacon of enduring change that fundamentally alters how agricultural risks are managed. This initiative aims to empower farmers, transforming them from victims of climate change to participants in a system that mitigates risks and enhances agricultural sustainability. The success of LCCC could serve as a blueprint for global strategies, potentially revolutionizing agricultural insurance and ensuring that smallholder farmers around the world have the resources to weather the storms of a changing climate.

How does it work? At the core of LCCC's model is the integration of smart contracts, which are programmed to automatically execute insurance payouts based on specific conditions such as weather anomalies indicative of drought or excessive rainfall. This approach not only removes the need for intermediaries, significantly reducing administrative costs, but also guarantees swift and reliable compensation for farmers suffering from crop losses. Moreover, the blockchain backbone ensures that each transaction is securely recorded on an immutable ledger, enhancing transparency and building trust among all parties involved.

Recognizing the necessity for user-friendliness, especially given that many of the target beneficiaries are not technologically sophisticated, LCCC has developed a simple interface that allows farmers to easily register and manage their insurance policies through commonly used mobile devices. This practical application ensures that the benefits of blockchain technology are accessible to those who need them most.

Under Confino's guidance, LCCC also places a strong emphasis on forming strategic partnerships with various local and international bodies. These collaborations are crucial for adapting to the complex regulatory environments of different countries, understanding specific local agricultural challenges, and building trust among the local farming communities. By working closely with nongovernmental organizations (NGOs), government entities, and agricultural specialists, LCCC ensures its solutions are precisely tailored to meet the distinct needs of each region it serves.

Yet, achieving financial sustainability remains a challenge for LCCC. Striving to move beyond dependency on donations and grants, the coalition is exploring various revenue-generating strategies such as offering tiered insurance products, monetizing the aggregated data for analytical insights, or forming partnerships with agricultural stakeholders who could benefit from the risk assessments facilitated by the LCCC platform.

Despite facing significant challenges, the LCCC achieved considerable success in its formative years, enrolling thousands of farmers across various countries. This initiative provided these farmers with vital insurance coverage against crop failures, fundamentally changing their relationship with climate unpredictability (see **Figure 12** for a picture of these farmers). Previously at the mercy of environmental fluctuations, these farmers now had a safety net that not only safeguarded their livelihoods but also empowered them to enhance their agricultural investments.

The broader implications of LCCC's initiatives were substantial, extending well beyond the individual farmers. By stabilizing the incomes of smallholder farmers, LCCC contributed to the economic resilience of entire rural communities. This stabilization had cascading benefits for local food security and broader economic development, highlighting the transformative potential of blockchain in sectors critical to human survival.

Strategic decisions were central to the success of LCCC, guided adeptly by Roy Confino. A crucial early decision involved selecting technology partners who not only possessed the necessary technical expertise but also shared LCCC's commitment to social impact. Partners like DAOstack, Chainlink, Etherisc, Avalanche, and Pula were instrumental, each contributing distinct capabilities from decentralized governance to reliable blockchain infrastructure, which collectively strengthened the foundation of LCCC's operations.

Figure 12   Cocoa farmers drying their crop in sub-Saharan Africa Roy Confino

Choosing the right regions for pilot projects was another strategic layer. Confino and his team selected these areas based on various factors, including the severity of climate risks, the prevalence of smallholder farming, and the availability of reliable data. These regions provided essential initial insights that shaped the scaling and refinement of LCCC's model.

Navigating regulatory landscapes posed additional complexities, as each country presented unique regulatory frameworks governing insurance and blockchain technologies. Confino's approach involved a careful balance between compliance and maintaining the efficiency and affordability of LCCC's offerings, necessitating continuous dialogue with regulatory bodies and ongoing adjustments to the coalition's processes and technology. This adaptive strategy ensured that LCCC not only met local regulations but also remained effective and accessible to the farmers it aimed to support.

The success of the LCCC serves as a compelling blueprint for other sectors seeking to harness the power of blockchain technology beyond the conventional confines of cryptocurrency. This initiative vividly demonstrates how blockchain can be strategically applied to solve complex, global issues, such as enhancing agricultural resilience against climate change. The principles of transparency, efficiency, and direct stakeholder engagement that underpin LCCC's model have broad applicability, offering valuable lessons for industries ranging from healthcare to supply chain management.

By adopting similar approaches, industries can leverage blockchain to not only streamline operations but also to address societal challenges through enhanced accountability and improved access to essential services. The scalable nature of LCCC's model showcases the potential for blockchain applications to be customized and expanded across different contexts and regions, potentially transforming how businesses and social enterprises operate. As industries continue to explore the diverse applications of blockchain, the work of LCCC stands as a testament to the technology's potential to drive significant social and economic change, setting a standard for future innovations.

5. Energy Consumption

One of the most debated issue about Bitcoin is its energy consumption and how PoW makes it extremely inefficient and costly.

Bitcoin's energy consumption is substantial, with estimates varying due to different methodologies but consistently showing high usage. For instance, in 2023, global electricity usage attributed to Bitcoin mining ranged from 67 TWh to 240 TWh, with a point estimate of 120 TWh, which approximates the total electricity consumption of countries like Greece or Australia. This represents about 0.2% to 0.9% of global electricity demand.[6]

Furthermore, Bitcoin mining energy use doubled as cryptocurrency prices rose, illustrating a direct relationship between the value of Bitcoin and its energy consumption. This rise in energy usage is linked with increased mining profitability, which incentivizes more intensive mining operations.[7]

Despite the high energy costs, Bitcoin mining generates significant economic value, approximately $13 billion annually worldwide, highlighting its importance as a growing industry. This economic activity not only supports technological innovation but also provides substantial revenue that can be reinvested into various sectors, including renewable energy.

Furthermore, a significant portion of Bitcoin's energy consumption comes from renewable sources. Reports suggest that a large fraction of the energy mix used in Bitcoin mining comprises sustainable sources, with estimates suggesting around 40% to 56% of Bitcoin mining energy being derived from non-fossil fuel sources. This is comparable to the global use of nuclear power and renewable energy for electricity.[8]

Finally, Bitcoin mining has been leveraged as a means to improve the viability of renewable energy projects. For example, in areas like West Texas, Bitcoin mining operations can absorb excess renewable energy production, which might otherwise go to waste due to mismatched supply and demand scenarios. This ability to act as an "energy off-taker" helps stabilize the grid and supports the financial health of renewable projects.[9]

The environmental impact of Bitcoin is a complex issue that involves high energy consumption, which can be concerning. However, the increasing integration of renewable energy sources and the economic incentives provided by mining can play a role in advancing energy sustainability. What I would like you to keep in mind is that the industry is evolving and is trying to find solutions to limitations such as the environmental impact of Bitcoin in ways that most people might overlook.

---

[6] The Cambridge Bitcoin Electricity Consumption Index provided estimates of Bitcoin-related electricity demand, indicating a significant range of energy use attributed to Bitcoin mining activities globally and specifically in the United States. This included a detailed discussion on the challenges of estimating and tracking this energy use due to the dynamic nature of cryptocurrency mining operations (U.S. Energy Information Administration: https://www.eia.gov/).

[7] Bitcoin mining's significant economic impact globally and specifically in the United States was highlighted with revenue figures amounting to approximately $13 billion annually worldwide, showcasing the substantial economic value generated through these mining activities (buybitcoinworldwide.com).

[8] A report from Bitstamp indicated that a considerable portion of the energy used in Bitcoin mining comes from renewable sources, comparing favorably with global averages of renewable energy use and helping to mitigate some of the potential negative environmental impacts associated with high energy consumption (Bitstamp.net and https://forkast.news/bitcoin-minings-green-mile-54-5-sustainable-energy-use/).

[9] See the discussion about the integration of Bitcoin mining with renewable energy projects, particularly how it can stabilize grids and financially support renewable energy sources (https://www.forbes.com/sites/digital-assets/2023/10/18/bitcoin-mining-catalyzes-growth-in-renewable-energy-and-infrastructure/)

6. Concluding Remarks

As we conclude this exploration into the realms of blockchain and Bitcoin, ideally it has become clear that the technology is foundational to the burgeoning digital economy. For the technical reader, the intricacies of blockchain's cryptographic safeguards, consensus mechanisms, and the decentralized ethos offer a blueprint for building secure, transparent, and resilient systems. Non-technical readers should appreciate understanding how blockchain facilitates trustless interactions, potentially transforming sectors beyond finance.

Bitcoin, as the first application of blockchain technology, demonstrated that digital currencies could function without central authorities. However, it's also important to acknowledge its limitations—scalability, volatility, and environmental impact. Scalability concerns have been addressed by newer blockchain technologies like Ethereum with its transition to proof of stake in Ethereum 2.0, which also aims to reduce the massive energy consumption associated with proof-of-work systems. Layer-2 solutions such as Lightning Network for Bitcoin and rollups for Ethereum further enhance transaction throughput and efficiency. These are all developments that we will explore in detail in the next chapters.

What I want to ensure comes across is that if you think that BTC or even blockchain is not perfect, you are right, but you should not underestimate the amount of collective work that has been done and is still ongoing that aims to improve it.

As blockchain technology continues to evolve, it faces ongoing challenges such as regulatory scrutiny, the need for technical scalability, and the quest for broader adoption. However, its potential to decentralize power, enhance transparency, and secure data integrity remains undiminished. Future avenues for blockchain technology will likely focus on enhancing user friendliness, integrating with traditional financial systems, and pioneering innovative applications that extend beyond cryptocurrencies.

In sum, blockchain and Bitcoin not only redefine our understanding of money but also challenge our approach to problems requiring trust and transparency. Their ongoing evolution will likely continue to inspire both incremental improvements and revolutionary changes across various domains.

Coding Exercises

Creating Blockchain on Python

In this script we are implementing a proof-of-work consensus to form our own blockchain.

We define the Block class and the Transaction class to represent transactions. And, the calculate_hash function takes a Block object as an argument.

The proof_of_work function first takes the last block and a list of transactions as inputs and then tries to find a suitable nonce (a number used once) that, when used to create a new block, results in a hash that meets a specific condition (e.g. starting with four zeros, as per if new_block.hash[:4] == "0000"). This is the core of the proof-of-work mechanism. It continuously increments the nonce and recalculates the hash until the condition is met. Once the correct nonce is found, the new block is returned, effectively adding it to the blockchain.

The is_valid_transaction checks whether a transaction is valid with a simplified validation mechanism where it checks only if the transaction amount is positive (transaction.amount > 0).

```python
import hashlib
import time

class Block:
    def __init__(self, index, previous_hash, timestamp, transactions,
hash, nonce):
        self.index = index
        self.previous_hash = previous_hash
        self.timestamp = timestamp
        self.transactions = transactions
        self.hash = hash
        self.nonce = nonce

class Transaction:
    def __init__(self, sender, receiver, amount):
        self.sender = sender
        self.receiver = receiver
        self.amount = amount

def calculate_hash(block):
    value = str(block.index) + str(block.previous_hash) + str(block
.timestamp) + str(block.transactions) + str(block.nonce)
    return hashlib.sha256(value.encode('utf-8')).hexdigest()

def create_genesis_block():
    transactions = [Transaction("genesis", "genesis", 0)]
    return Block(0, "0", int(time.time()), transactions, calculate_
hash(Block(0, "0", int(time.time()), transactions, 0, 0)), 0)
```

```python
def proof_of_work(previous_block, transactions):
    nonce = 0
    while True:
        new_block = Block(previous_block.index + 1,
                          previous_block.hash,
                          int(time.time()),
                          transactions,
                          calculate_hash(Block(previous_block.index + 1,
previous_block.hash, int(time.time()), transactions, previous_block
.hash, nonce)),
                          nonce)
        if new_block.hash[:4] == "0000":  # Adjust the number of leading
zeros for different difficulty
            return new_block
        nonce += 1


def is_valid_transaction(transaction):
    # Simplified validation: amount should be positive
    return transaction.amount > 0

# Create blockchain and add genesis block
blockchain = [create_genesis_block()]
previous_block = blockchain[0]

# Dummy transactions
transactions = [Transaction("Alice", "Bob", 50), Transaction("Bob",
"Charlie", 25)]

# Add blocks to the chain
for i in range(10):
    if all([is_valid_transaction(tx) for tx in transactions]):
        new_block = proof_of_work(previous_block, transactions)
        blockchain.append(new_block)
        previous_block = new_block
        print(f"Block #{new_block.index} has been added to the
blockchain!")
        print(f"Hash: {new_block.hash}\n")
    else:
        print("Invalid transactions")
```

End-of-Chapter Questions

Multiple-Choice Questions

1. **What cryptographic concept was critical to the early development of blockchain and was used for securing digital timestamps?**
   (A) Digital signatures
   (B) Hash functions
   (C) Encryption algorithms
   (D) Merkle trees

2. **Who proposed the proof-of-work system to combat email spam, which later influenced Bitcoin's mining process?**
   (A) Satoshi Nakamoto
   (B) Adam Back
   (C) Wei Dai
   (D) Nick Szabo

3. **What does the block header in a blockchain include?**
   (A) Only the hash of the previous block
   (B) A list of new transactions
   (C) Timestamp, nonce, and the hash of the previous block
   (D) The digital signatures of the participating nodes

4. **Which data structure used in blockchain helps to efficiently verify the integrity of large datasets?**
   (A) Encrypted hash chains
   (B) Distributed ledgers
   (C) Merkle trees
   (D) Peer-to-peer networks

5. **In blockchain, what mechanism ensures that nodes agree on the current state of the ledger?**
   (A) Proof of stake
   (B) Proof of authority
   (C) Proof of work
   (D) Proof of consensus

6. **What is the primary purpose of mining in a blockchain that uses proof of work?**
   (A) To secure the network and process transactions
   (B) To release new cryptocurrencies into the system
   (C) To create new blocks for storing data
   (D) All of the above

7. **Which early digital cash system directly influenced Satoshi Nakamoto's development of Bitcoin?**
   (A) Hashcash
   (B) b-money
   (C) DigiCash
   (D) E-Gold

8. **What is a node in the context of blockchain technology?**
   (A) A transaction with encryption
   (B) A user's digital wallet
   (C) A communication point in the network
   (D) A device that maintains a copy of the ledger and processes transactions

9. **Which feature of hash functions makes them suitable for blockchain transactions?**
   (A) Reversibility
   (B) Non-deterministic outputs
   (C) Fixed output size
   (D) Adjustable complexity

10. **How does proof of work contribute to blockchain security?**
    (A) By ensuring all transactions are reversible
    (B) By allowing instant transaction verification
    (C) By requiring computational work to validate transactions and blocks
    (D) By encrypting all the transactions

11. **What significant problem does blockchain solve compared to traditional banking systems?**
    (A) Transaction speed
    (B) Inflation control
    (C) Double-spending
    (D) Identity theft

12. **In what scenario would a blockchain fork occur?**
    (A) When two blocks are mined at the same time
    (B) When a transaction is rejected
    (C) When new regulations are applied to the blockchain
    (D) When there is an upgrade to the blockchain software

13. **What potential risk is associated with blockchain that uses proof-of-work consensus?**
    (A) 51% attacks
    (B) Phishing attacks
    (C) Data corruption
    (D) Software bugs

14. **How are transactions selected to be included in a block by miners?**
    (A) Based on the age of the wallet
    (B) Random selection
    (C) Transaction size and associated fees
    (D) Alphabetical order of the transaction data

Open Questions

- Explain the role of Merkle trees in the context of blockchain and why they are crucial for its efficient operation.
- Discuss the evolution of digital cash systems leading up to Bitcoin and how these systems influenced the design of Bitcoin.
- Describe the process of mining and how it contributes to the security and stability of a blockchain network.
- Discuss the implications of blockchain technology in non-financial sectors and give examples of potential applications.
- Discuss the ethical implications of blockchain technology. How does the decentralization of financial and data transactions impact privacy and security concerns?

Chapter 2

Ethereum

The "Windows" to the Blockchain Universe—Now Loading Smart Contracts and Oracle Magic

Preface

Ethereum and Bitcoin are like the A-list celebrities of the crypto world. Bitcoin is the OG, the granddaddy of all cryptocurrencies. It's like that classic rock band that paved the way for everyone else. It's a bit old-school, sticking to its roots, which is basically a fancy way of saying it doesn't do much more than just sit there and be valuable. Bitcoin is like the strong, silent type at a party—doesn't talk much, just stands in the corner looking cool, and gets asked to take a selfie with everyone.

Ethereum, on the other hand, is the life of the party. It's the guy who's got all the gadgets, can juggle, do card tricks, and somehow knows everyone's name. Ethereum took the blockchain concept and said, "What if we put a whole app store on this thing?" It's not just about digital gold; it's about smart contracts, decentralized applications (dApps), and a whole lot of other things that Bitcoin never signed up for. So, if Bitcoin is the *Mona Lisa*, Ethereum is like the Louvre—a place where you find everything from ancient sculptures to modern art.

Ethereum is always evolving, like a software update that actually works. Ethereum's move from proof of work (PoW) to proof of stake (PoS) is like trading in a diesel-powered monster truck for a Tesla: still plenty of power but now with less noise and

57

environmental impact. It's about as dramatic as moving from a bustling bazaar where everyone is shouting to a high-tech boardroom where validators sit quietly, sipping their stake-flavored lattes, keeping the network running like clockwork.

But don't let the switch from PoW to PoS fool you into thinking this is all calm waters and smooth sailing. Oh no, Ethereum's new playground is more like a high-stakes poker game, where validators ante up their tokens, hoping the blockchain dealer deals them a winning hand. If you mess up, though, it's not just a bad beat—it's slashing. You know when the network takes a chunk out of your staked tokens for bad behavior. It's like blockchain's version of a dunk tank, where you get soaked for not playing by the rules. Ethereum PoS is like a club where the entry fee is pretty steep, but once you're in, you have a say in the club's rules. You get to vote on proposals, earn block rewards, and maybe even tell your friends you're an Ethereum validator (which, let's face it, sounds pretty cool).

Ethereum brought smart contracts to the table for the first time. Now, when you hear "smart contracts," don't think about a bunch of lawyers sitting around a boardroom in suits, sipping expensive coffee. Nope, smart contracts are digital contracts written in code. They're like that friend who never forgets your birthday, always shows up on time, and won't let you forget you owe him 10 bucks for that pizza last week. You give a smart contract some instructions—like, "Hey, transfer 10 Ethereum to my buddy if he sends me this digital art"—and it does it, no questions asked.

Here's where it gets interesting, though. These smart contracts need information from the real world, like whether it rained in Seattle or if GameStop stock went up or down. But here's the thing: smart contracts live in their little blockchain bubble. They don't have the latest weather report or stock prices. That's where oracles come in. And no, not like the Oracle from *The Matrix*. These oracles are data providers that bring

Staking and slushing

real-world information into the blockchain. It's like having that one friend who's always on Twitter, Instagram, and TikTok at the same time, knowing everything that's happening. But let's get real for a second: oracles are like the weakest link in this whole setup. If an oracle starts giving fake data, your smart contract could go haywire. It's like if your GPS suddenly told you to take a left turn off a bridge. Not good, right? That's why it's crucial to have reliable oracles, usually with a decentralized structure, to ensure they don't lead your blockchain into a fiery crash.

So, you've got these smart contracts doing their digital thing and oracles bringing in the real-world scoop. The whole point? Automate things so you don't need some guy in a suit with a briefcase making decisions. In this way, Ethereum becomes like the Swiss Army knife of the crypto world: whatever you need, Ethereum has got a tool for it.

In the end, smart contracts and oracles are revolutionizing the way we think about contracts and data verification. No middlemen, no room for shenanigans—just code and data. But remember, just because it's smart doesn't mean it can't mess up, so keep an eye on your oracles and make sure your smart contracts don't start throwing tantrums. Because when they do, it's a whole new level of chaos.

1. Introduction

Historical Background

Ethereum was conceived as a revolutionary step forward in blockchain technology by Vitalik Buterin, who first detailed his vision in a white paper released in 2013. In this document, Buterin described a platform that would go beyond the primarily financial applications offered by Bitcoin, introducing a new blockchain framework designed to support dApps through a more versatile scripting language. Ethereum's proposed innovation was its ability to execute smart contracts—self-automated computer programs that operate without human intervention once conditions are predefined.

The concept quickly gained traction within the cryptocurrency community. To bring Ethereum to life, Buterin and other cofounders launched a crowdfunding campaign in 2014, which became one of the earliest and most successful initial coin offerings (ICOs). Investors were offered Ether, the native cryptocurrency of Ethereum, in exchange for Bitcoin, raising more than $18 million and setting the stage for Ethereum's development and future launch.

The Ethereum network officially went live on July 30, 2015, with its initial release called Frontier. This launch marked the beginning of an open-source, decentralized platform that enabled developers around the world to create and deploy smart contracts and decentralized applications. The programming language Solidity was introduced alongside the platform, specifically designed for developing smart contracts that run on the Ethereum Virtual Machine (EVM), an abstract layer running on top of the actual hardware.

Today, Ethereum remains a central figure in the blockchain space, not just as a cryptocurrency but as a foundational platform for a wide range of applications across different sectors. This flexibility and capability have cemented its position as a leading blockchain for innovation and development.

Ethereum was not the brainchild of a single individual but rather a group of vision-ary developers and entrepreneurs who came together to realize Vitalik Buterin's initial concept. While Buterin is often the most prominently associated with Ethereum due to his role in conceptualizing and advocating for the platform, several key figures played crucial roles in its early development. The group of cofounders includes Gavin Wood, who wrote the Ethereum Yellow Paper that specified the EVM, the runtime environ-ment for smart contracts. Wood's contributions were fundamental in translating Buterin's ideas into a technical blueprint that could be implemented.

Other notable cofounders include Anthony Di Iorio, who provided much of the initial funding for Ethereum; Charles Hoskinson, who played a significant role in estab-lishing the project's structure and business strategy before moving on to found Cardano; and Joseph Lubin, who is particularly significant due to his role in founding ConsenSys. ConsenSys is a blockchain software technology company based in Brooklyn, New York, founded in early 2015, just as Ethereum was about to be launched. It was established to focus on developing decentralized software services and applications that operate on the Ethereum blockchain.

ConsenSys has been instrumental in the wider adoption and development of Ethereum's infrastructure. It acts as both a venture studio and an incubator for decentral-ized applications, and it has played a significant part in funding and supporting various projects built on Ethereum. Lubin's vision with ConsenSys was to create a hub that would promote and support the development of a decentralized internet, often referred to as Web 3.0. By fostering various startups, ConsenSys has helped to expand the Ethereum ecosystem, making it more accessible and useful for a broader audience.

ConsenSys has developed several key products and platforms that have become inte-gral to the Ethereum landscape, including MetaMask, a popular Ethereum wallet and gateway to blockchain apps, and Infura, a service providing scalable access to Ethereum and IPFS networks. These tools have lowered the entry barriers for developers looking to build and deploy smart contracts and dApps on Ethereum.

2. Ethereum 1.0: Key Concepts

Improving on Bitcoin   Vitalik Buterin's conceptualization of the ledger of Bitcoin as a state-transition system is central to understanding its architecture.

In this system, shown in **Figure 1**, transactions modify the state of the system, which consists of all unspent transaction outputs (UTXOs). Each UTXO has a denomination and an owner, identified by a cryptographic public key. Transactions are formed by inputs (which reference UTXOs and provide a cryptographic signature proving ownership) and outputs (which establish new UTXOs).

The state transition function, APPLY(S,TX) -> S' or ERROR, updates the state by validating each transaction based on several criteria: the existence of the UTXO, the legitimacy of the signature, and the conservation of value across inputs and outputs.

State : ownership status of all existing BTC; accounts & BTC balances

Transaction : made of inputs (unspent BTC, sending address, signature) and outputs (receiving address, amount)

State	
Account	**Balance**
A	0
B	2
C	0
D	1
E	0

Transaction		
Spend		**Signature**
B	2	353456552151..
D	1	d0ad4e237f2b..
Add		
A	0	
C	2	

State'	
Account	**Balance**
A	2
B	0
C	2
D	0
E	0

Figure 1   Bitcoin as a state transition system

If these conditions are met, the transaction is applied, removing input UTXOs and adding new output UTXOs to the state.

As we discussed in the previous chapter, mining integrates this transaction system with a decentralized consensus mechanism essential for a secure and unified agreement on the state of the ledger. This process involves assembling transactions into blocks, which are linked through cryptographic hashes to form the blockchain. A valid block must reference a valid previous block, contain a valid proof of work, and successfully apply all included transactions to transition from the state at the end of the previous block to a new state. The proof-of-work mechanism, which involves solving a computationally intensive problem to validate blocks, ensures security and prevents fraudulent rewriting of the blockchain. Miners are incentivized through block rewards and transaction fees, both expressed in newly created or differential amounts of bitcoin.

Bitcoin's scripting system, often referred to as Bitcoin Script, is a stack-based execution language used to process and validate transactions on the Bitcoin network. It operates by processing commands in a last-in–first-out (LIFO) sequence, which is typical of stack-based languages. This means the last element added to the stack is the first one to be processed, allowing the script to execute commands as they are popped off the top of the stack.

The design of Bitcoin Script is intentionally restrictive, which is advantageous for a number of reasons. First, the lack of Turing completeness (the ability to perform arbitrary computations through features like loops) prevents scripts from executing indefinitely. However, the absence of loops and complex logic operations means that Bitcoin Script cannot support applications that require internal state management or more sophisticated transaction types beyond simple transfers and multisignature setups. For example, contracts that conditionally execute transactions based on external states or the outcome of previous transactions are not possible within the Bitcoin Script framework.

Bitcoin Scripting Example: Multisignature Wallet   Bitcoin's scripting language, known as Script, is designed with simplicity and security in mind. The primary role of Script is to validate transactions based on specific conditions, such as multisignature requirements or time-locked releases, rather than to support complex application development.

The absence of Turing-completeness in Script ensures that all script executions can be completed in a predictable amount of time, which is crucial for maintaining the stability and security of the Bitcoin network. By limiting the operations that can be performed, Bitcoin reduces the potential for security vulnerabilities, focusing solely on the conditions under which coins can be spent.

Here's a basic example of a Bitcoin script that creates a two-of-three multisignature wallet. This wallet requires two out of three designated people to sign a transaction before it can be executed.

OP_2 <pubkey1> <pubkey2> <pubkey3> OP_3 OP_CHECKMULTISIG

Explanation:

- **OP_2** and **OP_3:** These are opcode constants indicating that two out of three public keys are required to validate the transaction.
- **<pubkey1> <pubkey2> <pubkey3>:** These placeholders represent the public keys of the parties authorized to sign the transactions.
- **OP_CHECKMULTISIG:** This opcode checks that the signatures corresponding to the provided public keys are valid.

Ethereum   Ethereum allowed the simple "Transaction" on the blockchain ledger to be able to handle complex data packages, where they can include executable code and a wide array of possible inputs and outputs. This flexibility allowed for the creation of sophisticated decentralized applications that can manage complex operations, from automatic escrow releases to supply chain management, and even decentralized autonomous organizations (DAOs), executed on the blockchain.

In Ethereum, every application state is comprised of *accounts*, each identified by a unique 20-byte address. Accounts are divided into two types: externally owned accounts, controlled by private keys, and contract accounts, governed by their contract code. Each account includes four elements: a nonce to ensure each transaction is processed only once; the account's current ether balance; any contract code (if the account is a contract account); and storage, which is initially empty.

Ether, the principal internal crypto-fuel of Ethereum, not only facilitates the execution of these decentralized applications but also compensates transaction fees. Externally owned accounts can initiate transactions through creating and signing transactions. Conversely, contract accounts activate their embedded code upon receiving a message, which allows them to execute operations, send messages, and create contracts.

Transactions in Ethereum are signed data packages that specify a message from an externally owned account, encapsulating several details: the recipient's address, a signature identifying the sender, the amount of ether to be transferred, and optional additional data. These transactions are governed by a STARTGAS value, which limits the computational steps they can take, and a GASPRICE, which determines the fee per computational step. This model is critical in preventing denial-of-service attacks by ensuring that each operation has a cost proportionate to its resource consumption.

Furthermore, contracts can send "messages"—similar to transactions but generated internally by a contract. These messages can influence other contracts, thereby enabling intricate, contract-to-contract interactions within the Ethereum ecosystem.

The state transition function in Ethereum, APPLY(S,TX) -> S', therefore is slightly more complex than Bitcoin: it checks the transaction's form and signature, calculates the transaction fee, deducts this fee from the sender's account, and transitions the ether balance as specified. If a transaction triggers contract execution, the contract code runs until it is completed or the gas runs out, which may result in reverting the state changes except for the fee payment. Successful transactions update the state and refund any unused gas to the sender. **Figure 2** shows the state, transaction, and the new state on Ethereum.

3. Ethereum 2.0

Ethereum 2.0 marked a transformative upgrade from its original architecture, designed to enhance scalability, efficiency, and sustainability. Early Ethereum described in the previous section operated on a PoW system, which, while securing the network, led to significant energy consumption and limited transactions per second. Ethereum 2.0 transitions to a PoS mechanism, which will be described in the upcoming section. This transition had a pivotal role for the future of Ethereum.

The Beacon Chain

The Beacon Chain was launched in December 2020 and marked the first phase of the transition to PoS. It introduced the PoS consensus mechanism to Ethereum, but initially,

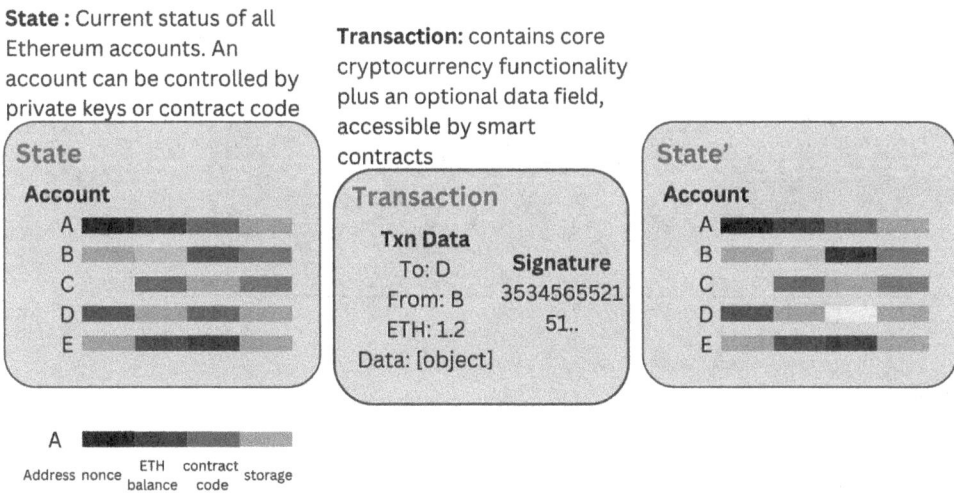

Figure 2   Ethereum as a state transition system

it operated separately from the main Ethereum chain, which continued to use PoW. Validators on the Beacon Chain are responsible for processing transactions and proposing and attesting to new blocks. Think of the Beacon Chain as Ethereum's high-tech lighthouse, guiding the way forward without yet handling the general traffic of transactions and smart contracts. It's the overseer of the PoS system, managing validators, keeping tabs on their stakes, and ensuring that everyone plays by the rules. In this new era, validators replace miners; instead of solving cryptographic puzzles, they are chosen to propose and validate blocks based on the amount of Ether they're willing to lock up as a stake.

The final phase of the transition, known as "the Merge," saw the existing Ethereum chain merge with the Beacon Chain, effectively ending Ethereum's reliance on PoW, shown in **Figure 3**. Post-Merge, the combined chain continues as a PoS blockchain. This transition reduced Ethereum's energy consumption by more than 99%, a significant milestone given the network's substantial carbon footprint under PoW, as **Figure 4** depicts.

The Merge: When Two Become One

The transition from Ethereum 1.0 to 2.0, which occurred on September 15, 2022, saw two worlds converge—one old and battle-worn (the current Ethereum mainnet) and the other young and promising (the Beacon Chain). Scheduled meticulously, this wasn't just a flick of a switch but a carefully orchestrated process where the entire state of Ethereum, including its history and all its worldly possessions (your precious ETH and dApps), migrated onto a shiny new PoS system. This transition marks the moment when the Beacon Chain became the main engine of the network, and PoW is retired.

Post-Merge, Ethereum aims to be faster, leaner, and greener. Performance improvements mean transactions that once trundled along like a horse-drawn cart can now zip

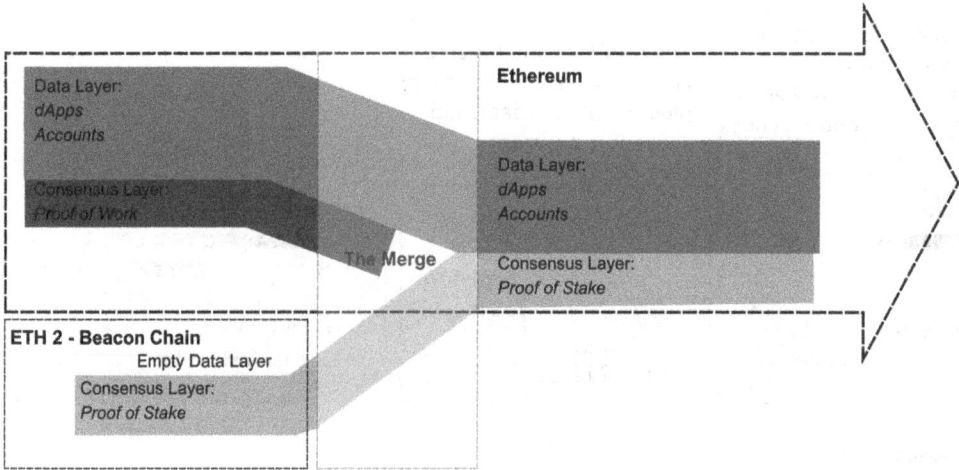

Figure 3   The Merge

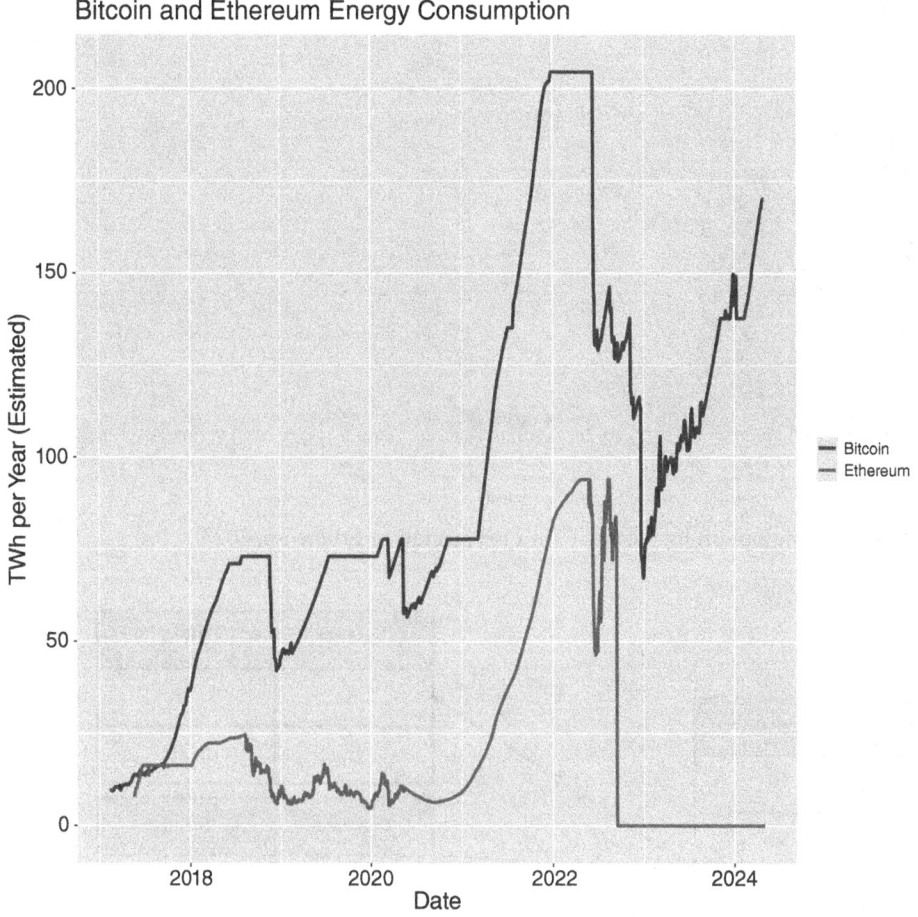

Figure 4   Bitcoin and Ethereum energy consumption over time (Adapted from Digiconomist, 2024)

around like sports cars—only without the gas emissions. Ethereum's new PoS protocol is not just about being environmentally friendly; it's about accommodating more transactions, reducing fees, and doing it all without handing over power to an elite few—a balancing act that would give a trapeze artist sweaty palms. **Figure 5** shows the annualized energy consumption values of different activities in comparison with Ethereum PoS, which is dramatically smaller than the others.

By drastically reducing its carbon footprint, Ethereum 2.0 seeks to silence critics who've long decried blockchain's environmental impact, aligning itself with a world that's increasingly conscious of sustainability. **Figure 6** compares energy consumption by some popular activities, showing that Ethereum post-merge consumes less than Netflix. Moreover, with increased transaction throughput, Ethereum is eyeing a future where it can support a global scale of decentralized applications—imagine everything from finance to gaming to social media running in a decentralized manner on Ethereum.

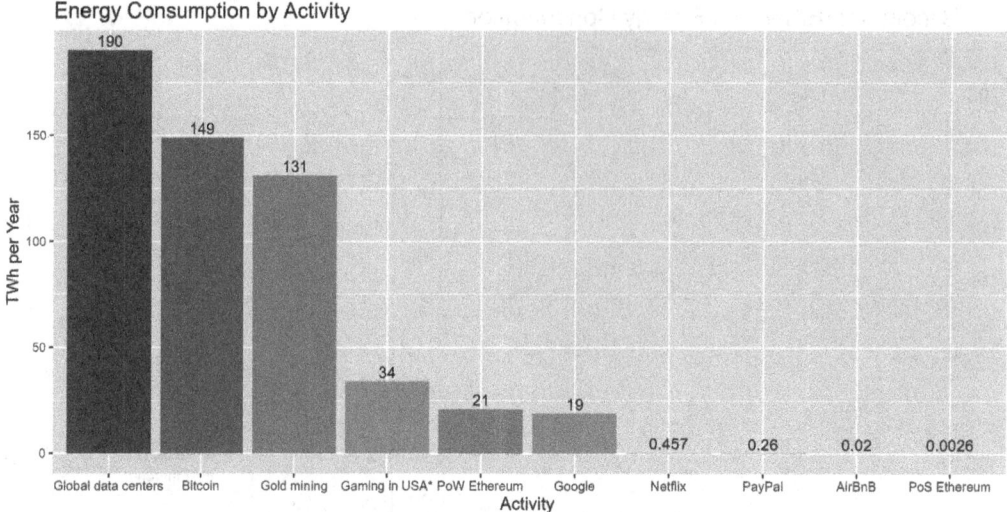

Figure 5   Energy consumption by activity (With permission of Ethereum, 2023)

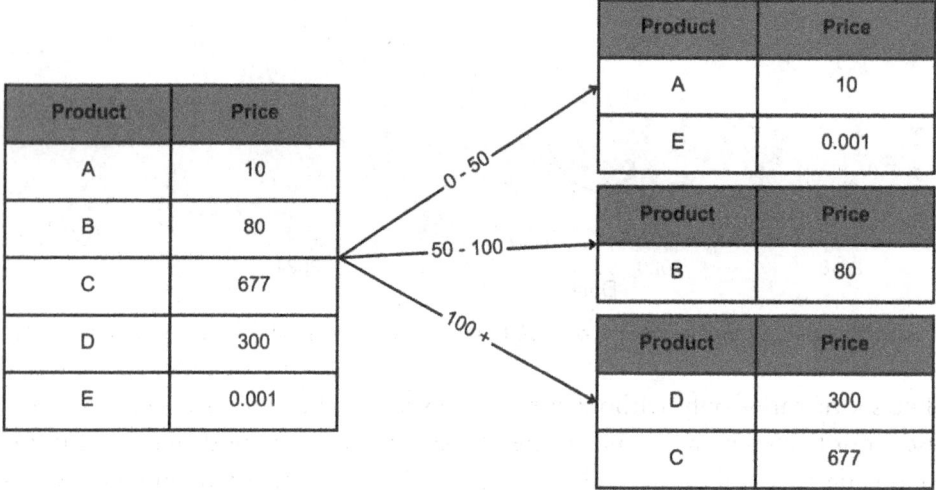

Figure 6   Basic example of sharding data

Sharding

Another one of the core components of Ethereum 2.0 is **sharding**, which plays a crucial role in addressing the scalability issues faced by the Ethereum network.

Sharding is a database partitioning technique adapted for blockchain technology to dramatically increase the efficiency of resource usage and transaction processing. In the context of Ethereum 2.0, sharding involves dividing the state and history of Ethereum's entire network into smaller, manageable pieces known as *shards*.

How Sharding Works

1. **Division of Data:** In Ethereum 2.0, the entire network is split into multiple shards. Each shard contains its own independent state and transaction history, which means that nodes need only process transactions for their specific shard rather than the entire network. In **Figure 6**, we show a simplified example of this process. This division reduces the workload on individual nodes and allows the network to process many transactions in parallel, significantly increasing throughput.

2. **Random Assignment of Validators:** Validators are randomly assigned to each shard. This randomization ensures security and prevents malicious actors from targeting specific shards. Validators are responsible for processing transactions, creating new blocks, and ensuring the integrity and security of their assigned shard.

3. **Crosslinking for Interoperability:** Shards regularly communicate with the main Ethereum blockchain, now referred to as the Beacon Chain, through a process known as *crosslinking*. Crosslinks are references to shard blocks (snapshots of their state) and serve as checkpoints that get logged on the Beacon Chain's Coordination Layer, as shown in **Figure 7**. This mechanism ensures that the state of each shard is coherent and that the shards remain part of a unified Ethereum network.

There are several benefits of sharding. By enabling multiple shards to process transactions simultaneously, Ethereum can handle significantly more operations than would be possible on a single-chain architecture. This parallel processing capability is akin to opening up additional lanes on a highway, reducing traffic congestion dramatically.

With sharding, individual nodes bear less burden as they no longer need to process the entire network's transaction load. Nodes can operate with lower computational and storage requirements, making network participation more accessible to individuals with

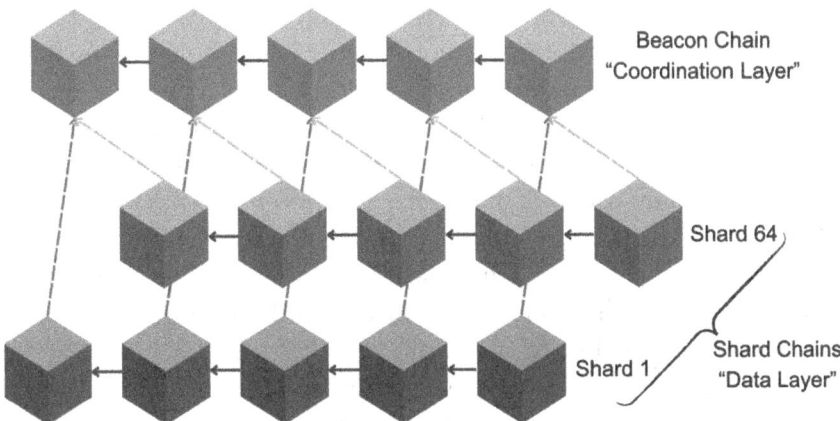

Figure 7   Shard chains on Ethereum

less powerful hardware. Sharding also improve throughput without sacrificing decentralization or security. It allows Ethereum to scale effectively as more users join the network and demand for decentralized applications grows.

Some additional challenges emerge due to Sharding though. Sharding introduces concerns about data availability and the integrity of cross-shard transactions. Ensuring that all data remains available and that transactions between shards are securely and reliably processed requires complex coordination and consensus mechanisms. Developing a secure, decentralized, and efficient sharding solution is technically challenging. The Ethereum development community has invested significant effort in research, testing, and community consensus to implement sharding correctly. Think about the Ethereum's community as a massive open-source flash mob, where everyone shows up to code instead of dance. There's a risk that certain shards may become isolated or more vulnerable to attacks, particularly if they end up processing a higher proportion of high-value transactions. Balancing the load and security of shards remains a critical area of focus.

Consensus Algorithm: Proof of Stake

In proof of work, we used computational power to make the system secure, by ensuring that the miner selected was selected at random and that miners could not control the process. What if we could accomplish this better without all that work? What if we could make it such that supporting the network and its operations is more economically rewarding than malicious activity? We could use *economic* incentives.

Proof of stake, unlike its computational heavyweight counterpart proof of work, doesn't require miners to solve complex puzzles using the brute force of expensive hardware that guzzles electricity like a sports car does premium fuel. Instead, PoS operates on a principle akin to a high-stakes raffle where the size of your ticket (the amount of cryptocurrency you hold and are willing to "stake" as collateral) increases your chances of being chosen to validate transactions and create new blocks. This method not only cuts down on the energy bill—making it Mother Nature's favorite—but also speeds up transaction validation processes without turning your computing rig into a room heater.

Let's look at an example. For a given block, three users stake tokens for the right to validate. User A stakes 10 tokens, user B stakes 20 tokens, and user C stakes 70 tokens. The system determines randomly which of the users will perform validation. User A has a 10% chance of being selected (10 tokens out of a total of 100 staked), user B has a 20% chance, and user C has a 70% chance. Once the validation is completed, the user chosen will receive a small amount of tokens as a fee. But if that user is later found to have validated a block fraudulently, they will lose their entire stake. While user C is more likely to be selected, they also have the most to lose if they commit fraud.

In PoS, the validators are like the responsible adults who are chosen based on how much they have invested in the network, figuratively and literally. This creates a system where the more you invest, the more you're incentivized to maintain the network's integrity—essentially turning economic stake into a form of security deposit.

The concept of PoS was a response to the growing outcry over the sustainability of PoW. Introduced by developers Scott Nadal and Sunny King in 2012 with Peercoin, the first cryptocurrency based on this concept, PoS was designed as an energy-efficient alternative to PoW. Peercoin, while not as famous as its big brother Bitcoin, served as the proving ground for PoS.

Over the years, as PoS matured, it began to be seen not just as an energy-efficient alternative but to address some of the inherent inefficiencies and centralization issues posed by PoW. With PoW, as seen in the Bitcoin network, the rise of mining pools had started to hint at a game rigged in favor of those who could afford massive computational power, turning the democratic dream of cryptocurrency into something a tad more oligarchic.

This narrative set the stage for Ethereum's ambitious move toward PoS with Ethereum 2.0, where the network left its gas-guzzling days behind to embrace a greener, faster future. It's akin to switching from an old steam engine to an electric bullet train, where the new track promises a smoother, quicker, and more environmentally friendly ride through the decentralized landscape.

In sum, PoS is not just a technical specification; it's a philosophical pivot toward more sustainable and equitable blockchain technologies. It's the community betting big on the power of staking over mining, hoping to hit a jackpot that pays off in scalability, security, and sustainability—all without putting the planet on the line.

Staking: The High Roller's Game

In the world of PoS, validators put up their own crypto as collateral, effectively saying, "Trust me, I have skin in the game." This act of staking is akin to a security deposit on an upscale apartment. Just as you wouldn't trash a place when you know your money is on the line, validators are motivated to act honestly because they stand to lose their stake if they don't. Think of it as a poker game where playing dirty can cost you your chips.

Consensus Mechanism: The Art of Blockchain Politics

If blockchain were a government, validators in a PoS system would be its senators, elected not by popular vote but by the weight of their stakes. These validators have the critical job of proposing and voting on the next block in the chain. It's a roundtable where each participant's voting power is proportional to their stake. The more you stake, the bigger your voice. It's democracy meets plutocracy in the digital realm, where consensus isn't just about agreement but about weighted influence, steering the blockchain away from potential forks in the road and toward continuity and integrity.

Rewards and Penalties: The Carrot and the Stick

In this high-stakes environment, validators are rewarded for their vigilance and participation. Like diligent bees in a hive, their efforts to maintain the blockchain's integrity are sweetened by rewards, typically in the form of transaction fees or newly minted tokens. It's a financial pat on the back for keeping the network robust and transparent.

However, where there's potential for reward, there's also risk of penalty. This is where the stick comes in—a mechanism known as *slashing*. Should a validator decide to take a digital nap and miss their turn at proposing a block or, worse, attempt to deceive the network, their staked coins can be slashed. It's the network's way of saying, "Play by the rules or pay the price." This slashing mechanism is crucial; it's the watchful parent ensuring that no one runs amok in the playground, preserving the network's security and reliability.

The Ghost of Inaction: Nothing at Stake Problem

Then there's the ghostly tale of the "Nothing at Stake" problem, a unique challenge in the PoS world where validators might find it tempting to endorse multiple blockchain histories, thereby preventing consensus because, unlike in PoW, creating multiple blocks costs them nothing extra. Why settle for one version of the truth when you can bet on all outcomes without additional cost? This scenario can lead to various forms of blockchain mischief and malfeasance, undermining the very trust and consistency the blockchain is supposed to ensure. Various PoS systems have come up with different solutions to combat this phantom—by introducing penalty mechanisms, where validators face a real risk of losing their stake for dishonesty, thus attaching a tangible cost to deception.

The Battleground of Network Security

Unlike PoW, where security is underpinned by the sheer computational power needed to dominate the network, PoS faces different battle conditions. For the security of PoS systems, the position and influence of validators—and their stakes—are critical. However, these systems are not without their Achilles' heel. They could potentially be more vulnerable to certain types of attacks, such as the long-range attack, where an attacker tries to rewrite a blockchain's history from a point far back in time, or the bribery attack, where validators are directly influenced to act maliciously.[1]

---

[1] A long-range attack happens when an attacker attempts to rewrite a blockchain's history starting from a point far back in time. This is feasible under certain conditions in PoS systems because, unlike proof of work, which requires substantial computational effort to rewrite historical blocks, a PoS system can potentially be compromised if an attacker gains control of a large number of old, inactive, or no longer used private keys that once had significant staking weight. The attack involves the following steps:

1. **Acquiring Old Keys:** The attacker gathers old private keys that had staking rights at some past time. These keys might be acquired from users who have exited the network and no longer need them.
2. **Forking the Chain:** Using these keys, the attacker starts a fork of the blockchain from a historical point where these keys were active.
3. **Building the Alternative Chain:** Since PoS validation can be less resource-intensive than PoW, the attacker can potentially build an alternative chain in secrecy that may outpace the current legitimate chain if the cumulative stake is significant.

Each type of attack vector in PoS requires a nuanced defense strategy. Networks bolster their defenses through combinations of technological safeguards, economic incentives, and community-driven governance models, aiming to shield their ecosystems from both internal and external threats.

Economic Incentives

We have seen that the idea behind PoS is that those with a more significant investment in the network are more likely to act honestly. Let's analyze how staking actually works in reality.

The actual staking process varies between different cryptocurrencies and may involve participating in a staking pool—a collective of token holders combining their assets to increase their chances of being chosen as validators. Staking pools, which are collaborative efforts where multiple stakeholders combine their cryptocurrency holdings to increase their chances of being chosen as validators, present a democratized approach to participation in the blockchain validation process.

For instance, **Lido,** one of the largest staking services, allows Ethereum holders to stake their ETH without needing to meet the full 32 ETH required to become a full validator. By pooling smaller amounts of ETH from multiple users, Lido can form a collective stake that meets the validator threshold, enabling all participants in the pool to share in the rewards proportional to their contribution. This not only lowers the entry barrier for individual investors but also enhances the security of the network by decentralizing the validation process further.

Another example is **Stakefish,** a decentralized staking provider that supports multiple cryptocurrencies. By offering a platform where users can contribute varying amounts of crypto assets into a collective pool, Stakefish provides a streamlined avenue for earning staking rewards without the need for each participant to operate their own validating node. This service is particularly appealing in networks where the technical or financial barriers to individual validation are high.

The advantages of using staking pools include increased chances of being chosen to validate blocks, resulting in more consistent rewards compared to solo staking efforts. Additionally, staking pools can offer more predictable returns and reduced risk of loss due to slashing, where penalties are imposed for malicious actions or failures by validators.

---

4. **Presenting the Alternative Chain:** Once the attacker's chain is longer, they can present it to the network. New nodes or nodes that have been offline for a long period might accept this longer chain as the valid one due to its length, thus rewriting the blockchain's history.

The severity of a long-range attack is mitigated by several factors:

- **Checkpointing:** Some networks implement checkpoints at which the blockchain's state is "locked in," and history before the checkpoint cannot be altered.
- **Key Activation Requirements:** Networks might require keys to show recent activity to participate in consensus, thus neutralizing old, inactive keys.
- **Social Consensus:** If an attack becomes evident, the community can come together to reject the attacker's chain, even if it technically has a higher stake.

However, a potential drawback of PoS is the risk of validator centralization through staking pools. Small stakeholders might pool their resources to increase their chances of being selected as validators. While this can democratize the validation process to some extent, it also introduces new risks, such as the potential for staking pool operators to become central points of failure or control within the network. Stake grinding is a potential security risk in some PoS systems. It refers to the manipulation of the blockchain by validators to increase their chances of being chosen to create new blocks and earn rewards. This manipulation is possible in some PoS designs where the future block validators can be predicted based on the current state of the blockchain. Knowing when they might be chosen next, these validators can then engage in behaviors like "stake grinding," where they attempt to influence the selection process. This might involve splitting their stake into multiple smaller stakes across different addresses, transacting in a specific way, or restructuring their holdings in a manner that increases their probability of being chosen.

Unintended Consequences: The Aristocracy of Cryptocurrency

PoS is not without its potential drawbacks, some of which have been the subject of much debate within the cryptocurrency community.

One of the most frequently cited concerns is the "rich get richer" dynamic that PoS can foster. Since the probability of being chosen to validate transactions and create new blocks in a PoS system is often proportional to the size of one's stake, those with larger holdings have a higher chance of being selected. This means the wealthiest stakeholders are likely to receive more transaction fees and block rewards, allowing them to increase their holdings and influence over the network further. This concentration of wealth and power could lead to a form of plutocracy, where only a few large stakeholders effectively control the network. It contrasts with the ideal of a decentralized system where power is distributed among many participants rather than concentrated in the hands of a few.

This potential issue is not just theoretical. In practice, smaller stakeholders may find it increasingly difficult to compete with larger, more established ones, who can leverage their substantial resources to maintain and grow their influence. Over time, this could lead to an ossification of the network's power structure, making it more resistant to change and possibly less secure. If a small group of validators were to collude, they could potentially exert undue influence over the network's governance and the direction of its development.

Another related concern is the **barrier to entry** for new validators. While PoS eliminates the need for energy-intensive mining rigs, it introduces the requirement for significant up-front capital to acquire enough tokens to participate meaningfully as a validator (e.g. 32 ETH). This financial barrier could deter small-scale participants and further entrench the positions of wealthier validators.

Ethereum's PoS model attempts to mitigate these issues through several mechanisms. For example, that's another reason for using *sharding* as it distributes the validation process across multiple smaller chains, which could lower the barrier to entry for validators and ensure a more equitable distribution of rewards.

PoS VULNERABILITIES

Proof-of-stake systems, while offering energy efficiency and scalability advantages over proof-of-work systems, introduce specific security vulnerabilities or attack vectors. Here are some key attack vectors with technical explanations and examples where applicable:

- **Long-Range Attacks:** As previously discussed, this involves rewriting a blockchain's history using old keys. Prevention includes techniques such as checkpointing and requiring key activation.
- **Nothing-at-Stake Problem:** In a situation where a blockchain forks, validators might be tempted to vote for multiple branches since doing so doesn't cost them anything (unlike in proof of work, where mining on multiple forks is cost-prohibitive). This can lead to security issues, such as double-spending. Solutions include penalizing behaviors that support multiple forks simultaneously (known as *slashing*).
- **Stake Grinding Attack:** In early PoS versions, attackers could influence their chances of being chosen to create a new block by "grinding" through numerous potential blockchain inputs until they found one that would select them as the validator. This has been largely mitigated by newer PoS algorithms that use randomization techniques less susceptible to manipulation.
- **Bribery Attacks:** An attacker may bribe validators to act maliciously, such as voting for a particular fork or participating in double-spending. Smart contracts on platforms like Ethereum have made such bribery more feasible by automating payments based on certain conditions being met.
- **Validator Centralization:** If a few validators hold a significant amount of the total stake, the system risks becoming centralized, similar to the concerns around mining pools in proof-of-work systems. This centralization can make the network more vulnerable to collusion and targeted attacks. An example of concerns around this issue surfaced with EOS, where allegations of vote-buying and central control by a few large stakeholders highlighted potential security risks.
- **Denial-of-Service (DoS) Attacks:** Validators in PoS systems are known entities (as opposed to anonymous miners in PoW). This can make them targets for DoS attacks, attempting to delay or block their ability to propose blocks or vote on consensus decisions.

Examples of Actual Incidents:

- **Ethereum Classic 51% Attack:** Although Ethereum Classic uses a PoW mechanism, similar principles apply to PoS in terms of consensus vulnerabilities. In January 2019, Ethereum Classic suffered several deep chain reorganizations due to a 51% attack, attributed to rented hash power,[2] demonstrating the potential for such scale attacks in PoS if validators collude or gain disproportionate control.
- **Steem Blockchain Takeover:** In 2020, the Steem blockchain was taken over by a group of exchanges and the Steemit team, led by Justin Sun, which used their large holdings to vote in new delegates, effectively centralizing control. While this was a governance attack more than a typical network security issue, it showed how large stakes could be used to influence network direction in PoS systems.

These incidents and vulnerabilities highlight the importance of careful design in consensus mechanisms and governance structures within PoS blockchains to prevent both technical and economic attacks.

Ethereum Improvement Proposals (EIPs)

As a dynamic and continuously evolving platform, Ethereum faces the challenge of integrating new technologies, standards, and functionalities while maintaining a decentralized governance structure. To manage this complexity, the Ethereum community relies on a structured mechanism known as Ethereum Improvement Proposals. These proposals are a pivotal aspect of Ethereum's ecosystem, allowing it to adapt, upgrade, and resolve issues systematically.

EIPs are documents that provide a standardized format for proposing changes and improvements to the Ethereum platform. They are a critical tool for the ongoing development of Ethereum, ensuring that all changes are thoroughly vetted and agreed upon by the community before implementation. This process is not just about technical updates but also encompasses the philosophical ethos of Ethereum, promoting open participation, transparency, and community consensus.

The importance of EIPs lies in their ability to facilitate the democratic involvement of all stakeholders in the Ethereum community—from core developers to individual users. Through EIPs, Ethereum can address the needs and concerns of its diverse user base, implement security enhancements, and integrate innovative technologies that keep it at the forefront of the blockchain sector.

Let's look at EIPs in more details. First, EIPs serve several critical functions within the Ethereum community.

---

[2] NiceHash is one of the most popular platforms for renting hash power. Users can rent hash power from miners all over the world and direct it to the mining pool of their choice. The platform offers a marketplace where users can bid for hash power, providing a competitive environment that can lead to more favorable rental rates.

- **Standardization:** EIPs help standardize features and processes so that developers and projects can adopt new functionalities knowing they align with the broader Ethereum ecosystem's standards and practices.
- **Innovation and Updates:** EIPs enable continuous innovation and improvements on the Ethereum blockchain by allowing anyone in the community to propose changes or enhancements.
- **Transparency and Openness:** The EIP process is open to anyone and is conducted transparently, typically through the Ethereum GitHub repository and associated discussions. This openness ensures that various stakeholders in the community can review, comment on, and contribute to the proposed changes or new features.

EIPs are categorized into three types, each serving a specific purpose.

- **Standard Track EIPs:** These involve changes that affect most or all Ethereum implementations, such as consensus algorithms (changes requiring a fork), changes to the network protocols, or any change that affects the interoperability between Ethereum applications built on top of the protocol. Examples include EIP-1559, which changed the transaction fee market, and EIP-20, the standard for fungible tokens known as ERC-20.
- **Informational EIPs:** These EIPs are designed for general guidelines or information improvement but do not necessarily propose new features. They are intended to influence the behavior of the Ethereum community or provide guidance and advice in a non-binding manner.
- **Meta EIPs:** This type of EIP describes processes surrounding Ethereum or proposes a change to (or an event in) a process. They are similar to Standards Track EIPs but apply to areas other than the Ethereum protocol itself. Meta EIPs might include changes to procedures, decision-making processes, or tools that are not directly tied to the blockchain's code.

EIP Process: The EIP process typically follows these general steps:

1. **EIP Draft:** An EIP is first written by any community member and submitted as a draft. This document must be detailed, providing a clear explanation of the proposed feature or change, the rationale behind it, and any technical specifications required.
2. **Community Discussion and Updates:** Once submitted, the EIP is discussed by the community. During this phase, feedback is gathered, and the original proposal may be updated to reflect community input and technical reviews.
3. **Last Call and Finalization:** If the EIP gains sufficient support and meets the necessary criteria, it enters a "Last Call" period, where the community is given a final review period. If no further issues are raised, the EIP can be finalized.
4. **Implementation:** For Standard Track EIPs, the final stage is implementation, which might require a consensus if it affects core protocol features, potentially resulting in a network upgrade or hard fork.

Through EIPs, Ethereum not only fosters innovation and continuous improvement but also ensures that these advancements are compatible with the decentralized and community-driven nature of the platform. This process allows Ethereum to adapt and evolve in response to new challenges and opportunities in the blockchain space.

4. Burn-and-Mint Model

The transition for Ethereum also includes a new rewards mechanism for validators. Instead of receiving block rewards as in PoW, validators earn transaction fees and "tips" for their role in processing transactions. This change also introduces a deflationary aspect to Ethereum's tokenomics, as a portion of transaction fees is "burned" or removed from circulation, with the objective of increasing scarcity over time.

The burn-and-mint model is a mechanism designed to control the supply of a cryptocurrency and, by extension, its value. The core principle involves removing (burning) a portion of tokens from circulation and creating (minting) new tokens, balancing the two actions to maintain a stable currency value or to achieve other economic goals such as deflation.

Token burning is a deflationary mechanism where a certain amount of cryptocurrency is permanently removed from circulation. This is usually done by sending the tokens to a wallet address (known as a *burn address*) that is verifiably inaccessible because the private keys are unobtainable. This means the tokens can never be spent or retrieved, effectively reducing the total supply. Token burning can happen under various circumstances.

A portion of the transaction fees paid in the native cryptocurrency can be burned. Ethereum's EIP-1559 upgrade introduced a mechanism where the base fee of each transaction is burned, removing ETH from circulation. Minting refers to creating new tokens and adding them to the total supply. This occurs when new tokens are minted as rewards for validators in PoS systems.

Transaction Fees Before EIP-1559

Before the introduction of EIP-1559, Ethereum operated on a simple yet often inefficient auction system for determining transaction fees. In this system, users would specify a gas price in Gwei, a smaller denomination of Ether, indicating how much they were willing to pay per unit of gas to have their transaction processed.[3] This gas price acted essentially as a bid in an open auction, where miners, the network participants responsible for confirming transactions, would prioritize those transactions that offered a higher bid.

This auction-based mechanism, while straightforward, had significant drawbacks, particularly regarding fee predictability and economic efficiency. During periods of high

---

[3] The ETH token has several denominations as it uses up to 18 decimal places. The smallest denomination is wei, equivalent to 10^{-18} ETH. Gwei is equivalent to 10^{-9} ETH and is commonly used for gas price. Similarly, satoshis are the smallest BTC denomination equivalent to 10^8.

network congestion—common during market volatility or high demand for certain dApps—users would find themselves in bidding wars, often guessing how much they needed to pay to ensure their transaction was processed in a timely manner. This guess-work led to highly variable transaction fees and often resulted in users significantly over-paying just to avoid transaction delays.

Moreover, this system did not just affect individual users but could also influence the entire network's economics. In times of congestion, as users jockeyed to outbid each other, the overall transaction fees on the Ethereum network could spike unpredictably. This not only made cost planning difficult for regular users and developers alike but also raised questions about the scalability and long-term viability of Ethereum as a host for dApps and smart contracts, especially those requiring frequent and cost-effective interactions.

The auction system thus created a user experience that was often fraught with uncertainty and inefficiency, with ripple effects that could impact the broader Ethereum ecosystem. These issues underscored the need for a more predictable and stable fee mechanism, which ultimately led to the development and adoption of EIP-1559.

The Mechanics of EIP-1559

EIP-1559 replaces this auction system with a base fee for transactions, which is algorithmically adjusted. Here's how it works:

1. **Base Fee:** Each block has a base fee, which is the minimum price per unit of gas for transactions to be included in the block. This fee is burned, meaning it is removed from circulation, which can create deflationary pressure on Ethereum's supply.
2. **Block Size Variability:** Blocks can now be up to twice as large as the previous fixed limit, but they target a size set by the protocol. If blocks are consistently full, the base fee increases, and if they are below the target size, it decreases. This happens at a predictable rate: the base fee can change only by a maximum of 12.5% from block to block.
3. **Burned Fees:** The base fee is burned in every transaction. This means that part of every transaction fee (the base fee portion) is permanently removed from Ethereum's circulating supply. The exact amount of ETH burned depends on the base fee at the time and the gas used by the transaction.
4. **Tip or Priority Fee:** To incentivize miners (and, now, validators) to include transactions, users can add a tip, also known as a priority fee. This is the only part of the transaction fee that miners receive.
5. **Adjustments for Network Congestion:** As the network becomes more congested, the base fee increases, making it more expensive to transact. Conversely, if the network is underutilized, the base fee decreases. This system aims to balance the demand for block space with the maximum block size, smoothing out transaction fee volatility and improving the user experience.

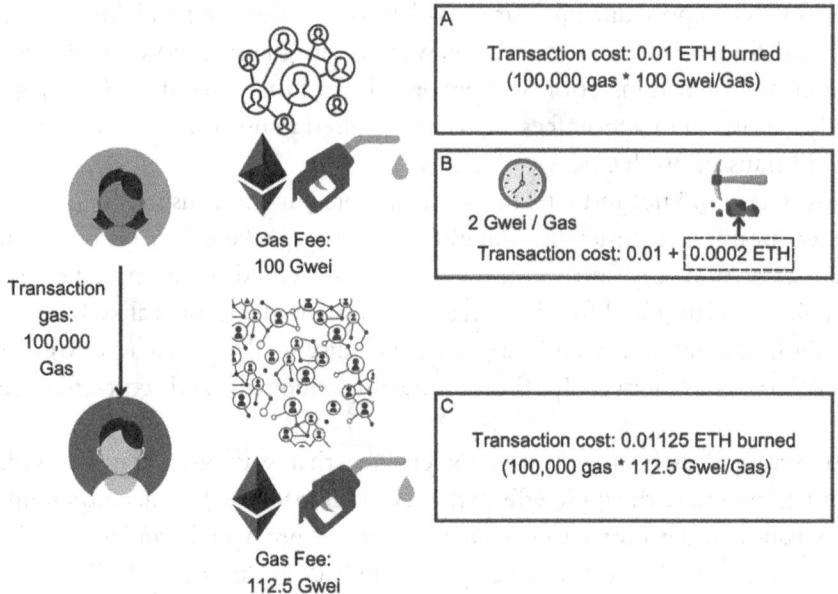

Figure 8   Burn and Mint on Ethereum transactions

Example of Burn and Mint in EIP-1559

Let's say the base fee is currently 100 gwei and a user wants to send a transaction that will use 100,000 gas. The base fee cost for this transaction is 0.01 ETH (100,000 gas ★ 100 Gwei/gas). This 0.01 ETH is burned, reducing the total supply of ETH, shown in **Figure 8A**.

If the user wants to ensure that their transaction is included promptly, they might add a priority fee of 2 Gwei per gas unit, adding an extra 0.0002 ETH to the transaction cost. This amount is paid to the miner, not burned, shown in **Figure 8B**.

If the network is busy and blocks are full, the base fee might increase by 12.5% for the next block, to 112.5 gwei, shown in **Figure 8C**. If the network is quiet and blocks are less than half full, the base fee might decrease by 12.5%.

Impact of EIP-1559

The introduction of EIP-1559 on August 5, 2021, has several intended impacts.

- **Predictable Fees:** Users can more reliably estimate the cost of their transactions based on the base fee.
- **Reduced Circulating Supply:** The burning of the base fee has the potential to make ETH deflationary, especially during times of high network usage.
- **User Experience:** Users can set a maximum fee they're willing to pay, and they get refunded any difference between the maximum fee and the actual fee (base fee + tip).
- **Security:** By burning the base fee, it reduces the ETH supply and aligns the long-term incentives of miners and users.

Dynamic Burn-and-Mint

Some projects implement a dynamic burn-and-mint mechanism where the rules for burning and minting are not fixed but adjust based on certain criteria. For example, a project might burn more tokens when the price is low to reduce supply and mint more tokens when the price is high to increase supply, with the goal of stabilizing the price. For Ethereum, each transaction under EIP-1559 burns the base fee, permanently removing that portion of ETH from the total supply. This burning reduces the circulating supply of Ethereum and, depending on the rate of network usage, could lead to a decrease in the total supply over time.

The dynamic interplay between the burning of the base fee and the minting of new ETH creates a unique economic model. If the amount of ETH burned through base fees exceeds the amount being minted as block rewards, Ethereum could become a deflationary asset. This possibility has significant implications:

- **Deflationary Pressure:** During periods of high network activity, if the base fees burned exceed the new issuance, Ethereum's supply decreases, which could exert upward pressure on the price per ETH, assuming demand remains constant or increases.
- **Predictability and Stability:** By automating fee adjustments and burning the base fee, EIP-1559 can make Ethereum's economic environment more predictable. This predictability is seen as a potential catalyst for further adoption and investment.

In summary, EIP-1559's introduction of a burn and mint model aims to make Ethereum's fee market more efficient, transparent, and fair, while also introducing a potentially deflationary mechanism to Ethereum's economy. This has wide-reaching implications for users, investors, and developers within the Ethereum ecosystem.

5. Ethereum as an Operating System: Smart Contracts

Where Bitcoin could be likened to a calculator—excellent at performing a specific task—Ethereum emerged as more of a smartphone: a versatile platform capable of running all manner of applications. Ethereum introduced the concept of a programmable blockchain. Through its Turing-complete programming language, Solidity, developers were given the tools to write smart contracts—self-executing contracts with the terms of the agreement directly written into lines of code. These contracts operate autonomously and irrevocably without needing intermediaries, reducing the potential for fraud while also cutting down on transaction and processing costs.

As we explore the transformative landscape of blockchain technology, Ethereum emerges not just as another digital currency but as a revolutionary platform that has fundamentally changed how we interact with digital agreements. This brings us to one of Ethereum's most notable contributions to the digital world: smart contracts. These autonomous scripts extend the utility of blockchain from mere financial transactions to complex, programmable agreements, embedding the logic of contractual obligations directly into code. Ethereum's integration of smart contracts has opened up unprecedented possibilities, transforming it from a platform of financial exchange to a foundational layer for decentralized applications across numerous industries. Next, we'll delve into how smart contracts work, their benefits, and the wide array of applications they support, illustrating why Ethereum is often referred to as the world computer.

Smart contracts represent a pivotal innovation in the realm of blockchain technology, extending its application beyond simple financial transactions to complex, programmable interactions. Essentially, smart contracts are self-executing contracts with the terms of the agreement directly written into lines of code. The following discussion will provide a technical overview of smart contracts, focusing on their key features, elements, and underlying principles.

A smart contract is a set of promises, specified in digital form, including protocols within which the parties perform on these promises. The concept was first proposed by Nick Szabo in 1996, long before the advent of blockchain technology. However, it wasn't until the emergence of blockchain platforms like Ethereum that smart contracts became a practical reality.

Smart contracts are executed by a computational network, typically a blockchain, ensuring that they run exactly as programmed without any possibility of downtime, censorship, fraud, or third-party interference. This is possible because the execution of smart contracts is managed by the nodes in the blockchain network; they automatically execute, control, and document legally relevant events and actions according to the terms of a contract or an agreement.

What makes smart contracts special?

The following are the key features of smart contracts:

- **Autonomy and Self-Sufficiency:** Once deployed on the blockchain, smart contracts operate without the need for human intervention. They autonomously execute actions when predefined conditions are met.
- **Trust and Safety:** They foster trust among parties who might not know each other. The blockchain's immutable record-keeping ensures that the contract cannot be altered once deployed, providing a secure environment for parties to transact.
- **Backup and Redundancy:** Every transaction and outcome is recorded on every node in the blockchain, creating an excellent backup mechanism and ensuring data redundancy.
- **Speed and Efficiency:** By automating tasks that traditionally require manual processing, smart contracts reduce the execution time while increasing efficiency.
- **Accuracy:** Automated contracts eliminate the errors that come from manually filling out heaps of forms.

Smart contracts are composed of the following:

- **Contractual Clauses:** The business logic includes rules under which the parties to the smart contract agree to interact with each other.

- **Digital Signature:** Each party to the contract must digitally sign the contract, agreeing to the terms and conditions laid out.
- **Subject of Agreement/Contract:** This includes the specific asset or currency being exchanged or the service being provided as part of the contract.
- **Terms and Conditions:** These are the specific conditions that trigger the execution of the contract.

At a technical level, a smart contract includes the following:

- **Variables:** These represent the state of the contract.
- **Functions:** Functions modify the state and handle the business logic of the contract. They are triggered by transactions or other functions.
- **Modifiers:** Conditions need to be met before executing a function.
- **Events:** These allow smart contracts to log actions and changes in state that the user interface or other contracts can listen for.

We are going to see a number of examples of smart contracts throughout the book. Hopefully by the end of it you will be able to write and develop your own.

Development Platforms

Ethereum is the most notable platform for developing smart contracts, utilizing Solidity as a programming language. However, other blockchain platforms like EOS, NEO, and Tezos also support smart contracts with different features and programming languages such as Vyper (an Ethereum-based language), C++, and Michelson, respectively.

The Birth of Smart Contracts

Smart contracts were more than just a new feature; they were a paradigm shift. Suddenly, developers could create sophisticated dApps for a wide range of uses from decentralized finance (DeFi) and games to complex voting systems and DAOs. Each application doesn't just transfer digital currency but automatically enforces the rules of an agreement based on predefined logic.

Imagine a vending machine for a moment—if you supply the right amount of money, it dispenses the item you selected. Smart contracts work under a similar principle: fulfill the conditions of the contract, and the contract automatically executes the agreed-upon action, be it transferring funds, issuing a ticket, or registering a vehicle.

In other words, smart contracts are self-executing contracts with the terms of the agreement directly written into lines of code. These contracts automatically enforce, execute, and manage the terms of legal agreements without the need for intermediaries. Here are the key components of smart contracts on Ethereum that are critical for understanding their function and utility:

- **Immutable Code:** Once a smart contract is deployed on the Ethereum blockchain, its code cannot be changed; it is immutable. This immutability ensures that the contract's behavior cannot be altered after deployment, providing trust and security for all parties involved.

- **Decentralization:** Smart contracts operate on a decentralized network of computers (nodes), making them resistant to censorship and downtime. This decentralization is crucial in a financial landscape where resilience and uptime are paramount.
- **Automated Execution:** Contracts automatically execute transactions and other specific actions when predefined conditions are met, without human intervention.
- **Transparency and Verification:** The terms and operations of smart contracts are visible and verifiable by all network participants. This transparency ensures that actions taken by the contract are always traceable and auditable, aligning with the principles of open-source technology and peer-reviewed methods in computer science.
- **Interoperability and Composability**: Ethereum's smart contracts can interact with each other through defined interfaces, allowing for complex operations and systems where contracts rely on other contracts to function. This composability is akin to building with LEGO blocks, offering flexibility and exponential utility.
- **Programmable Logic:** The ability to program logic into transactions opens up a myriad of possibilities in automated decision-making, complex financial instruments, and dynamic contract terms, which can adapt to real-world data inputs secured through oracles.

Ethereum Smart Contract Example: Simple Voting Contract   Solidity is a high-level, object-oriented, Turing-complete programming language designed to develop dApps on the Ethereum blockchain. Solidity's Turing completeness means it can support any computation, given the necessary resources, allowing developers to create programs with sophisticated logic and interactions.

Solidity enables smart contracts to maintain a state, meaning they can store data over time. This capability is essential for applications that need to track user interactions, manage complex transactions, or remember choices across different sessions. Additionally, Solidity supports features like inheritance, libraries, and complex user-defined types, which are instrumental in building advanced systems such as autonomous organizations or supply chain management tools.

Moreover, Solidity facilitates rich inter-contract interaction and composability. Contracts written in Solidity can communicate with one another, build on each other's functionalities, and even integrate external data via oracles. This interactivity extends the usability of Ethereum far beyond simple transactions, supporting a vibrant ecosystem of applications that leverage real-world data and complex algorithms.

The following is a simple example of a smart contract written in Solidity for a voting application:

```solidity
pragma solidity ^0.8.0;

contract SimpleVoting {
  mapping (address => bool) public voted;
  mapping (string => uint) public votes;
  string[] public candidates;
```

```
address public admin;

constructor(string[] memory candidateNames) {
    admin = msg.sender;
    candidates = candidateNames;
}

function vote(string memory candidate) public {
    require(!voted[msg.sender], "You have already voted.");
    require(isCandidate(candidate), "Not a valid candidate.");
    votes[candidate]++;
    voted[msg.sender] = true;
}

function isCandidate(string memory name) public view returns (bool) {
    for(uint i = 0; i < candidates.length; i++) {
        if (keccak256(abi.encodePacked(candidates[i])) == keccak256(abi.
encodePacked(name))) {
            return true;
        }
    }
    return false;
}
}
```

Explanation:

- **Contract Setup:** The contract starts with setting up the administrator and the list of candidates.
- **Voting Function:** This function allows each participant to vote once for a valid candidate. Votes are recorded in a mapping, and it checks if the user has already voted.
- **Candidate Validation:** There is a helper function to check if the provided name is a valid candidate.

When compared to the Bitcoin's Script, Ethereum's Solidity offers a robust framework for building a wide array of decentralized applications, making Ethereum a platform for innovation and complex decentralized systems. Each platform's scripting language is thus tailored to its primary objectives—Bitcoin ensuring secure and reliable transactions and Ethereum fostering a diverse and dynamic environment for decentralized application development.

Ethereum and Blockchain 2.0   The introduction of smart contracts on Ethereum created what is now referred to as blockchain 2.0. This wasn't just an upgrade in technology; it was an expansion of possibility. No longer was blockchain technology confined to financial transactions. Ethereum's framework enabled the creation of a decentralized platform that supported a multitude of applications and ventures, contributing significantly to the blockchain ecosystem's diversity and utility.

The Ripple Effect in the Blockchain Space   Ethereum's influence extends beyond its immediate ecosystem. It spurred innovation and competition, leading to the emergence of
numerous other blockchain platforms each proposing various improvements—from
speed and efficiency to interoperability and beyond (as we will see in the next chapter).
Ethereum's pioneering of smart contracts sparked a flurry of innovation in blockchain
technology, pushing other networks to evolve and adapt, which in turn led to new
blockchain generations like Polkadot and Cardano, each bringing their own contributions and enhancements to the table.

Moreover, by enabling developers to build on its platform, Ethereum facilitated the
creation of a decentralized financial system where users can lend, borrow, trade, and
invest without the traditional gatekeepers of finance. This democratization of finance has
had profound implications, potentially reshaping how we think about financial systems
and their accessibility.

BITCOIN VS. ETHEREUM: UNDERSTANDING THE CORE DIFFERENCES

	Bitcoin	Ethereum
Architectural Foundations and Objectives	• Engineered as a peer-to-peer digital currency system, where the primary function is to enable digital transactions without the need for centralized oversight. • Underlying blockchain serves primarily as a decentralized ledger for tracking ownership of Bitcoin. • Relatively simple compared to Ethereum, focusing on robustness and network security, with a rigid set of operations mainly around transaction processing and block validation.	• Designed as a programmable blockchain, it introduces a Turing-complete virtual machine, the Ethereum Virtual Machine (EVM), that executes scripts using an international network of public nodes. • Blockchain is designed to store not only transactions but also complex contract states, making it a platform for decentralized applications and smart contracts. This enables a wide range of applications from finance to gaming to be built on its network.
Block Time	• Maintains a block time of approximately 10 minutes, which inherently limits its transaction throughput to 7 transactions per second (TPS).	• A shorter block time — roughly 13-15 seconds pre-Merge — and has improved further post-Merge.

Consensus Mechanisms	• Proof of Work: Requires solving cryptographic puzzles to validate transactions and create new blocks. • Computationally exhaustive and energy consuming	• Proof of Stake: Achieves consensus by requiring validators to stake a certain amount of their tokens (ETH in this case) as collateral. • Consumes less energy
Script Languages	• Script, which is a simple, stack-based, Forth-like language that processes transaction validation rules. • It is purposely not Turing-complete, which means it doesn't support loops and is limited in functionality to prevent potential security risks that could arise from more complex computations. • Allows for the creation of various transaction types beyond simple sends, such as multisig transactions (where multiple signatures are required to confirm a transaction) or time-locked transactions (which only become valid after a certain time).	• Ethereum uses Solidity (along with other languages like Vyper), a high-level language that is Turing-complete, meaning it can theoretically perform any computation given enough resources. • Solidity is designed to enable developers to write smart contracts that control digital value through arbitrary computation. • It supports the creation of decentralized applications
Monetary Policy and Supply Mechanics	• Capped supply of 21 million coins, designed to introduce scarcity to its ecosystem and potentially increase its value over time.	• Initially without a fixed supply cap, now has a burn mechanism post-EIP-1559 where base transaction fees are burned, potentially leading to deflationary pressure if the burn rate exceeds the rate of new issuance.
Security and Network Stability	• The security model of PoW entails that the computational power (hashrate) distributed across a global network of miners secures the network.	• Security is ensured by the economic stake rather than computational power. This transition also mitigates the risk of centralized mining pools that dominate network mining power.

6. Important Components of Smart Contracts: Oracles

When we talk about smart contracts, oracles stand out as the indispensable messengers that bridge two seemingly incompatible worlds: the deterministic, secure blockchain, and the wild, unpredictable realm of real-world data. Without oracles, smart contracts on blockchains like Ethereum would be like deep-sea divers operating in the dark depths of the ocean with no communication line to the surface—they can do a lot down there, but they're blind to anything happening outside their immediate environment.

Oracles serve as the vital link, feeding blockchain networks with external data necessary for smart contracts to execute under specific conditions. These aren't your mythological oracles, ambiguous and cryptic; these digital oracles provide clear, concrete data whether it's the temperature from a weather station for an agricultural insurance contract, the closing price of a stock for financial derivatives, or the score of a sports game for betting applications. In a sense, oracles do what seemed impossible—they let blockchains communicate effectively with the outside world.

Beyond the Veil of the Blockchain

Imagine a smart contract as a scrupulous, rule-following bureaucrat who's great at managing processes but can't make a move without the right paperwork. Oracles are the runners who go out into the world to gather the necessary documents—the data—and bring them back so the contract can proceed. Without these runners, the bureaucrat is stuck, the processes halt, and the potential of smart contracts remains unfulfilled.

But here's the kicker: while oracles solve a major problem by connecting blockchains with external data, they also introduce a new layer of complexity and vulnerability. The blockchain is tamper-proof and operates with ruthless consistency, yet it relies on data that must pass through the murky waters of the internet, susceptible to manipulation, errors, or delays. Remember that issue is akin to the old saying "garbage in, garbage out." In other words, if the input on which the smart contracts are based upon are incorrect, the resulting transactions will also be wrong.

The Trust Conundrum

Here lies the oracle problem—how do you trust the messenger not to mess with the message? Various innovative solutions attempt to tackle this, from decentralized oracle networks like Chainlink, which aggregates data from multiple sources to mitigate the risk of any single point of failure, to cryptographic techniques like zero-knowledge proofs that enhance data privacy while still ensuring its veracity. The goal is to ensure that oracles are as reliable and secure as the blockchain systems they support.

To give you a sense of the breadth of information that oracles can provide, consider a DeFi platform that offers crop insurance. The platform uses smart contracts to automate the issuance of policies and the processing of claims, with payouts triggered by data feeds that report extreme weather conditions. Oracles play the critical role of retrieving and verifying weather data from various global sources, ensuring that farmers receive compensation quickly and accurately when drought or frost strikes.

What can go wrong?

Let me give you two examples that illustrate why oracles are a key component in the ecosystem.

bZx is a decentralized finance platform that allows for lending and trading with leverage. The platform utilizes oracles to fetch price data, which is crucial for maintaining the correct valuation of assets for trading and loan management.

In February 2020, bZx suffered from a sophisticated attack that exploited its reliance on a single oracle source. The attackers identified that bZx was using only one oracle for price feeds to determine the value of assets on its platform. Using this knowledge, they executed what is known as an *oracle manipulation* attack.

This is how the attack was carried out:

1. **Initial Loan:** The attackers took a large loan of ETH from a lending protocol.
2. **Market Manipulation:** They used a portion of this borrowed ETH to purchase a specific asset on another exchange, significantly driving up its price due to low liquidity.
3. **Exploiting bZx's Oracle:** Because bZx's oracle relied on the price from this single exchange, the inflated price was reported back to the bZx platform.
4. **Taking Out a Loan on bZx:** The attackers then used their remaining ETH as collateral to take out a massive loan on bZx, now significantly overvalued due to the manipulated asset price.
5. **Repaying and Profit:** Finally, they sold the overvalued asset on another market, repaid their original loan, and pocketed a substantial profit from the differences they created in the market.

This series of transactions resulted in a substantial financial loss for bZx and negatively affected its users, as the platform had to suspend operations temporarily to prevent further losses and address the vulnerabilities.

Following the incident, bZx moved to improve its oracle mechanisms by integrating additional oracle services to ensure redundancy and resilience against similar attacks. This event highlighted the dangers of relying on single-source oracles. It underscored the importance of using decentralized oracles that aggregate multiple data sources to provide a more stable and reliable feed, mitigating the risk of manipulation and providing better security for DeFi protocols.

Sometimes even in absence of malicious intent, oracles might be the weakest link due to errors. This is what happened to Synthetix. Synthetix is a DeFi platform that allows users to create and exchange synthetic assets, which are blockchain-based assets that provide exposure to real-world assets, such as currencies, commodities, stocks, and other financial instruments (we are going to have a deep dive into this platform later in the book in Chapter 9). The accurate valuation of these synthetic assets is crucial for the proper functioning of the platform, and it relies heavily on oracles to provide real-time price data.

In June 2019, Synthetix experienced a severe issue when an oracle error led to erroneous price data being fed into the system. Specifically, the price of the Korean won was reported incorrectly due to an error in the oracle feed, which caused drastic price discrepancies. This incorrect data allowed a trader to exploit the system by converting 1 billion synthetic Korean won (sKRW) into 1,000 times their actual value in synthetic Ethereum (sETH).

The exploit resulted in the trader accumulating more than $1 billion USD worth of sETH, which posed a significant risk to the system's liquidity and stability. The issue was exacerbated by the fact that Synthetix operates with a pooled collateral model, meaning that the exploit could potentially affect all users on the platform.

Upon discovering the exploit, Synthetix quickly halted trading and began an investigation. The platform's team reached out to the trader, who cooperated and agreed to reverse the trades at no profit to themselves. This cooperation was critical in managing the situation without further disruption to the broader Synthetix community. Following this incident, Synthetix took measures to enhance their oracle security, including implementing more rigorous checks and balances and exploring additional decentralized oracle solutions to prevent similar vulnerabilities in the future.

PROMINENT PROTOCOL: CHAINLINK

To better understand oracles, let's analyze the most used one.

Chainlink is recognized as a pivotal solution in the blockchain ecosystem, serving as a decentralized oracle network. Its primary function is to facilitate the secure and reliable transfer of tamper-proof data from external sources into various blockchain environments. This capability is crucial because, by nature, blockchains are closed systems with no inherent ability to access or verify the accuracy of external data. Chainlink addresses this limitation by providing smart contracts with a gateway to the outside world, thus significantly expanding their potential use cases.

Smart contracts on platforms like Ethereum are only as good as the information they rely on. If a smart contract is to execute automatically based on stock prices, weather data, or the outcome of a sports event, it needs a reliable connection to the current data in these fields. Chainlink serves this purpose, ensuring that the data fed into a blockchain is accurate and timely, thus enabling smart contracts to function effectively in a broad array of applications, from finance to insurance and beyond.

Solving the Oracle Problem: How Chainlink Ensures Security and Reliability

The "oracle problem" in blockchain refers to the security and reliability issues that arise when a blockchain must rely on an external data source. Traditional centralized oracles present a single point of failure; if the oracle is compromised, so too is the smart contract relying on it. Chainlink's decentralized approach mitigates this risk by aggregating data from multiple sources and thus ensuring that no single point of failure can compromise the integrity of data used in smart contracts.

Chainlink operates through a network of nodes, where each node acts as a point of communication between the blockchain and the external world. These nodes are responsible for retrieving data from external sources, processing it, and returning it to the smart contract in a usable form. To incentivize honesty and accuracy, Chainlink uses a reputation system and deploys mechanisms such as staking, where nodes must commit LINK tokens (Chainlink's native cryptocurrency) to participate in the network. Nodes that provide useful, accurate data are rewarded, while those that provide false data or act maliciously are penalized.

Moreover, Chainlink ensures that the data is not only decentralized but also comes from a variety of vetted sources. For instance, if a smart contract requires USD to EUR exchange rates, Chainlink doesn't rely on a single forex data provider. Instead, it might aggregate the data from multiple financial data services, ensuring that the rates are up-to-date and reflect a consensus across these providers, thus protecting against the manipulation of the data source.

Integration with Multiple Blockchains and Real-World Applications

Chainlink's architecture allows it to be blockchain-agnostic, meaning that it can function across different blockchain platforms. This flexibility is vital for broad adoption, as it provides capabilities for various blockchains to interact with the external data they need. Beyond typical data feeds, Chainlink also enables blockchains to interact with web application programming interface (APIs), facilitating a new level of functionality—from weather data integration into insurance contracts to real-time shipping data used in supply chain management.

Furthermore, Chainlink can connect blockchains with traditional bank payment systems. This ability bridges the gap between on-chain and off-chain financial systems, allowing, for example, smart contracts to trigger or verify bank payments automatically. Such functionality is indispensable for the blockchain to achieve meaningful integration with conventional financial infrastructures and for broadening the scope of DeFi applications.

Let's look at how Chainlink's data retrieval process works, as depicted in **Figure 9**.

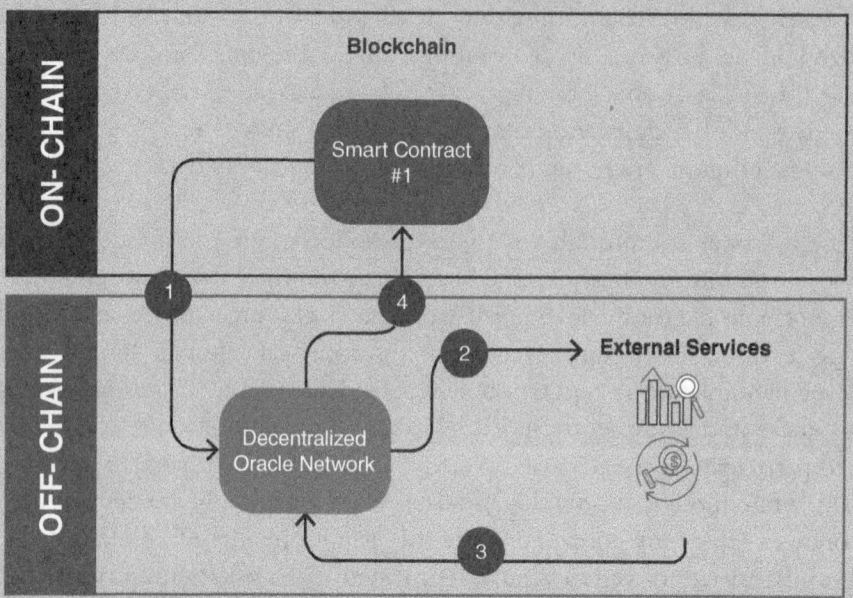

Figure 9   Chainlink's oracle process

1. *Smart Contract Requests Data via a Service Level Agreement (SLA):* The process begins when a smart contract on a blockchain platform, let's say Ethereum, requires data from the outside world to execute its terms. The developers of the smart contract create a service level agreement that specifies the type of data needed, the sources it should come from, and the conditions under which the data is valid. This SLA is essentially a set of requirements that ensures the retrieved data meets the specific needs of the smart contract, such as timeliness, accuracy, and reliability. The SLA is then published to the Chainlink network.

2. *Chainlink Nodes Register for the Request and Retrieve Data from External Sources:* Chainlink nodes, which are operated by independent entities, monitor the network for these requests. Once they detect an SLA that matches their capabilities or offerings, they register their intent to fulfill the request. Each node then independently connects to the specified external data sources. These sources could be APIs, databases, or other digital infrastructures that contain the required data. The node retrieves the data according to the parameters set in the SLA, ensuring that it accurately represents the current state of the data as requested.

3. *Data Is Aggregated and Reconciled Among Different Nodes to Ensure Consistency and Reliability:* After individual nodes have collected the data, Chainlink employs its aggregation model to compile and reconcile the data fetched by various nodes. This step is crucial as it mitigates risks associated with any single point of failure or manipulation within a single data source or node. The aggregation process involves comparing the data fetched by different nodes, checking for outliers, and using consensus mechanisms to determine the most accurate representation of the data. Methods like taking the median value or employing weighted averages based on node reliability scores are common.

4. *The Aggregated Data Is Fed Back into the Smart Contract:* Once the data has been aggregated to a consensus value, it is formatted as required by the smart contract and transmitted back to the blockchain. This returned data triggers the smart contract's execution logic, allowing it to proceed with its operations based on real-world data. The integration of external data into the blockchain environment is handled securely, ensuring that only verified and agreed-upon data impacts the smart contract's state. The data becomes part of the blockchain's immutable record, ensuring transparency and traceability of the operations conducted based on this data.

Through these steps, Chainlink provides a robust framework for data retrieval that bridges the gap between blockchains and the real world. This process not only expands the functionality of smart contracts but also enhances their applicability across various industries, enabling them to interact seamlessly with external systems and environments. Chainlink's decentralized approach ensures that the data integrity and security are maintained, reinforcing the reliability of blockchain technology for complex applications.

LINK as a Utility Token

Unlike Bitcoin, which was primarily designed as a digital alternative to traditional currencies, utility tokens are created to serve specific functions within a particular ecosystem. The LINK token is an essential part of the Chainlink network, serving multiple purposes that facilitate the decentralized oracle services. LINK is an ERC-20 token, meaning it follows the Ethereum standard for fungible tokens, but it also has an ERC-223 "transfer and call" functionality, which allows tokens to be transferred and executed in a single transaction.

Within Chainlink, LINK serves primarily as a utility token to incentivize node operators and facilitates the exchange of data between oracles and smart contract creators. The token's value comes from its role as the native currency used for transactions within the network, making it crucial for the ecosystem's functioning and sustainability.

One of the most critical aspects of Chainlink's decentralized oracle network is ensuring that nodes provide reliable and accurate data. The network achieves this by leveraging LINK tokens as incentives for honest behavior and disincentives for malicious or negligent actions. Node operators are required to stake a certain amount of LINK as collateral when they provide services. This staking mechanism aligns their incentives with the accuracy and reliability of the data they provide because if they supply inaccurate or fraudulent information, they risk losing their staked LINK.

This system encourages nodes to be honest and discourages malicious behavior because the potential penalties directly affect their financial holdings. Additionally, the network uses a reputation system where nodes that consistently provide high-quality data are rewarded with more opportunities to provide services and earn LINK tokens. This setup fosters a competitive environment where nodes strive to build and maintain a positive reputation to secure more lucrative contracts.

For smart contract creators who require external data, LINK also serves as the medium of payment for the services provided by Chainlink nodes. When a smart contract needs data from outside the blockchain, it sets up an SLA specifying the data requirements. The contract creators then deposit LINK tokens to pay for the oracle services based on the SLA terms.

The amount of LINK required for a specific service can vary based on several factors, such as the complexity of the data needed, the number of sources involved, and the reputation of the nodes. Once the nodes fulfill the SLA, they receive LINK as payment, which provides them with tangible incentives to participate in the network.

The dual role of LINK as both an incentive for nodes and a means of payment for services is aimed to create a self-sustaining economic ecosystem within Chainlink. By requiring smart contract creators to pay in LINK and having nodes stake LINK as collateral, Chainlink ensures that all parties are invested in the network's success and integrity.

7. Latest Developments in Ethereum: Account Abstraction

Account abstraction is one of the latest developments in the Ethereum ecosystem, aimed at enhancing the flexibility and functionality of Ethereum accounts. This development focuses on merging the functionalities of user accounts and smart contracts to create more versatile and user-friendly account management.

What Is Account Abstraction?

We saw that in Ethereum, there are two types of accounts:

- **Externally Owned Accounts (EOAs):** Controlled by private keys, typically representing individual users.
- **Contract Accounts (CAs):** Represent smart contracts, controlled by code rather than private keys.

Account abstraction aims to blur the lines between these two types of accounts, allowing EOAs to have smart contract-like capabilities and vice versa. This approach can simplify the user experience and enhance security and functionality.

Instead of relying solely on private keys for transaction validation, account abstraction allows for custom validation logic. This means transactions can be authorized based on various conditions set in smart contracts, such as multi-signature schemes, social recovery mechanisms, or biometric authentication. By enabling more complex authorization methods, account abstraction can reduce the risks associated with private key theft or loss. Users can implement more sophisticated security measures, making accounts less vulnerable to attacks.

Account abstraction can streamline the onboarding process for new users by allowing transactions to be signed in more intuitive ways. For instance, users could use email-based authentication or other familiar methods, reducing the barrier to entry for non-technical users. Traditionally, EOAs must hold ETH to pay for gas fees. With account abstraction, accounts could potentially pay for gas using other tokens or even allow third parties to cover gas costs, improving the flexibility and usability of the network. Also, with account abstraction, users can execute multiple transactions in a single batch. Traditionally, complex transactions involving multiple steps (e.g. token swaps on a decentralized exchange) require separate approvals and executions for each step. Account abstraction allows these steps to be bundled into one operation, simplifying the process and improving user experience. This makes DeFi transactions more efficient and user-friendly, similar to traditional financial transactions.

Account abstraction represents a significant step towards making Ethereum more user-friendly and secure. It has the potential to:

- Attract more mainstream users by simplifying the account management process.
- Enhance the security of user accounts through customizable authorization methods.
- Provide greater flexibility in how transactions are validated and paid for, fostering innovation in decentralized applications (dApps).

8. Concluding Remarks

This chapter has explored Ethereum's transformative role in the evolution of blockchain technology, moving far beyond the initial concept of digital currency exemplified by

Bitcoin, to a robust platform that enables complex decentralized applications through smart contracts. Ethereum has redefined what blockchain technology can achieve, providing a versatile infrastructure not only for cryptocurrency transactions but also for automating processes and agreements in an immutable and transparent manner.

Key Contributions of Ethereum:

- **Smart Contracts:** Ethereum's introduction of smart contracts marked a pivotal shift in the blockchain landscape. These self-executing contracts with the terms directly written into code enable automated, trustless transactions without intermediaries. This innovation has opened up possibilities across various sectors, including finance, real estate, healthcare, and more, reducing fraud, cutting costs, and increasing transparency.
- **Decentralized Applications (dApps):** The platform has fostered a burgeoning ecosystem of dApps that leverage its open-source nature, benefiting from the security and reliability of blockchain technology. These applications have diversified blockchain's potential uses, ranging from creating decentralized financial systems to new governance models.
- **Ethereum Virtual Machine:** The EVM lies at the core of Ethereum's functionality, enabling the execution of complex scripts worldwide on a single decentralized platform. It is instrumental in maintaining Ethereum's status as a true global computing engine.
- **Transition to Ethereum 2.0:** The upgrade to Ethereum 2.0 addresses significant issues such as scalability, energy consumption, and speed. Transitioning from a PoW to a PoS consensus mechanism not only decreases the network's energy consumption drastically but also allows for faster transactions, demonstrating Ethereum's commitment to innovation and sustainability.

Ethereum revolutionizes how we approach and execute digital agreements, with the potential to disrupt traditional methods of business and governance through decentralized solutions. By providing a platform for building decentralized applications, Ethereum has also paved the way for developers to explore new paradigms in software design and implementation.

As we continue to explore the evolution of Ethereum, it's evident that the ongoing development and potential widespread adoption of Ethereum 2.0 are poised to redefine standards for blockchain efficiency and scalability. This major upgrade, transitioning from proof-of-work (PoW) to a more energy-efficient proof-of-stake (PoS) consensus mechanism, not only promises significant reductions in energy consumption but also aims to enhance transaction throughput dramatically. These improvements are critical as Ethereum seeks to maintain its leadership in a rapidly expanding blockchain ecosystem.

The surge of interest in DeFi has been both a boon and a challenge for the Ethereum network. DeFi applications, which leverage Ethereum for financial services without traditional intermediaries, and stablecoins, which provide price stability in transactions, have driven unprecedented traffic and value through the network. This has highlighted

Ethereum's critical role in the future of finance, where its ability to execute and manage complex financial instruments in a decentralized manner becomes increasingly pivotal.

Moreover, Ethereum's flexible framework has facilitated a wave of innovation beyond traditional finance. Non-fungible tokens (NFTs), which enable the tokenization of digital and real-world assets, have opened new markets in art, music, and beyond. This expansion showcases Ethereum's capacity to support diverse applications, further cementing its position at the forefront of blockchain technology.

However, Ethereum's success has also highlighted its limitations. The network's scalability challenges have become increasingly apparent, with rising transaction costs and slower processing times during periods of high demand. Scaling Ethereum is like upgrading the internet from dial-up to broadband—necessary, inevitable, and a bit of a headache. This congestion undermines the network's ability to capitalize on network effects where increased usage should ideally lead to proportional value creation across the ecosystem.

In response to these challenges, the next chapter will delve into layer-2 solutions—innovative protocols built on top of the Ethereum blockchain that aim to alleviate congestion by handling transactions off the main chain. These solutions are designed to enhance scalability without compromising on security or decentralization, offering promising avenues to sustain Ethereum's growth. By exploring layer-2 technologies such as state channels, sidechains, and rollups, we will examine how the Ethereum community continues to innovate, ensuring that the network can scale effectively to meet user demands and support expanding use cases.

Example Solidity Smart Contract for an SLA

```
// SPDX-License-Identifier: MIT
pragma solidity ^0.8.0;

// Interface for Chainlink Oracle to fetch cryptocurrency prices
interface IChainlinkOracle {
    function getPrice(string memory symbol) external view returns (uint);
}

contract CryptoPriceSLA {
    address public owner;
    IChainlinkOracle public oracle;
    uint public lastPrice;
    string public constant SYMBOL = "ETH";  // Example for Ethereum
prices
    uint public constant UPDATE_INTERVAL = 1 minutes;
    uint public lastUpdateTime;
```

```
    // SLA terms
    uint public constant requiredAccuracy = 995; // 99.5%
    uint public constant maxLatency = 30 seconds; // 30 seconds maximum
latency
    uint public constant availabilityThreshold = 999; // 99.9%
availability

    // Monitoring performance
    uint public uptime;
    uint public totalChecks;
    uint public inaccurateDataCount;
    uint public lateDataCount;

    constructor(address _oracleAddress) {
        owner = msg.sender;
        oracle = IChainlinkOracle(_oracleAddress);
        lastUpdateTime = block.timestamp;
    }

    // Modifier to restrict certain functions to only the owner of the
contract
    modifier onlyOwner() {
        require(msg.sender == owner, "Only the owner can call this
function.");
        _;
    }

    // Function to update the price, simulating data retrieval
    function updatePrice() public {
        require(block.timestamp >= lastUpdateTime + UPDATE_INTERVAL,
        "Update interval has not passed.");
        uint price = oracle.getPrice(SYMBOL);
        uint delay = block.timestamp - lastUpdateTime;

        // Check latency
        if (delay > maxLatency) {
            lateDataCount++;
        }

        // Mock-up for accuracy check
        if (price < lastPrice * requiredAccuracy / 1000) {
            inaccurateDataCount++;
        }

        lastPrice = price;
        lastUpdateTime = block.timestamp;
        totalChecks++;
        uptime = (totalChecks - (lateDataCount + inaccurateDataCount)) *
1000 / totalChecks;
    }
```

```
    // Function to check SLA compliance
    function checkSLACompliance() public view returns (bool) {
        return uptime >= availabilityThreshold;
    }

    // Function to claim penalties or resolve disputes
    function resolveDispute() public onlyOwner {
        // Code to resolve any disputes according to SLA terms
    }

    // Fallback function to handle Ether sent to this contract
    receive() external payable {
        revert("This contract does not accept direct payments.");
    }
}
```

- **Oracle Interface:** We define an interface `IChainlinkOracle` that specifies how to interact with a Chainlink oracle to get cryptocurrency prices.
- **State Variables:** The contract stores variables such as the last price fetched, update intervals, and SLA metrics like required accuracy, maximum latency, and availability thresholds.
- **Constructor:** This sets up the contract with the address of the oracle and initial settings.
- **Update Price Function:** This simulates fetching the latest price from an oracle. It checks for data latency and accuracy against predefined thresholds, updating counters for performance metrics.
- **Check SLA Compliance:** This provides a method to check if the SLA terms regarding uptime and data quality are being met.
- **Dispute Resolution:** This is a placeholder function for handling disputes, which can be customized based on specific SLA terms and conditions.

This example gives a basic framework for how an SLA could be coded into a smart contract using Solidity, focusing on aspects such as performance monitoring and compliance checking.

Smart Contract Exercises

1: Basic Smart Contract: Hello World

Environment Setup: Use Remix, an online Solidity IDE, for writing and deploying the contract.

Writing the Contract:

- Start with a pragma directive to specify the compiler version.
- Declare the contract with **contract HelloWorld**.

- Inside the contract, declare a **string** variable **message**.
- Write a public function **setMessage** to set the message.
- Write a public function **getMessage** to retrieve the message.

Code

```solidity
pragma solidity ^0.8.0;

contract HelloWorld {
  string private message;

  function setMessage(string memory newMessage) public {
    message = newMessage;
  }

  function getMessage() public view returns (string memory) {
    return message;
  }
}
```

2: Basic Transaction Contract

Contract Setup:

- Use the same setup as Exercise 1.
- Add a payable function that allows sending ETH to the contract.
- Add a function to withdraw ETH from the contract to a specified address.

Code

```solidity
pragma solidity ^0.8.0;

contract Transaction {
  function deposit() public payable {}

  function withdraw(address payable recipient, uint amount) public {
    require(address(this).balance >= amount, "Insufficient funds");
    recipient.transfer(amount);
  }

  function getBalance() public view returns (uint) {
    return address(this).balance;
  }
}
```

3: Conditional Payments with Basic Validation

Adding Conditions:

- Implement a condition that allows withdrawals only if a certain condition, such as a minimum balance, is met.

```solidity
pragma solidity ^0.8.0;
```

```
contract ConditionalPayment {
  uint public threshold = 1 ether;

  function deposit() public payable {}

  function conditionalWithdraw(address payable recipient, uint amount)
public {
    require(address(this).balance >= threshold, "Balance does not meet
threshold");
    recipient.transfer(amount);
  }
}
```

4: Time-Locked Wallet

Implementing Time Lock:

- Add a **lockTime** variable that defines when funds can be withdrawn.
- Modify the **withdraw** function to check if the current time is past **lockTime**.

Code

```
pragma solidity ^0.8.0;

contract TimeLockedWallet {
  uint public lockTime;

  constructor(uint _lockTime) {
    lockTime = _lockTime;
  }

  function deposit() public payable {}

  function withdraw(address payable recipient) public {
    require(block.timestamp > lockTime, "Funds are locked");
    recipient.transfer(address(this).balance);
  }
}
```

5: Decentralized Finance Platform

1. Platform Setup:

- Develop a smart contract for a lending pool where users can deposit Ethereum or ERC-20 tokens to earn interest.
- Implement borrowing mechanisms where users can take out loans against their deposits, incorporating collateral management and liquidation processes.

2. Interest Calculation:

- Integrate an interest rate model that calculates accruing interest based on supply and demand dynamics within the platform.

```solidity
pragma solidity ^0.8.0;

import "@openzeppelin/contracts/token/ERC20/IERC20.sol";

contract DeFiPlatform {
  mapping(address => uint) public deposits;
  mapping(address => uint) public loans;
  uint public interestRate = 5; // Annual interest rate in percentage

  function deposit(uint amount) public {
    require(IERC20(token).transferFrom(msg.sender, address(this),
amount), "Transfer failed");
    deposits[msg.sender] += amount;
  }

  function borrow(uint amount) public {
    require(deposits[msg.sender] * 3 / 4 >= amount, "Insufficient
collateral");
    loans[msg.sender] += amount;
    require(IERC20(token).transfer(msg.sender, amount), "Transfer
failed");
  }

  function repay(uint amount) public {
    require(IERC20(token).transferFrom(msg.sender, address(this),
amount), "Transfer failed");
    loans[msg.sender] -= amount;
  }
}
```

End-of-Chapter Questions

Multiple-Choice Questions

1. **What is the primary purpose of Ethereum's transition from proof of work (PoW) to proof of stake (PoS) in Ethereum 2.0?**
   (A) To increase the number of tokens each miner can earn
   (B) To decrease the energy consumption of the network
   (C) To eliminate smart contracts
   (D) To reduce the speed of transactions

2. **Which feature of Ethereum allows for the creation of decentralized applications (dApps)?**
   (A) Bitcoin compatibility
   (B) Ethereum Virtual Machine (EVM)
   (C) Proof-of-work mining algorithm
   (D) External data retrieval through HTTP

3. **Smart contracts on Ethereum are:**
   (A) Executed by external servers to maintain decentralization
   (B) Self-executing contracts with terms directly written into code
   (C) Stored off-chain to ensure faster transaction times
   (D) Accessible only by the contract creator

4. **What role do oracles play in the Ethereum network?**
   (A) They predict token prices for investment purposes
   (B) They provide external data to smart contracts
   (C) They convert Ether into other cryptocurrencies
   (D) They act as external auditors for smart contract code

5. **Which type of Ethereum Improvement Proposal (EIP) involves changes that would affect all client implementations?**
   (A) Standard Track
   (B) Informational
   (C) Meta
   (D) ERC

6. **What is the main reason for Ethereum's implementation of sharding in Ethereum 2.0?**
   (A) To decrease transaction fees by reducing the amount of data each node needs to handle
   (B) To increase the block size
   (C) To ensure compliance with international data privacy laws
   (D) To make the network less secure

7. **Which statement best describes the concept of "gas" in Ethereum?**
   (A) It is a measurement of the computational effort required to execute operations
   (B) It is a fixed fee that users pay to miners for each transaction
   (C) It represents the storage space on the blockchain
   (D) It is the fee paid to developers when deploying new smart contracts

8. **Decentralized finance (DeFi) on Ethereum has grown due to its ability to:**
   (A) Allow anonymous transactions similar to Bitcoin
   (B) Replace traditional banking systems entirely
   (C) Enable transparent and permissionless financial services
   (D) Provide a centralized exchange for immediate liquidity

9. **What is the purpose of the Ethereum Improvement Proposal (EIP) 1559?**
   (A) To adjust the block size dynamically
   (B) To introduce sharding to Ethereum
   (C) To change the mechanism for calculating transaction fees
   (D) To upgrade the consensus mechanism from PoW to PoS

10. **Which Solidity keyword is used to define immutable variables, which cannot be changed after their initial assignment?**
    (A) Constant
    (B) Static
    (C) Immutable
    (D) Fixed

11. **How does the "require" function in Solidity contribute to smart contract security?**
    (A) It encrypts data stored in the contract.
    (B) It reverts the transaction if a condition is not met.
    (C) It prevents external contracts from accessing sensitive data.
    (D) It automatically updates the contract's state variables.

12. **In the context of Ethereum smart contracts, what is a "modifier"?**
    (A) A function that alters the behavior of other functions in the contract for reusable code
    (B) A variable type that can be modified after contract deployment
    (C) A special pragma that modifies the compiler's behavior
    (D) An operator used to change permission levels on functions

13. **What is the primary purpose of the Chainlink protocol on Ethereum?**
    (A) To facilitate faster block times
    (B) To provide external data to smart contracts via oracles
    (C) To serve as an alternative consensus mechanism
    (D) To enable the creation of proprietary tokens

14. **When deploying a new ERC-20 token on Ethereum, which function is necessary to initially assign all tokens to an address?**
    (A) transfer()
    (B) allocate()
    (C) distribute()
    (D) constructor()

15. **What mechanism in Ethereum ensures that smart contracts do not run indefinitely and consume excessive resources?**
    (A) Proof of stake
    (B) Gas and gas limits
    (C) Transaction fees
    (D) Block size limits

Open Questions

1. Discuss the implications of Ethereum's transition from proof of work (PoW) to proof of stake (PoS) on small-scale miners and the network's decentralization. How might this shift affect the security and participation in the network?

2. Explain how smart contracts on Ethereum can potentially transform the legal and contractual frameworks in traditional industries. Provide specific examples of industries where you foresee the most significant impact and justify your choices.

3. Ethereum's blockchain is often referred to as a *world computer*. What are the technical and practical challenges of scaling this computer to accommodate global demand, especially in the context of decentralized applications (dApps) and decentralized finance (DeFi) platforms?

4. Critically evaluate the role of oracles in Ethereum smart contracts. What are the potential risks associated with relying on external data feeds, and how might these risks be mitigated in a decentralized environment?

5. As Ethereum continues to evolve, layer-2 scaling solutions are becoming increasingly important. Discuss how these solutions work and their potential impact on Ethereum's performance and future development. Compare at least two different types of layer-2 solutions in your discussion.

Blockchain Explorer Project

Blockchain explorers are tools that allow people to view the data in blocks and transactions, parsed so that it is more easily understandable. For example, users can examine important block information like the block number, time, the number of transactions, the size, the miner/validator, and the reward earned by the miner/validator. When looking at transactions, one can see all the details such as ETH/token/NFT transfers, interactions with smart contracts and dapps, fees paid, and the wallet address involved. Knowing how to use a blockchain explorer is an important skill as it allows you to get a better understanding of the state of the blockchain and to understand how users are interacting with each other and with dapps.

The leading Ethereum block explorer is Etherscan. In this project, we will become familiar with the platform first and then analyze the data available. If you are already familiar with block explorers you can skip exercises 1-3. The goal of the project is to understand the fee dynamics of Ethereum especially with the various upgrades that have been implemented.

Exercise 1: Viewing Blocks

Navigate to `https://etherscan.io` to open the website. You'll be greeted with a plethora of numbers, indicators and information. Let's first familiarize ourselves with blocks. Look at the tab **Latest Blocks** and click on the block number. You should be able to see information regarding that particular block.

1. What is the block number?
2. What is the timestamp of the block?
3. How many transactions were included in the block?
4. Who is validator responsible for the block? How many ETHs did they receive as a reward?
5. What is the size of the block?

Exercise 2: Viewing Transactions

Return to the main page and look at the **Latest Transactions** tab, and click on one to view information about the transaction.

1. What is the transaction hash?
2. Which block was the transaction included in?
3. What is the address of the wallet that originated the transaction? What is the address of the recipient of the transaction?
4. What happened during this transaction? Describe in words what you see.
5. What is the fee that the originator paid for this particular transaction?

Exercise 3: Viewing Accounts

Click on the address of the originator or the recipient of the transaction that you just viewed. This action should bring up the details about this particular address or smart contract (specified in the header **Address** or **Contract**).

1. What is the ETH balance of this account? Does it hold any other tokens or NFTs?
2. How many transactions has this account been involved in?
3. If the account is a smart contract (if not, you can follow this step by searching for the smart contract address of USDT using its address 0xdac17f958d2ee523a220620

6994597c13d831ec7), navigate to the contracts tab. Many developers upload their smart contract code to Etherscan so that the source code can be viewed straight from the blockchain explorer. Can you see the source code? What language is it written in?

4. Navigate to the **Read Contract** tab. Here you can view some of the variables, parameters and metadata about the smart contract (if the source code has been published, if not use the USDT address above). Click on any dropdown menu and you should be able to interact with the smart contract and view some of its variables and functions. The **Write Contract** tab allows you to interact with contract functions that change the state of the blockchain, which requires you to have a wallet connected and some ETH to pay for transaction fees.

Exercise 4: Using the API for Data Analysis

Etherscan provides an API for developers to access blockchain data. To get started, you'll need an Etherscan account and API key. Let's understand the fee dynamics of Ethereum with various upgrades that it has received—most notably, EIP-1559 and The Merge. To do this, we'll need to use Etherscan's *getblockreward* endpoint described at https://docs. etherscan.io/api-endpoints/blocks#get-block-and-uncle-rewards-by-blockno. This endpoint provides data on the total reward earned by the miner/validator for the block, allowing us to understand how much users are paying for transactions on aggregate. To use the endpoint, you'll need to provide a block number. EIP-1559 went live on mainnet during the London Hard Fork on August 2021 (block height 12,965,000) and The Merge went live on September 2022 at block height 15,537,394. Create a window of block heights around these two events and use the API endpoint to download the fee reward data from Etherscan. For example, you could generate charts like the following:

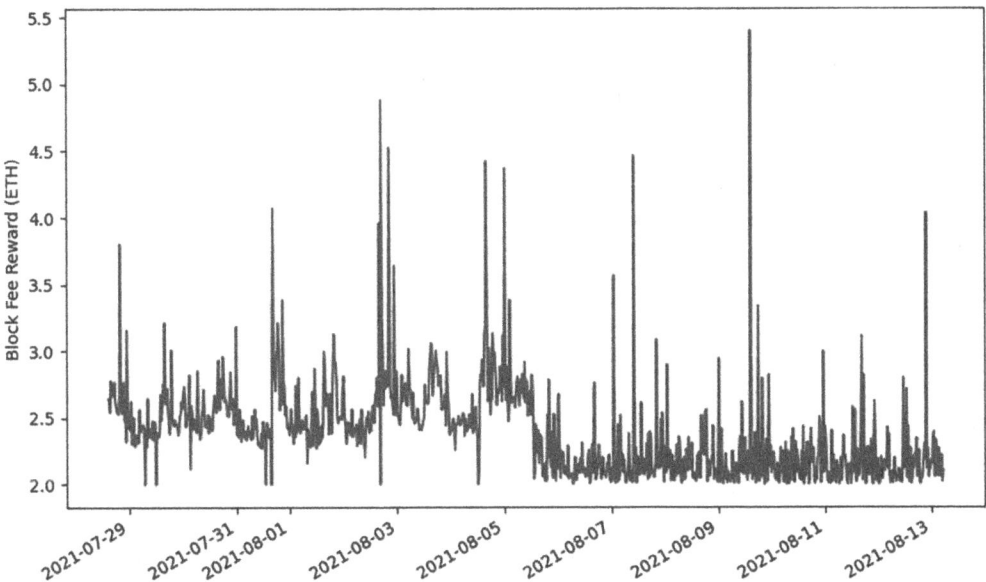

Ethereum Block Fee Reward Before and After the London Hard Fork (EIP-1559)

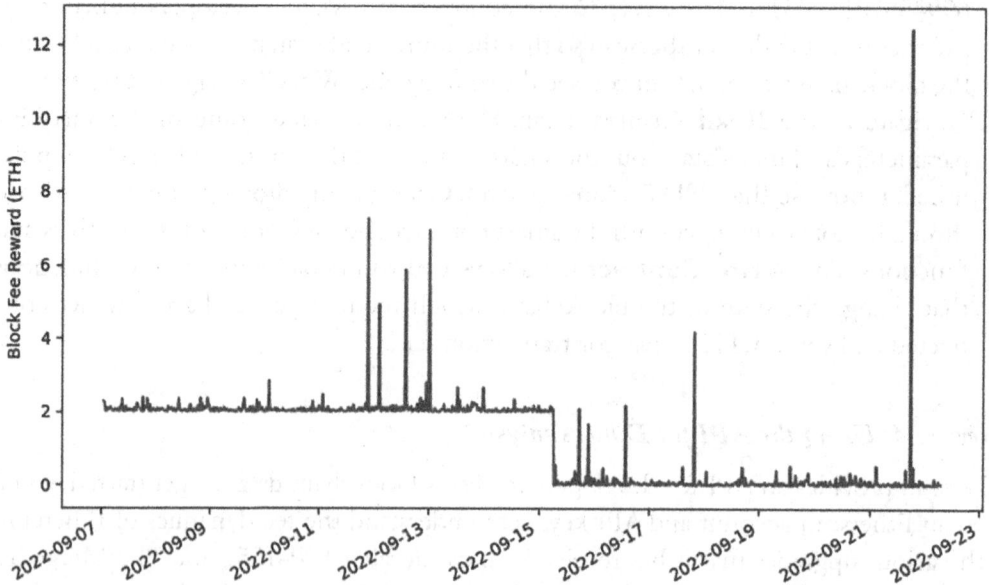

Ethereum Block Fee Reward Before and After the Merge

How did the fee dynamic change after each event? Is this behavior expected? Feel free to experiment with other windows. For instance, did FTX filing for bankruptcy in November 11, 2022, affect transaction fees? How did fees behave in the early years of Ethereum compared to today where it is more popular?

Chapter 3

Beyond Ethereum

A Gas-Guzzling Escape to the Holy Grail of Scalability

Preface

Welcome to the mystical world of blockchain technology, where the only thing growing faster than the transaction fees on Ethereum is the number of Layer 2 solutions popping up like mushrooms after a rainstorm. In this chapter, we dive headfirst into the rabbit hole of alternative blockchains and the wonderland of Layer 2 solutions, a tale so fantastical it makes Alice's adventures look like a trip to the DMV.

Imagine, if you will, a world where Ethereum, the blockchain of choice for everything from cat memes turned into NFTs to decentralized finance (DeFi) projects that make traditional banking look like playing Monopoly with Monopoly money, is facing a bit of a pickle. Yes, our beloved Ethereum, as revolutionary as it was, started showing the digital equivalent of middle-aged spread: slowing down and getting expensive.

Enter the heroes of our story: Layer 1 and Layer 2 solutions, along with a motley crew of alternative blockchains like Solana, which runs faster than Usain Bolt on a good day, and Polygon, the Swiss Army knife of scaling solutions. These intrepid adventurers embarked on a quest to solve the dreaded Scalability Trilemma, a challenge so daunting it could easily be the plot of the next big fantasy saga (move over, *Game of Thrones*).

Layer 1 solutions, with their fancy sharding techniques, are like the city planners trying to widen the highways in our blockchain city, making room for more transactions without turning the whole place into a giant parking lot. Meanwhile, Layer 2 solutions are the ingenious engineers building skyways and tunnels, keeping traffic flowing smoothly, without bothering the old city infrastructure below.

And oh, the competition for traffic! Blockchains vying for users' attention and transactions are like cities competing for the Olympics, each promising faster transaction times, lower fees, and more dazzling DeFi opportunities than the last. Ethereum, with its rich ecosystem and high fees, is like New York City: unbeatable in terms of attractions but oh-so-expensive. Solana and Polygon, with their speedy transactions, are like those up-and-coming cities, offering high-speed trains and affordable living to lure in the crowds. They put up billboards in the crypto space, advertising free transactions and instant confirmations like beach resorts promising sunny days and no rain.

The adventurous and interconnected nature of the blockchain ecosystem

Imagine if, in *The Lord of the Rings*, Frodo had the option to simply build a bridge from The Shire straight to Mount Doom, skipping all the fuss with orcs and dark lords. In the blockchain universe, this isn't just a daydream; it's the quest for interoperability, where different blockchain realms seek to connect in a harmonious Middle-Earth of technology. But instead of elves and dwarves, we have developers and cryptographers trying to make their blockchains play nice with each other, often with the same level of grudging cooperation.

Bridges in the blockchain world are akin to those rickety rope bridges in adventure movies—they promise a shortcut to untold treasures but wobble alarmingly with every step. These bridges aim to connect disparate blockchain ecosystems, allowing assets to flow freely between them like tourists hopping between countries. But like in those movies, there's always the risk of a plank giving way at the worst possible moment, leading to dramatic falls into the chasms of lost liquidity and broken smart contracts.

We'll explore these blockchain byways together, marveling at the ingenuity of those who seek to unite these digital lands in a grand, interconnected web of possibility. Whether you're a blockchain newbie or a seasoned crypto wizard, there's something in this chapter for you. You'll learn why trying to scale a blockchain is like trying to fit a whale through a revolving door and how to navigate this space without falling prey to the sirens of scalability or the pitfalls of platform partisanship.

1. Introduction

As we have seen, Ethereum emerged as a groundbreaking evolution in the blockchain space, introducing the world to smart contracts. This innovation extended blockchain applications far beyond financial transactions, paving the way for decentralized applications (DApps), decentralized finance (DeFi), and a host of other uses that have captivated the imagination and investment of millions worldwide. However, Ethereum's very success became a source of its most pressing challenges: network congestion and high transaction fees—symptoms of its underlying scalability issues.

Ethereum's current state can be analogized to a rapidly expanding city's road network that fails to keep pace with the surge in vehicular traffic. Just as roads become congested and travel times lengthen, the Ethereum network, too, has become clogged with transactions, leading to slow processing times and a less-than-optimal user experience.

A direct consequence of this congestion has been the surge in gas fees—the cost necessary to conduct transactions or execute smart contracts on the Ethereum network. These fees have seen significant spikes, particularly during periods of high demand, much like surge pricing models employed by ride-sharing services. For users, this means paying a premium for transaction processing, a cost that can be prohibitively expensive during peak times.

Furthermore, Ethereum's capacity, limited to processing about 15-30 transactions per second (TPS), pales in comparison to traditional payment processors like Visa, which can handle tens of thousands of TPS. This limitation not only exacerbates the issue of high fees but also results in slower transaction confirmations—akin to a restaurant struggling to serve a sudden influx of patrons.

At the heart of Ethereum's struggles lies the scalability trilemma, a fundamental challenge not unique to Ethereum but inherent to blockchain networks in general (**Figure 1**). This trilemma posits that a blockchain can optimize only two out of three key aspects at

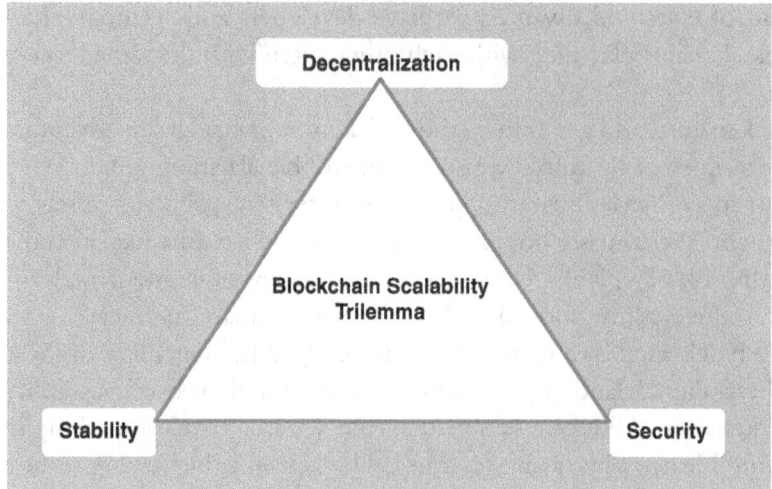

Figure 1 Blockchain scalability trilemma

any one time: security, decentralization, and scalability. Pursuing greater scalability, for example, to accommodate more transactions per second and reduce processing times, can inadvertently undermine decentralization, leading to a network that is potentially more vulnerable to attacks or manipulation.

The technical roots of the scalability trilemma can be explained as follows:

1. **Increasing Scalability:** Scaling the network, for instance by increasing block size or reducing block time, can strain nodes as they must process and store more data quickly. This requirement can lead to centralization, as only nodes with significant resources can keep up, diminishing the network's decentralized nature. Additionally, rushing the consensus process or simplifying validation to improve throughput could compromise security by making it easier for malicious actors to manipulate the network.

2. **Enhancing Security:** Bolstering security measures, such as by increasing the complexity of the consensus algorithm, or introducing more rigorous validation checks, can slow transaction processing and limit scalability. Additionally, to increase security by having more validators can inadvertently push toward centralization if the cost or technical requirements to participate become too high, excluding smaller participants.

3. **Maintaining Decentralization:** Preserving a high degree of decentralization by encouraging broad participation in the consensus process and network governance can limit scalability and security. With more validators, reaching consensus can take longer, reducing the network's ability to process transactions rapidly. Decentralization also means that compromising a single node or a small group of nodes doesn't jeopardize the network's integrity. However, it requires robust mechanisms to coordinate and secure a widely dispersed network.

Solving the trilemma involves innovative technical solutions that can provide a balance without compromising any one aspect significantly.

Ethereum's scalability challenges have led to the development of various solutions aimed at improving transaction throughput, reducing fees, and maintaining decentralization without compromising security. These solutions can be broadly categorized into Layer 1 and Layer 2 solutions, with a notable mention of emerging alternative blockchains designed for better scalability from the ground up.

1.1 Layer 1 Scalability Solutions

Layer 1 solutions involve changes to the Ethereum blockchain itself to increase its capacity to process transactions.

- **Sharding:** Sharding is a process that divides the Ethereum network into smaller pieces, or "shards," each capable of processing transactions and smart contracts independently. This parallel processing capability significantly increases the network's overall capacity. Sharding is a key feature of the upcoming the Ethereum 2.0 upgrade.
- **Proof of stake (PoS):** Ethereum transitioned from proof of work (PoW) to Proof of Stake (PoS) with its the Ethereum 2.0 upgrade. PoS improves scalability and energy efficiency by eliminating the computationally intensive mining process. Validators instead secure the network by staking their ETH, which requires far less power and enables faster transaction processing.

1.2 Layer 2 Scalability Solutions

Layer 2 solutions, including technologies like Arbitrum and Optimism, offer a promising approach by processing transactions off the main Ethereum chain (Layer 1) and subsequently recording the aggregated results back on it. This method can be likened to adding express lanes to a highway, where the overall capacity to handle traffic is significantly increased without altering the original road infrastructure.

Layer 2 solutions work on top of the Ethereum blockchain (Layer 1) to improve scalability without altering the blockchain itself using different mechanisms:

- **State Channels:** State channels allow multiple transactions to occur off-chain with only two transactions recorded on-chain – the opening and the closing of the channel. This is ideal for situations where participants need to perform numerous transactions privately, such as in gaming or recurring payments.
- **Plasma:** Plasma is a framework for building scalable applications by creating child chains that report back to the main Ethereum chain. It allows for the offloading of transactions from the main chain, improving throughput while leveraging the main chain's security.
- **Rollups:** Rollups perform transaction execution outside the main chain (off-chain) but store transaction data on-chain. There are two main types:
  - **Optimistic Rollups:** These assume transactions are valid by default and only execute computation on-chain in the event of a dispute.

- **Zero-Knowledge Rollups (ZK-Rollups):** These use zero-knowledge proofs to prove the validity of transactions in a compressed form, allowing for quicker verification on the Ethereum mainnet.

- **Sidechains:** Sidechains are independent blockchains that run parallel to Ethereum and have their own consensus mechanisms. They can process transactions and then relay them back to the main Ethereum chain, easing the burden on Ethereum while still being tethered to its security model.

1.3 Blockchain 3.0

Blockchain 3.0 represents the evolution of blockchain technology beyond its initial financial applications (Blockchain 1.0, exemplified by Bitcoin) and the advent of smart contracts and DApps (Blockchain 2.0, with Ethereum being the pioneering platform). Blockchain 3.0 encompasses technologies aiming to solve the issues still plaguing earlier blockchain iterations—namely scalability, interoperability, and sustainability—while expanding blockchain's applicability to fields like decentralized identity, governance, and beyond. While Ethereum continues to evolve, several Layer 1 and Layer 2 solutions are often highlighted as embodying the Blockchain 3.0 ethos by addressing these challenges more directly or introducing novel functionalities.

1. Polkadot (DOT)
   - Interoperability and Scalability: Polkadot stands out for its unique approach to interoperability, enabling different blockchains to communicate and share information through its relay chain and parachain structure. This not only enhances scalability by distributing transactions across multiple chains but also facilitates a more interconnected and efficient blockchain ecosystem.
2. Cardano (ADA)
   - Sustainability and Scalability: Cardano introduces a novel PoS algorithm called Ouroboros, designed to reduce energy consumption significantly. Its layered architecture separates the settlement layer from the computational layer, allowing for more scalable and sustainable operations. Cardano also emphasizes a research-driven approach, aiming to provide a more secure and robust infrastructure for DApps.
3. Solana (SOL)
   - High Throughput and Low Costs: Solana offers an impressive throughput of up to 65,000 TPS, achieved through innovations like proof of history (PoH) and a highly efficient consensus mechanism. This positions Solana as a high-performance blockchain capable of supporting demanding applications without the high costs and slow speeds associated with older platforms.

Blockchain 3.0 technologies strive to make decentralized networks more scalable, interoperable, and user-friendly, opening the door to mainstream adoption of blockchain technology. They address critical pain points that have hindered broader blockchain application, such as making transactions fast and affordable, ensuring different blockchains can work together seamlessly, and minimizing the environmental impact of blockchain operations.

The evolution from Ethereum's groundbreaking smart contract platform to these newer Blockchain 3.0 technologies represents a continuous effort in the blockchain community to create a more scalable, accessible, and sustainable decentralized internet. As these platforms mature and their ecosystems grow, they are expected to facilitate a new wave of decentralized applications that could redefine how we think about digital identity, finance, governance, and more, truly embodying the next generation of blockchain technology.

2. Layer 2 Solutions: How Do They Work?

We are going to see all the solutions mentioned above in detail.

2.1 State Channels

State Channels represent a critical advancement in Layer 2 scalability solutions, enabling multiple transactions to be conducted off the main Ethereum blockchain (off-chain) while ensuring the final state is securely settled on-chain. By establishing a "channel" between participating parties, state channels allow for rapid, free transactions with the security and decentralization guarantees of the underlying blockchain.

This mechanism is akin to tabulating a bar tab; rather than paying for each drink as it's ordered (equivalent to processing a transaction on the blockchain), patrons open a tab (a state channel), order their drinks throughout the night (conduct transactions off-chain), and settle the total bill at the end of the night (closing the state channel and settling the final state on the blockchain).

State channels have found practical applications in various sectors, notably in **micropayment platforms** and **gaming**, where they facilitate efficient, real-time transactions without the burden of gas fees.

- **Micropayment Platforms:** An example is the **Raiden Network**, often described as the Lightning Network for Ethereum. It enables scalable, low-fee, instant payments across a network of participants. This is ideal for IoT transactions, content monetization platforms, or any application requiring high-volume, low-value transactions.
- **Gaming: Connext** is another instance, providing scalable payment channels for DApps. In gaming, this allows for a seamless in-game economy where players can buy, sell, or trade items and currencies instantly without leaving the game environment or incurring high transaction costs. For example, a multiplayer online game could use state channels to handle in-game purchases and trades, significantly enhancing the user experience.

Despite their advantages, state channels come with several limitations:

- **Liquidity Concerns:** To open a state channel, both parties must commit funds to the channel, which are then "locked" until the channel is closed. This requirement can be a barrier to entry for some users or applications that do not wish to lock significant capital.
- **Availability Requirement:** Since state channels operate off-chain, participants must remain online to sign off on transactions and respond to state updates. This necessity can be cumbersome, especially in applications where continuous online presence is unrealistic.
- **Complexity in Dispute Resolution:** While state channels are designed to settle disputes on the blockchain, the actual mechanisms for doing so can be complex and daunting for users. This complexity can deter adoption, especially among less technically savvy users.

State channels and rollups collectively represent the forefront of efforts to scale Ethereum, catering to different needs and scenarios. While state channels excel in environments requiring rapid, numerous transactions between a set number of parties, rollups are more suited to general scalability improvements for the broader network.

Coding Example

Let's develop a basic smart contract that simulates opening and closing a state channel on Ethereum. This example will focus on a payment channel between two parties, allowing them to transact multiple times off-chain and only settle the final state on-chain.

Objective: Create a simplified Ethereum smart contract for a payment channel, demonstrating the opening, updating, and closing phases of a state channel.

Tools

- Remix Ethereum IDE for writing, compiling, and deploying the smart contract.

Step-by-Step Coding Example

1. Smart Contract Setup

```solidity
// SPDX-License-Identifier: MIT
pragma solidity ^0.8.0;

contract PaymentChannel {
    address payable public sender; // The party opening the payment
channel.
    address payable public recipient; // The party receiving the funds.
    uint public expiration; // Time when the channel automatically
expires.
```

```
constructor (address payable _recipient, uint duration) payable {
    sender = payable(msg.sender);
    recipient = _recipient;
    expiration = block.timestamp + duration;
}

// Function to extend the channel's expiration, for longer
transactions periods.
function extendExpiration(uint newExpiration) external {
    require(msg.sender == sender, "Only the sender can extend the
expiration.");
    require(newExpiration > expiration, "New expiration must be after
the current expiration.");
    expiration = newExpiration;
}

// Function to close the channel and release funds based on the off-
chain transactions.
// `_amount` is the total amount to be transferred to the recipient.
// `_signature` is the sender's signature over this amount, proving
they agree to the transfer.
function closeChannel(uint _amount, bytes memory _signature) external
{
    require(msg.sender == recipient, "Only the recipient can close
the channel.");
    require(isValidSignature(_amount, _signature), "Invalid
signature.");
    require(_amount <= address(this).balance, "Amount is more than
the contract's balance.");

    recipient.transfer(_amount); // Transfer the agreed amount to the
recipient.
    selfdestruct(sender); // Close the contract and return remaining
funds to the sender.
}

// Helper function to verify the signature.
function isValidSignature(uint _amount, bytes memory _signature)
internal view returns (bool) {
    bytes32 message = prefixed(keccak256(abi.encodePacked(this,
_amount)));
    return recoverSigner(message, _signature) == sender;
}

// Signature methods.
function splitSignature(bytes memory sig)
    internal
    pure
    returns (uint8, bytes32, bytes32)
{
    require(sig.length == 65, "Invalid signature length.");
```

```
    bytes32 r;
    bytes32 s;
    uint8 v;

    assembly {
        // first 32 bytes, after the length prefix.
        r := mload(add(sig, 32))
        // second 32 bytes.
        s := mload(add(sig, 64))
        // final byte (first byte of the next 32 bytes).
        v := byte(0, mload(add(sig, 96)))
    }

    return (v, r, s);
}

function recoverSigner(bytes32 message, bytes memory sig)
    internal
    pure
    returns (address)
{
    (uint8 v, bytes32 r, bytes32 s) = splitSignature(sig);

    return ecrecover(message, v, r, s);
}

// Builds a prefixed hash to mimic the behavior of eth_sign.
function prefixed(bytes32 hash) internal pure returns (bytes32) {
    return keccak256(abi.encodePacked("\x19Ethereum Signed Message:\
n32", hash));
    }
}
```

Explanation

- **Constructor:** Initializes the payment channel with a sender, a recipient, and an expiration date.
- **extendExpiration():** Allows the sender to extend the expiration time if more time for transactions is needed.
- **closeChannel():** The recipient can close the channel by presenting a signed message from the sender indicating the final amount to be transferred. This function ensures that only a valid signature from the sender can authorize the transfer, then self-destructs the contract to return any remaining funds to the sender.
- **isValidSignature():** Verifies that the provided signature corresponds to the signed message by the sender.

Then, this is how it works:

1. **Opening the Channel:** The sender deploys the contract, specifying the recipient and duration. The contract's deployment includes sending Ether to it, which is the maximum amount that can be transferred through the channel.
2. **Off-Chain Transactions:** The sender and recipient transact freely off-chain. For each transaction, the sender signs a message indicating the total amount of Ether that should be transferred to the recipient up to that point.
3. **Closing the Channel:** The recipient closes the channel by submitting the last signed message to the smart contract. The contract verifies the signature and transfers the specified amount of Ether to the recipient. The contract is then destroyed, returning any remaining Ether back to the sender.

This example simplifies many aspects of state channels, such as handling disputes and enabling multiple off-chain transactions, but it provides a foundational understanding of how state channels facilitate off-chain transactions with on-chain finality.

2.2 Plasma: Scaling Ethereum Through Hierarchical Blockchains

Plasma was first proposed in a whitepaper by Joseph Poon and Vitalik Buterin in 2017. The proposal came at a time when the Ethereum community was increasingly concerned about the network's ability to scale effectively. As Ethereum gained popularity for its smart contract capabilities, it became clear that its throughput was insufficient for the demand, leading to high gas fees and slow transaction times. Plasma was envisioned as a solution to these scalability issues, inspired by the Lightning Network's approach to Bitcoin scaling. It aimed to create a framework for executing scalable and autonomous smart contracts by establishing a series of child chains tethered to the Ethereum main chain.

The attraction to Plasma grew as the decentralized application (DApp) ecosystem on Ethereum expanded. Developers and users sought solutions to the network's scaling limitations, which became a bottleneck for DApp functionality and user experience. The promise of Plasma lay in its potential to multiply Ethereum's transaction capacity exponentially without sacrificing the network's decentralized security model. This was particularly appealing for developers looking to build complex, high-frequency DApps that were unfeasible on the Ethereum mainnet due to gas costs and throughput limitations.

At its core, Plasma is a framework for building nested blockchains, referred to as child chains, which are anchored to the Ethereum main chain. These child chains can process transactions independently of the main chain, aggregating them into a condensed form that is periodically committed to the main Ethereum blockchain. This hierarchical structure allows for significant increases in throughput by offloading the bulk of transaction processing to these child chains, while still leveraging the security and immutability of the main Ethereum chain.

Key Features of Plasma:

- **Child Chains:** Each child chain is a separate blockchain that can have its own consensus model, block validation mechanisms, and even operate different smart contracts. These chains report back to the main Ethereum chain, ensuring their state is secured by Ethereum's network.
- **MapReduce Technique:** Plasma utilizes a concept inspired by the MapReduce programming model to organize and process data on child chains before committing it to the main chain.[1] This technique enables efficient data handling and interaction across multiple child chains.
- **Fraud Proofs:** To maintain security, Plasma uses fraud proofs, allowing users to challenge invalid transactions recorded on child chains. If a fraudulent transaction is detected, it can be contested on the main Ethereum chain, ensuring that users' funds are protected.
- **Exit Mechanisms:** Users and assets can freely move between the main Ethereum chain and Plasma's child chains through a secure exit mechanism. This process ensures that users can retrieve their assets from child chains even in the case of disputes or child chain failures.

While Plasma presented a novel approach to scaling Ethereum, its implementation faced several challenges. Complexities associated with managing child chains, ensuring secure and efficient exits, and handling dispute resolutions have led to a reevaluation of its practicality. Over time, the focus within the Ethereum community has shifted toward alternative scaling solutions such as rollups, which offer simpler implementation and interaction models while still addressing the core scalability issues.

Despite these challenges, Plasma's conceptual framework contributed significantly to the ongoing dialogue and development of Layer 2 scaling solutions. It pushed the boundaries of what is possible in blockchain scalability, laying the groundwork for future innovations in the space.

Coding Example

Let's develop an example focusing on how assets can be locked in a smart contract on the main chain (simulating a deposit to a child chain) and how they can be withdrawn (simulating an exit from a child chain).

---

[1] The MapReduce programming model is a framework used for processing and generating large data sets with a parallel, distributed algorithm on a cluster. It simplifies the processing of vast amounts of data by breaking it down into manageable chunks, which can be processed in parallel across many nodes.

```solidity
// SPDX-License-Identifier: MIT
pragma solidity ^0.8.0;

contract SimplifiedPlasma {
    mapping(address => uint256) public deposits;
    address public owner;

    constructor() {
        owner = msg.sender;
    }

    // Event declarations
    event Deposited(address indexed depositor, uint256 amount);
    event Withdrawn(address indexed withdrawer, uint256 amount);

    // Modifier to restrict certain functions to the contract owner
    modifier onlyOwner() {
        require(msg.sender == owner, "Only the contract owner can perform
this action");
        _;
    }

    // Deposit function to simulate locking assets on the main chain
    function deposit() public payable {
        require(msg.value > 0, "Deposit value must be greater
than zero");
        deposits[msg.sender] += msg.value;
        emit Deposited(msg.sender, msg.value);
    }

    // Withdraw function to simulate exiting assets from a child chain
back to the main chain
    function withdraw(uint256 _amount) public {
        require(deposits[msg.sender] >= _amount, "Insufficient balance to
withdraw");
        deposits[msg.sender] -= _amount;
        payable(msg.sender).transfer(_amount);
        emit Withdrawn(msg.sender, _amount);
    }

    // Emergency withdraw function callable by the owner to handle
disputes or child chain failures
    function emergencyWithdraw(address _to, uint256 _amount) public
onlyOwner {
        require(deposits[_to] >= _amount, "Insufficient balance to
withdraw");
        deposits[_to] -= _amount;
        payable(_to).transfer(_amount);
        emit Withdrawn(_to, _amount);
    }
}
```

Then, this is how it works:

1. **Deposits:** Users can deposit Ether into the contract, simulating locking their assets into a Plasma child chain. The deposited amount is recorded in the contract's state.
2. **Withdrawals:** Users can withdraw their deposited Ether, simulating the process of exiting from the Plasma child chain back to the Ethereum main chain. The contract checks the user's balance before allowing the withdrawal.
3. **Emergency Withdrawals:** The contract owner can perform withdrawals on behalf of users, simulating a mechanism to resolve disputes or handle failures of the child chain.

This simplified example captures the basic interactions of depositing to and withdrawing from a Plasma-like framework but overlooks the full complexity of Plasma, such as handling multiple child chains, transaction verification within child chains, and fraud proof mechanisms.

2.3 Sidechains

Sidechains act as auxiliary blockchains that run alongside a main chain (like Ethereum) to offer expanded capabilities without overloading the primary network. By definition, sidechains are separate blockchains with their own consensus models and rules but are designed to communicate and interact with a main chain, enabling the transfer of assets and data back and forth.

The fundamental operation of sidechains involves two key processes: the locking and unlocking of assets on the main chain, and the corresponding issuance and burning of these assets on the sidechain. This two-way peg mechanism ensures that assets can move between the main chain and the sidechain without being duplicated or lost.

1. **Locking/Unlocking on Main Chain:** When assets are transferred from the main chain (e.g., Ethereum) to a sidechain, they are locked in a smart contract on the main chain, effectively taking them out of circulation.
2. **Issuance/Burning on Sidechain:** Corresponding assets are then created (issued) on the sidechain. These can be used freely within the sidechain's ecosystem. When transferring assets back to the main chain, the sidechain assets are burned (destroyed), and the original assets on the main chain are unlocked and returned to the user's control.

One of the hallmark examples of sidechain technology in action is Polygon (formerly known as Matic Network). Designed to alleviate the congestion and high fees associated with Ethereum's network, Polygon provides a faster, more cost-efficient environment for transactions and DApp interactions. It achieves this through a modified PoS consensus, which secures its network while enabling rapid processing. A notable application leveraging Polygon is Aavegotchi, a game that integrates DeFi concepts with crypto collectibles. By operating on Polygon, Aavegotchi facilitates a high volume of in-game transactions, from trading NFTs to managing DeFi stakes, without burdening the Ethereum mainnet.

Another example is the xDai Chain, which focuses on stable transactions by utilizing xDai, a stablecoin pegged to the US dollar, as its primary currency. The xDai Chain caters to payment and DeFi applications that benefit from predictable transaction costs. Platforms like Perpetual Protocol, which offers decentralized derivatives trading, utilize xDai to ensure users can trade with leverage efficiently and affordably, showcasing xDai's ability to support complex financial applications without the high costs associated with Ethereum's gas fees.

The introduction of sidechains represents a significant leap forward in blockchain development, addressing critical issues like scalability by offloading transactions from the main chain and enabling specific applications to function more efficiently. However, this innovation is not without its potential challenges. The security models of sidechains may differ from those of the main chain, introducing new vulnerabilities. Additionally, the complexity of managing assets across multiple chains adds a layer of difficulty for users and developers, necessitating a deeper understanding of the ecosystem, including the nuances of various wallets, tokens, and bridge mechanisms.

Despite these challenges, sidechains stand as a testament to the evolving landscape of blockchain technology, offering a pathway to scalable, versatile, and efficient applications. As we move forward, the continued development and refinement of sidechain technology will likely play a crucial role in expanding the capabilities and reach of blockchains like Ethereum, further integrating these systems into a wide array of applications and services.

Coding Example

This example is meant to provide a simplified asset transfer between the main chain and the sidechain.

Step-by-Step Example:

Smart Contract Setup:

```
// SPDX-License-Identifier: MIT
pragma solidity ^0.8.0;

contract AssetBridge {
    address public owner;
    mapping(address => uint256) public lockedAssets;

    constructor() {
        owner = msg.sender;
    }
```

```solidity
    // Event declarations for locking and unlocking assets
    event AssetsLocked(address indexed user, uint256 amount);
    event AssetsUnlocked(address indexed user, uint256 amount);

    // Modifier to restrict certain functions to the contract owner
    modifier onlyOwner() {
        require(msg.sender == owner, "Only the owner can perform this
action");
        _;
    }

    // Function to "lock" assets on the main chain, simulating a transfer
to the sidechain
    function lockAssets(uint256 _amount) external {
        require(_amount > 0, "Amount must be greater than zero");
        // In a real scenario, you would transfer tokens from the user to
the contract here
        lockedAssets[msg.sender] += _amount;
        emit AssetsLocked(msg.sender, _amount);
    }

    // Function to "unlock" assets on the main chain, simulating a
transfer back from the sidechain
    function unlockAssets(uint256 _amount) external onlyOwner {
        require(lockedAssets[msg.sender] >= _amount, "Insufficient locked
assets");
        // In a real scenario, you would transfer tokens from the
contract back to the user here
        lockedAssets[msg.sender] -= _amount;
        emit AssetsUnlocked(msg.sender, _amount);
    }
}
```

Explanation:

- The **AssetBridge** contract simulates an asset bridge between Ethereum and a sidechain.
- Users can "lock" assets in the contract, representing transferring assets to a sidechain. This is recorded in the **lockedAssets** mapping and emitted as an **AssetsLocked** event.
- The contract owner can "unlock" assets for a user, simulating the return transfer of assets from the sidechain to the main chain. This process is represented by the **unlockAssets** function and an **AssetsUnlocked** event.
- This simplified model does not include actual token transfers or interactions with a real sidechain. In practice, locking and unlocking would involve transferring ERC20 tokens or other assets into and out of the contract, and a corresponding sidechain mechanism would handle the mirrored operations on the sidechain.

This example abstracts the complexities of real sidechain interactions, focusing on the conceptual mechanism of locking and unlocking assets as a proxy for cross-chain transfers. A complete implementation would require mechanisms for securely verifying asset transfers between chains, handling disputes, and ensuring asset finality and consistency across both chains.

2.4 Rollups

Rollups work by executing transactions off-chain while ensuring that transaction data is securely recorded on-chain. This hybrid approach significantly increases the network's capacity to process transactions, reducing fees and improving transaction speeds without compromising the security and decentralization Ethereum is known for.

Rollups come in two primary flavors, each with its unique mechanism and advantages: Optimistic Rollups and Zero-Knowledge Rollups (ZK-Rollups). Though both types share the common goal of enhancing scalability, they diverge in their approach to transaction validation and security.

Optimistic Rollups take a trust-but-verify approach to transaction processing. By default, transactions executed within an Optimistic Rollup are presumed to be valid. This assumption allows for the off-chain execution of complex smart contracts and transactions without the computational overhead of immediate on-chain verification. Only in the event of a dispute—a challenge to the validity of a transaction—is the full computational power of the Ethereum mainnet invoked to adjudicate the claim. This model significantly reduces the amount of data and computation required on the mainnet for each transaction, enabling higher throughput and lower costs. However, the trade-off comes in the form of a delay in transaction finality, as transactions must wait out a *challenge* period before being conclusively confirmed. A prominent example of an Optimistic Rollup solution is Optimism, which has garnered attention for its compatibility with Ethereum's existing smart contracts and developer tools.

On the other side of the spectrum are Zero-Knowledge Rollups, or ZK-Rollups, which take a more cryptographic approach to scalability. ZK-Rollups use zero-knowledge proofs—a form of cryptographic proof that allows one party to prove to another that a statement is true without revealing any specific information about the statement itself. In the context of ZK-Rollups, this means that the validity of all transactions within the rollup can be verified in a compressed form on the mainnet without having to execute the transactions' full computational logic. This method not only ensures immediate transaction finality but also maintains privacy for the transactions' contents. ZK-Rollups are especially well-suited for applications requiring high throughput and strong privacy guarantees, such as financial transactions and voting systems. zkSync is a notable implementation of ZK-Rollups, offering Ethereum users and developers a scalable, secure platform for deploying decentralized applications.

While both Optimistic Rollups and ZK-Rollups offer significant improvements over Ethereum's baseline scalability, they each come with their own set of potential issues. Optimistic Rollups' reliance on a challenge period for dispute resolution introduces a delay in transaction finality, potentially impacting applications that require immediate settlement. Conversely, the complexity of generating zero-knowledge proofs in ZK-Rollups can present technical challenges, particularly for applications requiring fully general smart contract capabilities. Despite these challenges, the ongoing development and refinement of both types of rollups continue to push the boundaries of what's possible on Ethereum, paving the way for a more scalable, efficient, and versatile blockchain ecosystem.

Let's look at a few protocols as examples of these approaches.

PROMINENT PROTOCOL: ARBITRUM

Arbitrum is a leading example of an Optimistic Rollup solution designed to enhance the scalability of Ethereum by enabling high-throughput, low-cost transactions while maintaining the security and decentralization of the main Ethereum network. It's tailored to support the execution of smart contracts and general computation more efficiently than Ethereum's base layer.

At its heart, Arbitrum operates by assuming that transactions and smart contract executions conducted within its layer are valid by default. This assumption significantly reduces the immediate computational load on the Ethereum network because it bypasses the need for Ethereum to verify each transaction's computational correctness in real-time. Instead, transactions are batched together, and their collective state is periodically committed to the Ethereum mainnet.

When a transaction or smart contract execution occurs on Arbitrum, it's processed off-chain by validators who are responsible for maintaining the Arbitrum chain. These validators execute the transactions, keep track of the resulting state, and periodically post a summary or "rollup" of these states back to Ethereum. This summary includes a snapshot of the new state, effectively updating the Ethereum mainnet on the outcomes of the off-chain computations without burdening it with the computational load.

The "Optimistic" aspect of Arbitrum's rollup comes into play with its innovative approach to dispute resolution. Since computations are assumed to be valid, there needs to be a mechanism for challenging and verifying transactions when necessary. Arbitrum achieves this through an interactive dispute resolution protocol. If a party believes that a transaction has been executed incorrectly, they can challenge the computation on the Ethereum mainnet. Arbitrum then facilitates a game-like verification process where the challenging and defending parties isolate the specific point of contention in the computation. This process allows Ethereum to adjudicate the dispute by executing only the smallest necessary part of the computation, thereby verifying the transaction's correctness without the need for full on-chain execution.

By executing the bulk of its computation off-chain and only periodically committing state updates to Ethereum, Arbitrum can significantly increase transaction throughput and reduce transaction costs (gas fees) for its users. This efficiency does not come at the cost of security or decentralization because the Ethereum mainnet ultimately secures the assets and finality of the transactions. The ability to support EVM-compatible smart contracts allows developers to deploy existing Ethereum applications on Arbitrum without significant modifications, making it an attractive scalability solution for a wide range of decentralized applications.

Adoption Since its launch, Arbitrum has been adopted by various projects spanning DeFi, NFTs, and other sectors seeking scalability without compromising Ethereum's security. It has attracted protocols looking to scale their operations, reduce transaction fees for their users, and improve the user experience with faster transaction finality compared to the congested Ethereum mainnet. In DeFi, the most commonly used indicator for chains' activity is Total Value Locked (TVL). TVL represents the aggregate amount of assets that are currently locked within the smart contracts of a DeFi platform or a set of protocols on a blockchain. A higher TVL indicates that more users are willing to commit their funds, suggesting a higher level of trust and participation in that particular platform or ecosystem. In sum, TVL is a direct measure of how much capital is actively being used on a platform. For instance, in lending platforms, it includes the money lent out and staked as collateral. In yield farming, it includes the assets deposited in liquidity pools. The more the assets locked, the more active and potentially lucrative the platform is. TVL is also a useful comparative metric across different chains or platforms, giving investors and users a quick way to assess where the activity is concentrated at any given time. This can guide investment decisions and strategic moves within the DeFi space

According to DefiLlama, the most of the first DeFi projects to have TVL on Arbitrum were DEXs (Balancer V2, Swapr V2, SushiSwap, Uniswap V3, GMX V1 and MCDEX). **Figure 2** plots the TVL on Arbitrum since inception, based off computations by DefiLlama.

In summary, Arbitrum represents a practical implementation of Optimistic Rollups, addressing Ethereum's scalability challenges by balancing efficiency, security, and compatibility. Its innovative approach to computation and dispute resolution exemplifies how Layer 2 solutions can complement and extend the

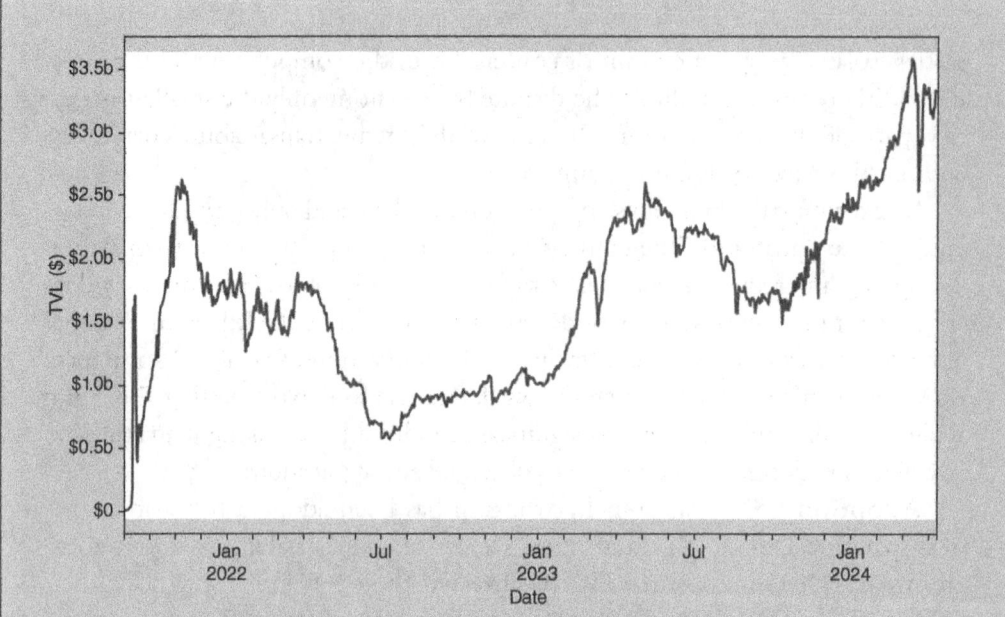

Figure 2   Arbitrum TVL (*source:* Adapted from DefiLama)

capabilities of existing blockchain infrastructures, paving the way for the broader adoption and growth of decentralized applications.

Let's look at another prominent protocol in this space: Optimism.

PROMINENT PROTOCOL: OPTIMISM

Optimism is another prominent example of an Optimistic Rollup, aiming to scale Ethereum by executing transactions off-chain while leveraging the security of the Ethereum mainnet. Like Arbitrum, Optimism optimizes the throughput and cost-efficiency of Ethereum transactions but with a keen focus on maintaining the Ethereum Virtual Machine's (EVM) compatibility. This compatibility allows developers to deploy existing Ethereum applications on Optimism with minimal changes.

Optimism processes transactions outside the Ethereum mainnet. Let's see a simplified breakdown of its operation:

1. **Transaction Execution:** Transactions are executed on the Optimism network, which runs parallel to Ethereum. This off-chain execution means that the Optimism network can handle many transactions quickly and at a lower cost than the congested Ethereum mainnet.
2. **State Commitment:** Periodically, the state of all transactions processed by Optimism (summarized as a single state root) is committed to the Ethereum blockchain. This state root represents a compressed version of the off-chain

transaction data, ensuring the Ethereum mainnet can remain the ultimate source of truth without being burdened by the details of every transaction.

3. **Assumed Validity and Dispute Resolution:** Following the Optimistic Rollup model, transactions processed by Optimism are assumed to be valid. If someone believes a transaction was fraudulent or incorrect, they can submit a fraud proof. Optimism then utilizes a challenge period during which disputes can be raised. If a transaction is successfully challenged, the network corrects the fraudulent activity.

Optimism helps Ethereum by significantly increasing transaction throughput and reducing fees. By moving the bulk of computational work off-chain and only periodically committing state updates to Ethereum, Optimism alleviates congestion on the mainnet. This approach enables more scalable DApps while still securing assets and computations using Ethereum's robust decentralized security model.

Handling Fraudulent Transactions in Optimistic Rollups

If to improve scalability, one assumes that all transactions are valid, isn't this a recipe for disaster?!

Fortunately, handling fraudulent transactions in Optimistic Rollups involves a unique mechanism that balances the efficiency of off-chain transaction processing with the security and integrity of the blockchain. In Optimistic Rollups, transactions are assumed to be valid unless proven otherwise. This assumption allows for high throughput and lower costs, making it an attractive layer 2 scaling solution for Ethereum. However, this approach introduces the possibility of fraudulent transactions being temporarily accepted by the system. To mitigate this risk, Optimistic Rollups employ a system of fraud proofs, dispute resolution windows, and specialized network participants known as watchers or verifiers.

When a batch of transactions from the rollup is submitted to the Ethereum mainnet, it triggers a dispute resolution window, often lasting several days. During this period, the batch is scrutinized by watchers whose role is to ensure the integrity of transactions. If they spot a discrepancy or a fraudulent transaction, they can challenge it by submitting a fraud proof. This proof acts as evidence that a specific transaction within the batch is invalid. The submission of a fraud proof initiates a verification process on the mainnet, where, if the challenge is validated, the fraudulent transaction is reverted, and the rollup's state is corrected to reflect the accurate transaction history.

This process ensures that, despite the initial assumption of transaction validity, there remains a robust mechanism for maintaining the ledger's integrity. The presence of incentives for identifying fraudulent transactions, alongside penalties for attempting to introduce them, further secures the network against manipulation.

The concept of fraud proof operates under the principle that while transactions are processed off-chain for efficiency, the security of the blockchain is never compromised. For instance, if Alice attempts to send Bob an amount of ETH that she does not own, and this transaction is included in a rollup batch, a verifier like Carol can identify this discrepancy by examining the available data on the rollup. She can then submit a fraud proof to the main chain, showcasing the invalidity of the transaction, leading to its reversion and ensuring the rollup's accurate reflection of account balances and transaction histories. Why would Carol spend time checking these transactions? Because she gets rewarded if she spots incorrect transactions.

This mechanism, though effective in maintaining security and integrity, introduces a trade-off in terms of transaction finality. The dispute resolution window necessary for challenging transactions means that finality on Optimistic Rollups is delayed compared to the main Ethereum chain or other scaling solutions like ZK-Rollups. However, this trade-off is often acceptable for many users and applications prioritizing scalability and cost-effectiveness over immediate finality. High transaction volumes are supported through off-chain computation and batch processing, enhancing the overall efficiency of the Ethereum network.

The system of handling fraudulent transactions in Optimistic Rollups exemplifies how layer 2 solutions can offer significant scalability benefits while ensuring the security and integrity of transactions through innovative mechanisms like fraud proofs and the active participation of network watchers. This balance between efficiency, security, and decentralization is at the heart of solving the scalability trilemma that blockchain networks face.

Balancing High Transaction Volume and Delayed Finality

Even with this delay in finality, Optimistic Rollups can still foster high transaction volumes, offering significant scalability benefits. Here's how:

1. Off-chain Computation: Transactions are processed off-chain, which significantly increases throughput and reduces congestion on the main Ethereum chain.
2. Batch Processing: Transactions are batched together before being submitted to the mainnet, allowing for efficient use of block space.
3. User Experience: For most users and transactions, the delay in finality is not a significant issue. Many transactions, especially smaller or routine ones, don't require immediate finality. Users generally accept a delay in exchange for faster and cheaper transactions.
4. Trust and Reputation: In practice, parties involved in a transaction on an Optimistic Rollup may operate based on a degree of trust. For instance, a reputable entity in the ecosystem may be trusted not to submit fraudulent transactions, thus reducing the perceived risk even within the challenge period.
5. Layer 1 for Critical Transactions: For transactions that require immediate finality, users might still prefer using the main Ethereum chain despite higher fees and lower throughput.

6. Risk Management: Applications and users can implement risk management strategies considering the finality delay. For example, a DeFi platform might delay withdrawal of funds until finality is achieved.

Let's outline a high-level pseudo-code to illustrate the conceptual process involved in submitting and handling a fraud proof within an Optimistic Rollup system. This example is simplified for explanatory purposes and does not represent actual code runnable on any blockchain.

PSEUDO-CODE FOR HANDLING FRAUDULENT TRANSACTIONS IN AN OPTIMISTIC ROLLUP

1. Submitting a Transaction Batch (by a Rollup Operator)

```
function submitBatch(batchHash, transactions) {
    // This function is called by the rollup operator to submit a batch
of transactions
    // to the main Ethereum chain. `batchHash` is a cryptographic hash
representing
    // the state of the rollup after applying the `transactions`.
}
```

2. Watching for Fraudulent Transactions (by Watchers/Verifiers)

```
function watchTransactions() {
    // Watchers monitor the transaction batches submitted to the Ethereum
chain.
    // They independently compute the state transitions based on the
transactions
    // and compare the result with the submitted `batchHash`.
}
```

3. Submitting a Fraud Proof (by a Watcher who Detects Fraud)

```
function submitFraudProof(batchHash, fraudulentTransaction, proof) {
    // If a watcher detects a discrepancy between their computed state
and the
    // `batchHash` submitted by the rollup operator, they can submit a
fraud proof.
    // The `fraudulentTransaction` is the specific transaction that is
disputed,
    // and `proof` contains evidence demonstrating the transaction's
invalidity.
}
```

4. Verifying the Fraud Proof (on the Main Ethereum Chain)

```
function verifyFraudProof(batchHash, fraudulentTransaction, proof) {
    // This function represents the smart contract logic on the Ethereum
chain
```

```
    // that verifies the submitted fraud proof. If the proof is valid,
indicating
    // the transaction was indeed fraudulent, the disputed batch is
rolled back,
    // and the state is reverted to before the fraudulent transaction.
}
```

5. Reverting the Fraudulent Transaction

```
function revertTransaction(batchHash, fraudulentTransaction) {
    // Based on a successful fraud proof verification, this function
reverts
    // the fraudulent transaction, restoring the rollup's state to its
valid
    // form before the fraud occurred.
}
```

Conceptual Overview

- **Rollup Operator Submits Batches:** Transactions are processed off-chain and submitted in batches by the rollup operator. Each batch submission includes a hash representing the new state of the rollup.
- **Watchers Monitor and Verify:** Watchers or verifiers independently compute the state transitions based on the transactions, and compare their results with the submitted batch hash.
- **Fraud Proof Submission:** If discrepancies are found, a watcher submits a fraud proof to the main chain, challenging the validity of the batch.
- **Main Chain Verification and Reversion:** The main Ethereum chain verifies the fraud proof. If validated, the fraudulent transaction is reverted, and the rollup's state is corrected.

This pseudo-code outlines the conceptual steps involved in detecting and resolving fraudulent transactions within an Optimistic Rollup framework.

Types of DApps on Arbitrum vs. Optimism *If there are several optimistic roll-ups available, which one should a developer choose to migrate to?*

Both Arbitrum and Optimism support a wide range of decentralized applications, from DeFi platforms to NFT marketplaces. However, differences in their technology, ecosystem development, and community support might make one more appealing than the other for specific use cases.

- **Arbitrum:** Has rapidly grown its ecosystem, attracting projects looking for high throughput and low costs. Arbitrum's significant adoption among DeFi protocols, like SushiSwap and Balancer, showcases its appeal for applications requiring complex smart contract interactions and high-frequency trading. Its capability to handle

sophisticated computations off-chain makes it a go-to for developers prioritizing flexibility and performance.

- **Optimism:** With its EVM compatibility, Optimism is a strong candidate for projects
that aim to leverage Ethereum's developer tooling and existing smart contracts with
minimal modifications. Optimism has been particularly attractive for applications
looking to maintain a close operational resemblance to Ethereum, such as Uniswap
and Synthetix. This makes it ideal for DApps seeking to offer their users the familiar
Ethereum experience with the added benefits of scalability.

In essence, the choice between Arbitrum and Optimism might come down to specific technical preferences, the existing user base of the DApp, and the types of interactions it requires. Both rollups are pivotal in Ethereum's scaling strategy, offering developers
the tools to build the next generation of decentralized applications without the limitations of the mainnet's current throughput and cost.

2.5 Zero-Knowledge Rollups (ZK-Rollups)

The term "Zero-Knowledge Proof" (ZKP) comes from the concept's ability to prove
the truth of a statement without conveying any information beyond the validity of the
statement itself, thus "zero knowledge" is transferred about the statement or the proof
beyond its truthfulness.[2] This might sound paradoxical at first—*how can you prove something without revealing any information about what you're proving?*

Yet, this is precisely what makes ZKPs so powerful and intriguing. The "zero knowledge" aspect refers to the minimal amount of information exchange necessary to establish trust: the verifier learns nothing but the fact that the statement is true. This principle
underpins ZKPs and highlights their potential for enhancing privacy and security in
digital transactions, where you can verify the authenticity of information without exposing the information itself.

Let's use an analogy to explain the concept of Zero-Knowledge Proofs (ZKPs), focusing on how they allow someone to prove they know a secret without revealing what it is.

Imagine a scenario (**Figure 3**) where a colorblind person and someone with normal
color vision are working together. The colorblind person has two balls, one red and one
blue, but to them, both balls appear identical because they can't perceive the difference
in color. Their task is to determine whether the sighted person can genuinely distinguish
the colors without explicitly revealing which ball is which. This setup can serve as an
analogy for Zero-Knowledge (ZK) proofs, where one party must demonstrate they
know something without disclosing specific information.

---

[2] Zero-knowledge proofs were introduced in a groundbreaking 1985 research paper titled "The Knowledge
Complexity of Interactive Proof Systems" by Shafi Goldwasser, Silvio Micali, and Charles Rackoff. This work
established a foundational definition for zero-knowledge proofs that remains influential:

"Zero-knowledge protocols allow one party (the prover) to demonstrate to another party (the verifier) the
truth of a statement without revealing any information beyond the veracity of the statement itself."

Figure 3   ZK Proof Figurative Illustration

To test the sighted person's ability to distinguish the colors, the colorblind person hides both balls behind their back. They may shuffle them, swap them, or leave them in the same position. The sighted person must then guess whether a swap occurred based on their ability to distinguish between red and blue. If the guess is correct, it indicates that the sighted person can identify the colors, even though they never explicitly say which ball is red or blue.

However, the sighted person could have guessed. This process is then repeated several times, with the colorblind person occasionally swapping the balls and sometimes leaving them as they were. Each time, the sighted person must correctly guess whether a swap occurred. If they can consistently guess correctly, it's strong evidence that they can tell the colors apart, even though the colorblind person never learns which ball is red and which is blue.

This analogy illustrates the concept of a Zero-Knowledge proof. The sighted person (the prover) can prove to the colorblind person (the verifier) that they possess specific knowledge (the ability to distinguish colors) without revealing any additional information (which ball is which). The repetition of the process and consistent correct guesses build confidence in the proof, demonstrating the ability to verify something without revealing sensitive details. This is similar to how Zero-Knowledge proofs are used in cryptography and blockchain technology to ensure security and privacy while proving the validity of certain information.

ZKPs in the blockchain context take this concept and apply mathematical structures to enable one party (the prover) to prove to another party (the verifier) that a statement (e.g., a transaction is valid) is true, without revealing any additional information other than the veracity of the statement itself.

Zero-knowledge rollups transform the traditional Layer 2 blockchain scaling paradigm by using zero-knowledge proofs to compress and secure transaction data. In a typical ZK rollup, a batch of transactions is reduced to a list of changes that reflect how Ethereum's state should be updated. This compressed batch, alongside a zero-knowledge proof, is sent to a smart contract on Ethereum, which oversees the state of the ZK rollup. The rollup node generates the proof, ensuring that the proposed state changes are consistent with the actual results of the batched transactions. Once verified, the smart contract implements these changes on Ethereum, updating the state and executing the transactions.

A critical aspect of zero-knowledge rollups is that they separate computation and storage from the Ethereum mainnet, performing them off-chain. The smart contract on Ethereum controls the transacted funds while the more resource-intensive tasks of computation and storage occur in a separate environment. This offloading of tasks allows ZK rollups to achieve significant efficiency gains.

Zero-knowledge rollups offer several notable advantages over other scaling methods, such as optimistic rollups. Firstly, ZK proofs rely on mathematical verification rather than incentivized actors in a dispute resolution system. This trustless approach provides a more secure and less vulnerable framework for validating transactions. In contrast, optimistic rollups depend on game-theory-based mechanisms to ensure validity, where actors might be incentivized to submit or challenge fraudulent transactions.

Secondly, the compression achieved by zero-knowledge rollups reduces the time-to-finality for transactions, making the process faster and substantially lowering fees. This compression involves summarizing the transaction data into a list of proposed changes that requires less bandwidth and computation to process.

Thirdly, zero-knowledge rollups have shorter withdrawal waiting periods compared to optimistic rollups. In optimistic rollups, funds are subject to a waiting period—sometimes up to a week—to mitigate the risk of fraud during the dispute resolution process. To circumvent this delay, users may turn to liquidity providers, but this comes with additional fees. In zero-knowledge rollups, the waiting period is significantly shorter, usually a few hours or even minutes, because verification relies on the quick processing of the zero-knowledge proof.

These advantages contribute to the growing appeal of zero-knowledge rollups, particularly in applications requiring high throughput, lower transaction costs, and improved security. As the technology evolves, ZK rollups are expected to play a more prominent role in scaling blockchain networks and enabling a broader range of decentralized applications. The inherent security and efficiency of zero-knowledge proofs pave the way for a more scalable and reliable blockchain ecosystem.

How does it look to use a ZK roll up? **Figure 4** shows a closer look at how this unfolds.

Transaction Batch Creation	In a ZK rollup, multiple transactions are combined into a single batch. Each transaction in the batch represents an operation on the Ethereum blockchain, such as a transfer of tokens or a smart contract interaction.
Generating a zk-SNARK Proof	The ZK rollup platform processes the batch of transactions to generate a zk-SNARK proof. This proof represents the result of executing all the transactions in the batch and provides a succinct way to summarize the changes to the Ethereum state. The proof includes mathematical commitments that ensure its security and integrity.
Submitting to a Smart Contract	The generated zk-SNARK proof is submitted to a smart contract on the Ethereum main chain. This smart contract is designed to verify zk-SNARK proofs and maintain the state of the ZK rollup.
Verifying the zk-SNARK Proof	The smart contract verifies the zk-SNARK proof by checking its mathematical correctness. This verification process ensures that the proof accurately represents the batch of transactions and the resulting changes to the Ethereum state. If the proof is valid, it indicates that the transactions in the batch are legitimate and consistent with the current state of the blockchain.
Updating the Ethereum State	Once the zk-SNARK proof is verified, the smart contract executes the state changes represented by the proof. This step updates the Ethereum blockchain to reflect the outcomes of the batched transactions. Because the zk-SNARK proof has already been verified, this process is efficient and secure.

Figure 4   High-level overview of how zk-SNARKs work in the context of a platform like zkSync

Initiation and Aggregation   When a user performs a transaction on a platform utilizing ZK-Rollups, that transaction is directed to an off-chain Rollup operator rather than being broadcast across the network. The operator gathers these transactions over a specified timeframe, bundling them into a single batch. This batch is then organized into a Merkle tree, a structure that effectively condenses the transaction data, facilitating the subsequent generation of a zero-knowledge proof that attests to the batch's validity.

The Role of Zero-Knowledge Proofs   Zero-knowledge proofs, specifically types like zk-SNARKs (Zero-Knowledge Succinct Non-Interactive Arguments of Knowledge) or zk-STARKs, are then computed for the batch. These proofs are pivotal, as they confirm the legitimacy of all transactions in the batch according to Ethereum's rules (such as ensuring no funds are double-spent and that all transactions are solvent) *without disclosing individual transaction details*. The computation of these proofs is performed off-chain by the Rollup operator.

Main Chain Interaction   Once the zero-knowledge proof is ready, it is submitted to a smart contract on the Ethereum main chain, along with a compressed version of the transaction data. This ensures that while the bulk of computational work is done off-chain, the essential data remains accessible on-chain for verification purposes.

Finalizing the Transaction Batch   The smart contract on Ethereum then verifies the submitted zero-knowledge proof. This verification process is significantly less resource-intensive compared to the traditional method of verifying each transaction individually. Upon successful verification, Ethereum's ledger is updated to reflect the batched transactions, cementing their finality and immutability within the blockchain's state.

Advantages Over Traditional Ethereum Transactions   The standard procedure on the Ethereum blockchain involves broadcasting each transaction to the network, where it is validated and added to a block by miners (or validators, with the advent of Ethereum 2.0). This demands that every node independently verifies every transaction, a process that can quickly become a bottleneck. ZK-Rollups streamline this by offloading most of the computational work off-chain. The Ethereum network, in turn, is tasked with verifying a singular proof representing hundreds or even thousands of transactions, markedly diminishing the computational burden. This is a benefit of batching, which is not really unique to ZK.

By conducting extensive transaction processing off-chain and employing zero-knowledge proofs for integrity assurance, ZK rollups significantly alleviate the load on the Ethereum network. This approach not only maintains the core tenets of security and decentralization but also heralds a scalable, efficient future for blockchain technology, ensuring its viability for a wide array of applications and higher transaction volumes.

ZKPs AND PRIVACY

Zero-Knowledge Proofs (ZKPs) have profound implications for privacy in digital transactions and beyond, by allowing the verification of data without revealing the data itself. This unique characteristic opens up a plethora of applications in various fields where privacy is paramount.

- **Financial Transactions:** In the realm of blockchain and cryptocurrencies, ZKPs can be used to facilitate private transactions. Unlike traditional blockchain transactions that are transparent and traceable, ZKPs enable parties to validate transactions without exposing sensitive information, such as the amount transferred, the identity of the parties involved, or even the asset type. This ensures financial privacy while maintaining the integrity and security of the transaction.

- **Identity Verification:** ZKPs allow individuals to prove aspects of their identity (e.g., age, nationality, or membership status) to third parties without revealing unnecessary personal information. For example, proving that one is over the legal age limit for purchasing alcohol without disclosing the exact age or date of birth. This application is incredibly useful in online verification processes, significantly enhancing privacy and reducing the risk of identity theft.

- **Voting Systems:** Implementing ZKPs in electronic voting systems can ensure the privacy and integrity of votes. Voters can prove that their votes have been cast correctly without revealing the vote's content, ensuring anonymity. Moreover, it can be used to verify that a voter is eligible to vote without disclosing their identity.

- **Selective Disclosure:** ZKPs enable selective disclosure of information within a dataset. For instance, one could prove they have a valid driver's license without revealing other personal information contained on the license, such as their address. This is particularly useful in scenarios where only specific pieces of data are required for verification.

- **Secure Multi-party Computation:** In scenarios where multiple parties need to compute an outcome based on their private inputs (e.g., bidding, negotiations), ZKPs can ensure that each party's input remains private. Only the final computation result is revealed, and no party gains knowledge about the other parties' inputs.

- **Access Control:** ZKPs can be used in access control systems to verify whether an individual has the right to access a resource without revealing their identity or the specific credentials that grant them access. This can be applied in both physical and digital security systems.

These applications represent just the tip of the iceberg for ZKPs. As research and technology advance, we can anticipate even more innovative uses for ZKPs, particularly in areas where privacy is critical. The ability to verify the truth of a claim while preserving the privacy of the underlying data has the potential to revolutionize how we handle sensitive information across industries.

To Wrap Up: Optimistic vs. ZK-Rollups?   The key difference between the two lies in their approach to transaction validation.

Optimistic Rollups: This approach assumes transactions are valid unless proven otherwise, significantly reducing the computational load on Ethereum. However, this comes with a challenge period, where transactions can be disputed before being finalized. This period is crucial for ensuring security but can introduce delays in transaction finality, which may not be suitable for all applications.

ZK-Rollups: It uses zero-knowledge proofs to validate all transactions off-chain before submitting a single proof to Ethereum for finality. This process ensures transactions are not only secure but also finalized almost instantly once the proof is accepted by the mainnet. zkSync can thus handle high transaction volumes with immediate finality, offering a significant advantage for applications that require speed and efficiency, such as financial services.

Current Challenges: Scalability Solutions in Practice

Challenges with Optimistic Rollups: The challenge period inherent to Optimistic Rollups, while a necessary security measure, poses operational challenges. For instance, during high network demand, such as a new token launch or during a DeFi protocol's liquidity event, the delay in transaction finality could impact users' ability to quickly access or trade assets. This delay necessitates balancing between security and operational efficiency in designing user experiences.

Complexity of ZK-Rollups: Despite their advantages, the complexity of developing ZK-Rollups, presents a significant challenge. Creating zero-knowledge proofs, especially for complex DApps requiring full EVM compatibility, involves sophisticated cryptographic techniques and a deep understanding of both blockchain technology and advanced mathematics. This complexity can slow down development and increase the resources necessary to launch and maintain ZK-Rollup-based solutions.

3. Alternative Blockchains (Ethereum Competitors)

With Ethereum's scalability issues becoming a bottleneck for decentralized applications, several alternative blockchains have emerged, focusing on high throughput, low fees, and scalability from the outset. Some of the most prominent examples include:

- **Polygon (MATIC):** While initially a Layer 2 scaling solution for Ethereum, Polygon has evolved into a framework for building interconnected blockchain networks, aiming to create a multi-chain Ethereum ecosystem.
- **Solana:** Solana uses a unique PoH consensus combined with PoS, achieving high throughput and low transaction costs.
- **Cardano:** Cardano is a decentralized blockchain platform that uses a unique PoS consensus mechanism, called Ouroboros to provide a secure, scalable and sustainable environment for smart contracts and decentralized applications.
- **Polkadot:** Polkadot is a blockchain platform designed to enable cross-chain interoperability, allowing multiple blockchains to connect and communicate through a shared network, while providing scalability and security through its innovative relay chain and parachain architecture.
- **Avalanche:** Avalanche features a unique consensus mechanism that allows for high throughput and quick finality, positioning itself as a highly scalable blockchain platform.

The choice between these solutions often depends on the specific requirements of the application, such as the need for speed, security, decentralization, or interoperability. Let's examine each in detail.

3.1 Polygon

Polygon, formerly known as Matic Network, is a multi-chain scaling solution for Ethereum. It was co-founded by Jaynti Kanani, Sandeep Nailwal, and Anurag Arjun in late 2017, with Mihailo Bjelic joining as a co-founder later. The project was initially developed to address the pressing issues of Ethereum's scalability, high transaction fees and slow transaction speeds, aiming to create a more accessible and user-friendly decentralized platform.

Development and Evolution   Polygon started as Matic Network, focusing on a single scaling solution for Ethereum through Plasma sidechains and a PoS blockchain. The initial vision was to improve the usability of DApps by providing faster and cheaper transactions while ensuring asset security is anchored to the Ethereum mainchain. Matic Network quickly garnered attention for its effective scaling capabilities, leading to its adoption by numerous DApps for improved performance.

In February 2021, Matic Network rebranded to Polygon, signaling a strategic shift toward creating a more ambitious and comprehensive framework for building and connecting Ethereum-compatible blockchain networks. This expanded vision included not just Plasma chains but also zk-Rollups, Optimistic Rollups, and other standalone chains, aiming to create a "Polkadot on Ethereum" that offers a multi-chain ecosystem with the interoperability, flexibility, and scalability needed for a decentralized future.

Polygon's Architecture   As captured in **Figure 5**, Polygon's architecture is as follows:

1. **Ethereum Layer:** At its core, Polygon maintains a tether to Ethereum, ensuring that assets and security mechanisms benefit from the robustness of Ethereum's network. This layer acts as the final arbiter and security guarantor for the entire ecosystem built on Polygon.
2. **Security Layer:** Operating alongside the Ethereum layer, this optional layer provides "security as a service," derived either from Ethereum directly or through a pool of professional validators. It's modular, meaning that chains can choose to subscribe for additional security or operate independently.
3. **Polygon Networks Layer:** This is where the various networks built using Polygon's SDK operate. Each network can have its own community, tokenomics, and governance models. These networks can be standalone blockchains or Layer 2 solutions, offering the flexibility for developers to choose the architecture that best suits their application's needs.

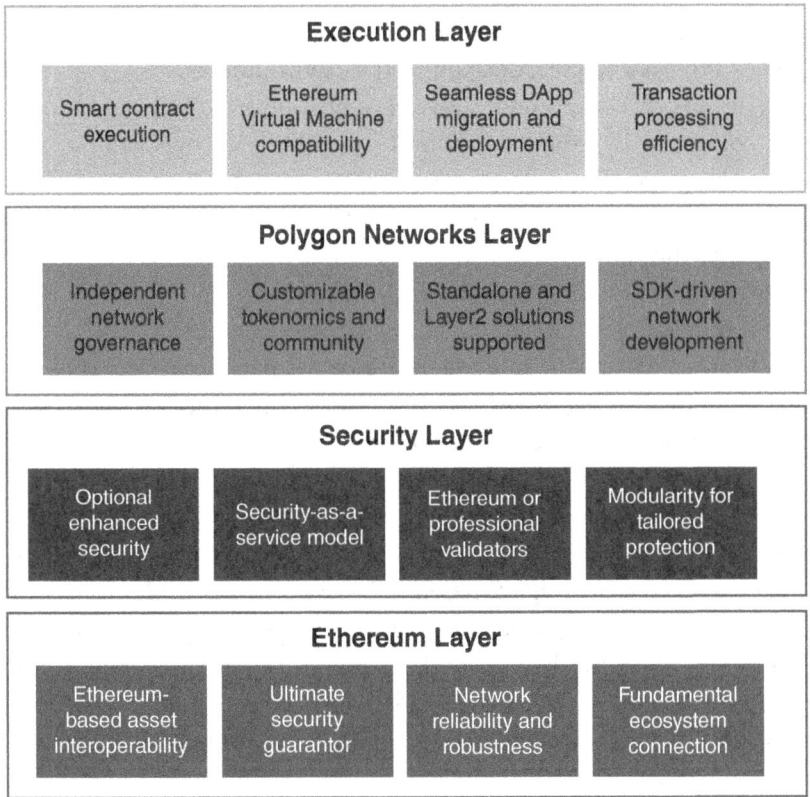

Figure 5   Polygon Architecture

4. Execution Layer: This layer is responsible for executing smart contracts and processing transactions. It's built on Polygon's Ethereum Virtual Machine (EVM) implementation, ensuring compatibility with Ethereum DApps and smart contracts, enabling developers to migrate or deploy their Ethereum DApps on Polygon with minimal changes.

Polygon's sidechains typically employ PoS as their consensus mechanism, striking a balance between speed, security, and decentralization. Validators stake MATIC tokens, Polygon's native token, to participate in the network's consensus process, validating transactions and creating new blocks. The PoS mechanism is designed to be energy-efficient while ensuring a high degree of security through economic incentives.

A critical component of Polygon's architecture is its bridging infrastructure, which facilitates asset transfers between Ethereum and Polygon's sidechains, as well as between different Polygon sidechains. The most commonly used bridge is the Polygon-Ethereum bridge, which supports both ERC-20 tokens and NFTs (ERC-721 and ERC-1155 tokens). This bridge operates by locking assets in a smart contract on the Ethereum network, minting corresponding assets on the Polygon network, and burning them on Polygon when they are transferred back to Ethereum.

Polygon's sidechains can achieve significantly higher transaction throughput than Ethereum's mainnet, with block times as low as 2 seconds and fees often a fraction of a cent. This is accomplished through the combination of PoS consensus and block architecture optimized for speed and efficiency, enabling Polygon to process up to 65,000 transactions per second (TPS) on a single sidechain in test environments.

The Polygon SDK is a core component allowing developers to build their own blockchains or scaling solutions. It provides modules for consensus, networking, and storage, among others, making it easier to develop custom blockchains suited to specific applications. Additionally, Polygon's full EVM compatibility means developers can deploy Ethereum smart contracts without any modifications, significantly lowering the barrier to entry for Ethereum developers looking to scale their DApps.

Polygon's technical infrastructure represents a comprehensive solution to Ethereum's scalability challenges, offering an adaptable framework for developers. By combining the security and interoperability of Ethereum with the high throughput and low cost of its own networks, Polygon stands as a pivotal platform in the broader blockchain ecosystem, facilitating the growth and scalability of DApps in ways previously constrained by Ethereum's limitations.

Polygon's scalability solutions have attracted a wide array of DApps, particularly from the DeFi and NFT spaces, seeking to leverage Ethereum's network effects without its scalability limitations. Projects ranging from QuickSwap, an AMM DEX; Aavegotchi, a crypto-collectibles platform; and OpenSea, the largest NFT marketplace, have integrated with Polygon to improve their transaction throughput and reduce costs. These integrations demonstrate Polygon's capability to support diverse applications, from high-frequency trading platforms to intricate NFT ecosystems, all while maintaining a user experience characterized by fast, low-cost transactions.

Polygon vs. Other Layer 2 Solutions   While Optimistic and ZK Rollups focus on batching transactions off-chain for later submission to Ethereum, Polygon's vision encompasses a broader approach by not only providing tools for building scalable DApps but also fostering an Ethereum-compatible multi-chain ecosystem. This distinction positions Polygon as a scaling solution and an infrastructure development platform, facilitating an internet of blockchains that are interoperable, scalable, and easy to build on.

Polygon, in its mission to resolve Ethereum's scalability conundrum, has developed a sophisticated platform that not only enhances throughput and reduces costs but does so without forsaking Ethereum's decentralized security model. Its technical architecture is a multi-layered system designed to support an array of scalable solutions, from sidechains to Layer 2 protocols like zk-Rollups and Optimistic Rollups. Below, we delve deeper into the technical fabric of Polygon and how it achieves its scalability objectives.

3.2 Solana

Solana was created by Anatoly Yakovenko, who introduced the project in a 2017 whitepaper titled "Solana: A new architecture for a high performance blockchain." Yakovenko's background as a former Qualcomm engineer influenced Solana's unique technological innovations. His vision was to create a blockchain capable of hosting DApps at scale, addressing the critical issue of blockchain scalability that hampered existing platforms like Ethereum.

Creation and Development   The foundational idea behind Solana involves combining PoH with a PoS consensus mechanism to improve throughput and efficiency without sacrificing security or decentralization. PoH is a novel concept introduced by Yakovenko, which acts as a cryptographic time-stamp mechanism, allowing the network to keep a trustless record of time between events. This innovation significantly reduces the need for communication between nodes about the state of the blockchain, which is a major bottleneck in traditional blockchain systems.

PoH is a novel consensus mechanism introduced by the Solana blockchain, designed to improve the scalability and efficiency of blockchain networks. At its core, PoH is not a consensus mechanism in the traditional sense (like PoW or PoS) but rather a method for encoding the passage of time on a blockchain, allowing for greater efficiency in the order and verification of transactions. It acts as a cryptographic clock that provides a way to automatically order events and transactions without relying on the coordination between nodes. This enables Solana to achieve high throughput and low latency.

How Proof of History Works   The fundamental idea behind PoH is to create a historical record that proves that a certain event occurred at a specific point in time. This is achieved through a sequential hashing process, where each hash is a function of the previous one, effectively creating a historical record that is computationally impractical to alter. PoH is not a consensus mechanism in the traditional sense but rather a cryptographic time-stamping technique that Solana uses alongside PoS to secure its network. The genius of PoH lies in its ability to create a historical record of transactions that proves that one event occurred before another, without requiring validators to communicate to agree on time. Each transaction and event on the Solana blockchain is hashed in a sequential manner, creating a verifiable order of events. This ordering allows validators to process and validate transactions more quickly because they have a cryptographically secure way to verify the timing of each transaction without having to witness it directly.

The Process

1. **Sequential Hashing:** At the heart of PoH is a sequence of computations where the output of one hash function becomes the input of the next. This sequence produces a chain of hashes, where each hash depends on its predecessor.
2. **Timestamping Transactions:** Transactions are timestamped by inserting them into the hash sequence. Because each hash is dependent on the one before it, the specific position of a transaction within this sequence acts as a cryptographic proof of when the transaction occurred relative to others.
3. **Verifiable Order:** The sequential nature of the hashing process ensures that the order of transactions is verifiable. Any attempt to alter the order or fabricate a transaction timestamp would require redoing the hash sequence from the point of alteration, a computationally infeasible task due to the time and resources required.

On Solana, PoH works alongside the PoS consensus mechanism to enhance the network's efficiency and scalability. PoH provides a decentralized clock that timestamps transactions, enabling the network to process thousands of transactions per second (TPS) by efficiently ordering and validating them without the need for extensive communication between nodes to agree on time or sequence.

PoH presents key benefits:

- **Scalability:** By providing a verifiable order of events and reducing the need for consensus on time, PoH allows the blockchain to process transactions more quickly and efficiently.
- **Efficiency:** The deterministic order of transactions simplifies the validation process, as validators can independently verify the timing and sequence of transactions without cross-referencing with other nodes.
- **Security:** The cryptographic nature of the sequential hashing process ensures the integrity of the blockchain's timeline, making it resistant to tampering or falsification of transaction times.

Example   Imagine a scenario where Alice sends 1 SOL to Bob, and shortly after, Bob sends 0.5 SOL to Charlie. In a traditional blockchain, reaching consensus on the order of these transactions might require complex coordination among nodes. However, in Solana's PoH system:

1. Alice's transaction is processed, generating a hash **H(Alice's transaction)** at timestamp **T1**.
2. The hash **H(Alice's transaction)** then serves as the input for the next hash in the sequence.
3. Bob's transaction is inserted into the sequence, generating **H(Bob's transaction)** at timestamp **T2**, using the hash from Alice's transaction as its predecessor.

Because of the sequential hashing, it is cryptographically verified that Alice's transaction occurred before Bob's. Any node or validator on the network can independently verify the order and timing of these transactions by looking at their position in the PoH sequence, significantly streamlining the validation process and improving the network's throughput and efficiency.

Key Advantages   *What are the key advantages of Solana compared to existing blockchains?*

High Throughput and Low Latency   One of Solana's most notable features is its ability to process many transactions per second (TPS) with low transaction costs. This is achieved through a combination of innovative technologies and architectural decisions, including the PoH consensus mechanism, which allows for greater scalability and efficiency. PoH creates a historical record that proves that an event has occurred at a specific moment in time, adding a layer of time verification to the blockchain's operation and significantly reducing the overhead needed for consensus.

Scalability   Solana's architecture allows it to support tens of thousands of transactions per second without sacrificing security or decentralization. This scalability is further enhanced by features such as Sealevel (a parallel smart contracts runtime), Gulf Stream (a mempool-less transaction forwarding protocol), and Turbine (a block propagation protocol). These technologies work together to optimize processing and reduce the bandwidth required for transaction validation, making Solana one of the fastest blockchains available.

Low Transaction Costs   The efficiency of Solana's network leads to significantly lower transaction costs compared to other blockchains, especially during times of high demand. This cost-effectiveness makes Solana an attractive platform for developers and users alike, particularly for applications requiring a high volume of transactions, such as decentralized finance (DeFi) platforms, high-frequency trading systems, and micropayment services.

Competitive Advantage Solana's primary competitive advantages include its unmatched processing speed and capacity, which address some of the most pressing scalability issues faced by legacy blockchains like Ethereum. Its ability to handle a large number of transactions swiftly and affordably opens new possibilities for blockchain applications, particularly in sectors where transaction speed and volume are critical.

Solana vs. Other Blockchains Compared to Ethereum's Layer 2 scaling solutions, Solana offers scalability as a native feature of its Layer 1 blockchain, providing a simpler developer experience and potentially more seamless user interactions. Additionally, Solana competes with other high-throughput blockchains like Binance Smart Chain (BSC) and Polkadot by offering unique features such as PoH, underlining its position as a leading solution for scalable blockchain applications.

In conclusion, Solana's innovative approach to blockchain scalability, speed, and efficiency establishes it as a formidable player in the blockchain space, offering developers and users a powerful alternative to more established platforms. Its continued growth and adoption across various sectors underscore its potential to shape the future of decentralized technology.

Solana represents a significant leap forward in blockchain technology, primarily through its unique consensus mechanism and several innovative protocols designed to maximize efficiency and throughput. At the heart of Solana's architecture is the PoH consensus, a novel approach that allows the network to process transactions at unprecedented speeds, significantly outpacing Ethereum and other blockchains in terms of transactions per second (TPS).

Parallel Processing with Sealevel Solana introduces Sealevel, a parallel smart contracts execution engine that maximizes the blockchain's processing capabilities. Unlike traditional blockchains where smart contracts are executed sequentially, Solana's Sealevel protocol allows for simultaneous processing of thousands of smart contracts. This parallelism is key to Solana's high throughput, enabling the network to handle many transactions across different smart contracts at the same time.

Gulf Stream Protocol for Mempool Management Another critical component of Solana's architecture is the Gulf Stream protocol, which optimizes the forwarding of transactions throughout the network. In traditional blockchain systems, transactions wait in a mempool until a validator includes them in a block. Gulf Stream allows validators on the Solana network to forward transactions to the edge of the network ahead of time, reducing confirmation time and improving the network's capacity to handle a high volume of transactions.

Turbine for Block Propagation Turbine is Solana's block propagation protocol, designed to break down data into smaller packets, making it easier and faster for nodes to process and transmit information. This protocol is akin to how torrent systems distribute large files efficiently by breaking them down into smaller pieces. By employing Turbine, Solana mitigates potential bottlenecks associated with transmitting large blocks of data, further enhancing its throughput.

Achieving Higher TPS and Advantages Over Ethereum The combination of these technologies—PoH for efficient time-stamping, Sealevel for parallel smart contracts execution, Gulf Stream for optimized transaction forwarding, and Turbine for effective block propagation—enables Solana to achieve a throughput of tens of thousands of TPS. This is a stark contrast to Ethereum's current capacity, which is constrained by its sequential processing model and has prompted the development of Layer 2 scaling solutions.

In essence, Solana's innovative design and technical advancements position it as a powerful alternative for building decentralized applications, particularly those requiring high transaction throughput and low latency, which are currently less feasible on Ethereum's base layer.

Solana Stood Out in 2021 As shown in **Figure 6**, Solana experienced explosive growth during the 2021 crypto boom, due to several reasons:

1. **High Performance and Low Costs:** Solana's promise of high throughput (reportedly up to 65,000 transactions per second) and low transaction costs resonated with developers and users frustrated by the high fees and network congestion on Ethereum, especially during peak DeFi and NFT activity periods.
2. **Proof of History:** Solana's unique PoH mechanism addressed scalability and throughput challenges head-on, setting it apart from other blockchains. This

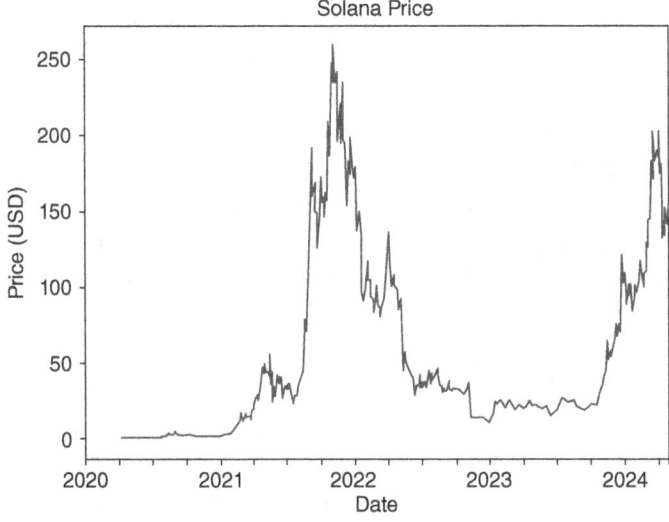

Figure 6 SOL Price Graph

technological innovation allowed Solana to process transactions at unprecedented speeds, making it an attractive platform for a wide range of applications, from decentralized exchanges (DEXs) to NFT marketplaces.

3. **Growing Ecosystem:** Throughout 2021, Solana rapidly expanded its ecosystem, attracting a multitude of projects spanning DeFi, NFTs, Web3, and more. The launch of successful projects on Solana, combined with developer initiatives and funding from the Solana Foundation, helped fuel its adoption and visibility in the crypto space.

4. **Community and Developer Support:** The Solana Foundation played a crucial role in fostering the community and supporting developers through grants, hackathons, and educational resources. This proactive approach helped build a vibrant ecosystem around Solana, contributing to its popularity and adoption.

5. **Market Sentiment and Speculation:** The bullish crypto market of 2021, along with speculative interest from investors looking for "the next Ethereum," drove significant capital into Solana's token, SOL. Positive market sentiment, driven by Solana's technological advancements and growing ecosystem, made it one of the best-performing assets of the year.

Solana's blend of innovative technology, strategic community engagement, and favorable market conditions in 2021 established it as a frontrunner in the next generation of blockchain platforms, aiming to solve the blockchain trilemma. Its performance during this period highlighted the crypto community's demand for alternatives to existing platforms that could offer scalable solutions for decentralized applications.

3.3 Cardano

Cardano was founded in 2015 by Charles Hoskinson and Jeremy Wood, two cryptocurrency enthusiasts and professionals who had previously worked together on the early development of Ethereum. The project is named after Gerolamo Cardano, a 16th-century Italian polymath, and its native cryptocurrency, ADA, is named after Ada Lovelace, a 19th-century mathematician often regarded as the first computer programmer.

From the outset, Cardano distinguished itself through its commitment to a scientific methodology and peer-reviewed research. This approach involved collaborating with academics and researchers worldwide to ensure that the foundation and development of the platform were based on rigorously tested and verified principles. The Cardano team aimed to address issues like scalability, interoperability, and sustainability that could hamper blockchain technology's broader adoption.

Cardano introduced a novel two-layer architecture to achieve its goals: the Cardano Settlement Layer (CSL) and the Cardano Computation Layer (CCL). The CSL is designed to handle the transfer of ADA, Cardano's cryptocurrency, with high security and efficiency. In contrast, the CCL is focused on the execution of smart contracts, enabling complex programmable transfers, and allowing developers to create decentralized applications with a range of use cases.

A cornerstone of Cardano's innovation is its consensus mechanism, Ouroboros. It is one of the first peer-reviewed, verifiably secure PoS algorithms. Ouroboros allows the network to achieve consensus without the significant energy consumption associated with PoW systems like Bitcoin. This not only makes Cardano more environmentally sustainable but also enables greater scalability and faster transaction processing times.

Since its launch, Cardano has undergone multiple development phases, each named after influential historical figures in literature and science, including Byron, Shelley, Goguen, Basho, and Voltaire. These phases have introduced significant upgrades to the network, including the implementation of the Shelley update that further decentralized the network and the Goguen phase that integrated smart contract functionality, broadening Cardano's capabilities for developers and end-users.

Cardano saw substantial growth in 2021, marked by increasing adoption, the launch of smart contracts, and growing interest from the developer community. This period was characterized by a significant rise in ADA's market value, driven by broader market trends in cryptocurrency and specific enthusiasm for Cardano's technological advancements and potential applications in finance, supply chain management, and governance.

Cardano's development continues with a strong focus on creating a robust, scalable, and interoperable blockchain platform. Its commitment to scientific research, formal methods in software development, and a community-driven approach positions Cardano as a leading platform in the pursuit of creating a more secure, transparent, and equitable global financial and social system.

The technical foundation of Cardano is structured around two main layers: the Cardano Settlement Layer (CSL) and the Cardano Computation Layer (CCL). The CSL acts as the balance ledger and is where all transactions involving Cardano's cryptocurrency, ADA, are directly recorded. This separation allows the Cardano network to handle the accounting of transactions with minimal overhead, enhancing the network's ability to scale and process transactions efficiently.

The CCL, on the other hand, is where the computational logic of the network resides. It's the layer that hosts smart contracts and DApps, enabling developers to create rules for transactions that go beyond simple transfers of value. This layer's flexibility and programmability are key to Cardano's vision of a more secure and robust platform for developing decentralized applications.

Ouroboros, the heart of Cardano's consensus mechanism, is the first PoS protocol proven to be secure through academic peer review. It operates in epochs and slots, where epochs are the overarching time frames and slots are fixed periods within epochs. In each slot, a slot leader is randomly chosen with probabilities proportional to their stake in ADA. These slot leaders are responsible for adding blocks of transactions to the blockchain. The security of Ouroboros comes from its rigorous cryptographic underpinning, ensuring that despite the randomness in slot leader selection, the network remains secure against attacks.

To enhance scalability and interoperability further, Cardano is developing sidechains based on the Kiayias, Miller, and Zindros (KMZ) sidechains protocol, allowing assets and information to flow seamlessly between the main Cardano chain and its sidechains. This will enable Cardano to support a wide range of use cases and applications without congesting the main blockchain.

Moreover, Cardano is committed to fostering a sustainable blockchain ecosystem. It has introduced a treasury system where a portion of transaction fees is pooled to fund future development projects voted on by the community. This not only ensures the long-term sustainability of the platform but also aligns with Cardano's philosophy of creating a more inclusive and democratically governed blockchain.

In terms of smart contract functionality, Cardano introduced Plutus, a smart contract platform that brings the benefits of functional programming to smart contract creation. Plutus contracts are written in Haskell, a functional programming language known for its high degree of fault tolerance. This choice reflects Cardano's emphasis on security and reliability, especially in applications that manage significant value or sensitive data.

In essence, Cardano's approach—characterized by a foundational commitment to peer-reviewed research, a layered architecture, and a pioneering PoS consensus mechanism—represents a significant advancement in the pursuit of creating a scalable, secure, and sustainable blockchain platform. Its ongoing developments in areas like interoperability, governance, and smart contracts underscore its potential to serve as a robust foundation for a new generation of blockchain applications.

Detailed Exploration of Cardano's Components

Ouroboros is the backbone of Cardano, enabling it to achieve consensus in a secure, decentralized manner without the significant energy consumption associated with PoW protocols. It segments time into epochs and slots, where epochs are overarching periods divided into shorter intervals called slots. A lottery system selects slot leaders for each slot, responsible for validating transactions and creating new blocks. The probability of being chosen as a slot leader is proportional to the amount of ADA (Cardano's cryptocurrency) the user has staked. This design not only secures the network but also incentivizes participation in the network's consensus process.

Smart Contracts and Plutus   Plutus is Cardano's smart contract platform, enabling developers to write high-assurance DApps with a strong focus on security. Smart contracts in Plutus are written in Haskell, a functional programming language that allows for the creation of verifiable, secure code. Plutus contracts consist of two parts: the off-chain code that runs on the user's machine and handles the user interface and blockchain interaction, and the on-chain code that executes on the blockchain.

DApps Suited for Cardano   Due to its secure, scalable, and sustainable design, Cardano is well-suited for a wide range of applications, including:

- **Financial applications:** DeFi platforms can leverage Cardano's security and scalability to provide services like lending, borrowing, and yield farming.

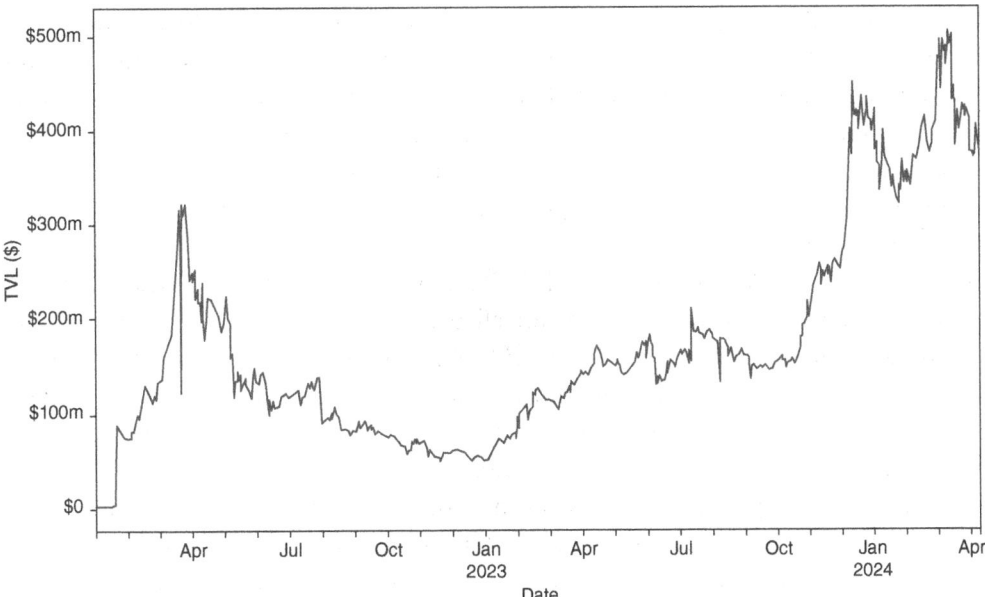

Figure 7 Cardano's TVL

- **Identity and credentials:** DApps focused on decentralized identity and verifiable credentials can benefit from Cardano's robust security features.
- **Supply chain tracking:** Cardano's ability to handle complex transactions and smart contracts makes it an excellent choice for supply chain management applications, offering transparency and traceability.
- **Governance:** The platform's focus on formal verification and security makes it a promising foundation for decentralized autonomous organizations (DAOs) and other governance-related applications.

Cardano's combination of a scientifically grounded approach, a focus on sustainability, and advanced features like Ouroboros and Plutus makes it a compelling platform for developing and deploying a broad spectrum of DApps, especially those requiring high levels of security and scalability. According to DefiLlama's TVL calculations, the first DApps on Cardano to have liquidity locked were mainly DEXs (MuesliSwap, SundaeSwap, ADAX Pro, Minswap, MeowSwapFi, WingRiders), and lending (FluidTokens, Lending Pond, Lenfi). **Figure 7** plots the TVL on Cardano using DefiLlama's definition:

3.4 Polkadot

Founded by Dr. Gavin Wood, one of the co-founders of Ethereum and the author of the Solidity programming language, Polkadot introduces a heterogeneously sharded model that enables different blockchains to transfer messages and value in a trust-free fashion, sharing their unique features and functionality while being secured under a unified network.

At its core, Polkadot operates on a sharded model where multiple blockchains (parachains) run in parallel, yet independently, to process transactions and operations. This model significantly increases the overall capacity and performance of the network. Unlike traditional sharding approaches that replicate the same blockchain structure across shards, Polkadot's heterogeneous sharding allows each shard, or parachain, to have its own unique characteristics, such as governance models, tokens, or consensus mechanisms, tailored to specific use cases.

The central chain, known as the Relay Chain, is Polkadot's heart, providing shared security, consensus, and interoperability for all parachains connected to it. The Relay Chain employs a nominated proof-of-stake (NPoS) consensus mechanism, where validators are selected based on the stake nominated to them by the network's token holders. This consensus mechanism is responsible for finalizing blocks added to parachains and ensuring the network's overall security and integrity.

Parachains are independent blockchains that connect to the Relay Chain and benefit from its security and interoperability features. They can have their own tokens, state, and governance mechanisms but rely on the Relay Chain for consensus and communication with other parachains. Parathreads operate similarly to parachains but on a pay-as-you-go model, ideal for blockchains that don't require continuous connectivity to the Polkadot network.

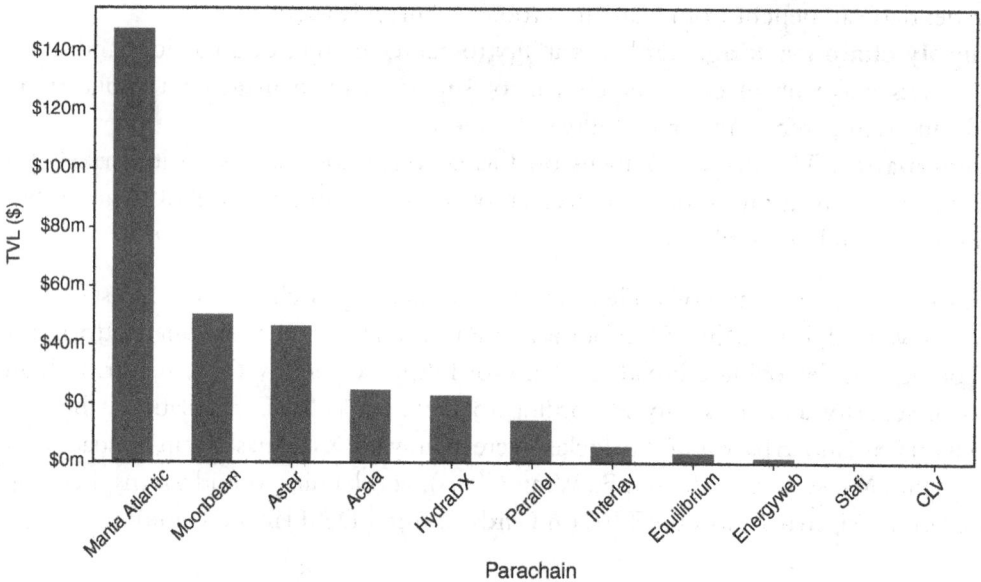

Figure 8   Polkadot's parachain TVL

One of Polkadot's standout features is its native support for cross-chain interoperability, enabled through the Cross-Chain Message Passing (XCMP) protocol. This protocol allows parachains to send and receive messages of any type, including token transfers, data, or function calls, without relying on a centralized intermediary. This level of interoperability is designed to foster a truly interconnected ecosystem where diverse blockchains can collaborate and share functionalities.

It also introduces the Substrate, which is a blockchain development framework created by Parity Technologies (also co-founded by Gavin Wood) that simplifies building custom blockchains tailored to specific needs or applications. Substrate-based blockchains can easily connect to Polkadot as parachains or operate independently, offering developers flexibility. It comes with a rich set of features, including modular consensus mechanisms, flexible governance structures, and upgradability without hard forks.

Polkadot's innovative architecture and emphasis on interoperability, scalability, and security position it as a foundational technology in the Blockchain 3.0 era. By enabling diverse blockchains to communicate and share functionalities, Polkadot paves the way for a more integrated and efficient decentralized web, where the strengths of individual blockchains can be leveraged across a unified ecosystem. **Figure 8** shows the TVL of the parachains tracked by DefiLlama. As of April 2024, Manta Atlantic has the highest TVL across all parachains on Polkadot.

Summary of Blockchains *We have discussed layer 2 solutions, alternative blockchains, and new technologies, but how do they stack up against each other?*

To gauge how different chains have developed over time, we plot the TVL of each of these chains using data from DefiLlama:

Ethereum reigns supreme with the highest TVL, completely dwarfing many of the alternative options (**Figure 9**). Many popular DApps, such as DEXs, lending protocols, NFTs, GameFi, were built solely for Ethereum as it has an established user base and is most well-known. However, as we have seen, there are new solutions that aim to solve problems inherent with Ethereum's design offering promising alternatives.

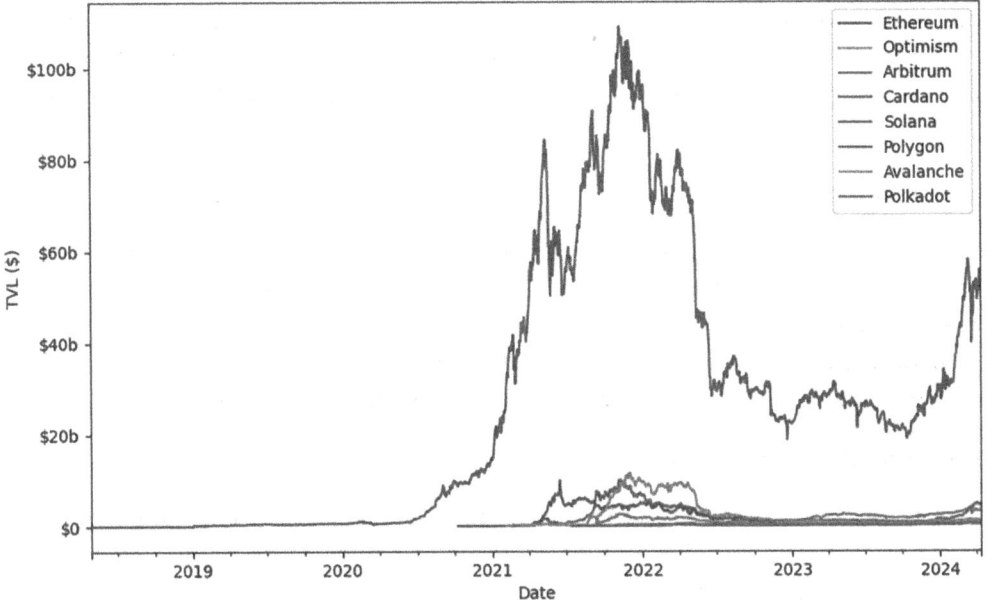

Figure 9   Layers 1 and Layers 2 TVL

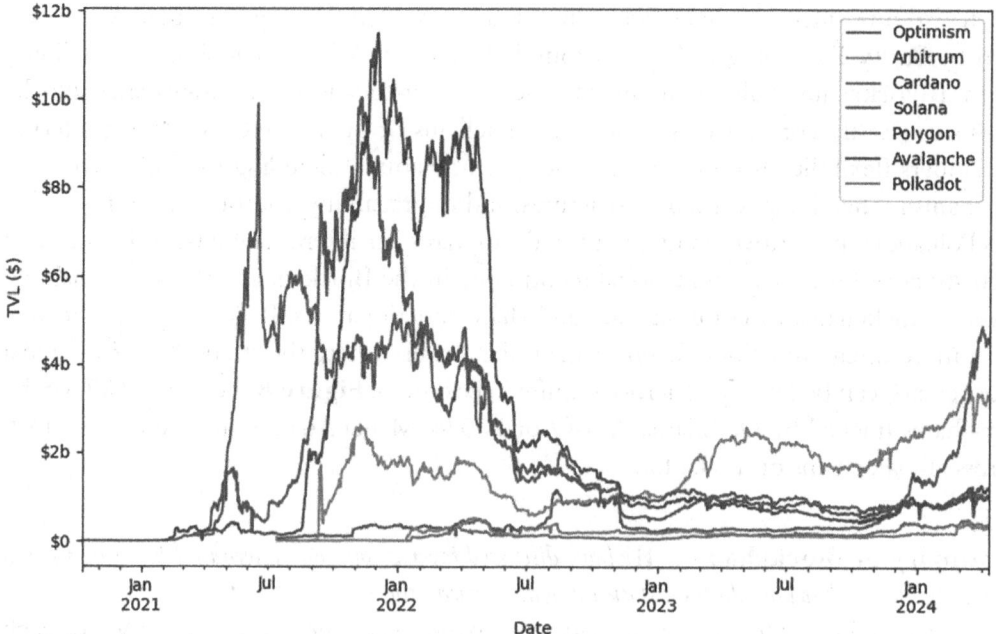

Figure 10   Layers 1 and Layers 2 TVL (excluding Ethereum)

Among these, Solana, Avalanche, and Polygon had the most TVL during the 2021 and 2022 highs in the cryptocurrency market. With recent advances in Layer 2 solutions, we have seen a surge in TVL on Arbitrum and Optimism (**Figure 10**).

To appreciate the differences among these chains, let's further compare how a simple transaction, such as Alice sending 1 token to Bob, is handled across different blockchain architectures and layer 2 solutions (**Figure 11**). This comparative illustration will highlight the unique operational mechanisms of Bitcoin (as a Blockchain 1.0 example), Ethereum (Blockchain 2.0), Cardano and Polkadot (Blockchain 3.0), and layer 2 solutions like Optimism (an Optimistic Rollup on Ethereum).

Bitcoin (Blockchain 1.0)

- **Process:** Alice broadcasts a transaction specifying Bob's address and the amount (1 BTC). Miners collect and verify transactions, solving a cryptographic puzzle (PoW) to add a new block to the blockchain.
- **Considerations:** Transaction throughput is limited (7 TPS), and confirmation times can be lengthy, depending on network congestion and transaction fees paid.

Ethereum (Blockchain 2.0)

- **Process:** Alice sends 1 ETH to Bob by creating a transaction in her Ethereum wallet. This transaction is included in a block by validators (post-Ethereum 2.0 upgrade) who execute the consensus mechanism.

Chain	Process	Considerations
Bitcoin (Blockchain 1.0)	Alice broadcasts a transaction specifying Bob's address and the amount (1 BTC). Miners collect and verify the transactions, solving a cryptographic puzzle (Proof of Work) to add a new block to the blockchain	Transaction throughput is limited (7 TPS), and, with an average block time of about 10 minutes, confirmation and finality times cab be lengthy, depending on network congestion and transaction fees paid.
Ethereum (Blockchain 2.0)	Alice sends 1 ETH to Bob by creating a transaction in her Ethereum wallet. This transaction is included in a block by validators (post-Ethereum 2.0 upgrade) who execute the consensus mechanism	Ethereum supports smart contracts, allowing for more complex transactions. However, it faces scalability issues, with higher gas fees and lower transaction speeds during peak times (~15-30 TPS, and 15 minute tx finality)
Cardano (Blockchain 3.0)	Alice sending 1 ADA to Bob involves her creating a transaction that validators (stake pool operators) verify. The Ouroboros protocol selects validators based on the size of their stake	Cardano introduces a layered architecture for separation of settlement and computation, aiming for higher scalability and lower transaction fees while maintaining security (~250-1,000 TPS, 1 day tx finality).
Polkadot (Blockchain 3.0)	Within Polkadot's ecosystem, Alice could send tokens to Bob across different parachains. The transaction would be verified by validators of the Relay Chain, ensuring interoperability and share security	Polkadot facilitates cross-chain transfers and interactions, with scalability achieved through parallel processing across parachains. The complexity of managing cross-chain transactions is abstracted by the Relay Chain (potentially >100,000 TPS)
Optimism (Layer 2 on Ethereum)	Alice's transaction is executed off the main Ethereum chain. The transaction data is bundled with others and submitted as a single batch to Ethereum for final verification, significantly reducing gas costs and improving speeds	Optimistic Rollups assume transactions are valid by default, with a challenge period for disputing fraudulent transactions. This model achieves scalability by offloading computation from Layer 1 while inheriting Ethereum's security

Figure 11 Layers 1 and Layers 2 TVL

- **Considerations:** Ethereum supports smart contracts, allowing for more complex transactions. However, it faces scalability issues, with higher gas fees and lower transaction speeds during peak times (~15-30 TPS).

Cardano (Blockchain 3.0)

- **Process:** Transactions on Cardano use a PoS model. Alice sending 1 ADA to Bob involves her creating a transaction that validators (stake pool operators) verify without the energy-intensive mining process. The Ouroboros protocol selects validators based on their stake.
- **Considerations:** Cardano introduces a layered architecture for separation of settlement and computation, aiming for higher scalability and lower transaction fees while maintaining security.

Polkadot (Blockchain 3.0)

- **Process:** Within Polkadot's ecosystem, Alice could send tokens to Bob across different parachains (independent blockchains). The transaction would be verified by validators of the Relay Chain, ensuring interoperability and shared security.

- **Considerations:** Polkadot facilitates cross-chain transfers and interactions, with scalability achieved through parallel processing across parachains. The complexity of managing cross-chain transactions is abstracted by the Relay Chain.

Optimism (Layer 2 on Ethereum)

- **Process:** On Optimism, Alice's transaction to send 1 token to Bob is executed off the main Ethereum chain (Layer 1). The transaction data is bundled with others and submitted as a single batch to Ethereum for final verification, significantly reducing gas costs and improving transaction speed.
- **Considerations:** Optimistic Rollups assume transactions are valid by default, with a challenge period for disputing fraudulent transactions. This model achieves scalability by offloading computation from Layer 1 while inheriting Ethereum's security.

Each platform's approach to handling transactions reflects its underlying technology and goals, from Bitcoin's emphasis on security and decentralization to Ethereum's support for complex DApps, and the advanced scalability and interoperability solutions offered by Blockchain 3.0 platforms and Layer 2 protocols.[3]

Case Study: "Ava Labs: Navigating the Next Blockchain"[4]

Avalanche was created by Ava Labs, a blockchain technology company founded by Emin Gün Sirer, Kevin Sekniqi, and Maofan "Ted" Yin. Emin Gün Sirer, a prominent computer science professor at Cornell University, has been a key figure in the blockchain and cryptocurrency space for many years, with significant contributions to peer-to-peer systems, decentralized networks, and consensus algorithms.

Avalanche is a decentralized blockchain platform known for its high throughput, low latency, and customizability. It aims to offer a versatile environment for a variety of decentralized applications, smart contracts, and subnets while addressing common blockchain challenges such as scalability and interoperability.

At the heart of Avalanche's architecture is its unique consensus mechanism, known as the Avalanche Consensus Protocol, designed to achieve rapid finality with a high degree of security. Unlike traditional consensus methods, Avalanche employs a system where validators sample a small, random subset of nodes to reach agreement, resulting in quicker consensus with fewer energy requirements.

---

[3] For more information about differences among chains in terms of how decentralized they are, please see the HBS note available at https://hbsp.harvard.edu/product/224048-PDF-ENG?Ntt=marco%20di%20maggio
[4] For more details about the case and additional resources to teach in the classroom, please see the HBS case I wrote with Wanyao Sha, and the corresponding teaching note, titled "Ava Labs: Navigating the Next Blockchain" available at https://hbsp.harvard.edu/product/223027-PDF-ENG?Ntt=marco%20di%20maggio

This approach allows Avalanche to process thousands of transactions per second, making it one of the fastest blockchains currently available.

Avalanche's architecture is based on three interconnected chains: the Exchange Chain (X-Chain), the Platform Chain (P-Chain), and the Contract Chain (C-Chain). Each chain serves a distinct purpose. The X-Chain is used for creating and exchanging assets, the P-Chain is responsible for managing validators and creating custom blockchains (subnets), and the C-Chain supports smart contracts compatible with Ethereum's Solidity language.

This multi-chain architecture is a significant differentiator for Avalanche, allowing it to support a wide range of applications and use cases. The ability to create custom subnets on the P-Chain provides developers with flexibility to design their own blockchains with specific rules and consensus mechanisms, catering to unique requirements. This level of customization is not typically available on other blockchain platforms.

Avalanche's compatibility with Ethereum smart contracts is another key advantage, allowing developers to easily migrate their Ethereum-based applications to Avalanche's C-Chain. This compatibility fosters interoperability with the broader Ethereum ecosystem while offering the benefits of Avalanche's high performance and scalability.

Avalanche also addresses interoperability through its subnet architecture, enabling different blockchains to communicate with each other. This feature opens the door to cross-chain interactions and broader collaboration within the blockchain ecosystem, a crucial step toward a more interconnected future.

In summary, Avalanche stands out due to its unique consensus mechanism, multi-chain architecture, high throughput, and customizability through subnets. Its ability to support a diverse range of applications, combined with compatibility with Ethereum, makes it a compelling option for developers seeking a scalable, high-performance blockchain platform.

Learning Objectives:

Exploring the case of Avalanche provides valuable insights into several key aspects of technology and business strategy. It sheds light on the factors that can make or break a new technology platform and helps understand the competitive landscape of a fast-changing industry. Here are the learning objectives that can help when diving into the Avalanche case:

- First, it enables a deeper understanding of the critical factors that determine whether a new technology platform succeeds or fails. These factors often include technical innovation, market demand, scalability, security, and user adoption. By examining Avalanche's unique consensus mechanism, multi-chain architecture, and rapid scalability, we can explore what differentiates a successful platform from those that struggle to gain traction. Understanding these elements provides a blueprint for evaluating emerging technologies in any field.

- Secondly, it allows us to evaluate the competitive dynamics within a rapidly evolving industry. The blockchain sector is characterized by intense competition and a continuous drive for innovation. Analyzing Avalanche's position within this landscape reveals how platforms compete for market share, attract developers, and build communities. This evaluation can also highlight the importance of differentiation, ecosystem development, and adaptability in staying ahead in such a competitive space.
- Finally, exploring Avalanche offers insights into the strategic options available to a new entrant in a crowded market. Given the dominance of established players like Ethereum, a new platform must adopt creative strategies to carve out its niche. Avalanche's approach—emphasizing scalability, customizable subnets, and Ethereum compatibility—demonstrates various paths a new entrant can take to gain a foothold. By understanding these strategic choices, students and professionals can better assess the potential success of a new technology in a competitive industry.

Overall, delving into the case of Avalanche provides a comprehensive understanding of the factors influencing the success of technology platforms, the competitive dynamics of evolving industries, and the strategic choices new entrants must consider. This knowledge is not only applicable to blockchain but also extends to a broader range of technology-based markets.

How does this new consensus mechanism work?   Let's start understanding how it works.

Unlike traditional consensus mechanisms that require global communication among all nodes or intensive computational work, Avalanche's approach involves validators randomly querying a small subset of other validators to reach consensus. This technique allows the network to converge quickly and with minimal communication overhead.

Specifically, in the Avalanche consensus mechanism, validators participate in a process called subsampling, where each validator randomly selects a small subset of other validators to query about the state of a transaction. This random sampling is repeated several times to increase confidence in the consensus outcome. If a validator's queries yield a consistent result (e.g., whether a transaction is accepted or rejected), it adopts that result as its own decision.

A key aspect of the Avalanche consensus mechanism is its reliance on quorum-based agreement. To reach consensus, a sufficient majority (quorum) of validators must agree on the outcome of a transaction. This approach allows the network to achieve consensus quickly, as it doesn't require all validators to communicate with each other directly.

The Avalanche consensus mechanism is part of a broader family of protocols that include Avalanche and Snowball. The idea behind Snowball is simple: When a validator queries other validators and reaches a consistent outcome, it increases its "confidence" in that outcome. As more validators agree, the confidence grows, reinforcing the consensus.

Avalanche consensus offers several key benefits:

- **Rapid Finality:** Due to its efficient subsampling process, consensus can be achieved quickly, allowing transactions to be finalized within seconds.
- **High Throughput:** The parallel processing capabilities enable the network to handle a large volume of transactions simultaneously.
- **Scalability:** The subsampling approach reduces communication overhead, allowing the network to scale efficiently with more validators.
- **Energy Efficiency:** Unlike PoW, which requires significant computational resources, Avalanche consensus relies on lightweight operations, reducing energy consumption.

Overall, the Avalanche consensus mechanism represents a significant advancement in decentralized consensus, providing a scalable, fast, and energy-efficient alternative to traditional consensus algorithms. Its unique approach to achieving agreement among a large number of validators has made Avalanche a compelling platform for decentralized applications and high-throughput use cases.

What makes a blockchain successful?   Let's do a deeper exploration of what drives the success of a blockchain platform. A common answer is the importance of building a robust ecosystem, encompassing both developers and users. A blockchain's growth and sustainability often hinge on this ecosystem, and Avalanche, like other platforms, faces various hurdles in this area.

Competition is one of the most significant obstacles, as Ava Labs enters a blockchain landscape where established players like Ethereum, Bitcoin, and Ripple dominate. These established platforms already have vast and active communities, creating a steep uphill battle for Ava Labs to attract attention, gain traction, and establish a competitive edge.

Brand recognition is another substantial challenge. Unlike industry veterans, Ava Labs lacks the reputation and familiarity that established platforms enjoy. This poses a significant hurdle in building trust among users and developers, who may be hesitant to engage with a relatively unknown brand. Overcoming this challenge requires a concerted effort in marketing, partnerships, and community engagement.

Network effects play a crucial role in the success of blockchain platforms. The value of a platform increases as more people use it, leading to a self-reinforcing cycle of growth. However, reaching this critical mass can be difficult. Ava Labs must find ways to encourage early adoption and motivate users and developers to join the platform. Without sufficient momentum, the network may struggle to attract the critical mass needed to drive further growth.

Technical complexity adds another layer of challenge. Blockchain technology, while innovative, can be daunting for developers and users unfamiliar with its intricacies. Avalanche's unique architecture and consensus mechanism might require developers to learn new programming languages, tools, and frameworks to build applications on the platform. This learning curve could deter adoption if not addressed through user-friendly resources and comprehensive support.

To overcome these challenges, Ava Labs must create a compelling value proposition that resonates with both developers and users. This includes offering a user-friendly platform, providing strong technical support, and creating incentives for early adopters. By simplifying the technical aspects and building a vibrant community, Ava Labs can establish itself as a trusted and appealing choice in a competitive market.

What strategic options are available to Ava Labs to gain market share and build a sustainable business model?   To gain market share and build a sustainable business model, Ava Labs has several strategic options that can guide its growth and position in the blockchain industry. These strategies offer unique pathways to establish a competitive edge, but each comes with its own set of risks and challenges.

One potential strategy for Ava Labs is to focus on specific use cases and industries where blockchain technology can offer substantial value. This approach allows Ava Labs to carve out a niche by addressing particular market needs, differentiating itself from other blockchain platforms. For instance, one such niche with substantial growth potential is GameFi, a combination of gaming and decentralized finance. GameFi leverages blockchain technology to create gaming experiences where players can earn real-world value through gameplay, typically via tokens or non-fungible tokens (NFTs). GameFi has gained traction because it allows players to own in-game assets and trade them on blockchain-based marketplaces (as we are going to explore in Chapter 13). This new model offers opportunities for players to earn rewards while engaging in gaming activities. Avalanche's high throughput, low latency, and ability to create custom subnets make it an ideal platform for GameFi applications, allowing developers to build complex gaming ecosystems with a decentralized backbone. A successful example of this approach is Square, which gained market share by catering to the payment processing needs of small businesses.

Another strategic option is partnering with established players in the blockchain industry. By collaborating with well-known platforms or services, Ava Labs can leverage existing user bases and benefit from the experience and expertise of these partners. For example, partnering with a major cryptocurrency exchange like Coinbase or Binance could increase visibility and attract more users. This strategy has been employed successfully by Apple, which partnered with major record labels to launch iTunes, thereby gaining immediate traction in the music industry.

A third option for Ava Labs is to offer competitive pricing and incentives to attract users and developers. By reducing transaction fees or providing grants and airdrops, Ava Labs can make its platform more appealing compared to other blockchains like Ethereum, which is known for their high costs. In addition to lower fees, Ava Labs could offer incentives to developers who build applications on the platform, creating a vibrant ecosystem. Uber is a notable example of a company that used incentives to motivate drivers and expand its service network.

Ava Labs could also choose to expand the Avalanche ecosystem by forming partnerships with other blockchain platforms or companies. This approach can increase the platform's network effects, making it more valuable and attractive to users and developers. Collaborating with major decentralized finance (DeFi) platforms like Uniswap or Aave, for example, could enable seamless interoperability between Avalanche and Ethereum, allowing users to transfer assets and data effortlessly. Amazon's expansion strategy, which included incorporating third-party sellers, serves as a successful precedent for this approach.

However, each of these strategic options carries inherent risks. Focusing on specific use cases might lead to over-specialization, making the platform vulnerable to shifts in market trends. A narrow focus could also limit its broader appeal, reducing its ability to attract a wider user base. Partnering with established players could lead to a loss of control over the platform's branding and direction. If a partner has significant influence, it might impact how Ava Labs is perceived or even constrain its strategic choices, ultimately affecting its independence.

Offering competitive pricing and incentives poses the risk of diminishing profitability. If pricing becomes too low, it could trigger a race to the bottom, affecting long-term sustainability. Excessive incentives might create dependency, leading to an unsustainable business model if users and developers rely too heavily on these perks. Expanding the ecosystem could dilute the brand and complicate focus. Maintaining a clear message and consistent strategy becomes challenging as the ecosystem grows. Resource allocation might also become a problem, as broader expansion could divert attention from core features and services.

In conclusion, discussing these options should highlight the fact that some of the strategic options available to blockchain platforms are not that dissimilar to those considered by Web2 companies.

4. Cross-chain Interoperability

The proliferation of diverse blockchain networks raises the critical question of whether the sector is becoming overly fragmented. Moreover, *how do the different ecosystems interact with each other?*

4.1 Bridges

Cross-chain interoperability allows different blockchains to communicate and share information, enabling assets and data to move seamlessly between them. The concept of "bridges" plays a crucial role in achieving this interoperability, serving as the connecting structure that links independent blockchains, allowing users to transfer tokens, assets, or other data across various networks.

A bridge is really like a highway connecting two cities, enabling traffic (in this case, data and assets) to flow between them. Bridges facilitate the transfer of tokens and data between different blockchains, typically involving a process of locking, minting, and burning tokens to ensure assets are accounted for on both sides of the bridge.

How Do Bridges Work?   Bridges typically work by creating a secure and verifiable method to transfer assets across blockchains. Here's an overview of the process:

1. **Locking Assets:** When a user wants to transfer an asset from one blockchain to another, the asset is first locked on the source chain. This step ensures that the same asset is not used or double-spent on both chains.
2. **Minting/Issuing Corresponding Tokens:** Once the asset is locked on the source chain, a corresponding token or asset is minted/issued on the destination chain. This new token represents the locked asset from the source chain and is usually of equal value.
3. **Verification and Security:** Bridges rely on a verification process to ensure the transfer's authenticity. This can involve validators, consensus mechanisms, or other security protocols to ensure that the transfer is secure and legitimate.
4. **Burning/Unlocking:** When the asset is transferred back to the source chain, the corresponding token on the destination chain is burned or locked, and the original asset is unlocked on the source chain. This step ensures that the asset's supply remains consistent and avoids duplication.

PROMINENT EXAMPLE: WORMHOLE

Wormhole, developed by the team behind Solana, was launched in November 2020 as a decentralized cross-chain bridge protocol. Wormhole gained significant attention within the blockchain community shortly after its launch due to its innovative approach to cross-chain interoperability. Solana Labs is known for its focus on building scalable and decentralized blockchain solutions, with Wormhole serving as a key component of its interoperability strategy. The protocol has been widely adopted by developers and users seeking to transfer assets and data across different blockchain networks.

At its core, Wormhole employs a network of "guardians" tasked with verifying and signing transactions, thereby establishing a secure mechanism for transferring assets across different chains. The functioning of Wormhole relies on a series of interconnected components:

1. **Guardians:** These are entities responsible for observing and validating messages from the Wormhole Core Contract, ensuring secure communication across different blockchains. Guardians play a crucial role in maintaining the integrity and security of the bridge by verifying the authenticity of transactions.
2. **Wormhole Core Contract:** This smart contract serves as the backbone of the Wormhole protocol, managing the issuance, transfer, and redemption of assets across chains. It acts as the central hub through which assets are transferred, and guardians validate transactions before they are executed.
3. **Relayers:** Operating off-chain, relayers are responsible for passing validated messages from the Wormhole Core Contract to the intended blockchain. They facilitate efficient cross-chain communication by relaying information between different networks, enabling assets to move seamlessly across chains.

The unique feature of Wormhole lies in its ability to support not only token transfers but also the movement of other digital assets such as nonfungible tokens (NFTs) and decentralized messages across different chains. This versatility expands the potential applications of Wormhole beyond simple asset transfers, allowing developers to build complex decentralized applications (DApps) that leverage cross-chain functionality.

For example, let's consider a scenario where an NFT created on the Ethereum blockchain needs to be transferred to the Solana blockchain. Using Wormhole, the NFT owner initiates a transfer request through the Wormhole Core Contract on Ethereum. Guardians validate the request, ensuring its authenticity and security. Once validated, relayers transmit the necessary information to the Solana blockchain, where a corresponding NFT is minted. This process enables the seamless transfer of the NFT between Ethereum and Solana, showcasing the interoperability provided by Wormhole across different chains.

Differences Among Bridges   Bridges can differ in their architecture, consensus mechanisms, and security protocols. Some key differences include:

- Consensus Mechanisms: Bridges can use various consensus mechanisms to validate transactions, including PoS, PoA, or other decentralized protocols. The choice of mechanism can impact the bridge's security and decentralization.

For instance, the bridge between Bitcoin and Ethereum utilizes a federated peg model, where a group of trusted custodians holds Bitcoin and mints corresponding WBTC tokens on Ethereum. This model relies on a centralized group of custodians to validate transactions and maintain the peg between Bitcoin and WBTC. The Cosmos Hub employs a decentralized consensus mechanism known as Tendermint, which utilizes a variant of PoS called Practical Byzantine Fault Tolerance (PBFT). The Inter-Blockchain Communication (IBC) protocol enables tokens to be transferred between different blockchains within the Cosmos ecosystem, allowing for decentralized cross-chain interoperability.

- Centralization vs. Decentralization: Some bridges rely on a centralized authority to manage the locking and unlocking of assets, while others use decentralized networks of validators. Decentralized bridges generally offer greater security and trust.

For example, Ripple utilizes a federated sidechain model, where a group of trusted validators, known as Unique Node Lists (UNLs), governs the consensus process for sidechains. These validators are selected by Ripple, leading to a centralized governance structure. While this model provides fast and efficient transactions, it relies on trust in the selected validators. In contrast, Chainlink provides decentralized oracle networks that facilitate the transfer of data between smart contracts and external sources. These networks operate in a fully decentralized manner, with multiple independent nodes providing data inputs and consensus. Chainlink's decentralized approach enhances security and trust by mitigating single points of failure and reducing the risk of manipulation.

- Security Risks: Bridges can be vulnerable to security risks, such as double-spending or replay attacks. The level of security varies based on the bridge's design and the robustness of its verification processes.

Cross-chain bridges have become prime targets for hackers due to the significant volume of funds they manage, resulting in some of the largest attacks in the blockchain world. Some of the key vulnerabilities include:

- *Centralization Risks:* If the bridge relies on a single or centralized entity to unlock assets, it creates a single point of failure.
- *Smart Contract Bugs:* Errors in the contract logic can lead to asset loss or unauthorized access.
- *Replay Attacks:* If the bridge does not have proper security measures, attackers might replay the same transaction to unlock assets multiple times.

- *Guardian Misbehavior:* In a system relying on validators (like Wormhole), if a majority of validators act maliciously, they could compromise the bridge's security.

Due to these vulnerabilities, there have been at least three notable hacks targeting bridges:

- **Ronin Bridge:** This bridge, connecting the Axie Infinity game to Ethereum (as we are going to see in Chapter 13), faced one of the largest attacks, with hackers stealing over $522 million. The attackers exploited a vulnerability in the bridge's smart contract security, allowing unauthorized withdrawals.
- **Wormhole Hack:** This high-profile attack on the Wormhole bridge resulted in a loss of $320 million worth of Wrapped Ethereum (WeETH). The hacker exploited a loophole in the bridge's validation process, creating unbacked tokens on Solana without providing the corresponding Ether on Ethereum.
- **Nomad Hack:** Nomad, a bridge connecting multiple blockchains, experienced a significant attack with over $200 million stolen on August 1, 2022. The vulnerability arose from a code error that allowed attackers to replicate and manipulate valid transactions, causing a "free-for-all" situation where multiple hackers exploited the same weakness. The problem arose from a contract update that failed to verify the legitimacy of messages before processing them, allowing the attacker to copy transaction data and replace it with their wallet addresses. This error caused a frenzied hack with hundreds of wallets exploiting the same vulnerability. The hack highlighted the importance of rigorous security measures and smart contract validation to prevent unauthorized access and asset loss.[5]

These examples underscore how bridges have become the connecting issue among blockchains but also one of the weakest link of the ecosystem.

Is there an alternative to bridges?   When considering the transfer of assets across blockchains, individuals may choose between bridges and exchanges, each offering distinct advantages. Bridges provide a cost-effective solution, as they typically charge lower fees for asset transfers compared to exchanges. This cost efficiency is particularly beneficial for large transfers or frequent cross-chain interactions. Additionally, bridges often facilitate faster asset transfers with fewer intermediate steps, compared to the potentially time-consuming process of swapping assets on an exchange and transferring them to another wallet.

Furthermore, bridges interact directly with blockchains, increasing users' eligibility for airdrops and other rewards based on their on-chain activity. In contrast, centralized exchanges may not offer such incentives, as they do not always reflect users' on-chain interactions. Moreover, bridges are inherently more decentralized than centralized exchanges, aligning with the ethos of blockchain technology and appealing to users who

---

[5] https://www.halborn.com/blog/post/the-nomad-bridge-hack-a-deeper-dive

prioritize decentralization and autonomy in their asset transfers. This decentralized nature of bridges provides users with a more native blockchain experience, reducing reliance on centralized entities for cross-chain transactions.

These reasons make bridges a compelling choice for users seeking efficient, low-cost, and decentralized asset transfers between blockchains. Although bridges can be vulnerable to security risks, their benefits in terms of cost, speed, eligibility for airdrops, and decentralization make them an attractive option for many crypto enthusiasts.

4.2 Layer Zero

A related approach is the one developed by Layer Zero. Similarly to bridges, the objective is to facilitate communication and interoperability between blockchains, but they differ in their approach and architecture.

Layer Zero is a network protocol designed to enable cross-chain communication at the foundational level. It allows different blockchains to interact and share data, enabling seamless interoperability. Layer Zero acts as a backbone, providing a common infrastructure for decentralized applications (DApps) to work across multiple blockchains.

Layer Zero focuses on scalability solutions at the protocol level, utilizing techniques such as sidechains and shard chains to increase transaction throughput. Integrating with existing blockchain networks at the protocol level means that Layer Zero establishes a direct connection and interaction with the underlying protocols of these blockchains. This integration allows Layer Zero to communicate with and leverage the functionalities of different blockchains in a native and efficient manner. At the protocol level, Layer Zero interacts with the consensus mechanisms, data structures, and communication protocols of existing blockchains. This integration enables Layer Zero to facilitate cross-chain communication, asset transfers, and data exchange between different chains. It operates as a layer on top of existing blockchains, aiming to create a unified ecosystem for seamless interaction between multiple chains. Decentralized infrastructure and governance are emphasized in Layer Zero, ensuring security through distributed consensus mechanisms.

In contrast, bridges like Wormhole primarily act as a token bridge protocol, facilitating the transfer of assets between different blockchains. It achieves this through smart contracts, allowing users to create wrapped tokens representing the same value across chains.

Let's consider a transaction involving Layer Zero and one involving Wormhole:

In Layer Zero: Alice wants to send Ether from the Ethereum blockchain to Bob on the BSC. She initiates the transaction using Layer Zero, which seamlessly transfers the Ether from the Ethereum main chain to a sidechain connected to BSC. The transaction is processed quickly and securely, utilizing Layer Zero's parallel processing capabilities.

---

[6] See the end of the chapter for more details about these two concepts.

In Wormhole: Alice wants to transfer USDT from the Ethereum blockchain to the Solana blockchain. She locks her USDT tokens in a smart contract on Ethereum, which mints an equivalent amount of wrapped USDT (wUSDT) on Solana using Wormhole. Once the wrapped tokens are received on Solana, Bob can access them by redeeming them through the Wormhole smart contract.

In both scenarios, interoperability between blockchains is achieved, but the mechanisms differ. Layer Zero facilitates seamless interaction between chains at the protocol level, while Wormhole enables token transfers through smart contracts and bridges.

At the technical level, let me emphasize a couple unique elements of this protocol. First, Layer Zero utilizes atomic swaps and Hash Time Locked Contracts (HTLCs) to enable trustless asset transfers between different blockchains.[6] Atomic swaps allow users to directly exchange assets across chains without relying on intermediaries. This process ensures that transactions occur securely and without the need for a trusted third party. Additionally, HTLCs play a crucial role in ensuring the security and irreversibility of transactions. These contracts require participants to fulfill specific conditions within a predetermined timeframe, preventing the risk of double-spending and ensuring that transactions are executed securely.

In terms of cross-chain validation, Layer Zero relies on a network of cross-chain validators to verify and validate transactions across different blockchains. These validators play a crucial role in maintaining the integrity and security of cross-chain transactions by ensuring that transactions are valid and consistent across all involved chains. By preventing double-spending and other malicious activities, cross-chain validators contribute to the overall security and trustworthiness of the Layer Zero protocol.

Layer Zero is governed by a decentralized network of nodes and validators, ensuring transparency and accountability in the decision-making process. Decentralized governance mechanisms allow community participation in protocol upgrades and changes, enabling stakeholders to have a say in the evolution of the protocol. This decentralized governance model fosters a collaborative environment where decisions are made collectively, ensuring that the interests of all participants are considered. By promoting transparency and accountability, decentralized governance enhances the trustworthiness and legitimacy of the Layer Zero protocol.

5. Concluding Remarks

The central theme of this chapter has been scalability and what we need to give up or live with to achieve it. We have seen how both Layer 1 solutions embodied by a new wave of more efficient blockchains, such as Solana and Avalanche, as well as Layer 2 solutions, including Optimistic Rollups and Zero-Knowledge Rollups, emerged to boost blockchain's capacity to handle increased traffic and more complex transactions. This focus on scalability highlights the commitment within the blockchain community to overcome limitations that have previously stymied broader use cases.

What I'd like to underscore is that no single approach is flawless, and recognizing the inherent limitations is crucial. Consider optimistic rollups, which enhance scalability but at the cost of finality. For some applications, this might not be a critical issue, but for others, it could be a deal-breaker. In contrast, zero-knowledge (ZK) rollups don't have this drawback but might face compatibility issues, like using different programming languages, and finding skilled developers in this specialized area can be challenging.

Several Blockchain 3.0 platforms have emerged in recent years, creating vibrant ecosystems. Solana and Avalanche are two notable examples, each offering unique features to compete with Ethereum's dominance. Solana provides faster transaction throughput, while Avalanche allows the creation of subnets for custom functionalities. Despite these innovations, Ethereum's network effects still make it the largest and most established ecosystem.

One key question to ponder from this chapter is whether the blockchain industry will become a "winner-takes-all" market or remain fragmented across multiple chains. In other words, is this diversity in blockchain platforms a lasting trend, or will the industry eventually consolidate around a single dominant chain? The answer might depend on the evolution of cross-chain interoperability, which could make switching between chains seamless for end users. If bridges between blockchains can be made more secure and compatibility issues resolved, users might not even notice which chain they're using, allowing for a more interconnected blockchain landscape.

Coding Examples

Simplified Optimistic Rollup Contract Example

This example simulates the submission of batched transaction states to the Ethereum mainnet. It's important to note that this does not encompass off-chain computation, fraud proofs, or the full Arbitrum protocol.

Smart Contract Code:

```solidity
// SPDX-License-Identifier: MIT
pragma solidity ^0.8.4;

contract SimplifiedRollup {
    address public owner;
    bytes32 public latestStateRoot;

    event StateUpdated(bytes32 newStateRoot);

    constructor() {
        owner = msg.sender;
    }
```

```
modifier onlyOwner() {
    require(msg.sender == owner, "Only the owner can update state");
    _;
}

// Function to simulate the submission of a new state root by the
rollup
    function submitStateRoot(bytes32 _newStateRoot) public onlyOwner {
        latestStateRoot = _newStateRoot;
        emit StateUpdated(_newStateRoot);
    }

// In a full implementation, there would be additional functions here
to handle:
    // - Verifying transaction execution off-chain
    // - Submitting and processing fraud proofs
    // - Dispute resolution mechanisms
}
```

Explanation:

- **Contract Initialization:** The contract is deployed by the owner, who will be responsible for submitting new state roots. In the context of an Optimistic Rollup like Arbitrum, the owner role would be played by the rollup's operator or validators responsible for batching and processing transactions off-chain.
- **State Submission:** The **submitStateRoot** function allows the owner to update the **latestStateRoot**, simulating the submission of a batch of transactions that have been executed off-chain. The state root is a hash representing the latest state of the rollup's off-chain ledger.
- **Event Emission:** The **StateUpdated** event is emitted every time a new state root is submitted, providing transparency and a way to track updates on-chain.

This simplified contract omits the complexity of handling off-chain computation, managing data availability, submitting fraud proofs, and resolving disputes, which are critical components of Optimistic Rollup solutions like Arbitrum.

Bridge Contract Example   We have seen that bridges facilitate cross-chain interoperability by allowing the transfer of assets between different blockchains. A simple example of a bridge involves locking an asset on one chain and minting an equivalent token on another. Here's a Solidity example that shows a basic bridge concept:

```
// SPDX-License-Identifier: MIT
pragma solidity ^0.8.0;
```

```
// This contract represents the bridge on the source chain
contract SourceBridge {
   address public destinationBridge; // Address of the destination bridge
   mapping(address => uint256) public lockedAssets; // Track locked
assets by user

   event AssetLocked(address indexed user, uint256 amount);

   constructor(address _destinationBridge) {
     destinationBridge = _destinationBridge;
   }

   function lockAssets(uint256 amount) external {
     require(amount > 0, "Amount must be greater than 0");

     // Lock the assets in the bridge
     lockedAssets[msg.sender] += amount;

     emit AssetLocked(msg.sender, amount);
   }
}

// This contract represents the bridge on the destination chain
contract DestinationBridge {
   address public sourceBridge; // Address of the source bridge

   event AssetUnlocked(address indexed user, uint256 amount);

   constructor(address _sourceBridge) {
     sourceBridge = _sourceBridge;
   }

   function unlockAssets(address user, uint256 amount) external {
     require(msg.sender == sourceBridge, "Only source bridge can unlock");

     emit AssetUnlocked(user, amount); // Mint equivalent tokens on
this chain
   }
}
```

In this example, the SourceBridge contract allows users to lock assets, while the DestinationBridge contract allows an authorized source (like a trusted validator) to unlock assets on the destination chain.

Additional Details: Atomic Swaps and Hashed Timelock Contracts (HTLCs)   Atomic swaps are a mechanism that allows users to directly exchange different cryptocurrencies or digital assets between two parties without the need for an intermediary or trusted third party. This process enables secure and trustless peer-to-peer transactions across different blockchain networks.

Here's how atomic swaps work:

1. **Setup Phase:**
   - Two parties, let's call them Alice and Bob, agree to exchange cryptocurrencies. Alice wants to exchange Bitcoin for Litecoin with Bob.
   - Alice and Bob generate unique cryptographic secrets known as preimages. Each party keeps their preimage secret.
2. **Contract Creation:**
   - Alice initiates the atomic swap by creating a contract transaction on the Bitcoin blockchain. This contract includes the details of the swap, such as the amount of Bitcoin to be exchanged and Bob's Litecoin address.
   - Alice also adds a condition to the contract: Bob can claim the Bitcoin if he reveals his preimage within a specified time window. Otherwise, Alice can reclaim her Bitcoin.
3. **Claiming the Funds:**
   - Bob sees the contract on the Bitcoin blockchain and agrees to the swap. He creates a similar contract on the Litecoin blockchain, specifying the amount of Litecoin to be exchanged and Alice's Bitcoin address.
   - Bob also adds a condition to his contract: Alice can claim the Litecoin if she reveals her preimage within the same time window. Otherwise, Bob can reclaim his Litecoin.
4. **Execution:**
   - Alice reveals her preimage to claim the Litecoin from Bob's contract on the Litecoin blockchain.
   - Bob uses the preimage revealed by Alice to claim the Bitcoin from Alice's contract on the Bitcoin blockchain.
5. **Completion:**
   - Both parties have successfully exchanged their assets without the need for a trusted intermediary. The atomic swap is completed, and Alice has received Litecoin while Bob has received Bitcoin.

Atomic swaps rely on cryptographic techniques such as hashed timelock contracts (HTLCs) to ensure that the exchange is atomic, meaning it either occurs entirely or not at all. If one party fails to reveal their preimage within the specified time window, both contracts become invalid, and the assets are returned to their original owners. This trustless and secure process makes atomic swaps a powerful tool for decentralized asset exchanges across different blockchain networks.

Hashed Timelock Contracts (HTLCs) are smart contracts that enable secure and trustless transactions between parties on different blockchain networks. HTLCs utilize cryptographic hashing and time-locking mechanisms to ensure that transactions occur securely and according to predefined conditions.

Here's how HTLCs work:

1. **Hash Locking:**
   - In an HTLC transaction, the sender (Alice) generates a cryptographic hash value and locks the funds with this hash. The hash value is derived from a secret known only to the sender and the receiver (Bob). This hash serves as a condition for releasing the funds.

2. **Time Locking:**
   - Additionally, the sender specifies a time lock, which determines the duration within which the recipient must claim the funds. If the funds are not claimed within this time frame, the transaction becomes invalid, and the funds are returned to the sender.

3. **Revealing the Secret:**
   - To claim the funds, the recipient (Bob) must reveal the preimage of the hash, which is the secret value used to generate the hash. This preimage is known only to the sender and the recipient.

4. **Conditional Execution:**
   - When Bob reveals the preimage, Alice can use it to verify that it matches the hash she provided earlier. If the preimage matches the hash, Alice can claim the funds within the specified time lock period.

5. **Refunding Funds:**
   - If Bob fails to reveal the preimage within the specified time lock period, Alice can refund the locked funds back to her own wallet. This ensures that funds are not locked indefinitely and allows for the resolution of expired transactions.

HTLCs are particularly useful in scenarios such as atomic swaps and payment channels, where parties want to ensure that transactions occur securely and according to agreed-upon conditions. By combining cryptographic hashing and time locking, HTLCs enable trustless and efficient transactions between parties on different blockchain networks while minimizing the risk of fraud or manipulation.

SIMPLIFIED ZK-SNARKS EXAMPLE

Imagine a transaction in a blockchain network where Alice wants to send 5 coins to Bob. The zk-SNARKs process needs to verify that Alice has enough balance and that the transaction is valid according to the network's rules.

Step 1: Encoding the Problem

- **Arithmetic Circuit:** Let's say Alice's balance is **x** coins. The transaction validity can be represented as an arithmetic circuit, which in a simplified form could be: $x - 5 >= 0$.

- **Polynomial Equations:** This is transformed into polynomial equations. For simplicity, consider the equation: $f(x) = x - 5$.

  Step 2: Trusted Setup

- **Public Parameters:** Suppose the setup generates public parameters **A**, **B**, and **C** for the zk-SNARKs system. The actual generation of these parameters is a complex cryptographic process.

  Step 3: Proof Generation

- **Witness Computation:** Alice, the prover, knows her balance **x**. She computes a witness **w** that satisfies $f(x) = w$. If Alice has 10 coins, then **w** will be **5** (since $10 - 5 = 5$).
- **Proof Construction:** Alice generates a proof using **w**, and the public parameters **A**, **B**, and **C** that shows she knows a value of **x** such that $f(x) = w$ without revealing **x**.

  Step 4: Proof Verification

- **Verifier's Role:** The verifier (a node in the network) checks the proof using the public parameters. If Alice's proof is correct, it shows she knows an **x** that makes the equation true, hence verifying the transaction validity.

Handling Invalid Transactions   If Alice tries to send more coins than her balance, the computation will not work:

- **Invalid Transaction Example:** Alice has 3 coins but tries to send 5.
- **Failed Computation:** For $x = 3$, the equation $f(x) = x - 5$ gives $f(3) = -2$, which does not satisfy the condition $x - 5 >= 0$.
- **Proof Generation Failure:** Alice cannot generate a valid proof for this transaction, as the witness **w** she computes will not match the criteria needed for a valid proof.

Punishment for Validators   In zk-SNARKs, the punishment mechanism is not directly tied to the proof system but rather to the blockchain protocol:

- **Validator Punishment:** If a validator (or miner) in a blockchain network tries to include an invalid transaction with an incorrect or fraudulent proof, they can be penalized.
- **Penalty Mechanism:** The exact mechanism depends on the blockchain's consensus protocol. In PoS systems, validators can lose their stake (slashing) for malicious actions. In PoW, they waste computational resources without gaining block rewards.

The zk-SNARKs process in a blockchain context involves creating proofs that a transaction meets certain criteria without revealing sensitive information. Invalid transactions fail at the proof generation stage, and validators are held accountable through the blockchain's consensus rules. The actual computation in zk-SNARKs is highly complex and involves advanced cryptographic techniques far beyond this simplified example.

Solana Coding Example   To give you a taste of coding on Solana, let's look at a basic Solana program (smart contract) written in Rust, which is the primary language used for Solana's on-chain programs. This example will illustrate a simple token transfer scenario on Solana, showcasing the process of writing, deploying, and interacting with a Solana program.

Example: Basic Solana Program for Token Transfer

1. Setting Up the Solana Project

First, ensure you have Rust and Solana CLI installed. Then, create a new project directory and initialize a new Rust project through the command line:

```
$ mkdir solana_token_transfer
$ cd solana_token_transfer
$ cargo init -lib
```

2. Writing the Program

Edit **src/lib.rs** to include the following code, which defines a basic program to increment a counter stored on the blockchain:

```
use solana_program::{
    account_info::{next_account_info, AccountInfo},
    entrypoint,
    entrypoint::ProgramResult,
    pubkey::Pubkey,
    program_error::ProgramError,
};

// Declare and export the program's entrypoint
entrypoint!(process_instruction);

// Program entrypoint's implementation
fn process_instruction(
    _program_id: &Pubkey, // Public key of the account the hello world
program was loaded into
    accounts: &[AccountInfo], // The account to say hello to
    _instruction_data: &[u8], // Ignored, all helloworld instructions are
hellos
```

```
) -> ProgramResult {
    let accounts_iter = &mut accounts.iter();

    let account = next_account_info(accounts_iter)?;

    let mut data = account.try_borrow_mut_data()?;

    let mut value = data[0];
    value = value.wrapping_add(1);
    data[0] = value;

    Ok(())
}
```

This program simply increments a value stored in an account by 1 each time it's called.

3. Building the Program

Compile your program:

```
cargo build-bpf --manifest-path=Cargo.toml --bpf-out-dir=dist/program
```

4. Deploying to Solana

Deploy your compiled program to the Solana devnet:

```
solana program deploy dist/program/solana_token_transfer.so
```

Remember, to deploy a program or interact with the Solana network, you'll need SOL (Solana's cryptocurrency) in your wallet for transaction fees.

5. Interacting with the Program

To interact with your program, you would typically use Solana's Web3.js library in a JavaScript application, creating transactions that call your program and sign them with the payer's private key.

Coding Example: Simple Plutus Contract

Given the functional nature of Haskell and the unique architecture of Plutus, a basic example of a Plutus contract might involve a simple transaction validator that only allows transactions under certain conditions. However, it's essential to note that setting up and running Plutus contracts requires a Cardano node and understanding of the Cardano blockchain's specific deployment processes, which are beyond this explanation's scope.

```
-- This is a highly simplified representation and not a functional
Plutus contract
module SimpleValidator where

import Ledger (Validator, validatorScript, mkValidatorScript)
import Ledger.Typed.Scripts (ValidatorTypes)
import qualified PlutusTx
import PlutusTx.Prelude

PlutusTx.makeLift ''MyDataType

validateTransaction :: MyDataType -> () -> () -> Bool
validateTransaction myData () () = -- Validation logic here

validator :: Validator
validator = mkValidatorScript $$(PlutusTx.compile [|| validateTransaction
||])

valInstance :: ValidatorTypes
valInstance = ValidatorTypes
    { vtValidator = validator
    , vtType = ...
    }
```

This pseudocode represents the structure of a Plutus contract, highlighting the separation between on-chain and off-chain code. The actual logic, data types, and conditions for transaction validation would need to be filled in based on the specific requirements of the DApp being developed.

End-of-Chapter Questions

Multiple-Choice Questions

1. **What is the main purpose of Layer 2 scaling solutions?**
   - (A) To decrease the security of the blockchain
   - (B) To increase transaction fees
   - (C) To increase transaction throughput and reduce costs
   - (D) To eliminate the need for Layer 1

2. **Which of the following is NOT a Layer 2 solution?**
   - (A) Sharding
   - (B) State Channels
   - (C) Plasma
   - (D) Rollups

3. **What is the primary benefit of using State Channels?**
   - (A) They allow for immediate transaction finality
   - (B) They increase the block size on the main chain
   - (C) They enable transactions to occur off-chain
   - (D) They eliminate the need for smart contracts

4. **What does "sharding" as a Layer 1 solution involve?**
   - (A) Splitting the network's data into smaller, manageable parts
   - (B) Encrypting the data on the blockchain
   - (C) Creating a single shard to process all transactions
   - (D) Decreasing the data storage on the blockchain

5. **Which of the following is a characteristic of Plasma?**
   - (A) Executes all transactions on the main chain
   - (B) Bundles state updates into single transactions
   - (C) Requires validators to stake cryptocurrency
   - (D) Creates child chains that report back to the main chain

6. **What differentiates Zero-Knowledge Rollups from Optimistic Rollups?**
   - (A) Zero-Knowledge Rollups require fraud proofs
   - (B) Optimistic Rollups use zero-knowledge proofs for transaction validation
   - (C) Zero-Knowledge Rollups offer instant transaction finality
   - (D) Optimistic Rollups increase transaction costs

7. **Which protocol is known for its use of PoH to achieve high throughput?**
   - (A) Ethereum
   - (B) Bitcoin
   - (C) Solana
   - (D) Ripple

8. **What does the term "interoperability" refer to in the context of block-chain technology?**
   (A) The ability of one blockchain system to perform transactions on another system without intermediaries
   (B) The isolation of one blockchain from another
   (C) The ability of a blockchain to operate without consensus
   (D) The ability of a blockchain to reject transaction requests from another chain

9. **Which Layer 2 solution is known for creating child chains that can operate independently?**
   (A) State Channels
   (B) Sharding
   (C) Plasma
   (D) Sidechains

10. **What is the main challenge associated with State Channels?**
    (A) They do not support smart contracts
    (B) They require all users to remain online to sign transactions
    (C) They only support cryptocurrency transactions
    (D) They require a large number of validators

11. **How do Rollups typically improve blockchain scalability?**
    (A) By processing transactions off-chain
    (B) By eliminating the need for consensus mechanisms
    (C) By increasing the block size
    (D) By using a different cryptographic algorithm

12. **What role does the 'relay chain' play in Polkadot's architecture?**
    (A) It executes all smart contracts
    (B) It manages consensus across parachains
    (C) It stores all transaction data
    (D) It is used for executing Plasma child chains

13. **Which of the following is a benefit of using a PoS consensus mechanism?**
    (A) It consumes more energy than PoW
    (B) It is less secure than PoW
    (C) It enables faster transaction processing
    (D) It requires validators to perform complex mathematical problems

14. **What potential risk is associated with bridges in blockchain interoperability?**
    (A) They guarantee transaction finality
    (B) They may lead to lost liquidity and broken smart contracts
    (C) They reduce transaction fees
    (D) They eliminate the need for native tokens

15. **Which project uses a modified PoS consensus to ensure rapid processing on its sidechain?**
    (A) Bitcoin
    (B) Ethereum
    (C) Polygon
    (D) Cardano

Open Questions

1. Discuss the implications of the scalability trilemma on the adoption of blockchain technology in mainstream business applications. How do Layer 2 solutions attempt to address these challenges? Consider factors like transaction speed, security, and decentralization in your discussion.

2. Analyze the potential impacts of blockchain interoperability on the future development of DApps. What role do newer blockchain technologies play in this ecosystem? Evaluate the benefits and challenges associated with interoperability between different blockchain platforms.

3. Evaluate the pros and cons of different Layer 2 solutions such as State Channels, Plasma, and Rollups. Which of these solutions do you think offers the most promising approach for large-scale implementation and why? Consider factors like transaction throughput, security, cost efficiency, and ease of integration.

4. How do developments in blockchain 3.0 technologies like Solana and Cardano challenge the current dominance of Ethereum in the DApp and smart contract markets? Discuss aspects like transaction fees, processing speeds, and the environmental impact of these blockchains.

5. Examine the long-term sustainability of PoS as a consensus mechanism in comparison to PoW. What are the potential benefits and drawbacks of PoS, especially in terms of security and network participation? Reflect on the transition of Ethereum to Ethereum 2.0 and how PoS may influence the scalability and security of the network.

6. Describe how sharding works and its potential impacts on blockchain performance and security.

7. Evaluate the advantages and potential risks associated with using sidechains as a scalability solution.

8. Discuss the differences between Optimistic and Zero-Knowledge Rollups and their use cases.

Exercise 1: State Channel Implementation

Objective: Implement a basic state channel contract that allows two parties to transact multiple times off-chain before settling on-chain.

Requirements:

- Develop a smart contract where two users can deposit ETH into the contract.
- Allow the users to sign off-chain messages to agree on the distribution of funds after multiple transactions.
- Provide a function to close the channel, where either user can submit the latest signed state to distribute funds accordingly.
- Ensure that only valid signed states can be submitted.

Steps to Approach:
1. **Contract Setup:** Start by creating a contract that allows two parties to deposit ETH. This establishes their ability to transact within the channel.
2. **Handling Transactions:** Implement a method to accept signed messages that represent transactions. These messages should include details like the amount and a nonce to prevent replay attacks.
3. **Closing the Channel:** Create a function that allows either party to submit the latest transaction for on-chain processing. The contract should verify the signatures against the public addresses of the participants.
4. **Security Considerations:** Ensure the function that processes the final state can handle disputes or incorrect submissions, possibly by allowing a challenge period during which the other party can submit a newer state if available.

Exercise 2: Rollup Contract for Batch Transactions

Objective: Create a smart contract that simulates a rollup mechanism for processing multiple transactions as a single batch.

Requirements:

- Design a contract that accepts multiple transactions in a single function call and processes them as a batch.
- Implement a mechanism to verify the legitimacy of each transaction within the batch (e.g., signatures, valid state transitions).
- Ensure that the contract updates the state only if all transactions in the batch are valid.
- Include a rollback mechanism in case any transaction in the batch fails.

Steps to Approach:
1. **Batch Input Handling:** Develop a function that takes an array of transaction details. Each transaction might consist of sender, receiver, amount, and a signature.
2. **Transaction Verification:** For each transaction in the batch, verify the signature and ensure that the transaction is valid (e.g., sender has enough balance, the transaction is not a duplicate).
3. **State Update:** If all transactions are valid, update the contract state accordingly. If any transaction in the batch is invalid, revert the entire batch to avoid partial updates.
4. **Optimizations:** Consider how gas costs can be minimized, such as by limiting the size of each batch.

Exercise 3: Cross-chain Asset Transfer

Objective: Develop a smart contract that enables asset transfers between two different blockchains (simulate with two different contracts).

Requirements:

- Create two smart contracts representing different blockchains.
- Implement a locking mechanism on the source blockchain contract where assets are locked when a transfer is initiated.
- Develop a proof verification system in the destination blockchain contract to unlock and distribute the assets once the transfer is confirmed.
- Include security features to prevent double-spending and replay attacks.

Steps to Approach:

1. **Locking Assets:** In the source chain contract, implement a function to lock assets pending transfer. Record details like the destination chain and recipient.
2. **Proof of Transfer:** On the destination chain, create a function that accepts proofs of locked funds (e.g., cryptographic proofs or security tokens).
3. **Asset Release:** Once a valid proof is submitted, unlock or mint the equivalent assets on the destination chain.
4. **Handling Disputes and Fraud:** Implement mechanisms to resolve disputes or fraud attempts, possibly through a timeout for the locked funds and a way to revert if the transfer fails.

Exercise 4: Plasma Chain Contract

Objective: Write a smart contract that represents a Plasma child chain, which can handle transactions independently and periodically commit the state to the main chain.

Requirements:

- Develop a Plasma child chain contract that processes transactions locally.
- Include a function to submit block headers to the main chain.
- Implement a challenge period mechanism for fraud proofs to dispute invalid transactions before finalizing commits.
- Ensure that users can withdraw their assets from the main chain if they decide to exit the Plasma chain.

Steps to Approach:

1. **Child Chain Operations:** Set up a contract to handle local transactions within the Plasma chain. This includes creating, signing, and verifying transactions.
2. **Committing to Main Chain:** Periodically, the child chain should commit its state to the main chain. This could be done by submitting the Merkle root of its latest state.

3. **Handling Exits:** Implement a mechanism for users to withdraw funds back to the main chain, including submitting proofs of their final state.
4. **Fraud Proofs:** Develop functions to challenge incorrect state commitments or fraudulent withdrawal attempts.

Exercise 5: Implementing a DAO with Layer 2 Scaling

Objective: Build a decentralized autonomous organization (DAO) that operates efficiently using a Layer 2 scaling solution.

Requirements:

- Create a DAO structure where proposals can be made, voted on, and executed within a Layer 2 framework to ensure scalability.
- Use a governance token for voting, where the token itself utilizes a Layer 2 solution for transfer and voting to minimize costs.
- Incorporate mechanisms for delegating votes and tallying them off-chain, with final results being committed on-chain.
- Design and implement security features that protect against common vulnerabilities in DAOs and Layer 2 solutions, such as short-range attacks.

Steps to Approach:
1. **DAO Setup:** Establish a basic DAO structure, where proposals can be created and voted on.
2. **Layer 2 Integration:** Integrate a Layer 2 solution for managing votes to reduce costs and increase transaction speed.
3. **Voting Mechanism:** Ensure that voting is secure and transparent, possibly using a Layer 2 scaling solution that supports data availability and integrity.
4. **Handling Proposals:** Develop methods to execute actions based on successful proposals, ensuring that only valid and approved actions are taken.

Chapter 4

Riding the Crypto Rollercoaster

How Stablecoins Keep Their Cool

Preface

In the kaleidoscopic carnival of crypto, where Bitcoin rides the roller coaster of market sentiment, reaching dizzying heights only to plummet into the depths of volatility, stablecoins stand at the cotton candy stand, offering a sweet taste of sanity. Amid the raucous laughter and screams from the crypto coaster, these unassuming tokens whisper, "Hey, how about something a bit more . . . stable?"

Imagine, if you will, a world where your digital dollars don't decide to take a nosedive just because Elon Musk tweeted about his new pet Shiba Inu. That's the utopia stablecoins promise—a currency as boring as your grandfather's savings account but as cutting-edge as that startup selling blockchain-based toothbrushes.

Stablecoins are the financial world's attempt at creating the perfect hybrid: a creature with the blockchain's heart, pulsing with decentralization and transparency, and traditional currency's steady hands at the wheel. They're pegged to the excitingly unexciting worlds of fiat currencies, gold, or even a basket of assets, ensuring that while everything else in crypto might be ready to party at a moment's notice, stablecoins have a curfew and a sensible bedtime.

The genius behind stablecoins lies in their thrillingly mundane stability mechanism. Some are backed by a vault full of dollars (or dollar-like substances), others by gold (presumably guarded by dragons), and a brave few by algorithms that are so complex they might as well be sorcery. This magical concoction provides a potion of predictability in the otherwise intoxicating brew of the crypto market.

In the DeFi kingdom, where traditional finance's rules are about as relevant as a pager in the age of smartphones, stablecoins strut their stuff. They grease the wheels of decentralized exchanges, make lending platforms hum, and give yield farming that je ne sais quoi. They're the reliable friend who holds your coat while you dive into the mosh pit of speculative trading.

But, as with any tale of innovation and daring, there's a twist. For all the promises of stability and security of stablecoins, they come with their own bag of worries. Regulation looms like a storm cloud, and whether the assets backing these tokens are as solid as claimed adds a delicious hint of mystery. It's like finding out that the haunted house might actually have real ghosts.

As we navigate this brave new world where digital and traditional finance collide with the subtlety of a wrecking ball, stablecoins offer a glimmer of hope—a bridge over troubled waters, if you will. They stand at the intersection of revolutionary zeal and a longing for the good old days when money was just money.

So here we are, at the edge of the crypto circus, with stablecoins holding our hand, promising us a future where digital finance can be both wildly innovative and comfortingly familiar. It's an odd couple that might just work, like pineapple on pizza or socks with sandals. In the constantly surprising crypto saga, stablecoins might not be the heroes we expected, but they're certainly the sidekicks we need.

Sweet taste of sanity

1. Introduction

Back in 2010, Laszlo Hanyecz figured 10,000 Bitcoins was a fair trade for two Papa John's pizzas. Today, that's known as the most expensive meal in history—it makes you wonder if they forgot his extra pepperoni.[1] The need for stablecoins emerges from the desire for "regret-free" transactions within the digital currency landscape. While Bitcoin was initially created as a medium of exchange with the vision of facilitating peer-to-peer transactions without the need for traditional banking systems, its utility in this aspect has been hindered by its volatility. The value of Bitcoin can fluctuate widely in short periods, making it a risky option for everyday transactions. It makes buying coffee a gamble. Today, a latte. Tomorrow, the whole coffee shop. This volatility undermines the fundamental requirement for a medium of exchange to have a stable value over time.

Enter stablecoins, the boring adults at the crypto party, ensuring your digital dollars don't go on a bender over the weekend. Stablecoins were introduced to mitigate this issue by pegging their value to more stable assets, such as fiat currencies or commodities, thereby offering the digital currency space a solution for conducting transactions without the fear of significant value changes post-transaction. This stability is crucial for wider adoption of cryptocurrencies in daily commerce and the evolving DeFi ecosystem, ensuring that digital currencies can be used for their intended purpose as a medium of exchange without the unpredictability associated with traditional cryptocurrencies like Bitcoin.

The first widely recognized stablecoin, Tether (USDT), was introduced in 2014.[2] Tether was created by Brock Pierce, Reeve Collins, and Craig Sellars, co-founders of the company Tether Limited. The primary motivation behind Tether was to bridge the gap between fiat currencies and cryptocurrencies, providing a stable digital currency pegged to the U.S. dollar's value, i.e., 1 USDT = $1. This pegging was designed to combine the best of both worlds: the stability and wide acceptance of fiat currencies with the technological advantages and borderless nature of cryptocurrencies.

Following Tether's success and the recognition of the benefits stablecoins offer, numerous other stablecoins were introduced, each with different mechanisms for maintaining stability. These include fiat-collateralized stablecoins like USDC (launched by Circle and Coinbase in 2018)[3], crypto-collateralized stablecoins like DAI (launched by MakerDAO in 2017)[4], and algorithmic stablecoins like Frax (launched in 2020), which used a sophisticated system of smart contracts to maintain its peg to the U.S. dollar without direct backing by fiat currency reserves. As shown in **Figure 1**, as of March 2024,

---

[1] At the time, the transaction was in fact worth about $41, marking the first known commercial transaction using Bitcoin. However, as Bitcoin's value skyrocketed over the years, the cost of those pizzas would be worth hundreds of millions of dollars today, illustrating the extreme volatility of cryptocurrencies.

[2] https://tether.to/en/about-us

[3] https://www.circle.com/en/usdc

[4] https://makerdao.com/en/

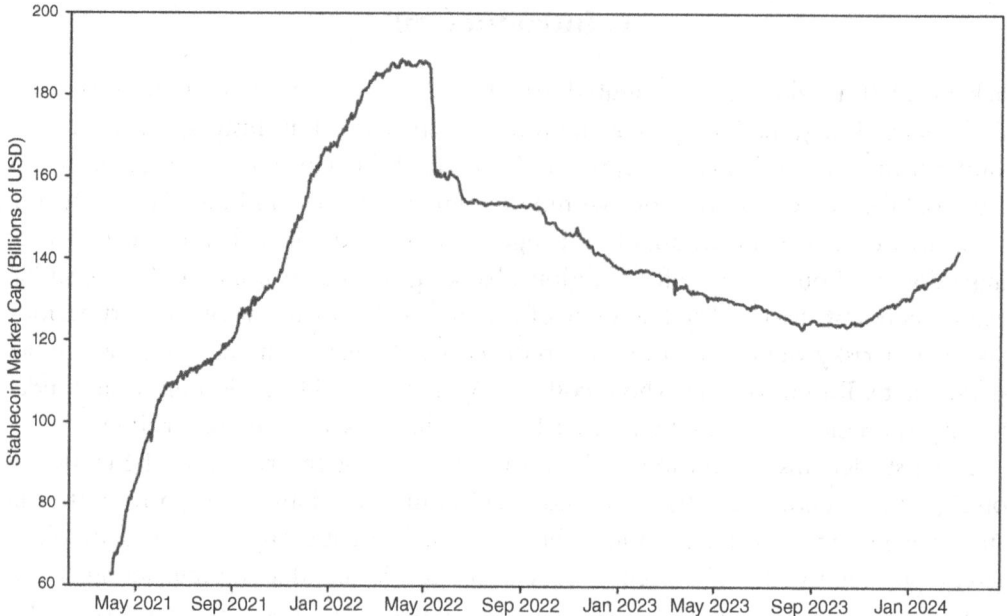

Figure 1   Stablecoins market cap (Adapted from DeFiLlama, 2024)

from DefiLlama, stablecoins' popularity has since skyrocketed and reached a peak of almost $200 billion USD during the 2021 bull market and in 2024 is at about $140 billion USD.

We will see that stablecoins are an indispensable tool, not only to purchase pizzas with digital tokens but for traders, investors, and decentralized finance (DeFi) participants, enabling smoother transactions, more predictable financial planning, and a safeguard against the notorious price swings of the crypto market.

Furthermore, the on-ramp and off-ramp processes, which refer to the methods of converting traditional fiat currencies into cryptocurrencies and vice versa, prominently feature stablecoins due to their stable value. When users want to enter the crypto market, they can use fiat to purchase stablecoins via exchanges or fiat-to-crypto platforms. Users can then trade these stablecoins for other cryptocurrencies, exploring the wider market without immediate exposure to its price fluctuations.

Conversely, when users wish to exit the crypto market, they can convert their volatile cryptocurrencies back into stablecoins. This conversion locks in the value of their assets, mitigating the risk of price volatility in the period between the decision to sell and the execution of the transaction. Subsequently, these stablecoins can be easily converted back into fiat currencies, completing the off-ramp process. This on-ramp and off-ramp mechanism provides a straightforward and less risky pathway for entering and exiting the crypto market, making stablecoins a crucial tool for integrating traditional financial systems with the burgeoning world of cryptocurrency.

2. Stability Mechanisms

We can break stablecoins into four main types based on how they maintain their peg. First, there are stablecoins that, similar to the pre-1971 dollar, are backed by gold or commodities, e.g. PAXG, even though they are not too important or popular within the digital assets market. Second, some stablecoins that are backed by other (volatile) cryptocurrencies, e.g. DAI, but maintain a buffer against volatility. Third, stablecoins, like Frax, that use smart contracts to influence the demand and supply of the token to maintain its value. Finally, the most used stablecoins are those backed directly by U.S. treasuries, cash, or other safe assets, such as USDT and USDC.

Let's examine each stability mechanism.

2.1 Gold-Backed Stablecoins

Gold-backed stablecoins tie their intrinsic value to real-world commodities, primarily gold, aiming to provide the stability and reliability often associated with precious metals. Among the various stablecoins, gold-backed ones like Paxos Gold (PAXG) and Tether Gold (XAUT) stand out for their direct correlation to the price of gold, marrying the physical asset's time-tested value with the digital era's efficiency and transparency.

Paxos Gold (PAXG), for example, is a digital token where each unit is backed by one fine troy ounce of a 400 oz London Good Delivery gold bar, securely stored in Brink's vaults. Ownership of PAXG represents a digital claim on physical gold and also grants the holder the right to take physical possession of the gold backing the token if they choose. This aspect of gold-backed stablecoins is governed by smart contracts on the blockchain, ensuring that ownership and transfer information is accurately and transparently recorded.

Similarly, Tether Gold (XAUT) provides ownership of one troy ounce of physical gold per token, with the gold stored in a secure vault in Switzerland. These tokens bridge the gap between traditional finance's tangible assets and the digital finance world's efficiency, offering a stable value pegged to the current gold price. This blend of blockchain's benefits with traditional financial assets like gold presents an appealing option for investors seeking tangible asset value while enjoying digital asset transactions' flexibility and global reach.

However, the adoption and usage of commodity-backed stablecoins, including those backed by gold, remain modest compared to their fiat-backed counterparts, such as USDC or USDT. Market capitalization and liquidity levels for PAXG and XAUT illustrate this point. Despite their innovative approach to combining physical gold with digital assets, these gold-backed stablecoins have not yet achieved widespread use or liquidity in the broader cryptocurrency market. For instance, as of March 2024, PAXG holds a market cap of $392 million USD with a 24-hour trading volume of nearly $17 million USD, compared to USDT's market cap of $99 billion USD and 24-hour trading volume of $66 million USD. Gold-backed stablecoins rank significantly lower than other more mainstream stablecoins.

The main allure of gold-backed stablecoins lies in their potential to provide investors with the best of both worlds: the reliability and intrinsic value of gold and the flexibility, efficiency, and transparency offered by blockchain technology. These stablecoins offer a digital method for owning, trading, and transacting with gold, all while maintaining a value closely pegged to the precious metal's current market price. This fusion aims to cater to those looking to diversify their digital asset portfolios with investments traditionally considered safe havens during economic turbulence.

In conclusion, while gold-backed stablecoins represent an innovative step forward in the world of digital finance, bridging traditional and digital financial worlds, their journey toward mainstream acceptance and liquidity is still underway. The future of these stablecoins will likely depend on broader market adoption, regulatory clarity, and their ability to offer tangible benefits over other forms of stablecoins and digital assets.

2.2 Crypto-Backed Stablecoins

Crypto-collateralized stablecoins represent an innovative approach to maintaining stability in the inherently volatile cryptocurrency market. The idea underpinning this type of stablecoins is that even volatile cryptocurrencies can be used as a reserve asset to ensure the stability of a different currency. With the advantage of leveraging other cryptocurrencies as collateral, these stablecoins aim to provide a stable value pegged to traditional fiat currencies, like the U.S. dollar, within a decentralized framework, meaning that both the stablecoin and their reserves are on-chain. Among the various stablecoin models, DAI, maintained by the MakerDAO protocol on the Ethereum blockchain, serves as a prime example of a crypto-collateralized stablecoin. We will delve into the mechanics of DAI, explore its collateralization process, and address potential challenges and solutions inherent in this model.

At its core, a crypto-collateralized stablecoin is backed by a basket of other cryptocurrencies rather than fiat money or physical commodities. This structure allows for the creation of a stable digital currency that can be used for transactions, savings, or as a hedge against the volatility of other cryptocurrencies. DAI, for instance, is pegged 1:1 to the U.S. dollar through an automated system of smart contracts on the Ethereum blockchain.

2.2.1 The MakerDAO Protocol and DAI   The MakerDAO protocol is the decentralized governance community that regulates DAI's issuance and stability. It employs a series of smart contracts to manage collateral assets, allowing users to generate DAI against their cryptocurrency holdings.

Users can mint DAI by locking their cryptocurrency assets, such as Ethereum (ETH), into a Maker Vault and creating a Collateralized Debt Position (CDP). The number of DAI one can generate is based on the collateral-to-debt ratio, a critical parameter that must be vigilantly maintained above a certain threshold to prevent the liquidation of the collateral.

How can you transform a volatile asset into a stable one? Overcollateralization is the mechanism that underpins the stability of DAI. By requiring users to deposit more collateral in value than the number of DAI they wish to generate, the system ensures a buffer against the price volatility of the collateral asset. For example, if an investor deposits $150 worth of Ethereum, they may be allowed to mint only $100 worth of DAI. This overcollateralization helps maintain DAI's peg to the U.S. dollar even as the value of Ethereum fluctuates, i.e. there are enough ETH to back up DAI.

The collateralization ratios in MakerDAO are dynamic, meaning they can change over time based on governance decisions and market conditions. The MakerDAO community, through its governance mechanism, votes on adjustments to these ratios to respond to changing market dynamics, such as volatility in the prices of collateral assets. For example, if the market becomes more volatile, the community might vote to increase the collateralization ratio to mitigate the risk of undercollateralization and ensure the system's solvency. Conversely, in more stable market conditions, the ratio might be lowered to make it easier for users to generate DAI. This flexibility allows MakerDAO to maintain the peg of DAI to the dollar while managing the risks associated with the collateral assets.

What happens in the case of a decline in the value of Ethereum? Rather than having margin calls, as happens in traditional finance, the MakerDAO protocol includes a liquidation mechanism to protect the stability of DAI against extreme volatility in the collateral asset. If the value of the collateral drops such that the collateral-to-debt ratio falls below the required minimum, the CDP is automatically liquidated to cover the outstanding DAI debt. Then, by selling when the value of the collateral is still above the value of the minted DAI, the protocol ensures that there are always enough reserves to back the stablecoin.

How does the liquidation process work? It includes different elements—let's go through them one by one.

1. **Auction:** The collateral in the liquidated Vault is sold to the highest bidder in exchange for DAI.
2. **Penalty Fee:** The Vault owner incurs a penalty fee, deducted from the auction proceeds.
3. **Debt Coverage:** Proceeds from the auction first go toward covering the outstanding DAI debt.
4. **Remaining Collateral:** Any excess funds after covering the debt and penalty fee are returned to the Vault owner.

When a Vault is flagged for liquidation, its collateral is placed into an auction system. The objective of this auction is to sell off the collateral to the highest bidder in exchange for DAI. This ensures that the system can recoup the DAI that was generated against the now-insufficient collateral, maintaining the overall stability of the DAI ecosystem. The auction mechanism is designed to be as transparent and efficient as possible, allowing participants to bid until a satisfactory exchange rate between the collateral and DAI is found.

A penalty fee is another integral part of the liquidation process. This fee is imposed on the Vault owner as a deterrent against risky behavior and to compensate the system for the operational risks and costs associated with the liquidation process. The penalty fee is deducted from the total proceeds of the auction, ensuring that the system recovers more than just the outstanding DAI debt. This additional fee is set by the governance of the MakerDAO community and can vary based on the type of collateral and other risk parameters.

The primary purpose of the auction's proceeds is to cover the outstanding DAI debt that was generated by the Vault owner. This means that before any funds are returned to the Vault owner or used to pay penalty fees, the generated DAI must be fully paid back. This ensures the integrity of the DAI stablecoin, as it guarantees that all DAI in circulation is properly backed by sufficient collateral, even in the event of market downturns.

Finally, any remaining collateral after the debt and penalty fee have been covered is returned to the Vault owner. This aspect of the liquidation process ensures fairness, as it allows Vault owners to recover any value that exceeds their DAI debt and the associated liquidation costs. It recognizes that while the Vault owner did not maintain a sufficient collateral-to-debt ratio, they are still entitled to any surplus value once their obligations to the system have been met.

Through these components, the MakerDAO liquidation process aims to balance the need for system stability with fairness to Vault owners. It provides a structured and predictable method for handling situations where the value of collateral falls, ensuring that DAI remains a stable and reliable stablecoin even in volatile market conditions.

Numerical Example: Understanding Collateral Ratios   **Figure 2** considers an investor who deposits $150 worth of Ethereum to generate $100 worth of DAI. This initial setup implies a 150% collateralization ratio ($150 in ETH / $100 in DAI). If the value of Ethereum increases to $200, the ratio improves, offering more buffer against volatility. Conversely, if Ethereum's value drops to $125, the ratio tightens to 125%, nearing the liquidation threshold, at which point the collateral will be liquidated to ensure that there are always enough reserves to cover the issue's DAI.

2.2.2 Potential Challenges and Advantages   There are two key inefficiencies in this system. First, the overcollateralization requirement, while providing stability, increases the opportunity costs and reduces liquidity as users need to lock up $150 to receive only $100 in DAI. To mitigate this issue, the MakerDAO community continuously adjusts the parameters governing collateralization ratios, liquidation thresholds, and penalty fees. Additionally, diversifying the types of accepted collateral can spread risk and enhance the system's resilience against price swings in any single asset.

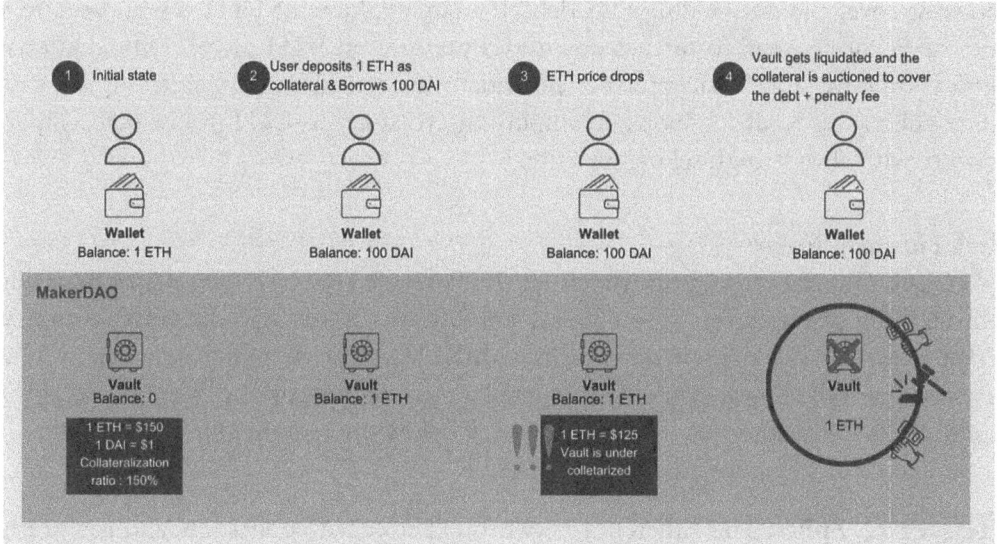

Figure 2 The figure outlines the process within a MakerDAO system when the ETH price falls, leading to the collateral becoming under-collateralized. Initially, 1 ETH is deposited ($150), and 100 Dais are borrowed. If the ETH price drops to $125, the vault becomes under-collateralized, triggering automatic liquidation

One might wonder *why an investor should go through the trouble of locking a larger amount of ETH to receive a smaller number of DAI.* There are several reasons why this might be a compelling proposition for investors. Investors with significant cryptocurrency holdings, such as Ethereum, might not want to sell their assets, anticipating future value appreciation. However, they might still need liquidity for various purposes, such as investing in other opportunities without losing their position in ETH. By using their ETH as collateral in MakerDAO to generate DAI, they can access liquid funds while maintaining their cryptocurrency investments. This process allows them to leverage their holdings to pursue additional investment opportunities or cover expenses without liquidating their assets. This is not dissimilar from borrowing against a real asset, such as a house, to increase one's liquidity.

The second important inefficiency generated by this system is its effect on the broader crypto market. If the collateral asset's price falls sharply, users risk having their collateral liquidated at potentially unfavorable rates. Even worse, the DAI liquidation system incorporates a **feedback loop** that interacts with the broader Ethereum market, especially during periods of significant price volatility: the DAI stability mechanism can exacerbate market movements in DAI and ETH.

Consider the following scenario. When the price of Ethereum decreases, the value of the collateral backing DAI (in Maker Vaults) also decreases. If the value of the collateral falls below a certain threshold (the liquidation ratio), the collateral is at risk of being liquidated. This is to ensure that the DAI issued against it remains adequately backed. However, the initiation of liquidations involves selling the collateral (ETH) on the open market to cover the outstanding DAI debt. If a large volume of ETH is liquidated in a short period, it can lead to further downward pressure on ETH prices. This additional pressure can lower ETH prices further, potentially triggering more liquidations in a cascading effect. This feedback loop can amplify the volatility in ETH prices, especially in a market with already high selling pressure.

Black Thursday Event

The "Black Thursday" event on March 12, 2020, serves as a stark example of how this feedback loop can operate under extreme conditions. On this day, the cryptocurrency market experienced a massive downturn, with ETH's price dropping significantly in a very short period. This rapid decline triggered a wave of liquidations in the MakerDAO system, as the collateral value of many Vaults fell below the required liquidation ratio.

Several factors compounded the situation:

- **Gas Price Spike:** The Ethereum network experienced congestion, and gas prices (transaction fees) spiked due to the high volume of transactions, including those triggered by liquidation and trading activities. This made it difficult for users to manage their positions efficiently.
- **Oracle Delay:** The price feeds (oracles) that MakerDAO used to get ETH prices were delayed in updating the rapidly falling market prices, leading to discrepancies between the collateral value in the system and the actual market value.
- **Zero-Bid Auctions:** The system's auction mechanism for liquidated collateral faced issues, with some auctions receiving zero bids due to network congestion and high gas prices. This meant that collateral was sold without recovering any DAI, exacerbating the liquidity issues.
- **DAI Depeg:** The combined effect of these factors led to a shortage of DAI liquidity, pushing its price above the $1 peg as demand for liquid DAI to close positions outstripped supply.

In response to Black Thursday, the MakerDAO community implemented several changes to improve system resilience, including adjustments to the liquidation system, improvements to auction mechanisms, and the introduction of new governance and risk management processes. These measures aim to mitigate the feedback loop's negative impacts during periods of extreme volatility and maintain the stability of both DAI and the broader Ethereum ecosystem.

Despite these inefficiencies, there is still hope for DAI. As we will discover in the next few chapters, DAI, being a stablecoin pegged to the U.S. dollar, serves as a bridge between traditional fiat currencies and cryptocurrencies, without the need for traditional financial intermediaries or centralized entities. Because of the unique transparency of blockchains, holders can verify the security of the system without needing to trust any central governing body—they can scrutinize the source code governing the protocol, examine the health of all CDPs, and participate in liquidation auctions to continuously ensure the safety of the protocol. The decentralized nature of DAI and other cryptocurrency-backed stablecoins is a powerful aspect of their stability mechanism that appeals to many users and incentivizes their participation in the ecosystem.

DAI allows investors to engage with the broader DeFi ecosystem, which offers a range of financial services, including lending, borrowing, and earning interest. By participating in DAI savings rates, liquidity pools, and other DeFi protocols, investors can earn interest on their DAI holdings. Additionally, by being part of the MakerDAO governance process through holding and using MKR tokens, investors can have a say in the development and future direction of the protocol, potentially earning rewards for their participation.

Furthermore, by converting volatile cryptocurrency holdings into DAI, a stablecoin, investors can protect themselves against market downturns and reduce their portfolio's volatility. This stability is particularly appealing for those looking to hedge against the inherent risks of the crypto market or for those seeking a stable store of value.

Crypto-collateralized stablecoins like DAI provide an innovative solution to the volatility challenge in the cryptocurrency market. By leveraging overcollateralization and automatic liquidations, these stablecoins offer a decentralized, stable medium of exchange. However, the complexity of managing collateralized debt positions, along with the risks of liquidation, has limited its adoption as it stands far behind USDT and USDC.

The alternative has different drawbacks. Consider what happened when in March 2022, the price of nickel surged by 250%, reaching more than $100,000 per ton. This spike was partly due to Russia's invasion of Ukraine, which raised fears of a nickel supply shortage. The London Metal Exchange (LME) suspended trading after Tsingshan, the world's largest nickel producer, faced massive losses and couldn't meet margin calls. China Construction Bank, Tsingshan's broker, was granted extra time by the LME to cover these margin calls, highlighting the challenges and risks in margin trading for large traders. This intervention was seen as unfair by many market participants because it deviated from standard margin call protocols, which usually require immediate settlement.

In contrast, in the crypto market, such discretion is typically not possible due to the decentralized and automated nature of most platforms. Margin calls and liquidations are executed automatically through smart contracts, ensuring that all participants are treated equally without the possibility of human intervention or preferential treatment. This automated system helps maintain transparency and fairness, as the rules are enforced consistently without exceptions.

2.2.3 Wrapped Cryptocurrencies Can stablecoins only be pegged to fiat currencies? No! For instance, we have discussed stablecoins that maintain a peg to commodities like PAXG. But there is a whole category of stablecoins that are pegged to other cryptocurrencies such as Wrapped ETH (WETH), and Wrapped BTC (WBTC). Why would people want to hold these stablecoins when they can hold the underlying asset? Keeping fiat currencies and gold in a digital wallet on a blockchain is impossible, which is why stablecoins are so powerful. *So why would someone want WBTC if they can have BTC?* The answer lies in the interoperability within a blockchain and across blockchains.

Let us motivate the existence of this group of coins with an example. Suppose you hold a diversified portfolio containing BTC, ETH, and other cryptocurrencies, and would like to use them as collateral to mint DAI and participate in the MakerDAO ecosystem. The smart contracts that govern the behavior of CDPs and DAI exist on the Ethereum blockchain, which is separate from the Bitcoin blockchain. The Ethereum blockchain has no information about your holdings on the Bitcoin blockchain, so how can you use BTC as collateral? You can use WBTC. WBTC is a stablecoin that is backed 1:1 by Bitcoin and can be freely used on the Ethereum blockchain like any another token.

At the most basic level, wrapped cryptocurrencies are simply stablecoins pegged to cryptocurrencies. These stablecoins are backed 1:1 with the underlying asset in a reserve that is either managed by a centralized party, like in the case of WBTC, or by a decentralized algorithm, like WETH. When the reserve is managed by a centralized party, wrapped cryptocurrencies operate similarly to fiat-backed stablecoins where the issuer holds custody of the underlying asset. In the case of WBTC, the underlying BTC is held by custodians like BitGo. A key difference with fiat-backed stablecoins is that the reserves can be verified on-chain because of the inherent transparency that blockchains have. Despite a greater transparency, risks still exist as these custodians are susceptible to attacks, hacks, and potential loss of funds. If a malicious actor gains access to the custodian's wallet, the reserve assets can be drained, leading to a depegging.

For decentralized algorithms, the reserve is usually held by a smart contract and governed by the source code. With WETH, the underlying ETH is held by a single smart contract on the blockchain that contains functionality for minting and burning. For instance, the source code for WETH is as follows:

```
pragma solidity ^0.4.18;

contract WETH9 {
    string public name     = "Wrapped Ether";
    string public symbol   = "WETH";
    uint8  public decimals = 18;

    event  Approval(address indexed src, address indexed guy, uint wad);
    event  Transfer(address indexed src, address indexed dst, uint wad);
    event  Deposit(address indexed dst, uint wad);
    event  Withdrawal(address indexed src, uint wad);

    mapping (address => uint)                        public  balanceOf;
    mapping (address => mapping (address => uint))   public  allowance;

    function() public payable {
        deposit();
    }
    function deposit() public payable {
        balanceOf[msg.sender] += msg.value;
        Deposit(msg.sender, msg.value);
```

```
    }

    function withdraw(uint wad) public {
        require(balanceOf[msg.sender] >= wad);
        balanceOf[msg.sender] -= wad;
        msg.sender.transfer(wad);
        Withdrawal(msg.sender, wad);
    }

    function totalSupply() public view returns (uint) {
        return this.balance;
    }

    function approve(address guy, uint wad) public returns (bool) {
        allowance[msg.sender][guy] = wad;
        Approval(msg.sender, guy, wad);
        return true;
    }

    function transfer(address dst, uint wad) public returns (bool) {
        return transferFrom(msg.sender, dst, wad);
    }

    function transferFrom(address src, address dst, uint wad)
        public
        returns (bool)
    {
        require(balanceOf[src] >= wad);

        if (src != msg.sender && allowance[src][msg.sender] != uint(-1)) {
            require(allowance[src][msg.sender] >= wad);
            allowance[src][msg.sender] -= wad;
        }

        balanceOf[src] -= wad;
        balanceOf[dst] += wad;

        Transfer(src, dst, wad);

        return true;
    }
}
```

As you can see, the contract contains functions that allow anyone to check the total supply of WETH, the balance held by all addresses, and the basic functionality like minting, burning, and transferring. In addition, anyone can verify the total ETH holdings that the contract has to ensure that all WETH tokens are backed 1:1. While the transparency of blockchain allows users to easily verify the health of the stablecoin, this mechanism is not free of risks. Because all functionality is determined by the source code, any errors or bugs in the code can be catastrophic to the token. Hackers can exploit these issues to drain the reserve or artificially increase the supply, leading to a loss of funds.

As mentioned, one important use case for wrapped cryptocurrencies, or stablecoins pegged to cryptocurrencies, is the ability to use a token on another blockchain without having to sell any of your holdings. For example, the Bitcoin blockchain does not have the smart contract functionality that Ethereum has, so investors cannot leverage their BTC holdings to earn a yield. Instead, they can use WBTC to earn a savings rate on their BTC by depositing WBTC into a decentralized lending program on Ethereum.

Another important use case is the standardization of smart contract code. As discussed in Chapter 2, the Ethereum blockchain has a system that allows people to propose improvements and standards called Ethereum Improvement Proposals (EIPs). In particular, the Ethereum Request for Comment (ERC20) standard was created to ensure that all tokens on the Ethereum blockchain adhere to a set of smart contract standards. The proposals dictate a set of functions and interfaces that each token must have so that decentralized finance (DeFi) applications can easily refer to a token's properties. Developing decentralized applications (dApps) would be highly time inefficient without the standard.

Suppose the developers of MakerDAO wanted to incorporate a dozen tokens as collateral for minting DAI. If each of these tokens had different functions and function names for transferring the token from one wallet to another, the code for minting DAI would have to consider each case, leading to inefficient code writing. Instead, with the ERC20 standard, developers can easily write the original code and subsequently integrate new tokens without having to make changes to the source code. Specifically, the ETH token was released before the ERC20 standard was proposed, so native ETH is not ERC20 compliant. Instead, the WETH token is a stablecoin that adheres to the standard and enables ease of use with ETH. dApp developers no longer need to write separate code for ETH and other ERC20 tokens like USDT and WBTC.

While wrapped cryptocurrencies function differently from other fiat and commodity pegged stablecoins, these tokens are a powerful tool, especially in DeFi, that allows greater interoperability and ease of use within and across blockchains.

2.3 Algorithmic Stablecoins

Unlike their fiat-collateralized counterparts, which rely on traditional currency reserves, or crypto-collateralized stablecoins, which depend on other digital assets as collateral, algorithmic stablecoins use a completely different approach. They are designed to maintain their peg to a particular value, usually one USD, through algorithms and smart contracts that automatically adjust the supply of the stablecoin in response to changes in demand. In other words, they create a *decentralized central bank* that adjusts the money supply to keep a fixed peg. In addition, rather than using other cryptocurrencies as collateral (e.g. ETH for DAI), these protocols might issue volatile currencies that act as reserve assets for the stablecoin.

The proposition of algorithmic stablecoins addressed several frictions in the digital currency space. First, they sought to reduce the reliance on centralized entities and the need for trust in these institutions to maintain collateral reserves, a necessity for fiat and crypto-collateralized stablecoins. This approach aligned more closely with the decentralized ethos of blockchain technology and cryptocurrency. Second, algorithmic stablecoins aimed to offer a more scalable and flexible solution to price stability, capable of adjusting the money supply in real-time without the need for manual intervention or the complexities involved in managing physical or digital reserves.

The popularity of algorithmic stablecoins grew as they promised to mitigate the volatility of cryptocurrencies without the regulatory, operational, and custodial challenges associated with maintaining collateral reserves. They offered a vision of a truly decentralized financial system, where stable digital currencies could facilitate everyday transactions, lending, and other financial services without the constraints of traditional banking systems or the risks of significant price fluctuations.

The primary stability mechanism is based on arbitrage. When the price of the stablecoin is higher than its target peg, the algorithm issues more stablecoins. This is done either by allowing users to mint more coins directly by interacting with the smart contract or by the protocol automatically increasing supply. The increased supply, according to supply and demand principles, should help bring the price back down to the peg. Conversely, when the price of the stablecoin drops below its peg, the algorithm decreases the supply. This could be achieved by incentivizing users to burn their stablecoins in exchange for a promise of future rewards or other tokens within the ecosystem, or by the protocol buying back and burning tokens itself. Reducing supply should, in theory, increase the price back to the peg.

We can represent the mechanism graphically through the standard supply and demand chart for the case of Frax which we will discuss next. In **Figure 3**, we see the current state of the market—the ideal situation where the token maintains its peg of $1.

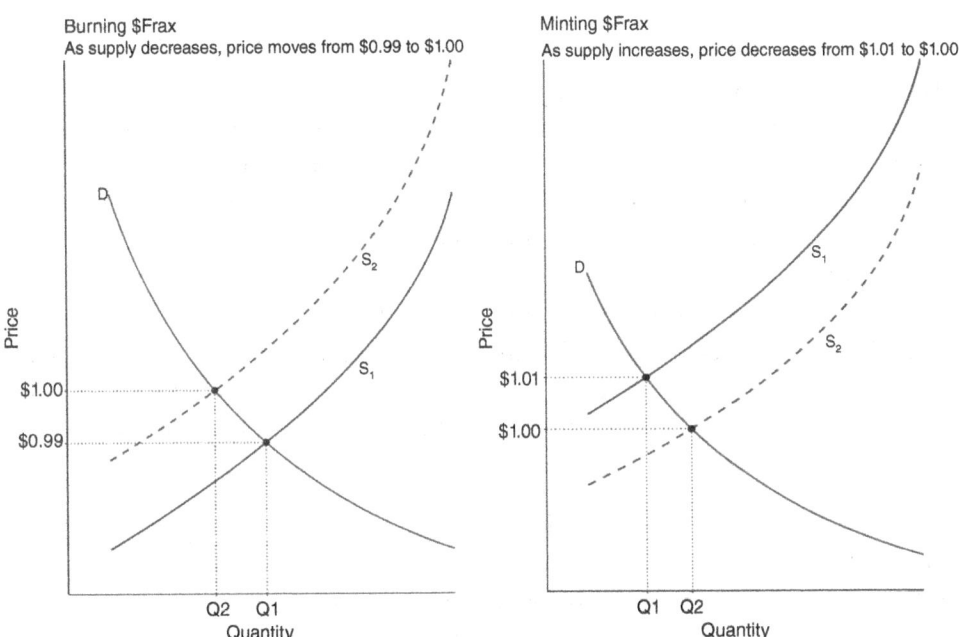

Figure 3 When the price is below the peg, the protocol incentivizes the burn of Frax, reducing the quantity from Q1 to Q2. When the price is above the peg, the protocol incentivizes the mint of $Frax increasing the quantity from Q1 to Q2

Suppose there is a sell-off such that the stablecoin loses its peg and now trades at $0.99. The smart contract is designated to automatically lead to a decrease of the supply so that the price is brought back to peg at $1. **Figure 3** depicts the contraction of supply in the event of a depegging where price is now below $1. Following standard supply and demand theory, these adjustments should maintain the stablecoin's peg. In reality, the peg is maintained through arbitrage opportunities that traders can take advantage of.

When the stablecoin's price deviates from its peg, traders can profit by buying low and selling high (or vice versa), moving the price toward the peg in the process. For example, if a stablecoin is pegged at $1 but is currently trading at $1.01, traders can mint (create) more coins at $1 and sell them at the market price of $1.01, making a profit and increasing the supply, which should help lower the price to $1. If the stablecoin falls to $0.99, traders can buy the stablecoin at this lower price from the market and redeem them at the peg value ($1) through the protocol, reducing the circulating supply and pushing the price back up.

The effectiveness of these arbitrage mechanisms depends on the responsiveness of the market participants, the liquidity of the market, and the efficiency of the underlying algorithms and smart contracts. The system assumes that there will always be enough market participants looking to exploit these arbitrage opportunities, thereby helping to stabilize the stablecoin's price. However, this may not always hold true, especially during periods of high volatility or when the confidence in the algorithmic system itself is shaken, leading to scenarios where the stablecoin can significantly deviate from its peg for extended periods.

Let's look at one real example.

Frax: Innovating Stablecoin Stability   Frax stands out in the world of stablecoins by introducing a mechanism that marries the concepts of collateralization and algorithmic regulation. This dual approach allows Frax to maintain a stable value against its target while also offering scalability, decentralization, and efficiency. Understanding how Frax operates requires a look at its two main components: the Frax stablecoin (FRAX) and the Frax Shares (FXS) token.

At its core, Frax is the world's first fractional-algorithmic stablecoin system. The term "fractional-algorithmic" refers to the fact that the stablecoin's backing comes partially from collateral (like cryptocurrencies or fiat currencies) and partially from algorithmic mechanisms. This hybrid model allows Frax to adjust its policies based on the market's behavior, ensuring stability and resilience against volatility.

1. **Collateralization:** A portion of FRAX's value is backed by collateral stored in smart contracts. Initially, this collateral consisted mainly of other stable assets such as USDC. The ratio of collateral to FRAX supply is not fixed and can be adjusted based on the governance decisions of the Frax community, primarily guided by holders of the Frax Shares (FXS) token.

2. **Algorithmic Regulation:** The remainder of FRAX's backing comes from algorithmic mechanisms governed by the Frax protocol. These mechanisms adjust the

supply of FRAX in response to changes in its price. If FRAX's price deviates from its peg, the protocol incentivizes users to expand or contract the supply through mechanisms like minting and burning, restoring equilibrium.

FXS is the governance token of the Frax ecosystem and plays a pivotal role in its operation and stability. Holders of FXS have voting rights on key parameters of the protocol, such as the collateral ratio and fee structures. Furthermore, FXS absorbs the volatility of FRAX's price deviations from its peg. In periods of high demand, when FRAX's price is above its peg, the protocol mints and sells FRAX, accumulating collateral and FXS, which can then be burned to reduce supply and increase its value. Conversely, when demand falls, the process reverses, with FXS being minted to purchase and retire FRAX from circulation, supporting its price.

Economic Incentives and Risks

The Frax ecosystem is designed with various economic incentives to maintain its peg and secure the system. Users are encouraged to participate in the minting and burning processes through mechanisms that offer arbitrage opportunities when FRAX deviates from its peg. These activities not only help stabilize FRAX but also provide users with a chance to profit from these interventions.

Let's see how this would work in the two relevant scenarios.

Scenario 1: FRAX Price Drops to $0.99   When the price of FRAX falls below its $1 peg, indicating an excess supply over demand, the Frax protocol employs a contractionary policy to reduce the supply and restore the peg. The protocol incentivizes users to buy FRAX from the market and burn it in exchange for a proportionate amount of the collateral (e.g., USDC) or newly minted FXS. This process is attractive to users because they can buy FRAX for $0.99 and redeem it for a value closer to $1 in collateral, making a profit through arbitrage. The act of burning FRAX reduces its supply, helping increase its price back to the $1 peg.

In parallel, if the governance decides, the protocol can adjust the collateral ratio to increase the amount of collateral backing each FRAX. This move can restore confidence in the stablecoin's value, encouraging users to hold or buy FRAX, thus pushing the price back up. The protocol's algorithmic functions also play a role, adjusting parameters such as redemption fees to make it more lucrative for users to participate in the contraction process.

Scenario 2: FRAX Price Rises to $1.01   When the price of FRAX exceeds its $1 peg, indicating higher demand than supply, the protocol adopts an expansionary policy to increase the supply and bring the price back down to $1. The protocol allows users to mint new FRAX by depositing collateral (and sometimes a combination of collateral and FXS, depending on the collateral ratio) at its current value. Since FRAX is selling for $1.01 in the market, users can mint it at $1.00 worth of collateral and sell it for a profit. This process increases the FRAX supply, which, according to the law of supply and demand, should help bring its price down to the peg.

If conditions allow, the governance may also lower the collateral ratio, making it cheaper to mint FRAX, thereby incentivizing more users to mint and sell FRAX, further aiding in price correction. Similar to the contraction scenario, algorithmic adjustments can be made to make the minting process more attractive or adjust the fees associated with minting and redeeming FRAX, further balancing supply and demand.

In both scenarios, the interplay between market participants exploiting arbitrage opportunities and the algorithmic adjustments by the Frax protocol work together to steer FRAX's price back to its $1 peg. The key to Frax's stability mechanism is its ability to dynamically adjust the supply of FRAX in response to its market price and the collateral ratio based on governance decisions and algorithmic rules, ensuring the stablecoin remains as close to its peg as possible under various market conditions.

However, as with any innovative financial mechanism, there are inherent risks. The effectiveness of Frax's hybrid model is subject to the overall health of the crypto market, the robustness of its algorithmic rules, and the governance decisions made by FXS holders. The interplay between collateralization and algorithmic regulation in response to market dynamics is a critical area of focus for ensuring the long-term stability and success of Frax.

Let's look at one case when things did not go as expected for an algorithmic stablecoin.

IRON (UN)STABLECOIN

The Iron Finance debacle, an event that sent shockwaves through the decentralized finance (DeFi) sector, serves as a cautionary tale about the inherent risks and complexities of algorithmic stablecoins and the DeFi ecosystem. Iron Finance's innovative yet ultimately unstable two-token system, consisting of the IRON stablecoin and TITAN, its collateral token, was designed to maintain IRON's peg to the U.S. dollar. The system allowed users to mint IRON by supplying a mix of USDC (a stablecoin) and TITAN tokens. This mechanism aimed to buffer market volatility and ensured IRON's stability.[5]

However, the model's partial collateralization became its Achilles' heel. A dramatic increase in TITAN's price, followed by a massive sell-off by large holders (whales), triggered a destabilizing effect. The sell-off led to a panic, creating a

---

[5] https://www.coindesk.com/markets/2021/06/17/in-token-crash-postmortem-iron-finance-says-it-suffered-cryptos-first-large-scale-bank-run; https://finance.yahoo.com/news/iron-finance-details-defi-bank-052135662.html; https://cointelegraph.com/news/iron-finance-bank-run-stings-investors-a-lesson-for-all-stablecoins.

"negative feedback loop" (or "death spiral") where the increasing supply of TITAN pushed its price toward zero, undermining IRON's peg to the dollar and causing what Iron Finance described as the crypto world's "first large-scale bank run."

The precipitous drop in TITAN's value—from around $10 to virtually zero—resulted in nearly $2 billion in losses. This event highlighted the vulnerability of partially collateralized stablecoins to market sentiment and the rapidity with which confidence in these digital assets can evaporate. The incident underscores the challenges of designing stablecoins that can withstand the speculative pressures and rapid liquidity shifts characteristic of cryptocurrency markets.

In response to the crisis, notable investor Mark Cuban, who was directly affected by the collapse due to his investment in TITAN, called for regulatory clarity around stablecoins and their collateralization standards. This event has spurred discussions on the need for better regulatory frameworks to ensure the stability and reliability of stablecoins, a critical component of the burgeoning DeFi sector. Moreover, it has prompted a reevaluation of the role of algorithmic mechanisms and collateralization strategies in maintaining stablecoin pegs.

The Iron Finance debacle not only highlights the potential for rapid financial losses in the volatile DeFi sector but also serves as a reminder of the complex interplay between innovation, regulation, and market dynamics in the cryptocurrency ecosystem. This example also illustrates the importance of thorough due diligence, robust design, and regulatory oversight in the development and adoption of stablecoins and other DeFi products.

2.4 Fiat-Backed Stablecoins

Let's now move on to the stablecoins with the widest adoption.

Fiat-backed stablecoins are digital tokens issued on a blockchain that represent a claim on a reserve of fiat currency held in trust by the stablecoin issuer. Each stablecoin unit is backed one-to-one by the corresponding fiat currency, meaning for every stablecoin issued, there is an equivalent amount of fiat currency held in reserve. This mechanism ensures the stablecoin's value remains closely tied to the value of the underlying fiat currency, minimizing price volatility compared to other cryptocurrencies. Fiat-backed stablecoins are basically saying, "Trust me, I have real money in the bank." It's like the digital version of showing off to your parents to prove you're responsible.

To maintain user trust, issuers of these stablecoins commit to regular audits and transparency reports, verifying the real-world currency reserves that back each token. Built on blockchain technology, fiat-backed stablecoins boast remarkable interoperability, allowing for seamless interaction with other digital assets and platforms, facilitating a more integrated and fluid digital economy. Moreover, they have the potential to revolutionize cross-border payments by enabling swift and cost-effective global transactions, circumventing the often cumbersome and expensive traditional banking system. This confluence of features makes fiat-backed stablecoins a cornerstone in the evolving landscape of digital finance, bridging the gap between the traditional financial world and the new, blockchain-based digital economy.

Fiat-backed stablecoins operate on a straightforward premise: for each stablecoin issued, there is a corresponding fiat currency (like the U.S. dollar) held in reserve. This direct backing by traditional currency ensures that the stablecoin maintains a stable value, closely mirroring the fiat currency to which it is pegged.

The process begins when an investor exchanges a dollar for a stablecoin, such as USDC, issued by Circle. Circle, in turn, holds this dollar in reserve and may invest it in highly liquid, low-risk assets like cash or government securities. This investment strategy is crucial for maintaining the liquidity necessary to manage withdrawals and maintain the stablecoin's peg to the fiat currency. Unlike crypto-collateralized stablecoins, which rely on overcollateralization to absorb market volatility, fiat-backed stablecoins rely on the stability and predictability of the underlying fiat assets to mitigate risks of liquidation.

Fiat-backed stablecoins, while offering a bridge between traditional finance and the crypto world, come with inherent challenges that stem from their centralized nature, regulatory scrutiny, and reserve management practices.

Centralization and Counterparty Risk

The centralization aspect of fiat-backed stablecoins introduces counterparty risk. Unlike decentralized cryptocurrencies like Bitcoin, which operate without a central authority, fiat-backed stablecoins rely on a centralized entity to hold and manage the fiat reserves that back the stablecoin's value. This setup necessitates trust in the managing organization to maintain the peg to the fiat currency. However, this central point of control is also a central point of failure. If the managing entity faces financial issues, legal problems, or operational challenges, the stability and reliability of the stablecoin could be compromised.

Regulatory Challenges

Fiat-backed stablecoins are subject to the regulatory environments of the jurisdictions in which they operate. This exposure to regulatory oversight can impact their functionality, acceptance, and even their existence. Regulations can vary significantly from one jurisdiction to another, creating a complex landscape for stablecoin issuers to navigate. For instance, in some countries, regulatory bodies may impose stringent requirements for anti-money laundering (AML) and know your customer (KYC) compliance, while others may have fewer clear guidelines. The evolving nature of cryptocurrency regulations adds another layer of uncertainty, as future regulatory changes could impose new restrictions or requirements on stablecoin issuers.

Reserve Management and Risks

The biggest issue in my opinion is the management of fiat reserves is critical to the stability and trustworthiness of fiat-backed stablecoins. These reserves must be managed prudently to ensure that each stablecoin token is adequately backed by fiat currency, maintaining the peg to the fiat currency's value. Mismanagement of these reserves, through inadequate auditing practices or outright fraud, poses a significant risk. For example, if a stablecoin issuer claims to have one-to-one backing for their stablecoin but is found to have less fiat reserve than claimed (or riskier assets as reserves), the trust in the stablecoin would erode, potentially leading to a loss of peg and a decline in the stablecoin's value. This scenario underscores the importance of transparent and regular audits of the fiat reserves, a practice that not all issuers follow rigorously.

At its core, there is an issue with the incentives. Stablecoins issuers receive $1 and promise $1 back at any moment. How would they make money if not by investing the dollars that they receive? Issuers have an incentive to look for a high yield on their reserves to keep them profitable (i.e. "reaching for yield" phenomenon). When U.S. treasury interest rates are high, everything is fine, and risk can be minimized. In fact, USDC amounted to $151 million in interest income (23% of the company's net revenue) in the second quarter of 2023 as it deposited the customers' funds in Treasuries and pocketed the yields.[6] However, when U.S. treasury rates are low, there may not be enough return to keep the company afloat, and there exists an incentive to shift from Treasuries to riskier commercial paper backed by corporations. If those riskier assets are then devalued because these companies might default, a stablecoin that has invested in them can then lose its peg.

Tether's first reserve breakdown, revealed in May 2021, showed that its reserves were composed of a mix of cash, equivalents, other short-term deposits, secured loans, corporate bonds, and other investments. Notably, a significant portion of these reserves was in commercial paper, a type of corporate debt that cannot be easily liquidated, accounting for about 49% of USDT's collateral.[7] This breakdown was part of Tether's efforts to comply with a settlement agreement with the New York Attorney General (NYAG), who investigated Tether and its sister crypto exchange Bitfinex over the cover-up of approximately $800 million in losses. The settlement required Tether to pay an $18.5 million fine and agree to provide quarterly breakdowns of its reserves.[8] This move toward transparency was aimed at addressing skepticism around USDT's backing and maintaining its peg to the U.S. dollar.[9]

This example of Tether's reserve management highlights the potential risks associated with fiat-backed stablecoins, particularly in terms of reserve transparency and asset liquidity. The reliance on commercial paper and other investments that may not always be liquid or fully transparent raises questions about the ability of such stablecoins to maintain their peg in all market conditions. This situation underscores the importance of clear, independent auditing and transparency in reserve management to maintain user trust and stability in the value of fiat-backed stablecoins.

---

[6] https://s27.q4cdn.com/397450999/files/doc_financials/2023/q2/Shareholder-Letter-Q2-2023.pdf

[7] View Tether's breakdown here: https://assets.ctfassets.net/vyse88cgwfbl/4EtXPBkmEPDNbIHNajz9vQ/bb47 66acfe36f5af0c4e54a2694c8a31/tether-march-31-2021-reserves-breakdown.pdf

[8] https://www.cnbc.com/2021/02/23/tether-bitfinex-reach-settlement-with-new-york-attorney-general.html

[9] You can view Tether's latest reserve breakdown on their website here: https://tether.to/en/transparency/#reports

However, with the interest rates being high, Tether posted a $4.52 billion profit in the first quarter of 2024, which makes it one of the most profitable companies per employee.[10]

One thing that can be implemented to limit distrust in the system is a **proof of reserves**. Proof of reserves is a method used by cryptocurrency exchanges and financial institutions to provide transparency and prove that they hold sufficient assets to cover their customers' deposits. This is crucial in building trust and ensuring solvency. How does this work?

1. **Snapshot of Holdings:** The exchange or the entity issuing the stablecoin takes a snapshot of all its cryptocurrency holdings.
2. **Auditor Verification:** An independent auditor verifies these holdings, ensuring they match customer balances.
3. **Merkle Tree Construction:** The auditor uses a cryptographic structure called a Merkle tree to aggregate all balances. Each user's balance is a leaf node, which is hashed and combined up to the root.
4. **Publishing the Root Hash:** The entity publishes the Merkle root, allowing users to verify their individual balances are included without exposing others' data.
5. **Periodic Audits:** Regular updates and audits are conducted to maintain transparency and accuracy.

The key benefit is that it provides assurance to users that the issuer holds sufficient reserves to back the stablecoins in circulation, ensuring that each token is fully collateralized by real assets.

Finally, if the mechanism behind fiat-backed stablecoins gives you a déjà vu, it is because there are parallels in the traditional markets.

Are Stablecoins Just Like Money Market Funds?

Money market funds are a type of mutual fund designed to offer high liquidity with a very low risk level. They invest in short-term, high-quality debt securities, including treasury bills, commercial paper, and certificates of deposit, aiming to yield returns slightly higher than those of a regular savings account without sacrificing liquidity. Money market funds are widely used by individual and institutional investors as a safe haven to park surplus cash, providing a stable asset with easy access and minimal credit risk. They play a crucial role in the traditional financial system, offering a mechanism for managing short-term liquidity needs. Until 2016, money market funds offered a fixed net asset value (NAV), that is, unlike other types of mutual funds or investment vehicles where the NAV fluctuates based on the underlying assets' market values, a fixed NAV aims to maintain a stable share price, typically at $1.00 per share. This stability is sought to reassure investors that their principal is protected and that they can redeem their shares at any time without facing a loss of value due to market fluctuations. This resembles a stablecoin

---

[10] See https://cointelegraph.com/news/tether-record-4-52-billion-profit-q1-2024.

a lot! There is an entity collecting fiat, parking it in safe securities, and promising a fixed exchange pegged to $1.

Stablecoins	Money Market Funds
• **Cryptocurrencies** whose value is **pegged to external assets** • Operations **executed over blockchain** network • **Traded 24/7** on exchanges • Decentralized (ex. DAI) • Backed by **a variety of assets** depending on the type • Regulation is **still evolving**	• **Financial institution** • Operate within **standard market hours** and offer daily liquidity to investors • **NAV** calculated **at the end of each trading day** • Aim to maintain **a stable NAV** of $1 per share • Backed **by diversified portfolio** of high-quality, short-term debt instruments • Subject to **well-established regulatory frameworks**

While both stablecoins and money market funds aim to provide stability and liquidity, they diverge significantly in their operational frameworks, regulatory environments, and risk profiles. Money market funds, being a well-established component of the traditional financial system, operate within a regulatory framework that mandates liquidity, quality, and diversification requirements. They are subject to oversight by financial authorities, such as the Securities and Exchange Commission (SEC) in the United States, which enforces rules to protect investors and maintain market stability. The regulatory environment for money market funds is designed to mitigate risks related to market conditions, issuer creditworthiness, and liquidity pressures, although they are not immune to market turmoil, as evidenced by instances of money market funds "breaking the buck" during financial crises. In 2009, the Reserve Primary Fund broke the buck because its reserves were no longer enough to guarantee $1 to the investors who had given them $1. Why? They had invested in commercial paper from Lehman Brothers. Similarly to stablecoins, the issuer might have an incentive to reach for yield and increase the riskiness of the reserves adversely impacting its stability.

The crisis of the Reserve Primary fund led the Fed to provide a backstop to the whole industry to guarantee that the investors were not losing their principal. Furthermore, money market funds in the United States transitioned from maintaining a fixed net asset value (NAV) to a floating NAV for certain types of funds because of rules adopted by the SEC in July 2014. These reforms were implemented to address risks revealed during the 2008 financial crisis, particularly the risks associated with redemption pressures on money market funds. The new rules, which became fully effective in October 2016, require institutional prime money market funds and institutional municipal money market funds to operate with a floating NAV, meaning the NAV fluctuates with market changes. Retail and government money market funds were allowed to continue using a fixed $1.00 NAV.

Narrow Banking and Stablecoins

Narrow banking, or 100% reserve banking, contrasts significantly with the traditional fractional reserve banking system. Originating from the turmoil of the Great Depression, narrow banking proposes that banks should maintain the entirety of their deposits as reserves at the central bank or in short-term U.S. Treasury bills, diverging from the fractional reserve system where banks are only required to keep a small fraction of deposits as reserves. This approach aims to address the inherent instability within the banking system, characterized by the practice of borrowing short-term from depositors and lending long-term to borrowers, a maturity mismatch that historically has led to bank runs and systemic crises.

The fundamental principle behind narrow banking is to eliminate the risks associated with fractional reserve banking, such as excessive risk-taking by banks under the safety net of federal deposit insurance—leading to moral hazard—and the potential for systemic contagion from bank runs. By ensuring that all deposits are fully backed by reserves, narrow banking seeks to provide a safer and more stable banking environment, eliminating the need for complex regulations designed to mitigate risk-taking behaviors.

Operational aspects of narrow banking suggest a shift toward banks primarily offering checking and savings services, with the possibility of engaging in lending through capital raised from investors, rather than depositors. This model, which requires a gradual transition due to the significant role banks play in providing private sector debt, has garnered support from numerous economists for its potential to enhance stability and reduce moral hazard in the banking sector. Notable endorsements include Milton Friedman, who articulated a coherent case for narrow banking in his 1959 book, "A Program for Monetary Stability."

Recent developments, such as the Federal Reserve beginning to pay interest on reserves in 2008, indicate a movement toward a system resembling narrow banking, with banks currently holding a significant portion of their deposits in reserve or Treasury bills. However, the current arrangement, characterized by subsidized deposit insurance and the ability to loan out deposits at rates higher than those offered by Treasury bills, continues to incentivize the traditional model over a fully reserved system.

Technological advancements and the speed at which information spreads today, exemplified by the "Twitter-fueled" bank run on Silicon Valley Bank, highlight the increased fragility of banks and the need for more robust regulatory frameworks. Yet, the current regulatory landscape seems incapable of effectively mitigating the inherent risks within the banking system.

Both narrow banking and stablecoins aim to provide a safe and stable store of value. Narrow banks achieve this by avoiding risky investments, while stablecoins maintain their peg through collateralization. While narrow banking is a regulatory proposal for traditional financial systems, stablecoin issuers often seek to comply with existing financial regulations and may be subject to future regulatory standards specifically designed for cryptocurrencies. By restricting investments to low-risk assets, narrow banking reduces the likelihood of bank runs and financial crises. Similarly, stablecoins aim to mitigate the volatility traditionally associated with cryptocurrencies, reducing investment risk for holders. Both narrow banks and stablecoins can facilitate payments, providing a medium of exchange that is stable and reliable. Narrow banks, through their risk-averse asset holdings, ensure depositors' funds are always available for withdrawal, while stablecoins provide a digital means for efficient, cross-border transactions without the volatility of typical cryptocurrencies.

Probably the most striking similarity between stablecoins and narrow banking has been the difficult path toward regulatory approval. Regulators have shown reticence toward approving narrow banks for several reasons, as evidenced by the Federal Reserve's reaction to the proposal of The Narrow Bank (TNB). Narrow banks propose a new banking model focused on taking deposits, particularly from institutional clients, and placing them directly in accounts with the Federal Reserve to earn interest. This interest would then largely be passed on to the bank's clients. TNB aimed to offer more safety for large institutional clients, positioning itself as a competitor mainly to Treasury bills rather than traditional bank lending, providing depositors the ability to withdraw funds at any time with a specific, pre-stated rate.

The Federal Reserve issued an advance notice of proposed rulemaking concerning the narrow banking model, suggesting limitations on the interest that could be paid to these "narrowly focused depository institutions." The concerns outlined include the potential for narrow banks to "complicate the implementation of monetary policy," "disrupt financial intermediation," and negatively affect "financial stability." Sound familiar? Such a model presents systemic issues by potentially draining deposits from traditional banks that would otherwise use them to fund loans, thereby affecting the broader financial system's liquidity and loan-making capacity. The Fed's apprehension also extended to the prospect of paying interest to large-scale institutional investors through narrow banks, which could lead to substantial payments from the central bank to these entities, diverting resources from activities that support the real economy.

Putting all of this together, there exists a trade-off between capital efficiency, decentralization, and price stability (see **Figure 4**). For instance, Terra, with its algorithmic stabilization mechanism, prioritized capital efficiency and decentralization. The model allowed for a more flexible and responsive system to market demands without requiring centralized control or excessive collateral.

On the other hand, crypto-backed stablecoins, like DAI and FRAX, exemplify a model that emphasizes price stability and decentralization. DAI maintains its peg through a system of overcollateralization and smart contracts, ensuring stability even in volatile market conditions. While this method effectively maintains stability and operates in a decentralized manner, it is less capital efficient. Users must commit a significant amount of extra capital as security, which could otherwise be utilized for investment or other purposes.

Finally, fiat-backed stablecoins such as USDT, USDT, and BUSD provide stability and capital efficiency with a 1:1 ratio between reserves and issued coins, at the expense of decentralization. Unlike cryptocurrencies like Bitcoin or Ethereum, which operate on

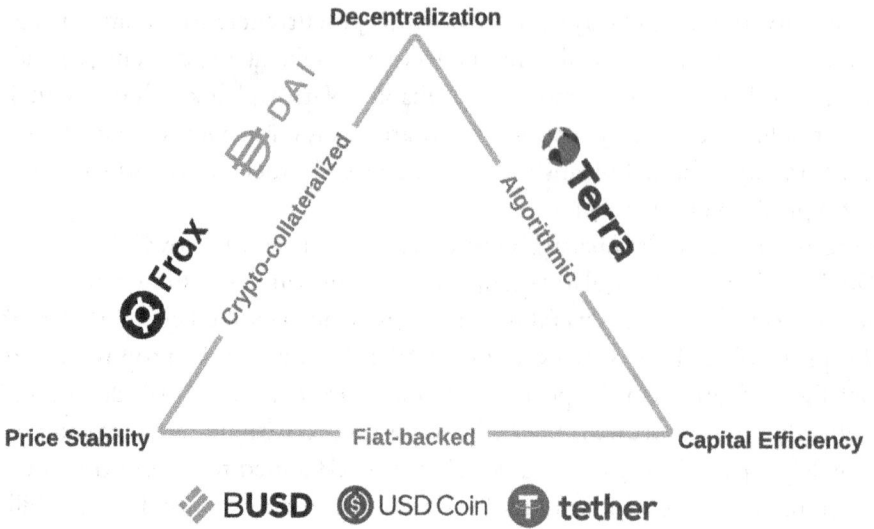

Figure 4   Stablecoin trade-offs

a decentralized network maintained by a global consortium of nodes, fiat-backed stablecoins are issued and managed by centralized entities. These entities, whether they are financial institutions or specific companies like Tether for USDT, Circle and Coinbase for USDC, or Binance for BUSD, hold the responsibility of managing the reserves that back the stablecoins. Users must place their trust in these entities to maintain the peg to the fiat currency, manage the reserves transparently, and ensure the ability to redeem stablecoins at any time.

This centralization raises concerns about oversight, regulatory compliance, and the potential for mismanagement of the reserves. It also introduces counterparty risk, where the stablecoin's value could be jeopardized by the issuer's financial instability or fraudulent activities. Despite these concerns, the utility and widespread adoption of fiat-backed stablecoins underscore their integral role in the crypto ecosystem, serving as a testament to their ability to provide stability, liquidity, and a bridge to the traditional financial system.

Case Study: "Private Money: The Case of Facebook"[11]

Facebook initially proposed in 2019 the creation of a new global stablecoin, that is not pegged to just the dollar, called Libra. Facebook basically thought, 'What could go wrong?' and decided to invent its own money. Because if there's anyone you trust with your financial stability, it's definitely the folks who thought poking was a good idea.

---

[11] For a more comprehensive treatment of Libra, and additional teaching resources, please see the Harvard Business School case titled "*Facebook's Libra: The Privatization of Money?*" by Marco Di Maggio, Ethan Rouen, George Serafeim, and Aldo Sesia (120021-PDF-ENG).

The stablecoin would be backed by a reserve of assets in different currencies designed to give it intrinsic value. The idea was that it would be governed by a consortium of companies under the Libra Association. As of summer 2019, the association had 27 founding members who were each expected to invest $10m in Libra to join (**Figure 5**). The goal was to have 100 founding members by the target launch of 2020.

The key intent was to create a global digital currency to facilitate low-cost, fast cross-border transactions and financial inclusion. The design would allow users to exchange fiat currency for Libra for use in online transactions for a negligible fee, and it would not require users to have a bank account or a line of credit to own and transact. One of the most important selling points was the possibility to improve financial inclusion, that is, reaching the 2 billion individuals with no access to a bank account but in possess of a smartphone.

To examine the key issues raised by Libra, consider these questions:

1. Why is Facebook developing Libra?
2. Does Libra complement Facebook's current business? What problems does it solve?
3. As a consumer would you use Libra? What concerns do you have?
4. Why is Facebook now looking to partner with other companies via the Libra association? Does the existence and structure of the Libra Association assuage your concerns?

Figure 5   Founding members of the Libra Association

a. Why would other companies want to join this oversight committee?

b. Put yourself in the seat of a company CEO (Amazon, JPMorgan, IBM, or American Express), would you join the Libra Association?

One of the key reasons behind this initiative is the possibility for Facebook to capture data about its users. That would allow Facebook to close the marketing loop by linking the ads viewed on the platform with the consumers' spending patterns when using Libra as a medium of exchange, such as what they buy, when, and from which brand.

In addition to collecting invaluable data about its users, Libra will further Facebook's attempts for a truly global reach. In many countries, Facebook was facing tougher competition from newer social media companies such as Tik Tok and was losing their edge with the younger generations. Facebook could better compete with other tech giants by leveraging its huge user base and entering the ecommerce space early.

On the technical side, Libra would be fully backed by a reserve of real assets, mainly based on a basket of bank deposits and short-term government securities held in the Libra Reserve for every Libra that was created to build trust in its intrinsic value. One important aspect of these reserves is that the interest on the assets in the reserve would be used to "cover the costs of the system, ensure low transaction fees, pay dividends to investors . . . and support further growth and adoption," which means the yield would be part of the revenue stream of the Libra association and not channeled back to the Libra token holders.

The governance of this project was delegated to the Libra Association Council, comprised of one representative per validator node operating the Libra Blockchain. All major policy and technical decisions were brought to the council and required the consent of two-thirds of council member's votes to pass. The association had 27 founding members, depicted in **Figure 3**, and were expected to invest $10 million each, and serve as validator nodes on the blockchain. Some were already partners with Facebook, so they simply continued to leverage their relationship. Members were the only ones allowed to add or remove Libra from circulation. The objective was to have about 100 validator nodes at launch and then increase this number as more members joined and Libra scaled. Among the initial members one can see crypto companies like Coinbase and Anchorage, as well as traditional firms like Visa and Mastercard, who might join to avoid been left behind.

One interesting question is: *Who isn't in the Association?* First, banks and any traditional financial institutions. The main reason being that a transnational currency like Libra presents unique challenges in terms of KYC and AML that might prevent banks from joining such an association to avoid reputational risk. Other tech giants such as Google, Amazon, and Apple are also missing. These are firms that are potential competitors of Libra, with their own strong user base. In fact, both Amazon and Apple are already involved in the payment business.

Libra is an interesting case to discuss to highlight the regulatory concerns that might arise with creating private money, a new currency fully governed by a private entity. First, regulators are concerned about privacy risks related to Facebook handling sensitive data, especially after the Cambridge Analytics scandal.[12] Allowing Facebook to collect and store purchasing data about millions of consumers would exponentially increase the risk of mishandling such sensitive information.

The second concern is related to financial stability. For-profit companies will control the Libra Association. These manage the reserves backing the stablecoin and might potentially be incentivized to invest in riskier securities to maximize their yields (like the Reserve Primary Fund), which would expose consumers to the risk of depegging. If adoption is successful, Libra might become too big to fail and induce regulators to step in and rescue the company with taxpayers' money. In addition, by buying and holding government debt issued by different countries, Libra could have significant macroeconomic impacts. Imagine having Libra decide that, for some reason, they will only purchase EU and Chinese government debts rather than U.S. debts. The decision has the potential to significantly increase the interest rates that the Fed must promise investors to hold its debt. Thus, the choice of government debt to hold in reserves, once Libra is used at scale, could have serious macroeconomic consequences.

Finally, another major concern is the influence private money, such as Libra, can have on central banks' ability to implement monetary policies. Private money projects, especially when backed by companies with large user bases, have the potential to become systemic financial infrastructures very quickly. Facebook, with its billions of users worldwide, could potentially introduce a new currency to a vast audience, enabling widespread adoption in a short period. This level of penetration and the possibility of Libra being used for daily transactions raised concerns about its ability to function as a parallel currency to national fiat currencies.

National currencies are tools through which central banks manage the economy by setting interest rates, controlling money supply, and implementing financial policy to influence inflation and employment levels. If a significant portion of economic activity in a country shifts to a privately issued currency like Libra, it could undermine the effectiveness of these tools. The need for a physical currency will significantly diminish and consumers might potentially begin to look at how the dollar moves in relation to Libra, rather than the other way around. Or, if

---

[12] The Cambridge Analytica scandal involved the misuse of Facebook data that was disclosed in 2018 by Christopher Wylie, a former Cambridge Analytica employee, in interviews with *The Guardian* and *The New York Times*. Facebook apologized for its role in the data harvesting, and CEO Mark Zuckerberg testified before Congress. In July 2019, Facebook was fined $5 billion by the Federal Trade Commission for privacy violations, and in October 2019, agreed to pay a £500,000 fine to the UK Information Commissioner's Office for exposing user data to a "serious risk of harm." Cambridge Analytica filed for Chapter 7 bankruptcy in May 2018.

people start saving in Libra instead of the local currency, and if businesses price goods and services in Libra, the central bank may find it challenging to manage economic cycles effectively.

Moreover, the stability of financial systems could be at risk. Traditional banking systems are heavily regulated to ensure stability, with mechanisms like deposit insurance and lender of last resort facilities. A global stablecoin, however, operates outside these traditional systems, and without the same level of oversight and control, it could introduce systemic risks, particularly in scenarios of large-scale redemptions or shifts in trust, e.g. a bank run on Libra.

Libra's proposal to back its currency with a basket of currencies and government securities also raises concerns about its impact on the global financial system. Such a reserve management strategy could influence interest rates and capital flows, especially in smaller economies. One can also observe a *"librarization"* of these economies, where the local currency is effectively substituted in everyday transactions by Libra, i.e. in a similar way in which developing countries observe dollarization. In extreme cases, if a significant number of people in a country prefer to use Libra over the national currency, it could impact the central banks' control over its currency and lead to destabilization.

Furthermore, the governance model of the Libra Association, which consisted of various companies and organizations, brought up issues of accountability and regulation. The decentralized nature of blockchain technology, combined with a governance model not tied to any specific national regulatory framework, created a regulatory gray area. Regulators were concerned about consumer protection, anti-money laundering (AML) standards, and the prevention of financing terrorism.

In summary, these concerns have led regulators around the world to scrutinize the project closely, resulting in delays and revisions to the original proposal.

On October 14, 2019, Booking.com revealed it was leaving the Libra Association days after similar announcements from eBay, Mastercard, Mercado Pago, PayPal, Stripe, and Visa.[13] Zuckerberg vowed that Libra would not proceed without full U.S. regulatory approval.

In April 2020, the whitepaper was updated to include offering stablecoins tied to individual currencies, making Libra a combination of different single-currency tokens rather than a separate cryptocurrency backed by a variety of global assets, which would appease the concern of creating a global currency. The new iteration also pledged that the Swiss Financial Market Supervisory Authority (FINMA)

---

[13] Two senators urged Visa, Mastercard, and Stripe to reconsider their involvement with Libra, saying it could have significant regulatory consequences for any payment processor involved. "If you take this on," the letters read, "you can expect a high level of scrutiny from regulators not only on Libra-related activities, but on all payment activities." (https://www.brown.senate.gov/newsroom/press/release/brown-schatz-warn-payments-providers-of-risks-with-libra-association)

would be responsible for regulatory oversight and promised to add heightened internal security measures and screen all digital wallets that joined the platform. By late 2020, Libra Association announced its intention to release its first offering, a single coin pegged to the USD, within the first few months of 2021. In December 2020, Libra changed its name to Diem to distance itself from the controversies that had dogged the project since inception.

Despite these efforts, Diem faced continued regulatory hurdles. In January 2022, the project announced the sale of its technological assets to Silvergate Capital Corporation, effectively ending the initiative to launch the Diem stablecoin. This sale marked the conclusion of Facebook's ambitious project to create a global digital currency. The project's dissolution underscores the complex regulatory and operational challenges faced by large-scale digital currency initiatives.

To conclude, *why did Libra fail?* Several reasons:

- Potential to circumvent national monetary policy: if widely adopted, Libra could diminish the effectiveness of national monetary authorities in controlling money supply, interest rates, and inflation within their jurisdictions.
- Currency substitution: there was concern that citizens might prefer using Libra over their national currencies in countries with unstable currencies or weak monetary policies.
- Impact on exchange rates and capital flows: widespread adoption could potentially affect exchange rates and capital flows, especially in smaller or emerging market economies.
- Monetary transmission mechanism: transmission mechanisms of monetary policy could be altered if Libra significantly impacted the demand for base money and other financial assets.
- Bank disintermediation: individuals and businesses could bypass traditional banks for financial services if Libra became a significant part of the financial system.
- Data privacy and financial surveillance: with Facebook's involvement, there were concerns about data privacy and financial surveillance.
- Lack of accountability and regulation: governance by a consortium of private entities raised concerns about accountability and regulation; Libra's initial structure lacked clear regulatory oversight.
- Competing with sovereign currencies: Libra was essentially creating a private synthetic currency that could compete with sovereign currencies and could potentially destabilize national currencies.

Does it mean that we should not expect any other effort in the creation of a similar stablecoin by other companies? Not really, in fact, Paypal recently announced a new stablecoin . . .

Example: Paypal Foray into the Stablecoin Space

PayPal decided to jump into the stablecoin pool with PayPal USD. It's like your uncle finally getting a smartphone—welcome to the 21st century, PayPal.

This innovative step by PayPal aims to bridge the gap between traditional financial systems and the digital financial ecosystem. This is great news for the integration of blockchain technology into mainstream financial services. PayPal is accepted almost everywhere and has a strong user base both in the retail and merchant space.

PYUSD is meticulously designed to provide a stable digital asset to PayPal's extensive user base, catering to a variety of use cases that extend from person-to-person payments to funding purchases on the platform. Furthermore, it facilitates the seamless conversion between PayPal's supported cryptocurrencies and PYUSD, thus enhancing the fluidity and flexibility of digital transactions for its users.

The foundation of PYUSD's stability lies in its backing by a reserve of USD deposits, short-term U.S. treasuries, and cash equivalents. This ensures that PYUSD is redeemable at a 1:1 rate with the U.S. dollar, providing a reliable and trustworthy digital currency option for users. Issued by Paxos Trust Company, PYUSD leverages PayPal's established infrastructure to foster its adoption in the Web3 space, thus promoting its use across a myriad of digital financial applications.

The introduction of PYUSD is poised to create waves in the stablecoin market, challenging the dominance of established players like USDT and USDC. This increased competition is anticipated to spur innovation, enhance service quality, and lead to a broader acceptance and utilization of stablecoins across various platforms and use cases. By diversifying the stablecoin options available to users, PayPal is not only expanding the choices for its customers but also contributing to the growth and maturity of the digital currency ecosystem.

PayPal's strategic foray into the stablecoin space with PYUSD reflects its commitment to remain at the forefront of the digital financial landscape. It recognizes the potential of stablecoins to facilitate a smoother transition for users from traditional finance to the digital realm, thereby ensuring PayPal's relevance and competitiveness in an increasingly digitalized world. Through PYUSD, PayPal is offering a stable digital asset and paving the way for a future where digital and traditional financial systems coalesce seamlessly, fostering a more inclusive and accessible global financial infrastructure.

3. Concluding remarks

Concluding this chapter on stablecoins, we've journeyed through the evolution of cryptocurrencies, pinpointing the volatility that often hinders their widespread adoption for everyday transactions. This volatility issue, exemplified by the story of Laszlo Hanyecz's 10,000 Bitcoin pizza purchase, has led to the emergence of stablecoins, a digital currency designed to offer stability in a space known for its unpredictability.

Stablecoins, by pegging their value to more stable assets like fiat currencies or commodities, present a solution for conducting transactions without the fear of significant value changes post-transaction. We observed the origins and motivations behind the creation of Tether (USDT), the first widely recognized stablecoin, aimed at bridging the gap between fiat and cryptocurrencies. Following Tether's success, various forms of stablecoins were introduced, demonstrating the diversity and adaptability of these digital currencies to meet the demands of a fluctuating market.

We delved into the mechanics and implications of different types of stablecoins, from gold-backed to fiat-collateralized and algorithmic stablecoins, each with unique mechanisms for maintaining stability. This exploration highlighted the critical role stablecoins play in the digital currency ecosystem, facilitating day-to-day transactions and serving as a cornerstone in the burgeoning field of decentralized finance (DeFi).

Furthermore, the chapter addressed the challenges and risks associated with stablecoins, including regulatory hurdles, the management of reserves, and the potential for systemic impacts due to feedback loops. Through case studies such as Frax, Iron, and the proposed Libra (later Diem) by Facebook, we've seen the complexities and potential pitfalls of implementing a stable digital currency on a global scale.

In conclusion, stablecoins represent a pivotal innovation in the quest for a more stable and usable digital currency. They stand at the intersection of traditional finance and the digital future, offering a glimpse into a world where digital and fiat currencies coexist. As the digital currency space continues to evolve, stablecoins will undoubtedly play a crucial role in shaping the future of finance, commerce, and how we perceive money in an increasingly digitalized world.

Code Example: Generating DAI with Depositing Collateral

Language: Solidity

Level: Intermediate

We can go through a simplified pseudo-contract in Solidity interacting with the MakerDAO system to generate DAI by depositing collateral (like ETH) into a Maker Vault.

```
// Specify the version of Solidity
pragma solidity ^0.8.0;
// Interface for the MakerDAO Vault (CDP) Manager

interface IVaultManager {
    function open(bytes32 _collateralType, address _owner) external
returns (uint256 vaultId);
    function deposit(uint256 _vaultId, uint256 _amount) external;
    function generateDai(uint256 _vaultId, uint256 _daiAmount) external;
    // Add other necessary functions here
}
// Interface for the ERC20 token (for DAI and collateral if it's an
ERC20 token)
```

```solidity
interface IERC20 {
    function approve(address _spender, uint256 _value) external
returns (bool);
    function transfer(address _to, uint256 _value) external
returns (bool);
    function transferFrom(address from, address to, uint256 value)
external returns (bool);
    // Add other necessary ERC20 functions here
}
contract GenerateDai {
    IVaultManager public vaultManager;
    IERC20 public daiToken;
    IERC20 public collateralToken; // If the collateral is an ERC20 token

    address public owner;

    constructor(address _vaultManager, address _daiToken, address
_collateralToken) {
        vaultManager = IVaultManager(_vaultManager);
        daiToken = IERC20(_daiToken);
        collateralToken = IERC20(_collateralToken);
        owner = msg.sender;
    }

    // Function to deposit collateral and generate DAI
    function depositAndGenerateDai(bytes32 _collateralType, uint256
_collateralAmount, uint256 _daiAmount) external {
        require(msg.sender == owner, "Only the owner can perform this
action");

        // Transfer collateral to this contract
        require(collateralToken.transferFrom(msg.sender, address(this),
_collateralAmount), "Transfer failed");

        // Approve the Vault Manager to use the collateral
        require(collateralToken.approve(address(vaultManager),
_collateralAmount), "Approve failed");

        // Open a new vault (CDP)
        uint256 vaultId = vaultManager.open(_collateralType, address(this));

        // Deposit collateral into the vault
        vaultManager.deposit(vaultId, _collateralAmount);

        // Generate DAI against the collateral
        vaultManager.generateDai(vaultId, _daiAmount);

        // Transfer the generated DAI to the owner
        require(daiToken.transfer(owner, _daiAmount), "DAI
transfer failed");
    }
    // Add other functions as necessary, such as for withdrawing
collateral, paying back DAI, etc.
}
```

The code demonstrates the basic process of depositing collateral into a MakerDAO Vault and generating DAI against it. It would be hard to test and deploy this contract as we do not have another vault manager contract defined on the blockchain, and DAI's own vault manager contract has a slightly different structure.

Code Example: Integrating DAI into Your Smart Contracts

Language: Solidity

Level: Beginner

In reality, MakerDAO utilizes a complex system of smart contracts on the Ethereum blockchain, and the process of generating DAI against ETH collateral is more nuanced than the previous example.

In this example, we will go through an implementable contract, which can be utilized in a situation where one wants to integrate the token itself into their own smart contracts and decentralized products.

DAI is an ERC-20 token, which means it adheres to a common standard for Ethereum tokens, ensuring compatibility with a wide range of wallets, exchanges, and other smart contracts, and has its own address on the blockchain. Developers can interact with this address within their own smart contracts to integrate DAI as a payment method or store of value. In decentralized applications, users actually prefer stablecoins as a medium of exchange because it ensures that the value of their transactions does not fluctuate wildly over short periods.

This will be a faucet smart contract. "Faucet" networks are test networks of blockchain where users can deploy and test their smart contracts with test coins. A DAI coin has an address on the Sepolia test network, which we will be using.

To actually deploy the contract on your own, you will need a Metamask wallet, Sepolia ETH, and Sepolia Dai (which you can get from Aave and will be explained at the end of the section).

```
// SPDX-License-Identifier: MIT
pragma solidity ^0.8.0;

// Adding only the ERC-20 functions we need
interface DaiToken {
    function transfer(address dst, uint wad) external returns (bool);
    function balanceOf(address guy) external view returns (uint);
}
contract owned {
    DaiToken public daitoken;
    address public owner;

    constructor() {
        owner = msg.sender;
```

```
        daitoken = DaiToken(0x68194a729C2450ad26072b3D33ADaCbcef39D574);
    }

    modifier onlyOwner {
        require(msg.sender == owner, "Only the contract owner can call
this function");
        _;
    }
}
contract Pausable is owned {
    bool public paused = false;

    modifier whenNotPaused() {
        require(!paused, "Contract is paused");
        _;
    }

    function pause() public onlyOwner {
        paused = true;
    }

    function unpause() public onlyOwner {
        paused = false;
    }
}

contract DaiFaucet is Pausable {

    event Withdrawal(address indexed to, uint amount);
    event Deposit(address indexed from, uint amount);

    // Give out Dai to anyone who asks
    function withdraw(uint withdraw_amount) public {
        // Limit withdrawal amount
        require(withdraw_amount <= 0.1 ether, "Withdrawal amount
exceeds limit");
        require(daitoken.balanceOf(address(this)) >= withdraw_amount,
"Insufficient balance in faucet for withdrawal request");
        // Send the amount to the address that requested it
        daitoken.transfer(msg.sender, withdraw_amount);
        emit Withdrawal(msg.sender, withdraw_amount);
    }

    // Accept any incoming amount
    receive() external payable {
        emit Deposit(msg.sender, msg.value);
    }
}
```

1. **Setting the Solidity Version:** We start by declaring the version of Solidity used for compiling the contract. This ensures compatibility and security with the features we'll use.

2. **Defining the DaiToken Interface:** To interact with the Dai token contract, we define an interface that includes only the necessary functions from the ERC-20 standard. This interface will be used to interact with the Dai token by calling its transfer and balanceOf functions, enabling our contract to send Dai and check balances.

3. **Implementing the "owned" contract:** We add the "owned" contract. The "owned" contract establishes the creator as the controller, setting up the DaiToken and owner variables. It uses the onlyOwner modifier to restrict function access. Upon deployment, it assigns the contract's owner and links to the Dai token on Sepolia using its address (0x68194a729C2450ad26072b3D33ADaC bcef39D574). This setup ensures that Dai-related functions affect the correct token contract.

4. **The "Pausable" contract, inheriting "owned," adds a kill switch:** This enables the owner to pause and unpause the contract, which can prevent actions when necessary, such as during maintenance or after discovering a vulnerability.

5. **Finally, The DaiFaucet contract, built on "Pausable" and "owned," manages Dai distribution and ownership control:** It logs transactions with Withdrawal and Deposit events. The withdraw function allows users to request up to 0.1 Dai, provided the contract has sufficient funds. It checks these conditions before transferring Dai using the defined DaiToken interface. Additionally, an unnamed function logs any Dai sent to the contract as deposits. This structure ensures controlled, transparent Dai transactions within the test network.

To try the script, you will first need to get a Metamask wallet. On your Metamask wallet you will need to change your network to Sepolia through test networks and use your account address to get some Sepolia ETH, which can be done in various websites. One of them as of 2024 is via Chainlink (https://faucets.chain.link/sepolia). Then Aave allows you to get Sepolia DAIs from https://staging.aave.com/faucet.

Then, you can compile and deploy the contract on Remix IDE. After successful deployment, you can interact with the contract through Etherscan.

End-of-Chapter Questions

Multiple-Choice Questions

1. **What was the primary motivation behind the creation of Tether (USDT) in 2014?**
   (A) To create a cryptocurrency with unlimited supply.
   (B) To bridge the gap between fiat currencies and cryptocurrencies by providing a stable digital currency pegged to the U.S. dollar.
   (C) To offer a decentralized governance model.
   (D) To facilitate high-volatility trading on crypto exchanges.

2. **Which type of stablecoin uses a sophisticated system of smart contracts to maintain its peg to the U.S. dollar without direct backing by fiat currency reserves?**
   (A) Fiat-collateralized stablecoins.
   (B) Crypto-collateralized stablecoins.
   (C) Gold-backed stablecoins.
   (D) Algorithmic stablecoins.

3. **What is the primary purpose of overcollateralization in crypto-collateralized stablecoins like DAI?**
   (A) To ensure liquidity in the crypto market.
   (B) To provide a buffer against the price volatility of the collateral asset.
   (C) To enable high-frequency trading.
   (D) To reduce the transparency of the blockchain.

4. **How does the MakerDAO protocol protect the stability of DAI against extreme volatility in the collateral asset?**
   (A) By requiring a membership fee for all DAI holders.
   (B) Through a liquidation mechanism that sells collateral to cover outstanding DAI debt.
   (C) By pegging DAI directly to gold reserves.
   (D) Using a fixed supply of DAI to control its market price.

5. **What was a major reason for the regulatory scrutiny faced by the Libra (now Diem) project initiated by Facebook?**
   (A) The potential to circumvent national monetary policies.
   (B) The lack of a blockchain technology foundation.
   (C) An oversupply of Libra tokens in the market.
   (D) The exclusive use of gold as a reserve asset.

6. **Which of the following was NOT a founding member of the Libra Association?**
   (A) Coinbase.
   (B) Mastercard.
   (C) Google.
   (D) Visa.

7. **What mechanism do algorithmic stablecoins use to maintain their peg?**
   (A) Direct backing by a reserve of cryptocurrencies.
   (B) Algorithmically adjusting the supply based on changes in demand.
   (C) Physical commodities like gold.
   (D) A fixed exchange rate established by government fiat.

8. **What does the MakerDAO system use to generate DAI?**
   (A) A fixed collateral-to-debt ratio of 1:1.
   (B) A variable interest rate on loans.
   (C) Collateral assets deposited in a Maker Vault.
   (D) A central bank's monetary policy.

9. **What was a significant factor in the "Black Thursday" event affecting the MakerDAO system?**
   (A) An increase in the value of Ethereum.
   (B) A decrease in the demand for DAI.
   (C) A massive downturn in the cryptocurrency market.
   (D) The introduction of a new stablecoin by a competitor.

10. **What is the primary goal of fiat-backed stablecoins like USDC and PYUSD?**
   (A) To achieve the highest returns on investment.
   (B) To offer a low-risk, low-return investment that prioritizes liquidity and stability.
   (C) To facilitate anonymous transactions.
   (D) To provide a platform for decentralized finance (DeFi) applications.

Open Questions / Numerical Exercises

1. Explain the role of overcollateralization in DAI's stability mechanism and calculate the collateralization ratio if an investor deposits $200 worth of Ethereum to generate $100 worth of DAI.

2. Discuss the implications of algorithmic stablecoins' supply adjustment mechanisms on market stability, using Frax as an example. Include how market demand influenced Frax's supply and price.

3. Given the volatility of cryptocurrency markets, evaluate the potential risks and benefits of investing in gold-backed stablecoins versus fiat-collateralized stablecoins. Consider factors such as market capitalization, liquidity, and the underlying assets.

Coding Exercises

Exercise 1: Implement a Basic Stablecoin Smart Contract

Objective: Write a simple Solidity smart contract for a fiat-collateralized stablecoin.

Requirements:
- Implement a basic ERC-20 token with functions for minting and burning tokens.
- Ensure that only the contract owner can mint new tokens, simulating the fiat collateral deposit.
- Implement a mechanism for users to "redeem" tokens, where tokens can be burned in exchange for a placeholder asset (simulated within the contract).

Exercise 2: Analyzing Stablecoin Price Stability

Objective: Write a Python script to analyze the price stability of a given stablecoin over the last year.

Requirements:
- Use the CoinGecko API to fetch historical price data for a chosen stablecoin (e.g., USDC, DAI).
- Calculate the price variance and standard deviation over the last year.
- Plot the price of the stablecoin over time and highlight any significant deviations from its peg.

Exercise 3: Simulate a Stablecoin Collateralization Mechanism

Objective: Create a simulation of a crypto-collateralized stablecoin mechanism in Python.

Requirements:
- Simulate a wallet holding ETH as collateral and issuing a stablecoin against it.
- Implement functions to handle collateralization ratio calculations, minting, and liquidation events based on simulated market price changes of ETH.
- Test the system by simulating various market conditions (e.g. a sudden drop in ETH price) and ensure the stability of the issued stablecoin.

Exercise 4: Smart Contract for Algorithmic Stablecoin

Objective: Develop a basic smart contract for an algorithmic stablecoin using Solidity.

Requirements:
- The contract should include mechanisms for expanding and contracting supply based on the token's price deviation from its peg.
- Implement a function that adjusts the supply algorithmically, mimicking a response to price changes.

- Include comments explaining how the supply adjustment aims to return the stablecoin to its target peg.

Exercise 5: Stablecoin Transaction Analysis

Objective: Write a Python script to analyze transactions involving a specific stablecoin on the Ethereum blockchain.

Requirements:
- Use the Etherscan API to fetch transaction data for a chosen stablecoin (e.g. USDT, USDC).
- Analyze the data to find the total transaction volume, average transaction size, and the number of unique wallets interacting with the stablecoin over a specified period.
- Visualize the transaction activity over time to identify any trends or patterns.

Chapter 5

The CBDC Saga

Rewriting the Rules of Money

Preface

Welcome to the grand ballroom of modern finance, where Central Bank Digital Currencies (CBDCs) are the latest guests to sashay through the door, turning heads with the promise of revolutionizing money itself. Picture this: the world's central banks, those venerable institutions often depicted in cartoons as stuffy old men with monocles, deciding to crash the crypto party. But instead of showing up in hoodies and flip-flops, they're decked out in digital tuxedos, bringing a level of respectability and, let's be honest, a whiff of government to the blockchain bash.

CBDCs are like the central banks' RSVP to the wild, wild west of cryptocurrencies. They've watched Bitcoin and its gang of digital outlaws from afar, eyebrows raised, murmuring, "Interesting, but what if we did it . . . with regulation?" And thus, the concept of CBDCs was born: digital currency, but with the kind of stability only a government can promise (or at least, strongly imply).

The developments around the world read like a finance thriller novel, with each country casting itself as the protagonist in its own saga of digital currency exploration. Some, like the Bahamas with its Sand Dollar, have leaped off the starting blocks, while others are still lacing up their sneakers, peering over at China's digital yuan with a mix of admiration and envy. It's a global race where everyone's trying to figure out not just how to run but where the finish line even is.

Central Bankers crashing the crypto party

Implementation challenges? Oh, there are a few. It's like deciding to build a digital Frankenstein's monster but realizing halfway through that you need it to do more than just scare villagers—it should also be able to do your taxes and make a mean espresso. These challenges range from the technical (how do you build a digital currency that a bored teenager can't hack?) to the philosophical (how do you ensure privacy in a world where every transaction is potentially visible to Big Brother?).

And then there are the design choices, where central banks must navigate the treacherous waters between innovation and stability. Do you go for a retail CBDC that lets citizens hold accounts directly with the central bank, effectively turning it into the world's most boring social media platform? Or do you opt for a wholesale version, which is less about jazzing up the public's wallet and more about making the financial system's plumbing so efficient that transactions happen at the speed of thought?

As we embark on this journey through the world of CBDCs, prepare for a tale about how the most traditional part of the financial system is dipping its toes into the future, sometimes reluctantly, sometimes eagerly, but always with an eye on rewriting the rules of money itself. Fasten your seatbelts—it's going to be a fascinating ride, with enough twists and turns to keep even the most jaded finance aficionados on the edge of their seat.

1. Introduction

The announcement of the Libra (later known as Diem) project by Facebook in June 2019 marked a pivotal moment in the digital currency landscape. It underscored the growing interest and potential of blockchain technology in transforming the financial sector and also acted as a catalyst, igniting a global conversation on the development of CBDCs.

As discussed in the previous chapter, Libra's ambitious goal was to create a global digital currency that would empower billions of people by facilitating low-cost, fast cross-border transactions. It aimed to offer financial inclusion to the unbanked and underbanked populations worldwide. However, the project quickly drew scrutiny from regulators and policymakers around the globe due to concerns over privacy, money laundering, and financial stability. The widespread reaction highlighted the challenges of introducing a digital currency with the potential to rival national currencies and to operate beyond traditional regulatory frameworks.

One of the most significant responses came from China, which accelerated its own digital currency project, the Digital Currency Electronic Payment (DCEP), also known as the *digital yuan*. China's move was partly driven by the desire to maintain control over its financial system, dominated by private companies such as Alipay and Tencent, and to compete with the global influence of the U.S. dollar. The digital yuan project, which had been in development for years, suddenly received renewed focus and urgency.

The ripple effect of Libra's announcement and China's aggressive push toward CBDCs prompted other central banks to explore and advance their digital currency projects. Countries like Sweden with its e-krona pilot, the Bahamas with the launch of the Sand Dollar, and the European Central Bank's exploration of a digital euro, embarked on their CBDC journeys. These initiatives aim to harness the benefits of digital currencies, such as enhanced efficiency in payments, increased financial inclusion, and the potential to streamline monetary policy implementation.

Moreover, the discussion around CBDCs and the Libra project has emphasized the need for a collaborative approach to regulation and development. The potential global impact of alternative forms of money necessitates international cooperation to address issues of interoperability, standards, and cross-border transactions. This collaborative effort is crucial to ensure that the benefits of digital currencies are realized while minimizing risks to financial stability and integrity.

As central banks around the world continue to explore the potential of CBDCs (see **Figure 1** for details about the status of CBDCs development around the world), the initial spark provided by Libra's announcement has evolved into a global movement toward the future of money. This transition to digital currencies represents a significant shift in the financial landscape, offering opportunities for innovation and improvement but also posing challenges that require careful consideration and global cooperation. The journey of CBDCs underscores the transformative potential of digital currencies and blockchain technology in reshaping the world's financial systems.

Definition

Central Bank Digital Currencies represent a groundbreaking evolution in the history of money and financial systems. As digital forms of fiat money, CBDCs are issued and strictly regulated by sovereign central banks, and are designed to coexist with or potentially replace traditional physical forms of currency. Unlike decentralized cryptocurrencies that operate without central authority, CBDCs are centralized, embodying the trust and authority of the issuing nation's central bank. CBDCs are what happens when central banks have a mid-life crisis and decide they're going digital, ensuring that even our money gets a taste of the existential dread that comes with the internet age.

Central Bank Digital Currencies Status

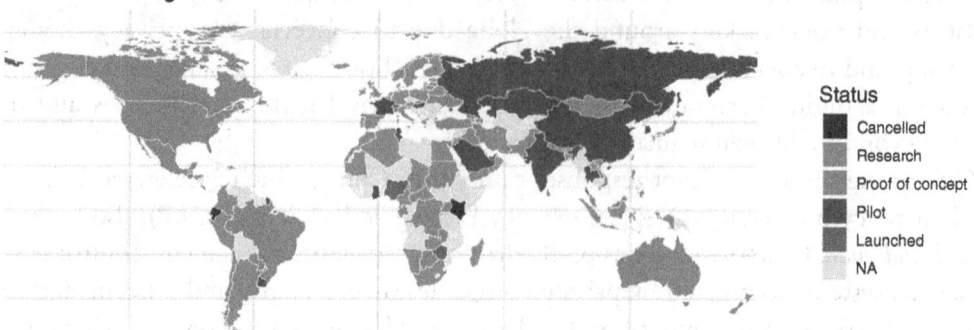

Figure 1 Status of CBDC development around the world. Adapted from DeFiLlama, 2024

The objectives behind the creation of CBDCs are multifaceted and ambitious. At the core, central banks aim to enhance payment efficiencies by reducing the cost and time involved in transactions, both domestically and across borders. This is particularly relevant in our increasingly globalized economy, where the speed and efficiency of payments can significantly impact economic growth and stability. The reason is that having a government issuing a digital currency would also naturally lead to the adoption of smart contracts with all the benefits in terms of efficiency that this would bring.

Furthermore, CBDCs are seen to ensure financial inclusion by providing accessible digital payment options to populations traditionally underserved by conventional banking systems. By offering a digital currency that does not require a bank account for transactions, central banks hope to integrate a larger segment of their population into the formal economy, promoting more equitable economic participation without requiring banks to open brick-and-mortar locations around the country. Lastly, securing financial stability is a paramount objective. In the face of rapidly evolving digital currencies and fintech innovations, central banks view CBDCs as tools to retain control over monetary policy, combat the rise of unregulated cryptocurrencies, and safeguard against systemic risks that could arise from the fragmentation of the monetary system.

To fully appreciate the significance of CBDCs, let's briefly explore the historical context and evolution of money, which has undergone profound transformations over millennia. The journey from the barter system to the advent of digital banking encapsulates humanity's relentless pursuit of more efficient, reliable, and scalable means of exchanging value. Initially, the barter system facilitated trade, allowing individuals to directly exchange goods and services. However, the limitations of this system, including the double coincidence of wants and challenges in storing value, led to the adoption of precious metals as a universal medium of exchange. Gold and silver, valued for their rarity and durability, became the standard means of trade, laying the groundwork for the development of fiat currency.

Fiat currency, money declared by a government to be legal tender despite not being backed by a physical commodity, represents a significant evolution in the concept of money. It relies entirely on the trust and confidence of its users in the government's ability to maintain its value. The transition to fiat currency enabled the development of modern banking systems and sophisticated monetary policies, further enhancing trade and economic growth.

The digital transformation of the banking system marks the latest chapter in this evolutionary journey. The advent of digital banking and electronic payments introduced unprecedented levels of speed, convenience, and accessibility. Online banking platforms, credit and debit card payments, and electronic fund transfers have become the backbone of the contemporary economy, setting the stage for the introduction of digital currencies. The proliferation of the internet and mobile technologies has paved the way for fintech innovations, challenging traditional financial models and prompting central banks to explore the potential of digital currencies.

In this context, CBDCs emerge as a natural progression in the digitization of money, aiming to blend the efficiency and innovation of digital currencies with the regulatory framework and stability of traditional fiat currency.

How does the current system work?

The current payment system, as overseen by central banks, is a multifaceted network that facilitates the flow of money between parties. This system is the backbone of economic transactions, supporting everything from simple retail purchases to complex international trades. Central to this system are the commercial banks and financial institutions that manage accounts for individuals and businesses, enabling them to deposit, withdraw, and transfer funds. These banks operate within a regulatory framework established by the central bank and other key regulators, which ensures the stability and integrity of the financial system.[1]

Transactions within this system can take various forms, including cash exchanges, electronic transfers, and card payments. Electronic payments have become increasingly prevalent, relying on an intricate infrastructure of payment processors, card networks, and clearinghouses. Payment processors and card networks facilitate the authorization and processing of card transactions, connecting merchants with cardholders' banks. Meanwhile, clearinghouses serve as intermediaries between banks, managing the reconciliation of transactions at the end of the day by ensuring that funds are appropriately transferred between parties' accounts.

---

[1] These regulations usually encompass multiple dimensions. For instance, banks are subject to capital adequacy requirements, which ensure that banks maintain a certain level of capital reserves relative to their current liabilities, such as those outlined in the Basel III international regulatory framework, and are designed to mitigate the risk of insolvency and enhance the stability of the financial system. Liquidity regulations require banks to hold a sufficient level of liquid assets to cover short-term liabilities. This is to ensure that banks can meet their financial obligations and withdrawal demands from depositors. The Liquidity Coverage Ratio (LCR) and Net Stable

The role of the central bank in this ecosystem is both foundational and regulatory. It issues the currency that underpins cash transactions and oversees the electronic payment systems to maintain their efficiency and security. One of the central bank's critical functions is operating the Real-Time Gross Settlement (RTGS) system, which allows banks to settle interbank transfers in real-time, ensuring the swift and secure movement of large sums of money.[2]

Despite its robustness, the current payment system has its limitations. The reliance on multiple intermediaries can introduce delays and costs, particularly for cross-border transactions, which must navigate disparate national systems and regulations.

Consider credit card transactions. **Figure 2** highlights how complex the current system is. When a cardholder presents their credit card for payment, the merchant uses a Point of Sale (POS) system or an online payment gateway to capture the card details and transaction amount. This information is then sent to the merchant's acquiring bank, which acts as an intermediary to facilitate the transaction. The acquiring bank forwards this transaction request to the card association, such as Visa or MasterCard, which routes it to the card-issuing bank. The issuing bank verifies the cardholder's account status and checks for sufficient funds. Based on this verification, the transaction is either approved or declined. The decision is sent back through the card association to the acquiring bank and finally to the merchant.

At the end of the business day, merchants typically batch and send all approved transactions to their acquiring bank for processing. The acquiring bank reviews these batched transactions and forwards them to the card association for settlement. The card association plays a pivotal role in facilitating the transfer of transaction details to the respective issuing banks, which then transfer the funds corresponding to the transactions back to the card association. The card association then passes these funds to the acquiring bank, which finally deposits them into the merchant's account.

Throughout this process, various fees are levied by each intermediary. The issuing bank charges an interchange fee, from 1.5% to 2.9%, which is a percentage of the transaction amount. This fee compensates the issuing bank for handling, fraud, and bad debt costs, and the risk involved in approving the payment. The card association charges an assessment

---

Funding Ratio (NSFR) are key liquidity requirements under Basel III. Consumer protection laws protect consumers from unfair banking practices, ensure the transparency of financial products and services, and promote financial literacy. Examples include the Truth in Lending Act (TILA) and the Fair Credit Reporting Act (FCRA) in the United States. Banks must also adhere to AML and CFT regulations, which include customer due diligence (CDD), know your customer (KYC) protocols, and reporting suspicious transactions. These measures are aimed at preventing the financial system from being used for illegal activities. With the increasing digitization of financial services, including the introduction of CBDCs, regulations around data protection and privacy have become increasingly important. These laws govern how banks collect, store, and process personal data and include regulations such as the General Data Protection Regulation (GDPR) in the European Union.

[2] Unlike traditional settlement methods that aggregate multiple transactions for end-of-day processing, RTGS operates on a transaction-by-transaction basis, ensuring that funds are transferred in real-time and on a "gross" basis, meaning that each transaction is settled individually without netting debits against credits.

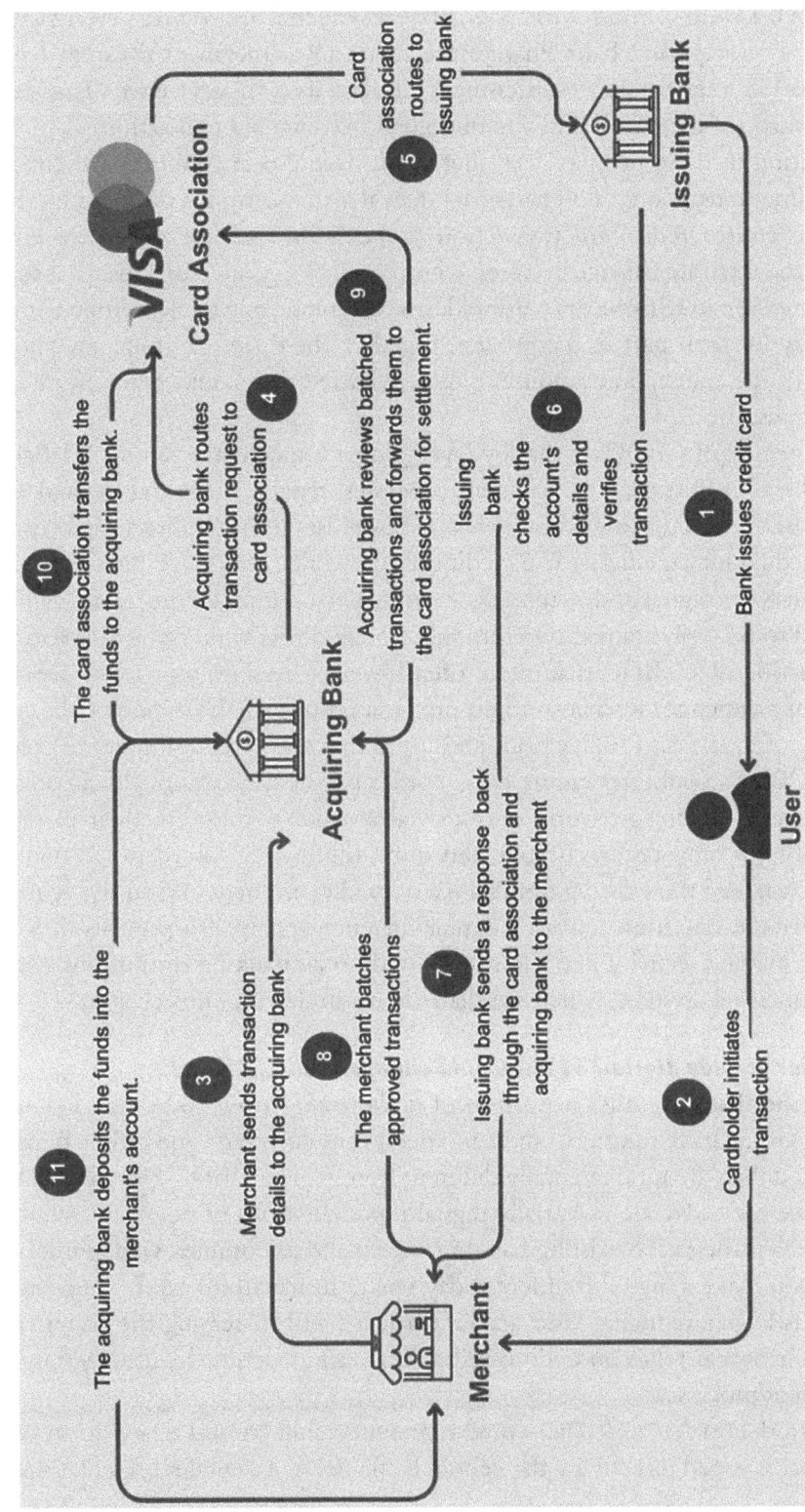

Figure 2 How payment processing works

fee, between 0.13% to 0.15%, for using its network, which is also a small percentage of each transaction. The acquiring bank charges the merchant a merchant discount fee, which encompasses the interchange fees, assessment fees, and its own service fees. This fee is usually a percentage of the transaction amount plus a fixed fee per transaction.

In addition to these primary fees, merchants may also encounter payment gateway fees for online transactions and chargeback fees if a transaction is disputed by the cardholder. The entire credit card transaction process, from authorization to settlement, underlines the intricate balance between security, efficiency, and cost, ensuring that funds are transferred securely from the cardholder to the merchant while compensating each intermediary for their part in the process. Together, these fees can total anywhere from 2% to 4% of the transaction amount, plus a fixed fee that could range from $0.10 to $0.30 per transaction.

The potential of CBDCs is that by leveraging advancements in digital ledger technologies, they could streamline payment processes, reduce costs, and expand financial access. A CBDC would allow consumers and businesses to make direct digital payments without needing intermediaries like credit card networks. This could reduce the reliance on credit cards for digital and potentially even in-person transactions, as a CBDC could be designed to be easily transactable through mobile devices and online platforms. With the introduction of a CBDC that might offer lower or even no transaction fees for certain types of payments, merchants might prefer accepting CBDCs, potentially reducing the volume of credit card transactions and impacting the revenue model of credit card networks. CBDCs could streamline cross-border payments, traditionally an area where credit cards and banking networks have played a major role due to their international reach. If CBDCs offer faster, cheaper, and more transparent international transactions, this could challenge the existing dominance of credit card networks in this space.

However, the transition toward a digital currency system also presents new considerations for privacy, security, and the role of traditional banking institutions within the broader financial ecosystem, which we shall discuss in detail in this chapter.

Isn't a dollar already digital? What would change with CBDCs?

While it's true that a significant portion of dollar transactions today are digital, in the form of electronic bank transfers, credit and debit card payments, and online transactions, these digital dollars are fundamentally different from what a CBDC represents. The digital dollars we use today are essentially digital representations of physical cash, managed and transacted through the existing banking system and its complex web of intermediaries. When you make a digital payment today, you're instructing a bank to update digital records in its ledger, reducing your account balance and increasing the recipient's. This process, while digital, relies on traditional banking infrastructure, regulatory frameworks, and settlement processes.

The introduction of a CBDC would represent a shift toward a new form of digital currency that is issued directly by the central bank, not as a digital representation of cash but as a distinct, standalone digital asset. This digital currency would be a liability of the central bank, just as physical cash is today, but in a digital form that can be used for both retail and wholesale transactions. Unlike the digital dollars that exist within the banking system, a CBDC would be designed to operate on a digital ledger or blockchain, providing several specific changes and benefits:

- **Direct Central Bank Liability:** CBDCs would be direct obligations of the central bank, not commercial banks. This means that individuals and businesses would hold digital currency that is a direct claim on the central bank, enhancing trust and security in the digital currency.

- **Improved Efficiency and Lower Costs:** By operating on a digital ledger, CBDC transactions could bypass many of the intermediaries that are currently involved in digital transactions, potentially reducing transaction times and costs. This is particularly relevant for cross-border payments, which currently involve multiple banks and clearing systems.

- **Increased Financial Inclusion:** CBDCs could be designed to work on simple digital wallets accessible via smartphones or smart cards, reducing barriers to access for unbanked or underbanked populations. This contrasts with the current system, where access to digital dollars often requires a bank account.

- **Enhanced Security and Privacy:** While the specifics would depend on the design, CBDCs could offer improved security features inherent in blockchain technology, with potential for privacy protections that are superior to those in the current banking system.

- **Programmable Money:** Unlike current digital dollars, CBDCs could be programmable, allowing for the integration of smart contracts that automatically execute transactions under certain conditions. This feature could enable new types of financial services and efficiencies.

- **Monetary Policy Implementation:** CBDCs could provide central banks with a new tool for implementing monetary policy directly through the currency, for example, by adjusting interest rates on CBDC holdings. This direct control contrasts with the more indirect tools central banks currently use to influence the economy through the banking system.

In summary, while dollars in their current digital form facilitate electronic transactions within the framework of traditional banking, CBDCs propose a new, direct form of digital currency that operates on a blockchain or digital ledger technology. This shift could bring about profound changes in transaction efficiency, cost, accessibility, and the overall structure of the financial system.

Case Study: The Digital Transformation of Island Economica

Before delving into the implementation details and the corresponding challenges, it is worthwhile to highlight the real benefits that might come from implementing a CBDC. To do so, we will consider a small island nation, like The Bahamas or a small economy in the Pacific, in our case study. The introduction of a CBDC in such a context can exemplify the concrete benefits impacting the economy, society, and the broader financial ecosystem.

Island Economica, a fictional small island nation, has long suffered from limited financial infrastructure, with a significant portion of its population lacking access to traditional banking services. The cost of maintaining physical cash across its dispersed archipelago is high, and remittance fees for its sizable diaspora are exorbitant. In response, the nation's central bank decides to introduce a CBDC, the Digital Economica Dollar (DED).

Enhancing Financial Inclusion

The first and most immediate benefit of the DED is its role in enhancing financial inclusion. By offering a digital wallet that can be accessed through smartphones or even basic feature phones, the central bank brings financial services directly to the unbanked population. This move dramatically expands access to financial services, enabling individuals to participate in the digital economy, receive direct deposits from employers, and access government services and benefits electronically. The simplicity and accessibility of the DED platform mean that even those residing in remote areas or without a formal bank account can now securely store and transact money.

Streamlining Remittances

For Island Economica, remittances from its diaspora are a vital part of the economy. However, traditional remittance channels are fraught with high fees and slow processing times. The introduction of the DED transforms this scenario. Leveraging blockchain technology, the DED facilitates instant cross-border transactions at a fraction of the cost of traditional services. This efficiency not only puts more money into the pockets of recipients but also encourages more frequent remittances, boosting the nation's economy.

Fostering Economic Resilience and Transparency

In the face of natural disasters, which are not uncommon for island nations, the DED provides a resilient and transparent mechanism for disaster relief and recovery efforts. Unlike physical cash, which can be difficult to distribute and track in the aftermath of a disaster, digital currency can be swiftly allocated to affected individuals' digital wallets. This rapid distribution is crucial for immediate relief efforts, and the digital nature of transactions ensures transparency and accountability in how funds are spent.

Reducing Operational Costs and Enhancing Efficiency

The operational costs associated with printing, distributing, and managing physical cash are significantly high for Island Economica. By transitioning to the DED, the central bank reduces these costs substantially. Furthermore, the DED's digital ledger technology allows for real-time tracking of money flow, aiding in monetary policy decisions and the fight against financial crimes such as money laundering and fraud. For businesses, the instant settlement of transactions improves cash flow management and reduces the reliance on costly credit facilities.

Catalyzing the Digital Economy

The DED acts as a catalyst for the digital economy, encouraging innovation in fintech and beyond. With a universally accessible digital currency, startups and established businesses alike innovate new services, from microloans and insurance to digital marketplaces that connect local producers with global consumers. This innovation spurs economic growth, creates jobs, and diversifies the nation's economic base.

Conclusion

The introduction of the Digital Economica Dollar in Island Economica showcases the multifaceted benefits of CBDCs. Beyond reducing transaction costs, the DED enhances financial inclusion, streamlines remittances, fosters economic resilience, reduces operational inefficiencies, and catalyzes the digital economy. While the path to implementing a CBDC involves navigating technical and social challenges, the potential benefits offer a compelling case for nations around the world to explore digital currencies as a tool for economic transformation.

2. How to Design it?

If you had the option to design a CBDC, one of the first choices you would have to make is to decide whether the main audience of your new form of money are retail users or financial institutions.

The distinction between retail and wholesale CBDCs reflects the two primary channels through which central banks are considering the implementation and distribution of digital currencies. This differentiation not only captures the target audience of each CBDC type but also indicates the unique set of objectives, challenges, and potential impacts these digital currencies are designed to address within the broader financial ecosystem.

2.1 Retail CBDCs: Democratizing Digital Currency Access

Retail CBDCs are aimed at the general public, including individuals, businesses, and government entities, facilitating everyday financial activities such as payments and transfers. This democratization of digital currency access is fundamentally about enhancing the efficiency and inclusivity of the financial system. By offering a digital currency directly from the central bank, these initiatives seek to ensure that all segments of the population have access to safe and reliable digital money, potentially transforming the landscape of financial inclusion.

The implementation of retail CBDCs can significantly reduce transaction times and fees compared to traditional banking systems. For example, the Digital Currency Electronic Payment (DCEP) project by China and The Bahamas' Sand Dollar illustrate pioneering efforts toward deploying retail CBDCs with the aim of streamlining domestic and cross-border transactions. These projects highlight the central banks' commitment to leveraging digital currencies in enhancing payment efficiencies, reducing operational costs, and ensuring broader economic participation across all societal segments.

However, the introduction of retail CBDCs is not without challenges. Ensuring universal access requires overcoming significant technical and logistical hurdles, including the development of user-friendly interfaces that cater to a wide demographic, including those with limited digital literacy. And note that central banks have never been in a customer-facing business, which creates operational nightmares, e.g. who would you call if a transaction needs to be reverted?

The digital divide, the gap between those who have ready access to computers and the internet and those who do not, could also be exacerbated by the roll-out of CBDCs. Ensuring equitable access to the digital infrastructure required to use CBDCs is critical to avoid further marginalizing those already underserved by the current financial system.

Additionally, privacy concerns remain paramount as the centralization of transaction data could potentially enable unprecedented levels of financial surveillance by state authorities. Balancing the need for security and privacy rights is thus a critical concern in the design and implementation of retail CBDCs.

2.2 Wholesale CBDCs: Streamlining Interbank Operations

In contrast, wholesale CBDCs are restricted to financial institutions holding reserve deposits with a central bank.[3] Their primary aim is to improve the efficiency and security of high-value transactions and settlements between these institutions. By leveraging blockchain technology or other forms of distributed ledger technology (DLT),

---

[3] https://www.federalreserve.gov/econres/notes/feds-notes/examining-cbdc-and-wholesale-payments-20230908. html: https://www.ecb.europa.eu/press/key/date/2022/html/ecb.sp220926~5f9b85685a.en.html

wholesale CBDCs offer a means to streamline interbank payments, reduce counterparty risks, and enhance the overall stability of financial markets. Currently, interbank transactions can take several days to clear and settle due to the involvement of various intermediaries and the need to reconcile accounts across different institutions. With a CBDC operating on a blockchain, transactions could be verified and settled in near real-time. For example, a blockchain's immutable and transparent ledger allows transactions to be instantly recorded and visible to all parties, eliminating the need for time-consuming reconciliation processes. This capability could be particularly beneficial for cross-border interbank payments, which are currently subject to even longer delays and higher costs due to the involvement of multiple banking systems and currencies.

In the current system, banks are exposed to the risk that a counterparty may fail to honor its obligations, a risk that is magnified in periods of financial instability. A CBDC, by facilitating instantaneous settlement, ensures that transactions are completed as soon as they are initiated, thereby reducing the window of exposure to counterparty failure. Furthermore, smart contracts—self-executing contracts with terms directly written into code—could be employed to automate and enforce the terms of interbank agreements, ensuring that obligations are met before a transaction can be finalized. This automation would further reduce the risk of default.

Lastly, the stability of financial markets stands to benefit from the enhanced liquidity management that a CBDC could offer. By enabling faster and more efficient interbank payments, banks would have greater control over their liquidity, being able to move funds more swiftly to meet demand without the need to hold excessive reserves. This enhanced liquidity management could prove critical in times of financial stress, allowing banks to respond to sudden liquidity shortages and contributing to the overall stability of the financial system more effectively.

Moreover, a CBDC could facilitate more direct and efficient implementation of monetary policy by central banks. For instance, a central bank could use a CBDC to directly adjust the reserves of commercial banks, thereby more precisely managing the money supply and influencing interest rates. When central banks adjust the reserves of commercial banks, they directly influence the amount of money that these banks can lend, thereby impacting the overall money supply and interest rates. Traditionally, central banks use methods like open market operations or adjusting reserve requirements to manage these reserves indirectly. For instance, they might buy government bonds to increase bank reserves, enabling more lending and potentially lowering interest rates.

With the introduction of a CBDC, this process can become more direct and efficient. A central bank could directly credit or debit CBDC to commercial banks' reserve accounts. By doing so, they can immediately increase or decrease the amount of money available for lending. This allows for more precise and timely adjustments to the money supply and interest rates, enhancing the effectiveness of monetary policy. For example, during an economic slowdown, the central bank could instantly increase reserves to stimulate lending and economic activity. Conversely, to curb inflation, it could reduce reserves to tighten the money supply. This direct intervention simplifies and accelerates the central bank's ability to manage economic conditions. This direct control over monetary policy tools could enhance the central bank's ability to stabilize the economy and respond to financial crises.

In summary, the introduction of a wholesale CBDC has the potential to fundamentally transform interbank settlements, making them faster, more secure, and less costly. By harnessing the efficiencies of blockchain technology and DLT, wholesale CBDCs could streamline the payment process, mitigate counterparty risks, and enhance liquidity management—all of which contribute to the stability and efficiency of financial markets.

Project Ubin in Singapore and the exploration of a digital Euro for wholesale transactions by the Eurosystem are indicative of growing interest in employing digital currencies to facilitate faster and more secure interbank settlements. These initiatives underscore the recognition of the inefficiencies in current financial market infrastructures and the belief that DLT and CBDCs can offer significant improvements.

Inefficiencies in Current Systems	Addressing Inefficiencies Through Wholesale CBDCs
• **High Transaction Costs and Times:** Traditional cross-border payments involve multiple intermediaries, leading to high transaction costs and processing times. This inefficiency is particularly pronounced in the correspondent banking model, which requires transactions to pass through several banks before reaching the destination.	• **Improved Transaction Efficiency:** By facilitating direct transactions between financial institutions on a shared ledger, wholesale CBDCs can significantly reduce the time and cost associated with cross-border payments. This efficiency stems from eliminating the need for multiple intermediaries, thereby streamlining the settlement process.
• **Operational Inefficiency and Risk:** The current infrastructure relies heavily on legacy systems that are not only slow but also prone to errors and fraud. This operational inefficiency is exacerbated by the layered complexity of transactions, where each intermediary adds time and cost.	• **Reduced Operational Risk:** DLT's inherent characteristics, such as transparency and immutability, reduce operational risks by providing a secure and tamper-proof system. This technology allows for real-time transaction tracking and reduces the potential for fraud and errors.
• **Liquidity Management:** In the existing system, managing liquidity across borders is challenging due to the fragmentation of financial markets. Banks need to hold reserves in multiple currencies across different jurisdictions, leading to inefficiencies in liquidity management.	• **Enhanced Liquidity Management:** Wholesale CBDCs can improve liquidity management by enabling more efficient allocation of funds. With CBDCs, financial institutions can transact directly in real-time, reducing the need for maintaining high levels of reserves in foreign currencies.
• **Counterparty and Settlement Risk:** The multistep process in traditional settlements increases counterparty risk—the risk that one party will not fulfill their payment obligation. This risk is a significant concern in high-value transactions typical of wholesale payments.	• **Decreased Counterparty and Settlement Risk:** The use of DLT and smart contracts in wholesale CBDC systems can automate the settlement process, reducing counterparty and settlement risks. Smart contracts ensure that transactions are executed only when certain predefined conditions are met, providing an additional layer of security.

Yet, the introduction of wholesale CBDCs also entails challenges. The integration of digital currencies into existing financial systems demands substantial technological alignment and regulatory oversight to ensure seamless interoperability and maintain financial stability. Moreover, while the direct benefits of wholesale CBDCs may not be immediately visible to the general public, their successful implementation is crucial for enhancing the underlying efficiency and security of the financial system at large.

2.3 Single-Tier or Two-Tier Systems

Another fundamental architectural design choice is the role that commercial banks are left to play in an economy with a CBDC. **Figure 3** depicts the two possibilities.

In a single-tier system, the central bank assumes a direct role in the issuance and distribution of the CBDC to consumers, businesses, and other entities. This model is akin to the central bank providing digital cash directly to the public, bypassing commercial banks and other financial institutions as intermediaries. The central bank also takes on the responsibilities of maintaining accounts, managing balances, and validating transactions for each user of the CBDC.

Implementing a single-tier system poses significant technical and operational challenges for central banks. It requires the development of a robust and scalable digital infrastructure capable of handling a high volume of transactions in real-time, ensuring security, privacy, and resilience against cyber threats. Moreover, the central bank must establish a user-friendly interface that allows easy access and transaction capabilities for the general public, which could significantly stretch its traditional operational focus.

The direct control afforded by a single-tier system could enhance the central bank's ability to implement monetary policy at the household level. For instance, it could allow for more precise targeting of inflation rates or employment levels by adjusting the supply of digital currency directly. However, this model might also lead to disintermediation of commercial banks, as consumers and businesses could prefer holding CBDCs directly with the central bank, potentially undermining the traditional banking sector's role in financial intermediation and credit creation.

Contrastingly, a two-tier system involves the central bank issuing the CBDC to commercial banks or other authorized financial institutions, which then distribute it to

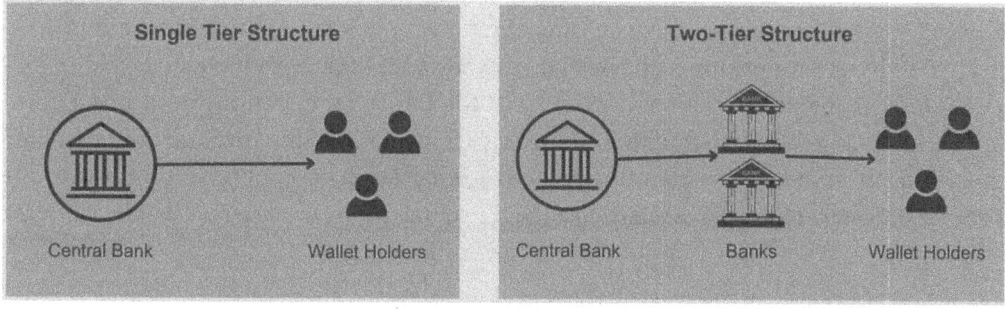

Figure 3 Comparing single-tier and two-tier CBDC systems

the public. In this model, the central bank focuses on the wholesale issuance of CBDCs, while retail distribution, account management, and customer service are handled by existing financial institutions.

A two-tier system leverages the existing infrastructure, expertise, and customer relationships of commercial banks and financial institutions, potentially facilitating a smoother rollout and wider adoption of CBDCs. This model minimizes the operational and technical burdens on the central bank, as it does not need to manage a vast number of retail user accounts or develop extensive customer-facing interfaces.

By incorporating commercial banks into the CBDC ecosystem, a two-tier system preserves the traditional role of banks in financial intermediation and credit creation, potentially mitigating the risk of disintermediation. This approach can also foster innovation in financial services, as banks and other institutions develop new products and services around the CBDC. However, it requires careful regulatory oversight to ensure that all participants in the system adhere to the necessary standards for security, privacy, and operational efficiency.

While the single-tier system offers central banks direct control over the CBDC and its distribution, potentially enhancing the effectiveness of monetary policy, it also poses significant challenges in terms of operational capacity and the risk of banking sector disintermediation. The two-tier system, conversely, capitalizes on the existing capabilities of commercial banks, potentially enabling a more efficient and user-friendly rollout of CBDCs, but it also necessitates rigorous regulatory oversight and coordination.

Countries exploring CBDCs are carefully considering these models based on their unique economic contexts, policy objectives, and financial landscapes. For example, the People's Bank of China (PBoC) is pioneering the Digital Currency Electronic Payment (DCEP) using a two-tier model, aiming to leverage the existing banking infrastructure to facilitate the distribution and management of its digital yuan.[4]

In this system, the central bank issues the digital yuan (e-CNY) and then distributes it to the public through commercial banks and other financial institutions, which act as the second tier. Commercial banks show a keen interest in joining this two-tier CBDC system for several reasons. Being part of the CBDC ecosystem provides commercial banks access to a new and rapidly growing market. As digital currency adoption increases, banks recognized as official distributors of the CBDC can tap into the demand for digital transactions, attracting new customers and transactions. For commercial banks, participating in this system means they can offer their customers faster, more secure, and cost-effective transaction options compared to conventional digital payments.

Gaining recognition as an approved bank for CBDC transactions positions a commercial bank as a forward-thinking, innovative institution. This can enhance its brand reputation, attract tech-savvy customers, and strengthen its competitive position in the financial industry. Through facilitating CBDC transactions, commercial banks can gain

---

[4] Similarly, the European Central Bank (ECB) is investigating a digital euro that could potentially adopt a two-tier system, recognizing the value of integrating with Europe's established financial institutions.

valuable data insights into consumer behavior, spending patterns, and financial needs. This data can inform product development, marketing strategies, and personalized customer services, deepening customer relationships and improving customer retention. Participating in the CBDC system also allows banks to work closely with the central bank and regulatory authorities, ensuring they are at the forefront of regulatory developments and compliance standards.

In conclusion, the choice between a single-tier and two-tier CBDC system involves a complex trade-off between direct control and operational feasibility, the potential impact on the banking sector, and the overarching goals of financial inclusion, efficiency, and stability.

2.4 Account-Based or Token-Based CBDC

Two additional fundamental models emerge when considering CBDC design: account-based and token-based systems, both of which have distinct implications for retail CBDC offerings.

In an account-based CBDC system, transactions are processed based on the verification of the identities of the transaction participants. This model requires central banks to maintain accounts for all users alongside a comprehensive digital identity system. The account-based architecture ensures a high level of security and enables central banks to directly manage and oversee transactions, thereby maintaining stringent control over the digital currency's integrity. However, this model raises concerns about privacy, as it necessitates the collection and storage of personal identity information by central banks or other managing entities.

Alternatively, the token-based CBDC model uses digital signatures and public-private key pairs for transaction validation, without directly linking transactions to the identity of users. This means that whoever holds the token is assumed to have the right to spend it, in the same way as someone owning a banknote. This approach offers enhanced privacy for users, as it mimics the anonymity of cash transactions in the digital realm. Nonetheless, the increased privacy comes at the cost of traceability, making it more challenging to monitor and prevent fraudulent transactions and money laundering activities.

2.5 Balancing Act: Navigating the Trade-Offs

The development and deployment of both retail and wholesale CBDCs represent a balancing act for central banks, requiring careful navigation of trade-offs between accessibility, efficiency, privacy, and security. The design choices made in the development of CBDCs will have significant implications for the future of monetary policy, financial stability, and economic inclusivity.

On the one hand, retail CBDCs can significantly enhance financial inclusion by providing access to digital payments for individuals without traditional bank accounts. They also allow central banks to directly implement monetary policies, such as interest rate adjustments, to the general public. Ultimately, retail CBDCs can spur innovation in the payments ecosystem, leading to faster, cheaper, and more secure transactions for consumers and businesses. However, implementing a retail CBDC raises significant privacy issues, as central banks could potentially have access to individuals' transaction data. There's a risk of disintermediation because individuals might prefer CBDCs over bank deposits, leading to disintermediation of commercial banks and impacting their ability to lend. Furthermore, the deployment of a retail CBDC requires a comprehensive and secure infrastructure to handle transactions directly with the public, posing significant operational and cybersecurity challenges.

Wholesale CBDCs can streamline interbank settlements and cross-border transactions, making them faster and more cost-efficient. By enabling real-time settlements, wholesale CBDCs can also significantly reduce counterparty risks in financial transactions. Finally, they offer central banks and financial institutions improved tools for liquidity management, facilitating more effective monetary policy implementation. Wholesale CBDCs do not come without implementation challenges. Integrating wholesale CBDCs into the existing financial infrastructure requires significant coordination among central banks, commercial banks, and other financial institutions. Additionally, the reliance on digital technology and the concentration of transactions among financial institutions may introduce new operational risks, including system failures and cyber-attacks.[5]

3. Detailed Examples of CBDC Initiatives

The Bahamas' Sand Dollar

The Bahamas launched Project Sand Dollar, the world's first fully deployed CBDC, in October 2020, following successful pilot testing on the islands of Exuma and Abaco starting in December 2019. The primary goals of the Sand Dollar are to promote financial inclusion across the archipelago's unbanked and underbanked populations, reduce service delivery costs, and increase the efficiency of financial transactions. The Sand Dollar is a centralized, regulated digital representation of the Bahamian dollar, backed by the nation's foreign reserves, making it a stable and secure means of exchange. The initiative also aims to achieve interoperability among payment services, support offline transactions, ensure near-instantaneous processing, and enhance transaction monitoring while protecting user confidentiality.

Despite its pioneering status, the Sand Dollar's circulation remains less than one percent of the currency issued, highlighting the challenges in achieving widespread adoption. To boost adoption it is critical to include building a network of merchants that

---

[5] https://cepr.org/voxeu/columns/cbdc-architectures-financial-system-and-central-bank-future;https://www.csis.org/analysis/central-bank-digital-currency-design-choices-and-impacts-currency-internationalization; https://101blockchains.com/retail-cbdc-architecture.

accept CBDCs, achieving interoperability with traditional banking systems, enlisting participation from banks and credit unions, and fostering user education and confidence.

Challenging Dollar Dominance through CBDCs: The Case of the Digital Yuan

China's DCEP, also known as the Digital Yuan, represents one of the most significant efforts by a major economy to develop and test a CBDC. Motivated by the desire to enhance the efficiency of its payment systems, increase the yuan's international presence, and potentially challenge the dominance of the U.S. dollar, China's approach to CBDCs is notable for its scale and speed of development. The DCEP is designed to replace some of the cash in circulation, offering features such as traceability, cost-efficiency, and real-time transaction processing. However, the initiative also raises concerns about privacy and the central government's increased ability to monitor financial transactions.

The ascent of digital currencies presents an innovative avenue for countries to enhance the global standing of their national currencies. 'Specifically, China's strategic initiatives to foster the adoption of the digital yuan in international trade through bilateral agreements with nations such as Brazil and other members of the BRICS consortium underscore the potential of CBDCs to challenge the hegemony of the U.S. dollar.

China's approach to internationalizing the digital yuan involves forging strategic partnerships and financial agreements that facilitate its use beyond its borders. A notable aspect of this strategy is China's engagement with Brazil and other BRICS countries, aiming to establish the digital yuan as a preferred currency for bilateral trade agreements. These efforts are not merely transactional but are part of a broader ambition to embed the digital yuan in the global financial system, thereby diversifying and expanding its international usage.

By signing agreements that prioritize the digital yuan in trade settlements, China is effectively creating a new ecosystem where its CBDC becomes a viable alternative to traditional fiat currencies, especially the U.S. dollar. This move is significant, considering the dollar's longstanding dominance in international trade and finance. The implications of these agreements extend beyond the involved parties, signaling to the global market that the digital yuan is a stable, government-backed digital currency ready for international commerce.

While the U.S. dollar has been the de facto global reserve currency, the entry of government-backed digital currencies into international trade introduces a new layer of complexity and competition. The digital yuan's adoption in countries like Brazil and other BRICS nations could gradually erode the dollar's supremacy in global finance, offering countries an alternative that circumvents the U.S. financial system and, by extension, its oversight and sanctions regime.

The journey of the digital yuan from a domestic digital currency to a tool of international trade policy illustrates the transformative potential of CBDCs in reshaping global economic relations. As China continues to expand its network of bilateral agreements to include the digital yuan in international trade, the world may witness a gradual reconfiguration of currency power dynamics. This development challenges other nations, especially those with significant stakes in the current financial order, to reconsider their positions and potentially accelerate their own CBDC initiatives.

For countries exploring the issuance of their own CBDCs, the trajectory of the digital yuan provides valuable insights into the strategic possibilities of digital currencies in enhancing national economic sovereignty and international trade influence. As the global financial landscape evolves, the interplay between emerging CBDCs and established fiat currencies like the U.S. dollar will undoubtedly be a key area of watch for policymakers, economists, and international traders alike.

Sweden's e-Krona

Sweden's exploration of a CBDC, the e-Krona, is driven by the country's rapid move toward becoming a cashless society. With cash usage in decline, the Riksbank is investigating the potential of a digital Krona to ensure public access to a safe and efficient payment method. The e-Krona project considers factors such as financial inclusion, the impact on the banking system, and the need for resilience in payment systems. Sweden's approach to CBDCs emphasizes careful planning and consideration of the implications for monetary policy, financial stability, and the payment market landscape.

PROJECT HAMILTON

Project Hamilton, a collaborative initiative between the MIT Digital Currency Initiative and the Federal Reserve Bank of Boston, embarked on a comprehensive exploration into the technical feasibility of a general-purpose CBDC tailored for the scale of the United States economy. This pioneering research project aimed to dissect the intricate technical challenges, opportunities, risks, and trade-offs associated with a hypothetical CBDC, providing valuable insights into its potential design and implementation.

One of the key outcomes of Project Hamilton was the development of a high-performance transaction processing system designed explicitly for CBDCs. This system was meticulously engineered to address three critical challenges: flexibility, performance, and resilience. To tackle these challenges, the project proposed decoupling transaction validation from execution, allowing for minimal data storage within the core transaction processor and facilitating independent scaling of various system components. The design also incorporated a secure transaction format and protocol to enable future programmability and self-custody functionalities, alongside a system architecture that efficiently executes transactions through two distinct architectures.

Both architectures achieved remarkable speed and throughput, significantly exceeding the project's initial requirements. The first architecture processed transactions in an ordered sequence, achieving over 99% completion in under two seconds for the majority of transactions but faced a bottleneck at approximately 170,000 transactions per second due to the ordering server. The second architecture, devoid of a singular ordering server, showcased superior scalability, handling up to 1.7 million transactions per second with the majority completing in under half a second. This architecture demonstrated linear scalability with the addition of more servers and maintained resilience by tolerating the loss of data-center locations without data loss or service disruption.

The project's findings also emphasized the potential for CBDCs to offer functionalities not currently feasible with either cash or traditional bank accounts. These include cryptographic proofs of payment, complex transfers involving multiple sources of funds, and flexible authorization mechanisms for transactions. The research underscored the importance of separating transaction processing into distinct stages to enhance system scalability and flexibility, allowing for innovative intermediary roles and functionalities in future CBDC designs.

Despite leveraging blockchain technology concepts, Project Hamilton concluded that a distributed ledger was not necessary to achieve its objectives, especially under the central administration of a single actor. This insight pointed to more granular design choices beyond the commonly discussed direct, two-tier, or hybrid models, highlighting the complexity of decisions regarding access, intermediation, institutional roles, and data retention in CBDC design. Adapted from[6]

3.1 Different Approaches and Challenges

The initiatives in The Bahamas, China, and Sweden illustrate the varied motivations and approaches to CBDC implementation around the world. While The Bahamas focuses on financial inclusion and transaction efficiency within a small island economy, China aims for broader impacts on monetary policy and international finance. Sweden's exploration of the e-Krona is driven by its societal shift away from cash, highlighting concerns about inclusion and payment system resilience. These examples underscore the importance of tailoring CBDC projects to national priorities and contexts, the potential benefits of improved transaction efficiency and reduced costs, and the challenges of achieving widespread adoption and integrating with existing financial systems.

---

[6] For more detailed information on Project Hamilton and its findings, you can visit the Federal Reserve Bank of Boston's executive summary and the MIT News article discussing the project's outcomes and future directions. Sources about Project Hamilton include: Federal Reserve Bank of Boston Executive Summary on Project Hamilton: Federal Reserve Bank of Boston

   MIT News article on Project Hamilton: MIT News

   MIT Digital Currency Initiative's release on Project Hamilton: MIT DCI

Implementing Central Bank Digital Currencies brings a suite of technical, economic, and social challenges that must be carefully navigated to ensure their successful deployment and adoption. Let's delve into the technical hurdles such as scalability, privacy, and security, as well as the broader economic and social implications, including impacts on traditional banking systems, privacy concerns, and the digital divide.

4. Technical Challenges in Implementing CBDCs

Scalability

A key technical challenge for CBDCs is ensuring they can handle the volume of transactions that a national economy demands. Scalability involves the capability of the system to process a high volume of transactions quickly and efficiently without compromising performance. Traditional blockchain platforms, like those used for cryptocurrencies, can struggle with scalability due to their consensus mechanisms, which can slow down as more nodes participate in the network. CBDCs aiming for scalability is like trying to fit the entire internet into a floppy disk. Sure, it's ambitious, but you might as well be trying to stream Netflix on a toaster.

For example, Ethereum can process about 15–30 transactions per second (TPS), far below the thousands of TPS processed by major credit card networks. As discussed in Chapter 3, solutions such as layer 2 scaling (e.g. rollups) and sharding exist, but implementing these at the scale required for a national currency presents significant technical hurdles. CBDCs are likely to be run on proprietary networks, that are permissioned in nature as the central banks are responsible for its maintenance, but also for its scalability, e.g. no interruption in service when millions (potentially hundreds of millions) of individuals use it daily.

Privacy

Privacy in CBDCs involves a delicate balance of ensuring transaction anonymity while allowing for regulatory compliance and anti-money laundering measures. Unlike cryptocurrencies such as Bitcoin, which offer pseudonymity, CBDCs must navigate stricter regulatory environments. Ensuring privacy while maintaining the ability for oversight by relevant authorities is a complex challenge. The key question is whether the central bank can credibly commit not to use its visibility into the households' spending patterns in any way.

These concerns are quite real for some people. In March 2023, Florida introduced legislation expressly prohibiting use of a federally adopted CBDC as money within Florida's Uniform Commercial Code (UCC). It instituted protections against a central global currency by prohibiting any CBDC issued by a foreign reserve or foreign sanctioned central bank. The main reason for such a legislative action was the belief that CBDCs would be the first step toward a pervasive "surveillance state."[7]

---

[7] See more about the announcement here: https://www.flgov.com/2023/03/20/governor-ron-desantis-announces-legislation-to-protect-floridians-from-a-federally-controlled-central-bank-digital-currency-and-surveillance-state/.

One potential solution that is currently explored is the use of zero-knowledge proofs (ZKPs), a cryptographic method that allows one party to prove to another party that a statement is true, without conveying any additional information (see Chapter 3 for more details). This could enable the verification of transactions without revealing the parties involved. In fact, there are many layer 2 protocols, categorized as zero-knowledge rollups (zk-rollups), that are experimenting with ZKPs as a solution to the scaling problem that layer 1s have. The mechanism involves bundling transactions off-chain and periodically submitting these bundles to the base layer for execution. A smart contract on the layer 1 network uses ZKPs to ensure the validity of the bundles. Zk-rollups aim to significantly improve the classic issues of scalability, transaction throughput, and transaction costs while maintaining the same security that layer 1s have.

Security

CBDCs face more security threats than a celebrity's Twitter account. Security concerns for CBDCs encompass a wide range of issues, from cybersecurity threats to the integrity of the underlying blockchain architecture. As centralized digital currencies, CBDCs could be targets for hacking, fraud, and cyber-attacks. Ensuring the security of CBDC transactions and the protection of users' data are paramount. While there is always a risk that a single bank is the target of such nefarious attempts, the ripple effects of a successful attack on a commercial bank pale compared to the consequences of an attack on a centralized payment system such as that provided by a CBDC.

Furthermore, smart contracts are likely to be a critical component of CBDC platforms. However, they can contain vulnerabilities that might be exploited by malicious actors. Regular audits and the development of best practices in smart contract design are essential to mitigate these risks.

Legal Tender Status of CBDCs

Legal tender status is a critical attribute that differentiates CBDCs from other forms of digital assets, such as cryptocurrency. This status ensures that CBDCs are recognized by law as acceptable means of payment mandatory for settling debts and financial obligations. The conferral of legal tender status on CBDCs thus aligns with a government's endorsement, providing a layer of security and trust that is absent in most digital currencies not backed by a central authority.

The government-backed assurance that comes with the legal tender status of CBDCs serves as a cornerstone for their acceptance and use within the economy. This assurance underpins the trust of both consumers and businesses in CBDCs as a stable, reliable form of money. Unlike cryptocurrencies, which are prone to volatile fluctuations in value, the value of CBDCs is stabilized by the central bank's regulatory mechanisms and monetary policies, offering a less risky digital alternative to cash and bank deposits. The government backing CBDCs is supposed to comfort us like a security blanket. But let's face it, that blanket has seen more patches and fixes than a Windows 95 operating system.

Official Medium of Exchange

By being designated as legal tender, CBDCs become an official medium of exchange, facilitating daily financial transactions. This official status is instrumental in integrating CBDCs into the existing financial ecosystem, allowing for seamless transactions between digital and fiat currencies. It enables consumers and businesses to use CBDCs for a wide range of transactions, from purchasing goods and services to paying taxes and settling debts, thereby enhancing the efficiency and convenience of the monetary system.

Legal Framework Amendments

The integration of CBDCs into the financial system and their recognition as legal tender necessitate significant legal and regulatory considerations. Many countries' existing legal frameworks do not account for digital currencies, particularly with regard to issues such as digital identity verification, privacy, cybersecurity, and anti-money laundering (AML) measures. Consequently, the introduction of CBDCs requires careful examination and, in many instances, amendments to current laws or the creation of new legislation to address these challenges adequately.

This legislative process involves clarifying the legal status of CBDCs, defining the rights and obligations of users and issuers, and establishing regulatory oversight mechanisms. For instance, adjustments may be needed to central bank acts, financial service regulations, and electronic money laws, among others, to accommodate the unique characteristics of CBDCs. Furthermore, cross-border considerations are crucial for international transactions involving CBDCs, necessitating international cooperation and harmonization of legal standards.

The journey toward the full integration of CBDCs into the global financial system is complex and multifaceted, requiring a concerted effort from lawmakers, financial institutions, and international bodies. As the world moves increasingly toward digitalization, the evolution of legal frameworks to accommodate CBDCs will be a pivotal aspect of ensuring their successful implementation and the continued stability and security of the financial system.

A Potential Solution: The Canton Network

The Canton Network is designed to enhance interoperability across financial institutions and facilitate the seamless exchange of tokenized assets. Developed by Digital Asset, known for its DAML smart contract language, the Canton Network aims to address the challenge of siloed blockchain networks by enabling a network of blockchain networks. This approach allows for the efficient and secure transfer of assets and information across various platforms, promoting collaboration and innovation among participating organizations.[8]

The network was unveiled with participation from thirty organizations, including notable entities like BNP Paribas, Deutsche Börse Group, Goldman Sachs, and Equilend.

---

[8] https://www.canton.network/

It focuses on providing a decentralized infrastructure that maintains privacy and control over data without relying on central intermediaries. This balance between decentralization and privacy is crucial for regulated financial institutions that deal with sensitive data and require compliance with regulatory standards.[9]

One of the key features of the Canton Network is its ability to connect previously siloed financial systems, enhancing the potential for growth and innovation in the financial sector. By utilizing unique smart contract technology, the network ensures that privacy is preserved during transactions, allowing participants to confidently exchange data and value. This opens up new possibilities for synchronized financial markets.

The Canton Network's pilot demonstrated its capabilities by simulating the use of 22 different DLT (Distributed Ledger Technology) applications, involving 45 institutions. This highlighted the network's potential to address the limitations posed by numerous institutional permissioned blockchains, which often operate in isolation. The Canton Network facilitates transactions across these networks, enabling the use of tokenized assets on one network as collateral for transactions on another, for example.

The pilot programs focused on several key areas, including:

- **Tokenization of Real World Assets:** Demonstrating the tokenization process for real-world assets, making them more accessible and liquid on digital platforms.
- **Cross-Network Transactions:** Testing the ability to use tokenized assets on one network as collateral for transactions on another network, a crucial capability for creating more integrated and efficient financial markets.
- **Regulatory Compliance and Privacy:** Ensuring that the interconnectedness facilitated by the Canton Network does not compromise privacy or regulatory compliance, which are critical concerns for financial institutions.

Moreover, the network's relevance to CBDCs has been underscored by its focus on interoperability. Interoperability is deemed essential for the success of CBDCs, ensuring they can seamlessly integrate into existing financial systems and support cross-border transactions. Digital Asset has been actively working with central banks to explore how the Canton Network can support the implementation and operation of CBDCs, leveraging the network's capacity for privacy, scalability, and interconnectivity.[10]

In summary, the Canton Network offers a practical solution to the challenges of interoperability, privacy, and regulatory compliance.

5. New Monetary Policy Transmission

Traditionally, a central bank manipulates its policy rates to influence economic activity; these adjustments impact the interest rates that commercial banks offer to their customers.

---

[9] https://www.ledgerinsights.com/30-firms-canton-network-for-institutional-blockchain-interoperability/
   https://blog.digitalasset.com/blog/the-canton-network-a-regulatory-perspective
[10] https://www.ledgerinsights.com/digital-asset-central-banks-cbdc-interoperability/

However, this transmission from central bank policy adjustments to tangible effects in the broader economy can often encounter significant friction, dampened by the existing financial system's inherent limitations.

Central banks rely on commercial banks to act as intermediaries, transmitting policy changes to the economy. If interest rates are increased, banks are expected to increase both the rates on the loans they extend as well as the rates offered on deposits.[11] These actions discourage households from borrowing and investing and, instead, encourage more depositors to save, which will ultimately cool down the economy.

However, the efficiency of this transmission is subject to various factors that can limit responsiveness. For example, a bank's liquidity position, its capital adequacy, and the competitive landscape within the banking sector can all influence how quickly and effectively it adjusts its lending rates in response to changes in central bank policy rates. If the central bank lowers interest rates to stimulate borrowing and spending, the intended effect might be muted if banks become risk-averse due to economic uncertainties, i.e. if they do not expect to be able to invest in profitable lending opportunities. Such risk aversion often leads to stricter lending standards, making it challenging for households and firms to secure credit even amid lower interest rates.

Moreover, information asymmetries between lenders and borrowers can exacerbate adverse selection and moral hazard problems, further obstructing the smooth transmission of monetary policy. The extent to which changes in policy rates are passed on to various types of loans or deposits can also differ significantly. For instance, rates on long-term loans might adjust more sluggishly compared to those on short-term loans. Furthermore, the economic expectations of households and firms regarding future conditions can influence their spending and borrowing decisions. If they anticipate worsening economic conditions, they may opt to save more and borrow less, irrespective of lower interest rates. The balance sheet conditions of these entities also play a crucial role, as those with high levels of debt might be less responsive to reductions in interest rates.

The traditional mechanisms for transmitting monetary policy are also hindered by prices and wages that may not adjust immediately to changes in policy, delaying the impact of interest rate adjustments on spending and investment decisions.

The introduction of a CBDC, however, could dramatically alter this landscape. With a CBDC, the central bank gains a direct digital conduit to every citizen and business that holding the digital currency. This direct connection means that when the central bank adjusts its policy rates, the effects can be transmitted almost instantly to CBDC holders. This immediacy could significantly enhance the precision and effectiveness of monetary policy measures. For example, a central bank could implement negative interest rates on CBDC holdings to encourage spending during deflationary periods, or adjust the interest rates paid on CBDC deposits to influence saving and spending behaviors directly. This new model of monetary policy transmission via CBDCs promises a level of

---

[11] See Drechsler, Itamar, Alexi Savov, and Philipp Schnabl. "The deposits channel of monetary policy." *The Quarterly Journal of Economics* 132.4 (2017): 1819–1876.

directness, speed, and efficiency previously unattainable, potentially revolutionizing the central bank's role in economic stewardship.

In a nutshell, a CBDC turns the central bank into a financial Santa Claus, knowing who's been naughty or nice with their spending, and ready to adjust your interest rates while you sleep.

6. Who Opposes the Introduction of CBDCs?

The banks. The core function of traditional banks as intermediaries between savers and borrowers could be fundamentally challenged by the advent of CBDCs. With CBDCs, individuals and businesses could hold their funds directly with the central bank, potentially reducing the need to maintain deposits in commercial banks. This shift could lead to a significant reduction in the deposit base of traditional banks, affecting their primary source of funding for lending activities. This reduction in deposits could force banks to seek alternative, more expensive sources of funding, such as wholesale funding, which carries higher risks and costs compared to insured deposits.

Moreover, if deposits are moving out of traditional banks, these are likely to finance their operations by relying on alternative forms of funding. The reliance on more expensive and riskier funding options could increase banks' exposure to default risk, raising the cost of funding further and potentially reducing the profitability and financial stability of these institutions. This scenario could be particularly disruptive for smaller banks, which rely more heavily on deposits for funding and may have limited access to alternative funding sources.

The introduction of CBDCs could also have profound effects on credit markets. By reducing the deposit base and increasing the cost of capital for banks, CBDCs might constrain the banks' ability to extend credit, particularly to small and medium-sized enterprises (SMEs) and individuals. This contraction in credit availability could dampen economic growth and innovation, particularly in sectors that rely heavily on bank financing.[12] The distributional implications across the firm size distribution are crucial, as small firms disproportionately rely on small banks for credit, suggesting that CBDCs could exacerbate financial inequalities within the economy.

---

[12] A model exploring the impact of CBDC on banks, depositors, borrowers, and the central bank, highlighting the potential reduction in bank deposits and its effects, is detailed in "How Might Central Bank Digital Currency Affect Banks?" by The FinReg Blog, Duke University (https://sites.duke.edu/thefinregblog/).

The International Monetary Fund (IMF) discusses the ongoing exploration and experimentation with CBDCs by central banks worldwide, emphasizing the potential benefits of CBDCs in terms of resilience, safety, and efficiency compared to private forms of digital money (https://www.imf.org/en/News/Articles/2022/02/09/sp020922-the-future-of-money).

The Bank Policy Institute provides an overview of the existing U.S. payment systems and discusses how a CBDC could impact these systems, focusing on the security issues related to private key management and the implications of account-based versus token-based CBDCs (https://bpi.com/central-bank-digital-currencies-costs-benefits-and-major-implications-for-the-u-s-economic-system/).

News from the Ivory Tower

Most of the academic work on CBDCs is theoretical in nature because there have been very few instances of pilots that have been run, which makes data about CBDC transactions close to non-existent.

The theoretical landscape surrounding the introduction of CBDCs and their impact on the financial system's stability is rich and varied. Schilling et al. (2020) break new ground by addressing the CBDC trilemma, evaluating its effects on efficiency, financial stability, and price stability. Meanwhile, Luu et al. (2023) posit that CBDCs can bolster financial stability by mitigating leverage and portfolio risks within the banking sector. A number of studies, including those by Fernández-Villaverde et al. (2021), Ahnert et al. (2023), and Skeie (2021), delve into the potential for CBDCs to influence bank run risks, with Fernández-Villaverde and colleagues observing that in times of banking crises, central banks may offer a more stable repository for deposits than commercial banks, potentially leading to a preemptive shift from bank deposits to CBDCs.[13]

Furthermore, the transition to CBDCs could introduce new dynamics in monetary policy transmission and financial stability. For instance, in times of economic uncertainty, individuals and businesses might prefer the safety of CBDCs, leading to rapid outflows from bank deposits to CBDCs. Such shifts could exacerbate liquidity pressures on banks, increasing the risk of bank runs and systemic financial crises. The Bank Policy Institute highlights the potential for a CBDC to destabilize banks' deposit bases, particularly in times of crisis, when the liquidity and safety of CBDCs might be more attractive than commercial bank deposits.

In sum, traditional banks view CBDCs like a vampire views a sunrise. Suddenly, their cozy world of hidden fees and 3-day transfer times is melting away faster than a snowman in Vegas.

To mitigate these risks and ensure a smooth transition to a CBDC-enabled financial system, policymakers and regulators will need to carefully design CBDCs with safeguards to protect against undue disintermediation of commercial banks and to maintain financial stability. Options such as limiting the amount of CBDC an individual or business can hold or designing CBDCs to complement rather than substitute bank deposits, could help alleviate some of the pressures on traditional banking systems. Additionally, fostering innovation in banking services and ensuring that banks can play a role in the

---

[13] Hemingway (2023), Chiu et al. (2022), Gross and Schiller (2021), Whited et al. (2023), and Chang et al. (2023) have all crafted theoretical frameworks to scrutinize the influence of CBDCs on banking and the extent of disintermediation they introduce. For instance, Chiu et al. (2022) discover that CBDCs that bear interest escalate competition, prompting banks to offer higher deposit rates, whereas a non-interest- bearing CBDC could enhance bank intermediation by pushing up deposit rates. Whited et al. (2023) present a model predicting that a non-interest-bearing CBDC significantly cuts into bank deposits. Di Maggio et al. (2024) is the first empirical study on CBDCs, which exploits transactional data from a pilot program in India to show that an increase in CBDC usage indeed leads to a reduction in bank deposits.

CBDC ecosystem, for instance, through the provision of digital wallet services, could help banks adapt to the new digital currency landscape.

Furthermore, one should think about these concerns as mainly motivated by what economists call a partial equilibrium approach: banks are likely to respond to the threat of losing depositors by increasing the interest rate offered on deposits. Then, an additional benefit of the introduction of CBDCs can be a better rate of return for savers in the economy. Central banks might also decide to implement a tiered remuneration system for the CBDC, where holdings of CBDC up to a certain threshold would earn a competitive interest rate, encouraging the use of the CBDC for daily transactions and as a means of payment. However, holdings of CBDC above this threshold would earn a significantly lower interest rate, discouraging individuals and businesses from converting all their bank deposits into CBDCs. A tiered remuneration system would incentivize individuals and businesses to continue to keep their savings and larger deposits with commercial banks, helping to preserve the deposit base and lending capacity of the banking sector.

Let's get our hands dirty with some basic CBDC code.

Code: Basic Transaction Mechanism

Language: Solidity

Level: Intermediate

The following is a simple Solidity example that illustrates a basic transaction mechanism, which could be adapted for use in a CBDC context:

```solidity
// Specify the version of Solidity
pragma solidity ^0.8.0;

contract CBDC {
    address public centralBank;
    mapping(address => uint256) public balances;
    uint256 public interestRate;  // e.g. a value of 5 represents a 5%
    annual interest rate
    mapping(address => uint256) public lastInterestClaimTime;

    constructor(uint256 _interestRate) {
        centralBank = msg.sender;
        interestRate = _interestRate;
    }

    function deposit(uint256 amount) public {
        require(msg.sender == centralBank, "Only the central bank
        can mint");
        balances[centralBank] += amount;
    }
```

```
function transfer(address to, uint256 amount) public {
    require(balances[msg.sender] >= amount, "Insufficient balance");
    applyInterest(msg.sender);
    applyInterest(to);
    balances[msg.sender] -= amount;
    balances[to] += amount;
}

function applyInterest(address account) internal {
    uint256 timeSinceLastClaim = block.timestamp -
lastInterestClaimTime[account];
    if (timeSinceLastClaim > 0) {
        uint256 newInterest = balances[account] * interestRate *
timeSinceLastClaim / (365 days) / 100;
        balances[account] += newInterest;
        lastInterestClaimTime[account] = block.timestamp;
    }
}

function claimInterest() public {
    applyInterest(msg.sender);
}
}
```

The above code is a simple example that establishes a central bank with the authority to mint new digital currency units and set an interest rate. The balance of every individual is stored in a mapping called *balances*. Individuals can transfer the currency themselves and receive interest on their balance during each transaction. The mint function allows the central bank, and only the central bank, to issue new currency units to a specified address. The *transfer* function enables peer-to-peer transactions between users. The *applyInterest* function computes the interest earned by an account since the last time they claimed interest. The *claimInterest* function allows an individual to claim interest in its own separate transaction. This example smart contract illustrates how a central bank could implement a CBDC with the functionality of calculating and applying interest payments. Since the CBDC is programmable, a central bank has the option to include additional functionality, improving the efficiency of payments, and facilitating compliance with regulations.

---

7. Concluding Remarks

The development of CBDCs is a response to the evolving needs of modern economies and the digitalization of financial systems. Whether through retail or wholesale applications, or via single-tier or two-tier frameworks, CBDCs offer the potential to enhance monetary policy implementation, increase financial inclusion, and improve the efficiency and security of payment systems. However, these benefits come with significant challenges, including technical hurdles, privacy concerns, and the need for robust regulatory frameworks. In addition, banks might suffer negative consequences due to the introduction of CBDCs, which might ultimately destabilize the financial system. As countries navigate these challenges, the choices they make regarding the structure and implementation of CBDCs will have lasting impacts on their economies and societies. Let me conclude with a summary of a report by the Bank of International Settlements (BIS), the so called central banks of central banks on CBDCs.

THE CENTRAL BANK OF CENTRAL BANKS (BIS) ON CBDCs

The BIS has recently published a report on the lessons learned about CBDCs, which highlights the following takeaways: Data from[14]

- **API Design and Benefits:** A well-designed API can facilitate retail payments in CBDC, allowing for interoperability with other payment systems and supporting a diverse range of use cases. It can be applied across central bank ledger types and third-party applications, enhancing compatibility in a multiledger technology environment.
- **Privacy and Security:** Balancing privacy with features like financial integrity and security is challenging, but emerging privacy-enhancing technologies, such as blind signatures, show promise. These technologies can enable the issuance of CBDCs without compromising the identity of the holder, potentially resisting quantum computer attacks while maintaining scalability.
- **Offline Payment Functionality:** Offering offline payments with CBDCs could significantly enhance digital payment instruments' utility, especially in areas with unreliable internet connectivity. However, implementing offline payments involves addressing complex technological, security, and operational considerations.
- **Public–Private Partnership Model:** The experiments support the promising CBDC model of a two-tier system involving public-private partnerships. This model emphasizes the fundamental importance of privacy and the challenge of ensuring cyber security.
- **Cross-Border CBDC Use:** Cross-border CBDC arrangements need to mitigate negative macroeconomic spillovers and financial stability risks. Designing CBDCs with features like restrictions on non-resident holdings and specific monitoring systems can help manage these risks.
- **Interoperability for Cross-Border Payments:** Ensuring interoperability between CBDC systems, either through compatibility, interlinking, or a common platform, is crucial for enhancing cross-border payments. This can help reduce costs, increase speed, and improve transparency and inclusiveness.

---

[14] The report is available here https://www.bis.org/publ/othp73.pdf.

- **Legal and Governance Frameworks:** Cross-border CBDC platforms must navigate complex legal and regulatory environments across jurisdictions. Establishing a robust legal basis and governance framework is essential for managing multiple legal frameworks and ensuring the rights and obligations of all parties are clearly defined.
- **Further Experimentation:** It is vital to continue experimenting and exploring additional business cases, transaction types, and interoperability with domestic payment systems. This includes introducing liquidity management tools and addressing legal and regulatory issues in a cross-border context.
- **Economic Implications:** Cross-border use of CBDCs involves careful consideration of potential impacts on monetary sovereignty, currency substitution, exchange rate volatility, and financial stability, particularly in emerging markets and developing economies. International cooperation is critical to addressing these challenges.
- **Flexibility in Design and Operation:** Experiments suggest that central banks have options in designing CBDC systems that accommodate different policies, legal, and regulatory frameworks. A modular approach to system design could provide the flexibility needed to adapt to evolving technical, business, and regulatory requirements.

These lessons highlight the complexities and trade-offs involved in designing and implementing CBDCs for domestic and cross-border use. They underscore the importance of careful policy consideration, technical innovation, and international cooperation in advancing the development of CBDCs.

End-of-Chapter Questions

Multiple-Choice Questions

1. **What catalyzed the global interest in developing CBDCs?**
   (A) The invention of Bitcoin
   (B) The announcement of Facebook's Libra project
   (C) The financial crisis of 2008
   (D) The creation of the European Union

2. **Which country accelerated its CBDC project in response to the Libra announcement?**
   (A) The United States
   (B) China
   (C) Sweden
   (D) The Bahamas

3. **What is a fundamental difference between CBDCs and cryptocurrencies like Bitcoin?**
   (A) Cryptocurrencies are digital forms of fiat money
   (B) CBDCs are issued and regulated by central banks
   (C) Cryptocurrencies offer higher privacy
   (D) CBDCs operate on a decentralized network

4. **Which of the following is NOT a goal of CBDCs?**
   (A) Ensuring financial stability
   (B) Promoting financial inclusion
   (C) Replacing physical cash entirely
   (D) Enhancing the efficiency of payments

5. **The Sand Dollar project is associated with which country?**
   (A) Sweden
   (B) China
   (C) The Bahamas
   (D) The European Union

6. **What unique feature do CBDCs potentially offer over traditional bank accounts?**
   (A) Interest on deposits
   (B) Cryptographic proofs of payment
   (C) Higher transaction fees
   (D) Anonymity

7. **Project Hamilton focused on exploring the technical feasibility of CBDC for which economy?**
   (A) Global
   (B) The European Union
   (C) China
   (D) The United States

8. **What was a key outcome of Project Hamilton?**
   (A) Development of a new cryptocurrency
   (B) Implementation of a single-tier system in the United States
   (C) Development of a high-performance transaction processing system for CBDCs
   (D) Launch of a CBDC in the United States
9. **Which CBDC model involves direct interaction between the central bank and the public?**
   (A) Two-tier system
   (B) Single-tier system
   (C) Wholesale CBDC
   (D) Retail CBDC
10. **Legal tender status of CBDCs means they are:**
   (A) Optional for settling debts
   (B) Not recognized by law for financial transactions
   (C) Recognized by law as acceptable for settling debts
   (D) Only usable for digital transactions

Open Questions

1. How might the introduction of a CBDC impact monetary policy tools and central banks' ability to implement them?
2. Discuss the implications of CBDCs on cross-border payments and international financial cooperation.
3. Analyze the potential risks and advantages of implementing a CBDC in a developing economy versus a developed economy.
4. Explain the difference between retail and wholesale CBDCs and their intended uses.
5. Discuss the significance of legal tender status for CBDCs and its implications for their acceptance in the economy.
6. Describe the potential challenges and benefits associated with the introduction of CBDCs into the financial system.

Coding Exercises

Exercise 1: Creating a CBDC with a Variable Interest Rate (Solidity)

Objective: Develop a Solidity smart contract for a CBDC that includes functionality to adjust the interest rate based on total supply, simulating a basic monetary policy tool.

Detailed Instructions:
1. Initialize Contract Variables:
- Define a **centralBank** address variable to represent the issuer of the CBDC.
- Create a mapping to store balances of CBDC holders.
- Implement a variable to store the current interest rate.

2. Issue CBDC:
- Write a function that allows the central bank to issue CBDCs to any address.
- Ensure that only the **centralBank** can call this function.

3. Transfer Functionality:
- Implement a transfer function that enables CBDC holders to send currency to others.
- Include checks to ensure the sender has enough balance.

4. Interest Rate Adjustment:
- Create a function to adjust the interest rate, modifiable only by the central bank.
- Simulate conditions for changing the interest rate, such as adjusting it based on the total CBDC supply.

Exercise 2: Privacy-Preserving CBDC Transactions (Solidity)

Objective: Implement a Solidity smart contract for CBDC transactions that enhances user privacy using zero-knowledge proofs (ZKP) or similar cryptographic techniques.

Detailed Instructions:
1. Smart Contract Setup:
- Create a basic structure for holding CBDC balances and transaction logs.

2. Implement Privacy Mechanism:
- Integrate a simplified version of a ZKP mechanism or hash-based method to obscure transaction details while ensuring they are valid.
- Provide functions for users to generate and verify transactions without revealing their balance or transaction amounts publicly.

3. Transaction Validation:
- Develop a function that validates transactions using the privacy mechanism, ensuring they are legitimate without disclosing sensitive information.

4. Testing and Analysis:
- Write test cases to demonstrate how privacy is maintained during transactions.
- Discuss potential challenges and limitations of implementing ZKP in CBDC systems.

Exercise 3: Implementing a Tiered Interest Rate System for CBDC (Solidity)

Objective: Create a Solidity smart contract that implements a tiered interest rate system for CBDC, encouraging spending over hoarding.

Design a smart contract named InterestCBDC.

Implement a function to adjust CBDC balances based on a tiered interest rate system (e.g. lower rates for higher balances).

Simulate changing interest rates based on macroeconomic indicators.

Setup and Initial Variables

1. **Initialize the Smart Contract:** Create a Solidity smart contract named **InterestCBDC**. Use pragma solidity ^0.8.0; or a more recent version to ensure compatibility with the latest Solidity features.
2. **Define State Variables:**
   - **centralBank:** A public address variable to represent the central bank's address.
   - **balances:** A mapping to track the CBDC balances of each address.
   - **tierRates:** An array of structs, where each struct contains the minimum balance threshold for that tier and the corresponding interest rate.

Function to Adjust Interest Rates Based on Tiers

1. **Implementing Tier Rates:**
   - Define a struct named **InterestTier** with two properties: **uint256 minBalance** and **uint256 interestRate**.
   - Initialize an array of **InterestTier** structs within the contract to define different tiers. For example, balances less than 1,000 units might receive a higher interest rate compared to balances greater than 10,000 units, encouraging users to spend or distribute their holdings rather than hoarding.
2. **Adjusting Balances:**
   - Create a function named **applyInterest** that loops through each account's balance, checks which tier it falls into based on its current balance, and applies the appropriate interest rate.
   - Ensure this function can only be called by the central bank to prevent unauthorized interest rate applications.

Dynamic Interest Rate Adjustments

1. **Macro Indicator Input:**
   - Add a function that allows the central bank to adjust the **tierRates** based on current macroeconomic indicators. This could be based on inflation rates, economic growth, or other relevant indicators.
   - This function should update the **tierRates** array to reflect the new interest rates applicable to each tier.
2. **Interest Application Schedule:**
   - Implement a mechanism to regularly apply interest to all accounts, possibly through a scheduled call to the **applyInterest** function. This could simulate a monthly or yearly interest application, mimicking real-world banking systems.

Chapter 6

Money Grows on Distributed Trees

The DeFi Forest of DAOs and DApps

Preface

Imagine the financial world as a vast, sprawling garden. Traditionally, this garden was meticulously curated by a select few gardeners (banks and financial institutions), who decided what would grow and where. Now, enter DeFi, a magical beanstalk sprouting in the midst of this well-ordered plot, reaching toward the sky with wild abandon, nurtured by the collective hands of internet denizens rather than the iron grip of the gardening elite. This isn't just any beanstalk; it's a vibrant ecosystem teeming with new forms of life (protocols, platforms, DAOs) that challenge the very nature of the financial flora below.

In this chapter, we'll skip down the yellow brick road of DeFi, past the singing flowers of Aave and Compound, where your digital coins can bloom into interest-bearing blossoms or be staked as seeds for future growth. It's a bit like lending money to a stranger on the internet, except here, smart contracts replace handshakes, and algorithms dictate the terms. But every enchanted garden has its peculiarities. Here, the flowers manage themselves through the mystical powers of smart contracts, and the bees (users)

DeFi beanstalk in the garden of finance

buzz from one bloom to another, cross-pollinating assets without the oversight of the head gardener.

But what's a revolution without its revolutionaries? Enter Decentralized Autonomous Organizations (DAOs), the poster children of DeFi's democratic ethos. DAOs are not just a new way to organize corporate structures but a radical experiment in collective decision-making and resource allocation. It's as if your local bank suddenly said, "You know what, let's let our customers decide how to run things." It sounds a bit chaotic, and sometimes it is, but it's also profoundly liberating.

Through it all, we're reminded that DeFi isn't just about creating a new financial system—it's about challenging our assumptions of what a financial system can and should be. It's about inclusivity, transparency, and empowering individuals.

Yet, for all its wonders, this garden is not without its thorns. The blossoms of DeFi can sometimes attract pests—smart contract bugs and parasitic attackers who drain the nectar without contributing to the ecosystem. Navigating this space requires a green thumb, a keen eye, and perhaps a good pair of gardening gloves.

Through this whimsical exploration, remember that DeFi isn't just about reshaping the garden of finance. It's about questioning why we garden in the first place and who gets to enjoy the fruits of our labor. It's a story of growth, risk, and the pursuit of a more colorful, inclusive, and fragrant financial world. Navigating this landscape requires a careful balance of innovation, security, and perhaps a healthy dose of skepticism.

So, welcome to the enchanted garden of DeFi. Mind the talking flowers, beware the thorns, and always keep an eye out for magic beans. Who knows? The next one you plant might just grow into a beanstalk that reaches the clouds.

1. Introduction

Decentralized Finance (DeFi) represents a revolutionary shift in the paradigm of financial services, offering a peer-to-peer (and peer-to-contract) alternative to the traditional, centralized financial systems. At its core, DeFi utilizes blockchain technology to enable financial applications and services that operate without intermediaries, thereby removing banks, brokers, and other go-betweens from the equation. This ecosystem thrives on core principles such as *openness*, *permissionless access*, *transparency*, and *interoperability*, which collectively aim to democratize finance, making it more accessible to a global audience.

DeFi encompasses a wide range of financial services, including lending and borrowing platforms like Aave and Compound, where users can lend their cryptocurrency to earn interest or borrow against their crypto assets in a decentralized manner. Another key application of DeFi is decentralized exchanges (DEXs) such as Uniswap and 1inch, which allow for the peer-to-peer trading of cryptocurrencies without the need for a central exchange. These platforms leverage liquidity pools rather than traditional market order books, facilitating seamless and efficient trading.

The innovation and flexibility offered by DeFi have the potential to redefine the financial landscape, challenging the traditional centralized financial institutions and systems by promising to unlock a plethora of opportunities, making financial services more accessible to people worldwide, irrespective of their geographic location or economic status.

2. Key Benefits of Making Finance Decentralized

Let's start by analyzing the key benefits. Then, we will provide a variety of examples to illustrate the differences between traditional markets and DeFi in practice, which are captured in **Figure 1**.

In traditional markets, accessing financial services often involves navigating a maze of paperwork, regulatory compliance, and gatekeeping institutions. The process can be especially daunting for the unbanked and underbanked populations, who find themselves sidelined due to lack of access or stringent requirements.[1] DeFi dismantles these barriers with its fundamental promise: "Got internet? Got a digital wallet? Congratulations, you're now financially savvy in the world of DeFi. Who needs a finance degree anyway?" This simplicity echoes the transformative leap from letter-based communication to emails, where the latter democratized access to global communication.

Creating a digital wallet in the DeFi space is as straightforward as setting up an email account, marking a stark departure from the extensive verification processes in traditional finance. This ease of access brings financial services to those previously excluded and encourages innovation. In this open ecosystem, anyone can develop and launch decentralized applications (dApps), similar to how the internet allowed for the creation

---

[1] According to a report from the World Bank in 2018, there are about 1.7 billion people with no bank access and about 1.1 of the 1.7 billion have access to a smartphone and an internet connection. View the report at https://www.worldbank.org/en/news/press-release/2018/04/19/financial-inclusion-on-the-rise-but-gaps-remain-global-findex-database-shows.

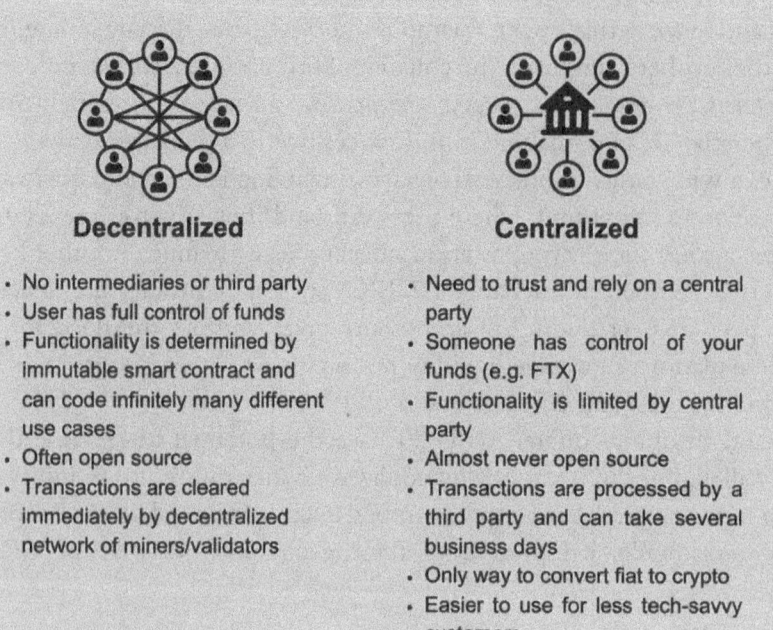

Decentralized

- No intermediaries or third party
- User has full control of funds
- Functionality is determined by immutable smart contract and can code infinitely many different use cases
- Often open source
- Transactions are cleared immediately by decentralized network of miners/validators

Centralized

- Need to trust and rely on a central party
- Someone has control of your funds (e.g. FTX)
- Functionality is limited by central party
- Almost never open source
- Transactions are processed by a third party and can take several business days
- Only way to convert fiat to crypto
- Easier to use for less tech-savvy customers

Figure 1   Decentralized and Centralized Finance Differences

and dissemination of countless digital platforms and services. Powered by blockchain technology and smart contracts, DeFi has unleashed a new era of **financial inclusivity** and innovation, allowing anyone with internet access to engage in a myriad of financial activities without the intermediaries that dominate traditional finance.

The impact of DeFi also extends deeply into regions where conventional banking services are scarce or non-existent. Here, DeFi is not just an alternative, it's often the only avenue for engaging with financial services. This democratization of finance mirrors the early days of mobile banking in parts of Africa, where technology leapfrogged traditional banking infrastructures, providing essential financial services to millions.

Moreover, DeFi returns control of financial assets to the individual allowing for self-custody. In traditional finance, your funds are often under the custody of institutions like banks, which act as intermediaries in every transaction. DeFi eliminates this reliance, using smart contracts to execute transactions directly between parties. This shift toward self-sovereignty in finance is akin to the rise of peer-to-peer file-sharing services, which disrupted traditional media distribution channels by allowing direct transfers between users.

In addition, DeFi's reliance on smart contracts for automation reduces human error and inefficiencies, a notable advancement over the often cumbersome and error-prone processes in traditional finance. Transactions in DeFi can be tracked on the blockchain with a level of **transparency** and security unmatched in conventional systems. This openness is revolutionary, akin to the transition from closed-source software to open-source projects that galvanized software development by allowing community scrutiny and contributions.

Despite these advancements, the DeFi ecosystem is not without its challenges. The accessibility of blockchain data, while a boon for transparency, might also present a steep learning curve for those unfamiliar with parsing complex information. Services have emerged to simplify this data, offering analytics that make understanding DeFi's complex transactions as user-friendly as checking a bank statement online. One of the most widely used platforms on Ethereum blockchain is Etherscan.

These transactions can be observed online on Etherscan or in trades conducted on DEXs. These transactions show us the tokens and the corresponding quantity being swapped and the exchanges. Each transaction includes the account hashes of the transaction. If the transaction is from or to a contract, it is also specified (**Figure 2**).

Each wallet address and a contract address have a dedicated page, which does look like a bank statement open to anyone (**Figure 3**).

In addition to that, each transaction can also be analyzed in detail. In **Figure 4**, one can view the block details (other transaction, block number, reward, size) and the gas information of the transaction, which is the ETH value of the resources that were consumed.

Services like blockchain explorers pull back the curtain on the technical details of blockchain transactions, allowing users to easily understand every minute detail of their

▸ **From** Uniswap V3: OHM-USDC 3 **To** 0x767C8bB1...9D43C5121 **For 1,048.177571683** ($13,584.38) ⓖ Olympus (OHM)

▸ **From** 0x2D722C96...2906CE9f8 **To** Uniswap V3: OHM-USDC 3 **For 13,317.497856** ($13,450.67) ⓢ USDC (USDC)

▸ **From** Uniswap V3: OHM 3 **To** 0x2D722C96...2906CE9f8 **For 5.792513049306042813** ($13,735.60) ⊝ Wrapped Ethe... (WETH)

▸ **From** 0x767C8bB1...9D43C5121 **To** Uniswap V3: OHM 3 **For 1,048.177571683** ($13,584.38) ⓖ Olympus (OHM)

Figure 2   Transactions on Etherscan

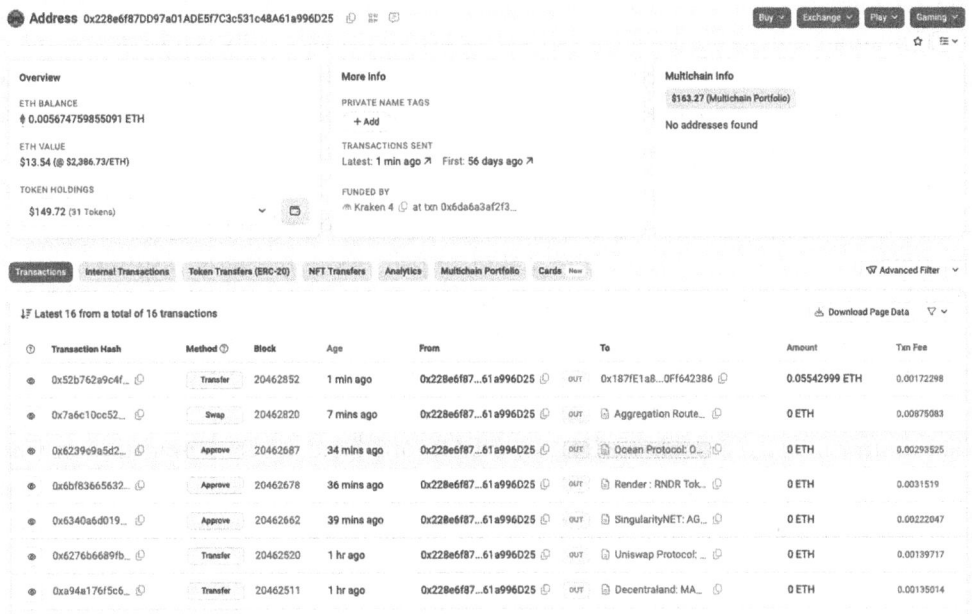

Figure 3   Wallet address history of transactions on Etherscan

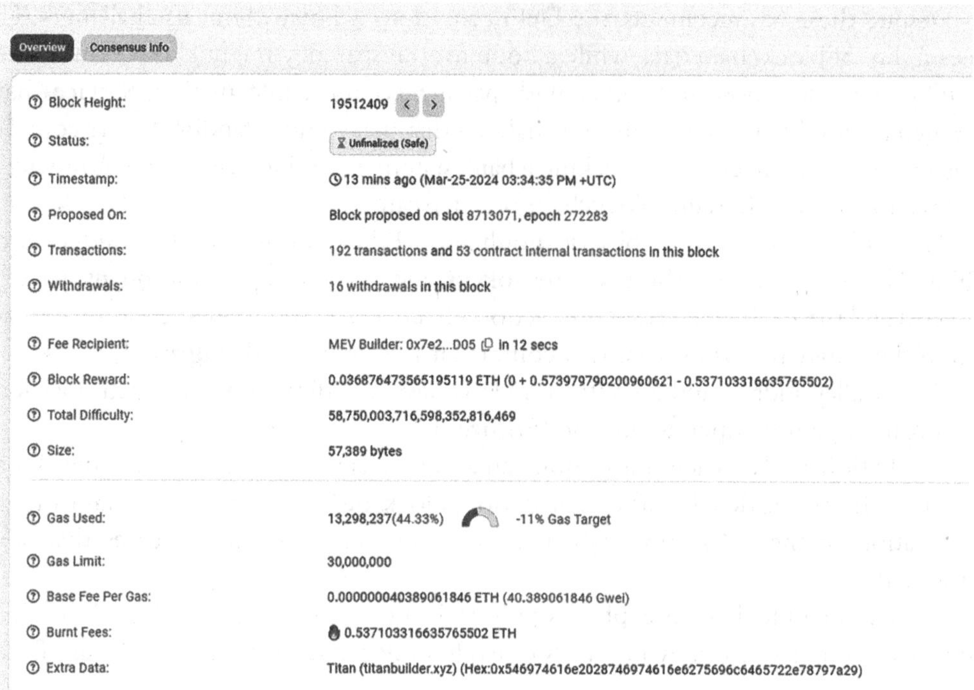

Figure 4 Transaction details on Etherscan

own transactions. The transparency principle of DeFi and blockchains means that these block explorers provide the details for all transactions, so anyone can view any transaction details at any time. We can even see the transactions included in the very first block! Despite the efforts, the information provided can be hard to follow, as it still uses some technical jargon.

In addition, in the traditional financial realm, if you accidentally send money to the wrong account, there's a procedure—albeit a painstakingly slow one. Now, enter the DeFi space. Here, intermediaries are as rare as a courteous internet troll. The whole system prides itself on cutting out the intermediaries, running on smart contracts that execute automatically. So, what happens if you, in a moment of distraction, send your precious digital assets to the wrong address? Well, prepare for a reality check.

In DeFi, there's no 1-800 number to dial in despair, no sympathetic customer service agent to hear your tale of woe. Your attempt to reverse a mistaken transfer would find as much success as shouting into the void. Why? Because transactions on the blockchain are immutable. Once done, they're etched in digital stone, unchangeable without the consensus of the network, which, spoiler alert, is not an easy feat.

This immutability is a double-edged sword. On one hand, it's the foundation of trust in the system, ensuring that transactions cannot be tampered with once they're confirmed.

On the other hand, it means that a slip of the finger could lead to a permanent financial facepalm. Mistakenly sent your crypto to the digital abyss? Congratulations, you've just made an irreversible donation to the unknown.

This lack of a fail-safe for user errors puts a spotlight on the importance of personal responsibility in DeFi. Every click, every transaction, is yours and yours alone to confirm. It's the financial equivalent of "measure twice, cut once." Except, in this case, it's more like "triple-check that address, because there's no going back."

In conclusion, while DeFi offers unparalleled freedom from traditional financial intermediaries, it also demands a high level of vigilance from its users. The lack of accountability mechanisms means that every transaction is final, pushing the ethos of personal responsibility to the forefront. It's an exciting, yet cautionary tale of finance's future, where the power is in your hands, but so is the responsibility.

Another important feature of Defi is its **interoperability**. At its core, it allows for various decentralized applications (dApps) to interact with one another seamlessly, akin to using Legos to construct an intricate structure. This flexibility and openness offer a stark contrast to the siloed nature of traditional financial systems, where operations between different institutions or services often involve complex and inefficient processes.

A tangible example of interoperability within DeFi is a user borrowing assets from a lending dApp, such as Aave, to then trade on a decentralized exchange (DEX) like Uniswap, and finally staking the acquired tokens on a yield farming platform like Yearn Finance—all in a single, streamlined transaction. Don't worry, we are going to see all of these in the next chapters. This sequence of actions, which taps into the unique offerings of three distinct platforms, exemplifies the fluidity and efficiency that interoperability brings to the DeFi ecosystem.

In traditional markets, attempting a similar operation would involve multiple steps: obtaining a loan from a bank, executing trades through a brokerage, and seeking out investment opportunities, each requiring separate applications, account setups, and possibly days for transaction settlements. DeFi's interoperability eliminates these hurdles, enabling users to optimize their financial strategies in real-time, without the need for intermediaries.

Moreover, the **open-source** nature of DeFi projects encourages innovation and collaboration, allowing developers to build upon existing dApps to enhance user experience or create entirely new services. This ethos of openness and cooperation is reminiscent of the early internet's development, where shared protocols and open standards laid the foundation for the web's exponential growth.

In conclusion, this ecosystem, built on the principles of openness, permissionless access, and transparency, democratizes finance and paves the way for a future where financial services are more inclusive, efficient, and interconnected.

IN SUM, THESE ARE THE KEY POINTS HIGHLIGHTING THE TRANSFORMATIVE NATURE OF DeFi:

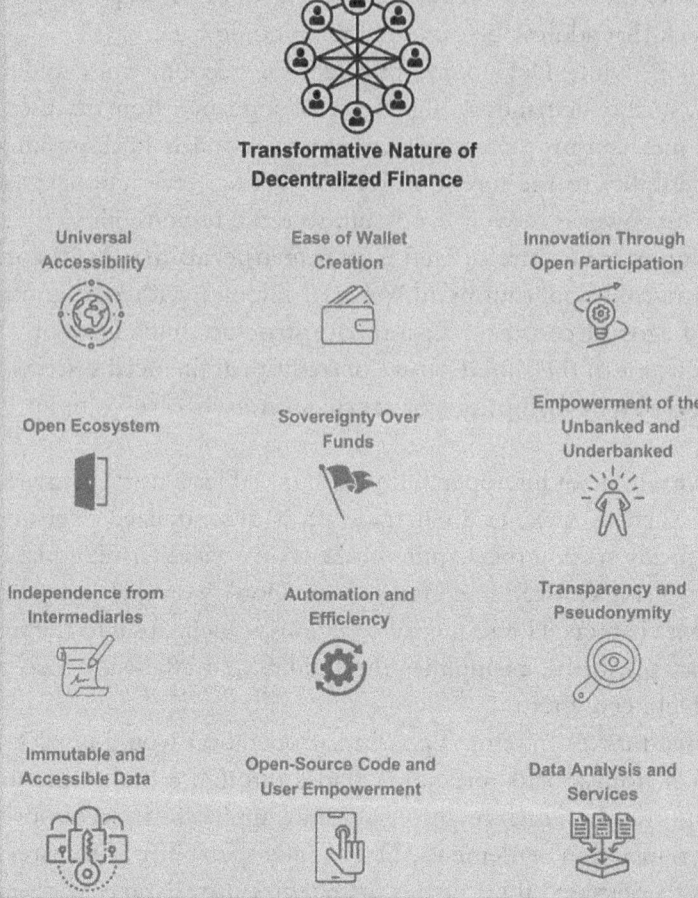

Figure 5 Key Points of the Transformative Nature of DeFi

- **Universal Accessibility:** DeFi applications are open to anyone with internet access. By simply creating a digital wallet, users worldwide can engage with DeFi platforms without the need for traditional bank accounts or undergoing exhaustive sign-up processes. This universality breaks down barriers to financial inclusion, particularly benefiting those who are unbanked, underbanked, or in regions where financial services are scarce or heavily regulated.
- **Ease of Wallet Creation:** Setting up a digital wallet is straightforward and free from the cumbersome paperwork and verification processes required by

traditional financial institutions. This ease of setup ensures that anyone can participate in the DeFi ecosystem quickly and without entry barriers.

- **Innovation Through Open Participation:** DeFi stands out for its open-source nature, allowing anyone to develop and deploy smart contracts. This openness encourages innovation and diversity in decentralized applications (dApps), enabling developers to address a wide array of financial needs and opportunities.
- **Empowerment of the Unbanked and Underbanked:** For individuals without access to conventional banking services, DeFi provides an invaluable platform for engaging in financial activities such as saving, lending, borrowing, and trading. This empowerment fosters financial inclusion at a global scale.
- **Sovereignty Over Funds:** In DeFi, users maintain full control over their funds without relying on intermediaries for custody. This autonomy allows for the immediate movement of assets, enhancing the efficiency and security of financial operations.
- **Open Ecosystem:** The DeFi ecosystem supports unrestricted interaction with various dApps for diverse purposes. This flexibility fosters a vibrant and dynamic financial landscape.
- **Independence from Intermediaries:** DeFi eliminates the need to trust third-party institutions with your assets. The reliance on smart contracts ensures that transactions are executed as programmed, minimizing the risk of fraud and reducing dependency on traditional financial intermediaries.
- **Automation and Efficiency:** Smart contracts automate financial agreements, reducing the potential for human error and inefficiencies inherent in manual processes. This automation streamlines transactions and enhances the reliability of financial operations.
- **Transparency and Pseudonymity:** All transactions within the DeFi space are recorded on the blockchain and can be pseudonymously tracked. This transparency ensures accountability while protecting individual privacy.
- **Open-Source Code and User Empowerment:** The open-source nature of DeFi applications allows users to audit the code themselves, identifying potential bugs and vulnerabilities. This collective scrutiny contributes to the security and reliability of DeFi platforms.
- **Immutable and Accessible Data:** Blockchain technology ensures that data is immutable and freely accessible. Users can analyze transaction histories, wallet balances, and other activities, fostering transparency and trust in the ecosystem.
- **Data Analysis and Services:** While blockchain data is publicly accessible, parsing and understanding this information can be challenging. Several services simplify the retrieval and analysis of blockchain data, enhancing the user experience, e.g. DefiLama.

3. Overview of DeFi Protocols

The landscape of Decentralized Finance (DeFi) is vast and varied, offering a range of services that challenge the traditional financial system's status quo. The current chapter will focus on DAOs and lending and borrowing protocols. We will then devote the next four chapters to decentralized exchanges, yield farming, tokenization, and NFTs.

Below is a brief overview of some pivotal types of DeFi protocols that are reshaping the world of finance, which will be presented in detail.

LENDING AND BORROWING PROTOCOLS

Examples: Compound, Aave

These protocols utilize smart contracts to automate the process of lending and borrowing digital assets. Interest rates are dynamically adjusted based on supply (deposits) and demand (loans), enabling a decentralized credit market. Users can earn interest on their deposits or take out loans without going through a traditional bank, all governed by transparent and immutable code.

DECENTRALIZED EXCHANGES (DEXs) AND AUTOMATED MARKET MAKERS (AMMs)

Examples: Uniswap, Sushiswap

AMMs and DEXs represent a revolutionary approach to trading, where trades are matched peer-to-peer (or, more precisely, peer-to-contract as we will see in the next chapter) without the need of a centralized party taking custody of funds. AMMs are an innovation that eliminates the need for order books used in traditional exchanges. Users provide liquidity by depositing tokens into pools, and these pools automatically set market prices based on a mathematical formula. This model facilitates trading without intermediaries, offering greater inclusivity and accessibility to financial markets.

ASSET TOKENIZATION AND SYNTHETIC ASSETS

Example: Synthetix

Asset tokenization protocols like Synthetix allow for the creation of digital representations of real-world assets, such as currencies, commodities, or even real estate, on the blockchain. This enables users to trade and invest in these assets without owning the physical asset, opening up new markets and opportunities. Synthetic assets, a subset of tokenized assets, mimic the value of these real-world assets, providing exposure to their price movements without direct ownership.

AND MORE. . .

The flexibility and programmability of smart contracts mean the potential applications of DeFi are nearly limitless. From yield farming and insurance to DAOs (Decentralized Autonomous Organizations) and prediction markets, innovative developers continuously expand the DeFi ecosystem, creating novel financial products and services that are more

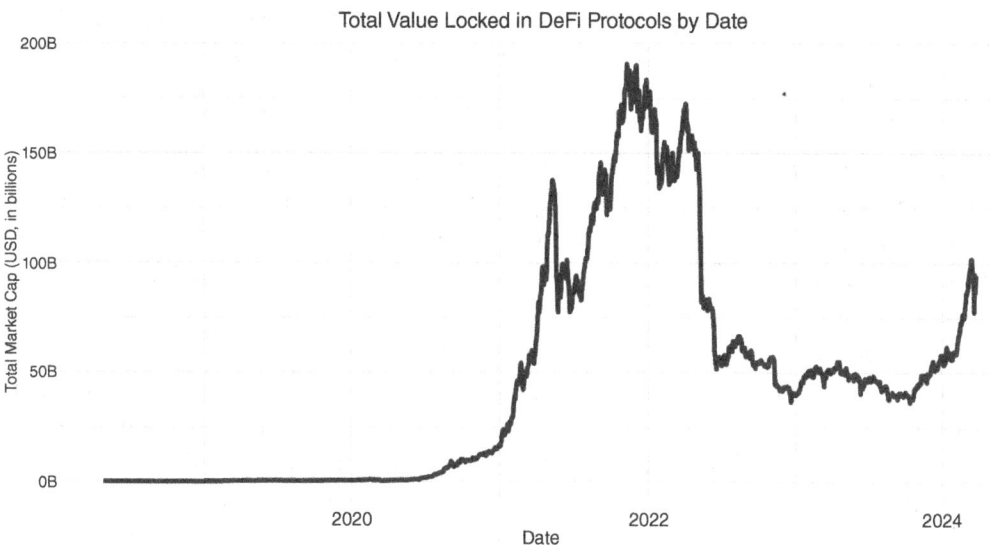

Figure 6 Total value locked in DeFi

accessible, efficient, and transparent. **Figure 6** shows the total value locked, a measure of how big the market is, for DeFi is at $95.1 billion as of March 2024, after reaching its peak during the 2021 bull run at almost $200 billion.

4. Decentralized Autonomous Organizations (DAOs)

Before diving into the intricacies of financial applications, let's delve into the world of DAOs. These decentralized autonomous organizations stand at the heart of the democratization ethos that fuels the DeFi movement, embodying the revolutionary shift toward a more open and equitable financial ecosystem. Unlike traditional organizations, which are hierarchical and governed by boards of directors and regulatory bodies, DAOs operate on a flat, democratic model. They are governed by smart contracts on blockchain platforms, which enforce rules, execute decisions, and manage resources without the need for central authority. This means that DAOs are not only transparent and immutable but also inclusive, enabling stakeholders to directly participate in decision-making processes.

Ethereum creator Vitalik Buterin described DAOs in a 2014 Ethereum blog as:

"The idea of a decentralized organization takes the same concept of an organization, and decentralizes it. Instead of a hierarchical structure managed by a set of humans interacting in person and controlling property via the legal system, a decentralized organization involves a set of humans interacting with each other according to a protocol specified in code, and enforced on the blockchain. [. . .] The ideal of a decentralized autonomous organization is

easy to describe: it is an entity that lives on the internet and exists autonomously, but also heavily relies on hiring individuals to perform certain tasks that the automaton itself cannot do."   •

From managing DeFi protocols and treasury funds to curating digital art collections and funding public goods, DAOs are being employed in increasingly creative and impactful ways. The flexibility and democratic nature of DAOs make them a potent tool for organizing around shared goals and interests, transcending geographical and cultural barriers.

The introduction of DAOs into the DeFi landscape has profound implications. First, it democratizes finance, allowing individuals to have a say in the operations and governance of financial protocols and projects. This is a stark contrast to TradFi, where decisions are often made behind closed doors. Secondly, DAOs facilitate a level of automation and security that was not previously possible. Through smart contracts, operations are executed precisely as coded, reducing the risk of fraud and eliminating intermediaries. Lastly, DAOs embody the spirit of innovation inherent in DeFi, pushing the boundaries of what is possible in financial services.

This section aims to explore the intricacies of DAOs, setting the stage for a comprehensive examination of DeFi's transformative power.

Blockchain developers and dapp creators have experimented with various organizational forms to support their projects' growth and governance. Some, like the Ethereum Foundation, chose to structure themselves as non-profit foundations, providing stewardship for open-source projects and fostering ecosystems without a central authority. The Ethereum Foundation, for instance, plays a critical role in supporting the Ethereum blockchain, funding research, development, and community engagement activities.

However, a novel approach came to the fore with the advent of DAOs. Through governance tokens, participants can propose, vote on, and implement changes within the DAO, from protocol upgrades to funding decisions. The underlying principle is that end-users should steer the direction of a protocol, as their interests are intrinsically aligned with the protocol's success.

Yet, the blockchain world is nothing if not diverse. Some projects have combined several governance models to leverage their unique strengths. Uniswap, a leading decentralized exchange, provides a compelling case study. Governed by the Uniswap DAO, decisions about protocol changes and treasury allocations are made through community voting, embodying the decentralized ethos. However, Uniswap's ecosystem also includes Uniswap Labs, an incorporated startup that focuses on developing the interface and supporting tools for the Uniswap protocol, alongside other public contributors. This hybrid approach ensures the Uniswap ecosystem benefits from both decentralized governance and focused development efforts.

As DAOs continue to evolve, they challenge us to rethink the essence of organization, ownership, and community. By distributing power among their members and automating governance through smart contracts, DAOs are paving the way for a more inclusive, participatory, and transparent model of collective action. Whether managing billions in assets or fostering niche communities, DAOs stand as a testament to the transformative potential of blockchain technology to reshape societal structures.

In essence, DAOs are not just a technological innovation; they are a cultural and philosophical exploration into the very nature of collaboration and governance in the digital age. As this exploration continues, the blockchain space remains a fascinating frontier of human coordination and creativity.

4.1 A Little Bit of History: The DAO

One of the most notable, and arguably the most pivotal, instances in the history of DAOs is the story of The DAO, launched in 2016. This project wasn't just another venture in the blockchain space; it was a grand experiment in decentralized governance and collective investment that captured the imagination of the crypto world.

Roughly a year after Ethereum itself went live, The DAO emerged as the first real attempt to utilize the blockchain's capabilities for decentralized crowdfunding. The vision was to create a venture capital fund without the traditional venture capital, entirely run and managed by its investors. Using smart contracts, The DAO created a structure where ownership and voting rights were distributed among users who invested Ethereum (ETH) into the project. This was a groundbreaking concept at the time, leveraging the power of smart contracts to democratize investment decisions and project funding.

The DAO's initial fundraising was nothing short of phenomenal. It managed to raise over $150 million worth of ETH, which amounted to approximately 12 million ETH at the time. This massive influx of funds was indicative of the community's belief in The DAO's vision and the potential of decentralized investment platforms. Investors, now token holders, were given the power to propose and vote on potential investment projects, embodying the principles of decentralized governance and community-driven decision-making.

However, The DAO's ambitious journey encountered a significant setback. A vulnerability in its smart contract code was exploited, leading to the loss of nearly a third of its funds. This incident not only highlighted the risks associated with smart contract-based systems but also sparked a major controversy within the Ethereum community. The debate centered around the principles of immutability and intervention, eventually leading to a hard fork of the Ethereum blockchain to recover the lost funds. This fork resulted in two separate chains: Ethereum (ETH) and Ethereum Classic (ETC).

Despite its failure, The DAO's impact on the Ethereum ecosystem and the broader blockchain community has been profound. It served as a critical learning experience, underscoring the importance of security in smart contract design and the complexities of decentralized governance. The DAO's ambitious attempt at creating a decentralized investment platform paved the way for future innovations in the space, inspiring a new generation of DAOs that have since iterated on its foundational ideas while incorporating robust security measures and more refined governance mechanisms.

In reflection, The DAO represents both the potential and the pitfalls of pioneering decentralized systems. It stands as a testament to the community's resilience and commitment to exploring new paradigms of collective organization and investment.

CONSTITUTIONDAO   ConstitutionDAO represents another fascinating chapter in the evolution of Decentralized Autonomous Organizations (DAOs), demonstrating the power of collective action through blockchain technology for a unique and ambitious purpose. In 2021, a diverse group of individuals, united by a novel idea, set out to do something unprecedented: purchase one of the rare remaining copies of the U.S. Constitution.

The initiative was born from a daring vision: to use the power of decentralized finance to acquire a historical artifact of profound significance. The DAO's creators believed that by pooling resources from individuals around the world, they could democratize ownership of a piece of American history, ensuring that it belonged to the people, in the spirit of the constitution itself, rather than to a billionaire hedge fund manager.

To achieve this goal, ConstitutionDAO launched a crowdfunding campaign, leveraging its token, PEOPLE, as the medium for raising funds. The campaign quickly captured the imagination of thousands, raising approximately $47 million. This remarkable achievement underscored the potential of DAOs to mobilize resources for collective goals on a scale and speed that traditional fundraising methods could scarcely match.

The climax of ConstitutionDAO's effort came at the auction, where the collective bid to win one of the remaining 13 copies of the U.S. Constitution. Despite the enormous sum raised and the widespread support from the community, ConstitutionDAO was outbid by a mere $200,000 . . . a bid submitted by Ken Griffin . . . a billionaire hedge fund manager. This outcome was a bittersweet moment for the DAO and its supporters, showcasing both the potential and the limitations of such decentralized endeavors.

In the wake of the auction, ConstitutionDAO faced the challenge of addressing the contributions of thousands of supporters who had rallied to its cause. Demonstrating transparency and integrity, the team offered two options to its investors: they could either claim their PEOPLE tokens, retaining a stake in the DAO's future endeavors, or opt to burn them in exchange for the value of their original deposit. This approach allowed participants to decide their level of continued engagement with the DAO, reflecting the principles of autonomy and choice that underpin the DAO concept.

Though ConstitutionDAO did not achieve its immediate goal of purchasing the constitution, its story remains a powerful example of what decentralized collective action can aspire to achieve. It highlighted the strengths of DAOs in quickly mobilizing large sums of money and generating widespread engagement around a shared objective. At the same time, it revealed challenges such as navigating the competitive dynamics of auctions and managing the logistics of decentralized governance on a large scale.

4.2 How Does a DAO Work?

From the previous examples, it should be clear that participating in a DAO offers a novel and democratic way to engage in collective decision-making processes. So, let's explore how this works, using a hypothetical DAO, "EcoChain DAO," dedicated to funding renewable energy projects, as our example. This step-by-step guide will hopefully make the process more understandable, highlighting the intricacies of participating in a DAO.

Eligibility   In EcoChain DAO, like many DAOs, the ability to submit proposals requires holding a certain amount of the DAO's governance tokens, "ECO tokens." This requirement ensures that those proposing decisions have a stake in the outcomes, aligning interests toward the DAO's success. For instance, to propose a new project funding, a member might need to hold at least 1,000 ECO tokens.

Drafting Proposals   A member of EcoChain DAO, Alex, believes in a new solar farm initiative and decides to draft a proposal. Alex's proposal includes detailed plans, expected environmental impact, and a budget request. It follows EcoChain's proposal template, outlining clear objectives to ensure it meets the DAO's guidelines for consideration. That's not very different from what a business plan would look like.

Submission Process   Alex submits the proposal through EcoChain's platform, staking 100 ECO tokens as a deposit. This deposit is a measure to prevent spam and is returned to Alex after the voting concludes, provided the proposal meets the community's engagement criteria.

Community Review   Once submitted, Alex's proposal enters a review period where all EcoChain DAO members can access it. This phase is crucial for gathering feedback, sparking discussions on the DAO's forums. Alex can then make any necessary revisions to the proposal based on community input.

Documentation   The proposal, along with all supporting documents and revisions, is documented on the Ethereum blockchain. Remember that blocks can also be used to communicate. This ensures transparency and creates an immutable record of the proposal, accessible for historical reference and future learning.

Voting Rights   In EcoChain DAO, as in most DAOs, voting power is proportional to the number of ECO tokens held. Sarah, a member with 5,000 ECO tokens, has more influence over the decision-making process than a member with 1,000 tokens. This system ensures that the most invested members have a significant say in the DAO's direction. Token holders can also delegate their votes to another user who might share the same views. For example, Charlie only holds 100 tokens and would like to participate but is unsure of the governance procedure. An option available to all token holders is to delegate votes to another voter—Charlie could delegate his 100 votes to Sarah without having to lose custody of his tokens if he believes that Sarah will represent his ideas or will make sound decisions that benefit the protocol. Delegating allows token holders to contribute to the governance process without having to be a full contributor on forums and voting systems.

Voting Process   When the voting period opens, members like Sarah cast their votes on Alex's proposal via the DAO's platform. Their votes are securely recorded through smart contracts on the Ethereum blockchain, ensuring both accuracy and transparency in the process.

Types of Voting Systems   EcoChain DAO uses quadratic voting, a system designed to prevent power centralization.[2] This means Sarah's influence, while substantial, doesn't overshadow the collective decision. The system requires more consensus for a proposal to pass, aiming to reflect the broader community's interest.

Execution of Decisions   Alex's proposal, having achieved the necessary consensus, is automatically enacted by the DAO's smart contracts. Funds are allocated from EcoChain's treasury to the solar farm project, demonstrating how approved decisions are implemented efficiently and in accordance with the community's will.

Transparency and Record-Keeping   The entire voting process, from submission to execution, is recorded on the blockchain. This ensures transparency and accountability and allows any member to audit the process, outcomes, and the DAO's adherence to its governance protocols.

Through this example, we can see how DAOs like EcoChain facilitate a transparent, democratic, and efficient mechanism for collective decision-making. By leveraging blockchain technology and smart contracts, DAOs empower individuals to contribute to shared goals and initiatives, marking a significant evolution in how we think about organizational governance and community participation. The vision is that the best ideas might come from everywhere, but especially from users.

Regulation   It is worth mentioning that DAOs also face regulatory challenges. At the crossroads where DAOs meet the keen eye of regulatory bodies, particularly the U.S. Securities and Exchange Commission (SEC), we uncover a web of intricacies and hurdles that epitomize the growing pains of the DeFi universe. One notable flashpoint in this ongoing dialogue was the SEC's 2017 report on "The DAO," which cast a spotlight

---

[2] Quadratic voting is a mechanism used by many decentralized autonomous organizations to create a more equitable and representative decision-making process. Unlike traditional voting, where each person has one vote per issue, quadratic voting allows participants to allocate multiple votes to express the intensity of their preferences, with the cost of additional votes increasing quadratically. This system helps capture the strength of individual preferences and prevents the tyranny of the majority by giving minority groups with strong opinions proportionate influence. Participants are given a set number of voting credits, and casting multiple votes for a single option becomes increasingly costly, encouraging a more balanced distribution of votes. This method ensures that decisions reflect the collective will and diverse preferences of the community, fostering fairer and more nuanced outcomes. See https://vitalik.ca/general/2019/12/07/quadratic.html for more details.

on the regulatory implications of DAOs by suggesting that their issued tokens might be securities, thereby bringing them within the ambit of federal securities laws. This assertion emphasized that blockchain technology-based securities must be registered with the SEC unless a valid exemption applies, setting a precedent for the regulatory scrutiny of DAOs and their token offerings. This is something we will explore in detail in Chapter 11.

The SEC has continued to express concerns over the lack of transparency and potential for investor manipulation within DeFi and DAOs. This stance is reflected in their recent enforcement actions and statements, highlighting the regulatory hurdles that these organizations must navigate. For instance, the SEC's settlement with BarnBridge, a DeFi platform, for failing to register its offering and misleading investors, serves as a cautionary tale for DAOs operating within the securities domain. This enforcement action, along with others, signals the SEC's commitment to applying existing securities laws to the DeFi space, emphasizing the need for compliance and transparency.

Furthermore, the SEC's recent action against CryptoFed for attempting to register its tokens while claiming they were not securities illustrates the complexity of navigating the regulatory framework for DAOs. This case highlights the challenges DAOs face in balancing regulatory compliance with their innovative models.[3]

However, it is not just a matter of securities. The Commodity Futures Trading Commission (CFTC) employed a novel approach to serve process on the Ooki DAO and its members. This case highlighted significant and novel issues regarding service and liability in the context of decentralized organizations. The CFTC pursued enforcement actions against bZeroX, its founders, and the Ooki DAO, alleging violations related to operating without proper registration and failing to adopt a customer identification program, among other charges. Interestingly, the order found that the founders and individual members of the Ooki DAO could be personally liable as members of what was deemed an unincorporated association. This determination rested on criteria such as being a voluntary group without a charter, formed by mutual consent for promoting a common objective, and organized for profit, which could, theoretically, apply broadly to many DAOs.

One of the most notable aspects of the CFTC's approach was its method of serving process on the DAO and its members. The CFTC claimed to have served the Ooki DAO

---

[3] CryptoFed was a project that aimed to operate as a decentralized autonomous organization (DAO) and issued its own tokens. The SEC took action against CryptoFed for several reasons, primarily focusing on the issuance of tokens that the SEC considered to be unregistered securities. The SEC's main contention was that CryptoFed had failed to register its tokens as securities or qualify for an exemption from registration. The regulatory body argued that the tokens issued by CryptoFed were offered and sold to the public, which necessitated registration under U.S. federal securities laws. The lack of registration meant that investors were not provided with the information typically required for securities offerings, information that's considered crucial for making informed investment decisions. The SEC's action against CryptoFed underscores the agency's stance on digital assets and DAOs, particularly highlighting the importance of complying with existing securities laws. It serves as a cautionary tale for other DAOs and crypto projects about the importance of understanding and adhering to regulatory requirements, especially when issuing tokens that could be considered securities by regulatory authorities.

and its members by submitting the complaint and other documentation through the DAO's Help Chat Box and providing notice through the DAO's online forum. This method was approved by the court, setting a precedent for how decentralized organizations and their participants can be served legal notices, especially when members are anonymous or pseudonymous and spread across the globe.

The actions and methodologies employed in the Ooki DAO case represent a pivotal moment in the legal treatment of DAOs and provide a crucial reference point for understanding the regulatory landscape facing decentralized organizations, especially concerning service of process and personal liability of DAO members.[4]

RECENT DAOs DEVELOPMENTS

Recent advancements in DAO models have showcased the versatility and broad applicability of decentralized governance across various sectors. Here are some examples of recent DAO models that have been adopted, each serving unique purposes and communities:

- **Protocol DAOs:** These DAOs focus on governing decentralized protocols, such as decentralized exchanges (DEXs) and lending platforms. A prominent example is **MakerDAO**, which governs the DAI stablecoin, allowing MKR token holders to vote on key parameters like collateral types and stability fees. Another example is **ENS DAO**, which oversees the Ethereum Naming Service, enabling decentralized domain name management.
- **Investment DAOs:** Investment DAOs pool resources to fund early-stage startups or other investment opportunities. **Orange DAO** is an example, consisting of over 1300 members collaborating to accelerate web3 development. **The LAO** operates as a venture capital fund on the Ethereum blockchain, funding new projects with a collective approach.
- **Service DAOs:** These DAOs offer services akin to traditional firms but operate on decentralized principles. **IndieDAO** provides design and development services, acting as a decentralized collective of freelancers. **SuperteamDAO** supports Solana-based projects with a range of services from design to development, leveraging the collective expertise of its members.
- **Media DAOs:** Media DAOs aim to democratize content creation and distribution, reducing censorship and advertiser influence. **BanklessDAO** is focused on promoting the adoption of cryptocurrencies and DeFi through education and media. **RugDAO** governs RugRadio, a platform for creators to own and monetize their content directly.

---

[4] See Skadden's Insight on the CFTC's Novel Theory of Liability and Service.

- **Social DAOs:** These DAOs serve as virtual communities for people with shared interests. **Friends with Benefits (FWB)** is a platform uniting creators and thinkers in web3, offering a space for collaboration and innovation. **DeveloperDAO** aims to support web3 developers by providing resources, education, and community engagement.

Each of these DAO models represents a different approach to utilizing blockchain technology for collective governance and decision-making. By leveraging the unique advantages of DAOs, such as transparency, inclusivity, and decentralization, these organizations are exploring new frontiers of collaboration and community-driven initiatives.

5. Traditional Finance vs. DeFi Lending

As we pivot from the groundbreaking realm of DAOs, with their approach to governance and decentralized decision-making, we transition into another vital cornerstone of the DeFi ecosystem: borrowing and lending protocols. While DAOs reconfigure the very fabric of organizational structure and collective action, borrowing and lending protocols tackle the financial services industry head-on. These protocols dismantle traditional barriers to access, democratizing the ability to lend and borrow assets through the power of smart contracts. Here, participants can engage directly with each other, bypassing traditional financial intermediaries and unlocking new possibilities for yield generation and financial management. As we delve into the mechanics, benefits, and challenges of these protocols, we continue our exploration of how DeFi is reshaping the financial world, offering unprecedented access and opportunities to users across the globe.

Let's delve deeper into how these protocols address the shortcomings of traditional finance and offer enhanced benefits to users, exemplifying with real-world DeFi platforms like Aave and Compound.

In the conventional banking system, obtaining a loan or earning interest on deposits can be cumbersome. Applicants undergo rigorous credit checks, provide substantial collateral, and navigate a sea of paperwork—processes that are time-consuming and geographically and economically limiting. Centralized financial institutions, acting as intermediaries, introduce additional layers of complexity, resulting in slower transactions, higher fees for borrowers, and reduced yields for lenders.

Think about what the challenge is in DeFi: how does lending occur if credit risk cannot be assessed? In addition, the decision to lend and at which rate, as well as the repayment of the loan, needs to be automated.

DeFi lending protocols like Aave and Compound streamline the traditional processes through blockchain technology. These platforms offer:

- **Permissionless Access:** Unlike traditional banks that require proof of identity and credit history, DeFi platforms are open to anyone with an internet connection. For example, a user in Kenya with access to Ethereum can lend or borrow assets on Aave without undergoing a credit check, democratizing access to financial services.
- **Efficiency and Speed:** Transactions on DeFi platforms are executed almost instantaneously, thanks to smart contracts that automate the loan origination, servicing, and enforcement of terms. On Compound, for instance, users can lend their Ethereum and start earning interest within minutes, a stark contrast to the days or weeks required for traditional loans to process.
- **Transparency:** Every transaction and smart contract is visible and verifiable on the blockchain, providing unparalleled transparency. Users can audit Aave's or Compound's smart contracts to understand precisely how interest rates are calculated and how funds are allocated.
- **Improved Rates:** With no intermediaries and reduced overhead costs, DeFi platforms often offer more attractive interest rates for both lenders and borrowers. Borrowers can access lower rates than traditional loans, while lenders receive higher yields on their deposits.
- **Collateralization and Liquidation:** DeFi loans typically require over-collateralization to mitigate default risk. If a borrower's collateral value falls below a certain threshold, platforms like Aave automatically liquidate the collateral to repay the lenders, ensuring lenders' funds are protected.
- **Interoperability:** Users can seamlessly move assets across different DeFi platforms to maximize yields. For example, a user might borrow DAI on Aave, trade it for another asset on Uniswap, and then stake the acquired asset on a third platform like Yearn. finance for additional earnings.
- **Programmability:** DeFi protocols allow for the creation of customized financial products. Users can engage in complex strategies, such as using borrowed funds to leverage positions or providing liquidity to earn yield, options that are programmable and tailored to individual needs.

5.1 Real Examples and Impacts

Consider the scenario of Alex, a cryptocurrency enthusiast. Alex decides to lend 10 ETH through Aave to earn interest. Simultaneously, Jordan, a trader looking to leverage a market opportunity, borrows this ETH against their stablecoin holdings. The process is quick, transparent, and does not require a traditional credit assessment, enabling Jordan to capitalize on the trading opportunity and Alex to earn passive income on their ETH holdings.

In another example, Mia, a liquidity provider, uses Compound to borrow assets to supply liquidity to a decentralized exchange (DEX) like Uniswap. Mia's assets are interoperable across platforms, allowing her to maximize her yield by engaging in liquidity mining while maintaining her borrowing position on Compound. Traders like Jordan can then trade directly with Uniswap to take advantage of market opportunities without needing to create an account, undergo KYC, and deposit funds in a centralized exchange like Coinbase.

These platforms created a system where lenders (or depositors) offer their assets to earn interest, while borrowers access these assets by placing their own as collateral. The operation hinges on smart contracts, which meticulously enforce loan terms, manage interest distribution, and guarantee the security of deposited funds through a process known as **over-collateralization**. Let's look at the mechanics of interest rate determination, utilization rates, and their implications for both borrowers and lenders.

Over-Collateralization and Smart Contracts   In DeFi platforms like Aave or Compound, over-collateralization is essential to safeguard lenders' assets. Borrowers must deposit assets of higher value than the amount they wish to borrow. This extra collateral acts as a buffer against market volatility, ensuring that lenders can be repaid even if asset prices drop. You might wonder, *why would someone choose to deposit more collateral on platforms like Compound than they are able to borrow? Why not simply sell the collateral to raise funds directly?* This concept mirrors the traditional mortgage process, where banks typically loan a fraction (e.g. 80%) of the collateral's value. Many holders possess tokens they're reluctant to sell, perhaps anticipating future appreciation. Yet, immediate financial needs persist, such as covering daily expenses or settling bills. In such scenarios, utilizing tokens as collateral to secure capital emerges as a strategic choice.

Algorithmic Interest Rates   Crafting a smart contract essentially entails automating the complex decision-making process traditionally handled by a loan officer, based solely on the data derived from on-chain activities. The pivotal challenge here is setting interest rates. In conventional settings, a lender would scrutinize a loan application, credit score, and payslip to gauge the borrower's risk profile and determine a suitable interest rate. *How, then, can this nuanced assessment be replicated autonomously within a blockchain environment?* This question underscores the initial hurdle in transitioning lending practices to a decentralized framework, requiring innovative approaches to risk assessment and interest rate determination without human intervention.

Interest rates in DeFi lending need to be based on what can be observed on chain, e.g. assets. Rates are in fact dynamically adjusted by algorithms based on the current supply and demand for each asset. This mechanism ensures that rates are fair and reflective of market conditions. When the demand to borrow a specific asset increases relative to its supply, interest rates rise, incentivizing more lenders to deposit that asset. Conversely, if there is an excess supply, interest rates will fall to encourage borrowing.

5.2 Utilization Rate and Interest Models

The utilization rate is a key metric in DeFi lending, representing the proportion of available assets that are currently being borrowed. It's calculated as the total borrowed amount divided by the total liquidity (the sum of funds available for borrowing plus already borrowed funds). This rate is crucial for determining the interest rates applied to borrowers and lenders.

A common model for setting interest rates involves the utilization rate and is expressed as:

$$I = I_{base} + U \cdot \left(I_{max} - I_{base} \right)$$

- I_{base} is the base interest rate applied when the utilization rate is zero, essentially the minimum interest rate.
- I_{max} is the maximum interest rate that applies when the utilization rate is at its peak.
- U is the utilization rate.

Through this model, the interest rate for borrowers increases linearly with the utilization rate, ensuring that rates adjust in real-time to the lending-borrowing dynamics of the platform. In other words, because the loans are over-collateralized, the interest rates are not based on the borrower's characteristics (since those are mostly unobservable as the users are anonymous on the chain) but on the demand to borrow the collateral.

Lenders earn interest as a portion of what borrowers pay, after the protocol deducts any fees or reserves. This system ensures that lenders are compensated for providing liquidity, with their earnings directly tied to the borrowing demand for the assets they've deposited. The interest received by lenders increases as more of the asset is borrowed (i.e. as the utilization rate increases), making lending especially lucrative during high demand periods.

NUMERICAL EXAMPLE   Consider a scenario where the DeFi platform has set I_{base} at 0.5% and I_{max} at 10%. If half of the platform's liquidity is being utilized (U=0.5), the interest rate for borrowers would be calculated as:

$$I = 0.5\% + 0.5 \cdot \left(10\% - 0.5\% \right) = 5.25\%$$

Lenders, in turn, receive a portion of this 5.25%, ensuring that both parties are incentivized correctly within the ecosystem. The dynamic nature of these calculations allows DeFi platforms to adapt swiftly to changes in market conditions, offering a flexible and efficient alternative to traditional financial institutions.

In conclusion, the intricate mechanisms of collateralization, interest rate determination, and the utilization rate at the heart of DeFi lending and borrowing protocols represent a paradigm shift in financial services.

The table below shows the rates for a variety of cryptocurrencies on Aave V3, as of March 2024.

Token	Lending Rate (%)	Borrowing Rate (%)
ETH	1.67	2.49
WBTC	0.08	0.94
USDC	14.68	18.04
USDT	10.76	13.31
LINK	0.01	0.1
DAI	21.69	26.65
PYUSD	7.79	12.21
CRV	0.76	6.78
LUSD	12.51	17.26
BAL	1.4	10.34
FRAX	9.1	11.27
crvUSD	3.6	5.08

Notice that the interest rates are not static but fluctuate in response to the shifting balance between supply and demand.[5] This fluid approach to interest rates plays a pivotal role in maintaining the equilibrium of the lending ecosystem, serving dual purposes that are foundational to the operation and health of DeFi platforms.

5.2.1 Dynamic Interest Rates: A Market-Responsive Mechanism

Unlike traditional finance, where interest rates may adjust periodically based on central bank policy or banking decisions, DeFi protocols utilize algorithms to adjust rates in real-time. This ensures that the rates accurately reflect the current market conditions, offering a transparent and fair system for both lenders and borrowers.

One of the critical roles of dynamic interest rates is to incentivize deposits. When the demand to borrow a particular asset surges, the algorithm automatically increases the interest rates. This rise in rates serves as an enticement for potential lenders to deposit more of that asset into the protocol, thereby increasing the supply available for borrowing. For example, if a DeFi platform like Aave sees a spike in demand for borrowing ETH, the interest rates for lending ETH will increase, attracting more lenders to deposit ETH to earn higher yields.

Conversely, dynamic interest rates also play a crucial role in balancing borrowing activities. As more of an asset is borrowed, driving up the utilization rate, the interest rates also rise. These higher borrowing costs naturally encourage borrowers to repay their loans sooner than they might under lower rates, aiming to avoid the increased interest expenses. This mechanism helps prevent the over-leveraging of assets and ensures that capital is not excessively tied up in loans, maintaining liquidity within the platform.

---

[5] To see updated rates on Aave, you can visit their app at https://app.aave.com/markets/. To view rates across various DeFi protocols and blockchains, visit an aggregator at https://defillama.com/yields.

The interplay between deposit incentivization and borrowing balance creates a feedback loop that is highly sensitive to market conditions. This loop allows DeFi protocols to self-regulate, automatically adjusting to changes in user behavior and external market factors. The model is designed to ensure that the platform can dynamically respond to shifts in demand and supply, maintaining a healthy ecosystem that is both robust and flexible.

For instance, during a market downturn, borrowers may be less inclined to take out new loans, leading to decreased demand. The algorithmic model will respond by lowering interest rates, making borrowing more attractive while simultaneously reducing the incentive for new deposits, thereby helping to stabilize the platform's liquidity and utilization rates.

In summary, the dynamic nature of interest rates in DeFi lending and borrowing protocols creates a balanced, self-regulating ecosystem responsive to the nuances of market conditions. This adaptability not only enhances the platform's efficiency and stability but also aligns closely with the decentralized ethos of DeFi, promoting a more inclusive and equitable financial landscape.

THE KINK MODEL   The function setting the interest rate does not need to be linear. In fact, it can incorporate a "kink," adding an additional layer of complexity and control to the way interest rates adapt to changes in utilization rates.

The "kink" model is a sophisticated approach where the relationship between the utilization rate (the ratio of borrowed assets to total liquidity) and the interest rate undergoes a change at a predetermined point, known as the "kink utilization rate." This design aims to create a more stable lending environment by moderating the pace at which interest rates increase as demand for borrowing grows. An example of the interest model with the kink might look like:

$$I = \begin{cases} I_{base} + U \cdot \left(I_{kink} - I_{base} \right) & \text{when } U \leq U_{kink} \\ I_{kink} + \left(U - U_{kink} \right) \cdot \left(I_{max} - I_{kink} \right) & \text{when } U > U_{kink} \end{cases}$$

Where I_{base} is the base interest rate, I_{kink} is the interest rate at the kink, I_{max} is the max interest rate and U_{kink} is the kink utilization rate.

Under this model, the interest rate progression is divided into two segments by the kink utilization rate:

- **Below the Kink:** Interest rates rise gradually with utilization rates to encourage lending without making borrowing prohibitively expensive.
- **Above the Kink:** Past the kink point, interest rates spike more sharply to quickly discourage excessive borrowing and promote the return of liquidity to the system.

Graphically, we can more clearly see a drastic change in the rate of change of interests. For example, Compound's interest rate model looks like the following (**Figure 7**):

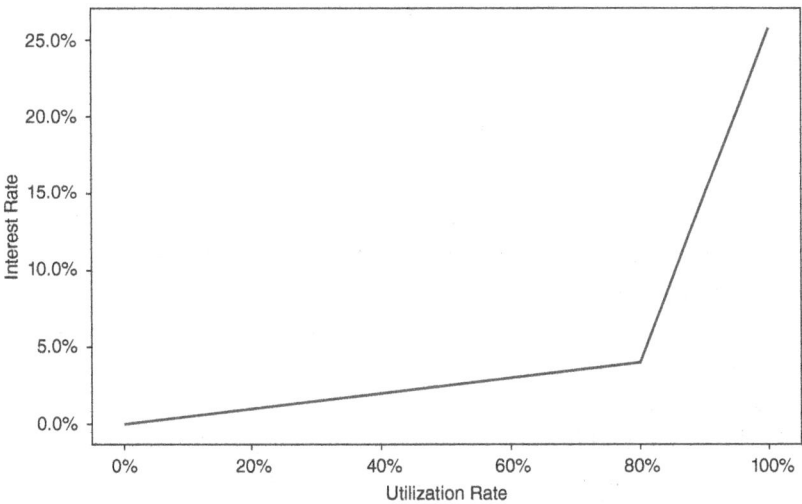

Figure 7 Graphical Representation of Compound's Kink Interest Rate Model

This dual-segment approach serves several crucial functions:

- **Moderation of Interest Rate Increases:** By controlling the slope of the interest rate curve before and after the kink point, the system can prevent sudden spikes in borrowing costs, ensuring that rates remain manageable for borrowers while still encouraging lenders to deposit more assets.
- **Encouragement of Lending:** In periods of high borrowing demand, the initial gentler increase in rates up to the kink point ensures that lenders are incentivized to contribute liquidity without deterring borrowers with steep interest rates.
- **Balancing Borrowing Demand:** Beyond the kink utilization rate, the sharp increase in interest rates acts as a deterrent to excessive borrowing. It encourages borrowers to repay loans, thus freeing up liquidity and maintaining the system's stability.

EXAMPLE OF THE KINK MODEL IN ACTION   Consider a scenario where a DeFi platform has set the following parameters for its kink model:

- Base interest rate I_{base} = 2%
- Interest rate at kink I_{kink} = 10%
- Maximum interest rate I_{max} = 50%
- Kink utilization rate U_{kink} = 80%

If the total liquidity in the system is $10 million and $6 million is currently borrowed, the utilization rate is 60%. This is below the kink point, and the interest rate would be calculated as:

$$I = 2\% + 0.6 \cdot \left(10\% - 2\%\right) = 6.8\%$$

However, if borrowing increases to $9 million, pushing the utilization rate to 90% (above the kink), the interest calculation shifts to reflect the higher segment:

$$I = 10\% + (0.9 - 0.8) \cdot (50\% - 10\%) = 14\%$$

THE KINK AS A RISK MANAGEMENT TOOL   The introduction of a kink in the interest rate model acts as a proactive risk management strategy for DeFi platforms. It prevents liquidity shortages by ensuring that even during high demand periods, the system remains balanced and functional. This mechanism underscores the innovative approaches DeFi protocols employ to manage the complex dynamics of lending and borrowing, providing a stable, efficient, and user-friendly financial ecosystem.

By adopting the kink model, DeFi platforms can fine-tune their systems to handle fluctuations in market activity, ensuring that both lenders and borrowers can operate with confidence, knowing that measures are in place to maintain stability and prevent the pitfalls seen in traditional financial systems.

Benefits	Risks
Accessibility: Anyone can participate	**Smart contract vulnerabilities:** Funds can be lost or stolen
Yield opportunities: Lenders can earn interest rates higher than traditional savings accounts	**Market volatility:** Sudden price drops can lead to the liquidation of collateral
Financial inclusion: Borrowers can access funds without a credit check	**Liquidity risks:** In extreme market conditions, there might not be enough liquidity to cover all loans

6. Case Study: Lending in the Digital Age: The Compound Blockchain Solution[6]/with permission of President & Fellows of Harvard College

Compound, founded in 2017 by Robert Leshner and Geoffrey Hayes, has been a trailblazer in the DeFi space, particularly in lending and borrowing cryptocurrencies. This DeFi lending protocol enables users to deposit cryptocurrencies to earn interest or borrow other crypto assets against them, leveraging smart contracts to automate the management and storage of the capital added to the platform. Users interact directly with Compound's protocol, which autonomously handles collateral and interest rates, removing the need for traditional financial intermediaries.

---

[6] For more details about this case and additional teaching resources for instructors, see my Harvard Business School case titled "Compound: Lending on the Blockchain" #224041 available at https://hbsp.harvard.edu/product/224041-PDF-ENG?Ntt=marco%20di%20maggio%20.

As discussed, interest rates on Compound are algorithmically determined based on the supply and demand for each asset, dynamically adjusting to maintain balance within the ecosystem. For example, if there is a surplus of funds in the Compound wallet, interest rates decrease, incentivizing borrowing. Conversely, smaller pools offer higher interest rates to attract more deposits, ensuring liquidity and competitive borrowing costs.

Compound also introduced COMP tokens, awarded to lenders and borrowers, grant voting rights on proposals affecting the protocol, such as interest rates and supported assets, moving toward a fully decentralized governance model. Compound's conservative approach to asset support, focusing on high-quality cryptocurrencies, and its token-based governance system, where COMP holders vote on protocol upgrades, mark its distinction in the DeFi landscape.

The platform's open and permissionless nature means that anyone with an internet connection and a crypto wallet can access its services, lending or borrowing without traditional financial gatekeepers. This democratizes access to financial services, allowing for a more inclusive financial ecosystem. However, despite its innovative contributions to DeFi, Compound, like any other platform in this emerging field, faces risks associated with smart contract vulnerabilities, reliance on external price oracles, and market volatility, which are inherent challenges in the decentralized nature of DeFi.

Overall, users might find interacting with Compound Finance compelling for various reasons, each addressing distinct demands within the DeFi ecosystem:

- **Earning Interest on Crypto Holdings:** Compound allows users to earn interest by depositing their crypto assets into liquidity pools. This is akin to earning interest from a savings account but with crypto assets instead of fiat currency. The interest rates are algorithmically adjusted based on supply and demand for each asset.

- **Permissionless Access and Efficiency:** The platform is accessible to anyone with an internet connection, removing geographic and economic barriers that are common in traditional finance. Transactions and loan management are executed almost immediately thanks to the automation provided by smart contracts, enhancing efficiency and speed.

- **Borrowing Against Crypto Holdings:** Users can borrow against their crypto assets by depositing them as collateral. This provides flexibility for traders and investors looking to leverage their holdings for liquidity without selling their assets.

- **Risk Management:** Over-collateralization ensures that loans are backed by more value than they represent, protecting the system and its users from market volatility and reducing credit risk. Additionally, Compound's conservative approach to supporting assets focuses on high-quality, less volatile cryptocurrencies, providing a stable environment for lending and borrowing.

- **Governance Participation:** COMP token holders have a say in the governance of the protocol. They can propose changes or vote on proposals, influencing the direction and functionality of Compound. This level of engagement and influence is not typically available in traditional finance.
- **Integration with Other DeFi Services:** Due to Compound's interoperability, users can easily move assets across different platforms to maximize their yields and borrowing capabilities. This creates a more fluid DeFi ecosystem where Compound acts as a foundational layer for other applications and services.

These points underscore how Compound meets the demand for a decentralized, efficient, and user-engaged financial platform, differentiating itself from traditional markets by offering transparency, reduced dependency on intermediaries, and innovative financial mechanisms that empower users.

However, DeFi protocols, including Compound, are not without their risks. A significant concern is smart contract vulnerabilities, which can arise from coding errors or unforeseen interactions between contracts, leading to security breaches or loss of funds. The reliance on external price oracles introduces another layer of risk, as oracle manipulation or failure can destabilize the protocol. For instance, if an attacker inflates the price of a low-liquidity asset on a few exchanges, the oracle might report this inflated price to the Compound protocol. This could allow the attacker to borrow more assets than they should be able to, based on the artificially high collateral value, leading to potential bad debt for the protocol. Market volatility and the associated risk of liquidation pose additional challenges, where abrupt price fluctuations can trigger collateral sell-off, often at times disadvantageous to the borrower. Comparatively, traditional financial systems grapple with credit, operational, and market risks, but the decentralized nature of DeFi introduces unique challenges that demand innovative risk management strategies.

We can start the case discussion by asking, *why have platforms like Compound become popular, and what benefits do they offer?*

- Accessibility and inclusivity
  - Operate on blockchain technology, which is inherently borderless and open to anyone with internet access.
- Interest earnings
  - DeFi platforms provide significantly higher returns on investments due to elimination of intermediaries and efficient allocation of capital within the ecosystem.
- Transparency and security
  - Blockchain's public ledger ensures that all transactions are transparent and immutable.

The initial business model is described by its founder as "When the protocol was first launched, the idea was that it would function like a smart contract-driven, decentralized autonomous bank. There would be some sort of net interest margin between what the system was paying for liquidity and what it was allowing people to borrow, and it would collect the difference."

Then, it might be worthwhile highlighting how the protocol has evolved over time, as it marks several milestones in the DeFi landscape.

Initial Launch and Supported Tokens

- Compound made its debut in 2018, initially supporting borrowing and lending of ETH, 0x Protocol (ZRX), Basic Attention Token (BAT), and Augur (REP). These assets were chosen based on their active market presence and the reputations of the projects behind them, ensuring that users had access to liquid markets and reputable assets from the start.
- **Community-Driven Token Selection:** Early on, Compound introduced a novel approach to governance, proposing that new supported tokens would be selected via community vote. This democratic approach aimed to decentralize decision-making and align the protocol's evolution with the interests of its users.
- **Incorporation of Stablecoins:** Recognizing the need for stable assets in lending and borrowing activities, Compound added support for stablecoins like USDC and DAI in the months following its launch. This was a strategic move to attract a broader user base and provide more stability in the lending markets.

Financial Milestones and Algorithmic Interest Rates

- **Seed Funding and Avoidance of ICO:** Compound raised $8.2 million in a seed funding round and made a pivotal decision not to hold an Initial Coin Offering (ICO), a common fundraising method in the crypto space at the time. This decision highlighted a commitment to regulatory compliance and a long-term vision.
- **Algorithmic Interest Rates:** A key innovation of Compound was the introduction of algorithmically set interest rates across each market. This system dynamically adjusted rates based on supply and demand, representing an innovative approach to financial markets in the DeFi space.

Governance Token and Market Expansion

- **Launch of COMP and Market Reaction:** In May 2020, Compound launched its governance token, COMP, which was listed on Coinbase the following month. This move significantly increased Compound's market capitalization, reaching approximately $700 million shortly after listing, and peaking at nearly $4 billion in May 2021.

- **Protocol Governance and New Markets:** Through community governance, Compound expanded its offerings in 2022 to include new markets like TrueUSD, SushiToken, Aave, and Maker tokens. It also allowed borrowing of stablecoins using various cryptocurrencies as collateral, demonstrating the protocol's adaptability and growth.

Gateway: A Vision for Cross-Blockchain Liquidity

- **"Gateway" and Its Implications:** "Gateway" represents Compound's ambition to bridge liquidity across various blockchains, potentially revolutionizing how assets are moved and utilized in the DeFi ecosystem. Governed by its own native token, this move could significantly expand Compound's reach and utility across different networks.

Having discussed the evolution of the protocol, we can now focus on one of the key dimensions of the case that perfectly puts together the topics of this chapter:

- *Reflect on the key benefits and challenges of having a protocol governed in a decentralized manner.*

Pros and Cons of Decentralization in Compound

- **Decentralized Development:** Ensures that no single authority can abuse the system, fostering trust among users. The open-source nature allows for community auditing and approval of changes, enhancing security and transparency.
- **Governance by COMP Holders:** COMP holders can vote on governance changes, embedding a democratic decision-making process within the protocol. This encourages a sense of ownership and participation among users.
- **Slower Innovation Process:** The requirement for community consensus can slow down the approval of changes, potentially leading to a slower innovation rate compared to centralized counterparts. This could hinder the protocol's ability to quickly adapt to new challenges or opportunities.
- **Monetary Incentives:** Initially, there was no direct monetary incentive for users to acquire and hold COMP tokens, as they did not receive additional rewards from the network. This lack of financial incentives impacts the token's attractiveness and the willingness of users to participate in governance.
- **Centralized Solutions for Monetization:** In response to the challenges of value capture for COMP holders, Compound launched Compound Treasury, a centralized solution targeting institutional investors. While this move aimed to create a revenue stream and bridge DeFi with traditional finance, it also highlighted the limitations of purely decentralized systems in capturing value and generating revenue.

In conclusion, in the words of Robert Leshner: "When development was centralized, there were no problems with Compound. Moving to a model with distributed control over the code has led to two major errors in governance. First, someone introduced a bug that made the protocol create more COMP than it was supposed to—$60 million of COMP was given to 20 different users. The second bug temporarily bricked the price feed of ETH. Accounts were frozen for 7 days. It didn't lead to a loss of funds to users, but it was terrifying. Both of these were community-driven changes." This example really shows the drawback of decentralization. Imagine being the protocol developer and founder and finding out that you let somebody else insert a crucial bug into your protocol. It must be frustrating to say the least.

Another key discussion point is the economic model behind the COMP token.

Holding COMP Tokens and Economic Profit

- **Governance vs. Economic Incentives:** COMP tokens primarily grant governance rights, allowing holders to propose and vote on changes to the protocol. This model aligns with decentralized finance's ethos, emphasizing community control and decision-making. However, the absence of direct economic benefits (e.g. dividends or profit sharing) from holding these tokens raises questions about their long-term value proposition. Without financial incentives, the motivation to acquire and hold COMP might diminish, potentially affecting its market demand and price.

Community's Role in Incentive Restructuring

- **Restructuring Incentives:** Any changes to the incentive structure to possibly include economic benefits for COMP holders would require community consensus. This democratic process ensures that the protocol remains aligned with its users' interests but also introduces complexities and potential delays in implementing new strategies. The necessity to achieve broad agreement may slow the pace at which Compound can adapt to evolving market dynamics and user needs.

Regulatory Considerations

- **SEC Attention:** Introducing profit-sharing or other forms of economic incentives could attract scrutiny from regulatory bodies such as the SEC. The SEC's interest would likely stem from concerns over whether COMP tokens could be considered securities under certain incentive schemes. This potential regulatory oversight adds a layer of complexity and risk to modifying the protocol's incentive structure.

Strategic Directions and Separate Ventures

- **Leshner's Strategic Move:** Robert Leshner, one of the protocol's founders, has explored creating separate ventures that leverage the Compound protocol to generate economic value. This approach allows for the development of businesses that can directly monetize the protocol's capabilities without altering its fundamental governance model or directly involving the protocol itself in profit-sharing mechanisms.
- **Building atop Compound:** The strategy of building businesses on top of the Compound protocol reflects a broader trend in DeFi, where the foundational technologies facilitate a range of services and applications. This approach seeks to create value indirectly, benefiting from the protocol's infrastructure while navigating around the direct economic incentivization challenges associated with governance tokens.

The discussion surrounding COMP tokens' economic incentives versus governance rights highlights the delicate balance between maintaining a decentralized governance model and providing sufficient value to token holders to sustain interest and investment in the protocol. The potential regulatory implications of modifying incentive structures add a layer of complexity to these considerations. Meanwhile, the exploration of separate ventures to monetize the protocol's capabilities represents an innovative approach to value creation within the DeFi ecosystem, albeit one that operates adjacent to the protocol's core governance and incentive mechanisms.

What Happened?   Despite Compound's roots in decentralized finance, which is characterized by peer-to-peer transactions without the need for traditional financial intermediaries, Compound Treasury was introduced as a somewhat centralized product. This new product was launched to cater to institutional investors who might be unfamiliar with or cautious about the complexities and risks associated with DeFi. Compound Treasury offers these investors a more familiar, centralized interface through which they can earn interest on their USD deposits. These deposits are then converted into stablecoins and invested in the Compound protocol to generate returns. The service combines the yield-generating capabilities of DeFi with the regulatory compliance and ease of use that institutional investors require.

The launch of Compound Treasury saw significant interest from various fintech and financial services firms, demonstrating the demand for DeFi products among institutional investors. Clients like Yotta, Current, Genesis, HashKey, and Nansen represent a broad spectrum of the financial services industry:

- Yotta and Current are fintech companies that offer banking services and seek innovative ways to offer their customers higher yields on deposits.
- Genesis is a digital currency trading and lending platform, indicating how firms within the crypto space itself are looking to leverage such products.
- HashKey is a digital asset management and financial technology firm, showing the interest from asset managers in DeFi opportunities.
- Nansen is a blockchain analytics platform, which suggests that even companies focused on blockchain data are interested in the financial products offered by Compound Treasury.

This expansion into offering services to institutional clients represents a significant step for Compound and the DeFi sector, indicating a growing acceptance and integration of DeFi services within the broader financial ecosystem. Through Compound Treasury, Compound aims to provide a secure, compliant, and user-friendly platform for institutional investors to access the benefits of DeFi, such as higher yields compared to traditional savings accounts, while mitigating some of the risks associated with direct participation in the DeFi space.

7. AAve

Aave introduced several groundbreaking features that have significantly influenced the sector's evolution. Founded in 2017 by Stani Kulechov as "ETHLend," it initially served as a Swiss-based decentralized financial marketplace on the Ethereum blockchain. As Compound, this platform enabled cryptocurrency holders to access liquidity without selling their assets, marking a significant departure from traditional financial mechanisms.

ETHLend's innovative approach was underpinned by its utility token, LEND, launched through an Initial Coin Offering (ICO) in December 2017. The ICO successfully raised $16 million by selling 1 billion LEND tokens, with an additional 300 million allocated for user adoption incentives, project development, and founding team rewards. By April 2018, ETHLend had processed over 12,000 ETH in loans, reflecting the growing demand for decentralized lending solutions. The success of ETHLend set the stage for the emergence of Aave, Finnish for "ghost," symbolizing a new era of transparency and innovation in DeFi.

Aave revolutionized the DeFi space by introducing a unique liquidity pool model, where each asset has its dedicated pool. This design allows for more accurate and algorithmically determined interest rates based on the supply and demand for each asset. Unlike traditional open marketplaces for lenders and borrowers, Aave's liquidity pools facilitated a more efficient and secure lending environment across multiple blockchain networks, including Ethereum, Avalanche, and Polygon.

In 2020, the LEND token underwent a migration to a new protocol, resulting in the creation of the AAVE cryptocurrency. This token serves not only as a governance tool but also symbolizes Aave's commitment to overseeing decentralized liquidity markets. As of March 2024, Aave had achieved a market capitalization of $1.85 billion with $11.41 billion of liquidity participating across seven blockchain networks and thirteen markets. The company's growth is also reflected in its team expansion to 105 employees and the raising of $49 million through a Series A funding round, inclusive of the initial ICO.

Innovations and Contributions

- **Rate Switching:** Aave introduced the capability for borrowers to switch between stable and variable interest rates. This flexibility empowered users to manage their borrowing costs more effectively, adapting to market conditions to optimize their financial strategies.
- **aTokens:** Representing a user's stake in a liquidity pool, aTokens accrue interest in real-time. These tokens can be utilized within the broader DeFi ecosystem, enhancing the composability and interconnectivity of financial applications.
- **Decentralized Governance:** Aave's governance model is a testament to its commitment to decentralization. AAVE token holders have significant influence over key decisions and protocol updates, ensuring that the platform evolves in alignment with its community's needs and preferences.
- **Diversification:** Under the Aave umbrella, a portfolio of projects was developed to expand the ecosystem's capabilities. This includes Aave Pocket for programmable bank accounts and debit cards, Aave Lending as a service solution, Aave Custody for digital asset custody, Aave Clearing for OTC cryptocurrency conversion, and Aave Gaming, pushing the boundaries of blockchain gaming.

Aave, however, pioneers a groundbreaking innovation with its introduction of **Flash Loans**. These allow investors to borrow substantial sums without any collateral, revolutionizing access to sophisticated financial strategies typically reserved for institutional investors. These loans have democratized access to significant capital without the need for upfront collateral, enabling a wide array of financial maneuvers that were previously out of reach for many retail investors. Capital is usually thought of as scarce, concentrated, and slow. It is scarce because it is risky to lend, so capital is expensive and difficult to raise. It is concentrated as only large institutions have access to large amounts of capital. It is also slow, as it usually takes time to raise capital from traditional institutions. Flash loans solve all three of these problems.

7.1 How Flash Loans Work

Flash loans leverage the power of smart contracts to provide users with access to large sums of capital for the duration of a single transaction on the blockchain. This means that funds can be borrowed and must be repaid, along with a small fee, *within the same block*. If the borrower fails to repay the loan within this extremely short timeframe, the transaction is automatically reversed, as if it never happened, thanks to the atomicity of blockchain transactions. See **Figure 8** for the key innovations offered by flash loans.

Flash loans are the DeFi equivalent of time travel. You borrow money you don't have, do something with it, and pay it back in the same transaction. It's like borrowing a cup of sugar from your neighbor, baking a cake, selling a slice to the same neighbor, and returning the sugar before they even knew it was gone.

Examples of Use Cases   Flash loans can be used for a variety of purposes, including:

- **Arbitrage:** Exploiting price differentials between different exchanges or assets.
- **Collateral Swapping:** Quickly swapping the collateral backing a loan without closing and reopening it.
- **Self-Liquidation:** Paying off a loan on the brink of liquidation to avoid penalties.

The typical process for executing a flash loan involves these steps:

1. **Identifying an Opportunity:** For example, a trader notices a price discrepancy in DAI between two exchanges.
2. **Borrowing:** The trader borrows a large amount of DAI via a flash loan from Aave's liquidity pool.

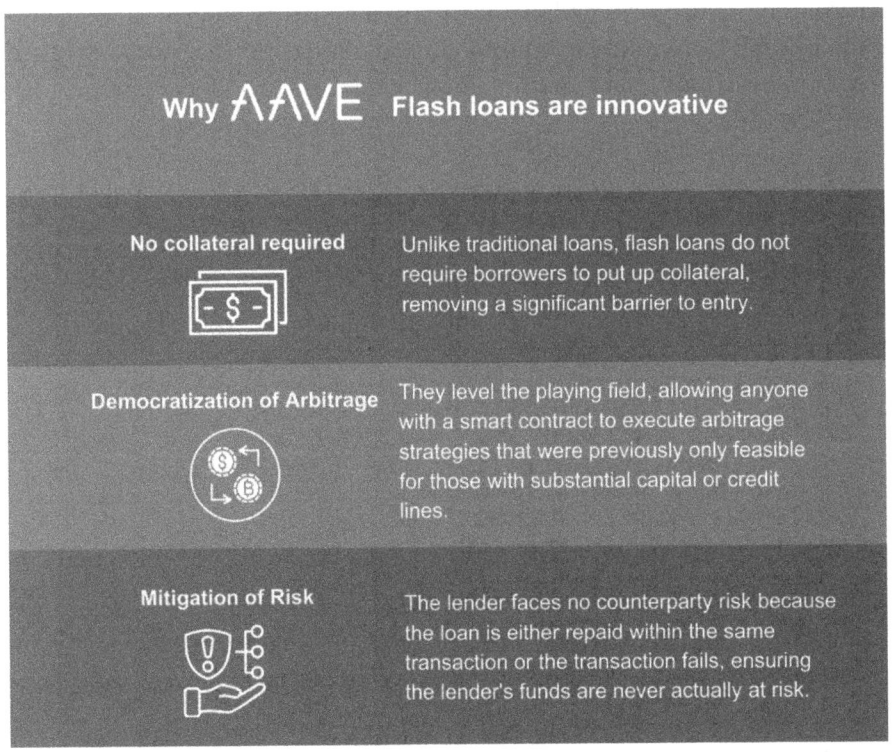

Figure 8   Why flash loans are innovative

3. Executing Trades: The trader sells DAI at the higher price on one exchange and buys it back at the lower price on another, all within the same transaction.

4. Repayment: The trader returns the borrowed DAI plus fees to Aave. If successful, the profit from the arbitrage covers the fees and generates income for the trader.

To utilize flash loans, traders must write and deploy smart contracts that can interact with the Aave protocol, initiate the loan, execute the trading strategy, and ensure repayment within the same transaction. This process requires careful planning and precision, as incorrectly coded contracts can result in failed transactions or financial losses due to slippage or other transaction fees. Additionally, since smart contracts are immutable and public, there's a risk that attackers could exploit any vulnerabilities.

Flash loans by Aave thus offer a powerful tool for retail investors to engage in activities typically dominated by larger financial institutions. By removing the need for collateral and providing access to significant capital, Aave's flash loans have opened new possibilities for arbitrage, liquidity provision, and financial management within the DeFi ecosystem. **Figures 9** and **10** show the growing popularity of flash loans. Their usage spiked during the latest bull market in 2021. In particular, it seems that investors tend to borrow large quantities of USDC, even if borrowing other stablecoins is also popular.

Flash loans, while being a revolutionary feature of the decentralized finance (DeFi) ecosystem, have, unfortunately, also been utilized for malicious purposes. These loans provide users with significant capital without any upfront collateral, which can be leveraged to exploit vulnerabilities within DeFi protocols. Here's a deeper look into how flash loans can be used for malicious intent and the implications for the DeFi landscape.

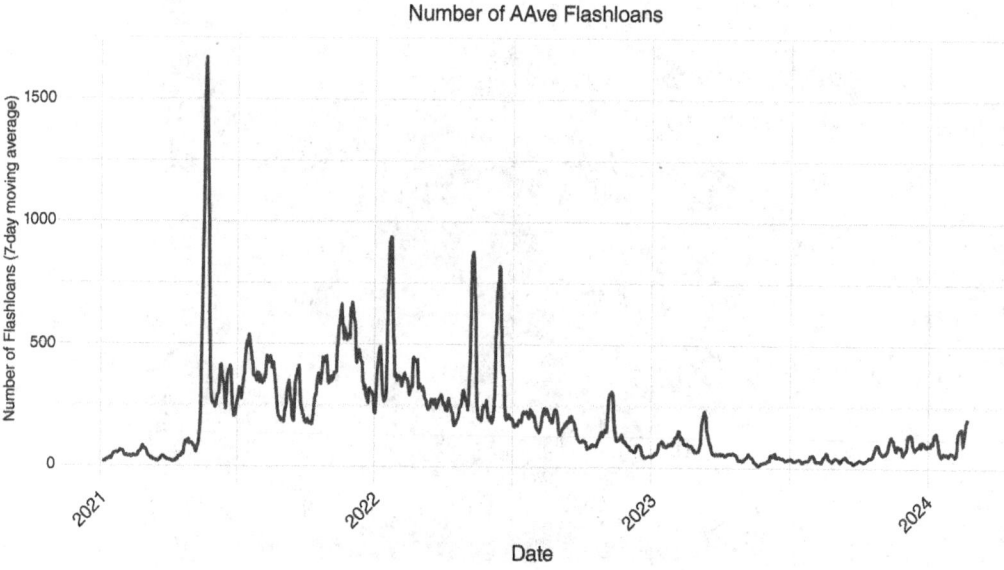

Figure 9   Daily number of flash loans

Process of a Malicious Flash Loan Attack The process of a malicious flash loan attack is as follows:

1. **Acquisition of a Large Sum:** An attacker takes out a flash loan for a substantial amount of money.
2. **Exploitation of Vulnerabilities:** The attacker then targets a DeFi protocol known to have certain vulnerabilities, such as issues with pricing oracles or susceptibility to reentrancy attacks.[7]

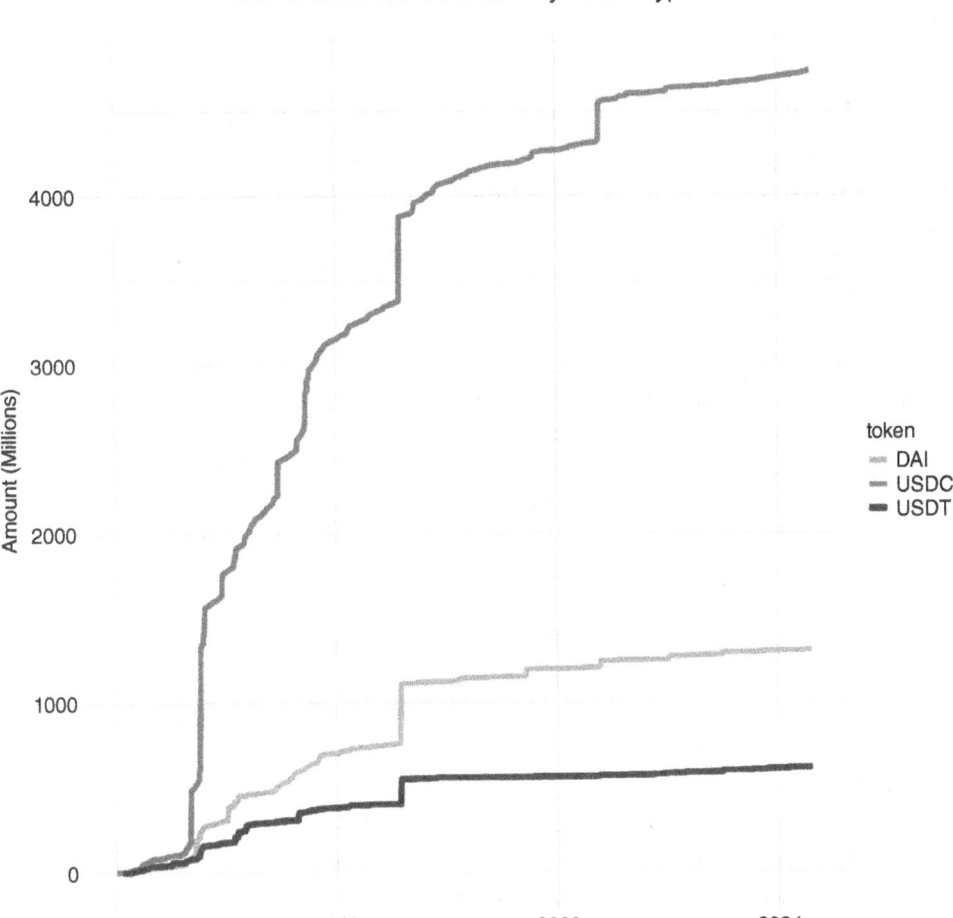

Figure 10 Cumulative flash loan amounts for stablecoins

---

[7] A reentrancy attack is a common exploit specific to smart contracts in blockchain technology. It involves an attacker making a function call to a contract and exploiting its external calls to re-enter and call the function repeatedly before it completes its execution. This can lead to unauthorized withdrawals or other unintended actions. The 2016 DAO hack is a notorious example, where attackers drained 3.6 million Ether, highlighting the critical importance of secure contract design.

3. **Market Manipulation:** With the funds obtained from the flash loan, the attacker manipulates the market. For example, they could exploit a DeFi platform relying on a single-source price oracle by artificially inflating the price of an asset, leading to inaccurate price reporting.

4. **Profit Generation:** Leveraging the manipulated market conditions, the attacker executes trades against the platform or calls vulnerable contract functions to extract profits.

5. **Loan Repayment and Profit Securing:** After securing profits from the exploit, the attacker repays the flash loan and retains the excess as profit, completing the attack without having invested any personal capital.

How can these risks be mitigated?

- **Checks-Effects-Interactions Pattern:** This design pattern ensures that all checks and state changes occur before external calls, reducing the risk of reentrancy.
- **Reentrancy Guards:** These are mechanisms within smart contracts that prevent a function from being called again before it completes its execution.
- **Pull Over Push for Withdrawals:** Instead of automatically transferring funds to users (push), contracts can require users to initiate withdrawals (pull), reducing the attack surface for reentrancy.

In conclusion, while flash loans present an innovative financial tool within DeFi, their potential for misuse serves as a reminder of the ongoing challenges in ensuring the security and integrity of smart contracts and protocols. The DeFi community must remain vigilant and proactive in addressing these challenges to foster a safe and robust decentralized financial landscape.

8. Concluding Remarks

In weaving together the multifaceted narrative of DeFi and its underpinning structures, such as DAOs and innovative borrowing and lending protocols, we traverse a landscape ripe with transformative potential yet not devoid of significant challenges. This journey through the intricacies of DeFi reveals an ecosystem that seeks to redefine our engagement with financial systems, promising a future where finance is more accessible, transparent, and equitable.

As we stand at the confluence of technological innovation and financial services, it becomes increasingly clear that the journey of DeFi is not merely about creating alternatives to traditional financial systems but about reimagining the very fabric of economic interactions and governance. DAOs, in this narrative, emerge not only as a novel organizational structure but as a symbol of the shift toward a more democratized and participatory approach to financial decision-making. The exploration of lending and borrowing protocols underscores a move toward efficiency and inclusivity, challenging the entrenched barriers of traditional finance.

However, this journey is not without its perils. The challenges of security vulnerabilities, regulatory uncertainties, scalability issues, and environmental concerns cast long shadows on the path ahead. Yet, it is within these challenges that the resilience and innovative spirit of the DeFi community shine brightest. Efforts to bolster security, engage constructively with regulators, enhance scalability, and mitigate environmental impact are testaments to the community's commitment to not only advancing the DeFi ecosystem but doing so responsibly and sustainably.

Before we conclude, I want to emphasize the transformative potential of flash loans within DeFi. A fundamental barrier in traditional finance is the scarcity of capital for retail investors, who cannot access funds on the scale available to large institutions—a reality often accepted as inevitable. Yet, flash loans challenge this status quo by enabling any investor to leverage market opportunities without significant capital upfront. This isn't a result of reckless lending akin to the practices observed during the 2008 subprime mortgage crisis. Instead, it's a near-riskless proposition for lenders. They can safely extend millions of dollars to borrowers with the confidence that their capital is protected, as these loans are structured to be repaid within the same transaction.

This innovation isn't just intriguing; it's a radical shift in how we think about financing and liquidity, debunking myths that DeFi lacks novelty. I bet skeptics, including many finance professionals and academics (I have met a few arrogant ones), arguing that there is nothing new in DeFi have never heard of flash loans.

Code Example : AAve Flash Loans

Language: Solidity

Level: Expert

Flash loans are designed to be interacted with through smart contracts initially. Therefore, this example is a very applicable one. This uses the Goerli test network, where you can get Faucet tokens to test the contract.

```
Credits to @jspruance on GitHub
pragma solidity >0.8.0;

import {FlashLoanSimpleReceiverBase} from "@aave/core
v3/contracts/flashloan/base/FlashLoanSimpleReceiverBase.sol";
import {IPoolAddressesProvider} from "@aave/core-v3/contracts/interfaces/
IPoolAddressesProvider.sol";
import {IERC20} from "@aave/core-v3/contracts/dependencies/openzeppelin/
contracts/IERC20.sol";

interface IDex {
    function depositUSDC(uint256 _amount) external;

    function depositDAI(uint256 _amount) external;

    function buyDAI() external;

    function sellDAI() external;
}
```

```
contract FlashLoanArbitrage is FlashLoanSimpleReceiverBase {
    address payable owner;

    // Aave ERC20 Token addresses on Goerli network
    address private immutable daiAddress =
        0xDF1742fE5b0bFc12331D8EAec6b478DfDbD31464;
    address private immutable usdcAddress =
        0xA2025B15a1757311bfD68cb14eaeFCc237AF5b43;
    address private dexContractAddress =
        0xD6e8c479B6B62d8Ce985C0f686D39e96af9424df;

    IERC20 private dai;
    IERC20 private usdc;
    IDex private dexContract;

    constructor(address _addressProvider)
        FlashLoanSimpleReceiverBase(IPoolAddressesProvider
(_addressProvider))
    {
        owner = payable(msg.sender);

        dai = IERC20(daiAddress);
        usdc = IERC20(usdcAddress);
        dexContract = IDex(dexContractAddress);
    }

    /**
        This function is called after your contract has received the
flash loaned amount
     */
    function executeOperation(
        address asset,
        uint256 amount,
        uint256 premium,
        address initiator,
        bytes calldata params
    ) external override returns (bool) {
        //
        // This contract now has the funds requested.
        // Your logic goes here.
        //

        // Arbirtage operation
        dexContract.depositUSDC(1000000000); // 1000 USDC
        dexContract.buyDAI();
        dexContract.depositDAI(dai.balanceOf(address(this)));
        dexContract.sellDAI();

        // At the end of your logic above, this contract owes
        // the flashloaned amount + premiums.
        // Therefore ensure your contract has enough to repay
        // these amounts.

        // Approve the Pool contract allowance to *pull* the owed amount
        uint256 amountOwed = amount + premium;
        IERC20(asset).approve(address(POOL), amountOwed);
```

```
            return true;
    }

    function requestFlashLoan(address _token, uint256 _amount) public {
        address receiverAddress = address(this);
        address asset = _token;
        uint256 amount = _amount;
        bytes memory params = "";
        uint16 referralCode = 0;

        POOL.flashLoanSimple(
            receiverAddress,
            asset,
            amount,
            params,
            referralCode
        );
    }

    function approveUSDC(uint256 _amount) external returns (bool) {
        return usdc.approve(dexContractAddress, _amount);
    }

    function allowanceUSDC() external view returns (uint256) {
        return usdc.allowance(address(this), dexContractAddress);
    }

    function approveDAI(uint256 _amount) external returns (bool) {
        return dai.approve(dexContractAddress, _amount);
    }

    function allowanceDAI() external view returns (uint256) {
        return dai.allowance(address(this), dexContractAddress);
    }

    function getBalance(address _tokenAddress) external view returns
(uint256) {
        return IERC20(_tokenAddress).balanceOf(address(this));
    }

    function withdraw(address _tokenAddress) external onlyOwner {
        IERC20 token = IERC20(_tokenAddress);
        token.transfer(msg.sender, token.balanceOf(address(this)));
    }

    modifier onlyOwner() {
        require(
            msg.sender == owner,
            "Only the contract owner can call this function"
        );
        _;
    }

    receive() external payable {}
}
```

To interact with Aave's flash loan service, the *FlashLoanArbitrage* contract incorporates key functionalities from the Aave V3 protocol and establishes an interface for decentralized exchange operations. This contract utilizes the *FlashLoanSimpleReceiverBase* for handling flash loans and sets up interfaces for ERC-20 token interactions, specifically targeting **DAI** and **USDC** tokens.

The contract begins by setting the owner to the deployer and linking the necessary token and DEX addresses. The *executeOperation* function, critical to the contract, is called post-flash loan reception and outlines the arbitrage strategy—depositing USDC, buying and selling DAI, then repaying the loan with interest. This ensures the contract leverages price differentials effectively while adhering to the flash loan's repayment requirements.

Further functionalities include requesting flash loans (*requestFlashLoan*), managing USDC and DAI allowances (*approveUSDC, approveDAI, allowanceUSDC, allowanceDAI*), and tracking balances (*getBalance*). Additionally, the contract provides a withdrawal function, restricted by the *onlyOwner* modifier, to transfer tokens back to the owner, ensuring control over the funds within the contract.

Code Example: DAOGovernance

Language: Solidity

Level: Expert

Most of the protocols we mention throughout this book are initially Decentralized Autonomous Organizations, and if one checks out their technical documentation, they will realize that all of these organizations have a "Governance" contract commonly. Governance contracts play a crucial role within these organizations, acting as the backbone for decision-making processes. They typically include mechanisms for proposing, voting on, and implementing changes within the ecosystem. These contracts ensure that token holders can exercise their rights and influence the direction of the protocol, promoting a democratic and transparent environment. Moreover, governance contracts often incorporate safety features, such as time locks and quorum requirements, to protect against hasty or malicious actions, ensuring that decisions are well-considered and representative of the community's consensus.

This example is a simplified version of a Governance contract with limited functionalities, but it definitely highlights how these contracts work in real life for decentralized governance.

```solidity
pragma solidity ^0.8.0;

interface IERC20 {
    function balanceOf(address account) external view returns (uint256);
}
```

```
contract DAOGovernance {
    // Structure for each proposal
    struct Proposal {
        string description;
        uint voteCount;
        bool executed;
        mapping(address => bool) voters;
        ProposalType proposalType;
    }
    // Enum for proposal types
    enum ProposalType { Governance, Financial, Project }
    // Mapping from proposal IDs to Proposal structures
    mapping(uint => Proposal) public proposals;
    // Total number of proposals
    uint public proposalCount;
    // Address of the token used for voting
    IERC20 public votingToken;
    // Quorum required for a proposal to pass
    uint public quorumPercentage;
    // Event to emit when a vote is cast
    event VoteCast(uint indexed proposalId, address indexed voter,
    uint votes);
    // Event to emit when a proposal is created
    event ProposalCreated(uint indexed proposalId, string description,
    ProposalType proposalType);

    // Constructor
    constructor(address _votingToken, uint _quorumPercentage) {
        votingToken = IERC20(_votingToken);
        quorumPercentage = _quorumPercentage;
    }

    // Function to create a new proposal
    function createProposal(string memory _description, ProposalType
    _proposalType) public {
        proposalCount++;
        Proposal storage newProposal = proposals[proposalCount];
        newProposal.description = _description;
        newProposal.proposalType = _proposalType;
        emit ProposalCreated(proposalCount, _description, _proposalType);
    }

    // Function to vote on a proposal
    function vote(uint _proposalId) public {
        Proposal storage proposal = proposals[_proposalId];

        // Ensure proposal exists and has not been executed
        require(bytes(proposal.description).length > 0, "Proposal does
        not exist");
        require(!proposal.executed, "Proposal already executed");

        uint voterBalance = votingToken.balanceOf(msg.sender);
        require(voterBalance > 0, "No voting tokens held");
```

```
    require(!proposal.voters[msg.sender], "Already voted");

    proposal.voteCount += voterBalance;
    proposal.voters[msg.sender] = true;

    emit VoteCast(_proposalId, msg.sender, voterBalance);
}

// Function to check if proposal has passed
function checkIfProposalPassed(uint _proposalId) public view
returns (bool) {
    Proposal storage proposal = proposals[_proposalId];
    uint totalSupply = votingToken.totalSupply();
    return ((proposal.voteCount * 100) / totalSupply) >=
    quorumPercentage;
}
}
```

The DAOGovernance first utilizes the ERC-20 interface, as usually voting rights are managed with the governance tokens. Then the contract facilitates the organization of proposals into Governance, Financial, and Project segments.

When the contract is initiated, it establishes the voting token's address and sets the required quorum percentage necessary for any proposal's approval. The introduction of new proposals is streamlined through the *createProposal* function, which augments the proposal count. This pivotal step is accompanied by the triggering of the *ProposalCreated* event. This event functions as a critical mechanism for recording and tracking the inception of proposals within the DAO ecosystem, ensuring that each new proposal is logged and accessible for future reference.

Voting on proposals is organized by the *vote* function. This function first performs essential checks: it confirms the proposal's validity, verifies it has not already been executed, and ascertains the voter's eligibility based on their token holdings and voting history. The voting power is proportional to the voter's token balance, integrating equity into the voting process. Each vote cast triggers the *VoteCast* event, cementing the action in the blockchain's immutable ledger, thereby offering a transparent and indelible record of each member's participation and stance.

Additionally, the contract's *checkIfProposalPassed* function provides a systematic approach to determining the success of each proposal, evaluating the gathered votes against the total supply of voting tokens. It should be noted that there are many other functions that can be added, like delegated voting, timelocks, proposal thresholds, and a logic that allows upgrades.

End-of-Chapter Questions

Multiple-Choice Questions

1. **What is the primary function of a Decentralized Autonomous Organization (DAO)?**
   (A) To facilitate peer-to-peer transactions without intermediaries.
   (B) To act as a central governing body for blockchain networks.
   (C) To enable community-driven decision-making and governance.
   (D) To provide a platform for trading digital assets.

2. **What mechanism(s) do DeFi protocols commonly use to ensure loans are paid back?**
   (A) Credit checks and reporting.
   (B) Collateralization with other digital assets.
   (C) Personal guarantees from the borrower.
   (D) Insurance funds paid by the borrower.

3. **In a DeFi borrowing and lending protocol, what is "liquidation"?**
   (A) When a borrower repays their loan in full.
   (B) The process of converting digital assets to fiat currency.
   (C) The act of selling collateral to cover an unpaid loan.
   (D) Increasing the liquidity pool with more funds.

4. **Which of the following is a benefit of DeFi over traditional finance?**
   (A) Higher fees for transactions and services.
   (B) Slower transaction speeds.
   (C) Accessibility and inclusivity regardless of geography.
   (D) Centralized control over assets.

5. **What role do governance tokens play in a DAO?**
   (A) They serve as the only currency accepted for transactions within the DAO.
   (B) They grant holders the right to vote on decisions and proposals affecting the organization.
   (C) They are symbolic and have no real use or value.
   (D) They act as collateral for borrowing activities within the DAO.

6. **In smart contract development, what is a "reentrancy attack"?**
   (A) A method for optimizing gas fees.
   (B) An exploit where a fallback function is used maliciously to drain funds.
   (C) A standard for token creation.
   (D) A way to ensure transaction privacy.

7. **What mechanism do DAOs typically use to prevent malicious proposals from being passed?**
   (A) Unlimited token minting.
   (B) Mandatory KYC for all voters.
   (C) Quorums and voting thresholds.
   (D) Locking tokens in a vault with a time delay.

8. **What innovation did Aave introduce to the DeFi lending market?**
   (A) Fixed interest rates for all loans.
   (B) The use of physical assets as collateral.
   (C) Flash loans that require no upfront collateral.
   (D) A ban on the use of governance tokens.
9. **What is the primary risk associated with smart contracts in DeFi platforms?**
   (A) The high cost of transactions.
   (B) Volatility of cryptocurrency prices.
   (C) Vulnerabilities that can lead to exploits or fund losses.
   (D) The requirement for manual execution of contracts.
10. **Which aspect of DeFi aims to improve accessibility to financial services?**
    (A) The high barriers to entry for new users.
    (B) Permissionless access, allowing anyone with an internet connection to participate.
    (C) Centralized control over funds and transactions.
    (D) Limited interoperability with traditional banking systems.

Numerical Exercises

Exercise 1: If a user deposits 10 ETH in a DeFi lending protocol offering an annual interest rate of 5%, calculate the amount of ETH the user will have after one year.

Exercise 2: A liquidity provider contributes 100 ETH and 300,000 DAI to a liquidity pool. If the price of ETH rises and the pool's new composition is 90 ETH and 330,000 DAI, calculate the provider's impermanent loss compared to simply holding the assets.

Exercise 3: A borrower takes a flash loan of 1,000 DAI with a 0.3% fee. They use the loan in an arbitrage opportunity, earning a profit of 5 DAI. Calculate the total amount the borrower needs to repay and their net profit after repaying the loan and fee.

Exercise 1: Understanding Over-Collateralization

Objective: Determine the minimum collateral required for taking out a loan in a DeFi protocol.

Given:
- Loan amount desired: 2,000 DAI
- Over-collateralization ratio: 150%

Task: Calculate the minimum amount of collateral required in DAI to secure the loan.

Exercise 2: Flash Loan Arbitrage Opportunity

Objective: Calculate the potential profit from a flash loan arbitrage opportunity between two exchanges.

Given:

- Amount borrowed with flash loan: 10,000 DAI
- Purchase price of ETH on Exchange A: 1,500 DAI
- Selling price of ETH on Exchange B: 1,550 DAI
- Flash loan fee: 0.09% of the borrowed amount

Task: Determine the net profit after buying ETH on Exchange A and selling it on Exchange B, including the repayment of the flash loan and fee.

Open Questions

1. Explain how flash loans work and provide an example of a legitimate use case for them in the DeFi ecosystem.
2. Describe the process and significance of over-collateralization in DeFi borrowing and lending protocols.
3. Analyze the potential impact of regulatory actions, like those from the SEC on DeFi platforms and DAOs. How can these entities navigate regulatory challenges?

Coding Exercises

Exercise 1: Deploy a Simple Lending Contract

Objective: Develop and deploy a basic Ethereum smart contract for lending that allows users to deposit Ethereum and earn interest over time. Upon withdrawal, users should receive their initial deposit plus accrued interest.

Detailed Instructions:

1. Smart Contract Setup:

- Start by initializing your project using Hardhat or Truffle, which are development environments for compiling, testing, and deploying your Solidity smart contracts.
- Create a new smart contract named **SimpleLending.sol** using Solidity.

2. Deposit Functionality:

- Implement a **deposit()** function that allows users to send Ethereum to the contract. Use the **payable** modifier to allow the function to accept ETH.
- Track each user's deposit amount and the time of deposit using a mapping and struct, respectively.

3. Interest Calculation:

- Define a fixed annual interest rate within the contract.
- Implement a function to calculate the interest earned by a deposit over the period it's been in the contract, using the formula for simple interest.

4. Withdrawal Functionality:

- Create a **withdraw()** function that allows users to withdraw their initial deposit plus the interest earned. Ensure that only the deposit amount plus interest is withdrawable.

5. Testing and Deployment:

- Write test cases using JavaScript to test the deposit, interest calculation, and withdrawal functionalities.
- Deploy your contract to a test network (e.g. Rinkeby) using Hardhat or Truffle. Test the deployed contract with a wallet like MetaMask.

Exercise 2: Implement a Borrowing Functionality with Collateral

Objective: Extend the lending contract from Exercise 1 to allow users to borrow funds by locking in collateral.

Detailed Instructions:

1. Collateral Management:

- Add a new struct to track borrowings, including the amount borrowed, the collateral locked, and the borrowing time.
- Implement a **lockCollateral()** function for users to deposit ERC-20 tokens as collateral. Use the ERC-20 **transferFrom** method to transfer tokens from the user to the contract.

2. Borrowing Function:
- Define a borrowing limit based on the collateral's value (e.g. users can borrow up to 50% of their collateral's value in ETH).
- Create a **borrow()** function that checks if the user has sufficient collateral and allows borrowing up to the specified limit.

3. Liquidation Process:
- Implement a function to check if the value of the collateral falls below a certain threshold (e.g. due to price fluctuations). If it does, allow the contract or other users to liquidate the collateral to cover the loan.

4. Repaying the Loan:
- Allow users to repay the borrowed amount plus interest. Upon repayment, unlock and return the collateral to the user.

Exercise 3: Create a DAO for Lending Protocol Governance

Objective: Develop a DAO that allows token holders to vote on key parameters of the lending protocol, such as interest rates.

Detailed Instructions:
1. Governance Token Creation:
- Use OpenZeppelin contracts to create an ERC-20 governance token for your DAO, named **GovernanceToken.sol**.
- Distribute these tokens to users based on their interaction with the protocol (e.g. depositing, borrowing).

2. Proposal Mechanism:
- Implement a proposal system where token holders can submit proposals for changes to the protocol. Proposals could include changing the interest rate or loan terms.
- Require a minimum number of tokens to submit a proposal.

3. Voting System:
- Create a voting system where token holders can vote on active proposals. The number of tokens held should determine voting power.
- Implement a time limit for voting on proposals.

4. Proposal Execution:
- After a proposal wins (based on predefined criteria like majority approval), automatically apply the changes to the lending protocol.

Chapter 7

The AMM Time Machine

Back to the Future of Finance

Preface

Welcome to the chapter where we dive headfirst into the psychedelic whirlpool of Automated Market Makers (AMMs). If you've ever wished to mingle in the same circles as the high priests of finance, like Goldman Sachs or Citadel, but found your invitation was lost in the mail, fret not. In the domain of AMMs, anyone with an internet connection and a dream can rub virtual elbows with these titans, all from the comfort of their own living room, wearing pajamas, no less.

Here, in this financial Narnia, you don't need a fancy degree or a Wall Street desk to play the game. The AMM platforms have democratized the art of market making, turning every Tom, Dick, and Harry into the potential next big thing in finance. It's like suddenly discovering you can sing as well as Freddie Mercury but in the world of liquidity provision. Who knew?

But, as with all great tales of adventure and power, there's a dragon to be faced: the beast known as impermanent loss. It sounds like a condition you'd argue with your gym instructor over, doesn't it? "Sorry, can't do more squats today; I'm suffering from a severe case of impermanent loss." Yet, in the DeFi saga, it's the sneaky villain lurking in the shadows, ready to snatch away your profits when the prices of your pooled assets decide to throw a party and forget to invite you.

Playing in the big league

Remember the days when "liquidity" was something you worried about with your drink, not your investments? Well, strap in because AMMs are here to turn that notion on its head, creating pools of liquidity so vast and deep that even Scrooge McDuck couldn't dive to the bottom. And the best part? You, yes YOU, sitting there with your third cup of coffee, could potentially set the financial world on fire by providing liquidity from your modest crypto stash. Throw your digital hat into the ring, and voilà, you're not just a spectator; you're playing in the big leagues now. It's a realm where the phrase "let your money work for you" takes on a whole new dimension, occasionally veering into "let your money take a wild Vegas trip without you."

But it's not all rainbows and sunshine in the land of DeFi. Enter the stage, vampire attacks, where protocols engage in a battle royale for liquidity, siphoning off users and funds faster than you can say "SushiSwap." It's a tale of intrigue, strategy, and, dare we say, a touch of malevolence. Yet, it's also a testament to the resilience and innovative spirit that defines the DeFi ecosystem.

Prepare to be amused, bemused, and (hopefully) illuminated as we embark on this journey together. By the end, you might not look at your digital wallet the same way ever again. Welcome to the club, the future market makers of the world. Goldman Sachs and Citadel, eat your hearts out.

1. Introduction

The essence of cryptocurrencies and tokens lies not just in their speculative value or as a medium for financial investment, but also in their capacity to facilitate a decentralized economy, where assets can flow freely without the need for traditional financial intermediaries. Without the means to easily swap tokens, these digital assets risked becoming isolated silos of value, significantly limited in their utility and broader applicability. Before the advent of Automated Market Makers (AMMs), the ability to exchange tokens was largely confined to centralized exchanges, a reality that shaped the utility and value of digital tokens in profound ways.

Centralized exchanges, operating similarly to traditional stock exchanges, provided a necessary bridge in the digital asset ecosystem, allowing for the exchange of tokens and cryptocurrencies. However, this came with its own set of challenges, including issues related to custody, security, and accessibility.[1] Traders and investors had to rely on these centralized entities to hold their assets, making them susceptible to hacking, fraud, and regulatory restrictions. Moreover, the process of listing a new token on a centralized exchange could be cumbersome and expensive, limiting the accessibility of newer or smaller projects to a broader market.

The introduction of AMMs enhanced the security and sovereignty of users' assets and dramatically increased the accessibility and liquidity of a wide range of tokens. Suddenly, tokens that might have been sidelined due to the constraints of centralized exchanges found a new lease on life, contributing to a more vibrant and interconnected digital asset ecosystem.

By democratizing access to token exchange and reducing the barriers to liquidity, AMMs have underscored the inherent value of digital tokens as not merely speculative instruments but as fundamental building blocks of a new, decentralized economic system. This shift has broadened the utility of existing tokens while simultaneously inspiring the development and dissemination of new ones, thereby fueling innovation and growth throughout the cryptocurrency ecosystem. This is largely because innovators found it easier to attract investment by offering tokens, knowing that investors were reassured by the prospect of being able to sell these tokens in the future.

This chapter takes you on an exploration into the heart of AMMs, peeling back the layers to reveal the mechanisms that power decentralized exchanges.

Traditional Financial Markets

To better understand how markets work in DeFi, let's first outline how traditional markets ensure that assets can be easily traded.

When exploring the mechanics of trading in traditional markets, the concept of **an order book** is fundamental. It represents the cornerstone of how trades are executed, and prices are determined in these environments. An order book is essentially a ledger that lists all pending orders for a particular asset, such as stocks, bonds, or currencies. **Figure 1** depicts an example of an order book from a centralized exchange collecting Bitcoin orders. These orders are divided into two main categories: buy orders (bids) and sell orders (asks). Each order lists the price at which a buyer or seller is willing to transact,

---

[1] The collapse of CeFi entities like Celsius, FTX, and others highlights significant issues within centralized crypto platforms, including poor risk management, lack of transparency, and inadequate regulatory oversight. For instance, Celsius faced liquidity crises due to unsustainable high-yield promises and risky lending practices, leading to its bankruptcy. Similarly, FTX's downfall was triggered by alleged mismanagement of customer funds and lack of internal controls, which culminated in a sudden liquidity crunch and subsequent bankruptcy filing.

Sell Orders			Buy Orders		
Price (USDT)	Size (BTC)	Total (USDT)	Price (USDT)	Size (BTC)	Total (USDT)
7500	17.355	130,162.50	6700	22.594	151,329.09
7400	0.02	147.18	6650	447.251	2,984,777.77
7350	4.539	33,134.70	6600	457.673	3,030,868.70
7250	1	7,249.90	6550	158.721	1,043,469.27
7200	269.144	1,931,154.50	6500	182.293	1,185,954.21
7150	283.813	2,028,520.76	6450	181.141	1,172,942.57
7100	314.581	2,228,138.87	6400	364.811	2,340,689.17
7050	229.299	1,611,827.44	6350	350.398	2,231,186.14
7000	395.468	2,760,509.15	6300	388.057	2,326,869.17
6950	159.534	1,105,208.98	6250	313.984	1,342,399.67
6900	166.535	1,146,085.85	6200	345.874	2,151,905.53
6750	960.836	6,463,149.97	6050	0.002	12.15

Figure 1 Example order book

along with the quantity of the asset. The order book is organized by price levels, with buy orders arranged from highest to lowest price and sell orders from lowest to highest. This organization allows participants to quickly see the highest price someone is willing to pay (the highest bid) and the lowest price someone is willing to sell (the lowest ask).

The size and number of orders at each price level within the order book provide insights into the market depth. A deep market is characterized by many orders at each price level, indicating high liquidity. This liquidity means that large transactions can occur without significantly impacting the market price. Conversely, a shallow market has fewer orders at each level, suggesting that large orders could more dramatically move the market price.

Trades occur when a buy order and a sell order match in price. For instance, if there's a buy order for 100 shares at $50 each and a corresponding sell order for 100 shares at $50, the trade is executed at this price. This matching process is central to the concept of price discovery, where the current market price of an asset is determined through the interactions of buyers and sellers in the market. The order book dynamically changes as orders are added, modified, or executed, constantly reflecting the current state of market supply and demand.

The order book is a real-time, transparent record of market activity. It shows not only the prices at which participants are willing to buy and sell but also the sentiment and expectations of market participants. A densely packed order book on the buy-side might indicate bullish sentiment, while a similar pattern on the sell-side could suggest bearish expectations. Traders and analysts closely monitor these patterns and movements in the order book to make informed decisions.

In essence, an order book is the mechanism through which supply and demand are balanced, prices are set, and liquidity is gauged. Understanding how order books function is essential for anyone participating in these markets, whether they are individual traders, institutional investors, or market analysts.

That's not all. In the structure of traditional financial markets, **a clearing agency** also plays a vital and multifaceted role in ensuring the efficiency and integrity of exchanges. It ensures that the frenetic dance of buy and sell orders doesn't descend into chaos: after the traders have taken their positions and the orders matched, there's still the monumental task of swapping assets and cash. This intermediary function is crucial for the successful completion of transactions and the maintenance of market stability.

A clearing agency acts by validating the details of each trade, confirming that the terms agreed upon by the buyer and seller match. This process, known as clearing, involves several key activities, including the calculation of obligations for each party, ensuring that securities and cash are appropriately allocated, and managing the risk that one party may default on their part of the transaction. By doing so, the clearing agency provides a crucial layer of security and trust, reinforcing the market's integrity.

One of the core responsibilities of a clearing agency is to mitigate counterparty risk. Counterparty risk refers to the possibility that one side of the transaction might fail to fulfill their financial obligations, either by not delivering the traded security or not providing the payment as agreed. The clearinghouse minimizes this risk through a mechanism known as the settlement guarantee. This guarantee ensures that, even in cases of default by one party, the transaction will still be completed as intended, protecting the other party from financial loss.

Additionally, clearing agencies are responsible for the accurate and secure record-keeping of all transactions. This administrative role includes maintaining detailed logs of trades and ensuring compliance with regulatory reporting requirements. By systematically recording transaction data, clearing agencies contribute to the transparency and oversight of financial markets, facilitating regulatory bodies' efforts to monitor and manage systemic risk.

The operational framework and services provided by clearing agencies are integral to the smooth functioning of financial markets. They enable the reliable exchange of securities and funds, uphold market integrity by managing and mitigating risks, and ensure regulatory compliance through meticulous record-keeping. Without the foundational support of clearing agencies, the traditional market infrastructure would face significant challenges in maintaining the level of trust and efficiency that participants rely on.

Liquidity is crucial for the efficient functioning of the markets, as it affects the ease with which transactions can be executed. **Market makers** play an indispensable role in financial markets by ensuring liquidity, which is the ability to buy or sell securities without causing a significant movement in the price. By always being ready to buy and sell securities at publicly quoted prices, market makers contribute to this liquidity, making it easier for other participants to execute their trades promptly and at predictable prices.

Market makers provide two-sided markets by continuously offering to buy (bid price) and sell (ask price) securities. This action creates a known price at which trades can be executed, contributing to market transparency. The presence of market makers on a platform ensures that there is enough trading volume, meaning that securities can be bought and sold in sufficient quantities. This availability of securities helps in maintaining an active market where participants can enter and exit positions easily. By fulfilling buy and sell orders, market makers help prevent large swings in securities prices. Their willingness to trade narrows the bid–ask spread (the difference between the buying and selling prices), which, in turn, stabilizes the price of securities and reduces market volatility.

For retail and institutional investors alike, market makers facilitate transactions by acting as the counterparty. When an investor wishes to sell, they can do so immediately to a market maker if no other buyer is available, and vice versa. This instantaneity removes the need for traders to find a matching order, significantly reducing the time it takes to execute trades. The activities of market makers improve market efficiency by ensuring that securities prices reflect available information more accurately and quickly. The constant buying and selling activity helps incorporate new information into prices, keeping them updated.

Market makers assume a significant amount of risk by holding positions in the securities they trade, betting on their ability to manage the bid-ask spread and turn a profit. Despite this risk, their activities are vital for the overall health and efficiency of the financial markets. Their role supports not just individual traders but the market ecosystem as a whole, contributing to its vibrancy and resilience.

To make traditional markets work, we also need institutions ensuring the safekeeping of investors' securities and assets. These institutions, such as banks or trust companies, act as **Custodians** for a wide range of financial assets, including stocks, bonds, and commodities. By entrusting assets to custodians, investors are shielded from the risk of theft, loss, or mismanagement that could arise if these assets were held personally or in less secure environments. Custodians in finance are like that friend who insists on holding your valuables at a party. You're grateful but also slightly nervous they'll join the conga line and forget your stuff.

The role of custodians extends beyond mere storage. They also provide a suite of critical services that facilitate the smooth operation of the post-trade process. This includes settling trades by transferring securities and funds between parties, collecting dividends or interest payments on behalf of the investor, and executing other corporate actions such as stock splits or mergers. Custodians ensure that investors' assets are correctly registered and that all legal and operational requirements are met, which is especially crucial in cross-border transactions where different jurisdictions and regulations come into play.

Moreover, custodians play a pivotal role in maintaining the integrity of the financial markets. Their responsibility in accurately holding and reporting the ownership of assets provides transparency and trust, foundational elements for the functioning of modern financial systems. This clarity about the actual ownership of assets reduces the likelihood of disputes and enhancing market confidence.

In summary, custodians are central to the infrastructure of the financial markets, providing security, operational efficiency, and regulatory compliance. Their services enable investors to participate in the markets with confidence, knowing that their assets are safeguarded and managed with the utmost care.

Finally, **Brokers** bridge the gap between individual investors and the broader securities markets. Their role encompasses a variety of functions aimed at facilitating the investment process for their clients, making it more accessible, efficient, and aligned with investors' goals. Brokers provide investors with access to various trading platforms, which are critical for executing buy and sell orders in the market. These platforms range from basic web interfaces for casual investors to sophisticated software offering real-time data and analysis tools for professional traders. By acting as the gatekeepers to these platforms, brokers enable investors to participate in financial markets that would otherwise be inaccessible to them.

One of the brokers' main functions is to execute trades on their clients' behalf. When an investor decides to buy or sell a security, the broker routes the order to the appropriate market or exchange where the transaction is completed. This process involves a deep understanding of market dynamics and the rules of different trading venues to ensure that clients' orders are executed at the best possible prices.[2]

Many brokers go beyond mere execution of trades and offer value-added services such as investment advice and portfolio management. They may provide clients with recommendations based on research and analysis of the market, individual securities, or broader economic trends. Some brokers offer managed accounts, where they make investment decisions on behalf of their clients based on a predefined strategy or set of goals. Beyond trading and investment management, brokers may offer a wide range of additional services aimed at meeting the diverse needs of investors. These can include retirement planning, tax advice, access to margin trading, and more. By offering a comprehensive suite of services, brokers aim to be a one-stop solution for investors' financial needs.

Brokers are subject to strict regulatory requirements designed to protect investors and ensure the integrity of the markets. They must comply with the regulations set forth by financial regulatory bodies, such as the U.S. Securities and Exchange Commission (SEC) or the Financial Conduct Authority (FCA) in the United Kingdom. This regulatory framework includes requirements for transparency, fair dealing, and protection of client assets.

---

[2] The broker has an actual obligation to execute customer orders at the most favorable terms available under prevailing market conditions. This regulation ensures that brokers act in their clients' best interests when executing trades.

In summary, brokers play a multifaceted role in the financial markets, acting as intermediaries that provide access to trading platforms, execute trades, offer investment advice, and ensure regulatory compliance. Through their services, brokers facilitate individual investors' participation in the financial markets, helping them achieve their investment objectives while providing safeguards against the risks associated with trading and investing.

2. The Core of AMM Mechanics

Having laid out the extensive list of intermediaries required for traditional markets to function correctly, it seems almost absurd to imagine a world where they are nonexistent (or nearly so). The pressing question then becomes: *how can we design a protocol that facilitates direct interaction between traders and efficient price formation without relying on numerous intermediaries?* We need a system that operates seamlessly on its own, i.e. self-executing, coded to execute transactions without the need for any manual input.

Imagine, if you will, a realm where the hustle of calling your broker is replaced by a few clicks, the arcane ritual of interpreting dense order books is rendered obsolete, and the age-old tradition of paying tribute to a cadre of intermediaries is but a distant memory. Sounds like a financial fable, doesn't it? Yet here we stand at the threshold of Automated Market Makers — a marvel not of fiction, but of blockchain ingenuity.

AMMs defy the conventional structure of traditional markets, where trades are tethered to the human-centric processes of brokerage firms, clearinghouses, and custodians. In this innovative landscape, algorithms take center stage, matching trades with unparalleled efficiency and transparency. These digital conjurers facilitate trading by creating liquidity pools, allowing assets to flow freely without the need for a direct counterparty, thus democratizing access to finance in a way previously unimaginable.

So, let us delve deeper into the mechanics and marvels of AMMs.

AMMs use algorithms to determine the price of assets within a liquidity pool. This mechanism is fundamentally different from the order book model, as it does not require orders to be matched. Instead, trades are executed against the liquidity available in the pool, with prices determined through predefined formulas, called **Bonding Curves**.

A bonding curve is a mathematical curve that determines the relationship between the price and the supply of a given asset. In the context of AMMs, these curves are used to set the price of assets in a liquidity pool. The curve ensures that the price adjusts as the supply of tokens in the pool changes. When a trade is executed, the quantities of the tokens in the pool change, which in turn, shifts the price according to the bonding curve. This mechanism allows the AMM to maintain a balanced value within the pool. It seems complicated, but let's keep going, and it will become clearer.

Uniswap, one of the most popular AMMs, utilizes the constant product formula $x \cdot y = k$, where x and y represent the quantity of two different tokens in a liquidity pool, and k is a constant value.

The price of the tokens in the pool is determined by the ratio of the reserves of the two assets. It is like a foreign exchange ratio, the price of x is relative to y. As depicted in **Figure 2**, when a trade occurs, the amount of one token is reduced, and the amount of the other need to increase, ensuring that the product of the two quantities remains constant. This change in the ratio determines the new price of the tokens. AMMs can provide liquidity at any price point, as long as there is enough liquidity in the pool. In other words, unlike traditional markets, where buying and selling rely on the presence of matching orders (someone willing to sell at the price you're willing to buy, and vice versa), AMMs use a mathematical formula to determine prices. This formula ensures that as long as there's liquidity (funds) in the AMM's pool, it can facilitate trades at *any* price. This is because the price is not set by order books but by the ratio of the two assets in the pool.

The limitation is that the ability of an AMM to facilitate trades smoothly depends on the pool having enough funds, e.g., a high k. If the pool is too small, large trades could drastically shift prices (due to the formula used), leading to less favorable rates for traders. However, with sufficient liquidity, the impact of individual trades on the overall price is minimized, making it more stable and predictable.

In traditional exchanges, a trade only happens if there's someone on the other side willing to take the opposite position at the same time. AMMs eliminate this requirement because the liquidity pool itself acts as the counterparty to all trades. This means that as long as you're willing to accept the price the AMM's formula gives you, you can trade

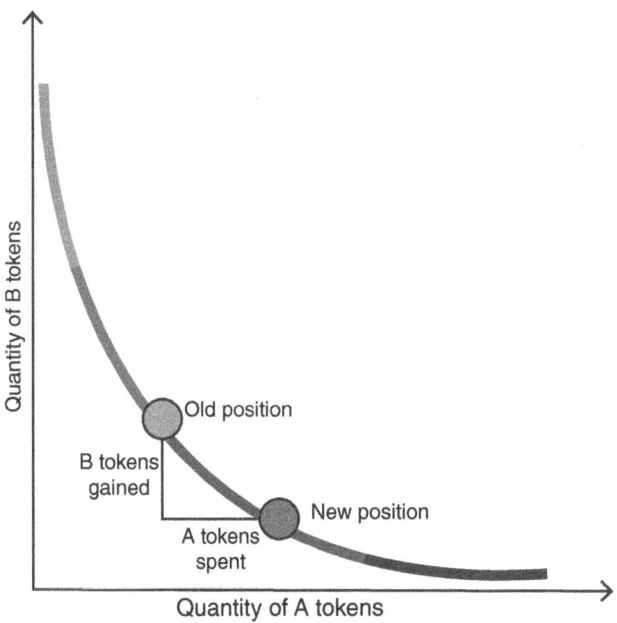

Figure 2   Constant product curve illustrated

any amount at any time without waiting for someone else who wants to trade the exact opposite of what you're offering. This characteristic is vital for ensuring that trades can be executed even without a direct counterparty and make it a **peer-to-contract**, rather than a peer-to-peer market. The investors interact directly with the smart contract governing the exchange of tokens x and y.

2.1 Advantages of AMMs

Having explained the basics, let's highlight the key benefits of AMMs:

- **Accessibility:** AMMs lower the barrier to entry for liquidity providers and traders, as anyone can contribute to a liquidity pool or trade against it.
- **Continuous Liquidity:** Unlike traditional exchanges, which may suffer from low liquidity during off-hours, AMMs provide continuous liquidity, thanks to the automated mechanism.
- **Decentralization:** AMMs operate on decentralized platforms, reducing the need for centralized authorities and intermediaries.

AMMs have fundamentally changed how trades are executed in decentralized finance (DeFi), relying on algorithms to determine asset prices and execute trades directly against a pool of funds rather than matching individual buy and sell orders.

The AMM's pricing algorithm calculates the amount of the output token given for an input token, based on the current state (i.e. the quantity of the two tokens) of the liquidity pool. If a trader specifies a desired amount of the output token, the algorithm determines the required amount of the input token to achieve this trade.

Every trade affects the price by altering the balance of the reserves in the liquidity pool. Since AMMs use formulas like the constant product model to set prices, the act of buying or selling tokens changes their ratio in the pool, thus shifting the price. This dynamic pricing mechanism ensures liquidity but also means that prices can fluctuate with each trade.

Let's dive into a simplified example to understand how AMMs work, using two real tokens, Ethereum (ETH) and DAI, in a liquidity pool. For simplicity, we'll use round numbers and ignore transaction fees to focus on the core concept. **Figure 3** captures this example.

Initial State:
- The liquidity pool contains 10 ETH and 10,000 DAI.
- This implies an initial price ratio of 1 ETH = 1,000 DAI (10,000 DAI / 10 ETH).

Assume that the AMM uses a constant product formula for price determination: $x \times y = k$, where:

- x = amount of one token (ETH in this case),
- y = amount of the other token (DAI),
- k = a constant value.

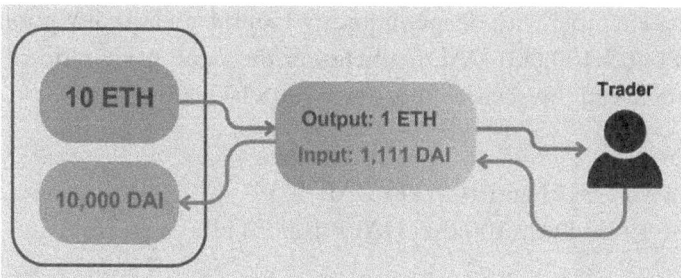

Figure 3 How liquidity pool works

In our example, $k=10\times10,000=100,000$.

Suppose a trader wants to purchase 1 ETH from the pool. To maintain the constant k, the AMM calculates how much DAI the trader needs to add to the pool.

After the purchase, the pool will have 9 ETH. To find the new amount of DAI in the pool ($ynew$), we rearrange the constant product formula to solve for $ynew=k/xnew$ $=100,000/9$

$ynew \approx 11,111.11 DAI$

To find out how much DAI is required for the purchase:

• Initial DAI in the pool = 10,000
• DAI after purchase = 11,111.11

DAI required for the transaction = 11,111.11 – 10,000 = 1,111.11 DAI

Amazing. . .but not free. On top of the blockchain's transaction fee (gas fee), AMMs charge an exchange trading fee for each trade. This fee is a percentage of the trade amount, intended to compensate liquidity providers for the risk of impermanent loss and to incentivize liquidity provision. More importantly, large trades, relative to the size of the pool's reserves, can significantly impact the execution price, leading to **slippage** — the difference between the expected price of a trade and the executed price. High slippage often occurs in pools with low liquidity (i.e. low number of tokens in the pool) or during highly volatile market conditions. Pools with higher liquidity typically offer lower slippage, as larger trades have a smaller relative impact on the reserve balances and, consequently, on the price. Venturing into a low-liquidity pool for a big trade is like trying to sneak out of a party through a squeaky door. Everyone's going to notice, and it won't be smooth.

In the example, the new price of 1 ETH in terms of DAI after the transaction can be observed as the ratio of DAI to ETH in the pool:

• New price of 1 ETH = 11,111.11/9 $\approx 1234.57 DAI$

The price of ETH in DAI has increased from 1,000 DAI to approximately 1234.57 DAI, showing the impact of the trade on the price due to the AMM's constant product formula. This change in price is known as "slippage," and it generally increases with the size of the trade relative to the size of the liquidity pool.

Let's work through the same example with deeper liquidity. Consider a liquidity pool that initially contains 100 ETH and 100,000 DAI, maintaining the same price ratio of 1 ETH = 1,000 DAI. The constant k in this scenario becomes 100×100,000=10,000,000.

Initial State with Higher Liquidity:
The liquidity pool contains 100 ETH and 100,000 DAI.
Initial price ratio: 1 ETH = 1,000 DAI (100,000 DAI / 100 ETH).

Trader's Purchase:
Assuming a trader wants to purchase 1 ETH from this higher liquidity pool. To maintain the constant k, we find the new amount of DAI in the pool: 100 − 1 ETH =99 ETH will be left in the pool. DAI amount in the pool needs to be 10,000,000 / 99 ≈101,010.10 DAI

To calculate the DAI required for this transaction:
Initial DAI in the pool - DAI after purchase = 101,010.10−100,000=1,010.10 DAI
New price of 1 ETH after the transaction: 101,010.10 / 99 ≈1,020.30 DAI

The price of ETH in DAI increased from 1,000 DAI to approximately 1,020.30 DAI.

In the first pool (10 ETH, 10,000 DAI), purchasing 1 ETH caused a significant price increase to approximately 1,234.57 DAI per ETH, which is a clear example of slippage. In the higher liquidity pool (100 ETH, 100,000 DAI), purchasing the same amount of ETH led to a smaller price increase to approximately 1,020.30 DAI per ETH. This shows how larger pools provide deeper liquidity, which is equivalent to say that larger trades can be executed with lower movement in prices.

2.2 Market Manipulation and Attacks

In addition to explicit transaction costs, traders also need to be wary of *sandwich attacks* and *front-running*, where other market participants exploit the transparency of pending transactions. While a transaction is pending, it is visible to others on the network, making it susceptible to various attacks. These can affect the execution price unfavorably, leading to a less advantageous outcome for the trader.

In the world of DeFi, a sandwich attack isn't lunch plans going awry. It's more like someone cutting in line at the deli and making off with your pastrami. It's called a sandwich attack because a malicious trader places orders on both sides of a pending transaction to profit from the price movement caused by the victim's trade. There might then be the risk of front-running, which occurs when someone sees a pending transaction and quickly submits their own transaction with a higher gas fee, ensuring it is executed first and capitalizes on the knowledge of the impending trade.

Let's explain the concept of a sandwich attack using the earlier AMM example with Ethereum (ETH) and DAI. A sandwich attack is a type of manipulation carried out by a trader who aims to capitalize on an upcoming transaction in a decentralized exchange (DEX) that uses an automated market maker (AMM) model.

Imagine there's a pending transaction from Trader A who intends to buy 1 ETH with DAI, as in the previous example. The trader is willing to accept slippage up to a certain percentage, knowing that their trade will impact the price due to the liquidity pool's mechanics.

The Attack:

1. **Initial Observation:** An attacker, let's call them Trader B, notices Trader A's pending transaction that will buy 1 ETH for approximately 1,111.11 DAI (increasing the price of ETH) as the price is deterministic and fully known ex ante.

2. **First Move, Front-Running:** Before Trader A's transaction is processed, Trader B places a transaction to buy ETH with DAI at the current rate, let's say 0.5 ETH to simplify, causing the price of ETH to increase slightly more than if only Trader A's transaction was processed. Trader B pays a higher gas fee to ensure their transaction is processed first.

3. **Trader A's Transaction:** Trader A's transaction is processed next. Due to the increased price from Trader B's front-running transaction, Trader A now pays even more for the 1 ETH, further increasing the ETH price.

4. **Second Move, Back-Running:** Finally, Trader B sells the ETH they previously bought back into the DAI pool, taking advantage of the increased ETH price caused by their initial purchase and Trader A's subsequent purchase.

Trader A ends up purchasing ETH at a higher price than initially expected due to the added slippage caused by Trader B's actions. Trader B (the attacker) profits from the price differential created by sandwiching Trader A's transaction with their buy and sell orders. Trader B is effectively buying low, before Trader A's transaction, and selling high, right after Trader A's purchase order is executed. This attack relies on the attacker's ability to predict and exploit the price impact of large pending transactions. It is considered malicious as it deliberately worsens the execution price for other traders to make a profit.

To mitigate these risks, traders can:

- **Select High Liquidity Pools:** To reduce slippage, a trader should focus on pools with high liquidity relative to the trade size.
- **Adjust Slippage Tolerance:** Most trading interfaces allow users to set a maximum slippage tolerance, canceling the transaction if the slippage exceeds this level.
- **Use Time-Weighted Average Price (TWAP):** For large trades, using TWAP strategies can help spread the trade over time to minimize price impact.[3]

---

[3] A TWAP strategy divides a large trade into smaller, more manageable chunks that are executed incrementally over a specified time frame, preventing the entire order from being placed at once and significantly moving the market price (or revealing too much information, which might lead to front-running). The TWAP algorithm determines the execution schedule for these smaller orders, which can be evenly distributed or adjusted based on market conditions (e.g. as a fraction of trading volume) to achieve a price close to the average during the trading period. By spreading out the trades, the TWAP strategy minimizes market impact and reduces the risk of price slippage, ensuring that the execution price remains close to the initial price without exerting undue influence on supply and demand.

Finally, AMMs introduce a unique set of dynamics to trading in the DeFi ecosystem, offering opportunities for liquidity provision and access to a wide range of tokens. However, the inherent characteristics of AMM platforms require traders to be mindful of factors like slippage, fees, and potential market manipulation tactics.

2.3 Liquidity Providers and Impermanent Loss

As we have seen, AMMs facilitate trading by maintaining liquidity pools for pairs of assets (e.g. ETH and DAI). Unlike traditional exchanges, where trades require a matching buy or sell order, AMMs allow trades to occur directly with the pool at prices determined by a mathematical formula. *But who creates the pools and ensures that there are assets to be exchanged?*

Liquidity Providers (LPs) are individuals or entities that deposit assets into these pools, effectively funding the market. By providing liquidity, they enable traders to buy and sell assets more smoothly. The role of LPs in AMMs is akin to that of market makers in traditional finance, as they both supply the market with the necessary liquidity for trading activities.

LPs are incentivized to deposit their assets into liquidity pools through rewards, often in the form of transaction fees generated from trades within the pool or other incentives specific to the protocol. These rewards can offer an attractive return on idle assets, encouraging participants to contribute liquidity to the pool.

In AMM platforms, trade fees are assessed on each transaction and are distributed to liquidity providers proportional to their share of the pool's liquidity. This distribution mechanism rewards LPs for the risk of providing liquidity by offering them a portion of the trading fees generated by the platform. However, the accrual of trading fees is not straightforward, primarily due to the implications of impermanent loss.

Impermanent loss describes the phenomenon where the value of assets provided by liquidity providers to a liquidity pool decreases compared to holding the assets outside the pool. This loss occurs when the prices of the assets in the pool diverge significantly from their prices at the time they were deposited. The term "impermanent" suggests that this loss is not realized unless the LPs withdraws their liquidity from the pool. If the asset prices return to their original ratio, the loss can be reversed. It is like lending your favorite shirt to a friend and getting it back shrunk. Sure, it might stretch back out, but until then, you're not rocking that look.

The root of impermanent loss lies in the AMM's pricing formula (e.g. the constant product formula $x \cdot y = k$), which automatically adjusts asset prices based on their supply and demand dynamics within the pool. As the price of an asset changes in the external market, arbitrageurs will buy or sell that asset in the AMM until its price aligns with the market price, altering the ratio of assets in the pool and potentially leading to impermanent loss for the LPs. This effect is exacerbated by larger price divergences.

Impermanent loss calculation often involves comparing the current value of an LP's share in the pool (accounting for the changed asset ratio) with the hypothetical current value of those assets had they been held instead of contributed to the pool. The difference represents the impermanent loss, excluding earned fees.

Let's look at a numerical example.

Assume you deposit an equal value of two tokens, Token A and Token B, into a liquidity pool that follows the constant product formula. Let's say 1 Token A = $10 and 1 Token B = $10, so you deposit 10 of each token, totaling $200 in value.

The price of Token A doubles to $20 in the external market.

Impermanent Loss Calculation:

- Initially, the pool contained 10 Token A and 10 Token B.
- After the price change, arbitrageurs adjust the pool to maintain the constant product, ending with fewer Token A and more Token B in the pool. For simplicity, let's assume the new balance is approximately 7.07 Token A and 14.14 Token B to maintain k.
- The value of your share in the pool is now roughly 7.07 Token A ($141.4) + 14.14 Token B ($141.4) = $282.8.
- If you had not provided liquidity and simply held your tokens, you would have 10 Token A ($200) + 10 Token B ($100) = $300.
- The impermanent loss, excluding trading fees, is $300 - $282.8 = $17.2.

This $17.2 represents the impermanent loss experienced due to the change in the price ratio of the assets. Despite the total value in the pool increasing due to the price increase of Asset A, the liquidity provider would have been better off by $17.2 if they had just held onto their assets instead of providing liquidity.

Impermanent loss is the difference between holding the tokens and the value of your withdrawal from the pool:

$$Impermanent\ Loss = \left(Value\ of\ holding\right) - \left(Value\ of\ Withdrawal\ from\ Pool\right)$$

If you withdraw your liquidity while the price disparity exists, the loss becomes permanent. This example shows how the non-linear nature of the constant product formula leads to impermanent loss when the price of one token changes relative to the other.

Impermanent loss is a risk for liquidity providers in AMMs, particularly in volatile markets. Notice that here the price of the underlying token increased and still the LP suffered! The reason is that impermanent loss captures the opportunity costs of providing those assets as part of the liquidity pool. This concept is crucial for understanding the trade-offs of participating in AMM liquidity provision.

The impermanent loss can be formally derived using the constant product formula, which gives this $2 \cdot \frac{\sqrt{R}}{R+1} - 1$ where R is the change in the ratio of prices.[4] **Figure 4** shows that when the relative change in "relative" price — the reserve ratio — moves away from 0, impermanent loss increases.

---

[4] The full derivation is shown in Appendix.

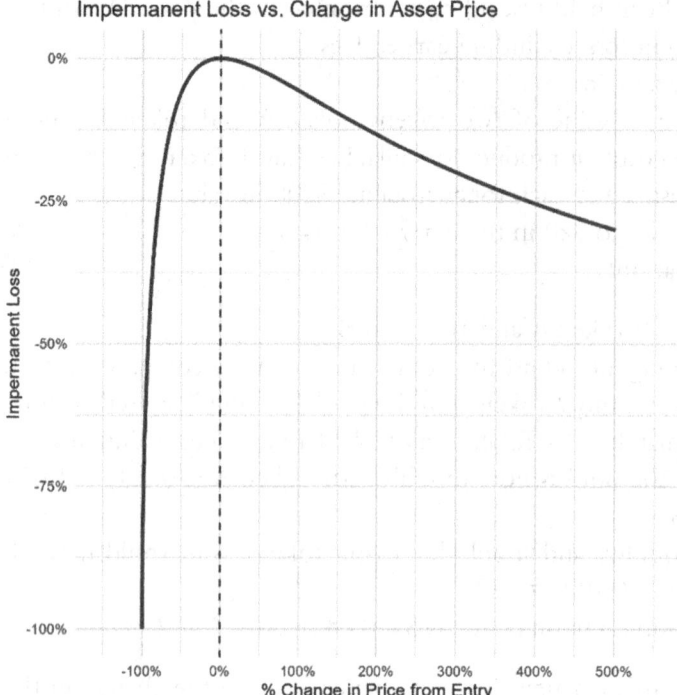

Figure 4   Impermanent loss with the change in asset price

Mitigating Strategies   To mitigate the risks of impermanent loss, LPs should consider several factors before providing liquidity to a pool:

- **Price Volatility:** LPs should assess their comfort with the price volatility of the assets in a pool. Pools with assets that have stable price relationships are less likely to result in significant impermanent loss.
- **Pool Liquidity:** High liquidity in a pool can reduce the impact of large trades on the price of assets, potentially mitigating the extent of impermanent loss. However, LPs should also be aware that pools with very high liquidity might offer lower fee returns per liquidity unit than those with moderate liquidity.
- **Asset Selection:** Choosing pools with assets that are less prone to high volatility can reduce the risk of impermanent loss. Stablecoin pools, for example, are generally considered lower risk in terms of impermanent loss.

3. What Is Better: AMMs or Traditional Markets?

Given the various direct and indirect costs associated with using AMMs for both token swappers and liquidity providers, it naturally leads us to question whether AMMs truly represent an advancement over traditional order books. The choice between AMMs and traditional order books impacts retail consumers, traders, and market makers in different ways, depending on their priorities, such as liquidity, price discovery, and the risk of market manipulation.

AMMs revolutionize trading by providing constant liquidity to the market. They allow for permissionless trading, where anyone can become a liquidity provider or trader without needing approval from a central authority. This democratization of finance aligns with the ethos of decentralized finance (DeFi) by making markets more accessible.

Anybody can be a LP then. . .but would you? As we have seen, AMMs are not without their risks. Impermanent loss poses a significant challenge to liquidity providers, particularly in volatile markets. Additionally, the reliance on smart contracts introduces vulnerabilities to bugs and exploits, which could lead to loss of funds. In addition, let's analyze some additional drawbacks to AMMs.

3.1 Limitations on Price Discovery

The first drawback of AMMs, affecting investors, is that they are not a venue for price discovery. Price discovery is the process through which the price of an asset is determined by the interactions of buyers and sellers in the market, reflecting all available information about the asset's value. In traditional financial markets, this process involves the matching of buy and sell orders, with prices adjusting based on new information, supply, and demand dynamics.

In AMMs, however, price adjustments are formula-driven, based on the changes in asset ratios within the pools rather than direct buyer and seller interactions. This means that AMMs do not inherently provide an avenue for price discovery in the traditional sense; they adjust prices based on the ratio of assets in the pool, which changes as traders arbitrage differences between the AMM prices and external market prices.

CENTRALIZED EXCHANGES LEAD PRICE DISCOVERY   In contrast, centralized exchanges (CEXs) play a significant role in price discovery for cryptocurrencies and tokens. They operate on an order book model, where prices adjust dynamically based on the matching of buy and sell orders. When new information emerges about a protocol or asset, it is often reflected first in the prices on centralized exchanges, where traders quickly incorporate this information into their trading strategies.

Decentralized exchanges (DEXs) and AMMs, on the other hand, rely on arbitrage traders to adjust the prices in the liquidity pools to reflect the prices found on centralized exchanges or other external price sources. This means that price information typically flows from centralized to decentralized platforms, making DEXs followers rather than leaders in price discovery.

3.2. Adverse Selection and Liquidity Providers

The second drawback, affecting mainly LPs, is the presence of adverse selection. Adverse selection refers to a situation where traders have different information about the value of an asset, leading those with superior information to profit at the expense of those with inferior information. In the context of AMMs, this dynamic is particularly relevant for liquidity providers.

When the value of a token increases due to new, positive information, traders will quickly buy this token on AMMs, exchanging it for the other token in the pool. This process continues until the price in the AMM adjusts to reflect the new information. However, because the price change in the AMM is formula-driven and reactive, LPs often find that the asset increasing in value is drained from their pool in exchange for the other asset, which is relatively less valuable. This means that LPs are effectively "selling low and buying high," which can lead to impermanent loss, as discussed earlier.

In other words, because arbitrageurs are the ones who adjust the price in the AMM by taking advantage of the discrepancy between the AMM and external market prices, LPs are exposed to adverse selection. They are left holding more of the asset that has decreased in relative value, while the more valuable asset is removed from the pool by traders capitalizing on the mechanics of the AMM's price adjustment.

In summary, the deterministic nature of price changes in AMMs, coupled with their role as followers in the price discovery process, exposes liquidity providers to adverse selection. This dynamic underscores the importance of understanding the mechanisms of AMMs and the market forces at play for anyone considering becoming a liquidity provider in these decentralized platforms.

3.3 Which Is Better Then?

It depends. See **Table 1** for a summary of the key benefits and drawbacks.

For Retail Consumers: AMMs may offer a more accessible and straightforward entry point due to their constant liquidity and permissionless nature. Retail consumers might find AMMs more user-friendly, especially those who are not deeply versed in complex trading strategies. However, the risk of impermanent loss and potential smart contract vulnerabilities are important considerations.

For Traders: The choice largely depends on the trader's strategy. Traders looking for quick, arbitrage opportunities might favor AMMs for their instant liquidity. On the other hand, those employing more sophisticated strategies that require nuanced price discovery might lean toward traditional order books. Additionally, traders concerned about the impact of their trades on the market might prefer the transparency and control offered by order books.

For Market Makers: Traditional order books may be more appealing due to the ability to employ various strategies and potentially profit from bid-ask spreads and market inefficiencies. However, market makers in AMMs can benefit from fees collected on trades, despite the risks of impermanent loss. The choice might depend on their risk tolerance and the specific market dynamics of the assets involved.

4. PROMINENT PROTOCOL: UNISWAP

Uniswap stands as a cornerstone in the decentralized finance (DeFi) landscape, exemplifying the innovative potential of AMMs.

Launched in November 2018, Uniswap V1 was a groundbreaking step for AMMs within DeFi, introducing the constant product formula $x \cdot y = k$ to determine prices within liquidity pools. This first version was revolutionary, yet it came with notable limitations:

- **Limited Token Support:** Initially, it only supported pools between Ethereum (ETH) and individual ERC-20 tokens. This design meant that direct ERC-20 to ERC-20 swaps were not possible without ETH as an intermediary, doubling the transaction fees for such trades.
- **Native ETH and WETH:** The protocol only supported native Ethereum transactions, not recognizing Wrapped Ethereum (WETH) as an ERC-20 token, which added an extra layer of complexity for users and developers.

Despite these constraints, V1 laid the foundational work for decentralized exchange on Ethereum, proving the concept of AMMs could indeed facilitate automated trading within the DeFi ecosystem.

In May 2020, Uniswap V2 was rolled out, addressing many of the initial version's limitations and introducing several key features:

- **ERC-20 to ERC-20 Swaps:** Direct trading between two ERC-20 tokens was enabled, significantly enhancing the protocol's flexibility and usability.
- **Wrapped ETH (WETH):** V2 simplified interactions with Ethereum by supporting WETH, making it easier for users to trade with ETH in a more ERC-20 compliant manner.
- **Protocol Charge Mechanism:** A new fee structure was introduced, including a protocol charge of 0.05% per trade, which could be activated in the future to support the development fund, illustrating an innovative approach to protocol sustainability.
- **Improved Oracle System:** The update included an enhanced oracle system, allowing for the on-chain accumulation of time-weighted average prices, which expanded Uniswap's utility beyond trading into more complex financial applications.

4.1 Uniswap V3: Concentrated Liquidity and Innovation

However, the most consequential innovation was launched in May 2021 with Uniswap V3. It represented a significant leap forward, introducing features that greatly increased capital efficiency and flexibility for liquidity providers (LPs):

Concentrated Liquidity: This feature allowed LPs to allocate their capital to specific price ranges, providing greater control over their exposure and potential returns. This innovation aimed to maximize fee generation and minimize impermanent loss within chosen price bands.

Multiple Fee Tiers: Recognizing the varying degrees of volatility among different asset pairs, and so different risk of impermanent loss, V3 introduced multiple fee tiers, enabling LPs to be compensated according to the expected risk and volatility of their chosen pools.

NFTs for LP Positions: Each LP's position, defined by their specific price ranges and fee tiers, was represented as a unique Non-Fungible Token (NFT), a novel approach to track and manage liquidity contributions in a decentralized environment.

Active Capital Management: With concentrated liquidity, LPs are encouraged to actively manage their positions to optimize their returns, marking a shift toward a more engaged form of liquidity provision within the AMM model.

To appreciate the importance of this development, let's compare slippage and impermanent loss between Uniswap V2 and V3 as depicted in **Figure 5**.

Uniswap V2:

- Suppose liquidity pool has 10,000 DAI and 100 ETH and that a trader wants to swap 1,000 DAI for ETH. The constant $k = 10,000 \cdot 100 = 1,000,000$
- After the trade, we need $11,000 \cdot y = 1,000,000$, solving for y gives us approximately 90.9 ETH left. The trader then receives about 9.1 ETH for their 1,000 DAI, and the price per ETH is roughly 110 DAI after the trade.

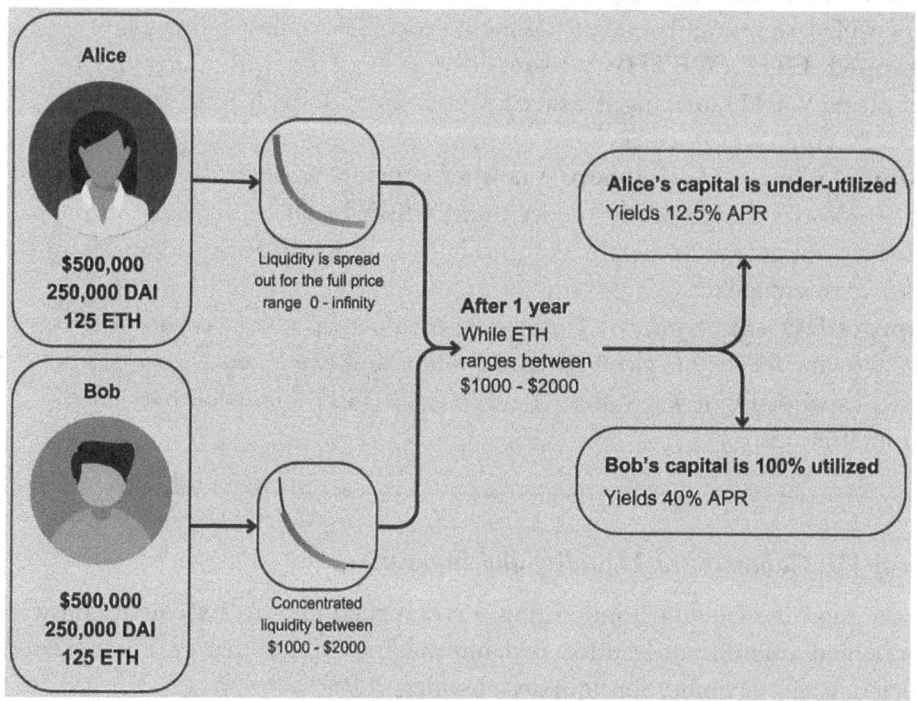

Figure 5   Concentrated liquidity example

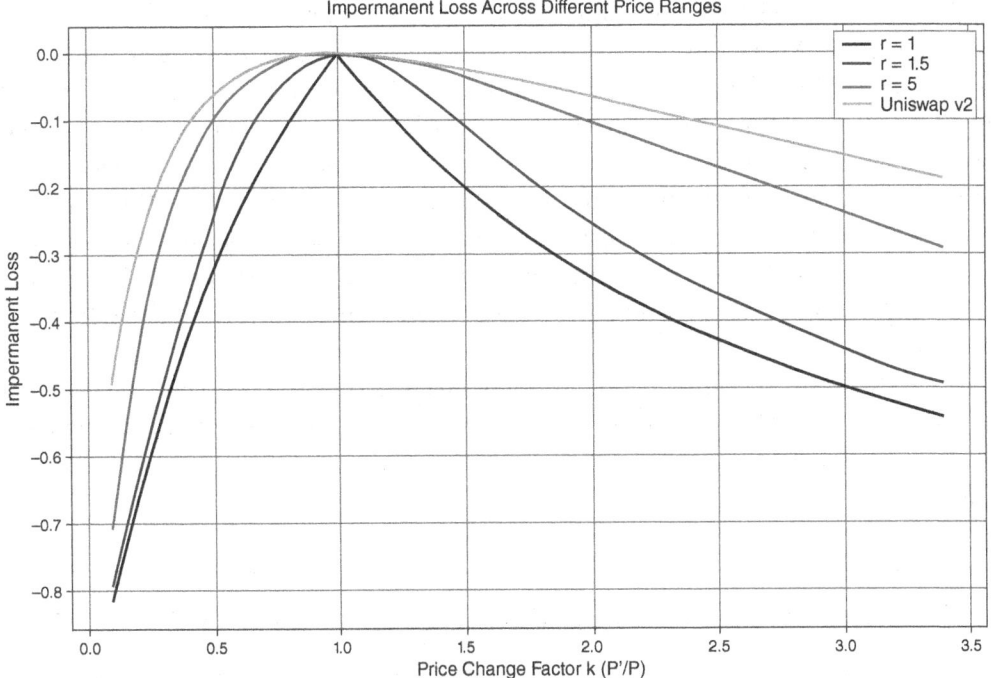

Figure 6   Impermanent loss in Uniswap V3

In Uniswap V3, an LP decides to deposit 500 DAI and 5 ETH between the price range of 100 DAI/ETH to 200 DAI/ETH. A trader executing the same 1,000 DAI trade for ETH would find less slippage if the price is within the concentrated range due to higher liquidity in that range. However, if the price moves out of that range, the LP's capital is not used, and the trader might experience higher slippage compared to V1 or V2.

Impermanent loss can be minimized in V3 if the LPs price range does not exceed the market price. The LP can adjust their price ranges actively, potentially reducing impermanent loss. This can be shown by expanding on the impermanent loss formula shown in Figure 4. In **Figure 6**, "*r*" corresponds to the price range. As *r* goes to infinity, impermanent loss converges into V2. [5]

Uniswap V3 aimed to provide greater capital efficiency and reduce slippage for traders executing trades within those ranges. For instance, if an LP deposits 500 DAI and 5 ETH within the price range of 100 to 200 DAI/ETH, trades within this range benefit from reduced slippage due to the concentrated liquidity. Furthermore, as a liquidity provider you would be compensated if there were more trades occurring within your specified range (i.e. it is as if the swappers were to interact with that specific smart contract rather than with the overall liquidity pool). However, should the price move outside this range, the LP's capital becomes inactive, potentially leading to higher slippage for traders than in previous versions.

---

[5] The full derivation is shown in the appendix.

The concentrated liquidity feature in V3 also introduces a nuanced dynamic to impermanent loss. While LPs can actively adjust their price ranges to mitigate some risks of impermanent loss, if the market price moves out of their selected range, they cease to earn fees, and their capital isn't utilized until the price returns to their designated range. For example, an LP providing liquidity for ETH/DAI between 100 and 200 DAI/ETH will see their position automatically rebalanced if the price moves to 150 DAI. However, if the price escalates beyond 200 DAI, all of the LP's ETH would be converted to DAI, leaving them with only DAI in their position. Should the LP have simply held onto their 5 ETH and 500 DAI, they would have realized more significant gains due to the price appreciation of ETH.

LPs can concentrate liquidity which can reduce slippage for traders and offer higher fees with less capital. They are effectively trading-off of a higher risk of impermanent loss if price moves out of range. Effectively, it requires a more active LP position management strategy.

4. Real Case Study: Monetization Strategy at Uniswap[6]

Uniswap also offers the possibility to delve into its efforts to generate revenue. It can be used to accomplish the following learning objectives:

- To understand the unique challenges of monetizing open-source projects within the DeFi space
- To explore the dynamics of competition and cooperation in a rapidly evolving ecosystem marked by frequent forks and clones
- To critically evaluate the effectiveness of decentralized governance models in guiding the development and strategic direction of DeFi platforms

This case centers around the following key questions:

- **Monetization:** How can Uniswap balance its open-source nature with the need to generate revenue? What innovative monetization strategies could be sustainable?
- **Competitive Landscape:** How should Uniswap navigate the competitive pressures from both centralized exchanges and other DeFi platforms engaging in vampire attacks?
- **Governance Dynamics:** What are the key challenges of decentralized governance for Uniswap, and how can it ensure that governance decisions are in the best interest of all stakeholders?

---

[6] For more details about this case (and if you are an instructor about how to use it in the classroom), see the Harvard Business School case coauthored with Wenyao Sha and titled "Uniswap: Decentralized Crypto Trading" N9-223-025 and the corresponding teaching note.

Monetization Challenges for Open Protocols Uniswap operates in a unique position within the decentralized finance (DeFi) ecosystem, primarily because it is built on an open-source codebase. This openness fosters innovation and collaboration, allowing developers worldwide to contribute to or build upon Uniswap's technology. However, this same openness poses a significant challenge for revenue generation. Traditionally, companies protect their intellectual property to create and maintain revenue streams, something inherently difficult for a platform like Uniswap, where the code is freely available. This scenario prompts a fundamental question: how can Uniswap generate sustainable revenue without compromising its open, permissionless ethos? There are a few options.

TRANSACTION FEES One of the most straightforward strategies for monetization involves instituting transaction fees on trades executed through Uniswap's platform. This approach has a clear precedent in both traditional finance (TradFi) and centralized crypto exchanges, where transaction fees are a primary revenue source. However, implementing fees in a decentralized setting requires careful consideration of several factors.

- **Competitive Balance:** Uniswap competes not just with other decentralized exchanges (DEXs) but also with centralized platforms. Any fee structure must be competitive enough to retain and attract users in this diverse marketplace. What would prevent the existing users from migrating to a different (cheaper) platform?
- **Community Acceptance:** As a platform deeply rooted in the DeFi community, any changes to the fee model need widespread support from Uniswap's users and stakeholders, particularly since these changes could be proposed and voted on through its governance model.
- **Dynamic Structuring:** Uniswap could explore a dynamic fee structure that adjusts based on market conditions, trading volumes, or even the type of assets being traded, ensuring that the platform remains competitive and adaptable.

VALUE-ADDED SERVICES Given the limitations and potential pushback on implementing transaction fees, Uniswap might consider developing and offering value-added services or products. These could provide additional revenue streams while enhancing the platform's overall value proposition. Potential avenues include the following:

- **Institutional Services:** Catering to the needs of institutional investors by offering bespoke trading solutions, analytics, and integration services. Given the growing interest of traditional finance in DeFi, Uniswap could position itself as a bridge between these two worlds, leveraging its open-source infrastructure to offer secure, scalable solutions.

- **Premium Features:** For retail users, Uniswap could introduce premium features that enhance the trading experience. These could range from advanced trading tools and analytics to personalized support. While the base layer of Uniswap would remain open and accessible, these premium features could attract users willing to pay for a more enriched experience.
- **Developer Ecosystem Support:** Recognizing the value that developers bring to the ecosystem, Uniswap could offer specialized services that support the development and deployment of third-party applications built on its protocol. This could include access to advanced APIs, deployment tools, and even funding or incubation programs for promising projects.

Each of these strategies presents its own set of challenges and opportunities. Implementing transaction fees requires careful balance to avoid alienating users, while developing value-added services demands a deep understanding of user needs and market dynamics. However, if executed thoughtfully, these strategies could not only ensure Uniswap's financial sustainability but also strengthen its position as a leader in the DeFi space.

Vampire Attacks: The Case of SushiSwap   Implementing any of the aforementioned strategies has its own challenges, especially because the protocols can be subject to what are called *vampire attacks*. A vampire attack in the context of decentralized finance (DeFi) refers to a strategy where a competing platform siphons off liquidity from another by forking (copying) its codebase and then offering greater incentives to attract its users and liquidity providers. This term gained prominence with the launch of SushiSwap, which executed a classic vampire attack by forking Uniswap's open-source code and then enticing its liquidity providers with the promise of SUSHI tokens, in addition to the usual transaction fee earnings.

The impact of such attacks can be profound, as seen in the case of SushiSwap. In a short period, SushiSwap managed to migrate a significant portion of Uniswap's liquidity onto its platform, challenging Uniswap's dominance in the DeFi space. This not only demonstrated the vulnerability of open-source DeFi platforms to such strategies but also underscored the competitive dynamics within the DeFi ecosystem, where the barriers to entry are low, and user loyalty is highly incentive-driven.

Uniswap's response to the vampire attack by SushiSwap involved a combination of immediate actions and long-term strategic initiatives to safeguard its position and foster innovation while protecting its interests:

- **Introduction of UNI Governance Token:** In response to the liquidity migration, Uniswap launched its own governance token, UNI, distributing it broadly to past users of the protocol through an airdrop, as well as to liquidity providers. This helped to incentivize liquidity provision and platform usage and aimed to create a stronger sense of community and stakeholder ownership, countering the narrative that Uniswap was less community-focused compared to SushiSwap.

- **Modifications to Licensing:** Learning from the experience, Uniswap introduced modifications to its licensing for the v3 iteration of the protocol. By adopting a Business Source License (BUSL), Uniswap sought to balance openness with the need to protect its intellectual property for a certain period. This license allowed Uniswap to keep its code open-source while restricting commercial use of the code for two years, giving Uniswap a temporal protection window against immediate forks of its latest innovations.

Vampire attacks are not unique to Uniswap and SushiSwap; they are a recurring theme within the DeFi industry, where the open-source nature of many projects makes them susceptible to such strategies. Another notable example includes the forking of Compound and Aave by platforms looking to replicate their success in the lending and borrowing domain, often by offering additional incentives or governance tokens to attract users.

These attacks highlight a common challenge within the DeFi industry: balancing the ethos of decentralization and open-source development with the need for projects to protect their innovations and sustain their ecosystems. The response to vampire attacks, as demonstrated by Uniswap, often involves a combination of incentivizing user loyalty, adopting strategic licensing measures, and continually innovating to stay ahead of competitors.

Uniswap's experience underscores the importance of community engagement and innovation as key defenses against vampire attacks. By fostering a loyal user base and continuously improving the platform, DeFi projects not only can survive such challenges but also thrive, contributing to the overall resilience and dynamism of the DeFi ecosystem.

Decentralized Governance in Action   Uniswap's decentralized governance model symbolizes the broader DeFi movement's commitment to democratizing financial systems and ensuring decisions are made transparently. At the heart of Uniswap's governance system are the UNI tokens, which not only represent a financial stake in Uniswap's ecosystem but also confer voting rights on their holders. This model empowers UNI token holders to participate in the governance process, including proposing changes, voting on new features, upgrading protocols, and using the community treasury.

The governance process typically begins with discussions within the community, followed by the formulation of proposals that are then put to a vote. For a proposal to be eligible for voting, it must first meet certain criteria, including a minimum threshold of UNI tokens backing the proposal. This mechanism ensures that only proposals with significant community support reach the voting stage, reflecting a collective interest in the platform's development.

One of the key decisions taken by the UniDAO was the decision to introduce stablecoin liquidity pools with a 0.01% fee in Uniswap v3. This represented a strategic move to enhance Uniswap's competitiveness in the stablecoin exchange market. This low fee structure was specifically designed to attract more liquidity and trading volume for stablecoin pairs, which are a critical component of the DeFi ecosystem due to their reduced volatility (and then lower impermanent loss) and widespread use for trading and value transfer.

By lowering fees to 0.01% for stablecoin pairs, Uniswap directly challenged other DeFi platforms specializing in stablecoin exchanges, such as Curve Finance. This move made Uniswap an attractive platform for users seeking to trade stablecoins with minimal cost, thus drawing liquidity away from competitors.

The introduction of the 0.01% fee pools incentivized liquidity providers to allocate more of their assets to Uniswap, knowing that their contribution would facilitate a high volume of trades at a lower cost. Increased liquidity for stablecoin pairs not only benefits traders in terms of reduced slippage but also solidifies Uniswap's position as a leading liquidity provider in the DeFi space.

Because of the attractive fee structure and the subsequent increase in liquidity and trading volume, Uniswap captured a significant portion of the stablecoin market. This strategic decision played a crucial role in Uniswap's growth, enabling it to maintain and even expand its market share in a highly competitive environment. It is even more surprising that such a decision was not taken by a board of directors but by a DAO!

Uniswap's decision to introduce the 0.01% fee tier demonstrates its agility and responsiveness to the needs of the DeFi community and market dynamics. It reflects a broader strategy of using governance mechanisms to adapt the platform's offerings to remain at the forefront of the DeFi space. By actively engaging its community through the UniDAO governance model, Uniswap can make data-driven decisions that align with its users' preferences and market trends.

While decentralized governance offers a path toward a more open and equitable financial system, it also introduces several challenges and complexities:

- **Coordinating Community-Driven Governance:** One of the main challenges is coordinating a large, diverse group of stakeholders, each with their own perspectives and interests. Ensuring effective communication and consensus-building among UNI token holders is crucial for the smooth functioning of the governance process. Platforms like forums and social media play a vital role in facilitating discussion and debate among community members.

- **Ensuring Fair Representation:** Another challenge is ensuring that all voices within the Uniswap community are heard and considered. There's a risk that larger token holders could disproportionately influence decisions, potentially sidelining smaller participants. Mechanisms such as delegation, where token holders can delegate their voting rights to representatives who share their views, have been implemented to address this concern. However, ensuring that this does not lead to centralization of power remains a critical issue.
- **Making Effective Decisions:** Decentralized governance must also contend with the challenge of making timely and effective decisions. The open, participatory nature of the process can sometimes lead to delays or gridlock, especially on contentious issues. Balancing speed and inclusivity is a delicate task, requiring careful structuring of the governance framework to facilitate efficient decision-making while still respecting the principle of community involvement.
- **Aligning with the Platform's Long-Term Vision:** This is probably the biggest challenge. Ensuring that governance decisions align with Uniswap's long-term vision and values is crucial. This involves not only strategic thinking and foresight from the community and its delegates but also mechanisms to guide decision-making toward sustainable, long-term objectives rather than short-term gains. The governance process must be designed to support the platform's mission to democratize finance, encourage innovation, and foster a healthy ecosystem.

The experience of Uniswap with decentralized governance illuminates both the potential and the pitfalls of community-driven decision-making in DeFi. It underscores the need for continuous innovation in governance mechanisms to address these challenges, ensuring that the platform can adapt and evolve in response to the needs of its users and the broader ecosystem. The journey of refining decentralized governance is ongoing, with each challenge presenting an opportunity to strengthen the foundations of the DeFi movement.

4.2 Uniswap V4

A Uniswap V4 by the end of 2024 has also been announced. It introduces significant innovations aimed at enhancing the decentralized trading experience through advanced customization, efficiency, and reduced operational costs.

CUSTOMIZATION WITH HOOKS Uniswap V4 improves liquidity pool customization through the introduction of "hooks." These are smart contracts that can be attached to liquidity pools, enabling developers to implement specific functionalities at various stages of a pool's lifecycle, such as before or after swaps or liquidity modifications. Hooks allow for unprecedented flexibility, including the ability to introduce dynamic fees, on-chain limit orders, specialized automated market maker (AMM) curves, and more tailored oracles. This level of customization opens the door to a wide array of innovative trading strategies and pool behaviors.

SINGLETON CONTRACT FOR EFFICIENCY   A significant architectural change in V4 is the consolidation of all liquidity pools into a single smart contract, known as a Singleton contract. This model contrasts with previous versions, where each token pair required a separate contract, leading to higher gas costs. The Singleton contract greatly reduces gas costs for trading and creating new pools, making multi-hop trades more efficient and significantly lowering the barrier to entry for setting up new pools.

The architectural shift to a Singleton contract in Uniswap V4, which consolidates all liquidity pools into a single smart contract, addresses several limitations present in earlier versions of Uniswap and similar DeFi platforms. Previously, each liquidity pool required its own contract, which not only increased the complexity of the system but also raised the gas costs associated with trades and pool creation. This model made it especially cumbersome and expensive for users to engage in multi-hop trades (trades that require swapping through multiple pools to get from the initial token to the desired token).

BEFORE SINGLETON CONTRACTS   Consider a user wanting to swap Token A for Token C, where no direct A–C pool exists, and the most efficient path is through Token B. In earlier Uniswap versions or other AMMs without a Singleton contract model, this user would need to execute two separate transactions:

1. **Swap Token A for Token B:** The user interacts with the A–B liquidity pool contract, executing a swap that incurs gas fees.
2. **Swap Token B for Token C:** The user then interacts with the B–C liquidity pool contract, incurring a separate set of gas fees for this second transaction.

Each interaction involves not only the gas costs of executing the swaps but also the overhead of transferring tokens between different contracts, leading to higher overall costs and inefficiencies.

WITH SINGLETON CONTRACTS   In contrast, with Uniswap V4's Singleton contract model, all liquidity pools are contained within a single contract. This consolidation significantly reduces the complexity and gas costs associated with trades, particularly for multi-hop trades.

Imagine a scenario in the new Singleton contract system where a user still wants to swap Token A for Token C via Token B. With V4, the process becomes more streamlined and cost-effective:

• **Single Contract Interaction:** The user submits a transaction that specifies the desire to swap Token A for Token C through Token B. This is processed within the single Singleton contract, reducing the transaction to a singular, more efficient operation.

- **Reduced Gas Costs:** Because all the pools are within one contract, the tokens do not need to be transferred between contracts; only their balances within the Singleton contract are updated. This significantly reduces the gas costs.
- **Efficient Routing:** The Singleton model facilitates more efficient routing algorithms for determining the best swap paths, further optimizing gas usage and potentially providing better rates for the user.

This architectural change not only lowers the barrier for users to engage in complex trades but also democratizes the creation of new liquidity pools. Creating a new pool in a system where each requires a separate contract is not just costly but daunting for smaller liquidity providers. With the introduction of the Singleton contract, the cost of creating new pools drops dramatically, encouraging more diverse and abundant liquidity provision on the platform.

Previous Model: Separate Contracts for Each Pool   In earlier versions of Uniswap, each liquidity pool required its own smart contract. For example, if a developer wanted to create a new liquidity pool for a token pair like ETH/DAI, they had to deploy a new smart contract specifically for that pair. This process involved several steps:

1. **Deployment:** The developer needs to interact with the Uniswap router contract to create and deploy a new smart contract on the Ethereum blockchain incurring gas fees for the deployment.
2. **Liquidity Provision:** Liquidity providers then add their assets to the pool by interacting with this newly deployed contract, paying gas fees for each transaction.
3. **Trading:** Traders swap tokens through this contract, with each swap transaction incurring gas fees.

This model made the creation of new pools costly due to the gas fees associated with deploying each new smart contract. Additionally, for liquidity providers, especially smaller ones, the costs and technical barriers could be prohibitive, limiting the diversity and number of new pools created.

The Singleton contract architecture significantly reduces the overhead associated with creating and managing pools. Here's how it changes the scenario:

- **Reduced Deployment Costs:** Instead of deploying a new contract for each pool, a developer simply registers a new token pair within the Singleton contract. This process requires far less gas, making it cheaper and faster.
- **Efficient Liquidity Provision:** Liquidity providers interact with one contract regardless of the number of pools they participate in, reducing transaction costs and complexity.

This architectural shift democratizes the creation of liquidity pools, enabling more participants to contribute to the Uniswap ecosystem, fostering a more inclusive and vibrant DeFi landscape.

FLASH ACCOUNTING SYSTEM   Uniswap V4 introduces a "flash accounting" system, which allows for the chaining of multiple actions (like swap-and-add-liquidity) in a single transaction. This system ensures that only net balances of inbound and outbound tokens are settled at the end of the transaction, enhancing security and efficiency. If debts aren't settled, the entire transaction reverts, ensuring that operations within the pool are secure and cost-effective.

The "flash accounting" system introduced in Uniswap V4 is a sophisticated mechanism designed to streamline and secure transactions within the protocol by allowing multiple actions to be executed within a single transaction (it should remind you of flash loans). This feature is particularly beneficial for complex operations that would traditionally require several individual transactions, thus improving both user experience and gas efficiency.

In traditional finance and earlier versions of Uniswap, operations like swapping tokens and then adding liquidity with those tokens would require separate transactions. Flash accounting enables these to be chained together seamlessly. For instance, a user can swap ETH for DAI and then use that DAI to provide liquidity to a DAI/USDC pool, all in one go.

At the core of flash accounting is the principle of net balance settlement. Instead of processing and finalizing each action's token transfers immediately, the system calculates the net amounts of tokens that should be inbound or outbound by the end of the transaction.

The system enhances security by ensuring that if the calculated net balances are not properly settled by the transaction's end—if, say, there's a deficit in what was supposed to be paid out versus what was actually available—the whole transaction is automatically reverted. This reversion mechanism protects against incomplete or fraudulent activities within a pool.

By consolidating multiple steps into a single transaction, flash accounting significantly reduces the cumulative gas costs associated with executing several blockchain transactions. This efficiency not only benefits users in terms of lower fees but also contributes to less congestion on the Ethereum network, where Uniswap operates.

Practical Example   Imagine a scenario where a trader wants to take advantage of a sudden market opportunity by swapping tokens and then immediately using those tokens to enter a liquidity pool. Without flash accounting, this trader would need to execute at least two separate transactions: one for the swap and another to add liquidity, each incurring its own gas fees and waiting times.

With flash accounting, these actions are combined. The trader initiates a swap from ETH to DAI and uses the DAI to add liquidity to a DAI/USDC pool in one transaction. If for any reason the liquidity provision can't be completed as intended (for example, if there isn't enough DAI post-swap to meet the liquidity provision requirements), the entire operation is undone, protecting the trader from partial execution that could result in a less favorable position.

This system represents a significant step forward in the evolution of DeFi platforms, offering users more flexibility and security while optimizing the network's overall gas efficiency. Flash accounting is a clear example of how Uniswap V4 continues to innovate within the blockchain space, enhancing the protocol's functionality and user experience.

4.3 Additional Trading Strategies

One innovative trading strategy that can be implemented with the introduction of hooks in Uniswap V4, which was not feasible in earlier versions, involves the use of on-chain limit orders. Before Uniswap V4, AMMs like Uniswap primarily facilitated swaps through a pooled liquidity mechanism without the ability for traders to set specific prices at which they wished to buy or sell tokens. This limitation meant that traders had to manually monitor the market and execute trades at moments when the price met their desired criteria, a process that could be both time-consuming and imprecise.

With the introduction of hooks in Uniswap V4, developers can now create smart contracts that attach to liquidity pools and introduce the functionality of on-chain limit orders. Here's a high-level overview of how this trading strategy could be implemented:

1. **Limit Order Logic:** A developer writes a hook that implements the logic for on-chain limit orders. This hook could specify conditions under which a trade should be executed, such as a target price point.
2. **Integration with Pools:** The hook is attached to specific Uniswap V4 liquidity pools. When a trader wants to place a limit order, they interact with the hook, specifying the desired price and the amount of the token they wish to buy or sell.
3. **Execution Conditions:** As trades occur within the pool and affect the price of the assets, the hook monitors these changes in real-time. When the price meets the conditions specified in a limit order, the hook automatically executes the trade.
4. **Enhanced Trading Strategy:** This capability allows traders to employ more sophisticated trading strategies, setting precise entry and exit points without needing to constantly monitor the market. It also enables the possibility of executing complex sequences of trades based on conditional logic defined within the hook.

This example demonstrates just one of the many possibilities that hooks open up for Uniswap V4, allowing for a richer, more diverse array of trading strategies that were previously not possible on AMM platforms.

5. Other Prominent AMMs

The diversity of mathematical formulas used by AMMs is a response to the varying needs of liquidity providers and traders and the unique characteristics of different types of assets. Let's delve into why other formulas exist beyond the constant product formula and explore the benefits of these alternative approaches.

Curve's StableSwap: $An^n \sum x_i + D = AD\,n^n + \dfrac{D^{n+1}}{n^n \prod x_i}$

- **Overview:** Curve's StableSwap formula is designed for pools of stablecoins or assets with very similar values. It combines elements of the constant product formula with adjustments that significantly reduce slippage for trades between assets of equivalent value. The formula is optimized for assets expected to have equal value, making it ideal for trading between different stablecoins with minimal price impact. It allows for much greater capital efficiency when dealing with similar assets, enabling larger trades without significant price deviation.

Balancer's N-dimensional Surface: $V = \prod_t B_t^{W_t}$

- **Overview:** Balancer generalizes the concept of AMMs by allowing for pools with more than two assets (N-dimensional), where Bt represents the balance of each token t, and Wt is the weight of each token. This formula allows for the creation of custom liquidity pools with multiple assets having different proportions. The flexibility in setting weights for each asset allows liquidity providers to create pools that can better manage risk and provide liquidity to a broader range of assets. It's particularly advantageous for creating index-like pools or for accommodating assets with different volatilities.

Why Do Other Bonding Curves Exist? Different assets and asset pairs have unique characteristics, including volatility and correlation. The choice of formula can be tailored to these characteristics, optimizing for stability, capital efficiency, or risk management. Different trading strategies and market conditions may benefit from specific liquidity pool behaviors. For instance, pools designed for highly volatile assets might prioritize price stability and risk mitigation.

The diversity of AMM formulas demonstrates the adaptability and innovation within the DeFi ecosystem, catering to a wide range of assets, trading strategies, and market conditions. This variety allows users to choose the AMM platform that best fits their needs, whether they are trading stablecoins, seeking investment exposure through index-like pools, or trading volatile crypto assets.

5.1 PROMINENT PROTOCOL: CURVE FINANCE

Curve Finance is specifically tailored for the trading of stablecoins and other pegged assets. Its innovative approach addresses some of the limitations found in traditional AMM models, such as those used by Uniswap, especially when dealing with assets that are designed to have stable values.[7]

---

[7] https://academy.moralis.io/blog/defi-deep-dive-what-is-curve-finance

Curve was initially designed to optimize the trading of pegged assets, like stable-coins (USD Coin, DAI, etc.), which are intended to maintain a stable value, typically pegged 1:1 with another asset like the U.S. dollar. In theory, these assets should always trade at or near their peg, but in practice, market dynamics can cause deviations.

Traditional AMMs, like Uniswap, use a bonding curve formula that ensures liquidity across a wide range of asset prices. However, this design is not optimized for stablecoins or pegged assets, where the value is expected to remain relatively constant. The general bonding curve used by Uniswap could lead to inefficient pricing and higher slippage when trading assets that are supposed to have a stable value.

To address these inefficiencies, Curve introduced a specialized bonding curve designed to facilitate more effective trading of pegged assets. This curve allows for minimal price impact trades when the assets' prices are close to their peg, which is often the case with stablecoins. As shown in **Figure 7**, the bonding curve is a combination of the constant product and constant sum $(x+y=k)$ bonding curves. The flatter segment of the bonding curve is around the 45-degree line, where the quantity of the token x is equal to the quantity of the token y. Why? Remember this is specifically designed for swapping stablecoins, for instance USDC for USDT, which should always trade 1:1.

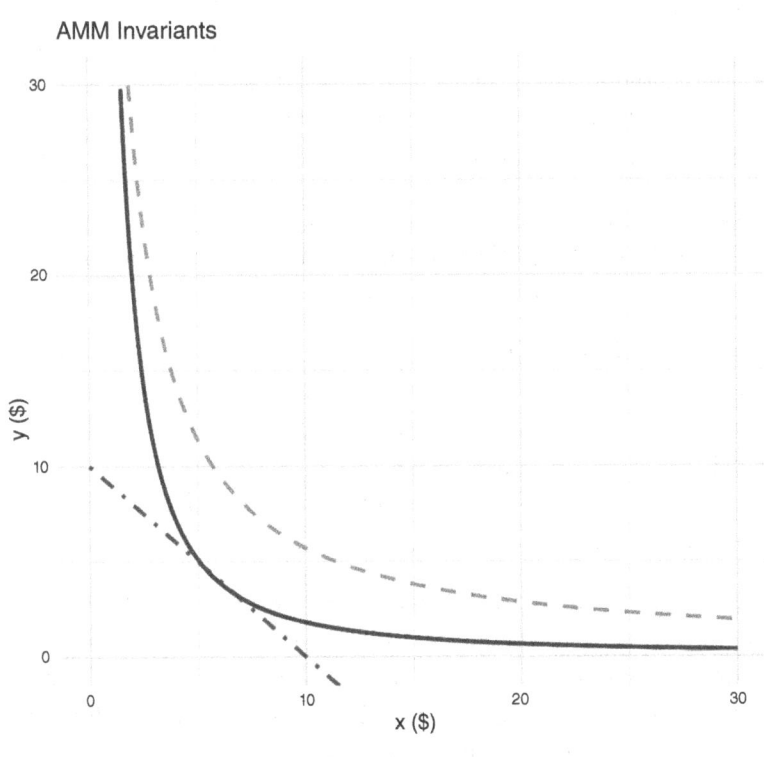

Figure 7   Curve finance's bonding curve

One of the key innovations in Curve's design is the addition of an amplification parameter to its bonding curve. This parameter is a dynamic factor that can adjust the curve's shape, allowing for near one-to-one exchanges between pegged assets, even if the liquidity pool becomes slightly unbalanced. The amplification parameter helps maintain tight spreads and low slippage for trades between stable values. For stablecoins it is really important to have very deep liquidity pool, where investors can swap even hundreds of millions of dollars' worth of tokens without affecting its price, i.e. in the same way as submitting a wire transfer for millions of dollars does not affect the relative value of the dollar.

The Curve mechanism ensures that as long as the pool's imbalance remains within a range determined by the amplification parameter, the exchange rate between the assets remains stable, promoting efficient one-to-one trades. However, once the pool's imbalance surpasses this threshold, the exchange rates begin to adjust more rapidly to correct the imbalance, preventing excessive deviation from the peg.

This innovative approach by Curve offers significant advantages for trading stablecoins and other pegged assets by minimizing slippage and maintaining more consistent pricing, compared to traditional AMMs. It reflects a tailored solution for a specific market segment within the DeFi ecosystem, showcasing the adaptability and evolution of AMM designs to meet diverse trading needs.

Let's look at a numerical example.

Imagine a Curve liquidity pool containing two stablecoins, DAI and USDC, designed to be pegged 1:1 with the U.S. dollar. Let's say the pool starts perfectly balanced with 10,000 DAI and 10,000 USDC.

Curve introduces an amplification parameter (A) to its formula, which essentially "flattens" the bonding curve when trading assets close to their intended peg. This parameter can be thought of as a way to "tune" the pool's sensitivity to imbalances. For this example, let's use an amplification parameter of $A = 100$, a simplified choice for demonstration purposes.

Scenario 1: Balanced Trade   A user wants to swap 1,000 DAI for USDC. Given the amplification and the current balance, the pool can facilitate this swap with minimal slippage, meaning the user gets very close to 1,000 USDC for their DAI.

Scenario 2: Slightly Unbalanced Pool   Before any trades, another user had swapped in a way that left the pool with 11,000 DAI and 9,000 USDC. Despite this imbalance, due to the amplification parameter, swapping 1,000 DAI for USDC would still result in receiving slightly less than 1,000 USDC, but much closer to 1:1 than without the amplification mechanism. The exact number would depend on the detailed calculations involving the amplification parameter.

Scenario 3: Exceeding the Amplification Parameter's Tolerance   If the pool becomes heavily imbalanced, say 20,000 DAI and 500 USDC, the amplification parameter can no longer maintain the 1:1 efficiency. Swaps now result in more significant slippage, and the price to swap DAI for USDC increases sharply. The formula adjusts to protect the pool's liquidity and encourage rebalancing trades.

The amplification parameter allows Curve to maintain efficient, low-slippage trades for pegged assets even in the face of minor imbalances. It achieves this by effectively making the liquidity "deeper" around the 1:1 peg. The amplification parameter (**A**) essentially "compresses" the liquidity around the 1:1 peg for stablecoins, making it behave as if there were more liquidity than there actually is, which in turn reduces slippage for small deviations from the peg. However, there are limits to this mechanism, and in cases of significant imbalance, the pool reverts to behaving more like traditional AMMs, with increased slippage to encourage trades that rebalance the liquidity pool.

In sum, Curve is primarily designed for stablecoin and pegged asset trading. Its specialized bonding curve and amplification parameter allow for efficient, low-slippage swaps between assets that are meant to have stable values relative to each other. This focus on stablecoins enables Curve to offer better rates and lower slippage for these types of assets compared to more generalized AMMs.

In contrast, Uniswap employs a more generalized approach, using a constant product formula ($x*y=k$) across a broad range of tokens, not just stablecoins. This allows for a wide variety of tokens to be swapped but can lead to higher slippage, especially for stablecoin pairs or assets with similar values. Curve's use of the amplification parameter adjusts liquidity depth around the 1:1 peg, optimizing the trading of stable assets.

Both platforms offer liquidity providers (LPs) the chance to earn from trading fees. However, as we will discuss in more detail in the next chapter, Curve's focus on stablecoins can lead to different risk and reward profiles, particularly because of its integration with other DeFi protocols for yield generation. This integration also means that Curve LPs might be exposed to additional risks from the underlying protocols. Curve pools often include incentives and bonuses, providing further opportunities for yield beyond transaction fees.

Curve has introduced CRV as its governance token, allowing liquidity providers to be rewarded based on their contribution and participate in the platform's governance. This model encourages active involvement from its community in decision-making processes. Similarly, Uniswap uses its UNI token for governance, enabling token holders to vote on proposals and protocol changes.

In summary, Curve and Uniswap serve different but complementary roles within the DeFi landscape. Understanding the nuances of each platform allows users to better navigate the DeFi space and optimize their trading and liquidity provision strategies.

5.2 PROMINENT PROTOCOL: BALANCER OVERVIEW

Is swapping just two tokens all that investors can do? That might seem quite basic at first glance. However, Balancer elevates this concept, offering a platform where you can do far more. Balancer is a multi-token AMM that allows users to create or add liquidity to customizable pools with up to eight tokens in any proportion. It extends the concept of an index fund and automates the process of portfolio rebalancing, thereby serving both as an AMM and a self-balancing portfolio manager.

Key Features

- **Custom Weighting:** Balancer pools can have custom token weightings, not just the 50/50 or fixed ratios seen in some AMMs. This allows for the creation of pools that can mimic a wide range of financial instruments or portfolios.
- **Multiple Tokens:** Each pool can contain up to eight different tokens, providing greater flexibility compared to many other AMMs that limit pools to two tokens.
- **Smart Pool:** Balancer also supports "smart pools," which are Balancer pools controlled by smart contracts, allowing for dynamic adjustments to the pool's parameters (such as fees or token weights) based on programmable logic.

Key Differences with Uniswap

- **Token Flexibility:** Balancer offers more flexibility with up to eight tokens per pool and customizable weightings, whereas Uniswap is restricted to two tokens with a fixed 50/50 ratio (except in V3 where liquidity can be concentrated).
- **Purpose and Use Cases:** Balancer's design allows it to serve additional use cases such as customizable index funds and portfolio rebalancing, beyond just being an AMM. Uniswap focuses on simplicity and efficiency in token swapping.
- **Smart Pools:** Balancer's smart pools allow for dynamic adjustments to pool parameters a feature not present in Uniswap's model.
- **Capital Efficiency:** Uniswap V3 introduced concentrated liquidity, which can offer greater capital efficiency than Balancer's broader pools, especially for popular trading pairs within specific price ranges.

While both Uniswap and Balancer platforms play crucial roles in the DeFi ecosystem, Balancer's flexibility and portfolio management features make it suitable for a wide range of financial strategies, whereas Uniswap's simplicity and efficiency appeal to users looking for straightforward swap mechanisms and concentrated liquidity options.

Let's dive into a numerical example to illustrate how a user might interact with Balancer, focusing on creating a liquidity pool and trading within that pool.

Creating a Liquidity Pool on Balancer   Alice decides to create a Balancer pool with the following tokens and weights:

- ETH: 50%
- DAI: 30%
- LINK: 20%

She wants to invest a total of $10,000, distributed across these tokens according to their weights. Assuming the current prices are:

- ETH = $2,000/ETH
- DAI = $1/DAI (since DAI is a stablecoin pegged to the USD)
- LINK = $20/LINK

Alice calculates her initial investment as follows:

- **ETH:** $10,000 ⋆ 50% = $5,000 → 2.5 ETH
- **DAI:** $10,000 ⋆ 30% = $3,000 → 3,000 DAI
- **LINK:** $10,000 ⋆ 20% = $2,000 → 100 LINK

Alice deposits these amounts into the pool.

Understanding Balancer's Formula Balancer pools maintain a constant weighted product of the token balances, which is described by the formula $V = \prod_i Balance_t^{\{Weight_i\}}$, where V is the invariant, $balance_i$ is the balance of token i in the pool, and $weight_i$ is the weight of token i (expressed as a fraction of 1).

Executing a Trade in the Pool Bob wants to trade 1 ETH for DAI in Alice's pool. To calculate the outcome of this trade, we follow these steps, incorporating Balancer's trading fees (let's use a 0.3% fee for this example):

1. **Calculate the Trading Fee:** A portion of Bob's ETH will be set aside as the trading fee. The fee is calculated on the input token (ETH in this case).
2. **Adjust the ETH Balance:** Add Bob's ETH (minus the trading fee) to the pool's ETH balance.
3. **Maintain the Invariant:** Adjust the DAI balance so that the product of the balances raised to their respective weights remains constant. This step involves solving for the new DAI balance that keeps the invariant the same as before the trade.
4. **Determine the Amount of DAI Received by Bob:** This is the difference between the pool's DAI balance before and after the trade.

Let's dive into the math using our setup. For simplicity, I'll illustrate the calculation for step 3, as it's the most complex part of the process.

1. **Initial State:**
   - ETH balance: 2.5 ETH
   - DAI balance: 3,000 DAI
   - LINK balance: 100 LINK
   - Weights: ETH (0.5), DAI (0.3), LINK (0.2)
   - Bob wants to trade: 1 ETH
2. **Apply the Trading Fee:**
   - Fee for 1 ETH = 1 ETH ⋆ 0.3% = 0.003 ETH
   - Amount of ETH for trading = 1 - 0.003 = 0.997 ETH

3. Update ETH Balance:
- New ETH balance = 2.5 + 0.997 = 3.497 ETH

4. Maintain the Invariant:
- This requires using the Balancer formula to solve for the new DAI balance, it involves iterative calculation or solving a non-linear equation that keeps the value of V constant.

Since the actual calculation for step 4 involves complex math that's best handled programmatically (due to the non-linear nature of the equation and the need for precision), let's proceed with a simplified approach to understand the outcome conceptually.

In our simplified example, after trading 1 ETH (considering a 0.3% trading fee), Bob would receive approximately 950 DAI from the pool. This calculation is a rough estimate meant to illustrate the process conceptually. In reality, the exact amount of DAI Bob would receive depends on the complex formula used by Balancer, shown in the equation below, which maintains the invariant by adjusting token balances within the pool to reflect the trade and fees:

$$V = \left(3.497^{0.5}\right) \times \left(newDAIBalance^{0.3}\right) \times \left(100^{0.2}\right)$$

This example demonstrates the interaction with a Balancer pool, highlighting the flexibility and complexity of managing multi-token pools with custom weightings. The real strength of Balancer lies in its mathematical model, which efficiently handles liquidity provision and trading across diverse asset types and weights, ensuring the pool remains balanced according to predefined parameters.

6. Concluding Remarks

As we conclude this chapter on AMMs, let me emphasize a few takeaways.

One of the most revolutionary aspects of AMMs is their ability to democratize the role of market making. Unlike traditional finance, where market making is typically the domain of specialized firms with significant capital, AMMs allow virtually anyone to become a liquidity provider (LP). This openness broadens participation in financial markets and can potentially lead to more inclusive financial systems.

AMMs utilize mathematical formulas, known as bonding curves, to determine the price of assets in a liquidity pool. These bonding curves adjust prices based on the ratio of assets in the pool, facilitating trading without the need for a traditional order book or a counterparty directly matching each trade. Remember that AMMs are effectively creating a peer-to-contract market, where no interaction among buyers and sellers is needed. The chapter explored various bonding curves used by AMMs, each with its advantages and application scenarios. For example, the constant product formula is widely adopted for its simplicity and effectiveness in providing liquidity across a wide price range. Meanwhile, specialized curves like those used by Curve Finance are optimized for assets expected to maintain a stable relationship, such as stablecoins, reducing slippage and improving capital efficiency for these specific trades.

A significant challenge for liquidity providers in AMMs is the risk of impermanent loss, which occurs when the price ratio of assets in a pool changes after they have been deposited. This phenomenon is primarily driven by adverse selection, where traders capitalize on price discrepancies between the AMM and external markets. While the potential for earning transaction fees exists, LPs must be cognizant of the risks of impermanent loss, especially in volatile markets.

The open and transparent nature of blockchain transactions can lead to adverse selection, with informed traders potentially exploiting pending transactions for profit. This aspect underscores the need for LPs and traders to be aware of the risks and dynamics at play within AMMs.

When asked what the real innovations developed in the crypto space are, AMMs always come to my mind. Creating a way to provide liquidity and effectively create markets for any type of token, without relying on intermediaries but just on economic incentives, is simply astonishing. They work around the clock and might also be more resilient in turbulent times than more centralized exchanges. The reason being that liquidity might be more easily withdrawn from centralized exchanged than from decentralized ones. Furthermore, they reduce counterparty risk, because traders do not give up custody of their assets to a centralized exchange, which can mishandle them as in the case of FTX. Obviously, they also introduce complexities such as impermanent loss and the need for careful consideration of bonding curves. Understanding these mechanisms is crucial for participants in the DeFi space, whether they are seasoned traders, prospective liquidity providers, or enthusiasts exploring the frontiers of decentralized finance.

I want to conclude with one more thought. There is some unintended consequence of too much liquidity: VCs no longer need to wait for a company to reach the initial public offering (IPO) stage to cash out. Instead, they can sell the tokens associated with their investment as soon as these tokens are listed on decentralized exchanges. This shift encourages shorter investment horizons and potentially reduces the focus on long-term company growth and sustainability. The ease of liquidating tokens immediately after their issuance can lead to a more speculative market environment, where quick profits take precedence over building lasting value. This dynamic can undermine the traditional role of VCs in nurturing startups through their growth phases, as the quick exit opportunities provided by AMMs can incentivize early sell-offs and reduced commitment to the long-term success of the projects.

As we part ways, keep your wallet close, your spirits high, and your sense of adventure alive. The DeFi landscape is ever-changing, and who knows? The next chapter in this thrilling saga could be written by you. Until then, happy trading, dear market maker of tomorrow. The world of AMMs awaits your next move.

First, the contract interacts with ERC-20 tokens (token0 and token1) using the IERC20 interface, allowing it to call standard functions like transfers and balance queries. It maintains reserves (reserve0 and reserve1) for each token, representing the liquidity pool's current state.

Coding Example: Constant Product AMM

Language: Solidity

Level: Intermediate

This example is a standard constant product AMM contract, that you can try to deploy with two tokens you also create.

```solidity
// SPDX-License-Identifier: MIT

pragma solidity >0.8.0;

import {IERC20} from "@aave/core-v3/contracts/dependencies/openzeppelin/
contracts/IERC20.sol";

contract CPAMM {
    IERC20 public immutable token0;
    IERC20 public immutable token1;

    uint public reserve0;
    uint public reserve1;

    uint public totalSupply;
    mapping(address => uint) public balanceOf;

    constructor(address _token0, address _token1) {
        token0 = IERC20(_token0);
        token1 = IERC20(_token1);
    }

    function _mint(address _to, uint _amount) private {
        // Code
        totalSupply += _amount;
        balanceOf[_to] += _amount;
    }

    function _burn(address _from, uint _amount) private {
        // Code
        totalSupply -= _amount;
        balanceOf[_from] -= _amount;
    }

    function _update(uint res0, uint res1) private {
        reserve0 = res0;
        reserve1 = res1;
    }

    function swap(address _tokenIn, uint _amountIn)
        external
        returns (uint amountOut)
```

```
    {
        require(
            _tokenIn == address(token0) || _tokenIn == address(token1),
            "token not available"
        );
        require(_amountIn > 0, "amountIn = O");

        bool isToken0 = _tokenIn == address(token0);
        (IERC20 tokenIn, IERC20 tokenOut, uint resIn, uint resOut) =
isToken0
            ? (token0, token1, reserve0, reserve1)
            : (token1, token0, reserve1, reserve0);

        tokenIn.transferFrom(msg.sender, address(this), _amountIn);
        uint amountInWithFee = (_amountIn * 997) / 1000;

        // dy =  ydx / (x + dx)
        amountOut = (resOut * amountInWithFee) / (resIn + amountInWithFee);
        tokenOut.transfer(msg.sender, amountOut);

        _update(
            token0.balanceOf(address(this)),
            token1.balanceOf(address(this))
        );
    }

    function addLiquidity(uint _amount0, uint _amount1)
        external
        returns (uint shares)
    {
        // x / y = dx / dy
        token0.transferFrom(msg.sender, address(this), _amount0);
        token1.transferFrom(msg.sender, address(this), _amount1);

        if (reserve0 > 0 || reserve1 > 0) {
            require(
                reserve0 * _amount1 == reserve1 * _amount0,
                "x / y != dx / dy"
            );
        }

        // s = (dx * T) / X = (dy * T) / Y
        if (totalSupply == 0) {
            shares = _sqrt(_amount0 * _amount1);
        } else {
            shares = _min(
                (_amount0 * totalSupply) / reserve0,
                (_amount1 * totalSupply) / reserve1
            );
        }
```

```
        require(shares > 0, "shares = 0");
        _mint(msg.sender, shares);
        _update(
            token0.balanceOf(address(this)),
            token1.balanceOf(address(this))
        );
    }

    function removeLiquidity(uint _shares)
        external
        returns (uint amount0, uint amount1)
    {
        uint bal0 = token0.balanceOf(address(this));
        uint bal1 = token1.balanceOf(address(this));

        // dx = (X * s) / T and dy = (Y * s) / T
        amount0 = (_shares * bal0) / totalSupply;
        amount1 = (_shares * bal1) / totalSupply;

        require(amount0 > 0 && amount1 > 0, "amount0 or amount1 = 0");

        _burn(msg.sender, _shares);
        _update(bal0 - amount0, bal1 - amount1);

        token0.transfer(msg.sender, amount0);
        token1.transfer(msg.sender, amount1);
    }

    function _sqrt(uint y) private pure returns (uint z) {
        if (y > 3) {
            z = y;
            uint x = y / 2 + 1;
            while (x < z) {
                z = x;
                x = (y / x + x) / 2;
            }
        } else if (y != 0) {
            z = 1;
        }
    }

    function _min(uint x, uint y) private pure returns (uint) {
        return x <= y ? x : y;
    }
}
```

totalSupply tracks the total issued liquidity tokens, and *balanceOf* maps user addresses to their owned liquidity tokens. The contract's constructor sets up the tokens within the pool via inputting the addresses of the token. Internal functions *_mint* and *_burn* manage liquidity tokens, either issuing them when liquidity is added or destroying them when liquidity is removed. The *_update* function adjusts the reserves after transactions.

The swap function allows users to trade one token for another, deducting a 0.3% fee and adjusting reserves accordingly. The *addLiquidity* function enables users to add to the pool, receiving liquidity tokens based on their contribution relative to the pool's total size or through a square root formula for initial additions. The *removeLiquidity* function lets users withdraw their contribution in both tokens proportional to their pool share by surrendering their liquidity tokens.

Functions *_sqrt* and *_min* support liquidity token calculations and minimum value determinations. An important point here is that there's no straightforward square root calculation in Solidity, as there are no floats. Numbers should be integers so square root function is built in a way that the result converges to an integer representation of the square root of a given number. This is called the Babylonian method.

Now, you can try this contract out completely on Remix, without any additional faucet networks or tokens.

1. *Create ERC-20 Token Contracts*: Begin by drafting two ERC-20 token contracts for Token 0 and Token 1. Utilize the IERC20 interface standard in Solidity, defining functions for token minting, transferring, and approval, among others. Ensure these contracts include functionalities to mint new tokens.
2. *Mint Tokens:* Use the mint function in your Token 0 contract to create 500 tokens. Similarly, mint 100 tokens from the Token 1 contract. Verify the successful minting by checking the total supply of each token, ensuring the quantities (500 for Token 0 and 100 for Token 1) are accurately reflected.
3. *Approve Token Transfer:* Access the approve function in the Token 0 contract, which requires a spender address and an amount (uint256). Enter the CPAMM contract's address as the spender and set the amount to the total tokens minted, in this case, 500 for Token 0. Repeat the process for Token 1, setting the amount to 100. This step authorizes the CPAMM contract to move tokens on your behalf.
4. *Initiate Liquidity Provision:* Navigate to the addLiquidity function within the CPAMM contract. Input the previously approved amounts of Token 0 and Token 1 (500 and 100, respectively) as the parameters for the amounts to add to the pool.
5. *Verify Reserves and Total Supply:* Following the addition of liquidity, examine the CPAMM contract's reserves to ensure the transaction was successful. You should see reserve 0 holding 500 tokens and reserve 1 with 100 tokens. Additionally, check the total supply of liquidity tokens, which should now reflect a value of 223, confirming the correct execution of liquidity provision.

End-of-Chapter Questions

Multiple-Choice Questions

1. **What is the primary function of an Automated Market Maker (AMM) in the DeFi ecosystem?**
   (A) To provide a centralized exchange platform for cryptocurrencies.
   (B) To automatically match buy and sell orders from users.
   (C) To facilitate decentralized trading by using liquidity pools instead of traditional order books.
   (D) To offer banking services such as loans and savings accounts.

2. **Which of the following best describes the concept of impermanent loss?**
   (A) The loss incurred from trading fees while making transactions on an AMM.
   (B) The temporary loss experienced by liquidity providers due to volatility in the prices of the assets in a pool.
   (C) The permanent loss of assets due to hacking or exploits in smart contracts.
   (D) The depreciation in the value of governance tokens over time.

3. **What role do liquidity providers (LPs) play in the AMM ecosystem?**
   (A) They ensure the security and integrity of transactions on the blockchain.
   (B) They provide the capital in the form of cryptocurrency pairs to liquidity pools, facilitating trading on the platform.
   (C) They act as auditors, verifying the legitimacy of trades and swaps.
   (D) They serve as regulatory bodies, overseeing the compliance of AMMs with financial laws.

4. **Which formula is most commonly used by AMMs to ensure liquidity and determine prices within a pool?**
   (A) The quadratic formula.
   (B) The constant sum formula.
   (C) The constant product formula.
   (D) The linear progression formula.

5. **How does the introduction of different bonding curves affect AMMs?**
   (A) It reduces the overall security of the DeFi platform.
   (B) It allows for the optimization of trade execution and capital efficiency based on the specific characteristics of the assets.
   (C) It eliminates the possibility of impermanent loss.
   (D) It standardizes the pricing mechanism across all types of assets.

6. **What is a 'vampire attack' in the context of DeFi AMMs?**
   (A) A security breach where hackers drain funds from liquidity pools.
   (B) A strategy where a new AMM platform entices liquidity providers from another platform with better incentives.
   (C) An internal attack by governance token holders to manipulate prices.
   (D) A rapid decrease in liquidity due to mass withdrawal by LPs.

7. **Why is adverse selection a concern for liquidity providers in AMMs?**
   (A) Because it can lead to an unequal distribution of governance tokens.
   (B) Because informed traders can exploit price discrepancies at the expense of LPs.
   (C) Because it prevents LPs from withdrawing their funds.
   (D) Because it increases the cost of transaction fees on the platform.

8. **Which type of bonding curve is particularly suited for assets expected to maintain a stable price relationship, such as stablecoins?**
   (A) Constant product curve.
   (B) Constant sum curve.
   (C) Specialized or adapted curves designed for low volatility.
   (D) Exponential growth curve.

9. **How do AMMs handle the issue of slippage in high-volatility trades?**
   (A) By pausing all trading during periods of high volatility.
   (B) By utilizing oracle services to adjust prices according to external market conditions.
   (C) By adjusting the price according to the size of the trade and the liquidity available in the pool.
   (D) By requiring additional collateral from traders engaging in large transactions.

10. **What mechanism do AMMs use to facilitate trades without requiring a traditional buyer and seller to match?**
    (A) Derivative contracts.
    (B) Liquidity pools where assets are traded against the pool's reserves.
    (C) Peer-to-peer lending agreements.
    (D) Futures contracts.

Open Questions

1. Explain the concept of impermanent loss in the context of AMMs. How does the price volatility of assets in a liquidity pool contribute to impermanent loss for liquidity providers?

2. Describe the function and importance of bonding curves in AMMs. How do different types of bonding curves (e.g. constant product, constant sum) impact the efficiency and functionality of a liquidity pool?

3. Discuss the role of liquidity providers (LPs) in the AMM ecosystem. What incentives are typically offered to encourage users to supply liquidity to pools, and how do these incentives affect the AMM's overall liquidity?

4. Evaluate the implications of 'vampire attacks' on the DeFi ecosystem. How do these strategies influence competition among AMMs, and what measures can platforms take to retain their liquidity providers and users?

5. Analyze the trade-offs between decentralized governance and centralized decision-making in the context of managing AMMs. How does the governance model affect the adaptability and resilience of AMMs in the rapidly evolving DeFi landscape?

Numerical Exercises

Exercise 1: Calculating Price Impact in an AMM

Suppose you have a liquidity pool on an AMM using the constant product formula, which currently contains 5,000 units of Token A and 10,000 units of Token B. Calculate the new price of Token A in terms of Token B if a trader wants to swap 500 units of Token A for Token B. Assume no transaction fees for simplicity.

Exercise 2: Understanding Impermanent Loss

A liquidity provider adds liquidity to a 50/50 ETH/USDC pool in an AMM. At the time of deposit, 1 ETH = 2000 USDC, and the liquidity provider contributes 2 ETH and 4000 USDC.

After some time, the price of ETH rises to 1 ETH = 4000 USDC in the external market. Calculate the impermanent loss suffered by the liquidity provider if they decide to withdraw their liquidity at this new price ratio. Compare the value of their withdrawal to the scenario where they had simply held onto their 2 ETH and 4000 USDC without providing liquidity to the AMM.

Coding Exercises

1. Implementing Flash Loan Attack Prevention in an AMM
- **Objective:** Using the AMM smart contract example provided in the previous section, develop a mechanism within the contract to detect and prevent potential flash loan attacks.
- **Instructions:**
    1. Implement a function within your AMM smart contract that can detect a rapid increase in trade volume and liquidity withdrawal within the same transaction block, which are indicative of a flash loan attack.
    2. Once a potential flash loan attack is detected, design and implement measures to prevent the attack from affecting the pool's prices or liquidity adversely. This could involve temporarily freezing the pool, adjusting the price calculation to mitigate the impact, or rejecting the transactions that are likely part of the attack.
    3. Create a series of tests to simulate normal trading activity and flash loan attack scenarios. Validate that your prevention mechanism can differentiate between the two and only activates during an attack scenario.
- **Focus Areas:** DeFi security, Attack detection, LP protection, Contract testing, Monitoring tools

2. Simulating Trades and Calculating Slippage with Python:
- **Objective:** Write a Python script to simulate trades against an AMM pool and calculate the slippage for each trade.
- **Instructions:**
    1. Define an initial liquidity pool with 10 ETH and 10,000 DAI.
    2. Write a function to simulate trades of different sizes against this pool. For each trade, calculate the new price after the trade and the slippage compared to the initial price.
    3. Output the results showing how larger trades increase slippage.
- **Focus Areas:** Trade simulation, slippage calculation, and the impact of trade size on AMM pools.

3. Designing a Liquidity Provider Reward System in Solidity:
- **Objective:** Build a smart contract that rewards liquidity providers based on the amount and duration of liquidity provided.
- **Instructions:**
    1. Implement a system within your AMM smart contract to track the amount of liquidity each provider contributes and the time it remains in the pool.
    2. Calculate rewards based on liquidity provided and time, with longer durations and larger amounts receiving more rewards.
    3. Allow liquidity providers to claim their rewards through a function in the smart contract.

- **Focus Areas:** Reward system logic, smart contract functionality, and incentive structures in DeFi.

4. Implementing a Dynamic Fee Structure in an AMM:
- **Objective:** Create an AMM that adjusts its trading fees based on pool liquidity or trading activity.
- **Instructions:**
  1. Design a fee adjustment mechanism within the AMM smart contract. This could be based on total liquidity in the pool or the volume of recent trades.
  2. Write functions to automatically adjust fees within specified limits based on these criteria.
  3. Include a way for users to view the current trading fee before executing trades.
- **Focus Areas:** Dynamic fee algorithms, smart contract state management, and enhancing AMM efficiency.

Appendix

1. Impermanent Loss in Uniswap V2

x = the reserves of token X

y = the reserves of token Y

The constant product formula makes sure that:

$$x \cdot y = L^2$$

Define p as the price of token x in terms of y. V is the value of the pool:

$$V = x.p + y$$

Since the values of the total amount of each token are equal we can define p as:

$$p = \frac{y}{x}, \; y = x \cdot p, \; x = \frac{y}{p}$$

Therefore:

$$y = L \cdot \sqrt{p} \text{ and } x = \frac{L}{\sqrt{p}}$$

So the value can be shown as:

$$V = x \cdot p + y = 2L\sqrt{p}$$

Now assume the price of x in terms of y has changed by k: (in the text we call this R)

$$p' = p \cdot k$$

$$V_{held} = x' \cdot p + y = L \cdot p' \cdot k + \frac{L \cdot p \cdot k}{\sqrt{p'}} = L\sqrt{p'} \cdot k + L\sqrt{p'}$$

$$V_{held} = L\sqrt{p} \cdot \left(1 + k\right)$$

If we plug in P' to the initial V formula,

$$V_1 = 2L\sqrt{p'} = 2L\sqrt{p \cdot k}$$

Thus, impermanent loss can be shown as:

$$IL(k) = \frac{V_1 - V_{held}}{V_{held}} = \frac{L\sqrt{p} \cdot \left(2\sqrt{k} - 1 - k\right)}{L\sqrt{p} \cdot (1+k)} = \frac{2\sqrt{k}}{(1+k)} - 1$$

2. Impermanent Loss in Uniswap V3

With concentrated liquidity the liquidity provider selects the price range $[P_a, P_b]$ at time t. This resembles the constant product model, with additional "virtual" reserves to enhance the pool's capital efficiency. The LP must provide assets x and y, amplified by virtual reserves to maintain the desired liquidity.

$$\left(x + \frac{L}{\sqrt{P_b}}\right)\left(y + L\sqrt{P_a}\right) = L^2$$

$$x = \frac{L}{\sqrt{P_t}} - \frac{L}{\sqrt{P_b}}$$

$$y = L\sqrt{P_t} - L\sqrt{P_a}$$

Now, assume P is the price at which liquidity is initially provided, and $P' = P_k = P_t = P(k)$

$$x = L\left(\frac{1}{\sqrt{P'}} - \frac{1}{\sqrt{P_b}}\right)$$

$$y = L\left(\sqrt{P'} - \sqrt{P_a}\right)$$

If the liquidity had not been provided, the asset's value would be

$$V_h = xP' + y$$

when liquidity is provided is:

$$V_h = L\sqrt{P'}(1+k) - L\left(\frac{\sqrt{P_a} + k\sqrt{P_b}}{\sqrt{P_b}}\right)$$

For $P' = Pk$ consider three cases:

$P_b < P'$ (upper bound is smaller than the relative price change)

$$y' = L\left(\frac{P_b}{\sqrt{P'}} - \sqrt{P_a}\right)$$

$$IL\left(k, P, P_a, P_b\right) = L\left(\sqrt{P_b} - \sqrt{P_a}\right) - LV_h$$

$$IL\left(k, P, P_a, P_b\right) = L\left(\sqrt{P_b} - \sqrt{P_a}\right) - L\sqrt{P'}\left(1+k\right) + L\left(\frac{\sqrt{P_a} + k\sqrt{P_b}}{\sqrt{P_b}}\right)$$

$$IL\left(k, P, P_a, P_b\right) = \frac{\sqrt{P_b}}{P} - k\left(1 - \frac{P}{\sqrt{P_b}}\right)^{-1}$$

$P_a \leq P' \leq P_b$ (relative price change is within the range)

$$x' = L\left(\frac{1}{\sqrt{P'}} - \frac{1}{\sqrt{P_b}}\right)$$

$$y' = L\left(\sqrt{P'} - \sqrt{P_a}\right)$$

$$IL\left(k, P, P_a, P_b\right) = 2\sqrt{k} - 1 - k\frac{\sqrt{P_a}}{P'} - k\frac{P}{\sqrt{P_b}}$$

If $P' < P_a$ (lower bound is larger than the relative price change):

$$x' = L\left(\frac{1}{\sqrt{P_a}} - \frac{1}{\sqrt{P_b}}\right)$$

$$IL\left(k, P, P_a, P_b\right) = L\left(\frac{1}{\sqrt{P_a}} - \frac{1}{\sqrt{P_b}}\right)kP - LV_h$$

$$IL\left(k, P, P_a, P_b\right) = L\sqrt{P'}\left(1+k\right) - L\left(\frac{\sqrt{P_a} + k\sqrt{P_b}}{\sqrt{P_b}}\right)$$

$$IL\left(k,\, P,\, P_a,\, P_b\right) = k\left(\frac{P}{P_a} - 1\right) + 1 + \frac{\sqrt{P_a}}{P'}$$

If we simplify by $P' = P_k$ and $P/P_a = P_b/P = r$

$$IL\left(k,\, P,\, P_a,\, P_b\right) = \begin{cases} \dfrac{\sqrt{r} - k}{k+1}, & \text{if } r < k \\[2ex] \dfrac{\sqrt{r}}{\sqrt{r}-1}\left(\dfrac{2\sqrt{k}}{k+1} - 1\right), & \text{if } \dfrac{1}{r} \le k \le r \\[2ex] \dfrac{k\sqrt{r} - 1}{k+1}, & \text{if } k < \dfrac{1}{r} \end{cases}$$

Chapter 8

Liquidity Pools

Dive Deep into the Ocean of DeFi
(Lifebuoys Not Included)

Preface

If traditional finance is a well-trodden path through the woods, DeFi is the jungle—wilder, denser, and where the trees have eyes. Well, not really, but you get the picture. It's a place where the bold forge new paths, and the not-so-bold follow breadcrumbs hoping they don't lead to a bear's den. This chapter? Consider it your machete through the DeFi jungle, crafted even for those who thought "liquidity pool" was a new type of spa treatment.

Imagine this: a universe where your digital assets hustle harder than a caffeinated squirrel in a nut factory. Here, the notion of "passive income" is given a nitrous boost by the blockchain, launching it into realms so fantastical, traditional finance looks like it's still using a flip phone.

As we flip through these digital pages, we're embarking on a quest that's part Indiana Jones, part The Wolf of Wall Street. This treasure hunt is unlike any other—because this treasure has legs. It doesn't just sit in a chest; it multiplies, dances, and occasionally throws a tantrum. You'll master the arcane arts of becoming a liquidity provider, a title that in the DeFi kingdom is akin to knighthood, minus the horse and the shiny armor but with all the digital glory. It signals your brave contribution to the swirling cauldrons of decentralized exchanges. But hold onto your keyboard—where there's the scent of digital gold, there's also the risk of digital quicksand. Tales of impermanent loss and market mood swings serve as our bedtime stories, gently whispering that even in a land where finance is decentralized, economic gravity still exists. So, as we set sail on this adventure, remember, in DeFi, fortunes are made, lost, and sometimes, just sometimes, found again in the couch cushions of the blockchain.

Next up, grab your popcorn for the blockbuster drama: the Curve Wars. Picture a realm where the clang of combat echoes not with the ring of steel, but with the clickety-clack of keyboards. Here, governance tokens are the swords, and smart contracts the shields, in an epic struggle for the throne of liquidity. It's like Game of Thrones meets Silicon Valley, but with less backstabbing and more back-end coding. Alliances form over cups of artisanal coffee and disband with the speed of a 404 error, all in the noble quest to be crowned the liquidity king. So, lace up your digital boots, for in the Curve Wars, the only thing sharper than the strategies are the wit of its participants.

So, dear reader, as you flip through these pages, prepare to be enchanted by the magic of DeFi, where every transaction is a spell, every smart contract a charm, and every liquidity pool a potion. May your journey be fruitful, your crops plentiful, and may you always find the optimal yield in the vast, verdant fields of decentralized finance.

Liquidity pools

1. Introduction

In the DeFi landscape, two concepts have emerged as foundational pillars, reshaping how investors interact with digital assets and opening new avenues for financial growth and inclusion: liquidity provision and yield farming. We have touched upon them in the previous chapter, but there is much more to analyze because these mechanisms not only fuel the DeFi ecosystem but also represent a paradigm shift in the democratization of finance, enabling anyone with an internet connection to participate in market-making and earn passive income. This chapter aims to demystify these concepts, exploring their significance, mechanics, and the transformative role they play within DeFi.

At its core, liquidity provision is about making assets available for trading in decentralized exchanges (DEXs) through liquidity pools. This process is crucial because it addresses a fundamental challenge in any financial market: ensuring that assets can be easily bought or sold without causing significant price impacts. In traditional finance, market makers fulfill this role, but DeFi democratizes the process, allowing anyone to become a liquidity provider (LP). By contributing to liquidity pools, LPs facilitate smoother and more efficient market operations, enhancing the overall utility and stability of the DeFi ecosystem. Moreover, liquidity provision serves as a gateway for individuals to engage with DeFi, providing them with the opportunity to earn returns on their crypto assets beyond mere speculation.

Yield farming, often considered the next evolutionary step after liquidity provision, involves strategically moving assets across different protocols to maximize return on investment. This practice has become synonymous with the DeFi movement, highlighting the innovative and dynamic nature of this space. Yield farmers leverage various DeFi protocols to earn rewards in the form of transaction fees, interest, or governance tokens. This boosts the liquidity and usability of DeFi platforms and creates complex financial ecosystems where participants can optimize their earnings through savvy asset allocation and risk management.

1.1 The Bigger Picture Within DeFi

Liquidity provision and yield farming are more than just mechanisms for earning; they are the linchpins of the DeFi ecosystem, driving innovation and attracting capital. These practices embody the spirit of decentralization, challenging traditional financial models by offering more accessible and potentially lucrative alternatives for asset management. Moreover, they spur the development of new financial products and services, from automated portfolio managers to decentralized insurance models, further expanding the DeFi landscape.

However, as with any financial endeavor, these activities come with their own set of risks and complexities. From impermanent loss to smart contract vulnerabilities, participants must navigate a landscape fraught with challenges. Understanding these risks and the strategies to mitigate them is crucial for anyone looking to dive into the world of DeFi.

In conclusion, liquidity provision and yield farming are not just pivotal for the functioning of DeFi; they represent a broader shift toward a more open, inclusive, and innovative financial system. This chapter will explore these concepts in depth, providing you with the knowledge and insights needed to navigate the DeFi ecosystem effectively and responsibly. As we peel back the layers of these mechanisms, we'll uncover the transformative potential they hold for reshaping the future of finance.

We'll begin by dissecting the mechanics of liquidity provision and yield farming, exploring the diverse ways these services manifest across leading protocols. Following this, we'll delve into the competitive landscape of liquidity acquisition, uncovering how this competition fosters a novel interplay among liquidity, token economics, and value creation.

1.2 The Advent of Liquidity Provision

Liquidity provision, at its core, involves investors depositing assets into a pool to facilitate trading on decentralized exchanges (DEXs). This concept was a groundbreaking departure from traditional finance, where market making was typically the domain of specialized firms. The innovation of liquidity pools in DeFi democratized access to market making, allowing anyone to become a liquidity provider (LP) and earn fees from the trading activity their capital facilitated.

The historical roots of liquidity provision in DeFi can be traced back to the launch of Ethereum in 2015, which provided the foundational smart contract infrastructure necessary for DeFi applications. However, it was the introduction of Bancor in 2017 and, more significantly, Uniswap in 2018 that popularized the automated market maker (AMM) model. Uniswap's AMM model allowed assets to be traded in a decentralized manner without the need for traditional order books, using liquidity pools instead. This model incentivized users to become LPs by offering them a share of transaction fees, setting a precedent for future protocols.

1.3 The Emergence of Yield Farming

Yield farming, also known as liquidity mining, emerged as an extension of liquidity provision, taking the concept a step further by offering additional incentives for liquidity providers. Yield farming involves LPs receiving rewards, often in the form of the platform's native tokens, in addition to the usual transaction fees, for staking or lending their cryptocurrency assets.

The term "yield farming" was popularized in the summer of 2020, known as "DeFi Summer," largely due to the explosive growth of Compound. Compound's introduction of its governance token, COMP, and the subsequent distribution to users of the protocol, marked a significant moment in DeFi history. Users began to actively "farm" these rewards by strategically moving assets across platforms to maximize their returns, kick-starting a yield farming frenzy that attracted significant capital to the DeFi ecosystem.

Since these early developments, liquidity provision and yield farming have evolved significantly, with numerous protocols introducing innovative mechanisms to attract liquidity and incentivize participation. Protocols like SushiSwap, Aave, and Yearn.finance have introduced various improvements and new concepts, such as optimized yield strategies, leveraged farming, and risk mitigation techniques, further expanding the scope and appeal of DeFi.

These mechanisms have not only contributed to the explosive growth of the DeFi sector but also to the maturation of the space, with increasingly sophisticated financial products and services being developed. The evolution of liquidity provision and yield farming reflects the broader DeFi ethos of innovation, democratization of finance, and the creation of an open, inclusive financial system.

As DeFi continues to grow and mature, liquidity provision and yield farming will undoubtedly remain at the heart of this transformative sector, driving innovation and accessibility in the decentralized financial markets.

2. How to Build a Liquid Market?

As we have seen in the previous chapter, in traditional finance, market makers and financial institutions often provide liquidity, ensuring that assets can be bought and sold easily. However, in the DeFi space, liquidity needs to be decentralized, transparent, and accessible to all participants. Liquidity mining and yield farming achieve this by rewarding users who deposit their assets into liquidity pools with governance tokens or interest, effectively turning the provision of liquidity into a competitive and rewarding activity. In a nutshell, protocols purchase (or more precisely *rent*, as we are going to see later) liquidity by paying LPs for their services.

Imagine embarking on the journey of creating your own Ethereum lending protocol, one that enables users to borrow USDC using ETH as collateral. At the heart of this venture lies the need to attract and retain users by encouraging them to deposit both ETH and USDC into your carefully crafted smart contract. The success of your platform hinges not just on its functionality but also on its ability to incentivize participation. Here's how you might go about it.

To incentivize users to deposit crypto into your protocol, you could offer rewards for their deposits. This could manifest in several forms, such as interest earned from the loans taken out by borrowers. However, the realm of DeFi offers even more innovative ways to reward participation, such as through tokenization and liquidity mining.

In return for their contribution, users earn rewards in the form of the platform's native tokens by staking their Liquidity Provider (LP) tokens. These LP tokens represent their share of the pool and are a testament to their contribution. This model serves a dual purpose: it bootstraps liquidity, ensuring there's enough volume for seamless platform functionality, and fosters a sense of community and ownership among participants.

Moreover, the native tokens earned as rewards often carry governance rights, allowing token holders to participate in the decision-making processes of the protocol's decentralized autonomous organization (DAO). This imbues participants with a voice in the platform's future direction, aligning user incentives with the long-term health and the protocol's evolution.

To further enhance liquidity and attract capital, many protocols launch liquidity mining programs. These programs offer additional rewards, usually in the form of native protocol tokens, for a limited time or for specific pools. Such initiatives draw in more capital and stimulate community engagement and loyalty. More importantly, they provide liquidity for the token, which makes it more attractive for investors to trade.

By participating in these liquidity mining programs, users can stake or lock up their coins in the smart contract that governs the release of rewards. This amplifies their potential earnings and solidifies their stake in the platform's ecosystem. Beyond serving as a reward mechanism, the native protocol tokens are often pivotal in governing the platform's DAO, enabling users to help steer the protocol toward success.

In summary, the journey to creating a successful Ethereum lending protocol is paved with innovative incentivization mechanisms. By offering rewards through interest, tokenization, and liquidity mining, you can attract and retain users, ensuring both the liquidity necessary for your platform's operation and the active participation of your community in its governance and future development.

Let's delve into an illustrative numerical example that encapsulates the incentives and mechanics behind providing liquidity and participating in yield farming programs, alongside the potential returns and risks involved.

Imagine a nascent DeFi protocol, CryptoFarm, aiming to boost liquidity for a newly introduced ETH/DAI trading pair. To attract liquidity providers (LPs), CryptoFarm offers transaction fees as a reward and additional incentives in the form of its own governance token, XYZ.

Suppose you, an investor, decide to support this initiative by depositing $10,000 worth of ETH and an equivalent $10,000 in DAI into the pool. Over a month, the trading volume for this pair escalates to $1,000,000, and your contribution secures you a 1% share of the pool. Given the protocol's transaction fee rate of 0.30%, your share from the fees alone amounts to $30.

To further sweeten the deal, CryptoFarm has introduced a liquidity mining program. For every $1,000 generated in transaction fees across the platform, 100 XYZ tokens are distributed among the LPs. This month, with the pool accruing $3,000 in fees, a total of 300 XYZ tokens are dispersed, and your 1% stake entitles you to 3 XYZ tokens. If XYZ is currently trading at $50 per token, this translates to an additional $150 in liquidity mining rewards, bringing your total monthly earnings to $180.

To calculate the annual percentage yield (APY) from fees alone, we use the formula:

$$APY = (\$30 \ / \ \$20{,}000) \times 12 \times 100 = 1.8\%$$

Including the liquidity mining rewards, the APY becomes significantly more attractive:

$$APY = (\$180 \ / \ \$20{,}000) \times 12 \times 100 = 10.8\%$$

Expanding our scenario, let's say CryptoFarm also hosts an ETH/USDT trading pool with a similar yield farming opportunity. You decide to provide liquidity here as well, contributing 2 ETH and 6,000 USDT (with ETH priced at 3,000 USDT each). Following your contribution, the pool's total stands at 10 ETH and 30,000 USDT.

Assuming a monthly trading volume of 500,000 USDT and a fee rate of 0.30%, the total fees collected amount to 1,500 USDT. With your share being 20%, you earn 300 USDT in fees. Moreover, CryptoFarm disperses its native token, CFARM, at a rate of 1,000 tokens daily to ETH/USDT LPs. Given your pool share, you accumulate 200 CFARM tokens daily. If each CFARM token is valued at 5 USDT, your daily earnings from CFARM token distribution reach 1,000 USDT, amounting to 30,000 USDT over the month when assuming a constant price.

While the returns from transaction fees and CFARM token distribution appear lucrative, they come with the inherent risk of impermanent loss, especially in volatile markets. For instance, if the price of ETH rises to 4,000 USDT, your holdings in the pool might not capture ETH's full price appreciation, leading to potential opportunity costs.

Upon deciding to withdraw your liquidity at month's end, the final amounts you receive will reflect the current state of the pool, adjusted for any price changes and the accrued fees and rewards. Such yield farming opportunities are undeniably attractive, offering an APY far beyond traditional financial products.

However, these returns are not without their risks. Impermanent loss is a critical concern, particularly in volatile markets. For example, if the price of ETH rises to 4,000 USDT, LPs like those in CryptoFarm's ETH/USDT pool could miss out on the asset's price appreciation due to their funds being locked in the liquidity pool. Upon withdrawing their liquidity, the actual amounts received back, in terms of ETH and USDT, would depend on the current state of the pool, potentially resulting in less ETH than initially deposited if its price has increased significantly.

Liquidity mining serves to enhance the returns from yield farming, making it an attractive proposition. **Figure 1** represents the interaction between liquidity mining and yield farming. However, the value of the reward token itself is subject to market fluctuations, introducing a level of unpredictability to the overall yield. During the DeFi summer, many platforms offered APYs exceeding 100%, driven largely by the soaring value of their governance tokens. Yet, as the initial excitement waned and token prices normalized, these astronomical APYs became unsustainable.

Moreover, the allure of high returns can sometimes overshadow the complexities and risks involved in yield farming, including impermanent loss. This phenomenon, where the value of assets deposited in a liquidity pool diverges from holding the assets outside the pool, can significantly impact the net return, especially when asset prices are highly volatile.

In conclusion, while liquidity mining and yield farming offer compelling opportunities for earnings within the DeFi ecosystem, participants must navigate these waters with caution. Understanding the mechanisms at play, the potential for impermanent loss, and the volatility of reward tokens is crucial for anyone looking to engage in these activities.

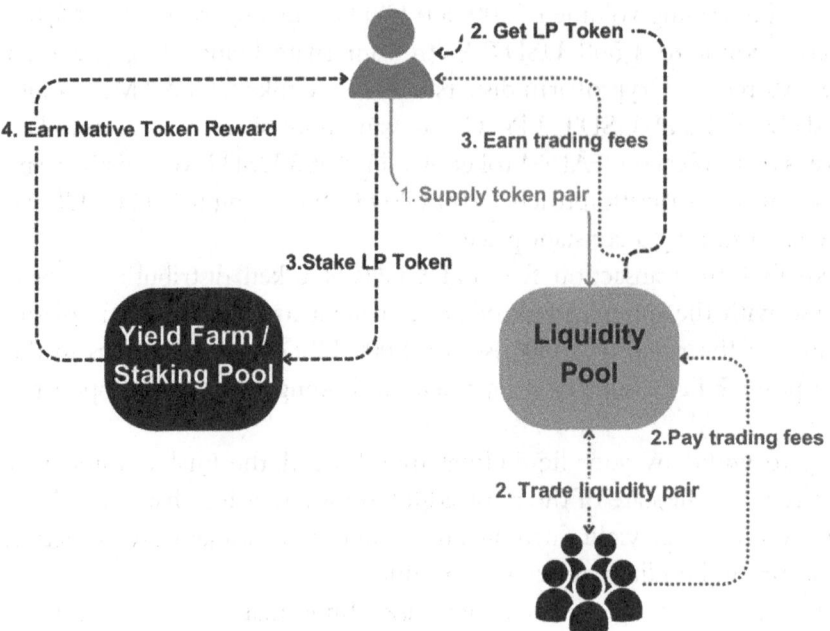

Figure 1   Liquidity mining (short dashed) and yield farming (long dashed)

2.1 Differences and Complementarities in a Nutshell

Liquidity mining and yield farming have distinct characteristics and serve complementary roles within DeFi.

Strategy Optimization: At its core, liquidity mining focuses on rewarding users for providing liquidity to specific pools, enhancing the ecosystem's overall fluidity. Yield farming, however, extends beyond liquidity provision, employing sophisticated strategies that might involve leveraging, staking in various protocols, and optimizing the allocation of assets to maximize returns.

Incentive Structure: While both models offer incentives in the form of tokens, liquidity mining is straightforward, offering rewards directly linked to the liquidity provided by the user. Yield farming's incentives are multi-faceted, combining interest, fees, and bonus tokens, which may derive from multiple activities across the DeFi landscape.

Risk Profile: Yield farming typically involves a higher risk and complexity level, given its reliance on various strategies and protocols, which may include leveraged positions and frequent asset reallocation. Liquidity mining presents risks primarily related to impermanent loss and the volatility of reward tokens. Let's look at some real-world examples:

- **Liquidity Mining on SushiSwap:** Users who provide liquidity to any trading pair on SushiSwap earn SUSHI tokens in addition to a share of the trading fees. This is a clear example of liquidity mining, where the primary goal is to incentivize liquidity provision.
- **Yield Farming on Curve Finance:** Curve offers sophisticated yield farming opportunities, especially for stablecoin pairs. Users can deposit stablecoins to earn trading fees, CRV tokens (Curve's governance token), and additional rewards when staked in Yearn.finance's yVaults, showcasing the intersection of yield farming strategies that leverage multiple protocols.

The choice between liquidity mining and yield farming depends on the user's risk tolerance, investment goals, and familiarity with the DeFi ecosystem.

- **New Entrants and Conservative Investors:** Liquidity mining in a stablecoin pool, such as USDC/DAI on Compound, might be more appropriate for those new to DeFi or with a lower risk appetite, offering predictable rewards with reduced exposure to volatile assets.
- **Experienced Users Seeking Higher Returns:** Yield farming, with its complex strategies and potential for higher returns, may be more suited to experienced users willing to navigate the DeFi ecosystem's intricacies, such as leveraging different protocols like Yearn.finance and SushiSwap to maximize earnings.

In summary, liquidity mining and yield farming represent vital cogs in the DeFi machine, each playing a unique role in enhancing liquidity, offering rewards, and fostering ecosystem growth. Whether prioritizing straightforward liquidity provision or diving into the intricate world of yield farming, users have a spectrum of opportunities to generate returns on their crypto assets within the DeFi ecosystem.

But how should an investor choose what to do in reality? Let's delve into a nuanced scenario where an investor, Alex, evaluates two distinct liquidity pools to determine an optimal investment strategy balancing risk and reward.

Alex has earmarked $10,000 for investment in DeFi liquidity pools, eyeing both traditional and more speculative opportunities. Pool A represents a pairing of Ethereum (ETH) and USD Coin (USDC), a stablecoin, known for its trading volume and relative price stability. Pool B, on the other hand, pairs ETH with a volatile small-cap altcoin, Token X, enticing investors with higher yield prospects but accompanied by increased risk.

- **Pool A:** This pool offers a 10% Annual Percentage Yield (APY) derived primarily from transaction fees, attributable to the high liquidity and trading volume characteristic of the ETH/USDC pair. For Alex, investing $10,000 into this pool, evenly split between ETH and USDC, projects an expected return of $1,000 over the year.
- **Pool B:** Here, the allure is a 30% APY, partly buoyed by additional incentives in Token X. The same $10,000 investment in this pool could potentially yield $3,000 over a year. However, the inclusion of a volatile altcoin introduces a significant risk factor, especially regarding impermanent loss.

The nature of Pool A inherently mitigates the risk of impermanent loss due to the pairing of ETH with a stable asset like USDC. Conversely, Pool B's exposure to a volatile token like X amplifies the risk of impermanent loss, especially if Token X's price diverges significantly from ETH.

For Alex, managing this risk requires a careful assessment of Token X's volatility and market liquidity. High volatility could erode the apparent high APY through impermanent loss, while liquidity concerns might affect the ability to exit the position without substantial slippage.

To navigate these waters, Alex considers a diversification strategy, pondering an allocation of 70% of the investment to Pool A for its stability and 30% to Pool B for the chance at higher returns. This approach aligns with Alex's moderate risk tolerance, seeking to capture the best of both worlds: the stable returns from Pool A and the growth potential of Pool B. *So, what should Alex (and you) consider as decision factors?*

- **Risk Tolerance:** Alex's inclination toward Pool A or B heavily depends on their risk tolerance. A conservative strategy favors Pool A for its stability and lower risk of impermanent loss, while a more aggressive stance might lean toward Pool B's higher yield potential, accepting the associated risks.
- **Market Outlook:** The decision also hinges on Alex's outlook on the crypto market, particularly the potential price trajectory of Token X and ETH. Optimism about Token X's appreciation could justify greater exposure to Pool B, despite its inherent risks.
- **Technical Considerations:** Beyond yields and risks, Alex must weigh technical factors such as transaction fees, the stability and security of the DeFi platforms hosting these pools, and the smart contracts' security.

Investors like Alex must navigate complex trade-offs between yield, risk, and liquidity as captured in **Figure 2**. Just looking at the overall yields, although attractive, might lead to negative consequences for investors.

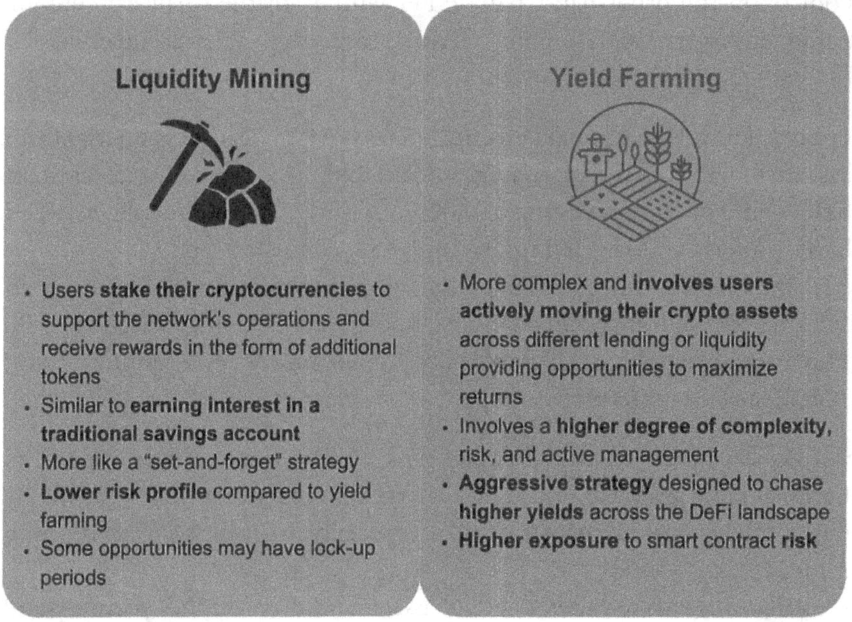

Figure 2 Yield farming vs. liquidity mining

PROMINENT PROTOCOL: YEARN.FINANCE

Does this all sound a tad complex? Fear not, every challenge finds its match in a protocol. Enter Yearn.finance, a platform ingeniously designed to navigate the intricate labyrinth of yield farming and liquidity mining with ease. Yearn.finance, often symbolized by its native token YFI, represents a cornerstone in the evolution of Decentralized Finance (DeFi) yield optimization. It offers a sophisticated, automated approach to yield farming that seeks to maximize Annual Percentage Yield (APY) for its users.

Yearn.finance emerged as a response to the increasingly complex DeFi landscape, where opportunities for yield farming were abundant but fragmented across numerous protocols. Navigating this landscape required considerable expertise and constant vigilance, as APYs would fluctuate based on market dynamics and protocol incentives. Yearn.finance innovated upon this premise by automating the process of moving users' assets across different lending and liquidity protocols to chase the best yields.

YFI was designed to be earned exclusively through liquidity provision, aligning incentives between the platform and its users. Holders of YFI tokens were granted governance rights, allowing them to vote on key protocol decisions, including changes to yield strategies, fee structures, and the addition of new liquidity pools. Yearn.finance's automated strategies alleviate the need for users to manually switch their assets between protocols to earn optimal yields. Instead, assets deposited into Yearn.finance vaults are automatically allocated to the most lucrative yield farming opportunities available, adjusted in real-time by the platform's algorithms. This not only maximizes potential returns but also democratizes access to sophisticated yield farming strategies, previously only accessible to highly experienced and active DeFi users.

Numerical Example Suppose Alice decides to deposit $10,000 into a Yearn.finance vault that strategically allocates funds between several DeFi protocols to optimize yield from lending and liquidity provision.

- **Initial Deposit:** Alice deposits $10,000 into the Yearn.finance DAI vault.
- **Strategy Execution:** The vault identifies that lending DAI on Compound is currently offering an APY of 8%, while providing liquidity to a DAI/USDC pool on Curve is offering an APY of 12% after accounting for trading fees and CRV token rewards.
- **Allocation:** Based on Yearn.finance's algorithms, 60% of Alice's deposit is allocated to Compound, and 40% to the Curve pool, aiming to balance risk and return.
- **Yield Generation:** Over a month, the allocation to Compound earns an equivalent annualized yield of 4.8% ($240), and the allocation to Curve earns 4% ($160) after fees and incentives.

- **Vault Optimization:** Midway through the month, Yearn's strategy identifies a new opportunity on Aave with an APY of 10%. The vault dynamically reallocates funds to capitalize on this higher yield, enhancing returns without any action required from Alice.
- **Total Returns:** By the end of the month, Alice's effective yield from the vault outperforms the individual returns from solely lending on Compound or providing liquidity on Curve, thanks to Yearn.finance's optimization.

Yearn.finance exemplifies the innovation and user-centric approach that defines DeFi's yield optimization segment. By automating the complex process of yield farming across multiple protocols, Yearn.finance not only maximizes APY for its users but also sets a benchmark in liquidity mining, governance, and community engagement. Through platforms like Yearn.finance, DeFi continues to evolve, offering more sophisticated, efficient, and accessible financial services.

PROMINENT PROTOCOL: SUSHISWAP

SushiSwap has emerged as a significant player, introducing various features and mechanisms that have enriched the ecosystem. Central to SushiSwap's innovation and functionality is the SUSHI token, which plays a multifaceted role within the platform.

The SUSHI token serves as the cornerstone of the SushiSwap ecosystem, embodying multiple functions—governance, fee sharing, and liquidity mining incentives. As a governance token, SUSHI grants its holders the power to participate in crucial decision-making processes that shape the future of SushiSwap. This includes proposals and voting on changes to the protocol, adjustments to fee structures, and the introduction of new features or pools, thereby decentralizing the platform's direction and aligning it with the community's interests.

Moreover, the SUSHI token facilitates a fee-sharing mechanism that rewards its holders and liquidity providers. A portion of the trading fees generated by the platform is distributed among SUSHI holders who stake their tokens in the SushiBar (xSUSHI), thereby incentivizing long-term holding and participation in the ecosystem. This mechanism not only enhances the token's value proposition but also fosters a more engaged and invested community.

Liquidity mining programs on SushiSwap further leverage the SUSHI token to incentivize liquidity provision. By supplying liquidity to selected pools, participants earn SUSHI tokens as rewards, promoting greater liquidity and facilitating smoother trades within the platform. This model has been pivotal in attracting assets to SushiSwap, bolstering its competitiveness and liquidity depth.

SushiSwap has introduced mechanisms such as boosted yield for long-term liquidity providers and special rewards for participating in targeted pools. These initiatives are designed to balance the liquidity across different pools, ensuring that even less popular assets maintain sufficient liquidity while providing lucrative opportunities for yield farmers.

ONSEN PROGRAM As a liquidity mining initiative, Onsen aims to attract new projects and liquidity by offering them enhanced visibility and rewards within the SushiSwap platform. Projects selected for the Onsen program receive SUSHI rewards allocated to their liquidity providers, encouraging the SushiSwap community to engage with and support emerging tokens and platforms. This program not only benefits new projects by facilitating their entry into the DeFi space but also enriches the SushiSwap ecosystem with increased diversity and liquidity.

KASHI LENDING AND BENTOBOX SushiSwap's foray into the lending sector with Kashi and the BentoBox vault represents a significant expansion of its services, broadening its appeal beyond exchange functionalities. Kashi is a decentralized lending platform that allows users to lend and borrow a wide array of assets, including those not typically supported by traditional lending platforms. Its isolated risk lending pairs model mitigates the systemic risk often associated with DeFi lending, offering a safer and more flexible borrowing environment.

The BentoBox token vault complements Kashi by serving as a novel yield strategy optimizer. Users can deposit their tokens into BentoBox, which then can be utilized across various applications, including Kashi, to maximize yield or lending opportunities. This integration streamlines the user experience and enhances capital efficiency within the SushiSwap ecosystem.

Together, these components—Sushi Token, yield farming and incentives, the Onsen program, Kashi lending, and BentoBox—illustrate SushiSwap's comprehensive approach to DeFi. Through continuous innovation and a commitment to community engagement, SushiSwap has established itself as a versatile and dynamic platform within the DeFi landscape, offering users a wide range of opportunities to engage, invest, and grow within the ecosystem. **Figure 3** highlights the key differences between SushiSwap and Uniswap.

Numerical Example: Leveraged Yield Farming on SushiSwap Imagine a trader named Alice who has $10,000 worth of Ethereum (ETH) and is looking to maximize her returns in the DeFi space. Alice is interested in yield farming but also wants to leverage her position to increase her potential earnings. She chooses SushiSwap for this strategy due to its integrated lending platform, Kashi, and yield farming opportunities.

Step 1: Leveraged Trading through Kashi

- Alice decides to use Kashi to enter a leveraged position. She uses her $10,000 of ETH as collateral to borrow $20,000 worth of USDC at an interest rate of 5% per annum.
- She now has $30,000 worth of capital to deploy ($10,000 of her own ETH and $20,000 in borrowed USDC).

Uniswap   **SushiSwap**

	Uniswap	SushiSwap
Governance 	Uniswap employs a governance model that allows UNI token holders to vote on key protocol decisions and changes. This model emphasizes community involvement in the platform's direction, though it has faced criticism regarding the concentration of voting power among larger holders.	SushiSwap, originating as a fork of Uniswap, introduced the SUSHI token not just as a governance token but also as an instrument for community reward and engagement. SushiSwap's governance extends to innovative proposals like the BentoBox and Kashi Lending, reflecting a community-driven approach to expanding its DeFi offerings.
Incentive Structures 	Uniswap's incentive model primarily focuses on liquidity provision rewards through transaction fees generated in the pools. While this model promotes a straightforward incentive for liquidity providers, it has been seen as less aggressive in attracting and retaining liquidity compared to SushiSwap.	SushiSwap, from its inception, adopted a more aggressive incentive model, rewarding liquidity providers with SUSHI tokens on top of the transaction fees. The Onsen program and yield farming opportunities further enhance SushiSwap's appeal to liquidity providers seeking additional rewards.
Additional Features and Expansion 	Uniswap has primarily focused on optimizing its core offering – exchange services through AMM. It has introduced versions with improved capital efficiency and user experience but has been more conservative in expanding beyond exchange functionalities.	SushiSwap, on the other hand, has aggressively expanded its services beyond simple AMM functionalities. The Kashi Lending platform and BentoBox are prime examples of SushiSwap's foray into lending and yield optimization, offering users a broader range of DeFi services within one ecosystem.
Community Engagement and Development 	Uniswap has a strong foundation and support from both the Ethereum community and institutional backers. Its development path reflects a focus on stability, user experience, and gradual improvement of its core exchange functionalities.	SushiSwap has cultivated a community-centric development ethos, where new features and projects are often community-proposed and supported. This approach has allowed SushiSwap to innovate rapidly, though not without facing challenges related to governance and protocol direction.

Figure 3   Comparison of Uniswap and SushiSwap

Step 2: Yield Farming on SushiSwap

- Alice then uses her $30,000 to provide liquidity to a high-yield Onsen program pool on SushiSwap, which offers an annual percentage yield (APY) of 20%.
- She receives SLP (SushiSwap Liquidity Provider) tokens in return for her liquidity provision, which she can stake to earn additional SUSHI tokens as rewards.

Profit Calculation

Yield Farming Earnings:

- From the Onsen pool, Alice earns 20% APY on her $30,000 liquidity provision over a year, totaling $6,000 in yield ($30,000 * 20%).

SUSHI Token Rewards:

- Let's assume the SUSHI rewards add an additional $1,000 in value over the year due to staking her SLP tokens.

Interest on Borrowed USDC:

- The $20,000 USDC borrowed through Kashi incurs a 5% interest rate over the year, totaling $1,000 in interest expenses ($20,000 * 5%).

Net Profit:

- Total Earnings from Yield Farming and SUSHI Rewards: $6,000 + $1,000 = $7,000
- Less Interest Expense on Borrowed USDC: $1,000
- Net Profit for Alice: $7,000 - $1,000 = $6,000

Alice's strategy of leveraging her position to amplify her yield farming returns, while simultaneously earning additional rewards and managing her risk through a single platform, is unique to SushiSwap.

This example underscores how SushiSwap's diverse ecosystem offers sophisticated strategies for traders looking to leverage their assets for higher returns, combining elements of lending, liquidity provision, and incentive-driven yield farming not concurrently available on Uniswap.

PROMINENT PROTOCOL: PANCAKESWAP

Another prominent example in this space is represented by PancakeSwap. Symbolized by its native token CAKE, the protocol stands as a beacon within the Binance Smart Chain (BSC) ecosystem. As the leading decentralized exchange (DEX) on BSC, PancakeSwap has carved a niche for itself, offering an attractive alternative to Ethereum-based protocols.

Launched in September 2020, PancakeSwap quickly ascended to prominence, capitalizing on the growing demand for DeFi services amid Ethereum network congestion and high gas fees. Built on Binance Smart Chain, a blockchain designed with high throughput and low transaction costs in mind, PancakeSwap offered users a seamless and cost-effective DeFi experience. This strategic positioning allowed PancakeSwap not only to attract a broad user base but also to amass significant capital, challenging the dominance of Ethereum-based DEXs.

At the core of PancakeSwap's ecosystem is the CAKE token, which plays a pivotal role in both incentivizing liquidity provision and empowering users with governance rights. CAKE rewards are distributed to users who provide liquidity to the platform's various trading pairs, fostering a robust and diverse liquidity pool that underpins the exchange's functionality. Beyond its utility in liquidity mining, the CAKE token allows holders to participate in PancakeSwap's governance, voting on proposals that shape the platform's development and future direction.

One of PancakeSwap's most compelling features is its ability to offer significantly lower transaction fees compared to its Ethereum counterparts. This advantage, coupled with BSC's fast block times, ensures swift trade execution and settlement, enhancing the overall user experience. These attributes make PancakeSwap particularly appealing to both new entrants in the DeFi space and seasoned traders looking to optimize their trading strategies without the burden of high costs and network delays.

Numerical Example   Imagine Bob, a DeFi enthusiast looking to maximize his returns through liquidity provision. Bob decides to allocate $5,000 of Binance Coin (BNB) and $5,000 of USDC to a PancakeSwap liquidity pool.

- **Initial Investment:** Bob contributes $5,000 of BNB and $5,000 of USDC to the BNB/USDC pool on PancakeSwap.
- **CAKE Rewards:** In return for his liquidity provision, Bob starts earning CAKE tokens as rewards. Let's say PancakeSwap offers an APY of 20% in CAKE rewards for this pool.
- **Yield Calculation:** Over a year, Bob's $10,000 investment yields $2,000 worth of CAKE tokens as liquidity mining rewards.
- **Transaction Costs:** Benefiting from BSC's low transaction fees, Bob's costs for entering and exiting the liquidity pool are minimal, significantly lower than they would be on Ethereum-based DEXs. While he spends only $0.20 on PancakeSwap, the same action on Uniswap costs him $50. This significant disparity can notably impact overall investment returns, especially for frequent transactions.
- **Settlement Speed:** All of Bob's interactions with PancakeSwap, from providing liquidity to claiming his CAKE rewards, are executed swiftly, thanks to BSC's fast

block times. Bob's transaction on PancakeSwap is settled almost instantly, allowing him to capitalize on trading opportunities without delay. On the other hand, the slower settlement on Ethereum means Bob has to wait longer for his transactions to complete, which could lead to missed opportunities in fast-moving market conditions.

This example underscores PancakeSwap's value proposition, combining efficient liquidity provision with attractive rewards, all within a user-friendly and cost-effective framework. By leveraging BSC's capabilities, PancakeSwap not only offers a viable alternative to Ethereum-based protocols but also enriches the DeFi ecosystem, providing users with more choices and opportunities to earn yield on their crypto assets.

In conclusion, PancakeSwap's emergence as the leading DEX on Binance Smart Chain epitomizes the dynamic and competitive nature of the DeFi sector. Through innovative features like CAKE token rewards, lower transaction fees, and fast settlements, PancakeSwap has successfully attracted significant capital and user engagement, highlighting the diverse opportunities available across blockchain platforms.

3. The Curve Wars

It should be clear by now that attracting liquidity providers by compensating them for their services is a crucial mechanism within decentralized finance. This approach allows DeFi platforms to ensure a consistent flow of liquidity, enabling trades, loans, and other financial activities to occur smoothly. However, this model also introduces a significant challenge: the mercenary nature of liquidity providers. These providers, motivated by the pursuit of the highest possible returns on their capital, are inclined to move their assets to whichever protocol offers the most lucrative rewards. This transient loyalty creates a highly competitive environment among DeFi protocols, each vying to offer more enticing incentives than the next.

Protocols at their inception are under considerable pressure to bootstrap liquidity rapidly to facilitate efficient market operations and attract user engagement. Liquidity is crucial because it allows users to execute trades efficiently without causing substantial price fluctuations, thereby ensuring market stability and confidence among participants. Offering elevated rewards to LPs emerges as a primary strategy for achieving this initial liquidity. This is not too dissimilar to Uber paying drivers to join the platform or WeWork offering free leases to tenants to fill the buildings. While effective in the short term, this approach raises questions about sustainability and the long-term value proposition of the protocol beyond mere incentives.

The strategic manipulation of fee structures within liquidity pools becomes a nuanced tool in this competition. By adjusting fees, a protocol can make its pools more appealing to liquidity providers without necessarily increasing the emission rate of rewards tokens. This delicate balance between attractive returns for LPs and sustainable economic models for the protocols themselves is at the heart of strategic decisions in DeFi development.

The phenomenon of protocols engaging in aggressive strategies to attract and retain liquidity is exemplified by the "Curve Wars." This term refers to the intense competition and strategic gameplay among DeFi protocols, particularly around the Curve Finance platform, to secure dominant positions in liquidity provision. Protocols engage in various tactics, including staking large amounts of governance tokens, to influence fee structures and rewards distributions in their favor. The objective is clear: to become the most attractive destination for liquidity providers and, by extension, to secure a significant share of the market's transaction volume and fees.

The Curve Wars highlight a broader theme in DeFi: the relentless pursuit of liquidity as a cornerstone of protocol success. While this competition drives innovation and growth, it also underscores the challenges of creating stable and loyal liquidity foundations in a space where incentives can shift rapidly.

The "Curve Wars" represent one of the most fascinating strategic battles within the Decentralized Finance (DeFi) ecosystem, showcasing the intricate dance of protocols vying for liquidity and influence. At the heart of these wars was Curve Finance, as we have seen, it is a decentralized exchange optimized for stablecoin swaps with minimal slippage, and Convex Finance, a platform designed to boost rewards for liquidity providers on Curve.

Curve Finance operates on an innovative model, utilizing its CRV token as a governance token and an incentive for liquidity provision. The protocol introduced a mechanism where liquidity providers could lock CRV tokens to boost their rewards, thereby aligning the interests of users with the long-term health of the platform. This system created a high demand for CRV tokens, as more locked CRV meant higher yields.

Enter Convex Finance, which ingeniously capitalized on Curve's model by offering liquidity providers on Curve an even more lucrative deal. **Figure 4** offers an overview of the interplay between Curve and Convex. Convex allows users to stake their Curve liquidity provider tokens on its platform, receiving boosted CRV rewards without the need to lock CRV tokens themselves. Instead, Convex aggregates its users' stakes, locks a massive amount of CRV on their behalf, and passes the amplified rewards back to its users, along with additional Convex tokens (CVX) as a cherry on top.

The result was a dramatic shift in the dynamics of liquidity provision on Curve. Protocols began to recognize the power of controlling a significant portion of CRV tokens, not just for the yield-boosting benefits, but also for the governance power it conferred within the Curve ecosystem. The ability to dictate which pools received the most lucrative CRV rewards meant protocols could direct liquidity toward their preferred assets (i.e. their *own* assets), significantly impacting their own platforms' liquidity and token value.

This realization sparked the Curve Wars, a fierce competition among DeFi protocols to accumulate and lock CRV tokens through Convex, aiming to gain a strategic advantage by steering Curve's liquidity incentives in their favor. The wars underscored the complex interdependencies within the DeFi space, where protocols not only collaborate but also compete for the vital resource of liquidity.

Convex Finance emerged as a kingmaker in this context, its platform becoming the battlefield on which the Curve Wars were waged. By enabling smaller players to compete

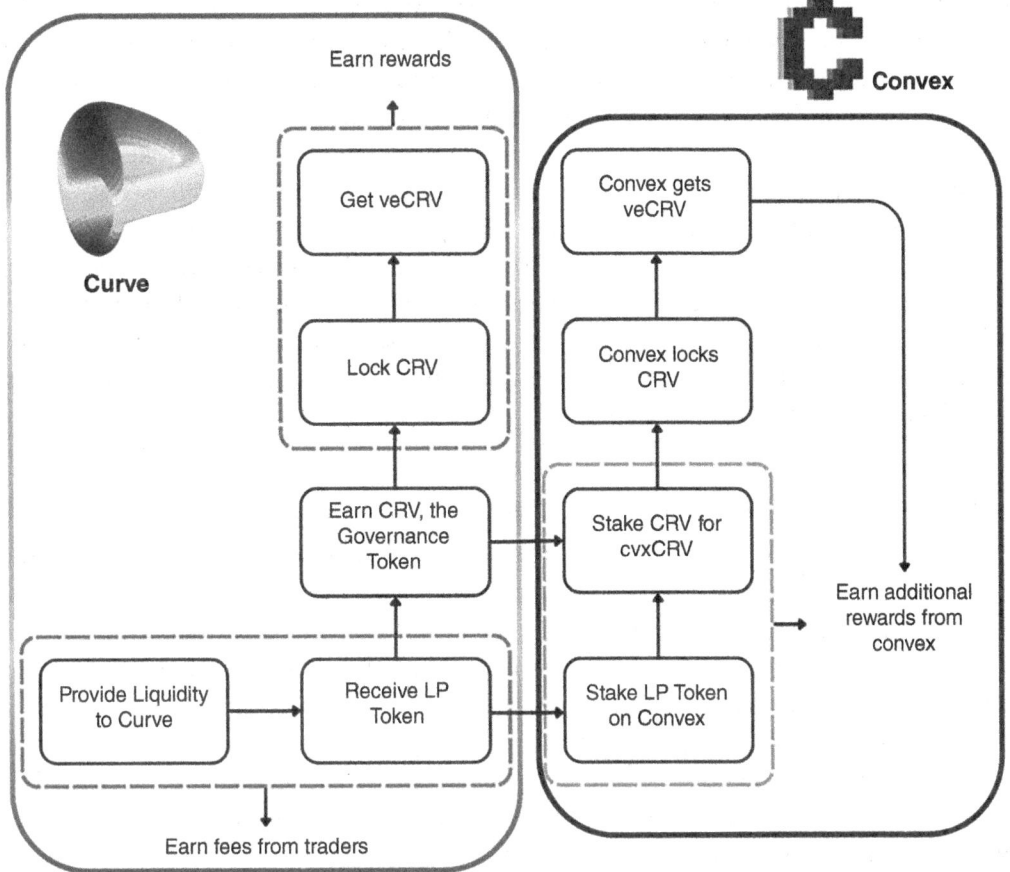

Figure 4   Curve and Convex staking mechanism, liquidity provider can lock LP tokens or CRV on Convex, and in return they earn higher rewards than they would on Curve.

with larger protocols in terms of CRV staking and rewards, Convex leveled the playing field and intensified the competition. The economic incentives of maximizing yield and governance influence drove protocols into a frenzied accumulation of CRV, with Convex acting as the conduit for their ambitions.

3.1 More Details about the Underlying Economic Incentives

CRV holders wield significant influence over the protocol's trajectory through their ability to propose and vote on critical changes. This includes adjustments to fee structures, the introduction of new liquidity pools, and broader protocol upgrades or modifications, empowering token holders to directly impact Curve's development.

By staking CRV tokens, users earn rewards and engage in a unique mechanism where locked CRV transforms into veCRV (*vote-escrow*ed CRV). This process not only enhances the users' rewards from liquidity provision but also amplifies their governance voting power, aligning long-term incentives between the protocol and its stakeholders. *Why?* This model incentivizes users to lock up their CRV tokens for extended periods. In return, they gain governance rights, a say in protocol decisions, and various rewards, such as increased trading fees or boosted yield farming rewards. This mechanism aims to mitigate the "mercenary" behavior of LPs by fostering a more committed and stable liquidity base.[1]

Curve incentivizes liquidity provision to its various pools through token rewards, ensuring the platform maintains robust liquidity levels. This mechanism is critical for facilitating efficient trading and minimizing slippage within the protocol.

Amidst this backdrop, a sophisticated system of incentives has evolved, leveraging governance power for strategic advantage through what is commonly referred to as the "bribing system." This system capitalizes on the governance framework by incentivizing veCRV holders to vote in ways that align with specific interests, often related to directing more rewards to certain liquidity pools.

3.2 The Bribing System and Its Implications

Protocols and projects can effectively "buy" governance influence within Curve by offering bribes or incentives to veCRV holders. This is usually done through platforms designed to facilitate these transactions, offering rewards to veCRV holders who vote in favor of proposals that increase rewards to particular pools. Such strategies aim to attract more liquidity providers by enhancing yields for specific pools.

Convex Finance allows Curve liquidity providers to stake their LP tokens and receive boosted CRV rewards, additional Convex (CVX) tokens, and potentially other incentive tokens. Convex achieves this by accumulating a significant amount of veCRV, using it to vote for increased rewards to pools where Convex LP tokens are staked, thereby amplifying the returns for its users.

A NUMERICAL EXAMPLE: CURVE AND CONVEX SYNERGY   Consider a Curve liquidity pool comprising two tokens, Token A and Token B, with a total liquidity of $10,000,000. Curve distributes 100,000 CRV as annual rewards to this pool's liquidity providers.

- **Without Convex:** A provider contributing 1% of the pool's liquidity ($100,000) would normally earn 1,000 CRV annually, equating to $2,000 at a CRV price of $2 per CRV.
- **With Convex:** The same provider stakes their LP tokens in Convex. Due to Convex's reward-boosting capabilities, they now receive 2,500 CRV annually (a 2.5x increase, worth $5,000), plus additional rewards in CVX tokens and any other incentives distributed through Convex.

---

[1] Other protocols have used a similar model. For instance, Frax Finance implemented a similar model with their veFXS token, aiming to stabilize their fractional-algorithmic stablecoin system. By locking FXS tokens into veFXS, users can influence governance decisions, earn additional rewards, and participate in yield farming incentives, aligning user actions with the protocol's long-term health and stability. Balancer introduced veBAL to incentivize long-term liquidity provision and governance participation. Similar to Curve's model, locking BAL tokens into veBAL grants users voting power in governance decisions and a share of the protocol's trading fees, promoting a vested interest in the protocol's success.

Incorporating Bribes: If a project offers a bribe of 50,000 tokens (valued at $1 each, thus $50,000) to veCRV holders through Convex to vote for proposals that benefit their pool, Convex leverages its veCRV holdings to secure the increased rewards allocation. This action elevates the yield for liquidity providers staked on Convex and rewards those veCRV holders who participated in the vote, enhancing their overall yield. Remember that anybody can check which addresses own certain assets.

The synergistic relationship between Curve and Convex, augmented by the strategic use of bribes, highlights a dynamic and competitive landscape within DeFi. Liquidity providers benefit from significantly higher returns through Convex, driven by enhanced CRV rewards and additional incentives. Meanwhile, the governance influence exerted through bribes shapes the distribution of rewards across Curve's pools, enhancing their liquidity and attractiveness. This intricate web of incentives and governance underscores the evolving nature of DeFi, where protocols and projects vie for liquidity and influence through innovative mechanisms, continually shaping the ecosystem's future.

4. Economic Implications and Game Theory

The mechanisms of liquidity mining and yield farming have important implications for token economics, the sustainability of rewards, and the distribution of wealth within decentralized finance (DeFi) ecosystems.

4.1 Tokenomics Implications

Although not all have a burning mechanism like ETH, most protocols incentivize users to "stake" their tokens, that is, to park the tokens they own in the protocol for a defined period in exchange for a reward. Staking enhances the security of the network because the staked tokens guarantee the legitimacy of any new transaction added to the blockchain, as required by a proof-of-stake consensus mechanism. The rewards of staking increase commensurate with the length of the lockup period. This additional benefit is particularly important for potentially volatile tokens, as holders will be unable to trade staked tokens even when prices shift.

Users might also stake what are called Liquidity Provider (LP) tokens, which are earned from supplying liquidity to a decentralized exchange. Users receive LP tokens, mathematical representations that they own those assets in the pool, which provide the claim for the return of those assets to the holder. These assets need not sit idly in the wallet. Users can stake the LP tokens they receive in the Curve staking pool, for which they will receive the CRV token. By staking LP tokens, users earn yield twice, as they are paid for supplying liquidity in LP tokens that they can then stake to earn more yield.

The Curve ecosystem is a prime example of the key ingredients requisite to creating a "deflationary" effect. A significant demand for staking is generated by the access afforded to the veCRV, which crucially affect the rewards to which one has access and the fees that can be earned by delegating the attendant voting rights. All this passive income makes it more convenient for users of Curve to hold the token (and by staking, keep it out of circulation, effectively reducing supply) rather than sell it.

4.2 Renting vs. Owning Liquidity

The foregoing discussion about the liquidity wars highlights one of the key objectives of nascent protocols, to attract liquidity for their tokens. Doing so means that investors are able to swap the token with others without incurring large transaction costs, i.e. slippage. In this way, the protocol makes sure that investors and users can effectively integrate the new protocol in the existing ecosystem. One of the key advantages enjoyed by traditional banks is the access to a sticky and cheap source of funding: deposits. In crypto, liquidity is much more mercenary. This means that it can be quickly acquired, can also be deployed and scaled efficiently, but is always fickle. The reason is that liquidity providers are always on the lookout for the protocol offering the highest yields. In traditional finance, the capricious nature of liquidity providers is not as damaging for banks. For instance, while Bank of America might try to attract new depositors by increasing the savings rate by a few basis points, the other banks are not substantially threatened by such a strategy.

EXAMPLE: OLYMPUSDAO   One response to this issue has been provided by the decentralized autonomous organization (DAO), Olympus. This new protocol has started acquiring its own liquidity. How? In a nutshell, by printing new tokens, OHM, in exchange for other assets (e.g. ETH or DAI), or liquidity providers tokens. The treasury can then use these newly acquired assets to provide liquidity directly to DEXs or investe them to earn returns. The parties on the other side of the transactions are incentivized because they can obtain OHM at a discount with respect to its market value. In other words, for every $1 worth of DAI they can acquire more than $1 worth of OHM. By implementing this design, Olympus has offered a solution to the "race to the bottom" where protocols are forced to provide higher and higher incentives to attract liquidity providers, which has the additional adverse effect of diluting the value of the protocols by increasing circulating supply.

OlympusDAO introduced a novel approach to liquidity management with its (3,3) game theory model and its native token, OHM, aiming to create a decentralized reserve currency. One of the key strategies OlympusDAO employed to attract and effectively purchase liquidity involves its "bonding" mechanism and the concept of protocol-owned liquidity. Let's see these new features in more detail.

Bonding Mechanism   The bonding mechanism is at the heart of OlympusDAO's approach to attracting liquidity. This process allows users to purchase OHM directly from the protocol at a discounted rate in exchange for providing liquidity to the protocol's treasury. Users can offer various assets, such as stablecoins or LP tokens, to the treasury via bonding. In return, they receive OHM after a vesting period, typically at a rate that's favorable compared to buying OHM on the open market. This mechanism serves multiple purposes:

- **Directly Increases Protocol-Owned Liquidity (POL):** By acquiring LP tokens through bonding, OlympusDAO directly adds to its treasury, increasing its POL. This approach contrasts with traditional liquidity mining, where liquidity may quickly migrate to other protocols once incentives dry up.
- **Attracts Long-Term Investors:** The bonding mechanism, coupled with the vesting period, incentivizes participants to invest in the protocol for longer periods, fostering a more stable and committed community.
- **Creates a Sustainable Economic Model:** The discounted OHM acquired through bonding encourages users to engage with the protocol's economy, including staking, further integrating them into OlympusDAO's ecosystem.

Staking Rewards and (3,3) Model   OlympusDAO's staking rewards are another critical component of its strategy to attract and retain liquidity. By offering attractive APYs for staking OHM, the protocol encourages users to lock up their tokens, reducing circulating supply and creating upward pressure on the token's price. The (3,3) model, often referenced in OlympusDAO's community, symbolizes the ideal scenario where all participants stake their OHM, leading to mutual benefit and protocol growth. In game theory, particularly in the context of a prisoner's dilemma, the choices made by individuals can lead to different outcomes based on the combination of choices. A choice can be to cooperate (3) or to defect (defecting would be represented by a different number, depending on the payoffs in a specific game theory model). When both parties choose to cooperate (3,3), it results in the highest collective reward. This game-theoretic model incentivizes cooperative behavior, aligning individual incentives with the long-term success of the protocol.

Protocol-Owned Liquidity (POL)   The concept of POL marks a shift from relying on external liquidity providers to the protocol itself owning a significant portion of its liquidity. This model offers several benefits:

- **Reduced Dependence on External LPs:** By owning its liquidity, OlympusDAO minimizes its reliance on external liquidity providers, who may withdraw their support if better opportunities arise elsewhere.
- **Increased Economic Security:** POL provides the protocol with a more stable foundation, ensuring liquidity is always available for users to trade OHM and reducing the impact of market volatility on the protocol's operations.
- **Enhanced Governance and Control:** With a significant portion of its liquidity owned by the treasury, OlympusDAO can better manage its monetary policy and adapt to changing market conditions, promoting a more sustainable ecosystem.

OlympusDAO's innovative approach to liquidity management, through bonding, staking, and the acquisition of POL, presents a new paradigm in DeFi, offering insights into how protocols can create more resilient and autonomous financial systems. Launched in May 2021, OlympusDAO's native token, OHM, was backed by a treasury of diversified assets, mainly stablecoins like DAI, attracted significant attention and rapid growth, propelling its market cap to more than $4 billion within months.[2]

However, the model's sustainability came into question as the price of OHM plummeted by more than 95% from its peak. Several factors contributed to this decline, including the inherent volatility of the crypto market and the sell-offs by large holders which triggered cascading liquidations. The high annual percentage yields (APYs), which were initially a draw, also became a liability as they were unsustainable in the long term, leading to excessive inflation of the OHM supply. Additionally, the emergence of numerous forks and copycat projects diluted the unique value proposition of OlympusDAO.[3]

4.3 Sustainability of Rewards

When evaluating the incentives provided to liquidity providers (LPs), it's crucial to assess the protocol's ability to maintain these rewards over the long haul.

Many DeFi protocols distribute their native tokens as rewards for liquidity mining and staking. However, if these tokens are minted at a high rate, it can lead to inflationary pressures, diluting their value and potentially leading to a loss of confidence in the protocol.

Example: SushiSwap (SUSHI)

SushiSwap faced challenges related to its token emission rate, especially during its early days when it offered high SUSHI rewards to attract liquidity providers away from Uniswap. The initial emission rate was 1,000 SUSHI per Ethereum block across all pools, leading to a rapid increase in SUSHI supply. To address inflation concerns and sustain the token's long-term value, SushiSwap later implemented a community governance decision to reduce the token emission rate, demonstrating how protocols can adjust their strategies based on community feedback and economic realities.

Aligning the distribution of rewards with the actual value created by participants ensures the sustainability of the rewards mechanism. This alignment can be achieved by developing mechanisms that limit the total supply of tokens or by tying the emission of new tokens to specific achievements within the ecosystem, such as milestones in protocol usage or liquidity provided.

Example: Aave (AAVE) and Compound (COMP)

Rather than distributing tokens at a constant high rate, **Aave** and **Compound** designed their tokenomics to reward users based on their contribution to the protocol's health and growth. For example, rewards might be scaled based on the amount of

---

[2] https://blockworks.co/news/the-investors-guide-to-olympusdao
[3] https://www.upside.gg/the-ledger/olympus-dao

liquidity provided or borrowed in less liquid markets, encouraging users to contribute where it's most needed.

Compound introduced "COMP farming," where users earn COMP tokens based on the interest generated in the protocol. This model incentivizes users to supply and borrow assets, directly contributing to the protocol's activity and liquidity, thereby aligning rewards with genuine value creation within the Compound ecosystem.

Incorporating mechanisms for dynamic adjustment of reward rates based on current protocol metrics and market conditions can further align rewards with value creation. These adjustments help maintain a balance between incentivizing participation and controlling token supply.

Example: Curve Finance (CRV)

- **Curve Finance** utilizes a sophisticated model for its CRV token, where the emission rate is adjustable based on governance proposals and the overall liquidity in the protocol. Curve's governance can decide to increase incentives for specific pools to attract more liquidity or decrease them if the market conditions change. This flexibility allows Curve to adapt its reward mechanisms to the current needs and goals of the protocol, ensuring that rewards are always aligned with actual value creation and contribution to the protocol's liquidity.

4.4 Impact on Token Distribution

While the aim of liquidity mining and yield farming is to democratize finance, the reality can sometimes be different. Participants with significant capital are often able to provide more liquidity, earning proportionately greater rewards. This dynamic can lead to an accumulation of wealth and governance power among the already wealthy, potentially undermining the principles of decentralization and equal opportunity that many DeFi protocols espouse. Such concentration of tokens and influence poses a risk to the ecosystem's health and integrity, as decisions may be swayed by a few at the expense of the broader community.

Example: Compound (COMP)

- **Compound** introduced its governance token, COMP, as a way to decentralize the decision-making process of the protocol. However, the distribution mechanism, which heavily rewards users based on the amount of capital they supply or borrow, has been criticized for favoring wealthier participants. Large holders of COMP tokens, as a result, have significant influence over governance decisions. This situation highlights the challenges DeFi faces in achieving truly democratic governance structures.

To mitigate the risk of wealth concentration and ensure a fairer distribution of tokens, several strategies and mechanisms can be adopted:

- **Capped Rewards:** Implementing caps on rewards for individual accounts or ensuring that rewards do not scale linearly with the amount of capital provided can help level the playing field for smaller participants.

- **Participation Incentives for Small Holders:** Protocols can design specific programs or incentives that encourage participation from smaller holders, ensuring they have a meaningful opportunity to contribute and earn rewards.
- **Governance Mechanisms:** Adjusting governance mechanisms to limit the influence of large token holders, such as through quadratic voting or delegation systems, can help ensure that the protocol remains responsive to the broader community.
- **Fair Launches and Airdrops:** Initiating protocols with a "fair launch" or distributing tokens through airdrops to a wide user base can also contribute to a more equitable token distribution from the outset.

5. Liquid Staking

What if all your tokens are staked? Can you still earn some additional rewards or are those assets locked away and idle? In traditional staking models, cryptocurrency holders lock up their tokens as a form of security deposit to participate in the network's consensus mechanism (such as in Proof of Stake (PoS) networks). These staked tokens help secure the network, and in return, stakers earn rewards proportional to their stake. However, these tokens are often locked and cannot be used for other purposes until they are unstaked, which can sometimes involve a cooldown period.

Liquid staking addresses this by issuing a representative token in exchange for the staked asset. This representative token can then be used within the DeFi ecosystem to earn additional yields, trade, or as collateral for loans, thus providing liquidity to stakers without requiring them to unstake their primary assets.

Liquid staking has become increasingly common for several reasons:

- **Increased Capital Efficiency:** It allows stakers to utilize their assets more efficiently. Instead of having capital tied up and idle, users can engage in other DeFi activities, maximizing their potential returns.
- **Enhanced Liquidity:** Users benefit from improved liquidity, as they receive a liquid representative of their staked assets that they can freely trade or use in the DeFi ecosystem, mitigating one of the significant drawbacks of traditional staking.
- **Risk Diversification:** By enabling participation in multiple DeFi protocols simultaneously, liquid staking allows users to spread their risk and take advantage of diverse investment opportunities.
- **Encourages Staking Participation:** The ability to earn additional yield on staked assets without sacrificing liquidity makes staking more attractive to a broader audience, potentially increasing the security and robustness of the network by encouraging broader participation.

Liquid staking is offered as an option to address the liquidity issue directly associated with traditional staking mechanisms and to harmonize the staking and DeFi ecosystems. By solving the liquidity challenge, protocols can ensure that the security and decentralization of the network are not compromised by the users' desire for liquidity. This innovation is particularly appealing in the rapidly evolving DeFi sector, where opportunities for yield and participation in various protocols can change swiftly.

Furthermore, liquid staking can also be seen as a response to the growing demand for more flexibility in how users can interact with their cryptocurrency holdings. It represents a natural evolution in the DeFi space, aiming to make staking and participation in network security more accessible and appealing to a wider user base. As the blockchain and DeFi landscapes continue to mature, innovations like liquid staking play a crucial role in bridging the gap between traditional staking benefits and the dynamic opportunities available in decentralized finance.

Lido (LDO) allows users to stake their assets, such as ETH on Ethereum 2.0, without locking up their capital and losing liquidity. In return, stakers receive stETH (staked ETH) on a 1:1 basis for the ETH they stake. This stETH can then be used across various DeFi protocols to earn additional yields, trade, or serve as collateral, all while still earning staking rewards from Ethereum 2.0.

Let's explore a numerical example that highlights the opportunities liquid staking opens up, particularly focusing on how it enables participants to leverage their staked assets to earn additional yields in the DeFi ecosystem. For this example, we'll use a hypothetical liquid staking protocol similar to Lido, where Ethereum (ETH) is staked, and staked ETH (stETH) is received in return.

Scenario: Staking ETH and Using stETH in DeFi

Initial Setup:

- **User's Initial Holdings:** 10 ETH (Assuming ETH price is $2,000 per ETH, total value = $20,000)
- **ETH Annual Staking Reward Rate:** 5%

The user decides to stake all 10 ETH using a liquid staking protocol and receives an equivalent amount of stETH (10 stETH) that represents their staked ETH plus future staking rewards.

Year 1: Earning Staking Rewards

- At the end of Year 1, thanks to the 5% staking reward, the user's effective holding in terms of stETH would increase to reflect these rewards. For simplicity, assume now the user effectively holds 10.5 stETH due to rewards.
- **Value of Staked Assets at the End of Year 1 (assuming ETH price remains unchanged):** $21,000

Leveraging stETH in DeFi:

The user now decides to use their stETH in the DeFi ecosystem to earn additional yields.

Example 1: Yield Farming with stETH

- The user contributes their 10.5 stETH to a DeFi protocol offering a yield farming pool that accepts stETH and offers an annual yield of 10%.
- **Additional Earnings Over a Year from Yield Farming:** 1.05 stETH (10.5 stETH * 10%)
- **Total stETH after 1 Year of Yield Farming:** 11.55 stETH

Example 2: Borrowing Against stETH

- The user chooses to use their stETH as collateral to borrow USDC in a lending protocol to invest in other opportunities within DeFi or to leverage their position.
- **Collateralization Ratio:** 75% (For every 1 stETH, the user can borrow up to 75% of its dollar value in USDC)
- **USDC Borrowed Against 10 stETH:** $15,000 (75% of $20,000)
- The user invests the borrowed USDC in another opportunity offering an annual return of 20%.
- **Return on Borrowed Capital after 1 Year:** $3,000

Summary

- **Original ETH Staked for 1 Year:** Gained 0.5 ETH in rewards (valued at $1,000 if ETH's price remains $2,000/ETH)
- **Yield Farming with stETH:** Earned additional 1.05 stETH (~$2,100)
- **Investing Borrowed USDC:** Earned $3,000 from investment returns

Total Value Created:

- **From Staking Rewards and Yield Farming:** $3,100 in equivalent ETH value
- **From Investing Borrowed Capital:** $3,000

This example demonstrates the power of liquid staking to earn traditional staking rewards and leverage staked assets for additional yield-generating opportunities in DeFi, significantly enhancing the user's earning potential beyond what would be possible through simple staking. It illustrates how liquid staking protocols open a myriad of opportunities for users to actively participate in the growing DeFi ecosystem without sacrificing the liquidity of their assets.

While liquid staking presents numerous opportunities within the DeFi ecosystem by enabling users to earn rewards on staked assets while retaining liquidity, it also introduces several risks and challenges:

1. Liquidity and Market Risks:
- The value of the liquid staking tokens (e.g., stETH) is meant to closely track the underlying staked assets. However, market conditions could lead to divergence in prices, causing the liquid tokens to trade at a discount or premium. This risk becomes particularly pronounced during market turmoil or when there's a sudden rush to redeem the liquid tokens for the underlying assets.

2. Slashing Risks:

- In Proof of Stake networks, validators are at risk of slashing penalties for misbehavior or network downtime. Since liquid staking pools aggregate users' stakes under validators, poor performance or malpractice by these validators could lead to slashing events that diminish the value of the pooled stakes, affecting all participants.

3. Centralization Risks:

- While liquid staking protocols aim to decentralize the staking process, there's a risk of centralization with a few large protocols or pools controlling a significant portion of the network's staked assets. This centralization can lead to security risks for the underlying blockchain network and potentially undermine the decentralized nature of the network.

4. Counterparty Risks:

- Depending on the design of the liquid staking protocol, there might be counterparty risks, especially if the protocol involves lending activities or if the liquid tokens are used as collateral. The failure of a counterparty to meet their obligations could lead to losses.

Understanding and mitigating these risks are crucial for participants in liquid staking protocols.

6. Concluding Remarks

As we conclude our exploration of Decentralized Finance (DeFi), particularly focusing on the innovative mechanisms of liquidity provision, yield farming, and the strategic complexities of phenomena like the Curve Wars, we can reflect on the key insights garnered.

First, liquidity provision and yield farming are central to the functioning of DeFi, offering mechanisms for decentralized market making and incentivizing participants with rewards that enhance the liquidity and efficiency of financial services on the blockchain. These are needed to create markets for the tokens.

Second, the Curve Wars illustrate the strategic depth within DeFi, highlighting how protocols compete and cooperate within a decentralized framework to secure liquidity, influence token economics, and shape the ecosystem's development. Relatedly, through examples like OlympusDAO and the evolving strategies of liquidity pools, we've seen how DeFi protocols innovate to attract and sustain liquidity, ensuring the ecosystem's vibrancy and long-term viability.

A key insight to grasp is that, despite their innovative edge, crypto protocols grapple with challenges reminiscent of those encountered by traditional Web2 companies. Chief among these is the necessity to bootstrap adoption or, more precisely, to secure sufficient liquidity for their token—a task that can prove to be a costly venture. This similarity underscores the importance of strategic planning and resource allocation in both realms. For crypto protocols, effectively attracting liquidity fuels their operational capabilities and enhances their attractiveness to potential users and investors, mirroring the growth dynamics of Web2 businesses as they strive to capture market share and user engagement.

Code Example: Interacting with Yearn Vault

Language: Solidity

Difficulty: Beginner

```solidity
// SPDX-License-Identifier: MIT
pragma solidity >0.8.0;

interface IERC20 {
    function approve(address spender, uint amount) external
returns (bool);
    function balanceOf(address account) external view returns (uint256);
}

interface IYearnVault {
    function deposit(uint _amount) external;
    function withdraw(uint _shares) external;
    function balanceOf(address account) external view returns (uint256);
}

contract YearnFinanceExample {
    IERC20 public token;
    IYearnVault public yearnVault;

    constructor(address _token, address _yearnVault)  {
        token = IERC20(_token);
        yearnVault = IYearnVault(_yearnVault);
    }

    // Deposit tokens into the Yearn Vault
    function depositIntoYearn(uint _amount) external {
        token.approve(address(yearnVault), _amount);
        yearnVault.deposit(_amount);
    }

    // Withdraw your original deposit based on the share growth
    function withdrawFromYearn(uint _shares) external {
        yearnVault.withdraw(_shares);
    }

    // Check your balance in the vault
    function checkBalance() external view returns (uint256) {
        return yearnVault.balanceOf(msg.sender);
    }
}
```

The **YearnFinanceExample** contract is a straightforward implementation designed for interaction with Yearn Finance Vaults, utilizing the capabilities of ERC-20 tokens. The contract initializes by setting the addresses for both the ERC-20 token and the Yearn Vault, which is essential for its operations.

Functionally, the contract allows for two main actions: depositing into and withdrawing from a Yearn Vault. The deposit function, *depositIntoYearn*, involves a preliminary step of token approval. This is a standard procedure in ERC-20 token management, ensuring that the contract has the necessary permissions to handle tokens on behalf of the user. Following approval, the specified token amount is deposited into the vault.

The withdrawal function, *withdrawFromYearn*, enables users to retrieve their deposits from the vault, adjusted for any interest earned. This reflects the underlying investment strategy's performance of the Yearn Finance Vaults, designed to optimize yield.

Moreover, the contract includes a *checkBalance* function to provide users with the ability to check their vault balance. This feature supports transparency and user engagement by allowing for easy access to investment information.

This is a very simple demonstration that can be implemented for interacting with any Vault in any platform essentially. However, it won't be possible to test this on a faucet network completely as it is dependent on an actual Vault.

Code Example: Yield Farming on Pancake Swap

Language: Solidity

Difficulty: Expert

```
// SPDX-License-Identifier: MIT
pragma solidity ^0.8.0;

// Import necessary interfaces and libraries
import "@openzeppelin/contracts/token/ERC20/IERC20.sol";
import "@openzeppelin/contracts/security/ReentrancyGuard.sol";

interface IPancakeRouter02 {
    function swapExactTokensForTokensSupportingFeeOnTransferTokens(
        uint amountIn,
        uint amountOutMin,
        address[] calldata path,
        address to,
        uint deadline
    ) external;

    function addLiquidity(
        address tokenA,
        address tokenB,
        uint amountADesired,
        uint amountBDesired,
```

```
        uint amountAMin,
        uint amountBMin,
        address to,
        uint deadline
    ) external returns (uint amountA, uint amountB, uint liquidity);
}

interface IMasterChef {
    function deposit(uint256 _pid, uint256 _amount) external;
    function withdraw(uint256 _pid, uint256 _amount) external;
    function emergencyWithdraw(uint256 _pid) external;
}

contract YieldFarmer is ReentrancyGuard {

    IPancakeRouter02 public immutable pancakeRouter;
    IMasterChef public immutable masterChef;
    uint256 public immutable pid; // Pool ID for the MasterChef contract

    // Addresses for the tokens involved
    address public immutable tokenA;
    address public immutable tokenB;
    address public immutable lpToken;

    // Constructor to set initial values
    constructor(
        address _pancakeRouter,
        address _masterChef,
        uint256 _pid,
        address _tokenA,
        address _tokenB,
        address _lpToken
    ) {
        pancakeRouter = IPancakeRouter02(_pancakeRouter);
        masterChef = IMasterChef(_masterChef);
        pid = _pid;
        tokenA = _tokenA;
        tokenB = _tokenB;
        lpToken = _lpToken;
    }

    // Swap tokenA for tokenB
    function swapTokens(uint amountIn, uint amountOutMin, address[]
calldata path) external nonReentrant {
        IERC20(path[0]).transferFrom(msg.sender, address(this),
amountIn);
        IERC20(path[0]).approve(address(pancakeRouter), amountIn);
        pancakeRouter.swapExactTokensForTokensSupportingFeeOnTransfer
Tokens(
            amountIn,
            amountOutMin,
            path,
```

```
        address(this),
        block.timestamp
    );
}

// Add liquidity to PancakeSwap
function addLiquidity(uint amountA, uint amountB) external
nonReentrant {
    IERC20(tokenA).transferFrom(msg.sender, address(this), amountA);
    IERC20(tokenB).transferFrom(msg.sender, address(this), amountB);

    IERC20(tokenA).approve(address(pancakeRouter), amountA);
    IERC20(tokenB).approve(address(pancakeRouter), amountB);

    pancakeRouter.addLiquidity(
        tokenA,
        tokenB,
        amountA,
        amountB,
        0,
        0,
        address(this),
        block.timestamp
    );
}

// Stake LP tokens in the MasterChef contract
function stakeLPTokens(uint256 _amount) external nonReentrant {
    IERC20(lpToken).transferFrom(msg.sender, address(this), _amount);
    IERC20(lpToken).approve(address(masterChef), _amount);
    masterChef.deposit(pid, _amount);
}

// Add more functions such as withdraw, harvest, etc.

}
```

This contract is a more advanced example for yield farming on Pancake swap. While the user interface for doing this exists, smart contracts may be useful if the user wants to perform further operations or automatize the procedure for a specific goal.

Something we are using here that we haven't shown previously is *ReentrancyGuard*. It is a critical security feature implemented to safeguard the contract against reentrancy attacks. A reentrancy attack occurs when an attacker takes advantage of the call to an external contract to re-enter the calling contract and drain funds or perform unauthorized actions before the first execution is completed. This type of attack exploits the asynchronous nature of blockchain transactions and the ability to call back into the contract before the initial function execution ends. *ReentrancyGuard* works by using a state variable to lock the contract's state when a function is being executed. If an external contract call within a protected function tries to re-enter the original function, the guard detects that the contract is already in the execution phase and blocks the re-entry, preventing any further actions until the first execution is complete. This mechanism is crucial in functions that interact with external contracts, like *swapTokens*, *addLiquidity*, and *stakeLPTokens*, ensuring that the contract's operations cannot be exploited to perform unauthorized withdrawals or duplicate actions that could compromise the security of the funds it manages.

The *swapTokens* function allows users to swap one type of token (tokenA) for another (tokenB) directly through PancakeSwap's router. This process is essential for yield farming, where specific token pairs are often required to participate in liquidity pools. The function ensures that the contract first receives the tokens from the user, approves the router to spend these tokens, and then performs the swap, adhering to the minimum amount of tokenB specified by the user to mitigate slippage risks.

The *addLiquidity* function enables users to contribute to liquidity pools on PancakeSwap by providing pairs of tokens (tokenA and tokenB). This contribution is a prerequisite for earning trading fees or rewards distributed by DeFi platforms. The contract automates the transfer of tokens from the user to the contract itself, grants the PancakeSwap router approval to use these tokens, and then adds them to the liquidity pool, thus simplifying the liquidity provision process for the user.

Once liquidity is provided, users receive liquidity provider (LP) tokens as proof of their contribution. The *stakeLPTokens* function allows users to stake these LP tokens in a MasterChef contract, which manages the distribution of farming rewards. This staking mechanism is where the actual "farming" happens, as users earn rewards based on the amount and duration of their staked LP tokens.

However, the current form of the *YieldFarmer* contract is not comprehensive for a fully operational yield farming strategy. To be practical and testable in a live environment, it requires additional functionalities, including withdrawal of funds, harvesting of rewards, and managing emergency withdrawals. These are essential for a complete yield farming cycle, allowing users to retrieve their stakes and earned rewards, thus providing a full suite of interactions with the underlying protocols. These can be easily added by following the same structure then deployed for testing.

End-of-Chapter Questions

Multiple-Choice Questions

1. **What does liquidity mining involve?**
   (A) Digging for physical resources.
   (B) Providing liquidity to a pool to earn rewards, typically in the form of tokens.
   (C) Mining Bitcoin.
   (D) Investing in water resources.

2. **Which of the following best describes yield farming?**
   (A) Cultivating crops on a farm.
   (B) Staking or lending crypto assets to generate high returns or rewards in the form of additional cryptocurrency.
   (C) Searching for yield signs on a road.
   (D) Farming simulation games on blockchain.

3. **What role do liquidity providers (LPs) play in AMMs?**
   (A) They create new tokens for the AMM.
   (B) They borrow funds from the AMM.
   (C) They contribute assets to liquidity pools, facilitating trading by providing market depth.
   (D) They regulate the AMM's operations.

4. **Which token is commonly associated with liquidity mining in the Curve protocol?**
   (A) ETH
   (B) BTC
   (C) CRV
   (D) USDC

5. **What is the primary risk associated with yield farming?**
   (A) Low yields in agricultural production.
   (B) Smart contract vulnerabilities.
   (C) Lack of digital identity.
   (D) Decreased internet speed.

6. **What does the term 'liquidity pool' refer to?**
   (A) A swimming pool filled with cash.
   (B) A collection of funds locked in a smart contract.
   (C) A pool of miners verifying blockchain transactions.
   (D) A database of all cryptocurrency transactions.

7. **What is the purpose of staking in the context of DeFi?**
   (A) To verify transactions and secure the network.
   (B) To lock up tokens in a smart contract to earn rewards.
   (C) To participate in blockchain mining.
   (D) To create new liquidity pools.

8. **What challenge does liquid staking aim to address?**
    (A) The energy consumption of blockchain networks.
    (B) The lack of liquidity due to assets being locked up in traditional staking.
    (C) The complexity of understanding blockchain technology.
    (D) The volatility of cryptocurrency prices.

Open Questions

1. Discuss the economic incentives behind liquidity mining and yield farming. How do these incentives drive user behavior, and what potential risks do they introduce to the DeFi ecosystem? Provide examples of strategies users might employ to maximize their returns from liquidity mining and yield farming.

2. Identify and elaborate on the main risks associated with participating in DeFi protocols, particularly focusing on liquidity provision and yield farming. How can users mitigate these risks, and what role do protocol developers have in ensuring the safety and security of participants' assets?

3. Explain the concept of liquid staking and its significance in the context of Proof of Stake (PoS) blockchain networks. What are the potential benefits and drawbacks of liquid staking for individual stakers and the overall network security and decentralization?

Coding Exercises

Exercise 1: Liquidity Mining Rewards Distribution Smart Contract

Objective: Develop a Solidity smart contract for a simplified liquidity mining program. The contract will distribute a predetermined amount of reward tokens to liquidity providers based on their contribution to the pool.

Detailed Instructions:

1. **Token Setup:** Begin by creating two ERC-20 tokens using OpenZeppelin contracts—one for liquidity provision (LP Token) and one for rewards.

2. **Adding Liquidity:** Implement a function **addLiquidity** that allows users to deposit a specified amount of LP tokens into the contract. Upon deposit, track the user's contribution percentage relative to the total liquidity pool.

3. **Reward Distribution:** Allocate a fixed number of reward tokens to be distributed over a set period (e.g. 100,000 tokens over 30 days). Implement a function **distributeRewards** that calculates each user's share of the rewards based on their liquidity contribution.

4. **Claiming Rewards:** Allow users to claim their accumulated rewards at any time via a **claimRewards** function. Ensure that claiming rewards updates their available rewards to prevent double claiming.

5. **Removing Liquidity:** Create a function **removeLiquidity** that enables users to withdraw their LP tokens from the pool, adjusting the total liquidity and each user's contribution percentage accordingly.

6. **Testing:** Write unit tests to verify that liquidity addition, reward calculation, reward claiming, and liquidity removal work as intended. Test cases should cover scenarios like adding and removing liquidity by multiple users, reward distribution accuracy, and rewards claiming process.

Exercise 2: Yield Farming Strategy Simulation

Objective: Simulate different yield farming strategies using Python or JavaScript to identify which strategy might be most profitable under varying market conditions.

Detailed Instructions:

1. **Strategy Definitions:** Define at least three distinct yield farming strategies. For example, Strategy A could prioritize pools with the highest APY, Strategy B might spread funds across various pools to mitigate risk, and Strategy C might focus on pools involving stablecoins to minimize volatility exposure.

2. **Market Conditions Simulation:** Create a synthetic dataset or use historical data to simulate various market conditions over a specified period. This dataset should include fluctuating APYs for different liquidity pools, changing token prices, and variable transaction fees.

3. **Strategy Simulation Engine:** Develop a simulation engine that applies each strategy to the dataset. The engine should account for factors such as compound interest, transaction fees, impermanent loss, and any strategy-specific actions.

4. **Performance Analysis:** For each strategy, calculate the total returns after the simulation period, factoring in gains from yield farming and any losses from impermanent loss or fees. Compare the net profitability of each strategy.

5. **Optimization and Insights:** Analyze the results to provide insights into how each strategy performs under different conditions. Discuss the trade-offs between risk and return for each strategy and suggest any potential optimizations.

Exercise 3: Liquid Staking Contract with Reward Optimization

Objective: Design and implement a Solidity smart contract for liquid staking that not only allows users to stake tokens and receive derivatives but also optimizes the distribution of staking rewards.

Detailed Instructions:

1. **Staking Token Setup:** Utilize an ERC-20 token as the staking token. Users will stake this token in exchange for a derivative token that represents their staked amount plus rewards.

2. **Issuing Staking Derivatives:** When users stake their tokens, issue them a derivative token (e.g. stETH for staked ETH) that reflects their staked amount. Use a 1:1 ratio for simplicity but adjust the derivative token's value over time to represent accrued rewards.

3. **Rewards Optimization Algorithm:** Implement an algorithm within the contract that dynamically allocates staked tokens to different validators or staking strategies based on performance metrics such as past reward rates and uptime. This algorithm aims to maximize overall rewards for the pool.

4. **Redeeming Derivatives:** Allow users to redeem their derivative tokens for the underlying staked tokens plus any accrued rewards. Ensure the redemption reflects the optimized rewards earned during the staking period.

5. **Handling Validator Performance:** Regularly update the performance metrics of validators or staking strategies. Include a mechanism to reduce exposure to underperforming validators.

6. **Safety Mechanisms:** Implement safeguards to protect against validator slashing events, such as distributing staking across multiple validators and incorporating insurance or slashing protection mechanisms.

7. **Unit Testing:** Develop comprehensive unit tests to ensure the contract functions as intended, particularly focusing on the accuracy of reward optimization, the issuance and redemption of derivative tokens, and the robustness of safety mechanisms.

Chapter 9

The Tokenization Transformation from Wall Street to Your Street

Preface

If 2021 was the year crypto threw a wild, glitter-strewn gala, captivating the world with its gallery of pixelated primate NFTs, an army of doge-inspired digital coins, and a parade of Hollywood's glitterati singing its praises, then brace yourself for the sequel—but not the kind you might expect. Picture this: the glitz and glam have left the building, replaced by the stern-faced seriousness of the financial elite.

Gone are the days when Dogecoin was king. Now, we're trading in meme coins for something even your accountant can't yawn at—Real World Assets (RWAs).[1] Yes, those bricks and mortar are getting a blockchain facelift. Imagine a world where tangible assets like real estate, art, and even intellectual property get a blockchain makeover. This shift isn't about catching a ride to the moon on the back of the latest sensation; it's about laying down the bricks for crypto's maturity into a pillar of modern finance.

So, say goodbye to the days of speculative tweets from tech moguls sending markets into a frenzy. The forthcoming wave of crypto innovation is set to don a suit and tie,

---

[1] Please let's agree here and now that RWA is the worst possible acronym for these as it will get confused with the older and more used acronym of risk-weighted assets in traditional finance!

rolling up its sleeves to tackle the nitty-gritty of asset tokenization. It's less about the flash and more about the substance, marking a pivotal chapter in the grand saga of digital currencies and blockchain technology—a transformation that could redefine the very foundations of investment, ownership, and asset management for generations to come.

Tokenization, with its promise to revolutionize ownership and investment in real-world assets through blockchain technology, is inadvertently bridging the gap between the anarchic spirit of early crypto enthusiasts and the buttoned-up world of traditional finance. So in a plot twist worthy of a soap opera, crypto and banks are now BFFs. Next thing you know, they'll be exchanging friendship bracelets and secret handshakes.

As we venture deeper into the era of tokenizing everything from buildings to Beethoven, the allure of blockchain's efficiency, security, and transparency has not gone unnoticed by the titans of Wall Street and beyond. The very mechanisms designed to democratize finance, cutting out intermediaries and reducing reliance on centralized authorities, are now catching the eye of major banks, investment firms, and financial institutions. These entities, once viewed as the antithesis of the crypto movement, are now keen to harness the power of blockchain for their own portfolios.

In an ironic twist of fate, the burgeoning field of asset tokenization might just roll out the red carpet for the very institutions that Satoshi Nakamoto's original vision sought to circumvent. Nakamoto's original manifesto for Bitcoin championed a peer-to-peer electronic cash system, one that would operate independently of any central authority. The goal was to disrupt the established financial ecosystem, providing an alternative to those disillusioned by the 2008 financial crisis. However, as tokenization gains momentum, it's these very institutions, with their regulatory prowess and financial clout, that are poised to play a significant role in shaping the future of crypto.

This pivot toward embracing traditional financial powerhouses could signal a departure from the grassroots, libertarian ethos that characterized the early days of cryptocurrency. The potential for blockchain to streamline processes, ensure the integrity of transactions, and open up new investment opportunities has proven too enticing to

The Tokenization Bridge from traditional finance to DeFi/Web3

ignore, even for the staunchest critics within the financial establishment (I am looking at you Larry Fink).

Yet, there's a silver lining. This convergence of crypto and traditional finance could also herald a new era of innovation, collaboration, and financial inclusion. By bringing the reliability and structure of established institutions into the fold, tokenization might just achieve what the early pioneers of cryptocurrency dreamed of: transforming the global financial landscape in a way that benefits everyone, from individual investors to multinational corporations.

In this unexpected alliance, we find the ultimate irony: Satoshi's vision of a decentralized financial system may well be realized through the participation of the very institutions it was meant to disrupt. As tokenization continues to blur the lines between old money and new, the blockchain revolution proves that, sometimes, to change the system, you must work from within it.

1. Introduction

At its core, tokenization is about converting rights to an asset into a digital token on a blockchain. Imagine your grandma's secret cookie recipe is a gold mine. Tokenization lets you turn that recipe into a digital "cookie token" everyone wants a piece of, without giving away the actual cookies. While the idea of representing real-world assets in different forms isn't novel, blockchain technology has supercharged this concept, propelling it into the future with unprecedented speed and versatility.

Stablecoins, such as USDT and USDC, stand as the vanguards of this movement. As you would remember from Chapter 4, these digital currencies are pegged to the U.S. dollar, ensuring that for every token issued, there is a corresponding dollar in the real world. This makes stablecoins a prime example of fungible tokens, where each unit is identical to the next, interchangeable and indistinct. This fungibility is akin to how we view traditional money, where each dollar bill holds the same value and utility as another.

However, the realm of tokenized assets isn't confined to the uniformity of stablecoins. It extends into the unique and varied world of non-fungible tokens (NFTs), where each token represents something distinct and irreplaceable, like a piece of art or a rare collectible. This duality within tokenization—between the fungible and non-fungible—opens the door to digitizing almost every conceivable asset in the real world, from the Mona Lisa to your neighbor's house.

The concept of breaking down assets into smaller, more accessible parts isn't a novelty brought about by blockchain. The financial world has been at it for years through instruments like Real Estate Investment Trusts (REITs) and Exchange-Traded Funds (ETFs), which have democratized access to investments that would otherwise require significant capital. With over $5 trillion managed in ETFs alone, the appetite for fractional ownership in public markets is undeniable. *Did crypto bros just ignore the existence of these widely available instruments?* Maybe, or maybe not. This traditional fractionalization has its confines, primarily thriving in the efficient, high-tech corridors of public markets. Here, trades are executed in milliseconds, and transparency is the order of the day. The private markets, by contrast, remain in the shadows—manual, slow, opaque, and burdened with overheads. These sectors, ripe with potential, have been left yearning for the innovation that tokenization promises.

Tokenization on the blockchain addresses these inefficiencies head-on. By digitizing assets, the process of matching capital with investment opportunities is streamlined, cutting through the bureaucratic red tape that has long stifled innovation in private markets. Blockchain technology enhances transparency and speed and significantly reduces the costs associated with transactions and asset management. The critical advantage is that this democratization of asset ownership could transform previously illiquid assets into liquid ones, opening up investment opportunities to a broader range of investors.

Consider the tokenization of real estate, an asset class traditionally marked by high entry barriers and a lack of liquidity. Through tokenization, investors can purchase tokens representing a fraction of a property, making real estate investment accessible to those previously priced out of the market. Real estate tokenization means you can own a piece of a building in Manhattan. The catch? It might just be the equivalent of a bathroom tile, but it's in Manhattan! Similarly, thanks to art tokenization, you can now own a piece of a Jean-Michel Basquiat. That's right, for the price of a latte, you can brag about being an art collector. Your piece might just be a pixel, but who's counting?

As we stand on the brink of this tokenization wave, it's clear that the fusion of traditional asset fractionalization with blockchain technology is not just an incremental improvement but a revolutionary leap forward. This synergy promises to unlock value in previously inaccessible markets, heralding a new era of inclusivity, efficiency, and transparency in asset ownership. The journey of tokenization is just beginning, and its potential to reshape the financial landscape is boundless.

2. How does it work?

Let me start by discussing in the abstract how the process would work; we can then analyze a number of different protocols and examples across different asset classes to better understand the benefits and limitations of tokenization.

The tokenization process of real-world assets such as art or real estate involves a series of critical steps, each meticulously executed to ensure the seamless bridge between the tangible asset and its digital representation. This intricate process, when applied to the examples of a piece of art or a real estate property, unfolds in a manner that meticulously aligns with both legal frameworks and market expectations, ensuring the assets' viability in the digital domain.

The journey begins with the assessment and appraisal of the asset to ascertain its market value. In the context of a piece of art, a professional art appraiser would evaluate the artwork based on its provenance, condition, market demand, and historical significance.

For a real estate property, a licensed real estate appraiser would conduct a comprehensive evaluation, considering factors like location, condition, market trends, and comparable property values. This step is foundational, establishing a credible baseline value for the asset before it enters the digital realm.

Securing the asset legally for tokenization is the next critical step. For an artwork, this might involve verifying the ownership and copyright status, ensuring no legal encumbrances prevent its tokenization. In real estate, this step could require structuring ownership through a specific entity, such as a trust or limited liability company that holds the property title, thereby facilitating its backing of the digital tokens.

A third-party audit is indispensable, providing an objective verification of the asset's existence and value. An independent auditor would examine the artwork, verifying its authenticity, condition, and appraised value. For real estate, the auditor would review property documents, appraisals, and legal structures to confirm the asset's valuation and legal readiness for tokenization. This verification process adds a layer of trust and transparency, crucial for potential investors.

The creation of legal and smart contract mechanisms ensures that the token accurately represents the asset's ownership or interest. For an artwork token, the smart contract might define the terms of ownership share, rights to future sale proceeds, or exhibition rights. In real estate tokenization, the smart contract would detail the ownership structure, distribution of rental income, or conditions for the property's future sale. These contracts serve as the binding agreement between the token holders and the asset, encoded on the blockchain to ensure immutability and enforceability.

Launching the token sale involves offering the digital tokens to qualified investors, highlighting the investment terms and potential returns. An art token sale might target collectors and investors, emphasizing the artwork's value, rarity, and investment potential. A real estate token offering would appeal to investors interested in property income or appreciation, providing detailed information about the property, expected returns, and token liquidity.

Ongoing management and compliance are also essential, ensuring that the token and underlying asset adhere to legal requirements and maintain their value proposition over time. For an art token, this could involve managing the artwork's storage, insurance, and exhibition to preserve its value. In the case of real estate, ongoing management includes property maintenance, tenant relations, and financial administration, alongside compliance with real estate laws and regulations.

As depicted in **Figure 1**, the pivotal step in the tokenization of a real-world asset and its subsequent integration into the blockchain ecosystem hinges on the assurance that the digital tokens being created are adequately collateralized. This foundational requirement necessitates that a company embarking on tokenization must not only possess but also demonstrate unequivocally that it holds sufficient reserves to underpin the value of their token. This mechanism of verification is crucial for several reasons, primarily aimed at fostering trust and stability within the token's ecosystem and upholding the financial system's integrity in which the token circulates.

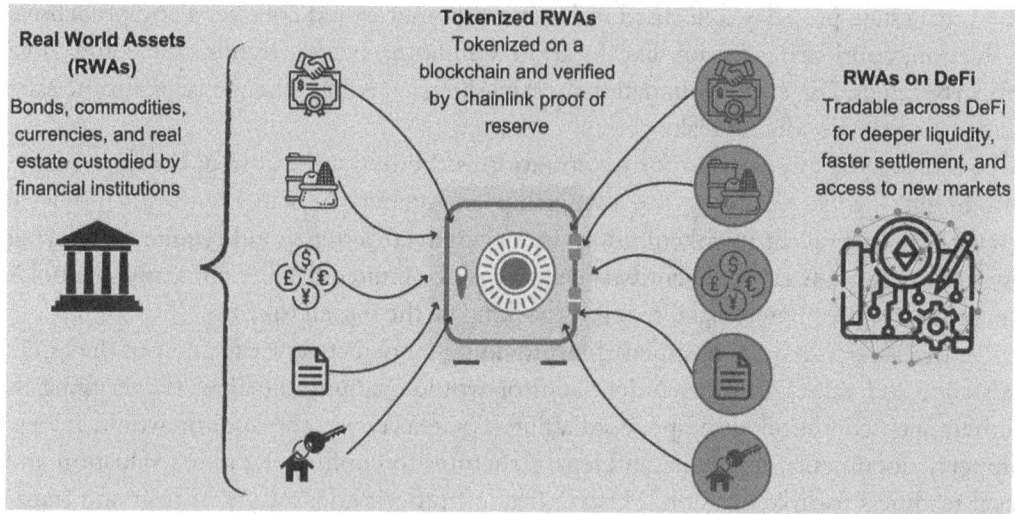

Figure 1   Tokenization of real-world assets

To operationalize this, for every digital token issued on the blockchain, there must be a corresponding real-world asset that backs it. This one-to-one correlation ensures that the digital representation on the blockchain accurately reflects a tangible asset, thereby grounding the token's value in the real economy. The importance of this direct linkage cannot be overstated, as it forms the bedrock upon which trust in the digital token is built. Without this tangible backing, tokens could be perceived as mere speculative instruments, detached from real value and susceptible to volatility, potentially undermining the stability and trust in the blockchain ecosystem. This is really similar to what we discussed in the case of stablecoins: if there is nothing in the vaults (physical or digital) to act as a reserve for the tokens, they become as useful as monopoly money.

This process of ensuring tokens are sufficiently collateralized is not merely a procedural step but a fundamental aspect that guarantees the token's legitimacy and viability. It serves to align the interests of token issuers with those of the investors and users, ensuring that the digital tokens hold intrinsic value mirrored by actual assets. Furthermore, it plays a crucial role in integrating digital assets within the broader financial system, allowing for a seamless interface between traditional financial mechanisms and the emerging digital economy.

The involvement of an independent auditor or a verification entity provides an unbiased assessment of the company's claims regarding its reserves, offering a layer of transparency that is vital for the token's credibility. This transparency is not merely a formality but a critical component that deters fraudulent activities and establishes a foundation of trust. By allowing independent verification, token issuers open their process to scrutiny, reinforcing the legitimacy of their tokens and, by extension, the integrity of the tokenization process itself.

The need for rigorous verification and the assurance of collateralization underscores the symbiotic relationship between real-world assets and their digital counterparts.

This relationship ensures that digital tokens are not just abstract digital constructs, but representations of value grounded in the physical world. Through this meticulous process, tokenization promises to bring about a revolution in how assets are managed, traded, and perceived.

2.1 Key Benefits

Traditional markets often grapple with inefficiencies stemming from the manual handling of securities, reliance on intermediaries, and protracted settlement times. For instance, purchasing a share in a real estate investment trust (REIT) or a piece of art through conventional channels involves multiple steps and parties, including brokers, lawyers, and banks, each adding their layer of complexity, cost, and time to the transaction.

In contrast, tokenization streamlines the investment process by leveraging blockchain to automate these transactions through smart contracts. Consider the example of a real estate property. Traditionally, investing in real estate directly requires significant capital, extensive paperwork, and a long duration from the initial agreement to the final settlement. However, when this asset is tokenized, its ownership can be divided into smaller, more affordable digital tokens. These tokens can be bought or sold on a blockchain platform, where smart contracts automate the exchange, eliminating the need for intermediaries such as brokers and lawyers, and significantly reducing transaction costs.

Furthermore, blockchain's inherent features enhance security and transparency in transactions. Traditional investment processes are vulnerable to fraud and errors, given the reliance on paper-based documentation and the opaqueness of intermediary operations. Blockchain technology, however, offers a transparent and immutable ledger of transactions, ensuring that every transfer of tokens representing asset ownership is recorded and verifiable by all parties at any time. This reduces the potential for fraud and builds trust among investors.

Reducing costs and increasing efficiency is another hallmark of tokenization. In traditional settings, the cost structure of transactions is inflated by fees for legal services, brokers, and regulatory compliance, not to mention the operational costs associated with managing and servicing the asset. By automating these processes and cutting out intermediaries, tokenization lowers the barrier to entry for investors, making it feasible to invest in assets with smaller amounts of capital. This efficiency extends to regulatory compliance, where blockchain can provide a more streamlined approach to KYC and anti-money laundering (AML) checks by securely storing verified investor information, accessible with permission, thus avoiding repetitive processes for each new investment. In essence, rather than going through these processes for all the institutions involved, one could do a proof of identity once that satisfies the requirements for all the parties involved.

Tokenization also democratizes investment opportunities, opening up markets that were previously accessible only to wealthy or institutional investors. Through tokenization, assets like commercial real estate, fine art, or even ownership stakes in private companies can be divided into tokens that represent a fraction of the total value, allowing individual investors to participate in investment opportunities with lower capital require-ments. This broader access can significantly increase the liquidity of traditionally illiquid assets like real estate or art, as tokens can be more easily and efficiently traded on second-ary markets.

Finally, probably the most evident benefit is that the increased market liquidity and unified investment platforms that blockchain enables can transform the investment landscape.

In other words, once something is tokenized, there might be a market for it, maybe thanks to an AMM!

Traditional illiquid assets suffer from long hold periods and a limited pool of poten-tial buyers. By facilitating fractional ownership and simplifying transactions, tokenization expands the investor base and enhances the liquidity of these assets. Moreover, block-chain platforms can serve as a one-stop shop for managing a diversified portfolio of tokenized assets, from real estate and art to stocks and bonds, further streamlining trans-action efficiency and reducing settlement times.

In essence, blockchain's impact on tokenization presents a paradigm shift from the traditional market infrastructure, characterized by its capacity to enhance efficiency, reduce costs, and broaden investment opportunities, marking a significant leap toward a more accessible, transparent, and efficient financial ecosystem.

2.2 What is the achievable market?

If only art or real estate were to be tokenized, you might not care much. However, tokenization is likely to redefine the boundaries of what constitutes a marketable asset. By converting rights to an asset into a digital token, virtually anything of value—from financial assets and real estate to collectibles, data, and even infrastructure—can be tokenized, unlocking a new universe of investment opportunities (see **Figure 2**). This transition broadens the scope of what can be considered an investable asset and signifi-cantly enhancing the liquidity and accessibility of these assets. Let's explore the potential of tokenization across various verticals, illustrating the vastness of the achievable market with examples of tokenization projects.

- *Financial Assets:* The tokenization of financial assets such as stocks, bonds, and deriva-tives represents a direct evolution of existing market structures, making these instru-ments more accessible and tradable. An example is tZERO, a platform that offers a regulated way to trade tokenized securities, thus broadening access to capital and investment opportunities while enhancing liquidity in the market.
- *Real Estate:* Real estate tokenization allows investors to buy shares in properties, mak-ing what was once the preserve of the wealthy or institutional investors accessible to a wider audience. RealT is a notable project in this space, enabling the purchase of tokens representing partial ownership in rental properties, thereby democratizing access to real estate investments and improving liquidity in a traditionally illiquid market.

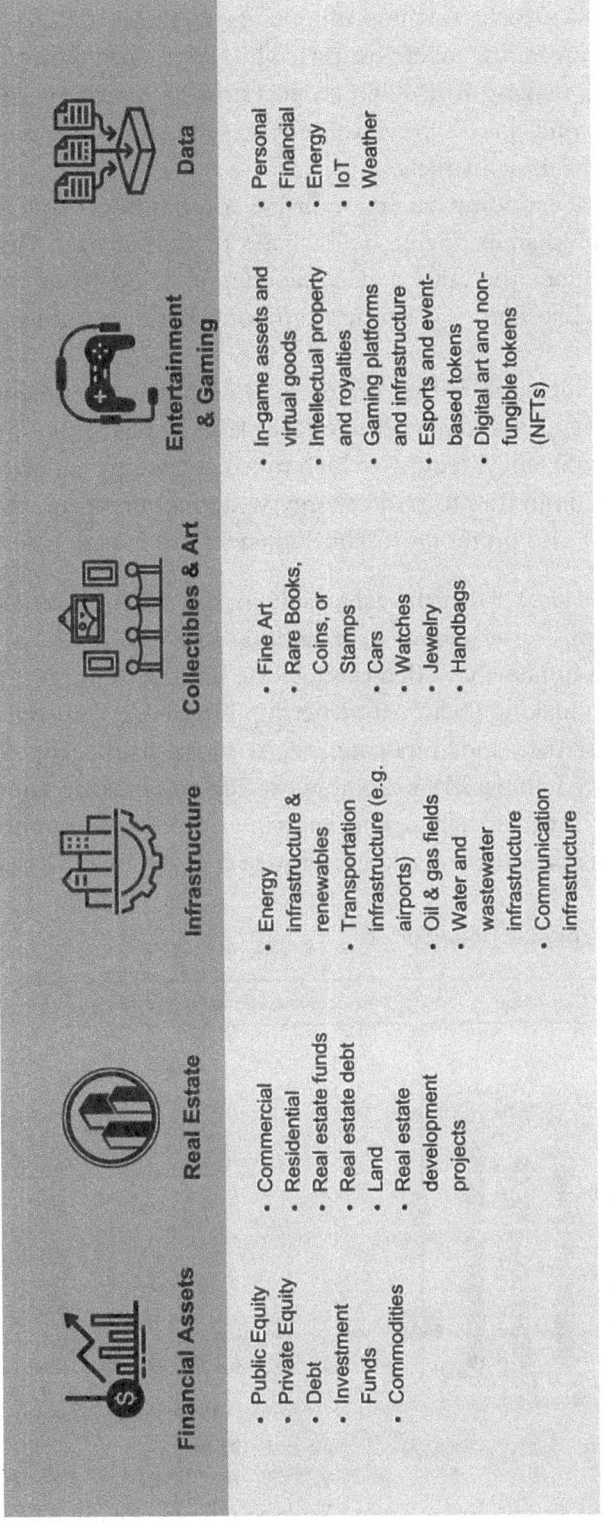

Figure 2 Use cases for Tokenization

407

- *Collectibles and Art:* The tokenization of collectibles and art opens new avenues for ownership and investment in these unique assets. Projects like CurioInvest enable users to invest in tokenized collectible cars, while Maecenas allows for fractional ownership of fine art, making it possible for investors to own a piece of a Picasso or a Warhol. This not only makes previously inaccessible assets accessible but also adds a layer of liquidity to these markets.
- *Data:* In the digital economy, data is a valuable commodity. Tokenization can facilitate the secure and transparent buying, selling, and trading of data. Ocean Protocol uses tokenization to unlock the value of data, allowing individuals and enterprises to monetize their data while ensuring privacy and control, thus creating a new market for data assets.
- *Infrastructure:* Tokenizing infrastructure projects can open investment opportunities in large-scale projects such as renewable energy plants or telecommunications networks. An example is Brooklyn Microgrid, which tokenizes energy generated by solar panels, allowing local communities to trade energy within a microgrid. This provides a new investment avenue and promotes sustainable energy solutions.

It should now be clearer that the achievable market for tokenized assets is expansive, transcending traditional asset classes to include a wide range of real-world assets and digital goods. The examples above demonstrate the breadth of opportunities that tokenization presents, from making fractional ownership possible in real estate and art to creating new markets for data and infrastructure. As blockchain technology continues to evolve and regulatory frameworks become more accommodating, the scope for tokenization is bound to expand further, making the achievable market not just big, but boundless, at least according to some consultants. **Figure 3** shows that the tokenization market

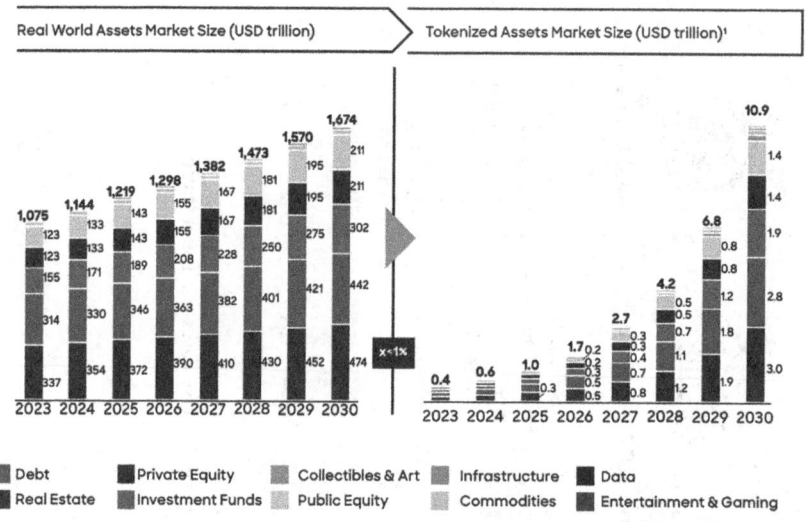

Figure 3 RWA market size estimation (*Source:* With permission of Roland Berger, 2023)

is expected to reach 11 trillion by 2030.[2] Tokenization promises to democratize access to investment opportunities, enhance asset liquidity, and revolutionize how we think about ownership and value in the digital age.

As argued by Larry Fink, the CEO of Blackrock, after the Bitcoin ETF, tokenization will be "the next generation for markets."[3]

Let's discuss a few recent examples to understand how the market is evolving and what the first applications might be.

2.3 The MakerDAO Transition toward RWA

MakerDAO has significantly focused on the tokenization of RWAs, particularly through the addition of U.S. Treasury bonds to its portfolio. This move is part of a broader strategy known as the "Endgame Plan," aimed at diversifying the assets backing MakerDAO's DAI stablecoin and enhancing the ratio of decentralized collateral. By incorporating traditional financial assets like government bonds, MakerDAO seeks to bolster the stability and reliability of DAI. For example, MakerDAO partnered with New Silver in 2021 to mint real-estate-backed DROP tokens. These tokens could then be used as collateral within the MakerDAO system to generate DAI.

The tokenization of RWAs by MakerDAO involves converting physical assets or traditional finance assets into on-chain counterparts. This strategy encompasses a wide range of assets, from bonds and real estate to various forms of debt instruments. MakerDAO's focus on RWAs has been a major revenue driver, accounting for a significant portion of its income. In particular, MakerDAO's investment in U.S. Treasuries has been a lucrative move, contributing to its position as a leader in the RWA sector within the cryptocurrency industry.

Recent initiatives by MakerDAO, such as injecting $100 million worth of RWAs through BlockTower Andromeda, primarily in short-term U.S. Treasury bonds, have further solidified this approach.[4] The protocol's cumulative RWA assets currently stand at approximately $2.7 billion, indicating the scale and significance of its investment in RWAs. This strategic focus on RWAs not only aids in revenue generation but also showcases MakerDAO's resilience in the face of a bear market, with annualized revenue nearing $150 million, much of which is derived from RWAs.

The growth of real-world asset tokenization, as seen in MakerDAO's activities, is part of a larger trend within the crypto industry that could potentially unlock trillions of dollars in global illiquid assets. MakerDAO, among other protocols, is leveraging this opportunity to provide traditional asset managers with new ways to tokenize their portfolios, thereby offering liquidity against these assets and opening additional credit avenues. The advantages of tokenizing RWAs include DeFi growth by adding TradFi assets' value to

---

[2] See https://web-assets.bcg.com/1e/a2/5b5f2b7e42dfad2cb3113a291222/on-chain-asset-tokenization.pdf.

[3] https://www.forbes.com/sites/davidbirch/2023/03/01/larry-fink-says-tokens-are-the-next-generation-for-markets/

[4] https://cryptopotato.com/makerdao-injects-100m-worth-of-rwas-via-blocktower-andromeda/

decentralized finance, enhanced liquidity through fractional ownership, transparency with blockchain's immutable ledger, efficiency in asset trading and management, and innovation in financial products.[5]

2.4 Art Tokenization Example

Another example of tokenization involves digitizing artworks. Art tokenization is reshaping the art market by offering new forms of ownership and investment. Consider the case of a famous Banksy's Girl with Balloon original painting valued at $5 million. Traditionally, such a treasure would be accessible only to VIPs like Robbie Williams or Chris Martin. However, tokenization breaks down these barriers.

In this process, the artwork is first appraised and authenticated, ensuring its value is well established. Next, digital tokens representing fractional ownership in the artwork are created. For instance, 50,000 tokens could be issued, each representing a 0.002% stake in the painting, priced at $100 per token. These tokens are then sold on blockchain platforms, making pieces of the painting available to a broader audience, including both art enthusiasts and investors.

Ownership of these tokens carries several benefits. Holders can receive a share of any profits if the artwork is sold in the future. Tokenization platforms may also offer additional perks, such as exclusive viewings or digital showcases of the artwork.

The tokenization process democratizes access to high-value investments and enhances the liquidity of art assets, allowing shares to be traded on secondary markets. The blockchain ensures a tamper-proof record of the artwork's history, ownership, and authenticity, thereby instilling trust and transparency. This also opens the art market to new investors, potentially increasing overall investment in art and cultural assets. Tokenization can even enhance the art experience by linking physical art with digital experiences, adding value to the ownership of art tokens.

Although there might be significant benefits, there are also several operational challenges:

- *Technological Challenges*: Creating a seamless user experience also poses significant challenges, particularly when considering the varying levels of technological literacy among users. Navigating the tech behind tokenization can feel like trying to assemble furniture without instructions—frustrating but oh-so rewarding when you finally get it right.
- *Regulatory Issues*: The art market is subject to a myriad of regulations that vary greatly by jurisdiction. The lack of clear regulatory frameworks for tokenized assets adds complexity, raising compliance risks and potential legal liabilities.
- *Art Valuation:* Determining the value of art is highly subjective and complex. Tokenization can strive to make the process more objective by relying on attributes like rarity and historical significance, but achieving an unbiased valuation, which happens

---

[5] https://cryptomarketcap.com/learn/real-world-assets-crypto

off-chain, remains a critical issue. Moreover, the valuation process needs to be transparent and asset-backing must be clear to maintain trust.

- *Liquidity:* While tokenization aims to increase the liquidity of art investments, there's a risk that individual tokens, especially those representing smaller stakes, may remain illiquid.

Some notable platforms and collaborations have emerged as leaders in the field of art tokenization. Sygnum, a Swiss digital banking and asset management platform, allows investment in iconic works from artists like Picasso and Warhol. They collaborate with Artory, a digital registry for the art market, to provide tokenization services and enable secure storage, transfer, and trading of digital tokens representing art ownership.

3. Completing the Security Market Line

There is also a bigger objective for tokenization. By bringing real-world assets onto the blockchain, tokenization offers a groundbreaking approach to diversifying the risk profile of digital asset investments. Traditionally, in finance, diversification strategies often include incorporating Treasuries and bonds into portfolios. These assets act as a "shock absorber," providing stability and safety even when the stock market faces downturns. They offer a predictable, albeit often modest, return, which is a cornerstone of risk management for investors looking to hedge against market volatility.

In the digital asset space, particularly within the crypto market, risk management practices have somewhat mirrored these traditional strategies, albeit with a unique twist. Instead of U.S. Treasuries, crypto investors have gravitated toward stablecoins as their

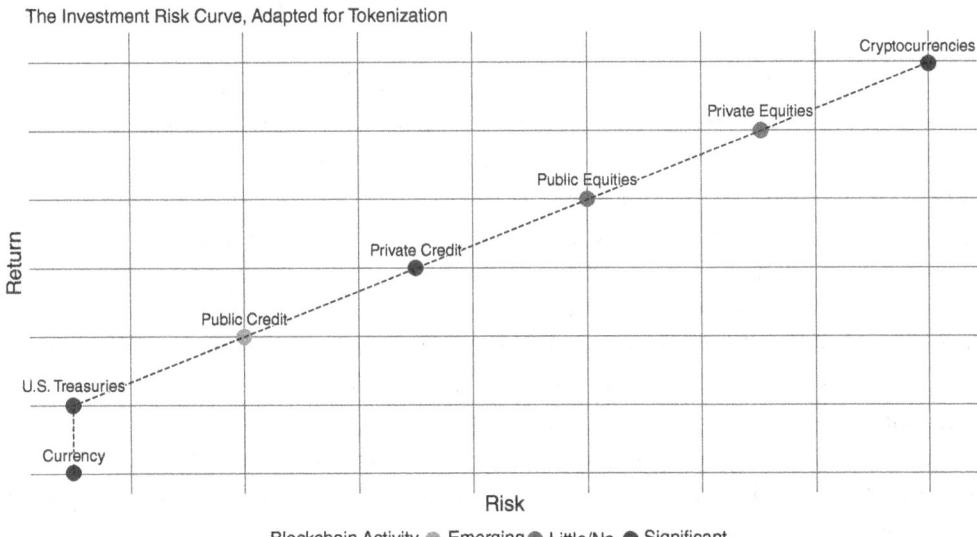

Figure 4   Investment Risk Curve for Tokenization. X axis shows the risk, Y axis shows return potential. The colors classify current blockchain activity. (*Source:* Adapted from RWA.xyz, 2023)

haven asset. While they serve a similar purpose to Treasuries in providing a safe harbor amid the tumultuous crypto seas, stablecoins typically offer no yield, presenting a dilemma for yield-seeking investors in the digital space.

This is where the potential of tokenized assets, such as tokenized Treasuries, becomes compelling. If investors can achieve a yield from these traditionally safe assets on-chain, the appeal is undeniable. Imagine being able to earn a 5% yield on tokenized U.S. Treasuries or corporate bonds, all while operating within the blockchain ecosystem. This not only provides the safety and predictability associated with these assets but also introduces a yield that is typically not available with stablecoins.

Tokenizing Treasuries seems a boring application of tokenization but expands the risk profile of offerings in the crypto space by incorporating assets on the left end of the risk spectrum. This diversification is crucial, especially considering the high volatility and speculative nature of many digital assets. By integrating traditional financial instruments in a tokenized form, investors can balance their portfolios, marrying the high-reward, high-risk profile of cryptocurrencies with the steady, dependable nature of government and corporate debt instruments.

Moreover, the on-chain availability of these tokenized assets enhances liquidity and accessibility, allowing for more dynamic portfolio management and opening up these traditionally exclusive investment opportunities to a broader audience. This evolution in asset tokenization not only broadens the investment landscape but also democratizes access to financial instruments that have been the mainstay of risk-averse investors.

The tokenization of Treasuries and similar assets provides a solution to the yield dilemma faced by crypto investors relying on stablecoins for risk management, offering a pathway to achieve not just risk diversification but also yield generation on-chain. This expansion of the risk profile for digital assets enhances the robustness and appeal of the crypto investment ecosystem, promising a more nuanced and balanced approach to investment strategy in the blockchain era.

The market for tokenized U.S. Treasuries is experiencing significant growth, reflecting a burgeoning interest in bridging traditional financial assets with blockchain technology. Franklin Templeton emerged as a leading issuer in this space, with its market cap growing by 203.5% or $210.8 million by the end of October 2023. This growth, despite being substantial, saw its market share drop to 44.6% due to the influx of new entrants. Ondo Finance, a relative newcomer, notably captured a 25.3% market share with a $178.4 million increase in the same period. Ethereum is the largest network for tokenized U.S. Treasuries, holding 48.4% of the total market cap at $340.8 million, closely followed by Stellar with 45.9%. The appeal for investors lies in seeking higher returns from government bond rates, as the average yield for all tokenized Treasuries stood at 5.25%.

Another notable project, Tradeteq, launched U.S. Treasury Yield (USTY) tokens, representing shares in a U.S. Treasury bond ETF, on the XDC Network. This move caters to professional investors seeking to capitalize on the benefits of blockchain, such as increased liquidity, faster settlement, and lower costs. Tradeteq's initiative, alongside the growing market cap, which reached $622 million, underscores the increasing adoption and potential of tokenized Treasuries. Banks and financial institutions are recognizing the value in creating blockchain-based tokens for traditional assets, signaling a shift toward a more digitized and efficient financial infrastructure.

The rising interest and investment in tokenized Treasuries highlight the expansive potential of the digital bond market. As the market continues to grow, driven by the demand for higher yields and the efficiencies offered by blockchain technology, tokenized U.S. Treasuries are poised to become a significant component of the digital asset landscape.

3.1 Isn't this just a fancy way of reinventing ETFs?

Indeed, the concept of buying shares of an ETF (Exchange-Traded Fund) shares similarities with the tokenization of assets, particularly in the context of democratizing access to investments and enabling fractional ownership. However, while both approaches aim to simplify and broaden investment opportunities, there are critical distinctions and limitations when comparing ETFs to tokenized assets, especially in terms of ownership, liquidity, and operational efficiency.

DIRECT VS. INDIRECT OWNERSHIP   When you buy an ETF, you're purchasing shares of a fund that holds the underlying assets, rather than owning those assets directly. ETFs are managed by entities that maintain custody of the actual securities or commodities. In contrast, tokenizing an asset like a treasury bond theoretically provides direct ownership of the asset in digital form. This direct ownership can offer clearer rights and potentially fewer layers between the investor and the asset, although it also comes with its set of regulatory, custody, and security challenges.

OPERATIONAL EFFICIENCY AND COSTS   ETFs are subject to management fees, which can vary significantly depending on the fund's strategy, provider, and size. These fees cover the costs of managing the ETF, including administrative expenses, portfolio management, and custody services. While ETFs offer the advantage of professional management, the associated costs can eat into investment returns over time. Tokenized assets, on the other hand, typically involve lower operational costs after their initial setup. The use of blockchain technology for issuing, trading, and settling tokenized assets can reduce the need for intermediaries, potentially lowering transaction costs and management fees.

MARKET HOURS AND LIQUIDITY   ETFs are traded on stock exchanges, meaning they're subject to the same trading hours and market conditions as stocks. This limits investors' ability to buy or sell ETF shares outside of market hours, which can be particularly restrictive for investors in different time zones or those looking to react quickly to market news. Tokenized assets, traded on decentralized platforms, can theoretically offer 24/7 trading, providing greater flexibility and potentially more opportunities for liquidity. However, the actual liquidity of tokenized assets can vary widely depending on the asset, platform, and market participation.

LEGAL AND REGULATORY FRAMEWORK   ETFs operate within a well-established legal and regulatory framework, providing investors with certain protections and recourse in case of disputes or fraud. The regulatory environment for tokenized assets is still evolving, with varying degrees of clarity and protection depending on the jurisdiction. Investors in tokenized assets may face uncertain legal rights, potential regulatory changes, and varying degrees of oversight and consumer protection.

TECHNOLOGICAL AND SECURITY CONSIDERATIONS While blockchain technology offers many potential benefits, including transparency, immutability, and efficiency, it also poses unique challenges and risks. Security vulnerabilities, technology failures, and the risk of losing access to digital wallets can pose significant risks to investors in tokenized assets. In contrast, ETFs, as traditional financial products, are supported by established financial institutions with rigorous security protocols and regulatory oversight.

3.2 Private Markets

If the appeal of tokenized treasuries is still somewhat obscure to you, let's see if applying tokenization to other asset classes is more compelling.

The private markets, characterized by a rich tapestry of assets including private equity, credit opportunities, and other alternative investments, are now being reimagined through the lens of blockchain technology.

Let's discuss a few recent developments in this space to better understand how this market is evolving.

Citigroup, in partnership with Wellington Management, WisdomTree, and other financial institutions, recently conducted a proof-of-concept (POC) simulation on the Avalanche blockchain. This experiment aimed to explore the tokenization of private equity funds, showcasing the potential of blockchain technology to revolutionize the private equity market by making it more transparent, efficient, and accessible. The simulation entailed the tokenization of a Wellington-issued private equity fund, bringing it onto a blockchain network, thereby illustrating the practical applications of smart contracts in automating and controlling the distribution and compliance of tokenized assets. The simulation tested key use cases such as the end-to-end transfer of tokenized assets, secondary trading, and utilizing these digital assets as collateral in lending scenarios. By employing Avalanche Spruce, a subnet designed specifically for institutional use, the project was able to test blockchain technology's application in automating various aspects of the investment process, including distribution rules and identity verification.[6]

The emerging trend showcases a significant stride toward tokenizing private funds. Their proof of concept illustrates the tangible benefits of utilizing smart contracts for private equity funds, such as operational efficiencies and new functionalities that traditional assets lack. This venture not only aims to streamline the complexities inherent in private markets but also to democratize access, enhancing rule enforcement and operational scalability within the digital sphere.

---

[6] https://cryptobriefing.com/citi-pilots-tokenization-private-assets-using-avalanche-infrastructure/ https://www.kitco.com/news/article/2024-02-14/citigroup-wellington-and-wisdomtree-successfully-tokenize-private-equity

The increasing involvement of traditional financial powerhouses in tokenizing RWAs points toward a paradigm shift. Notable entities such as BlackRock, Fidelity, BNY Mellon, JP Morgan, Goldman Sachs, UBS, and HSBC are actively leveraging blockchain to tokenize a diverse range of assets. This transition is not only about enhancing operational efficiencies but also about placing tokenized products directly with client bases, thereby expanding the reach and inclusivity of private market investments.

JP Morgan has been actively exploring the tokenization of funds and other assets through various initiatives and proofs of concept (PoCs), focusing on improving the efficiency, liquidity, and personalization of investment portfolios.

One of the most important initiatives is the creation of the Onyx platform. It is a bank-led blockchain platform established in 2020, designed to enhance the movement of money, information, and assets through digital means. It is known for pioneering blockchain solutions within the banking sector and operates several key components that facilitate a broad range of financial services and innovations. It has different components.

- **Liink:** Formerly known as the Interbank Information Network (IIN), Liink is a blockchain-based platform that allows banks and financial institutions to execute cross-border transactions and share information in a peer-to-peer manner. It helps to validate new accounts for cross-border payments, thereby reducing fraud risk and improving transaction efficiency.
- **Onyx Digital Assets:** This platform focuses on the tokenization of assets, enabling financial institutions and fintech companies to create tokenized versions of their financial products. It allows for the instant and atomic settlement of transactions, providing real-time transparency and automating operational processes. This enhances the utility and mobility of financial assets, which can be used as collateral for secured intraday financing or posted as collateral margin without affecting market positions.
- **JPM Coin:** JPM Coin is a digital currency fully backed by U.S. dollar reserves, created on the Quorum blockchain protocol. It is used to facilitate instant settlements between institutional clients. Unlike typical stablecoins, JPM Coin is designed for use within JP Morgan's ecosystem and offers the security and backing of the bank itself.
- **Digital Financing:** This application within Onyx provides access to secured financing by tokenizing cash and collateral, enabling the settlement of repo transactions within minutes. It reduces settlement and counterparty risk through the use of smart contracts, which ensure real-time transaction settlement and lifecycle transparency.

The idea behind Onyx is to leverage blockchain technology to offer a robust and secure infrastructure for financial transactions, aiming to increase efficiency, reduce risks, and open up new opportunities for financial institutions to utilize their assets more effectively. This is even more impressive since Jamie Dimon, CEO of JP Morgan, has been one of the most critical figures of crypto.[7]

---

[7] See https://finance.yahoo.com/news/jamie-dimon-calls-bitcoin-fraud-131026597.html.

Another notable initiative is their collaboration with Apollo Global Management as part of the Monetary Authority of Singapore's Project Guardian. This project aimed to tokenize funds, including alternative assets, to automate and personalize discretionary portfolios for wealthy clients, representing a significant opportunity within the $5.5 trillion space of personalized wealth management portfolios.[8]

The PoC tested the interoperability of JP Morgan's Onyx Digital Asset platform with permissioned layers of public blockchains, including the Cosmos-based Provenance Blockchain and an Ethereum-compatible subnet on the Avalanche blockchain. This initiative was not just about expanding client bases or improving liquidity but also about leveraging blockchain to automate and transform asset management processes through tokenization. By doing so, asset managers can achieve efficiencies and enable customization at levels previously unattainable.

Specifically, the approach taken by JP Morgan and Apollo involved tokenizing investment funds to allow for automated and personalized management of discretionary portfolios, which cater to the unique investment preferences and objectives of wealthy clients. This process of tokenization makes it easier to include alternative assets in investment portfolios alongside publicly traded assets, potentially unlocking a significant revenue opportunity by improving the distribution of alternative funds through wealth management channels.

For wealth managers, the process of rebalancing portfolios, which traditionally involves thousands of manual steps, can be condensed into a few clicks through the Crescendo prototype developed as part of this initiative. This not only reduces operational complexities but also introduces the possibility of real-time settlement, further optimizing the efficiency of asset management.

One of the surprising benefits discovered during the PoC was the potential reduction of portfolios held in cash, due to the efficiencies of real-time settlement enabled by blockchain technology. This could lead to significant improvements in the returns of investment portfolios by minimizing the opportunity costs associated with holding a portion of the portfolio in low-return cash positions.

Interoperability between blockchains was a critical aspect of this PoC, with technologies like Axelar used to facilitate interactions between the Provenance blockchain and Onyx, as well as LayerZero to connect Avalanche with the Onyx ledger. This allowed for the automatic redemption of fund assets and subscription to new ones across different blockchain platforms, streamlining the process of portfolio management and asset allocation.

This initiative by JP Morgan and Apollo under Project Guardian is seen as potentially setting a new standard for how investment portfolios are managed and how blockchain technology can be applied to solve complex challenges in institutional financial services. The success of this PoC showcases the potential for blockchain interoperability to revolutionize the financial sector, making asset management more efficient, personalized, and adaptable to the evolving needs of investors.[9]

[8] https://www.ledgerinsights.com/jp-morgan-apollo-fund-tokenization-personalized-portfolio.
[9] https://www.ledgerinsights.com/jp-morgan-apollo-fund-tokenization-personalized-portfolio/

This evolutionary step in the financial landscape signifies a broader acceptance and recognition of the benefits that tokenization brings to the table. With the capacity to operate round the clock, deliver real-time data availability, and significantly reduce transaction costs through direct transfers without intermediaries, blockchain technology is redefining how private assets are issued, traded, and managed. Moreover, the potential for fractional ownership through tokenization democratizes access to investments that were once gated behind high thresholds, making them accessible to a wider audience. This not only amplifies investment opportunities but also fosters a more inclusive financial ecosystem.

As the market for tokenized real-world assets continues to burgeon, driven by institutional adoption and regulatory advancements, the landscape of private markets is set to transform. With estimates suggesting a multi-trillion dollar market by 2030, the tokenization of private assets stands as one of the most promising frontiers in the convergence of traditional finance and blockchain technology.[10]

PROTOCOL EXAMPLE: GOLDFINCH

Goldfinch stands out in the decentralized finance (DeFi) landscape as a protocol that provides credit relying on RWAs without necessitating crypto collateral.[11] This mechanism is key in unlocking access to cryptocurrency capital for a much broader audience globally, especially for people who don't have enough crypto assets to use as collateral. By not requiring crypto collateral, Goldfinch can offer loans based on real-world assets and diversify lenders' exposure beyond just crypto assets.

Goldfinch's model works by allowing borrowers, particularly from emerging markets where the impact can be significant, to propose loan terms to the borrower pool. The community of Goldfinch investors then evaluates these terms and can contribute capital if they find the terms satisfactory. This collective assessment approach builds a foundation for a scalable lending model and creates an on-chain credit history that's vital for markets lacking this infrastructure.

The protocol caters to various businesses that drive economic growth in their regions, with all loans currently being collateralized by off-chain assets. This approach is particularly beneficial in regions with inefficient or inaccessible traditional finance systems, and where crypto can offer liquid, multinational benefits.

---

[10] https://www.citigroup.com/global/news/press-release/2024/citi-collaborates-with-wellington-management-and-wisdomtree-to-explore-tokenization-of-private-markets
https://www.kitco.com/news/article/2024-02-14/citigroup-wellington-and-wisdomtree-successfully-tokenize-private-equity
https://www.finextra.com/blogposting/25455/real-world-asset-tokenization-breakthrough-in-2024
[11] https://www.okx.com/learn/goldfinch-protocol

Goldfinch's reach is extensive, impacting individuals in over 28 countries and allowing for diversified investments across a global span of high-return markets that were previously exclusive to institutional insiders. The platform also features a native token, GFI, which serves multiple functions, including governance and staking, and incentivizes platform users.[12]

For investors looking to supply capital, Goldfinch offers options to optimize for yield or ease, such as investing directly in individual deals or depositing in the Senior Pool for an automated, diversified portfolio. Following the funding, the loan is tokenized into tradable token. The tokenization allows the creation of a secondary market where investors can buy and sell their stake in the loans, increasing liquidity.

Despite these advancements, the decentralized nature of the platform means that the community plays a crucial role in the protocol's operations. This includes a strong focus on due diligence and credit assessment, which is enhanced by Goldfinch's innovative approach to using real-world financial data and off-chain assets for loan collateralization.

Imagine a business, let's call it "AgriTech Inc.," based in an emerging market and specializing in agricultural technology. AgriTech Inc. seeks to expand its operations but requires capital to do so. Traditional banking solutions are not accessible or suitable due to high collateral requirements or interest rates.

This is how AgriTech Inc. might obtain funding through Goldfinch:

Proposal Submission: AgriTech Inc. prepares a loan proposal that includes the loan amount, the interest rate they're offering, the term of the loan, and the real-world assets they're willing to use as collateral. This proposal is then submitted to the Goldfinch protocol.

Backer Assessment: Backers on the Goldfinch platform review AgriTech Inc.'s proposal. Backers are usually more experienced investors or entities who provide the first-loss capital. They will assess the creditworthiness of AgriTech Inc., which could include reviewing financial statements, past credit history, the value of the collateral, and the business plan.

Funding the Loan and Tokenization: If backers are convinced of the potential and creditworthiness of AgriTech Inc., they provide part of the requested loan amount. This acts as a signal to the wider community of Goldfinch investors that the borrower pool is trustworthy. Once the loan is fully funded, it is tokenized into tradable tokens representing a portion of the loan and expected payments.

Liquidity Providers Participation: Following the backers' initial commitment, other liquidity providers in the Goldfinch protocol can participate by

[12] https://docs.goldfinch.finance/goldfinch/

supplying capital to the loan. These investors contribute to the Senior Pool, which is automatically diversified across all active borrower pools.

Loan Disbursement: Once AgriTech Inc.'s loan is fully funded, they can draw down the capital in USDC stablecoins. This cryptocurrency can then be converted to local currency to be used for real-world business needs.

Repayment and Interest Distribution: AgriTech Inc. will repay the loan over time according to the agreed-upon schedule. The repayments (in USDC) are made to the protocol, which then distributes them to the backers and liquidity providers as per their share of the loan.

Credit History on Blockchain: All transactions, repayments, and any defaults are recorded on the blockchain. This transparent history is key to building a decentralized credit score for AgriTech Inc., which can improve their terms on future loans.

Governance Token Incentives: Participants in the protocol may earn Goldfinch's governance token (GFI) as part of their rewards. This token can provide them with voting rights on future protocol decisions.

This is a simplified example, but it showcases the core mechanics of Goldfinch's decentralized lending platform. By allowing loans without crypto collateral and creating a trust-based system, Goldfinch aims to make DeFi lending more inclusive, especially for unbanked businesses in emerging markets.

Overall, Goldfinch's emergence as a DeFi lending protocol is a testament to the growing intersection between traditional finance and blockchain technology, aimed at creating a more inclusive financial system. It offers investors and borrowers a novel way to interact with global capital flows, potentially leading to significant financial and social impacts.

It's all about liquidity   One key aspect to note is that tokenization introduces a level of liquidity previously unattainable, transforming static investments into fluid, tradeable assets. Morgan Krupetsky, Director of Business Development for Institutions and Capital Markets at Ava Labs, emphasizes how tokenization facilitates smaller deal sizes and lower investment minimums, making investment opportunities economically viable for a broader audience. Beyond the apparent benefits of accessibility and reduced reliance on middlemen, tokenization's real triumph lies in its capacity to generate active markets for assets once locked away due to their inherent illiquidity. Remember that one of the key advantages of generating a token is the possibility to integrate it into a DEX like Uniswap and then generate a more liquid market for the underlying asset. This not only broadens investment horizons but also enhances the overall efficiency of capital allocation across the financial ecosystem. In this light, tokenization is likened by Krupetsky to the leap from Blockbuster to Netflix; where geographical constraints once limited market participation, tokenization, akin to Netflix's model, requires only connectivity to unlock global capital, turning the world's financial market into an expansive clearinghouse accessible to all.

4. On-Chain vs. Off-Chain Tokenization

As the landscape of digital assets continues to evolve, a clear distinction emerges between the tokenization of off-chain RWAs and the use of tokenization for native digital assets. This divergence underscores the vast potential of blockchain technology and the complexity and challenges inherent in bridging the digital and physical worlds. At the heart of this distinction are fundamental differences in asset origination, the role of blockchain in asset lifecycle, and the implications for investors, regulators, and the broader financial ecosystem.

The tokenization of off-chain RWAs involves converting rights or ownership of physical assets—such as real estate, art, or commodities—into digital tokens on a blockchain. This process promises to unlock liquidity, enhance asset transferability, and democratize access to investments traditionally reserved for the affluent or institutional investors. However, it also introduces challenges related to valuation, legal ownership transfer, regulatory compliance, and the physical asset's custody and management.

It is impossible to eliminate intermediaries then!

Conversely, tokenizing native digital assets—such as cryptocurrencies, virtual goods, or digital rights—represents a more straightforward application of blockchain technology. These assets are born digital, exist solely in the digital realm, and are designed to operate within a blockchain ecosystem. The process leverages the inherent advantages of blockchain, including transparency, security, and efficiency, without the complexities of translating physical asset attributes into digital representations.

Natively on-chain assets are designed and issued directly on the blockchain, integrating the technological advantages of this infrastructure from the outset. This approach allows for the complete realization of blockchain's benefits, including enhanced security through decentralization, increased transparency, and the elimination of intermediaries. By embedding legal ownership and rights directly within the token, these assets offer a more streamlined and efficient framework for recognizing ownership and executing transactions. The potential for automating historically manual and siloed components of the issuance and management process is significantly increased, leveraging smart contracts for activities ranging from compliance checks to dividend distribution, thereby reducing operational costs and improving capital efficiency.

Conversely, assets originating in traditional markets before being tokenized and brought onto the blockchain involve a translation process. Here, the digital token acts as a representation—or "digital twin"—of the real-world asset or fund ownership. While this approach extends some of blockchain's benefits to traditional assets, such as improved liquidity and accessibility, it may not fully capitalize on the technology's potential to streamline operations and reduce costs. The tokenization of such assets often requires maintaining parallel systems (on-chain and off-chain) to manage and reconcile the digital representations with their physical counterparts, potentially complicating compliance and auditing processes.

For this reason, there have been several attempts to issue on-chain assets by traditional institutions. For instance, in April 2021, the European Investment Bank issued a

€100 million two-year digital bond on the Ethereum blockchain, marking a milestone in the utilization of blockchain technology for the issuance of financial securities. This initiative, conducted in partnership with Goldman Sachs, Banco Santander, and Société Générale, showcased the viability of using distributed ledger technology (DLT) for the entire bond issuance process, including placement, settlement, and registration.

In January 2023, the EIB continued its exploration of digital bonds by issuing its first sterling-denominated digital bond, raising £50 million. This bond was issued using a combination of private and public blockchains and accessed via HSBC's Orion tokenization platform. This issuance followed the Luxembourg legal framework, tailored to accommodate the issuance, transfer, and custody of dematerialized securities on DLT.[13]

Another significant initiative by the EIB is Project Venus, which involved the issuance of a €100 million euro-denominated digitally native bond using private blockchain technology. This project represents the EIB's second euro-denominated digital bond issuance and highlights the institution's commitment to exploring private blockchain solutions for financial transactions. This project, involving the same key financial institutions, underscored the capability for same-day settlement and highlighted the use of central bank digital currency (CBDC) for payment. The bond represented a leap toward more consistent data structures across the industry and paved the way for future on-chain derivative solutions.

These developments underscore the tangible benefits of on-chain tokenization, particularly in reducing underwriting and borrowing costs. A report by the Hong Kong Monetary Authority suggested that tokenized bond issuances could see reductions in underwriting fees by an average of 0.22 percentage points of the bond's par value and in borrowing costs by an average of 0.78 percentage points compared to similar conventional bonds. This not only implies a lower cost of capital and administrative fees but also showcases the compelling value proposition for companies considering blockchain-native issuance. Additionally, tokenization improved liquidity by 5.3%, rising to 10.8% with access to retail investors.[14]

In 2023, Siemens issued a €60 million EUR, one-year bond directly to investors, showcasing the potential for direct, digital bond issuance. Additionally, UBS, SBI, and DBS collaborated on the first cross-border repo (repurchase agreement) using a natively issued digital bond. A repo is essentially a short-term borrowing mechanism where

---

[13] A key piece of legislation in this area is the amendment to the Luxembourg law on securities accounts, introduced in 2021. This amendment explicitly recognizes the use of secure electronic registration mechanisms, including DLT, for holding and transferring securities. The law allows securities to be recorded and transferred via DLT, making it legally possible for entities to issue, hold, and transact digital securities within a regulated and secure environment. This legislative move was designed to enhance the efficiency, transparency, and security of financial transactions, aligning with Luxembourg's ambition to become a leading European hub for fintech and digital finance. Ensuring that digital securities are subject to the same regulatory standards as traditional securities it also helps protecting investors and maintaining confidence in digital financial markets.

[14] https://www.ledgerinsights.com/tokenized-bonds-reduce-costs-hong-kong-monetary-authority/

securities are sold to an investor with an agreement to repurchase them at a higher price on a later date.[15] This transaction marks a significant step in utilizing blockchain for more complex financial transactions, highlighting the efficiency and versatility of digital bonds in institutional finance. These instances highlight the growing interest and confidence among traditional financial institutions in leveraging blockchain technology to tokenize a range of assets, pointing toward a future where blockchain-enabled finance could be the norm rather than the exception.

The advancements by the EIB, alongside efforts by Citigroup, Wellington Management, WisdomTree, and other institutions illustrate a broader industry trend toward embracing tokenization for private markets and beyond. As traditional financial powerhouses continue to explore and adopt blockchain technology for tokenizing real-world assets, the potential for transforming private equity, credit opportunities, and other alternative investments through digitalization becomes increasingly evident.

4.1 Mortgages

For anyone who's ever taken the plunge into homeownership, the mortgage process is like a rite of passage—but less of the "finding your spirit animal" variety and more "trudging through a bureaucratic swamp." It's an ordeal where time warps, paperwork multiplies, and patience is tested beyond the realms of sanity. Technology might help. Blockchain benefits both borrowers and lenders by making loans more affordable and processes faster and more secure. For borrowers, the use of blockchain can reduce origination costs dramatically, from thousands to just hundreds of dollars, and accelerate funding times to as little as five days, a significant improvement over the traditional process that could take over 45 days. For lenders, blockchain streamlines application processing, underwriting, and even reduces the need for third-party services, cutting down associated costs and risks.

To show you this is not just wishful thinking, let me talk about a specific protocol. Figure Technologies has improved the Home Equity Line of Credit (HELOC) experience by leveraging blockchain technology, positioning itself as a significant player in the United States' lending market. In 2022, Figure emerged as the country's largest non-bank HELOC lender, with over $1.6 billion in HELOC volume originated throughout the year.[16] By April 2023, Figure's cumulative origination volume of its HELOC product reached a substantial $5.3 billion, as per DBRS Morningstar.

Traditional HELOC lenders might take four to six weeks to complete the loan process; Figure, utilizing its high-tech blockchain-based system, can approve an application

---

[15] The incentive to enter into a repo transaction includes liquidity management and earning interest. For the seller (borrower), it's a way to raise short-term capital using securities as collateral. For the buyer (lender), it's an opportunity to earn interest on their cash with the added security of holding collateral, which they can sell if the borrower defaults. Repos are used by a range of financial institutions to manage short-term funding needs while providing lenders with a low-risk investment option.

[16] https://www.figure.com/blog/the-heloc-experience-has-been-forever-changed-by-figure/

in a matter of minutes and fund loans in as few as five days. This rapid turnaround is enabled by eliminating the back-and-forth transfer of hard copies of documents, as the blockchain technology allows for secure and immediate online processing.

Furthermore, Figure's approach to HELOCs is more cost-effective for consumers. Traditional loan processes involve significant origination costs, which can range into the thousands of dollars. With Figure, these costs are dramatically reduced to just hundreds, resulting in savings on account opening fees, maintenance fees, and prepayment penalties for customers.

The use of blockchain provides a secure, encrypted record that cannot be altered, thus adding a layer of security to the lending process and reducing the potential for fraud. For lenders, blockchain streamlines the application and underwriting processes, significantly reducing the need for third-party services and associated costs.

Despite these advantages, it is important to note that the integration of blockchain in the HELOC process is still a novel approach in the financial industry. The technology, while offering many benefits, is relatively new and has high implementation costs, which might explain the caution observed among lenders in widely adopting it. However, with companies like Figure demonstrating the efficiency and cost benefits, blockchain utilization in the lending process is likely to gain more traction.

Let's walk through a hypothetical example of a homeowner named Alex who wants to get a Home Equity Line of Credit (HELOC) to renovate his home and compare the process of doing so through Figure, which uses blockchain, and a traditional bank lender. **Figure 5** captures this comparison.

The blockchain process used by Figure reduces the time needed for Alex to access the funds from over a month to less than a week. The costs are also lower due to the elimination of certain fees and the digital nature of the process, which cuts down on overhead.

By using blockchain, Figure improves the speed, efficiency, and convenience of obtaining a HELOC compared to traditional methods, while also adding the security benefits of blockchain's immutable record-keeping.

4.2 Saving the Environment

Another interesting application of tokenization is the market for carbon credits. Tokenization might offer a solution to several persistent issues in the carbon market, significantly the Voluntary Carbon Market (VCM), which has seen rapid growth and is anticipated to reach over $50 billion by 2050. Tokenization addresses the need for greater transparency, liquidity, and efficiency within this market.

One major challenge in the current carbon credit system is the complexity and opacity of transactions. Carbon credits, representing a ton of carbon dioxide emissions reduced or removed from the atmosphere, vary widely in terms of their source, methodology, and impact. Similar to the real estate market where properties have unique features and varying market values, carbon credits differ based on attributes such as project type, country of origin, and verification year, leading to significant price disparities.

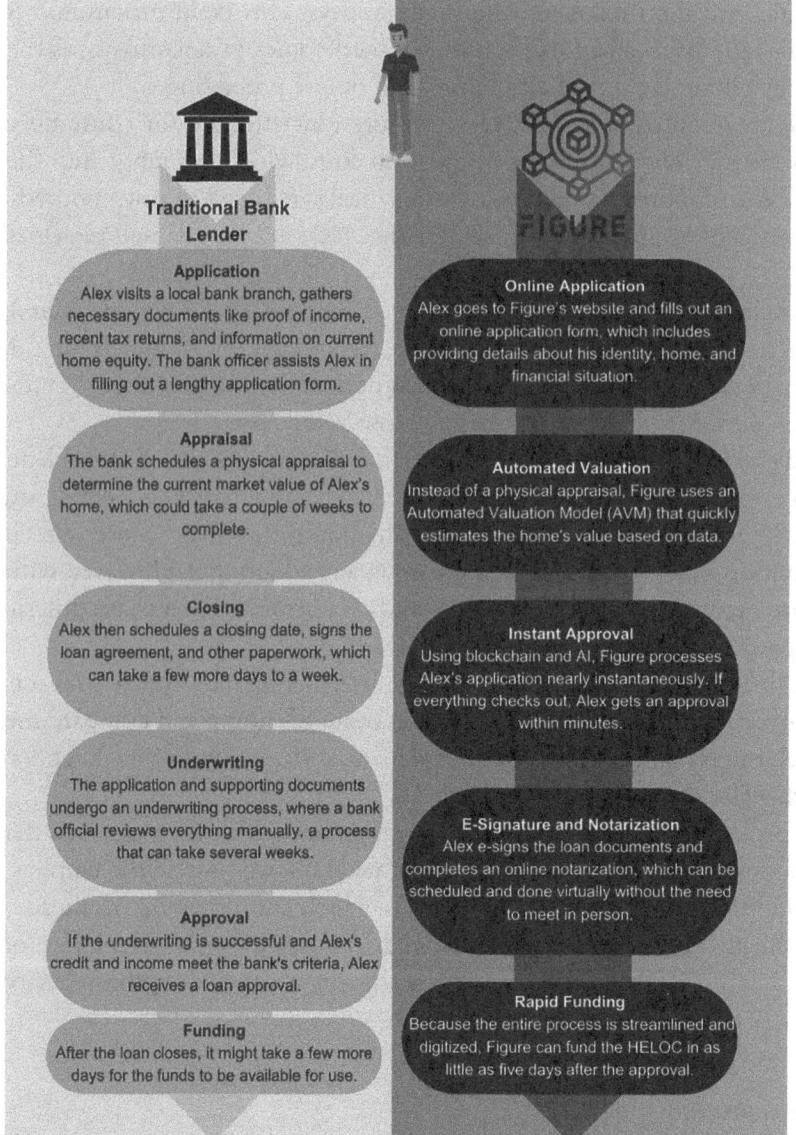

Figure 5 Mortgage process in traditional banks vs. HELOC on Figure

Tokenization on a blockchain offers a streamlined and transparent approach. By converting carbon credits into digital tokens, each transaction becomes traceable and immutable, recorded on a public ledger. This ensures that credits cannot be double-counted or fraudulently claimed, addressing a significant issue in the VCM. Moreover, blockchain enables the creation of a liquid marketplace where tokens representing similar carbon credits can be pooled, enhancing market efficiency and price discovery. In other words, having the carbon credits on chain allows a better match between buyers and sellers of such credits.

The process begins with verified carbon offset projects, like reforestation initiatives, generating credits by reducing or removing emissions. These credits are then digitized and issued as tokens on a blockchain, enabling direct interaction between buyers and sellers through smart contracts. This disintermediation cuts down on transaction costs and speeds up the funding process, from project inception to credit issuance, which traditionally takes years and significant financial investment.

Furthermore, blockchain's inherent transparency allows for better verification of carbon credits. Independent third-party verifiers assess the emissions reductions and the verification data is securely recorded on the blockchain. This creates a trustworthy and auditable record, fostering confidence among participants in the carbon market.

In essence, blockchain technology and the tokenization of carbon credits introduce a paradigm shift in how carbon markets operate. By improving transparency, liquidity, and access, blockchain paves the way for a more inclusive and efficient market, facilitating the global fight against climate change. This approach not only benefits the environment but also provides new opportunities for investment and participation in climate action initiatives.

The Toucan Protocol facilitates the tokenization of carbon credits, transforming them into digital assets that can be traded on the blockchain. The protocol starts by converting traditional carbon credits into blockchain-based tokens. This process involves verifying the authenticity of carbon credits and then issuing corresponding digital tokens that represent these credits on the blockchain. Once carbon credits are tokenized, they are made available on the Toucan platform for trading. This not only creates a more liquid market for carbon credits but also allows for smaller investors to participate, which wasn't as feasible in traditional carbon markets due to high entry barriers. Through blockchain's inherent properties, every tokenized carbon credit's origin, methodology, and impact can be tracked and verified by anyone on the network. This significantly reduces the risk of fraud and double counting, issues that have plagued traditional carbon credit markets.

Toucan Protocol enables the integration of carbon credits into the decentralized finance (DeFi) ecosystem. This opens up innovative use cases such as using carbon tokens as collateral for loans, or in decentralized autonomous organization (DAO) governance, thereby broadening the utility and demand for carbon credits. By making carbon credits more accessible and usable, Toucan aims to incentivize businesses and individuals to contribute more actively to climate action. It encourages the financing of projects that have a tangible impact on reducing carbon emissions through a market-driven approach.

4.3 Tokenizing IP

Is this only affecting the Wall Streeters? Thankfully, no.

Imagine the vibrant world of Luigi, an Italian chef with a flair for the dramatic and a talent for creating mouth-watering dishes. Luigi's YouTube channel, "Luigi's La Cucina," is a hit, blending humor, charisma, and culinary wizardry to entertain and educate a vast audience.

Through his engaging how-to videos on Italian cooking, Luigi earns a hearty $50,000 a month from YouTube ad revenue.

Now, let's stir in a pinch of innovation with a dash of finance and explore how tokenization can spice up Luigi's culinary empire. Tokenization, in essence, allows Luigi to convert the copyright of his YouTube channel into digital tokens. These tokens represent shares in the revenue generated by his cooking videos. A financier, enchanted by Luigi's sauce-simmering skills and business acumen, sees an opportunity to invest in Luigi's future earnings.

Here's how it cooks down: Luigi's annual royalties from "Luigi's La Cucina" amount to a delicious $600k. Our financier, seeing the potential for a lucrative investment, decides to buy the tokenized copyright for $550k. This transaction not only provides Luigi with a substantial upfront sum but also gives the financier a slice of the future revenue pie. It's a win-win: Luigi gets immediate capital to expand his culinary ventures, perhaps opening a trattoria or launching a line of gourmet ingredients, while the financier enjoys a built-in yield from the channel's ongoing success.

This concept of monetizing intellectual property (IP) isn't new; it's been a staple in the portfolios of large music companies and private equity firms (e.g. think about purchasing the rights to a Beatles' album). However, the world of tokenization brings this opportunity to the smaller creators like Luigi. By leveraging blockchain technology, tokenization democratizes access to financial tools that were previously out of reach for individual artists, chefs, and creators, opening up new avenues for investment and growth.

Though the space is burgeoning, several protocols and platforms are emerging to facilitate the tokenization of IP across various domains, not just YouTube channels but music, art, literature, and more. These platforms offer creators a way to secure funding, retain control over their work, and potentially reap greater rewards as their IP appreciates in value.

The added value of tokenizing IP lies in its ability to create more liquid, transparent, and accessible markets for creative works. For investors, it offers a novel way to support and profit from the success of creators like Luigi. For creators, it provides a mechanism to realize the value of their work upfront, enabling them to continue innovating and producing content that resonates with their audience.

As the world of tokenization expands, we can expect to see more creators like Luigi exploring how blockchain can serve up new financial opportunities, making the arts and entertainment industry a richer, more diverse, and more flavorful feast for all.

4.4 Synthetic Assets

A related but somewhat different concept is that of synthetic assets. Synthetic assets are financial instruments that *simulate* other assets' values using smart contracts, without requiring ownership of the underlying asset. They're created within the blockchain ecosystem, allowing exposure to various assets, including currencies, commodities, and stocks, in a decentralized manner. Tokenized real-world assets, in contrast, involve converting the value of tangible or intangible assets into digital tokens on a blockchain, providing direct or indirect ownership and investment opportunities in the actual assets, from real estate to art, through blockchain technology.

In other words, synthetic assets are digital representations of real-world assets, such as currencies, commodities, stocks, and even more abstract financial instruments like indices. These are created and managed entirely on a blockchain platform, allowing for the seamless creation, trading, and management of these assets without the need for traditional financial intermediaries. This process leverages smart contracts, which are self-executing contracts with the terms of the agreement directly written into code.

These digital assets are designed to mimic the value of their real-world counterparts, allowing users to gain exposure to various asset classes without the need to physically own them. This is achieved through complex financial mechanisms and algorithms embedded in smart contracts that adjust the value of the synthetic asset in real-time, based on data from external price feeds or oracles.

What makes them like tokenized assets are the benefits they might offer. Synthetic assets can, in fact, democratize access to investment opportunities, especially for those in regions with strict capital controls, high barriers to entry, or other forms of financial exclusion. For example, an investor in a country where buying foreign stocks directly is restricted can instead buy a synthetic version of a stock or index, gaining exposure to its price movements without owning the actual asset.

PROMINENT PLATFORM: SYNTHETIX

Synthetix is a protocol on the Ethereum blockchain that allows for the creation, trading, and management of synthetic assets, or Synths. Synths are ERC-20 tokens that provide exposure to the price movements of real-world assets, ranging from fiat currencies and commodities to cryptocurrencies and equities, without requiring ownership of the actual asset.

The foundation of Synthetix's system is its collateralization process, where users stake the platform's native token, SNX, as collateral to create Synths. This is achieved through a smart contract mechanism. The protocol has instituted a collateralization ratio—determined by community governance—to maintain system stability and to mitigate against market volatility and the risk of under-collateralization.

When a user stakes their SNX to mint Synths, they assume a portion of the debt pool proportional to the amount of Synths minted. This debt pool is a key innovation of Synthetix, representing the collective obligation of all Synth creators to back their Synths with SNX. The value of an individual's debt can fluctuate based on the changing exchange rates of all Synths within the system. As the value of the underlying assets represented by the Synths changes, so does the debt's value. If the underlying assets increase in price, the debt value rises, and vice versa.

This pooled risk structure requires users to attentively manage their collateralization ratios. Should their ratio drop too low—either due to a fall in the value of SNX or an increase in the value of the minted Synths—they must either provide more SNX as collateral or burn some of their Synths to rebalance the ratio. In contrast, if Synth values fall, they may unlock some of their collateral by burning a smaller amount of Synths.

Let me show you a comprehensive example:

Alice is interested in investing in gold, but she prefers not to purchase physical gold or ETFs. Instead, she opts to use Synthetix for price exposure to gold. She decides to stake $1,000 worth of SNX. If the platform's collateralization ratio is 750%, this means Alice can mint up to $133 of synthetic gold (sGOLD).

When Alice mints her sGOLD, she now holds a stake in the debt pool that reflects the value of her sGOLD. The price of this sGOLD is pegged to the real-world price of gold via oracles that provide updated price data to Synthetix.

Should the price of gold increase by 10%, her sGOLD's value increases correspondingly. Alice can choose to hold onto her sGOLD in anticipation of further price increases or trade it for other Synths such as synthetic USD (sUSD) or synthetic Bitcoin (sBTC) on the Synthetix exchange, without requiring an intermediary.

If Alice decides to close her position, whether to realize gains or limit losses, she does so by burning her sGOLD. The necessary amount of sGOLD to burn will depend on the current value of the sGOLD. If its value has risen, she needs to burn less to unlock her SNX collateral. If the value has fallen, she must burn more.

Upon completing the burning process, Alice's staked SNX collateral is unlocked. She can now withdraw it, having successfully closed her position.

The debt pool in Synthetix is a fundamental concept that underpins the creation and valuation of synthetic assets within the platform. It operates on the principle of shared risk and reward, ensuring that the network's synthetic assets (Synths) are backed by collateral.

When a user, say Alice, wants to mint a synthetic asset such as synthetic gold (sGOLD), she stakes the native token of the platform, SNX, as collateral. The amount of SNX she needs to stake is governed by a collateralization ratio set by the protocol, designed to account for volatility and price fluctuations of the underlying assets and SNX itself. Upon staking SNX and minting sGOLD, Alice incurs a debt equivalent to the value of the sGOLD minted. This debt is her portion of the total debt pool, which represents the cumulative value of all Synths minted by all users in the Synthetix system.

The debt pool is **dynamic**, meaning its total value fluctuates with the changing prices of the underlying assets represented by the Synths. If the price of gold rises, the value of sGOLD rises, and consequently, the total debt pool increases. This also means that Alice's share of the debt pool grows even if she has not minted additional sGOLD—her debt increases in sUSD terms because the Synth she holds has appreciated in value. The reverse is true if the price of gold declines.

To leave the system and unlock her staked SNX, Alice must "burn" her sGOLD, which is to say, she needs to pay back the equivalent value of her debt in the form of sGOLD. The specific amount required depends on the current value of the debt pool and her share of it. If the value of sGOLD has gone up since she minted it, she'll need to burn less sGOLD than she minted to settle her debt. If the value of sGOLD has gone down, she'll have to burn more.

This mechanism ensures that all Synths are backed by a proportionate amount of SNX, maintaining the system's stability. It also means that users are collectively responsible for maintaining the collateralization of the network, sharing the risks and rewards of price movements in the underlying assets. The debt pool system is crucial for the trustless and decentralized issuance of Synths, allowing Synthetix to provide exposure to various asset classes without requiring users to hold the actual assets.

The key components of Synthetix's operation include:

- Oracles: They provide real-time data to ensure Synth prices accurately reflect the prices of their real-world counterparts.
- Collateralization: This mechanism, requiring over-collateralization, is designed to account for price volatility and secure system stability.
- Synthetic Assets (Synths): These are blockchain-based assets that track the price movements of real-world assets.

Synthetix, therefore, represents a dynamic bridge between traditional and digital finance, allowing users to engage with a wide range of assets in a decentralized manner. It is an ecosystem that offers flexibility and exposure to global asset prices while emphasizing the importance of active risk management and collateralization to maintain a stable and secure trading environment.[17]

---

[17] https://docs.synthetix.io; https://www.gemini.com/cryptopedia/synthetix

Case Study. "Fluidity: How to Tokenize a Manhattan Building"[18]

Let me discuss a real attempt by a company to create a primary and secondary market for tokens representing a real estate asset.

In December 2018, well before the NFTs and tokenization boom, Brooklyn's Fluidity set out to transform real estate investment through blockchain. Their vision began with a tokenized offering for a Manhattan condo, aiming to raise $25 million. Partnering with Propellr, they navigated financial regulations by embedding smart contracts in tokens, which ensured AML and KYC compliance. These tokens, tradeable on Fluidity's AirSwap platform, represented debt interest rather than direct property ownership. This innovative approach promised to expedite the financing process, cut costs by bypassing traditional intermediaries, and open new revenue channels by facilitating easier, peer-to-peer transactions.[19]

The key questions inspired by this case are:

1. What are the key frictions in the real estate market that Fluidity aims to address?
2. What is Fluidity's business model? Is this a sustainable business?
3. As a developer, would you use tokenization as an alternative to a bridge loan?
4. What are the main challenges that might prevent making this firm successful?

To enhance the discussion on the challenges Fluidity addresses and the advantages of tokenization in real estate, the conversation could shift to identifying three main barriers in the current market: liquidity issues, accessibility constraints, and complex transaction processes. By tokenizing real estate assets, Fluidity introduces a solution that promises greater fluidity in investments for both developers and investors. For developers, tokenization through platforms like Fluidity provides a transformative approach to raising capital. It allows them to bypass traditional banking constraints, offering a faster, more flexible means of securing investment. Developers can tokenize and sell shares of their projects directly to a global pool of investors, significantly shortening the time and reducing the costs associated with issuing securities. This innovative method not only accelerates funding processes but also opens new avenues for financial growth, making it an appealing alternative to conventional financing methods.

This method notably democratizes access to capital, potentially reducing reliance on traditional bank loans and broadening the investor base. It simplifies transactions by using blockchain to eliminate intermediaries, reducing costs, and speeding up processes. Through tokenization, investors can purchase fractional

---

[18] For more details about the case, and a teaching note guiding the discussion in class, see my Harvard Business School case titled "Fluidity: The Tokenization of Real Estate Assets" available at https://hbsp.harvard.edu/product/219057-PDF-ENG?Ntt=marco%20di%20maggio%20fluidity
[19] It is worth seeing the video available on Bloomberg, "Blockchain Takes Manhattan," YouTube, published November 12, 2018, https://www.youtube.com/watch?v=Z-CZLuLPZwI&feature=youtu.be, for an entertaining explanation of the project.

ownership in properties, making investments more accessible and allowing for diversified portfolios at lower entry costs.

However, there are numerous nuances that limit the success of this platform. Specifically, the risks associated with tokenization for Fluidity's investors include the lack of collateralization, meaning that if a developer defaults, investors have no direct claim on the underlying asset, potentially lining them up with other creditors. Notice that this is not the case if the developer had to raise capital through a bank loan as that would have been collateralized. This risk could lead investors to demand higher returns, making tokenization less appealing to developers with access to traditional capital sources. For developers, a significant risk is whether tokenization can attract sufficient investment, particularly from smaller investors, to fund large projects.

The key challenge to scale Fluidity's business model, however, is the need to create a liquid secondary market. It is akin to a "chicken and egg" problem, where both buyers and sellers are hesitant to enter a market without the presence of the other. In the case of Fluidity, this issue is exacerbated by the presence of adverse selection. *What kind of developers would use Fluidity in lieu of a bank loan?* The platform may predominantly attract developers who are unable to secure traditional bank loans, indicating potentially higher risk projects. This adverse selection can lead to a lack of confidence among investors, resulting in low liquidity in the secondary market. Low liquidity undermines the model's viability, as the promise of easy entry and exit from investments is compromised, challenging the platform's ability to sustain a robust and attractive market for tokenized assets.

Despite Fluidity and Propellr's initial interest in projects valued at $3 billion, many deals were with developers lacking alternative financing, signaling fewer desirable investments. Consequently, the market's readiness for real estate tokenization was overestimated, with institutional investors showing little interest. This mismatch in market demand and supply led to the dissolution of the Fluidity and Propellr partnership in summer 2019.

Perhaps the project was simply too futuristic, launching in an era not yet ripe with NFT buzz and tokenization trends. It's a valuable case study, though, shedding light on the hurdles that need jumping before tokenization's full potential can be unleashed.

5. Satoshi's Vision?

The transformative power of tokenization in creating new markets far surpasses its ability to democratize access or eliminate intermediaries. By turning previously illiquid assets, like private equity funds, into tradable digital tokens, tokenization not only opens these investments to a wider audience but more crucially, it establishes a liquid market where none existed. This innovation is a game-changer, making the flow of capital more efficient and unlocking value in sectors previously constrained by their illiquid nature, thereby fundamentally altering investment landscapes.

Picture the private equity fund "Greed's Bounty Partners," as a collection of investors who've banded together to shepherd a company through its growth phase. Their strategy has always had a long-term horizon, but as the investment matures, so do the varying opinions on its future. It's a natural evolution in group dynamics where differing views on risk and timelines emerge.

Now, enter tokenization. Here's the essence of how this tech could elegantly navigate the divergent paths ahead for the fund:

- **Smart Contracts and Digital Tokens:** Every stake in the fund could be represented as a digital token, a unit of ownership that's programmed with the terms agreed upon by "Greed's Bounty Partners." These terms might include the fund's duration, rules for distribution of proceeds, or protocols for selling the stake.
- **Secondary Market Creation:** Smart contracts can facilitate a seamless secondary market, almost like a mini-stock exchange for the fund's tokens. This market gives liquidity to an asset class that is traditionally illiquid, allowing members to sell their tokens to other interested parties.
- **Diverse Exit Strategies:** When the investment horizon starts to wane, some members might wish to exit early. Tokenization allows these members to sell their tokens on the secondary market to either existing members who want to increase their stake or new investors looking to enter.
- **Valuation and Trading:** The value of these tokens could be updated based on the latest valuation of the company they own. Token holders can then trade these tokens at current market values, making the process dynamic and reflective of real-time sentiment.
- **Automation of Transactions:** As members trade tokens, smart contracts could automatically enforce rules around transactions, ensuring that all regulatory and fund agreement conditions are met without manual intervention.
- **Investor Flexibility:** Token holders gain flexibility, as they can choose to sell all or just a part of their stake, enabling them to adjust their investment to suit personal financial goals or react to market changes.
- **Democratization of Investment:** By lowering the entry and exit barriers through tokenization, "Greed's Bounty Partners" could potentially open the fund to a broader investor base, democratizing access to private equity investments.
- **Transparency and Security:** All token transactions would be recorded on the blockchain, offering transparency, security, and an immutable record of ownership and trades.

In summary, tokenization could offer "Greed's Bounty Partners" an elegant solution to address their internal divergence on investment timelines and strategies. It provides a nimble framework within which investors can act independently while still respecting the collective agreement of the fund. Through the power of blockchain and smart contracts, tokenization offers a path to greater liquidity, flexibility, and democratic access to the world of private equity investment.

Ironically, the advent of making investment processes more streamlined for the affluent—such as venture capitalists—was likely far from the egalitarian digital utopia envisioned by Satoshi Nakamoto. However, these advancements find themselves at the heart of traditional finance's power corridors, drawing interest from the sector's most influential figures. It's a pragmatic acknowledgment that the widespread adoption of blockchain and cryptocurrency technologies hinges, to some extent, on their endorsement.

One way to think about this is that the present cohort of DeFi enthusiasts doesn't have the numbers to propel the sector to its aspirational $10 trillion market potential. Then, if this is ever going to happen, this growth will need to be fueled by the entry of pension funds, banks, and legacy corporations into the DeFi ecosystem.

6. The Path Forward

Maybe we are going to reach a point where we won't need to use the (terrible) acronym RWAs anymore, because any asset will be tokenized. Why not?! There are still a few hurdles to face before we can get there.

Navigating regulatory challenges is a critical step toward the widespread adoption of RWA tokenization. Regulations vary by jurisdiction, creating a complex landscape for token issuers to navigate. Ensuring compliance with securities laws, anti-money laundering (AML) standards, and know your customer (KYC) protocols is essential. Additionally, establishing clear legal rights for token holders and defining the token's status (utility, security, or otherwise) requires careful legal consideration. Ambiguity in a token's classification can lead to regulatory complications, affecting everything from taxation to securities law compliance. If token holders' rights are not clearly defined, it may result in disputes over ownership, access, and control of the underlying assets, potentially undermining the token's value and utility. This necessitates a careful legal and regulatory approach to avoid potential pitfalls. Building a regulatory framework that accommodates the unique aspects of blockchain technology while protecting investors is crucial for the tokenization sector's growth and innovation.

Two additional fundamental changes are necessary for widespread crypto adoption: wallets must be user-friendly and assets should be secure yet recoverable. Passkeys by Apple and Google have effectively addressed the first change by integrating a secure signing mechanism into smartphones, like crypto hardware wallets. These Passkeys are deeply integrated into iOS and Android ecosystems, linked with Apple and Google accounts making them recoverable, and designed to be phishing-resistant.

The adoption of Passkeys by major companies like Amazon, PayPal, and Microsoft is turning them into a new standard for secure service sign-ins. Now, most people with a smartphone already possess a secure and recoverable hardware wallet. The remaining challenge is that these devices typically can't perform crypto transactions due to most blockchains supporting only specific types of signatures that Passkeys don't use.

This is where Account Abstraction comes into play. It separates the concepts of signers (like Passkeys or hardware wallets) and accounts. Accounts are managed on-chain with code that can be controlled and updated by the owner, while signers remain off-chain and serve as access keys to the account. The account holds tokens and interacts with smart contracts, acting on the signer's behalf.

A significant area of research is enabling Passkey signing for crypto transactions. This would allow transactions to be signed with a Passkey and sent on-chain via a relayer, with the Abstract Account confirming the Passkey signature to execute the transaction. Another research focus is social recovery for accounts, allowing for the recovery of accounts even if the signer's key is lost, similar to having a spare key with a trusted friend. This makes crypto assets more secure and reduces the barriers to entry, paving the way for broader adoption.[20]

Summing up, tokenization is like the financial world's latest diet craze—promising to slim down fees, beef up security, and somehow make everyone rich. Let's just hope it's not the financial equivalent of kale.

Code: Auto repayment for Goldfinch

Language: Solidity

Level: Intermediate

Most of the DApps are built with a modular structure and have complex architectures. For example, Goldfinch's smart contracts has the following architecture.

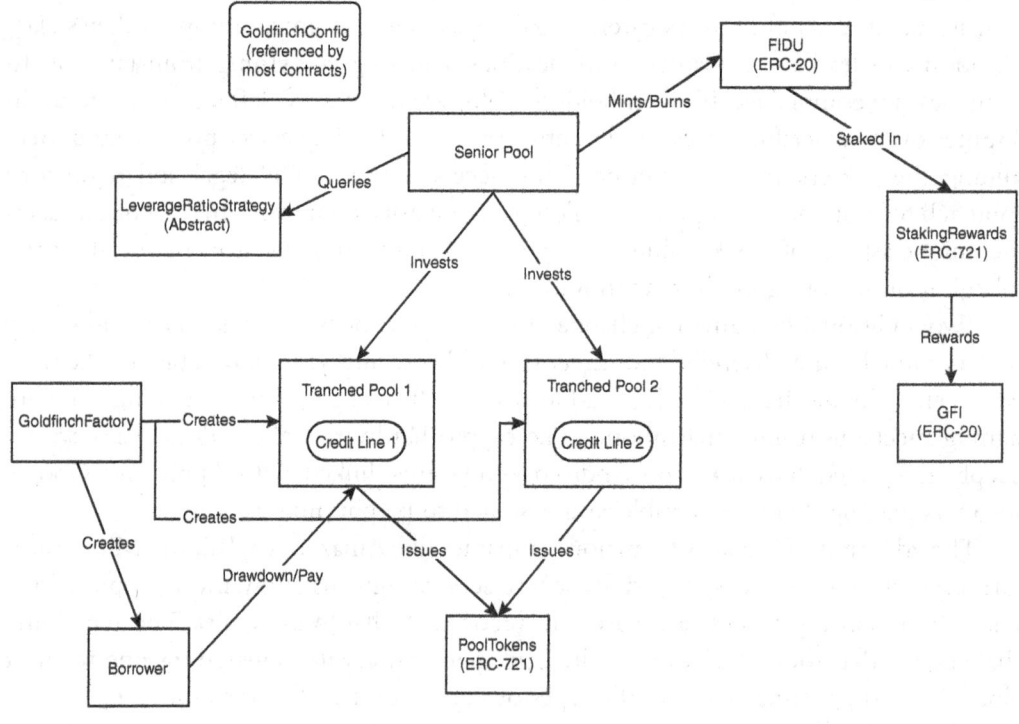

[20] CoinDesk: Tokenize Everything: Institutions Bet That Crypto's Future Lies in the Real World. Kitco News: Real-World Asset tokenization and the future of financial markets: Part 2 Cryptoglobe: What Is Real-World Asset Tokenization? The Next Institutional Megatrend Texture. Capital: Tokenization of Real-World Assets: Assessing Market Sentiment

- Borrowers interact with the *GoldfinchFactory*, which creates new tranched pools for them and a *Borrower* instance.
- *Tranched Pools* and *Credit Line* contain specific credit lines, establishing terms for borrowing.
- *Senior Pool* aggregates capital from various investors and invests in the tranched pools to provide the necessary funds for the credit lines.
- In exchange for the investment, tranched pools issue *PoolTokens*, representing the investment stake, back to the Senior Pool.
- *GoldfinchConfig* serves as a central reference point for system settings and is queried by the Senior Pool and potentially other parts of the system.
- *FIDU Tokens* represent investments within the Senior Pool. They can be minted or burned depending on the pool's activities.
- Investors can stake their FIDU tokens in a special contract (*StakingRewards*) to earn *GFI* tokens as rewards.
- Earned by staking FIDU, these ERC-20 tokens can be used within the ecosystem or traded via GFI Rewards.

And the actual interactions are usually from a user interface on the app's webpage, using your wallet.

```solidity
pragma solidity ^0.8.22;

import "@openzeppelin/contracts/token/ERC20/IERC20.sol";

interface IBorrower {
    function pay(uint256 amount) external;
}

contract AutoRepayment {
    address public owner;
    IBorrower public borrower;
    IERC20 public usdc;
    mapping(address => RepaymentSchedule) public repaymentSchedules;

    struct RepaymentSchedule {
        uint256 amount;
        uint256 dueDate; // Unix timestamp of when the payment is due
        bool oneOff;
        uint256 endDate; // Unix timestamp of when the repayment
        schedule ends
    }

    constructor(address _borrowerAddress, address _usdcAddress) {
        owner = msg.sender;
        borrower = IBorrower (_borrowerAddress);
        usdc = IERC20(_usdcAddress);
    }
```

```
modifier onlyOwner() {
    require(msg.sender == owner, "Caller is not the owner");
    _;
}

function setRepaymentSchedule(uint256 _amount, uint256 _dueDate, bool
_oneOff, uint256 _endDate) public {
    require(_dueDate > block.timestamp, "Due date must be in
    the future");
    require(_endDate >= _dueDate, "End date must be after due date");
    repaymentSchedules[msg.sender] = RepaymentSchedule(_amount,
    _dueDate, _oneOff, _endDate);
}

function setBorrowPool(address _borrowerAddress) external onlyOwner {
    borrower =IBorrower (_borrowerAddress);
}

function autoRepay() public {
    RepaymentSchedule storage schedule = repaymentSchedules
    [msg.sender];
    require(usdc.allowance(msg.sender, address(this)) >=
    schedule.amount, "Insufficient allowance");
    require(usdc.balanceOf(msg.sender) >= schedule.amount, "Insuffi-
    cient user balance");
    require(block.timestamp >= schedule.dueDate, "It is not yet time
    to repay");
    require(block.timestamp <= schedule.endDate, "Repayment period
    has ended"); // Check if the current time is before the end date

    usdc.transferFrom(msg.sender, address(this), schedule.amount);
    usdc.approve(address(borrower), schedule.amount);
    borrower.pay(schedule.amount);

    if (!schedule.oneOff) {
        if (block.timestamp + 30 days <= schedule.endDate) { //
        Ensure next due date is within the repayment period
            repaymentSchedules[msg.sender].dueDate += 30 days; // Set
            next due date for recurring payments
        } else {
            // If the next payment would be beyond the end date,
            adjust the schedule or mark as complete
            repaymentSchedules[msg.sender].amount = 0; // Optionally
            mark as complete or reset schedule
        }
    } else {
        repaymentSchedules[msg.sender].amount = 0; // If it's a
        one-off payment, reset the schedule
        repaymentSchedules[msg.sender].dueDate = 0;
    }
}
```

```
function withdrawUSDC(uint256 amount) public onlyOwner {
    require(usdc.balanceOf(address(this)) >= amount, "Insuffi-
    cient funds");
    require(usdc.transfer(msg.sender, amount), "Transfer failed");
}
}
```

In this example, we will write a simple example of interacting with TranchedPool as a borrower to repay our debt automatically. The contract will unfortunately not be deployable as it requires an existing borrower contract address, which is created after the pool is set. Another important aspect of the contract is that you would need to give access to the contract to withdraw funds from your wallet—which can be done via Etherscan. Also, in a real-life setting, it would need additional security and regulatory requirements.

The script again will start with the basic Solidity setup, and we are importing the OpenZeppelin IERC20 interface for interacting with ERC20 tokens mainly for USDC. Then we define an interface *IBorrower* that includes a pay function, which the contract will use to make payments on behalf of the user.

Then we have an important struct—which is a unique data type declaration argument—called the Repayment Schedule. The repayment schedule will either have the monthly payments or the one-off payment. The contract has to input the address of the Borrower contract we are referring to and the address of the USDC token.

The *setRepaymentSchedule* function allows the contract owner to manually input the repayment schedule, again if it will not be a one-off payment, _oneOff should be 0, and the amount should include the monthly payment, and the user has to provide the end date for the payments.

The *autoRepay* function starts by retrieving the repayment schedule for the user who called the function. It then checks several conditions: that the user has granted enough allowance for the contract to use their USDC, that the user has enough USDC to cover the payment, and that the current time is past the due date but not past the end date for repayment. If these conditions are met, the contract uses transferFrom to move the specified amount of USDC from the user's account to the contract. It then approves the borrower to withdraw this amount from the contract and calls the pay method on the borrower contract. If the payment is marked as a one-off, it clears the repayment schedule; if it's a recurring payment, it updates the due date for the next payment, ensuring it does not exceed the ending date.

The *withdrawUSDC* function is straightforward: it allows the contract's owner to withdraw a specified amount of USDC from the contract to their personal wallet. This function checks that there are sufficient funds in the contract before performing the transfer. This might be used for operational expenses or returning excess funds, under the assumption that only the trusted owner (who should be the deployer or an authorized entity) can execute this action.

In this example, we will explore a contract named "*Asset Tokenization*" used for creating and managing digital assets in the form of tokens, referred to here as "*Custom Asset Tokens*" (CAT). The contract is a simple general structure that can be used to tokenize any type of asset. The user needs to assign a custom Asset Id for the assets they want to tokenize. The contract does require an additional algorithm to generate Asset Ids—that can be developed on a different platform.

The script begins with standard Solidity setup and defines constants such as the token's name, symbol, and decimals for precision. The *totalSupply* indicates all available tokens, while *balanceOf* maps each address to its token balance, facilitating token distribution and management.

Code: Tokenization of an Asset

Language: Solidity

Level: Intermediate

```solidity
pragma solidity ^0.8.22;

contract AssetTokenization {

    address public immutable owner;
    string public constant name = "CustomAssetToken";
    string public constant symbol = "CAT";
    uint256 public constant decimals = 6;
    uint256 public totalSupply;

    mapping(address => uint256) public balanceOf;
    mapping(address => mapping(address => uint256)) public allowance;
    mapping(uint256 => address) public assetOwners;

    // Modifiers
    modifier onlyOwner() {
        require(msg.sender == owner, "Only the owner can perform
        this action");
        _;
    }

    constructor(uint256 _initialSupply) {
        owner = msg.sender;
        totalSupply = _initialSupply * 10 ** decimals;
        balanceOf[msg.sender] = totalSupply;
    }

    function transfer(address _to, uint256 _value) public returns (bool
    success) {
```

```
        require(balanceOf[msg.sender] >= _value, "Insufficient balance");
        balanceOf[msg.sender] -= _value;
        balanceOf[_to] += _value;
        emit Transfer(msg.sender, _to, _value);
        return true;
    }
    function approve(address _spender, uint256 _value) public returns
    (bool success) {
        allowance[msg.sender][_spender] = _value;
        emit Approval(msg.sender, _spender, _value);
        return true;
    }
    function transferFrom(address _from, address _to, uint256 _value)
    public returns (bool success) {
        require(_value <= balanceOf[_from], "Insufficient balance");
        require(_value <= allowance[_from][msg.sender], "Allowance
        exceeded");
        balanceOf[_from] -= _value;
        balanceOf[_to] += _value;
        allowance[_from][msg.sender] -= _value;
        emit Transfer(_from, _to, _value);
        return true;
    }

    function registerAsset(uint256 _assetId) public returns (bool
    success) {
        require(assetOwners[_assetId] == address(0), "Asset already
        registered");
        assetOwners[_assetId] = msg.sender;
        emit AssetRegistered(_assetId, msg.sender);
        return true;
    }

    function transferAsset(uint256 _assetId, address _newOwner) public
    returns (bool success) {
        require(assetOwners[_assetId] == msg.sender, "Only owner of the
        asset can transfer the asset");
        assetOwners[_assetId] = _newOwner;
        emit AssetRegistered(_assetId, _newOwner);
        return true;
    }

    function mint(uint256 _amount) public onlyOwner {
        totalSupply += _amount * 10 ** decimals;
        balanceOf[owner] += _amount * 10 ** decimals;
    }

}
```

Unique to this contract is the *assetOwners* mapping, associating unique asset IDs with owners' addresses, laying the groundwork for asset tokenization.

Functions such as transfer, approve, and *transferFrom* resemble standard ERC-20 token interactions, enabling users to exchange tokens and grant transaction permissions. The addition of asset management functions, *registerAsset* and *transferAsset*, allows for the registration and transfer of asset ownership, introducing a real-world element to the digital token framework.

Critical to this contract is the mint function, restricted to the contract owner (typically the deployer or an authorized entity), allowing the creation of new tokens, thereby increasing the total supply. This is akin to controlling the issuance of new assets or shares.

Security features and access control are enforced through modifiers like *onlyOwner*, ensuring sensitive actions are restricted to authorized users. However, it should be noted that for deployment in a real-world scenario, the contract would require enhancements in security, compliance, and user interface, such as integrating with user wallets and meeting regulatory standards.

End-of-Chapter Questions

Multiple-Choice Questions

1. **What is tokenization in the context of blockchain technology?**
   - (A) Converting real money into cryptocurrency.
   - (B) Converting rights to an asset into a digital token on a blockchain.
   - (C) Converting digital assets into physical assets.
   - (D) Converting blockchain data into encrypted tokens.

2. **Which of the following is NOT a benefit of tokenization?**
   - (A) Increased liquidity of assets.
   - (B) Democratization of access to investment.
   - (C) Higher volatility of asset prices.
   - (D) Enhanced transparency and security of transactions.

3. **What role do smart contracts play in tokenization?**
   - (A) They act as digital agreements that execute automatically based on predefined rules.
   - (B) They provide encryption for blockchain transactions.
   - (C) They serve as digital wallets for storing tokens.
   - (D) They convert digital tokens back into real-world assets.

4. **What is a significant challenge in the tokenization of real-world assets?**
   - (A) The creation of digital tokens.
   - (B) Blockchain scalability.
   - (C) Regulatory compliance and legal frameworks.
   - (D) Cryptocurrency mining.

5. **How does blockchain technology impact the liquidity of tokenized assets?**
   - (A) It decreases liquidity by making transactions more complex.
   - (B) It has no impact on liquidity.
   - (C) It increases liquidity by facilitating easier and faster transactions.
   - (D) It restricts liquidity to certain geographical regions.

6. **What is a synthetic asset in the context of blockchain and tokenization?**
   - (A) A real-world asset that has been digitized on a blockchain.
   - (B) A digital representation of a real-world asset, allowing for investment without owning the actual asset.
   - (C) A physical asset backed by a digital token.
   - (D) A type of cryptocurrency that mimics the behavior of traditional currencies.

7. **What distinguishes tokenized real-world assets from synthetic assets?**
   - (A) Only synthetic assets use blockchain technology.
   - (B) Tokenized real-world assets offer direct or indirect ownership, whereas synthetic assets provide exposure without ownership.
   - (C) Synthetic assets cannot be traded.
   - (D) Tokenized real-world assets are not based on blockchain technology.

8. **What challenge does tokenization address in the carbon credit market?**
   (A) Reducing the value of carbon credits.
   (B) Increasing the complexity of transactions.
   (C) Enhancing transparency and liquidity.
   (D) Decreasing the demand for carbon credits.
9. **What is a potential advantage of tokenizing intellectual property (IP)?**
   (A) It restricts access to the IP.
   (B) It decreases the IP's market value.
   (C) It enables direct investment and fractional ownership in IP.
   (D) It makes the IP less secure.
10. **How does Account Abstraction contribute to cryptocurrency adoption?**
    (A) By increasing the complexity of transactions.
    (B) By separating signers and accounts for more flexibility and security.
    (C) By eliminating the need for digital wallets.
    (D) By making cryptocurrencies less accessible.
11. **What technological development helps integrate secure signing mechanisms similar to crypto wallets into smartphones?**
    (A) Blockchain
    (B) Passkeys
    (C) Smart contracts
    (D) Digital signatures
12. **What is a challenge in tokenizing off-chain real-world assets?**
    (A) Simplifying the valuation process.
    (B) Ensuring digital tokens do not represent actual assets.
    (C) Navigating legal and regulatory frameworks.
    (D) Preventing the use of blockchain technology.
13. **How does the tokenization of U.S. Treasuries compare to traditional ETFs?**
    (A) By allowing 24/7 trading and eliminating management fees.
    (B) Tokenization is more expensive than ETF management.
    (C) ETFs offer direct ownership of assets, while tokenized Treasuries do not.
    (D) Tokenized Treasuries offer less liquidity than ETFs.

Open Questions

1. Describe the process of tokenization and its impact on asset liquidity.
2. How do smart contracts facilitate transactions in the tokenization ecosystem?
3. What challenges do companies face in tokenizing real-world assets, and how might these be addressed?
4. Discuss the benefits and potential drawbacks of synthetic assets as compared to tokenized real-world assets.
5. Explain the significance of regulatory clarity and legal frameworks in the adoption of tokenization technology.

Coding Exercises

Exercise 1: Creating a Basic ERC-20 Token

Objective: Write a Solidity smart contract for a basic ERC-20 token with standard functionalities including minting, transferring, and burning capabilities.

Tasks:
- Implement an ERC-20 token with a fixed supply.
- Add functions to mint (create) new tokens to an address, ensuring only the contract owner can mint new tokens.
- Include a function to burn (destroy) tokens from a holder's balance.
- Write unit tests in JavaScript or Solidity to test the minting, transferring, and burning functionalities.

Exercise 2: Developing a Token Sale Contract

Objective: Create a smart contract for a token sale, allowing users to buy your previously created ERC-20 tokens with Ethereum.

Tasks:
- Design a smart contract that accepts Ethereum in exchange for your ERC-20 tokens at a fixed rate.
- Implement a function to update the token price, restricted to the contract owner.
- Ensure that the contract can receive Ethereum and correctly update the buyer's token balance.
- Develop a function to withdraw the collected Ethereum to the owner's address.

Exercise 3: Tokenizing a Bond

Objective: Write a Solidity smart contract to tokenize a corporate bond, allowing investors to buy and sell fractional ownership of the bond.

Tasks:
- Design a smart contract that represents a bond with a fixed interest rate and maturity date.
- Implement functions to allow investors to buy and sell tokens of the bond, with each token representing a portion of the bond's value.
- Create a function to distribute interest payments to token holders proportionally based on their holdings.
- Ensure the contract automatically redeems tokens at maturity, paying back the principal to the token holders.

Exercise 4: Creating a Tokenized Mutual Fund

Objective: Develop a smart contract that simulates a tokenized mutual fund, enabling investors to purchase shares of the fund as tokens.

Tasks:
- Construct a smart contract that pools funds from investors to invest in a predefined basket of assets.
- Allow investors to purchase and redeem tokens of the fund, with the token value reflecting the net asset value (NAV) of the fund's holdings.
- Implement a mechanism to adjust the NAV of the fund as the value of the underlying assets changes.
- Include functions for managing the fund's assets, such as buying and selling assets, within the smart contract.

Chapter 10

Digital Da Vincis

The Renaissance of Art in the Age of NFTs

Preface

Ah, NFTs: the digital enigma that turned the art, gaming, and, quite frankly, the whole internet on its head. Imagine, if you will, a world where your cat's grumpy face, plastered on a digital token, can sell for the price of a small island. Welcome to the wacky world of non-fungible tokens (NFTs), or as I like to call it, "Seriously, that JPEG just sold for how much?"

In the beginning, there were cryptocurrencies, digital money that said, "Down with the system!" Then came NFTs, strutting onto the blockchain with the audacity of a peacock in a hen house, declaring, "But what if that system could make your weird doodle worth a fortune?" NFTs are the digital age's answer to "Why can't I just screenshot that?" Spoiler alert: It's because blockchain magic says your screenshot is as valuable as a counterfeit *Mona Lisa* drawn by your nephew.

Here's where it gets juicy: NFTs are more than just digital bragging rights. They're a visionary leap into how we perceive ownership and value. Remember when your parents said, "Those video games will never pay the bills"? Well, the joke's on them, because now, thanks to NFTs, virtual real estate in Decentraland is hotter property than downtown Manhattan. And those in-game assets? They're not just pixels; they're your ticket to potentially flipping digital sneakers for the price of a car.

"But it's all just digital!" you cry. Exactly. We live in a world where friendships are forged in pixels, love letters are sent with taps, and our most prized possessions can be stored in the cloud. Our lives are digital, and NFTs are just art imitating life. Or is it the other way around?

And for the critics who scoff, "It's just a passing fad!" let's not forget that once upon a time, people thought the earth was flat and that Bitcoin was just funny internet money. The truth is, NFTs represent something revolutionary: the undeniable proof of digital ownership. They're the art gallery for our digital renaissance, a new frontier where artists, gamers, and even celebrities can monetize their digital footprint in ways we're just beginning to explore.

So, the next time you see a pixelated punk or a bored ape selling for the GDP of a small country, remember, this isn't just about owning digital art. It's about being part of an ever-evolving digital narrative, a testament to human creativity and innovation. And if that means someone wants to pay top dollar for a virtual yacht or a tweet, who are we to judge? In the grand scheme of things, NFTs are just another reminder that value, much like beauty, is in the eye of the beholder—or, in this case, the eye of the digital wallet holder.

Welcome to the future, folks, where your digital dreams can become a reality, and yes, even your grandma's knitting patterns can be immortalized on the blockchain.

8-bit Mona Lisa: Now accepting art critiques in pixels only

1. Introduction

Building on the foundational exploration of decentralized finance (DeFi) that brought to light the transformative power of decentralized autonomous organizations (DAOs), automated market makers (AMMs), liquidity mining, and yield farming, we pivot to a domain that's reshaping the essence of digital interaction, ownership, and creativity— non-fungible tokens. While DeFi revolutionized finance by challenging traditional institutions with decentralized solutions, NFTs parallel this disruption within the digital and creative realms, ushering in an era of unparalleled digital ownership and novel economic models for artists, creators, and collectors alike.

NFTs stand out in the blockchain landscape, offering a distinct contrast to the fungible tokens that drive DeFi. These tokens embody uniqueness, with each NFT having a digital signature that prevents it from being interchangeable. This characteristic is pivotal, as it ensures that every NFT represents a specific asset or piece of content—be it a digital artwork, a piece of music, a video clip, or even interactive digital experiences. This indivisibility and uniqueness enable NFTs to support direct digital ownership, authenticated through blockchain technology, thereby creating a market for digital scarcity and collectability that was previously unimaginable.

Consider the meteoric rise of digital art NFTs, epitomized by Beeple's *Everydays: The First 5000 Days*, which sold for an astonishing $69 million.[1] This sale not only spotlighted NFTs on the global stage but also underscored the vast economic potential and the shift toward valuing digital art on par with traditional art. Beyond art, NFTs are redefining music distribution, exemplified by artists like Kings of Leon releasing their album as an NFT, providing buyers with exclusive perks, and thereby offering a new revenue model for musicians in the digital age.

Moreover, NFTs are at the heart of virtual real estate and gaming revolutions. Platforms like Decentraland and The Sandbox allow users to buy, sell, and develop virtual lands as NFTs, enabling a new form of digital real estate investment and interactive online communities. In the gaming world, projects like Axie Infinity leverage NFTs to create play-to-earn models, where players can generate real income through gameplay, transforming economic opportunities especially in regions with limited access to traditional financial systems.

NFTs, therefore, are not just a new class of digital assets; they represent the convergence of art, technology, and economics, creating a vibrant ecosystem where the digital signature of each token is a gateway to a world of possibilities. As we delve deeper into the realm of NFTs, we uncover a revolutionary space where ownership, creativity, and value are redefined, offering profound implications for creators, collectors, and investors. This chapter aims not only to navigate the technicalities and mechanics of NFTs but also to illuminate the remarkable stories and examples that showcase the importance and transformative potential of this space.

---

[1] https://www.nytimes.com/2021/03/11/arts/design/nft-auction-christies-beeple.html

In the great digital expanse of our time, where friendships can start with a swipe and currencies exist without ever touching the palm of your hand, the emergence of NFTs as valuable assets seems almost ... inevitable. But let's tackle the elephant in the room or, rather, the JPEG on the blockchain: *why on earth should digital images—NFTs—be worth anything at all?*

First off, calling NFTs "just JPEGs" is like calling the *Mona Lisa* "just some oil paint on a canvas." Sure, at a molecular level, you're not wrong, but you're also missing the forest for the memes. In a world where digital natives navigate virtual realities as fluently as physical ones, it's no leap of the imagination that art, collectibles, and, yes, even those cherished baseball cards (or in my case soccer figurines), find their new, pixelated leases on life.

Imagine, if you will, a world where your prized collection of baseball cards isn't relegated to a shoebox under your bed, vulnerable to the ravages of time, coffee spills, or an overzealous spring cleaning. Instead, each card, with its stats and player holograms, exists eternally pristine in the digital realm, as NFTs. Lost your physical card of the legendary Babe Ruth in a tragic vacuuming accident? Fret not, for its digital counterpart remains unscathed in the blockchain, forever mint condition.

But NFTs go beyond mere digital replacements for our physical collectibles. They represent a new frontier of digital ownership and authenticity. In a realm where copying and pasting could make anyone an "owner" of a digital file, NFTs stand as immutable proof of ownership, a blockchain-backed certificate of authenticity for the digital age. They're the art gallery invites in your virtual mailbox, the limited-edition sneakers in your digital wardrobe, and, yes, even the deeds to virtual lands in realms yet to be explored.

To argue that NFTs are "just JPEGs" is to overlook the essence of what art and collectability have always been about—appreciation, ownership, and the stories we attach to the objects we hold dear. Just as we once marveled at the first photographs, wondering how light and silver could capture a moment in time, we now stand at the precipice of a new era in art and ownership, marveling at how pixels and blockchain can capture the essence of digital creativity.

So, the next time someone dismisses NFTs as "just JPEGs," remember, even the most magnificent cathedrals were once "just stones." And in this grand digital cathedral we're building, NFTs are not only the stained glass windows but also the bricks, mortar, and very ground upon which we stand. And if someone still doesn't get it, well, perhaps offer them a digital baseball card and see if that swings for the fences.

2. How Do NFTs Work?

To truly grasp the magnitude of their impact and the breadth of their applications, one must start at the foundational level—understanding the various standards that govern their creation, interaction, and existence on the blockchain.

2.1 NFT Standards

NFT standards play a crucial role in the ecosystem by defining the rules for the creation, issuance, and transfer of NFTs on blockchain platforms. The most commonly used standards are ERC-721 and ERC-1155 on the Ethereum blockchain, although other blockchains have developed their own standards.

ERC-721: Introduced as the standard for creating non-fungible, unique tokens, ERC-721 enables each token to have distinct properties and values. It's widely used for digital art, collectibles, and other unique assets. This standard ensures that each NFT is distinguishable and supports a secure method of trading and ownership verification.[2] Let's look at two examples: CryptoPunks and Decentraland.

CryptoPunks, developed by Larva Labs, stands as one of the pioneering projects utilizing the ERC-721 standard. Launched in 2017, it features 10,000 uniquely generated characters, each with its own distinct attributes and aesthetics, ranging from humans to zombies and even apes. These digital characters quickly ascended to iconic status within the blockchain community, becoming highly sought after collectibles. CryptoPunks not only demonstrated the potential of blockchain technology to authenticate and secure digital ownership but also set the stage for the explosive growth of the NFT market. The project's use of ERC-721 ensured that each Punk could be individually owned, traded, and verified through the Ethereum blockchain, making it a landmark example of the standard in action.

Decentraland leverages the ERC-721 standard to tokenize parcels of virtual land in its expansive, decentralized virtual world. Each piece of land in Decentraland is a unique, tradable asset on the Ethereum blockchain, represented as an ERC-721 token. This setup allows users to own, develop, and monetize their digital real estate, creating an immersive virtual environment where businesses, social spaces, and interactive experiences thrive. The adoption of ERC-721 facilitates the distinct ownership and transferability of these virtual land parcels, underpinning the economic and social infrastructure of Decentraland's user-generated content platform.

ERC-1155: Developed as a more versatile standard, ERC-1155 allows for both fungible and non-fungible tokens to be represented within a single contract. This multitoken standard enables a single deployed contract to manage multiple token types, making it efficient for creating and managing collections of unique items, as well as fungible tokens, within the same framework. It offers the benefits of reduced transaction and storage costs while maintaining the ability to represent the uniqueness and ownership of each NFT.[3]

Enjin, a platform that provides an ecosystem for gaming, has been a pioneer in leveraging the ERC-1155 standard. Enjin utilizes ERC-1155 to represent both in-game

---

[2] To view the original proposal for this standard, see the Ethereum Improvement Proposals website at https://eips.ethereum.org/EIPS/eip-721.

[3] View the original proposal at https://eips.ethereum.org/EIPS/eip-1155.

items and currencies, enabling a more seamless and integrated approach to asset management within games. This standard allows for the creation of a vast range of assets, from swords and armor to special currencies, all within a single contract on the Enjin platform. The unique capability of ERC-1155 to handle multiple token types efficiently makes it ideal for gaming environments where players can truly own, trade, and utilize their digital assets across various games and applications within the Enjin ecosystem.

The Sandbox employs the ERC-1155 standard to facilitate its vibrant, user-generated content platform, where players can create, own, and monetize their gaming experiences. Within The Sandbox, everything from virtual land to in-game items and experiences is tokenized using ERC-1155, allowing for a unified, efficient approach to asset management. This standard enables The Sandbox to offer a diverse range of assets, fostering a rich, interactive world where players have the freedom to innovate and trade. The adoption of ERC-1155 by The Sandbox not only enhances the fluidity and scalability of transactions but also empowers users by providing them with true ownership and control over their creations.

These standards are foundational to the NFT ecosystem, providing the framework that facilitates the secure creation, buying, selling, and trading of non-fungible tokens. They ensure interoperability among various platforms and applications, allowing for a wide range of use cases and innovations in the digital asset space.

2.2 Uniform Resource Identifier

Another fundamental component in the architecture of NFTs is the token Uniform Resource Identifier (URI). It serves a pivotal role by linking the NFT to its associated metadata or digital asset. This metadata, often hosted externally, provides detailed information about the NFT, including its name, description, image, and other attributes that define or enrich the token's digital representation.

It acts as a bridge between the token itself, stored on the blockchain, and its descriptive metadata, which may reside off-chain. When an NFT is minted, its metadata is typically not stored directly on the blockchain due to storage limitations and costs. Instead, the metadata is hosted elsewhere (e.g. on a web server or a decentralized file storage system like IPFS), and the NFT smart contract contains a URI pointing to this metadata.

By enabling the storage of metadata off-chain and linking it through a URI, NFTs can be associated with rich, complex information without the burden of high blockchain storage costs. This setup not only economizes space and resources but also paves the way for the incorporation of dynamic content. Some innovative projects are already exploiting this capability to create NFTs whose attributes evolve over time or in response to certain triggers, adding a layer of interactivity and engagement previously unseen. Moreover, the use of decentralized storage solutions like IPFS to host this metadata, accessible via URIs, further bolsters the integrity and permanence of NFTs. This approach ensures that an NFT's defining information remains durable and resistant to censorship, reinforcing the decentralized ethos of the blockchain world and securing the longevity and relevance of digital assets.

The URI in the context of NFTs is a critical element that ensures each token's uniqueness and value is not just confined to the blockchain but extended to encompass rich, descriptive, and potentially evolving digital content. As the NFT space grows, the methods of managing and leveraging URIs continue to evolve, offering more sophisticated and decentralized ways to link NFTs with their metadata.

2.3 Minting, Storing, and Owning NFTs

Minting an NFT is more than just the digital equivalent of printing a unique artwork or recording a song; it is a sophisticated process that infuses digital content with the immutability and security of blockchain technology. Creators begin by crafting their digital content, whether it be visual art, musical compositions, digital collectibles, or interactive experiences. The subsequent step involves defining the metadata, the soul of the NFT, which encompasses vital details such as the asset's name, description, creator, and unique attributes or traits that distinguish it from any other digital asset.

The choice of a blockchain platform and a corresponding token standard, typically ERC-721 for unique digital items or ERC-1155 for a more versatile approach that accommodates both fungible and non-fungible assets, sets the stage for the minting process. Through interaction with a dedicated smart contract, the creator uploads the asset's metadata, which is then algorithmically assigned a unique identifier. This identifier, along with the ownership details, is securely recorded on the blockchain, immortalizing the asset as an NFT. The minting process, while facilitating the birth of an NFT, incurs a "gas" fee, a necessary expenditure that covers the computational effort required to execute these operations on the blockchain.

The storage strategy for NFT metadata plays a critical role in the asset's accessibility and longevity. While on-chain storage offers a high degree of security and permanence, ensuring that the metadata remains tamper-proof and inseparable from the blockchain, it is often constrained by the blockchain's storage capacity and the cost implications of such a method. Consequently, off-chain storage solutions like the InterPlanetary File System (IPFS), which provides a decentralized and resilient approach, or traditional web servers, have become the norm. These methods link the NFT to its metadata through a URI recorded on the blockchain, striking a balance between scalability and integrity.

Ownership of an NFT is more than a mere claim; it is a cryptographically secured right, enshrined within the blockchain and tied indelibly to the owner's wallet address. This level of security affords the owner absolute control over the asset, encompassing the rights to transfer, sell, or otherwise utilize the NFT. Peer-to-peer transfers underscore the decentralized nature of NFTs, allowing ownership to change hands without intermediaries, directly updating the blockchain's ledger. Furthermore, the proliferation of NFT marketplaces has streamlined the process of buying and selling NFTs, providing platforms where secure transactions are facilitated through smart contracts.

Moreover, the introduction of approval mechanisms within NFT standards offers an additional layer of flexibility in transactions, allowing owners to delegate the authority to transfer their NFTs, thereby broadening the scope for lending, staking, or collaborative endeavors without relinquishing control.

This integrated approach to minting, metadata storage, and ownership and transfer mechanisms underpins the unique, secure, and verifiable nature of NFTs, making them pivotal to the digital economy across art, gaming, collectibles, and more.

2.4 The NFT Ecosystem

The NFT ecosystem thrives through a network of digital marketplaces and platforms that facilitate the creation, sale, purchase, and trading of non-fungible tokens. These platforms not only serve as the primary venues for NFT transactions but also play a pivotal role in community engagement, artist discovery, and the broader integration of NFTs into the digital economy.

Exploring the landscape of NFT marketplaces reveals a rich tapestry of features and business models, particularly when examining industry leaders such as OpenSea, Rarible, and LooksRare. Each platform brings its own unique flavor to the world of digital collectibles, catering to various facets of the NFT community through distinct approaches to user engagement, transaction models, and ecosystem development.

OpenSea stands as a behemoth in the realm, not just by virtue of its expansive catalog that spans an array of digital assets like art, domain names, and virtual collectibles but also through its commitment to user accessibility. Its interface simplifies the complexities of NFT transactions, making it an inviting portal for both seasoned collectors and newcomers. The platform's strategic move to support NFTs from multiple blockchains, including Ethereum, Polygon, and Klaytn, further cements its position by offering users flexibility in managing gas fees and blockchain preferences. OpenSea sustains its operations through a 2.5% transaction fee on sales, a cost borne by sellers, while also fostering partnerships that enrich its offerings and community engagement.

Rarible, on the other hand, carves its niche through a strong emphasis on decentralization and community governance, allowing stakeholders to wield influence over the platform's evolution via the RARI token. This focus is complemented by Rarible's support for multiple blockchains such as Ethereum, Flow, and Tezos, which broadens its appeal across the NFT space. The platform is particularly attractive to creators, offering tools that empower them to mint and list NFTs with ease, fostering a vibrant ecosystem of digital creativity. Rarible's business model integrates a 5% transaction fee, evenly split between buyers and sellers, and leverages the distribution of RARI tokens to incentivize platform activity and loyalty.

LooksRare distinguishes itself by directly rewarding user participation through trading rewards in its native LOOKS token, crafting an ecosystem where the act of buying and selling NFTs is itself incentivized. This model is designed to cultivate a loyal and active user base, further augmented by the opportunity to stake LOOKS tokens for additional rewards, embedding a layer of investment and return into the user experience. With a transaction fee of 2% on sales, distributed among LOOKS stakers, LooksRare aligns its success with the prosperity of its users, offering a compelling value proposition for those engaged in the platform's economy.

3. Use Cases and Applications

High-profile NFT sales have garnered significant attention, both within and outside the art world, highlighting the substantial economic potential of digital art. For instance, the sale of Beeple's *Everydays: The First 5000 Days* for more than $69 million at Christie's auction house marked a watershed moment, underscoring the legitimacy and financial viability of NFTs in the traditional art market. Such landmark sales have not only catapulted digital artists to global recognition but have also encouraged galleries, institutions, and collectors to engage with digital art in new and meaningful ways.

To really understand the potential behind NFTs, let's explore some of the key projects using this technology.

3.1 Prominent Example: CryptoPunks

CryptoPunks are one of the earliest NFT projects on the Ethereum blockchain, launched in June 2017 by Larva Labs. The collection consists of 10,000 uniquely generated characters, which have become some of the most coveted and influential NFTs in the space. Despite their simple 24x24 pixel art format, CryptoPunks have sold for millions of dollars, becoming iconic symbols of the NFT revolution.

CryptoPunks stand as a seminal force in the NFT domain, marking a significant chapter in the evolution of digital collectibles on the Ethereum blockchain. As one of the inaugural NFT projects to grace the Ethereum network, CryptoPunks not only pioneered the modern NFT movement but also laid the groundwork that would shape the trajectory of countless NFT collections that followed. This groundbreaking project introduced the world to a digital canvas where art meets cryptography, capturing the imagination of collectors and enthusiasts alike and setting a precedent for the value and appeal of NFTs.

The allure of CryptoPunks is further enriched by the diversity and uniqueness of its characters (see **Figure 1** for a few examples). With a cast that spans humans, zombies, apes, and aliens, each Punk is imbued with its own distinctive set of attributes, from facial expressions to headgear and accessories. These attributes play a crucial role in defining the rarity and value of each character, creating a vibrant tapestry of digital personas that are as diverse as they are captivating. This diversity not only adds depth to the collection but also invites a wide range of personal connections and preferences among collectors, making the acquisition of a CryptoPunk a highly personalized venture.

Figure 1   Examples of CryptoPunks (*Source:* With permission of CryptoPunks)

Moreover, the influence of CryptoPunks on the NFT market cannot be overstated. Serving as both a bellwether and a benchmark, CryptoPunks have significantly shaped market perceptions and valuations within the NFT space. Their historical importance, coupled with their limited supply, has propelled them to the status of highly coveted digital collectibles, setting the standard for rarity, desirability, and market value. The enduring legacy of CryptoPunks as a pioneering project, their rich diversity of characters, and their profound impact on the market underscore their pivotal role in heralding the era of NFTs and continuing to inspire the evolution of digital collectability.

3.2 Prominent Example: Bored Ape Yacht Club (BAYC)

The Bored Ape Yacht Club is a collection of 10,000 unique Bored Ape NFTs—digital collectibles living on the Ethereum blockchain. Launched in April 2021 by Yuga Labs, each Bored Ape serves as a membership card to an exclusive virtual club, granting access to members-only benefits, the first of which is access to THE BATHROOM, a collaborative graffiti board. The Apes quickly became a status symbol within the crypto community, with owners including celebrities and tech entrepreneurs.

The Bored Ape Yacht Club (BAYC) stands as a hallmark in the NFT landscape, not only for its distinctive artistic flair but also for the rich set of features it offers to its owners. At the heart of BAYC's allure is the unique variety and rarity of each Bored Ape, which are algorithmically generated from a deep pool of more than 170 traits (example in **Figure 2**). These traits span a wide range of expressions, headwear, clothing, and other distinguishing features, weaving a complex matrix of rarity that directly influences the value of each NFT. This aspect of uniqueness and scarcity elevates each Bored Ape beyond mere digital artistry, imbuing them with a tangible sense of individuality and worth.

However, the essence of BAYC transcends the digital tokens themselves, as ownership ushers individuals into an exclusive community brimming with benefits. Being a Bored Ape holder unlocks access to a vibrant ecosystem where members enjoy exclusive parties, access to unique merchandise, and intellectual property rights over their Apes. This communal aspect fosters a sense of belonging and camaraderie among holders, transforming the collection into a dynamic social network with shared interests and a collective identity centered around the Bored Ape motif.

Figure 2   Example of a Bored Ape NFT (*Source:* Bored Ape Yacht Club)

Further enriching this community is Yuga Labs' strategic expansion of the BAYC universe through additional NFT drops, such as the Mutant Ape Yacht Club (MAYC) and the Bored Ape Kennel Club. These expansions not only broaden the narrative and universe surrounding the Bored Apes but also enhance the intrinsic value and utility of ownership. By continually introducing new elements and experiences into the ecosystem, Yuga Labs ensures that the Bored Ape Yacht Club remains a living, evolving community with growing appeal and engagement. This blend of variety, community, and an ever-expanding ecosystem cements BAYC's status as a pioneering force in the NFT space, offering a compelling mix of art, exclusivity, and communal experience that captures the imagination of collectors and enthusiasts alike.

The BAYC has emerged as one of the most influential and successful NFT projects to date, captivating the digital art and collectible market with its unique blend of art, exclusivity, and community. The smart contract was programmed so that a 2.5% royalty fee from every future sale would be automatically sent to the creators. At launch, all NFTs were sold for 0.8 ETH (roughly $190). The entire collection sold out in 12 hours. By 2022, many celebrities, like Eminem, Steph Curry, and Justin Bieber, had purchased Bored Apes for prices ranging from roughly $200,000 to $1.29 million.

The BAYC has captivated the digital art and collectible space with its ingeniously crafted ecosystem, marked by a blend of *scarcity, community engagement, utility,* and *mainstream allure.* The deliberate scarcity of these NFTs, coupled with the rarity of specific traits, has ignited a fervent demand among collectors and investors alike, each vying to secure their own distinct piece of this digital art phenomenon. This exclusivity is not just a matter of ownership but a gateway to a realm of rarity where the uniqueness of each Ape stands as a testament to the owner's individuality within the digital universe.

Ownership offers the privilege of access to an array of private events, both in the virtual sphere and in the physical realm, alongside exclusive merchandise and entitlement to subsequent NFT drops. This cultivation of an exclusive club atmosphere has proven to be a significant draw, knitting together a tight community bonded by shared interests and the prestige of membership. The allure of belonging to this select community has been instrumental in fostering a sense of unity and engagement around the BAYC brand, elevating the collection beyond mere digital assets to symbols of social standing and communal identity.

Furthermore, the utility and expansion of the BAYC ecosystem extend the value of these NFTs beyond the digital art realm into tangible, real-world experiences and benefits. Access to exclusive parties and events underscores the real-world applicability and advantages of Bored Ape ownership, blurring the lines between digital collectability and physical experiences. The creators, Yuga Labs, have adeptly fueled this ecosystem's growth through the introduction of new projects continually enriching the Bored Ape experience and enhancing the inherent value and appeal of these NFTs.

Adding to the fervor surrounding BAYC is the endorsement from high-profile celebrities and influencers who have not only invested in but also publicly championed their Bored Apes. This celebrity involvement has catapulted the project into the limelight, significantly amplifying its visibility and desirability. The intersection of mainstream attention with the intrinsic qualities of the BAYC collection has propelled it to the forefront of the NFT dialogue, attracting an expansive audience to the collection and, by extension, to the broader NFT space. This confluence of scarcity, community, utility, and celebrity endorsement harmonizes to underscore the Bored Ape Yacht Club's monumental impact on the digital collectible landscape, setting a benchmark for innovation, engagement, and cultural resonance in the NFT domain.

3.3 Why Were They So Successful?

The value and success of BAYC can be attributed to several key factors, each contributing to its significant impact on the overall NFT market. BAYC's success is not just a product of market dynamics but also of strategic branding and community engagement. The creators have masterfully leveraged social media, celebrity endorsements, and high-profile collaborations to build hype and demand. Moreover, the project's emphasis on community and utility has set it apart from many other NFT collections, offering tangible value beyond the digital asset itself.

BAYC's success story underscores the potential of NFTs not just to create financial value but also to foster strong communities and push the boundaries of digital art and ownership. Its impact extends beyond individual collectors to influence the entire NFT space, driving innovation and setting new standards for value, community, and utility in digital assets.

Given the price at which some of these NFTs were selling, it would be nice to be able to predict whether a collection is going to attract a similar level of attention.

Predicting the success of an NFT collection involves scrutinizing a variety of indicators that can signal its potential viability and appeal in the market. While no single indicator guarantees success, a combination of factors can provide insights into the collection's future performance. Here are key indicators to observe:

1. **Creator Reputation and Track Record**
   - The assessment of NFT collections extends beyond the artwork itself, delving into the creator's reputation, the project's uniqueness, community engagement, and additional utility, among other factors. Creators with a solid track record and a history of success in digital art, gaming, or related fields often bring their existing follower base and credibility into new ventures. Their active engagement with the community across various platforms not only showcases their commitment to the project's success but also fosters a sense of trust and reliability among potential buyers and enthusiasts.

2. **Artistic and Conceptual Uniqueness**
   - Artistic and conceptual uniqueness stand as pivotal elements that differentiate one collection from another. Collections featuring innovative, visually captivating art or those grounded in original concepts or themes that resonate with a particular audience tend to garner more attention and demand. This uniqueness is a crucial draw, appealing to collectors' desires for distinctiveness and personal resonance with the art.

3. **Community Support and Growth**
   - The strength and activity of a collection's community, especially before the mint, significantly influence its initial and sustained success. An active, growing community, coupled with a robust social media presence that's marked by increasing followers and interactions, signals broad market interest and a healthy level of engagement that can propel a collection's visibility and desirability.

4. **Utility and Benefits**
   - Moreover, collections offering additional utilities or benefits, such as exclusive event access, content, or decision-making participation, present enhanced value to holders. NFTs integrated into larger ecosystems or platforms that provide synergies or additional functionalities often stand out for their potential success, leveraging the broader ecosystem's features to enhance the NFT's appeal and utility.

5. **Rarity and Scarcity**
   - Rarity and scarcity also play critical roles in driving interest and competition among collectors. Collections with a well-defined rarity structure and limited editions, especially those in high demand, are seen as more valuable and desirable, creating a competitive environment that can drive up prices and collector interest.

6. **Market and Timing**
   - The broader market sentiment and timing of a collection's launch can significantly impact its success. Launching during periods of heightened market activity and interest may capture more attention, investment, and enthusiasm, benefiting from the positive market dynamics.

7. Roadmap and Future Plans

- Long-term value is often signaled by a collection's roadmap and future plans. A clear, achievable roadmap that outlines future developments, collaborations, and milestones provides potential investors with a vision of the collection's direction and growth potential. Sustainable growth strategies, community benefits, and ongoing innovation indicate a commitment to maintaining and enhancing the collection's value over time.

8. Partnerships and Collaborations

- Lastly, strategic partnerships and collaborations can substantially augment a collection's credibility, exposure, and reach. By aligning with well-known brands, artists, or platforms, a collection can leverage these relationships for increased visibility and credibility. Cross-promotional opportunities afforded by such partnerships can further expand the collection's audience, attracting a more diverse group of collectors and enthusiasts.

In sum, the evaluation of NFT collections through these lenses offers a comprehensive understanding of their potential value and appeal, guiding collectors and investors in making informed decisions in the dynamic NFT marketplace.

Both BAYC and CryptoPunks exemplify the diverse appeal and potential of NFTs, blending art, technology, and community into digital assets that carry significant cultural and financial weight. These collections have not only achieved high-profile sales but have also fostered robust communities and inspired a wide array of derivative works and projects. As landmarks in the NFT landscape, BAYC and CryptoPunks continue to influence the direction and perception of digital collectibles and blockchain art.

The influx of NFTs has democratized art collection, enabling a broader audience to participate in the art market. It has also prompted a reevaluation of what constitutes value in art, shifting some focus from physical to digital works and from traditional to blockchain-based provenance and ownership models. One of the best examples is the experiment run by Damien Hirst.

Case Study: Damien Hirst "The Currency"

Damien Hirst's "The Currency" is a pioneering exploration at the intersection of art, technology, and economics, challenging the conventional boundaries between physical and digital art forms. Launched in 2021, this avant-garde project consists of 10,000 unique pieces, each existing simultaneously as a tangible work of art and an NFT see (**Figure 3** for one of this unique pieces). Crafted on handmade paper in 2016, each artwork is adorned with Hirst's distinctive dot design, a motif that has become synonymous with his exploration of color and form.

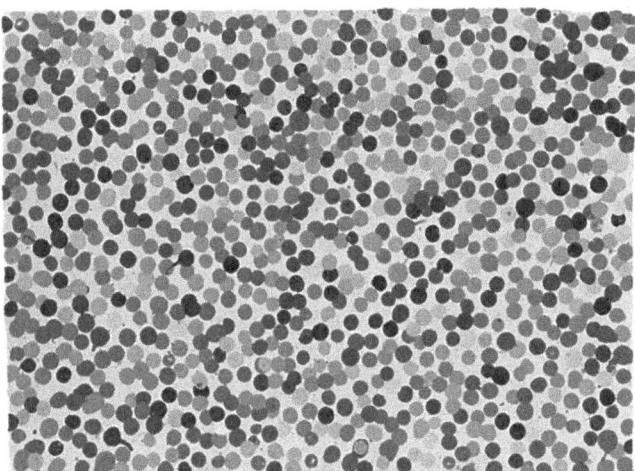

Figure 3 An artwork in "The Currency" Gallery named *Run like a man*

A compelling aspect of "The Currency" is the decision it imposes on its buyers, presenting them with a choice between retaining the NFT or exchanging it for its physical counterpart. This decision is not merely transactional but deeply philosophical, prompting participants to contemplate the essence of value and ownership within the art world. It asks whether the value of art resides in its physicality, its digital representation, or the conceptual intention behind it.

The titles of these artworks derive from lyrics of Hirst's favorite songs, infusing each piece with a layer of personal and cultural significance that extends beyond its visual appeal. This choice of titling adds another dimension to the project, intertwining Hirst's personal influences with the broader cultural narratives encapsulated in music.

By introducing each piece at $2,000 through a lottery system, Hirst democratized access to his work, breaking away from traditional art market barriers and inviting a broader audience to participate in this experimental fusion of art and blockchain technology. This project not only sparked immediate interest, generating $47 million in sales within its first month, but also maintained a dynamic presence in the art market, witnessing fluctuations in trading volumes and prices that mirrored the broader volatility of the NFT space. Cumulatively, "The Currency" has generated approximately $89 million, making a significant financial mark and prompting ongoing discussions about the future of art, the evolving role of NFTs, and the comparative value of physical versus digital works. These conversations have furthered the debate on the digitization of art and its broader implications for collectors, artists, and the art market at large.

At the conclusion of the exchange period in July 2022, a fascinating split emerged among the collectors: 5,149 opted for the physical artworks, while 4,851 chose to retain the NFTs. This division reflects a diverse range of perspectives on the value and significance of art in its physical and digital incarnations, highlighting the project's success in sparking dialogue and reflection on these themes.

Hirst's personal investment in the project, retaining 1,000 NFTs for himself, signals his firm belief in the enduring potential of the NFT space. Meanwhile, plans to exhibit the remaining physical artworks, in partnership with HENI, promise to bring the project's scope and impact into sharper relief. The anticipated burning event for unclaimed physical pieces stands as a potent symbol of the irrevocable choice between digital and physical mediums, highlighting the project's role in challenging traditional notions of art ownership, value, and authenticity.

"The Currency" stands as a referendum on the evolving nature of art in the digital age, blurring the lines between traditional art collecting and the emergent realm of digital assets. Through this project, Hirst not only navigates the fluid boundaries of art and currency but also invites the global art community to reconsider the foundations of artistic value and ownership.

3.4 PROMINENT PROTOCOLS: DECENTRALAND

NFTs are not just about digital art but can also involve real estate. Yes, real estate.

One prominent example of a platform facilitating the ownership of virtual land through NFTs is **Decentraland**. Decentraland is a decentralized virtual reality platform powered by the Ethereum blockchain, where users can purchase, develop, and sell parcels of virtual land in a digital world. This innovative platform stands out as one of the first and most successful examples of integrating blockchain technology with virtual real estate, offering a glimpse into the potential future of digital ownership and community engagement.

How Decentraland Works   Decentraland encompasses the following components:

- **Land Ownership:** In Decentraland, virtual land is represented as NFTs called LAND, each corresponding to a parcel of virtual real estate within the Decentraland metaverse. Each LAND token is a unique, non-fungible asset that grants its owner control over the content published to their portion of land within the Decentraland universe. This model of digital land ownership is a direct application of NFTs, where the scarcity and uniqueness of each parcel are secured on the Ethereum blockchain. **Figure 4** shows the location of Parcel -59,-20 on Decentraland.
- **Marketplace:** Decentraland features a marketplace where users can buy and sell LAND, along with other digital assets and creations, such as wearables for avatars or content to populate land parcels. Prices for LAND in Decentraland vary based on location, size, and proximity to high-traffic hubs or districts.

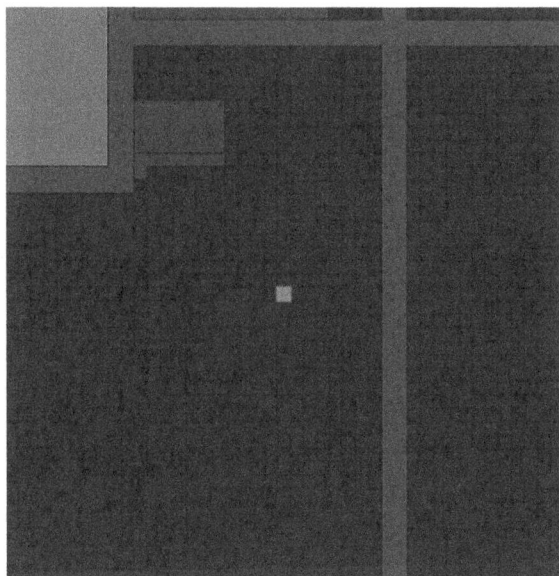

Figure 4   Example of a parcel on Decentraland

- **Development and Customization:** Owners of LAND in Decentraland have the freedom to develop their parcels as they see fit, creating anything from simple 3D structures to complex, interactive experiences. This flexibility has led to the development of a wide range of virtual spaces, including art galleries, gaming zones, virtual storefronts, and social hubs.
- **Community and Governance:** Decentraland is governed by a DAO, where LAND owners and holders of the platform's native token, MANA, can vote on policy updates, land auctions, and the types of content allowed within the metaverse. This community-driven approach ensures a level of democratic governance over the platform's development and direction.

Decentraland has attracted a diverse array of users, from individual creators and hobbyists to large companies and brands looking to establish a presence in the virtual world. High-profile collaborations and events, including virtual concerts, art exhibitions, and conferences, have taken place within Decentraland, demonstrating its potential as a platform for entertainment, commerce, and social interaction.

3.5 Prominent Example: NBA Top Shot

NBA Top Shot represents a pioneering convergence of blockchain technology, sports entertainment, and digital collectibles, marking a significant evolution in how fans engage with their favorite sports moments. Developed by Dapper Labs on the Flow blockchain, NBA Top Shot offers a unique platform where fans can buy, sell, and trade officially licensed NBA highlight clips as NFTs, known as "Moments." These Moments capture iconic in-game plays and achievements, packaged in digital form and authenticated on the blockchain, ensuring ownership and scarcity (see **Figure 5** for an example).

The choice of the Flow blockchain for NBA Top Shot is pivotal to its success. Designed for high scalability and user-friendliness, Flow facilitates a seamless experience for users, accommodating the vast transaction volumes associated with trading Moments without the steep transaction fees often seen on other platforms.[4] This blockchain architecture supports the creation of a vibrant marketplace that remains accessible to mainstream users, not just crypto-enthusiasts.

NBA Top Shot has successfully tapped into the mainstream sports fanbase, attracting users who may not have previously engaged with blockchain technology. This broad appeal can be attributed to several factors.

- **Official NBA Licensing:** By partnering directly with the NBA, Top Shot offers authentic, officially licensed content, lending credibility and attracting hardcore NBA fans.
- **Digital Scarcity and Ownership:** Each Moment is produced in limited quantities, creating scarcity that can increase the value of a highlight over time. Blockchain technology ensures that ownership is securely recorded and easily transferable, mirroring the traditional trading card market but with digital efficiency.

Figure 5   Examples of Moments (*Source:* NBA Top Shot)

[4] You can read Flow's technical papers at https://flow.com/technical-paper.

- **Engagement and Community:** NBA Top Shot has fostered a strong community of collectors and fans, leveraging social media and forums to engage users. Challenges, rewards, and special releases encourage active participation and continuous engagement within the platform.

NBA Top Shot exemplifies how NFTs can innovate the concept of sports memorabilia, shifting from physical cards or merchandise to digital assets that can be interactively traded, showcased, and even used in online competitions or games. This digital transformation allows for a more dynamic form of fandom, where fans can own a piece of the game's history and directly engage with the sport and its players in new ways.

The success of NBA Top Shot highlights the potential for expanding the NFT model to other sports and entertainment domains, offering a new revenue stream for leagues and a novel way for fans to connect with their passions. It also underscores the importance of user-friendly blockchain platforms and strategic partnerships in bringing NFTs to the mainstream.

As NFTs continue to evolve, the model established by NBA Top Shot may inspire similar initiatives across a range of sports and entertainment industries, further blurring the lines between physical and digital fandom, and enhancing the way fans celebrate and remember iconic moments.

3.6 Ordinals on Bitcoin: Revolutionizing Digital Ownership

Up to now, we have only considered NFTs that have emerged on Ethereum. Interestingly, one of the hottest areas that have emerged more recently is the one of NFTs on the Bitcoin chain.

The Ordinals protocol introduces a novel method for numbering and tracking individual satoshis, the smallest unit of Bitcoin, effectively allowing for the creation of unique digital assets directly on the Bitcoin blockchain. This development represents a significant shift in the utilization of Bitcoin, moving beyond its traditional role as a digital currency to a platform for hosting NFTs.[5]

The foundation for Ordinals was set by significant Bitcoin network upgrades such as Segregated Witness (SegWit) and Taproot. SegWit, implemented in 2017, introduced a way to separate witness data from transaction data, allowing for more efficient use of block space and paving the way for the inclusion of additional data types, such as those required for NFTs. Taproot further expanded Bitcoin's capabilities in 2021 by enhancing privacy, scalability, and the flexibility to include arbitrary data within transactions, directly benefiting the Ordinals concept.[6]

---

[5] https://academy.binance.com/en/articles/what-are-ordinals-an-overview-of-bitcoin-nfts, https://decrypt.co/resources/what-are-ordinals-a-beginners-guide-to-bitcoin-nfts
[6] https://chain.link/education-hub/ordinals-bitcoin-nfts

The Process of Inscription   Ordinals differentiate themselves from traditional NFTs primarily through their inscription method. Instead of minting new tokens on a separate layer or using smart contracts, Ordinals involve inscribing raw file data directly onto the Bitcoin blockchain. In other words, inscribing a satoshi to create an NFT involves marking a specific satoshi with a unique identifier, typically through the Ordinal Protocol. This identifier can contain images, text, or other data, transforming the satoshi into a non-fungible token. This method ensures that the data is fully on-chain, inheriting the security, immutability, and simplicity of Bitcoin. Each satoshi becomes uniquely identifiable, transforming it into a de facto NFT without departing from the Bitcoin protocol's fundamentals.[7]

Challenges and Considerations   While Ordinals open up new avenues for creativity and digital ownership on Bitcoin, they also present unique challenges. The lack of smart contract functionality on Bitcoin means trading Ordinals relies on over-the-counter (OTC) methods, often facilitated by dedicated communities. Additionally, the potential for inscriptions to include copyrighted or illicit content raises concerns about content moderation in a system designed to be permissionless and censorship-resistant.[8]

Differences from Ethereum-Based NFT Creation   These are the differences between Ordinals and Ethereum NFTs:

- **Smart Contracts:** Ethereum NFTs are typically created using smart contracts (e.g. ERC-721 or ERC-1155 contracts) that define the rules and behaviors of the NFTs. Ordinals do not use smart contracts; instead, they rely on the direct inscription of data onto satoshis.
- **Data Storage:** Ethereum NFTs often store metadata and links to digital content on decentralized storage solutions like IPFS, with the blockchain storing only the reference to this data. In contrast, Ordinals inscribe the raw file data directly onto the Bitcoin blockchain, making each inscribed satoshi fully self-contained.
- **Platform Capabilities:** Ethereum's design inherently supports the creation and trading of NFTs through its smart contract capabilities, facilitating a vibrant ecosystem of marketplaces and applications. Bitcoin's approach with Ordinals is more foundational, embedding digital assets directly into its blockchain without the need for additional layers or smart contracts.
- **Trading Mechanisms:** The lack of smart contract functionality on Bitcoin means that trading Ordinals often requires manual or OTC methods, whereas Ethereum NFTs can be easily traded on various decentralized exchanges and marketplaces through smart contract interactions.

Real-World Examples and Market Response   The advent of Ordinals has sparked the creation of Bitcoin-native NFT collections that mirror the enthusiasm seen on platforms like

---

[7] https://coinmarketcap.com/alexandria/article/what-are-bitcoin-ordinals-the-ultimate-guide-to-bitcoin-nfts
[8] https://coinmarketcap.com/alexandria/article/what-are-bitcoin-ordinals-the-ultimate-guide-to-bitcoin-nfts

Ethereum. Collections such as Ordinal Punks and Taproot Wizards, alongside Yuga Labs' TwelveFold, showcase the diversity of digital art and collectibles now possible on Bitcoin. These projects, along with the burgeoning interest in Bitcoin domain names and the experimental BRC-20 token standard, highlight the expanding ecosystem and the creative potential unleashed by Ordinals.[9]

The Future of Ordinals and Bitcoin NFTs The introduction of Ordinals marks a pivotal moment in the evolution of Bitcoin, bridging the gap between the original cryptocurrency and the dynamic world of NFTs. As the community explores this new frontier, the ongoing development of tools, wallets, and marketplaces will be critical in shaping the accessibility and utility of Bitcoin NFTs. With both excitement and controversy in equal measure, the Ordinals protocol undeniably adds a rich layer of complexity and opportunity to the Bitcoin ecosystem, heralding a new era of digital asset creation and ownership.

4. Strategies for Valuing and Trading NFTs

Now that we have seen some of the most successful and interesting projects in the NFT space, let's look at the financial side of things and try to understand how one could participate in this market as an investor. As usual, all disclaimers apply: I aim to give you the tools—no advice though!

Evaluating and investing in NFTs requires a multidimensional approach blending technical analysis, market insights, and an understanding of the broader cultural and social trends. The following is an expanded discussion on the methodologies used to assess NFTs, incorporating numerical examples and deeper insights into each process.

4.1 Metadata Analysis

Metadata analysis forms the cornerstone of NFT valuation, involving a thorough examination of the NFT's inherent attributes recorded in its metadata. This includes details such as the item's rarity, the creator's reputation, and its historical significance within the NFT space. For instance, an NFT from a series with 10,000 items might have certain traits that appear in only 100 of those items, making those particular NFTs 100 times rarer than others in the same series. Additionally, an NFT created by an artist with a substantial following and respected portfolio might inherently carry more value. Analyzing the smart contract code can also reveal functionalities or properties imbued in the NFT, such as unlockable content or proof of attendance, which could significantly affect its valuation. For example, an NFT granting access to exclusive virtual events or digital content upon ownership could be valued higher than a static digital asset.

---

[9] https://crypto.com/university/bitcoin-nfts-ordinals-protocol

Figure 6   CryptoPunk #7804

Real Example: Consider the CryptoPunks collection, one of the earliest and most prestigious NFT projects. An investor looking at CryptoPunk #7804, depicted in **Figure 6**, one of the rarest with only nine alien punks in existence, would note its distinctive attributes and scarcity, contributing to its high valuation. Furthermore, the NFT has three attributes—the cap, pipe, and shades—that all contribute to the rarity of the NFT.

4.2 Blockchain Data Analytics

Blockchain data analytics uses blockchain explorers and specialized analytics tools to scrutinize the ownership history and transactional behavior associated with an NFT. This process might uncover an NFT that has changed hands multiple times within a short period, indicating high demand or speculative interest. Tools like Etherscan or The Graph can help trace an NFT's provenance, revealing its first minting, previous owners, and sale prices. For example, discovering that an NFT was previously owned by a celebrity or influencer could enhance its perceived value due to its notable ownership history.

Real Example: An investor interested in an NFT from the Art Blocks Curated series might examine its transaction history to identify any patterns of ownership among prominent collectors or fluctuations in sale prices over time, providing insights into its market demand and liquidity. For instance, we can use Etherscan to view the transaction history of Chromie Squiggle #3806, depicted in **Figure 7**, to find that it has been sold five times and is now worth about $25,000.[10]

4.3 Liquidity and Market Depth Analysis

The liquidity of an NFT is crucial for investors and collectors, indicating the ease with which it can be sold at market price. This analysis focuses on the volume of active buyers and sellers within the market and the presence of liquidity pools that might support NFT collateralization. For instance, a market where thousands of transactions occur

---

[10] View the transaction history on Etherscan at https://etherscan.io/nft/0x059edd72cd353df5106d2b9cc5ab83a 52287ac3a/3806.

Figure 7 Chromie Squiggle #3806

monthly demonstrates higher liquidity than one with only a handful of sales. Moreover, platforms like Uniswap or Aave, which have started experimenting with NFT collateralization, contribute to the liquidity by allowing NFT holders to borrow against their assets. High liquidity generally signifies a healthy market, but it's also essential to assess market depth, understanding how large transactions might affect the NFT's price.

Real Example: An investor might analyze the trading volume and listing prices of Bored Ape Yacht Club (BAYC) NFTs on OpenSea. By observing trends in sales volume and price changes, the investor could gauge market sentiment and liquidity, aiding in the decision of when to buy or sell. For instance, BAYC #935, depicted in **Figure 8**, has more than 100 different sales and transfers since it was minted in 2021, with its most recent sale of about $42,000. Investors can view past transactions, price history, and ongoing offers on the OpenSea website.[11]

4.4 Algorithmic Valuation Models

Algorithmic valuation models employ a mix of quantitative and qualitative factors to compute an NFT's estimated market value. These models might consider rarity scores—numerical representations of an item's scarcity within its collection—and artist recognition alongside historical sale prices and market trends. For instance, an NFT with a rarity score in the top 1% of its collection might be valued significantly higher than those in the lower 50%. Programming skills, along with a deep knowledge of market dynamics, are essential to develop and refine these models, which can adapt over time as new data and trends emerge.

---

[11] View details at https://opensea.io/assets/ethereum/0xbc4ca0eda7647a8ab7c2061c2e118a18a936f13d/935.

Figure 8   BAYC #935

Real Example: By employing a model that analyzes rarity scores, social media mentions, and previous sale prices of NFTs within the World of Women collection, an investor could identify undervalued pieces that are likely to appreciate in value based on historical data trends and current market sentiment.

4.5 Sentiment Analysis

Sentiment analysis leverages natural language processing (NLP) tools and algorithms to sift through social media posts, community forums, and other digital platforms, gauging the public sentiment toward specific NFTs or collections. For example, a surge in positive social media mentions about a particular NFT series could precede a spike in demand and value. Tools like Brand24 or Sentiment Viz can quantify the sentiment, offering insights into potential market movements before they happen, based on the community's mood and interest levels.

Combining these analytical methods provides a comprehensive framework for assessing NFTs, balancing the technical specifics of blockchain analytics with broader market and social indicators. This holistic approach empowers collectors and investors to make informed decisions in the dynamic and often unpredictable NFT market.

Real Example: Before investing in an NFT from the Meebits collection, an investor might analyze social media sentiment and discussions on platforms like Twitter or Discord. A spike in positive sentiment following the announcement of a new utility for Meebits owners (e.g. integration into a popular virtual world) could signal a good investment opportunity.

Coding Example

Let's get our hands dirty and see if we can build a relatively simple valuation model. The following example incorporates a mechanism to compute and adjust rarity scores based on the number of transactions and a market-based indicator such as the total sales volume. This creates an interactive and responsive valuation model for NFTs.

```solidity
pragma solidity ^0.8.0;

import "@openzeppelin/contracts/token/ERC721/ERC721.sol";
import "@openzeppelin/contracts/access/Ownable.sol";

contract DynamicRarityNFT is ERC721, Ownable {
    using SafeMath for uint256;

    struct NFTAttributes {
        uint256 rarityScore;
        uint256 transactionCount;
        uint256 totalSalesVolume;
    }

    uint256 private nextTokenId = 0;
    mapping(uint256 => NFTAttributes) public nftAttributes;

    constructor() ERC721("DynamicRarityNFT", "DRNFT") {}

    function mintNFT(address recipient, string memory tokenURI) public
onlyOwner {
        uint256 tokenId = nextTokenId++;
        _mint(recipient, tokenId);
        _setTokenURI(tokenId, tokenURI);
        nftAttributes[tokenId] = NFTAttributes({rarityScore: 1000,
transactionCount: 0, totalSalesVolume: 0});
    }

    function recordSale(uint256 tokenId, uint256 salePrice) public {
        require(_exists(tokenId), "NFT does not exist.");
        NFTAttributes storage attributes = nftAttributes[tokenId];
        attributes.transactionCount += 1;
        attributes.totalSalesVolume += salePrice;

        // Dynamically adjust rarity based on transaction count and total
sales volume
        adjustRarityScore(tokenId);
    }

    function adjustRarityScore(uint256 tokenId) internal {
        NFTAttributes storage attributes = nftAttributes[tokenId];

        // Example adjustment logic: Increase rarity score by 1% of total
sales volume
```

```
        // and decrease by 2 points for each transaction to simulate
supply and demand effect
        uint256 volumeIncrease = attributes.totalSalesVolume.div(100);
// 1% of total sales volume
        uint256 transactionDecrease = attributes.transactionCount.mul(2);
        uint256 newRarityScore = attributes.rarityScore.add(volumeIncrease).
sub(transactionDecrease);

        // Ensure rarity score does not fall below a minimum threshold
        attributes.rarityScore = newRarityScore > 500 ?
newRarityScore : 500;
    }
}
```

In this example, the mintNFT function creates a new NFT with initial attributes, including a rarity score. The recordSale function is called to record each sale of the NFT, adjusting the total sales volume and transaction count. The adjustRarityScore function then dynamically adjusts the NFT's rarity score based on these factors, simulating the impact of market activity on the NFT's perceived rarity and value.

This model introduces an approach to valuing NFTs, where market activities directly influence an NFT's rarity score and, by extension, its desirability and valuation. By factoring in sales volume and transaction frequency, this system reflects real-world supply and demand dynamics, offering a nuanced method for assessing NFT value that evolves with market conditions.

News from the Ivory Tower[12]

The burgeoning market for non-fungible tokens (NFTs) has attracted significant attention from both practitioners and academics. Two recent studies, "The Economics of Non-Fungible Tokens" and "Selection-Neglect in the NFT Bubble," provide insights into the characteristics, dynamics, and economic implications of the NFT market.

The first study employs a comprehensive dataset and repeat sales regression methods to construct an aggregate NFT market index. This approach helps controlling for the unique attributes of individual NFTs, revealing that the NFT market index, sort of a time component, explains a significant portion of the variation in NFT returns. One of the critical insights is the importance of unique NFT characteristics in valuation. NFTs, by definition, are non-fungible, meaning each token is unique and cannot be replaced

[12] Huang, D., & Goetzmann, W. N. (2023). Selection-Neglect in the NFT Bubble. NBER Working Paper No. 31498. National Bureau of Economic Research.
Korteweg, A., Kräussl, R., & Verwijmeren, P. (2023). The Economics of Non-Fungible Tokens. SSRN Electronic Journal.

with another token. This non-fungibility is often tied to the distinct visual features and rarity of the NFTs, which play a significant role in their valuation. The authors demonstrate that visual attributes such as color, composition, and thematic elements significantly impact the prices of NFTs. It also reveals that these unique characteristics explain a substantial portion of the variation in NFT returns. This finding underscores the high degree of non-fungibility and the critical role of aesthetic and rarity factors in determining NFT value.

The relationship between NFT prices and the underlying cryptocurrency used for transactions is also explored. Both papers highlight the "money illusion" effect, where NFT prices are influenced by the recent performance of the denomination cryptocurrency, such as Ethereum. This relationship suggests that fluctuations in cryptocurrency values can significantly impact NFT market dynamics, adding another layer of complexity to the market's behavior.

"Selection-Neglect in the NFT Bubble" by Huang and Goetzmann, explores the NFT market's behavior during the COVID-19 era bubble. This paper highlights how behavioral biases, such as selection-neglect and extrapolative beliefs, contributed to the rapid rise and subsequent fall of NFT prices. The authors document that during the boom, optimistic beliefs were fueled by macroeconomic shocks, leading to aggressive trading behaviors. When liquidity declined, prices were subject to significant selection bias due to seller loss aversion, which delayed the market's crash. This study provides a critical view of the psychological factors driving the speculative nature of the NFT market.

Huang and Goetzmann's study leverages rich transaction-level data from prominent NFT trading platforms, specifically using data from SuperRare, which covers all bids, asks, and sales from April 2018 to June 2022. This comprehensive dataset provides a detailed view of market activity during the NFT bubble. To address selection bias, the authors implement a data-augmented Markov Chain Monte Carlo (MCMC) algorithm. This technique estimates latent prices for untraded NFTs and adjusts observed transaction prices accordingly. Their findings indicate that the corrected price index declines much earlier than the uncorrected one, highlighting the impact of selection bias on market perception. The corrected index's early decline compared to the uncorrected index reveals the nuanced effects of behavioral biases on perceived market trends.

In conclusion, the empirical literature on the NFT market provides valuable insights into its complex dynamics and the significant role of behavioral biases. By leveraging detailed transaction data and robust econometric methods, these studies reveal how cognitive biases and market frictions contribute to the volatility and speculative nature of the NFT market. As the market continues to evolve, further research is needed to understand its long-term economic implications and potential for sustainable growth.

5. NFTs and DeFi Integration

NFTs are not just digital art, virtual land, and funny apes. The underlying technology is helpful in DeFi as well. This convergence expands the utility of NFTs beyond collectibles and art, embedding them into financial applications that offer novel ways to interact with digital assets.

As we have explored in detail in the previous chapters, DeFi platforms utilize smart contracts on blockchain networks to provide financial services without traditional intermediaries. When NFTs are integrated into DeFi, they gain functionalities that enhance their liquidity, utility, and value proposition.

One of the most impactful use cases is the collateralization of NFTs to secure loans or other financial instruments. In this scenario, an NFT holder can lock their asset into a DeFi lending platform's smart contract as collateral to borrow cryptocurrency or stablecoins. This process adds liquidity to NFTs, which are typically less liquid than fungible tokens. For example, platforms like NFTfi and Arcade allow users to put their NFTs as collateral for loans, providing immediate liquidity while retaining ownership of their digital assets.

In addition, fractional ownership of NFTs, facilitated by DeFi protocols, allows multiple investors to hold a share of a high-value NFT. This democratizes access to expensive digital assets by lowering the entry barrier for investment. Platforms such as Fractional and Unicly use smart contracts to divide an NFT into several fungible tokens representing ownership shares, enabling a new form of community ownership and investment in NFTs.

Automated market makers (AMMs) are central to DeFi, providing liquidity through algorithm-driven trading pools instead of traditional order books. The integration of NFTs with AMMs introduces unique challenges and opportunities for liquidity in NFT markets.

The primary liquidity challenge for NFTs in DeFi stems from their non-fungible nature. Each NFT is unique, making it difficult to find buyers or sellers at a given time, which is a stark contrast to the high liquidity seen in fungible token markets. This uniqueness complicates their integration into traditional DeFi protocols, such as those relying on liquidity pools and AMMs, which are designed for interchangeable assets.

Moreover, the valuation of NFTs is inherently subjective, influenced by factors such as rarity, artist reputation, and community sentiment, rather than clear market fundamentals. This subjectivity can lead to wide price disparities and volatility, further exacerbating liquidity challenges.

Innovative Solutions for NFT Valuation and Exchange   To address these challenges, several innovative solutions have been developed.

- **Fractional Ownership:** By dividing an NFT into several fungible tokens representing shares in the ownership of the asset, fractional ownership increases the liquidity of high-value NFTs. This not only makes it easier for investors to buy into expensive NFTs but also simplifies the process of pricing and trading these assets on DeFi platforms.
- **NFT-Specific AMMs and Liquidity Pools:** Platforms are emerging with liquidity solutions tailored to NFTs, allowing users to trade NFTs directly with liquidity pools. These NFT-specific AMMs, such as Sudoswap, bypass the need for a direct buyer-seller match by using algorithms to facilitate trades, improving liquidity.
- **Dynamic Pricing Models:** Some platforms employ dynamic pricing models that adjust NFT prices based on real-time market demand and supply, helping to mitigate the valuation challenge. These models can utilize machine learning algorithms to analyze market data, historical sales, and other indicators to more accurately price NFTs.
- **Rental and Leasing Mechanisms:** To improve liquidity without selling the NFTs outright, some platforms offer rental or leasing options. This allows NFT owners to earn passive income from their digital assets while providing access to users who may not want to purchase an NFT at full price. Platforms like reNFT enable users to lend or rent NFTs, facilitating a new form of liquidity in the market.
- **Interoperable Standards and Cross-Chain Solutions:** Enhancing liquidity through interoperability, some projects are working on standards and protocols that enable NFTs to move across different blockchains. This cross-chain functionality broadens the potential market for NFTs, increasing their liquidity and accessibility.

These innovative approaches are not only addressing the immediate liquidity and valuation challenges faced by NFTs in DeFi but are also paving the way for new forms of digital asset interaction and financialization. As the DeFi ecosystem continues to evolve, it's likely that more solutions will emerge, further integrating NFTs into the broader financial landscape.

Uniswap V3 LP Position as NFT NFTs are also used in DeFi to represent unique assets with specific attributes. A prominent example is Uniswap V3's liquidity positions, which are represented as NFTs. As we have seen in Chapters 7 and 8, in Uniswap V3, liquidity providers (LPs) can customize their liquidity ranges, making each position unique. These custom positions are tokenized as NFTs, allowing LPs to trade, transfer, or use them in DeFi protocols. This approach merges the concept of NFTs with DeFi, enabling a flexible and tradable representation of liquidity positions.

In this code example, we will discuss a guide released by Uniswap on creating a smart contract that can custody a Uniswap V3 LP position as the one depicted in **Figure 9**.[13] The full code is as follows:

```solidity
// SPDX-License-Identifier: GPL-2.0-or-later
pragma solidity =0.7.6;
pragma abicoder v2;

import '@uniswap/v3-core/contracts/interfaces/IUniswapV3Pool.sol';
import '@uniswap/v3-core/contracts/libraries/TickMath.sol';
import '@openzeppelin/contracts/token/ERC721/IERC721Receiver.sol';
import '../libraries/TransferHelper.sol';
import '../interfaces/INonfungiblePositionManager.sol';
import '../base/LiquidityManagement.sol';

contract LiquidityExamples is IERC721Receiver {
    address public constant DAI =
0x6B175474E89094C44Da98b954EedeAC495271d0F;
    address public constant USDC = 0xA0b86991c6218b36c1d19D4a2e9Eb-
0cE3606eB48;

    uint24 public constant poolFee = 3000;

    INonfungiblePositionManager public immutable
nonfungiblePositionManager;

    /// @notice Represents the deposit of an NFT
    struct Deposit {
        address owner;
        uint128 liquidity;
        address token0;
        address token1;
    }

    /// @dev deposits[tokenId] => Deposit
    mapping(uint256 => Deposit) public deposits;

    constructor(
        INonfungiblePositionManager _nonfungiblePositionManager
    ) {
        nonfungiblePositionManager = _nonfungiblePositionManager;
    }

    // Implementing `onERC721Received` so this contract can receive
custody of erc721 tokens
    function onERC721Received(
        address operator,
        address,
        uint256 tokenId,
        bytes calldata
```

---

[13] View the full guide at https://docs.uniswap.org/contracts/v3/guides/providing-liquidity/setting-up.

```
    ) external override returns (bytes4) {
        // get position information

        _createDeposit(operator, tokenId);

        return this.onERC721Received.selector;
    }
    function _createDeposit(address owner, uint256 tokenId) internal {
        (, , address token0, address token1, , , , uint128 liquidity, , ,
, ) =
            nonfungiblePositionManager.positions(tokenId);

        // set the owner and data for position
        // operator is msg.sender
        deposits[tokenId] = Deposit({owner: owner, liquidity: liquidity,
token0: token0, token1: token1});
    }
}
```

The main function that allows the contract to receive, custody, and store data on a position is the **onERC721Received** function, which is a part of the inherited ERC721Receiver contract from OpenZeppelin. The function allows the contract to receive an ERC-721 NFT while simultaneously retrieving information about the LP position using the **_createDeposit** function. The **_createDeposit** function calls the **positions** function in the **nonfungiblePositionManager** contract that governs

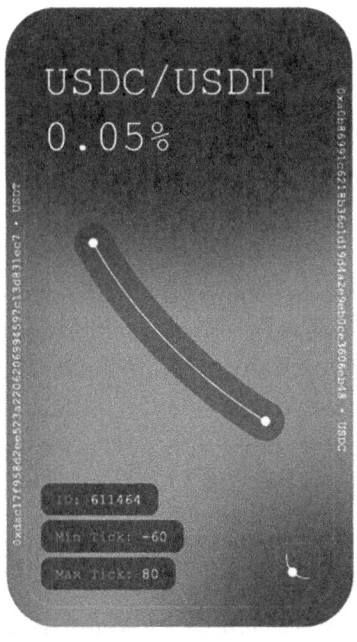

Figure 9   NFT representing an LP position in the USDC/USDT pool with 0.05% fee

Uniswap V3 LP positions. The **positions** function returns information for a particular position through the unique token ID that each NFT is assigned. Information like the pool tokens, fee tier, price range, liquidity deposited, uncollected fees, and more are returned by the function.[14] Our contract stores the pool token addresses and the liquidity of the position in the **deposits** mapping. Once the contract has custodied LP positions, any user can interact with it and find out more about the positions by providing the unique token ID to the **deposits** mapping.

6. Concluding Remarks

We have seen that NFTs are unique digital assets that represent ownership or proof of authenticity of specific items or content on a blockchain. Unlike cryptocurrencies, NFTs are not interchangeable, as each one has unique metadata. NFTs provide a transparent and immutable record of ownership and provenance, ensuring that creators and buyers can verify the authenticity of digital assets. This aspect is crucial for maintaining value and trust in digital markets. NFTs leverage smart contracts, allowing creators to set rules and conditions for their use. This enables complex interactions, such as royalty distribution, access control, and fractional ownership, which extends the utility of NFTs beyond static digital images.

One thing I'd like you to keep in mind is to remember what the technology allows, not just the specific applications that have emerged so far. While NFTs are popularly known for representing digital art, they have a wide range of applications, far beyond the (not so) nice ape pictures. NFTs can represent ownership of virtual real estate, digital collectibles, music, videos, and even real-world assets like event tickets, real estate deeds, or intellectual property. And we are going to see all of these in the next few chapters.

At this point, it is worth emphasizing one aspect: digital ownership through NFTs challenges traditional legal frameworks that govern property and copyright. One significant issue is the enforcement of rights across jurisdictions, given the global nature of blockchain networks. The decentralized and borderless characteristics of these networks complicate the application of national laws, requiring new legal interpretations and international cooperation.

However, NFTs intersect the legal system in other areas as well. While NFTs offer a novel way to certify and trade digital art and collectibles, they also raise questions about copyright ownership. For example, when an artist mints an NFT of their artwork, the buyer acquires a blockchain-based token of ownership, but this does not necessarily transfer the copyright of the artwork itself. The distinction between owning the token and owning the copyright to the underlying art remains a nuanced issue, as seen in cases like the lawsuit involving "MetaBirkins," where luxury brand Hermès

---

[14] View the full documentation at https://docs.uniswap.org/contracts/v3/reference/periphery/NonfungiblePositionManager#positions.

contested the unauthorized use of their Birkin bag trademark in an NFT collection (see Chapter 11).

The NFT space also grapples with issues of counterfeits, fraud, and market manipulation. The open and pseudonymous nature of blockchain can facilitate the creation and sale of counterfeit NFTs, challenging buyers to verify authenticity. Furthermore, instances of wash trading, where sellers trade NFTs with themselves to inflate prices, highlight the need for greater transparency and regulatory oversight.

Emerging technologies, such as layer-2 scaling solutions and interoperable blockchain protocols, promise to enhance the efficiency, scalability, and usability of NFTs. These advancements could address current limitations, enabling more sustainable practices and broader adoption. Furthermore, the development of new standards beyond ERC-721 and ERC-1155 could introduce features like enhanced rights management and improved interaction between NFTs and physical assets.

Regulatory clarity is crucial for the continued growth of the NFT market. Authorities worldwide are beginning to address the unique challenges posed by NFTs, focusing on consumer protection, copyright enforcement, and anti-money laundering (AML) compliance. The evolving regulatory landscape will likely influence market practices, with potential implications for creators, collectors, and platforms. Efforts to harmonize regulations across jurisdictions could foster a more stable and trustworthy environment for NFT transactions.

As digital ownership becomes more entrenched in our social and economic fabric, future market trends will likely reflect the diversification of NFT applications, including virtual real estate, gaming, and identity verification. The integration of NFTs with emerging technologies like augmented reality (AR) and virtual reality (VR) could further blur the lines between physical and digital worlds, creating new opportunities for interaction and commerce.

The trajectory of NFTs points toward a future where digital assets play a central role in our lives, challenging us to reconsider concepts of ownership, value, and community. As the ecosystem evolves, balancing innovation with ethical considerations and legal compliance will be crucial for harnessing the full potential of NFTs while ensuring a sustainable and equitable digital future.

Code Example: Dynamic NFT Valuation Algorithm

In this example we will go through a Python script that uses random forests to valuate an NFT. We will use the OpenSea API get the sales data of NFTs, where you need an API key from OpenSea. To get an API from OpenSea, you will need to create a profile with your wallet and then go to Profile > Settings > Developer.

Therefore, we will have two separate scripts, one to get the data and another to train our model.

The following script will scrape sales information from OpenSea:

```python
import argparse
import csv
from datetime import datetime, timezone
import requests
from time import sleep
import sys

# Manually input your OpenSea API key here
OPENSEA_APIKEY = 'your_opensea_api_key_here'

if OPENSEA_APIKEY == '':
    sys.exit('OPENSEA_APIKEY is empty. Please set your API key.')

def get_events(start_date, end_date, cursor='', event_type='successful',
**kwargs):
    url = "https://api.opensea.io/api/v1/events"
    query = {"only_opensea": "false",
            "occurred_before": end_date,
            "occurred_after": start_date,
            "event_type": event_type,
            "cursor": cursor,
            **kwargs
            }

    headers = {
        "Accept": "application/json",
        "X-API-KEY": OPENSEA_APIKEY
    }
    response = requests.request("GET", url, headers=headers,
params=query)

    return response.json()

def parse_event(event):
    record = {}
    asset = event.get('asset')
    if asset is None:
        return None

    record['collection_slug'] = asset['collection']['slug']
    record['collection_name'] = asset['collection']['name']
    record['collection_url'] = "https://opensea.io/collection/" +
asset['collection']['slug']
    record['vasset_id'] = asset['id']
    record['asset_name'] = asset['name']
    record['asset_description'] = asset['description']
    record['asset_contract_date'] = asset['asset_contract']
['created_date']
    record['asset_url'] = asset['permalink']
    record['asset_img_url'] = asset['image_url']
    record['event_id'] = event['id']
```

```
    record['event_time'] = event.get('created_date')
    record['event_auction_type'] = event.get('auction_type')
    record['event_contract_address'] = event.get('contract_address')
    record['event_quantity'] = event.get('quantity')
    record['event_payment_symbol'] = event.get('payment_token', {}).
get('symbol', None)

    decimals = event.get('payment_token', {}).get('decimals', 18)
    price_str = event['total_price']

    try:
        if len(price_str) < decimals:
            price_str = "0." + "0" * (decimals - len(price_str)) +
price_str
            record['event_total_price'] = float(price_str)
        else:
            record['event_total_price'] = float(price_str[:-decimals] +
"." + price_str[-decimals:])
    except Exception as e:
        print(f"Error processing price: {e}")
        print(event)

    return record

def fetch_all_events(start_date, end_date, pause=1, **kwargs):
    result = []
    next_cursor = ''
    fetch = True

    print(f"Fetching events between {start_date} and {end_date}")
    while fetch:
        response = get_events(int(start_date.timestamp()), int(end_date.
timestamp()), cursor=next_cursor, **kwargs)

        for event in response['asset_events']:
            cleaned_event = parse_event(event)

            if cleaned_event is not None:
                result.append(cleaned_event)

        next_cursor = response.get('next')
        if not next_cursor:
            fetch = False

        sleep(pause)

    return result

def write_csv(data, filename):
    with open(filename, mode='w', encoding='utf-8', newline='') as
csv_file:
        writer = csv.DictWriter(csv_file, fieldnames=data[0].keys())
        writer.writeheader()
```

```
        for event in data:
            writer.writerow(event)

def valid_datetime(arg_datetime_str):
    try:
        return datetime.strptime(arg_datetime_str, "%Y-%m-%d %H:%M")
    except ValueError:
        return datetime.strptime(arg_datetime_str, "%Y-%m-%d")
```

You can run the functions as follows:

```
# Setting the dates for fetching data
start_date = datetime.strptime("2023-04-01", "%Y-%m-%d")
end_date = datetime.strptime("2023-04-10", "%Y-%m-%d")

# Fetching the events
events = fetch_all_events(start_date, end_date)

# Saving the fetched events to a CSV file
if events:
    write_csv(events, 'output.csv')
    print("Data saved to 'output.csv'.")
else:
    print("No events fetched.")
```

Now, if everything works well, output.csv will have the columns we specify in the parse_event function. We will use random forests to estimate the sales price of a given NFT. Now we have our model:

```
import pandas as pd
from sklearn.model_selection import train_test_split
from sklearn.preprocessing import OneHotEncoder
from sklearn.compose import ColumnTransformer
from sklearn.pipeline import Pipeline
from sklearn.impute import SimpleImputer

# Load the dataset
data = pd.read_csv('nft_sales.csv')

# Fill missing numeric data
data.fillna({
    'event_total_price': 0,  # Assuming a missing price means no sale
    'event_quantity': 1  # Default to one if missing
}, inplace=True)

# Define categorical and numeric features
categorical_features = ['collection_slug', 'event_auction_type',
'event_payment_symbol']
numeric_features = ['event_quantity']
```

```
# Preprocessing for categorical data
categorical_transformer = Pipeline(steps=[
    ('imputer', SimpleImputer(strategy='constant',
fill_value='missing')),
    ('onehot', OneHotEncoder(handle_unknown='ignore'))
])

# Combine transformers
preprocessor = ColumnTransformer(
    transformers=[
        ('cat', categorical_transformer, categorical_features),
        ('num', 'passthrough', numeric_features)
    ])

from sklearn.ensemble import RandomForestRegressor
from sklearn.metrics import mean_squared_error
from sklearn.pipeline import make_pipeline

# Create a modeling pipeline
model = make_pipeline(preprocessor, RandomForestRegressor(n_estima-
tors=100, random_state=42))

# Split the data into training and testing sets
X = data.drop(['event_total_price', 'event_id', 'asset_id', 'collection_
url', 'asset_url', 'asset_img_url', 'event_time'], axis=1)
y = data['event_total_price']
X_train, X_test, y_train, y_test = train_test_split(X, y, test_size=0.2,
random_state=42)

# Train the model
model.fit(X_train, y_train)

# Predict and evaluate the model
y_pred = model.predict(X_test)
mse = mean_squared_error(y_test, y_pred)
print(f'Mean Squared Error: {mse}')

from sklearn.model_selection import GridSearchCV

# Parameter grid for Random Forest
param_grid = {
    'randomforestregressor__n_estimators': [50, 100, 200],
    'randomforestregressor__max_features': ['auto', 'sqrt', 'log2'],
    'randomforestregressor__max_depth': [None, 10, 20, 30]
}

# Grid search to find better parameters
grid_search = GridSearchCV(model, param_grid, cv=5)
grid_search.fit(X_train, y_train)
print(f'Best parameters: {grid_search.best_params_}')
print(f'Best cross-validation score: {grid_search.best_score_}')
```

Using joblib, we can save our random forests model and try to estimate the price for a given NFT.

```
import joblib

# Save the model
joblib.dump(grid_search.best_estimator_, 'nft_valuation_model.pkl')

# Function to load and use the model
def predict_nft_price(input_data):
    model = joblib.load('nft_valuation_model.pkl')
    prediction = model.predict(input_data)
    return prediction
```

This is a simple example of how you can use OpenSea API to gather data and build your own valuation model. To see what are the other endpoints that are available, you can visit OpenSea's developer section.

ERC-721: THE STANDARD FOR NON-FUNGIBLE DIGITAL ASSETS

The ERC-721 standard, in particular, has become the cornerstone for creating and managing NFTs. It provides a robust framework that ensures each token's uniqueness, ownership, and transferability, making it ideal for a wide range of applications from digital art to virtual real estate.

Design and Functionalities

The ERC-721 standard is designed to handle the unique needs of non-fungible tokens. Here are the key functionalities that make it the go-to standard for NFTs:

- **Uniqueness:** Each ERC-721 token is unique, represented by a unique identifier (token ID) within its contract. This uniqueness allows the token to represent distinct digital or physical assets, such as artwork, collectibles, or real estate.
- **Ownership:** The standard defines ownership details, ensuring that each token has a single owner at a time. Ownership is transferred through secure transactions, allowing for the safe buying, selling, and trading of NFTs.
- **Transferability:** ERC-721 includes functions for transferring tokens between accounts. It ensures that only the owner (or an approved delegate) can initiate a transfer, thereby securing the process.

- **Approval Mechanism:** Owners can approve another account to transfer a specific NFT on their behalf, facilitating interactions with marketplaces and other contracts without relinquishing ownership until the transaction is complete.

Technical Aspects

The following are the technical aspects:

- The standard specifies a set of required and optional methods and events. Key methods include **balanceOf, ownerOf, transferFrom, approve**, and **getApproved**.
- ERC-721 contracts keep track of the total number of tokens, and each token's owner, through mappings in the contract's state.
- Metadata extensions (optional) can link each token to external metadata (e.g. JSON files), providing detailed descriptions of the asset the NFT represents.
- In particular, the standard requires that contracts include the following functions and events[15]:

```solidity
pragma solidity ^0.4.20;
interface ERC721 {

    event Transfer(address indexed _from, address indexed _to,
uint256 indexed _tokenId);

    event Approval(address indexed _owner, address indexed _
approved, uint256 indexed _tokenId);

    event ApprovalForAll(address indexed _owner, address indexed
_operator, bool _approved);

    function balanceOf(address _owner) external view returns
(uint256);

    function ownerOf(uint256 _tokenId) external view returns
(address);

    function safeTransferFrom(address _from, address _to, uint256
_tokenId, bytes data) external payable;

    function safeTransferFrom(address _from, address _to, uint256
_tokenId) external payable;

    function transferFrom(address _from, address _to, uint256 _
tokenId) external payable;
```

---

[15] See the code from the ERC-721 proposal at https://eips.ethereum.org/EIPS/eip-721.

```
    function approve(address _approved, uint256 _tokenId) external
payable;

    function setApprovalForAll(address _operator, bool _approved)
external;

    function getApproved(uint256 _tokenId) external view returns
(address);

    function isApprovedForAll(address _owner, address _operator)
external view returns (bool);
}

interface ERC165 {
    function supportsInterface(bytes4 interfaceID) external view
returns (bool);
}
```

ERC-1155: A Multitoken Standard for Efficient Asset Management

The ERC-1155 standard introduces a versatile approach to managing various types of tokens within a single smart contract. This innovation is particularly beneficial for applications that require the handling of both fungible and non-fungible tokens, streamlining processes and reducing costs. ERC-1155 is designed to enhance efficiency and flexibility, making it a powerful tool for complex asset management systems.

Design and Functionalities

The ERC-1155 standard offers several key functionalities that set it apart from other token standards:

- **Multitoken Flexibility:** ERC-1155 enables a single contract to represent multiple token types, both fungible and non-fungible. This flexibility allows for the creation of complex assets systems, where a single contract can manage an entire collection of unique digital items, alongside fungible tokens (like currencies or points).
- **Batch Transfers:** One of ERC-1155's hallmark features is the ability to perform batch transfers, significantly reducing the gas costs associated with transferring multiple tokens and improving transaction efficiency.
- **Unified Interface:** The standard provides a unified, consistent interface for interacting with various token types, streamlining development and interaction processes across different applications.

Technical Aspects

The following are the technical aspects:

- **Methods and Events:** ERC-1155 defines a comprehensive API for interacting with the contract, including **balanceOf, balanceOfBatch, safeTransferFrom, safeBatchTransferFrom**, and approval mechanisms similar to ERC-721 but extended for batch operations.
- **Efficiency and Storage:** By enabling a single contract to manage multiple types of tokens, ERC-1155 optimizes the use of storage on the Ethereum blockchain, reducing the redundancy and inefficiency associated with deploying multiple single-type token contracts.
- **Metadata and URI Handling:** ERC-1155 supports a metadata URI that can be customized per token ID. This URI can point to metadata that differentiates each token, even when they are of the same type. The standard allows for on-chain and off-chain metadata, providing flexibility in how assets are described and presented.
- More specifically, the contract must include the following functions and events to comply with the standard[16]:

```solidity
pragma solidity ^0.5.9;

interface ERC1155 /* is ERC165 */ {

    event TransferSingle(address indexed _operator, address indexed
_from, address indexed _to, uint256 _id, uint256 _value);

    event TransferBatch(address indexed _operator, address indexed
_from, address indexed _to, uint256[] _ids, uint256[] _values);

    event ApprovalForAll(address indexed _owner, address indexed
_operator, bool _approved);

    event URI(string _value, uint256 indexed _id);

    function safeTransferFrom(address _from, address _to, uint256
_id, uint256 _value, bytes calldata _data) external;

    function safeBatchTransferFrom(address _from, address _to,
uint256[] calldata _ids, uint256[] calldata _values, bytes call-
data _data) external;

    function balanceOf(address _owner, uint256 _id) external view
returns (uint256);
```

---

[16] View the documentation at https://eips.ethereum.org/EIPS/eip-1155.

```
    function balanceOfBatch(address[] calldata _owners, uint256[]
calldata _ids) external view returns (uint256[] memory);

    function setApprovalForAll(address _operator, bool _approved)
external;

    function isApprovedForAll(address _owner, address _operator)
external view returns (bool);
}
```

Differences and Use Cases

These are use cases of the standards:

- **ERC-721** is ideal for scenarios where each asset needs to be distinctly identified and treated as a separate entity, with a focus on the uniqueness and individuality of each token.
- **ERC-1155** shines in use cases requiring a mix of fungible and non-fungible assets under a single contract, emphasizing efficiency, especially for gaming environments, where numerous types of assets (e.g. weapons, armor, currencies) need to be managed seamlessly.

Both ERC-721 and ERC-1155 have significantly contributed to the development and proliferation of NFTs, each serving distinct needs within the ecosystem and offering developers the flexibility to choose the most appropriate standard based on their specific use case requirements.

End-of-Chapter Questions

Multiple-Choice Questions

1. **Which token standard is most used for creating NFTs on the Ethereum blockchain?**
   (A) ERC-20
   (B) ERC-721
   (C) ERC-1155
   (D) ERC-777

2. **In the context of NFTs, what is the primary function of a "smart contract"?**
   (A) To facilitate high-speed internet connections
   (B) To automate the execution and enforcement of agreements without intermediaries
   (C) To encrypt NFT data for security purposes
   (D) To increase the transaction speed on the blockchain

3. **What mechanism allows NFTs to be uniquely identifiable and prevents them from being interchangeable?**
   (A) Blockchain hashing algorithms
   (B) Digital signatures
   (C) Metadata embedded in the token
   (D) Public-key cryptography

4. **How can NFT creators ensure their digital artwork remains accessible over time and is not lost due to web hosting issues?**
   (A) By storing the artwork on centralized servers
   (B) By utilizing decentralized file storage systems like InterPlanetary File System (IPFS)
   (C) By emailing copies to themselves for backup
   (D) By posting the artwork on social media platforms for public record

5. **What is the significance of the ERC-1155 token standard in the development of NFTs and digital assets?**
   (A) It allows for the creation of fungible tokens only
   (B) It enables a single contract to mint both fungible and non-fungible tokens, optimizing transaction and storage costs
   (C) It is used exclusively for creating digital currencies like Bitcoin and Ethereum
   (D) It restricts the creation of digital assets to only high-value items

6. **What makes an NFT different from a cryptocurrency like Bitcoin?**
   (A) NFTs can be used only for art transactions
   (B) Each NFT is unique and cannot be exchanged on a one-to-one basis like cryptocurrencies
   (C) NFTs have no monetary value
   (D) Cryptocurrencies are not supported by blockchain technology

7. **How can the ownership of an NFT be verified?**
   (A) Through a written certificate
   (B) By checking the blockchain
   (C) Via email confirmation
   (D) Ownership is anonymous and cannot be verified

8. **Which of the following is a use case for NFTs?**
   (A) Representing ownership of physical real estate
   (B) Digital art collections
   (C) Standardizing online payments
   (D) Facilitating high-speed internet connections

9. **What role do smart contracts play in the context of NFTs?**
   (A) They determine the internet speed required to download NFTs
   (B) They act as the legal paperwork for transferring real estate
   (C) They automate the execution of an agreement so that all participants can be immediately certain of the outcome, without any intermediary's involvement
   (D) They reduce the file size of digital art

10. **Which feature of NFTs has primarily contributed to their popularity in digital art markets?**
    (A) Anonymity of ownership
    (B) The ability to replicate the digital art an infinite number of times
    (C) Proof of ownership and authenticity
    (D) The requirement for physical storage

11. **What does "minting" an NFT mean?**
    (A) Printing a physical copy of a digital art piece
    (B) Creating a new NFT on the blockchain
    (C) Exchanging two NFTs between owners
    (D) Destroying an NFT

12. **How does the concept of "rarity" affect the value of an NFT?**
    (A) Rarity is not a factor in valuing NFTs
    (B) The rarer the NFT, the lower its value due to lack of demand
    (C) Rarity and uniqueness can significantly increase an NFT's value
    (D) All NFTs are equally rare, making rarity irrelevant

13. **What is one criticism often levied against NFTs?**
    (A) They simplify the art creation process too much
    (B) They are too similar to cryptocurrencies
    (C) The environmental impact of the energy consumption required for blockchain transactions
    (D) They can only be bought with traditional currencies

Open Questions

1. Discuss how NFTs have impacted the digital art market. Include examples of how artists have benefited from this technology.
2. Explain the significance of blockchain technology in verifying the authenticity and ownership of NFTs.
3. How do smart contracts contribute to the functionality and security of NFT transactions?
4. Analyze the potential environmental impacts of NFTs and discuss possible solutions to mitigate these concerns.
5. Explore the future possibilities of NFT technology beyond digital art. Consider areas such as gaming, real estate, and intellectual property rights.

Coding Exercises

Exercise 1: Representing Tickets to a Concert

Objective: Develop an NFT smart contract that represents a digital ticket to a concert. Each ticket should be uniquely identifiable with information regarding the artist, venue, date, and seating. The contract should have functionality for verification that allows the holder to enter the venue, and transfers so that the holder can resell the ticket on a marketplace.

Detailed Instructions:
1. **Contract setup:** Begin with OpenZeppelin's ERC-1155 smart contract framework so that your NFT adheres to all necessary standards.
2. **Concert Information:** Embed information about the concert in the metadata, such as the artist, venue, date of the concert, and seating information.
3. **Transfer:** Implement a function that allows the NFT to be transferred and sold on marketplaces in the event that the holder would like to resell the ticket.
4. **Verification:** Implement a function that allows concert staff to verify the authenticity of the ticket and ensure the ticket cannot be reused or transferred after it has been used.
5. **Testing:** Write tests to verify that all functions work as intended, especially the verification and usage of the ticket so that holders cannot "double spend" the ticket after use.

Exercise 2: Liquidity Provision on Uniswap V3

Objective: Develop a smart contract or adjust the Uniswap V3 LP custody example to allow a user to mint a new Uniswap V3 position, custody the NFT, adjust the liquidity and price range, collect fees, and remove all liquidity.

Detailed Instructions:
1. **Contract setup:** Begin with the Uniswap example or a new smart contract that can receive and custody ERC-721 NFTs.
2. **Adding liquidity:** Implement a function that allows users to deposit liquidity into a Uniswap V3 pool. The contract should have flexibility over the pair, fee tier, and price range. Upon deposit, receive and provide custody of the NFT.
3. **Tracking a position:** Include a function that allows the user to track information about the position, such as liquidity, and fees accumulated.
4. **Adjusting liquidity:** Allow the user to adjust the position through changes in liquidity, or changes in price range. When the price of the pool moves, investors may want to adjust the price range of their LP position to continue maximizing the efficiency of their capital, so including such a function is crucial.

5. **Collecting fees:** In Uniswap V3, fees are not accrued in the pool liquidity. Instead, they are set aside and allocated to each LP as unclaimed fees until they are specifically claimed in a transaction, or claimed automatically when liquidity is adjusted. Implement a function that allows the user to collect any unclaimed fees without having to adjust the position.

6. **Remove liquidity:** Finally, implement a function that allows the investor to exit their LP position completely and transfer all tokens back to the investor.

7. **Safety Mechanisms:** Implement safeguards against malicious actors and events such as hackers attempting to take control of the custodied positions, reentrancy guards, etc.

8. **Testing:** Include a comprehensive set of tests that ensure the contract functions as intended, such as ensuring that the contract is correctly adjusting liquidity, ensuring that functions that manage the LP position can only be called by the owner or allowed proxies, and ensuring that the information tracking the position is accurate.

Chapter 11

Regulatory Framework

Work in Progress

Preface

Picture this: the cryptocurrency landscape, a wild west of digital finance, buzzing with the electricity of innovation and the shadow of uncertainty. Into this fray steps the regulatory sheriff, tasked with the Herculean endeavor of taming the beast while fostering the growth of this financial frontier. At the heart of this epic saga is the eternal tussle between freedom and control, where the dreams of a bull market draw in legions of hopeful investors, only to be occasionally dashed by the spectacular implosions of crypto giants. FTX was like that guy who claims he can do a backflip, only to land on his face. And just like that, the regulators are suddenly interested in gymnastics.

To navigate this treacherous terrain, we embark on a quest to understand the Holy Grails of regulation: protecting the innocents (investors), ensuring the kingdom (market) remains pure (integrity), and banishing the dragons (financial crimes). Yet, our noble quest is fraught with peril. The crypto realm, with its arcane magics of decentralization, anonymity, and cross-border escapades, defies the conventional spells of regulation. The old scrolls of financial law, crafted in the age of traditional markets, find themselves ill-suited to the task.

Thus, the regulatory mages are tasked with crafting new spells—innovative regulatory strategies—that balance the twin mandates of oversight and fostering innovation. Their goal? To ensure the crypto realm is neither a lawless wasteland nor a stifled domain

The crypto wild west

where innovation fears to tread. As we stand on the precipice of change, watching regulatory bodies across the globe engage in this alchemical endeavor, we are reminded that the future of crypto is not merely in the hands of those who trade and invest but also in those who govern and guide.

We are witnesses to a grand experiment in financial history. The outcomes of these endeavors will shape not just the future of cryptocurrency but the very essence of global finance.

1. Introduction: Regulatory Objectives

From its inception, the regulatory stance on cryptocurrency has been a hotly debated topic, capturing the headlines, and keeping market professionals on their toes. The surge into a bull market, attracting scores of new retail investors, followed by the dramatic failures of prominent entities like FTX, has only intensified this discussion.

To set the stage for upcoming developments, we start by considering the core objectives of regulation in both traditional and crypto markets. These include safeguarding investors, maintaining market integrity, and thwarting financial crimes. However, the unique attributes of the crypto market—such as decentralization, anonymity, and the ease of cross-border transactions—pose distinct challenges to these goals. While existing regulations for traditional financial markets offer a foundational structure, the peculiar nature of crypto assets demands inventive regulatory strategies. These strategies must strike a careful balance between ensuring sufficient oversight and fostering technological innovation and financial inclusivity. Regulatory bodies across the globe are striving to achieve this equilibrium, with critical advancements anticipated as the crypto market continues its evolution. **Figure 1** presents the key regulatory objectives and how those are implemented in traditional markets and the difficulties to reach the same goal in the crypto markets.

In traditional finance, AML/CFT regulations are well-established, with financial institutions required to perform due diligence on their customers (Know Your Customer,

Objective	Traditional Markets	Crypto Asset Markets
Anti-Money Laundering/Counter-Financing of Terrorism (AML/CFT)	Well established regulatory frameworks for prevention	Decentralized nature creates challenges in providing a global framework
Investor Protection	Institutions try to ensure transparency and fair trading	Lack of disclosure requirements leads to risks
Market Integrity	Regulations attempt to limit market manipulation and improve efficient trading	Hard to maintain market integrity because of decentralization and global activity

Figure 1   Regulatory objectives and traditional markets versus crypto assets markets

or KYC), monitor transactions for suspicious activity, and report to regulatory authorities. These measures are crucial in preventing the financial system from being exploited for money laundering or financing terrorism. Whereas, the pseudo-anonymous nature of cryptocurrency transactions complicates AML/CFT efforts. While blockchain technology provides a transparent transaction ledger, identifying the parties involved without additional information is challenging. Regulators worldwide are extending AML/CFT regulations to crypto asset service providers (CASPs), mandating KYC processes, and monitoring and reporting suspicious activities. The primary challenge lies in creating a global standard, as the decentralized nature of cryptocurrencies allows for cross-border transactions outside the purview of national regulations.

Similarly, investor protection in traditional markets is achieved through regulations that ensure transparency, fair trading practices, and the provision of accurate information to investors. Regulatory bodies like the U.S. Securities and Exchange Commission (SEC) and the European Securities and Markets Authority (ESMA) in Europe enforce these regulations, which include disclosures by publicly traded companies, oversight of investment products, and actions against fraudulent activities. The lack of consistent disclosure requirements and the prevalence of scams and market manipulation in crypto markets, on the other hand, pose risks to investors. Even though regulators are beginning to address these issues by proposing regulations that would bring transparency and accountability to the crypto market, the sector's global and decentralized nature complicates enforcement.

Market integrity in traditional markets is maintained through regulations that prevent market manipulation, insider trading, and other unethical practices. Strict surveillance mechanisms and penalties are in place to detect and deter such activities, ensuring that markets operate fairly and efficiently. The crypto market's integrity faces challenges from high price volatility, thin liquidity in some assets, and potential for manipulation through tactics like "pump and dump" schemes.[1] The global and fragmented nature of the crypto market, along with the lack of a centralized regulatory authority, makes it difficult to monitor and enforce market integrity effectively. Some countries are beginning to implement regulations aimed at crypto market surveillance and fraud prevention, but global coordination is needed for comprehensive oversight.

U.S. Regulators　　One of the reasons behind the apparent difficulty to regulate the crypto market in the United States is that the regulatory landscape for crypto assets is multifaceted and governed by various regulatory bodies each with its distinct mandate and focus areas which create the splendid cacophony of U.S. crypto regulation. The primary regulators include the SEC, the Commodity Futures Trading Commission (CFTC), the Financial Crimes Enforcement Network (FinCEN), and the Internal Revenue Service (IRS).

The SEC plays a pivotal role in regulating and overseeing the securities markets in the United States, with its jurisdiction extending to digital assets deemed to be securities. The agency's approach to crypto assets primarily hinges on the application of the Howey Test, a 1946 Supreme Court decision criterion used to determine what constitutes an investment contract (and therefore a security). It is like using a VHS tape to explain streaming; it's charmingly outdated but somehow still in use. Under this framework, the SEC has pursued actions against various crypto projects and exchanges that it believes are offering unregistered securities. The agency focuses on investor protection, aiming to safeguard investors from fraud and market manipulation within the crypto space.

The CFTC regulates the U.S. derivatives markets, including futures, swaps, and certain types of options. For crypto assets, the CFTC's jurisdiction comes into play when a crypto asset is considered a commodity. Bitcoin, for example, has been classified as a commodity, and thus, derivatives contracts based on Bitcoin fall under the CFTC's purview. The CFTC aims to ensure the integrity of the markets it oversees, protecting against fraud and abusive trading practices. The CFTC and SEC sometimes have overlapping jurisdictions, especially in cases where a crypto asset can be considered both a commodity and a security.

FinCEN, a bureau of the U.S. Department of the Treasury, plays a crucial role in combating money laundering, terrorist financing, and other financial crimes. It requires

---

[1] A "pump-and-dump" scheme involves a coordinated effort to artificially inflate the price of a cryptocurrency by purchasing large quantities and spreading positive, often false, information to create hype around the token and attract unsuspecting investors. Once the price is sufficiently inflated, the orchestrators sell off their holdings, causing the price to plummet and leaving new investors with significant losses. These schemes typically target cryptocurrencies with low market capitalization and trading volume, making them easier to manipulate. In traditional financial markets, pump-and-dump schemes are illegal and actively prosecuted by regulators such as the SEC, but the decentralized and global nature of the cryptocurrency market poses regulatory challenges. To avoid falling victim to such schemes, investors should always conduct their own research, be skeptical of sudden price spikes accompanied by aggressive marketing, and prefer cryptocurrencies with higher liquidity and trading volumes.

businesses involved in the crypto industry, especially those considered money services businesses (MSBs), to comply with Anti-Money Laundering (AML) and Know Your Customer (KYC) regulations. This includes registering with FinCEN, implementing AML programs, and reporting suspicious activities. FinCEN's regulations aim to prevent the use of crypto assets for illicit activities while promoting financial transparency.

The IRS is responsible for tax collection and tax law enforcement and has issued guidance on the tax treatment of cryptocurrencies. According to the IRS, crypto assets are treated as property for tax purposes, meaning that transactions involving cryptocurrencies are subject to capital gains and losses rules. Crypto users are required to report transactions, including buying, selling, and exchanging crypto, on their tax returns. The IRS's approach highlights the importance of tax compliance for individuals and businesses engaged in crypto transactions.

Together, these regulatory bodies form the backbone of the U.S. regulatory framework for crypto assets, each with its specific focus area ranging from securities law compliance, market integrity, anti-money laundering efforts, to tax reporting and compliance. In this eclectic band of regulatory agencies, the challenge isn't just about playing in time; it's about figuring out the genre of music they're supposed to be playing. Each agency brings its own sheet music, based on its mandate and focus areas, leading to a multifaceted regulatory landscape that's as complex as a jazz fusion concert crossed with a symphony orchestra. And in this grand performance, the crypto market dances, trying to keep up with the ever-changing tempo and occasionally stepping on a regulatory toe or two.

So, when you wonder why regulating crypto feels like trying to catch a greased pig at a county fair, remember this symphony of regulatory powers, each playing to the tune of their own statutes and mandates. It's a performance you won't want to miss, complete with improvisations, solo acts, and the occasional cacophony that somehow, against all odds, produces a melody that guides the dynamic world of crypto assets.

2. Are Crypto Assets Securities?

The debate over whether cryptocurrencies are securities is a pivotal discussion with far-reaching implications for investors, developers, regulators, and the broader financial ecosystem.[2] At the heart of this debate is the question of how cryptocurrencies fit into existing regulatory frameworks, particularly those defined by the SEC and other global

---

[2] Many papers have been written about this subject, determining whether crypto assets are securities under various jurisdictions. See https://papers.ssrn.com/sol3/papers.cfm?abstract_id=3075820,
https://papers.ssrn.com/sol3/papers.cfm?abstract_id=4282385,
https://papers.ssrn.com/sol3/papers.cfm?abstract_id=4055585,
https://papers.ssrn.com/sol3/papers.cfm?abstract_id=3272975,
https://papers.ssrn.com/sol3/papers.cfm?abstract_id=3725395,
https://papers.ssrn.com/sol3/papers.cfm?abstract_id=3339551, and
https://faculty.westacademic.com/Book/Detail?id=270263.

financial regulatory bodies. This classification impacts everything from taxation to the legal responsibilities of those who issue, trade, and manage these digital assets.

The criteria for what constitutes a security in the United States hinge on the application of the Howey Test, a standard derived from a 1946 (!) Supreme Court case. According to this test, an investment contract (and thus a security) exists if money is invested in a common enterprise with the expectation of profit to be derived primarily from the efforts of others.

The Howey case involved W. J. Howey Co. and Howey-in-the-Hills Service, Inc., Florida corporations that owned large citrus groves. Howey sold real estate contracts for half of the groves to finance future developments, offering buyers the option to lease the land back to Howey-in-the-Hills for cultivation, harvesting, pooling, and marketing of the produce. This service contract granted Howey-in-the-Hills full possession and control over the land and its produce, with no rights for the purchaser to intervene.

Howey marketed these land sales through a resort hotel it owned, promising significant profits to potential investors, most of whom were not Florida residents or agriculturally knowledgeable. The scheme essentially involved investors buying land and then participating in a leaseback arrangement, expecting profits from the agricultural efforts managed by Howey-in-the-Hills. The Supreme Court needed to determine if the arrangement W. J. Howey was offering to his clients was a security product, regulated by the Securities Acts of 1933 and 1934 or whether it was only a real estate deal, followed by a lease agreement.

One way to better understand how the Howey Test originated from a case about oranges more than seventy years ago might impact the digital asset space today is to apply it to Bitcoin step by step[3]:

1. *Investment of Money*

   The first criterion is clearly met with Bitcoin, as individuals invest money to purchase Bitcoin. This is straightforward and aligns with the initial part of the Howey Test.

2. *Common Enterprise*

   A common enterprise typically refers to the pooling of funds or assets where the fortunes of the investor are interwoven with and dependent upon the efforts and success of those managing the enterprise. Bitcoin operates on a decentralized network without a central authority or party whose efforts are responsible for increasing the value of Bitcoin. Instead, the value of Bitcoin is determined by market supply and demand, making this criterion more complex to apply. The decentralized nature

---

[3] The SEC has provided some guidance through no-action letters, highlighting factors considered when a crypto token is not a security. These factors include the token not being used to build the platform (which must be fully operational at the time of token sale), tokens being immediately usable for their intended purpose, and the tokens being marketed for their functionality rather than investment potential. However, the SEC's guidance has been criticized for being limited and not addressing other types of crypto tokens that are commonly used, leaving many aspects of crypto regulation unclear.

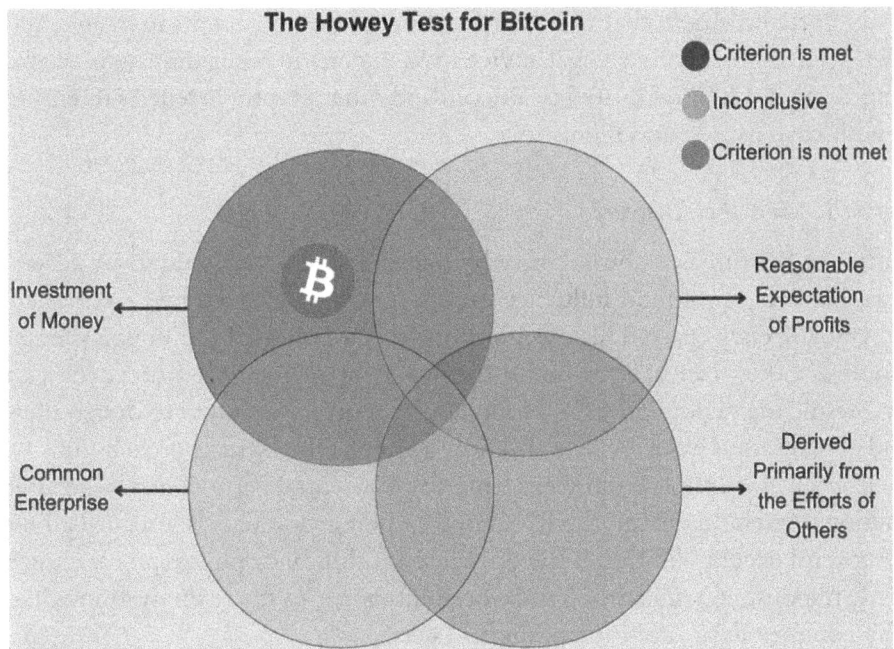

Figure 2   Application of the Howey Test to Bitcoin

of Bitcoin suggests it might not meet this criterion in the traditional sense of a common enterprise.

3. *Reasonable Expectation of Profits*

Investors in Bitcoin might have a reasonable expectation of profits due to the appreciation of Bitcoin's value over time. However, the expectation of profit is based on the market's dynamics—supply and demand—rather than the efforts of a third party or promoter. This distinction is crucial because the expectation of profits must be primarily from the efforts of others for an investment to be considered a security.

4. *Derived Primarily from the Efforts of Others*

This criterion is where Bitcoin distinctly diverges from being considered a security under the Howey Test. Bitcoin's value and operation are not reliant on the efforts of a specific entity or group. Instead, its decentralized protocol allows it to operate and be secured by a distributed network of miners and node operators. The efforts of these participants are not coordinated in a manner that would fulfill the "efforts of others" criterion as intended by the Howey Test; they are independent actors in a large decentralized system.

Applying the Howey Test to Bitcoin suggests that Bitcoin does not qualify as a security (**Figure 2**). The key differentiation lies in the decentralized nature of Bitcoin and the fact that its value and success are not primarily dependent on the efforts of a centralized party or group of promoters. This analysis aligns with the current stance of several regulatory bodies, including the SEC, which has not classified Bitcoin as a security.

However, it's important to note that the interpretation of these criteria can evolve, and regulatory perspectives can change. Legal advice from experts in securities law is crucial for entities engaging in activities related to Bitcoin and other cryptocurrencies to ensure compliance with current laws and regulations.

2.2 Is Decentralization the Answer?

The recognition of Bitcoin as a non-security by regulators, primarily due to its decentralized nature, has had a profound influence on the strategies adopted by practitioners within the cryptocurrency space. This classification has underscored the importance of decentralization as a key factor in avoiding the stringent regulations associated with securities. As a result, many developers and founders have been motivated to design their protocols and digital assets with decentralization at their core. This approach aims to mimic Bitcoin's regulatory treatment by ensuring that no central party controls the asset or its distribution, thereby reducing the likelihood of being classified as a security. This strategic shift toward decentralization is then not just a technical or philosophical choice but a pragmatic response to regulatory frameworks, intending to foster innovation while navigating the complex legal landscape of digital assets.

However, pursuing decentralization as a strategy to navigate securities law is not a catch-all solution. The concept of decentralization itself is nebulous and lacks a clear definition in the eyes of the law, making it a challenging defense against securities classification. This ambiguity becomes particularly evident when applying the Howey Test to Ethereum (ETH), one of the most decentralized cryptocurrencies (**Figure 3**). Despite Ethereum's widespread use and decentralized nature, the application of the Howey Test—which examines the expectation of profits from the efforts of others—illustrates the complexities and uncertainties in determining whether a highly decentralized asset like ETH should be classified as a security.

- **Investment of Money:** Ethereum clearly meets this criterion, as participants invest capital, either through purchasing Ether directly on exchanges or by acquiring and staking Ether in the PoS mechanism.
- **Common Enterprise:** Ethereum's network can be considered a common enterprise, particularly with the shift to PoS. In PoW, the argument for a common enterprise is weaker because miners work independently to validate transactions and are not necessarily dependent on each other's efforts. However, in PoS, validators stake their Ether to secure the network and validate transactions. This staking mechanism creates a more direct reliance on the network's overall success, as validators' rewards are directly tied to their participation in and the performance of the network.
- **Expectation of Profits:** In PoW miners expect profits from their independent efforts to solve cryptographic puzzles. In contrast, in PoS, validators' expectations of profits are more closely tied to the collective success of the Ethereum network.

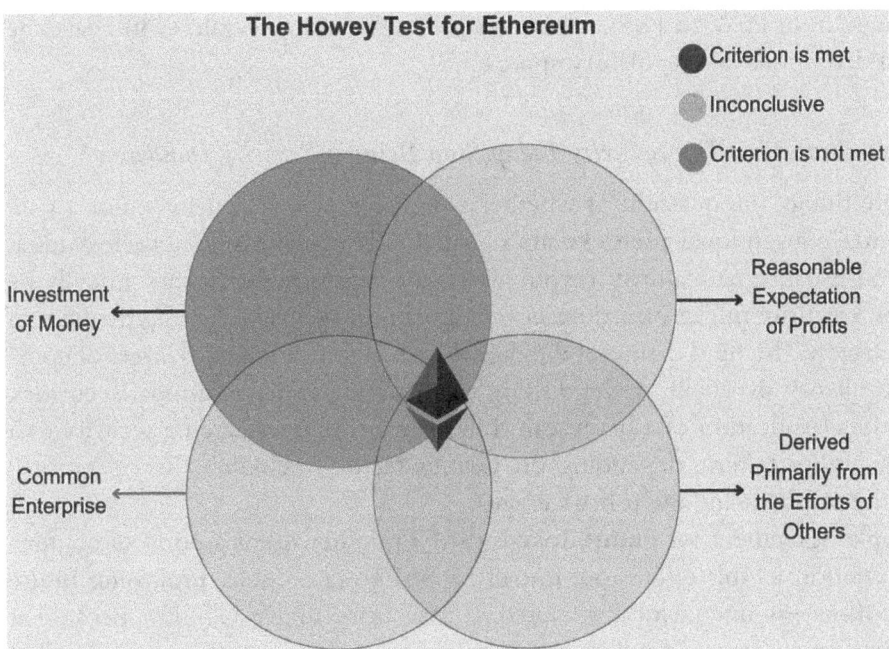

Figure 3 Application of the Howey Test to Ethereum after PoS

Validators receive transaction fees and network rewards, which depend not only on their individual staking and validation efforts but also on the overall functioning and adoption of the Ethereum network. This creates an expectation of profits derived significantly from the efforts of others, including the Ethereum developers and the broader Ethereum community.

- **Derived from the Efforts of Others:** This criterion sees a significant shift in the transition from PoW to PoS. In PoW, the effort is predominantly the miner's computational power. In PoS, while validators must still perform certain actions to participate, the return on investment heavily depends on the management, governance, and development of the Ethereum network by the Ethereum Foundation and other developers. Validators' profits are more directly tied to these third-party efforts in maintaining and improving the network's functionality, security, and adoption.

Thus, with the transition to PoS, Ethereum's reliance on collective participation and the expectation of profits based on the efforts of others (i.e. the Ethereum Foundation and developers) become more pronounced. This shift could make ETH more susceptible to being classified as a security under the Howey Test. The argument hinges on the increased role of the common enterprise's success (the Ethereum network) and the profits derived significantly from the efforts of parties other than the individual investor or validator.

This example highlights a broader issue within cryptocurrency regulation: the difficulty of applying traditional legal frameworks to new and rapidly evolving technologies (e.g. the change from PoW to PoS), where the principles of decentralization challenge conventional definitions and regulatory approaches.[4]

2.3 Can Something That Is a Security Today Stop Being a Security Tomorrow?

To complicate things, the question of whether a digital asset is a security is not a *static* question. Unlike conventional assets like stocks and bonds, which maintain their status as securities from issuance to maturity, crypto assets can transform. What may initially be recognized as a security might, over time, *morph* into a non-security, blurring the lines of regulatory purview. The fluid nature of the digital asset classification adds layers of complexity to regulatory oversight, distinguishing them starkly from traditional securities. Specifically, the classification of a token can shift from being considered a security to a non-security (utility token), depending on various factors including the operational maturity of the platform and the token's usage.

The Simple Agreement for Future Tokens (SAFT) framework is a point of contention and illustration in this discussion. Initially, a SAFT—a contract promising future delivery of tokens—is unequivocally treated as a security under U.S. law because it involves an investment contract where investors put in money with the expectation of profits predominantly from the efforts of others (e.g. the initial protocol's team). The expectation is that once the platform or project is fully functional and the tokens acquire utility apart from investment, the tokens can transition from securities to non-securities. However, this transition is nuanced and subject to regulatory interpretation and scrutiny.

This transition hinges on the decentralization of the network on which the tokens operate and the "economic substance of the transaction." For instance, the SEC and its officials have noted that a token's status as a security could change when it becomes sufficiently decentralized—where the fortunes of the purchasers are no longer dependent on the managerial efforts of a centralized group but on the network's participatory ecosystem. **Figure 4** succinctly depicts how this might occur depending on the characteristics of the transactions.

The morphing from a security token to a utility token is pivotal for several reasons. From the issuer's perspective, ensuring that the initial offering complies with securities registration requirements or falls within an exemption can mitigate concerns about the token's later utility status. However, the ongoing classification impacts exchanges and platforms that trade these tokens, particularly due to the regulatory implications of trading securities versus non-securities. Exchanges operating within or targeting customers

---

[4] Discussions around decentralization as an important factor in regulating crypto has becoming more prominent. Read more about these debates here: https://www.courthousenews.com/decentralized-crypto-platform-can-be-sued-as-general-partnership-judge-rules/#:~:text=Home%20Page-, Decentralized%20crypto%20platform%20 can%20be%20sued%20as%20general%20partnership%2C%20judge,damages%20from%20a%202021%20hack, https://www.quinnemanuel.com/the-firm/publications/sec-0010-aim-at-crypto-platforms-as-unregistered-exchanges/, https://www.coindesk.com/business/2023/03/29/the-liability-of-daos-and-their-founders-has-been-put-to-the-test-in-court/, and https://papers.ssrn.com/sol3/papers.cfm?abstract_id=4065143.

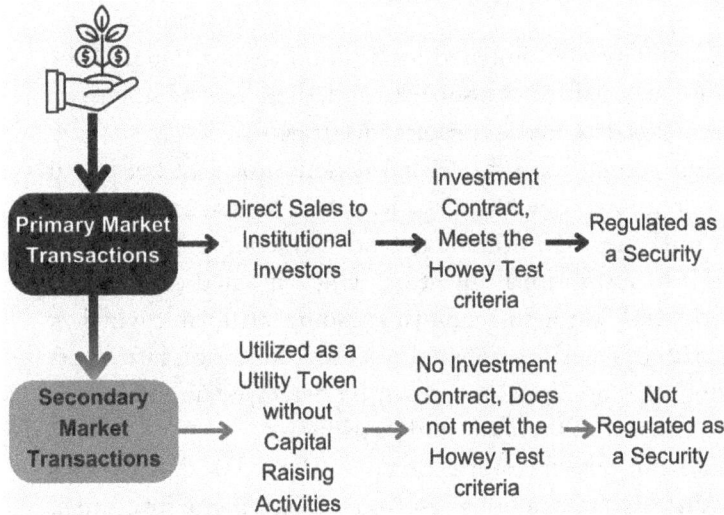

Figure 4   How tokens can be both securities and non-securities depending on the transactions

from jurisdictions like the United States are cautious about listing tokens that may be classified as securities to avoid regulatory breaches.

The morphing theory underscores a broader regulatory challenge: applying traditional securities laws to digital assets that can evolve in their functionality and purpose. This dynamic nature poses questions about how regulators can establish clear, consistent guidelines that accommodate the technological and operational realities of crypto assets while ensuring investor protection and market integrity.

For market participants, navigating this evolving regulatory landscape requires vigilance and adaptability. Entrepreneurs and developers in the crypto space must consider not only the current classification of their tokens but also how future developments might affect their regulatory status. This consideration is crucial for compliance planning, investor relations, and the broader strategic positioning of their projects within the market.

As the crypto market continues to mature, the dialogue between regulators, industry participants, and legal experts will be crucial in shaping a regulatory environment that supports innovation while protecting investors and the integrity of financial markets. While hoping that such a dialogue could be fruitful, the courts in the U.S. have been testing with several prominent cases, one of which is related to Ripple Labs.

RIPPLE CASE

The SEC vs. Ripple Labs case, particularly highlighted by the July 13, 2023 decision by Judge Analisa Torres, represents a landmark moment in the regulatory landscape of the crypto industry and an example of the morphing theory at work. This case centers on the classification of XRP, a digital currency created by Ripple Labs, and whether its distribution and sale constitute securities transactions under U.S. law. The SEC initiated legal action against Ripple Labs, arguing that XRP should be classified as a security and, therefore, be subject to strict regulatory requirements designed to protect investors.

Judge Torres' decision is significant for several reasons, not least because it provides clarity on a contentious issue: the classification of digital assets in secondary market transactions. The court found a crucial distinction between Ripple's direct sales of XRP to institutional investors, which it ruled as securities transactions, and sales of XRP through secondary trading platforms, which it determined did not constitute securities transactions. This bifurcation introduces a nuanced understanding of how digital assets can be perceived and regulated differently based on the context of their sale and distribution.

For direct sales to institutional investors, the court aligned with the SEC's perspective, suggesting that such transactions involved the offering of investment contracts. This is because these sales were directly managed by Ripple and targeted at investors looking to profit from the future efforts of Ripple Labs to increase XRP's value. This classification leans on the application of the Howey Test, a Supreme Court ruling from 1946 that defines a security as an investment of money in a common enterprise with a reasonable expectation of profits to be derived from the efforts of others.

Conversely, the court's stance on secondary market sales is groundbreaking. By ruling that these transactions do not automatically qualify as securities transactions, Judge Torres challenged the SEC's broad application of securities laws to digital assets. This part of the decision underscores the importance of transaction context in determining the regulatory status of crypto assets. It implies that the mere act of buying or selling digital tokens on secondary platforms does not inherently involve an investment contract if those transactions do not directly implicate the issuer's efforts in a way that would qualify them as securities.

The implications of this decision are profound for the crypto industry. It provides a legal precedent that could influence the regulatory treatment of digital assets beyond XRP, affecting a wide array of cryptocurrencies and tokens, especially those whose issuers might fear similar legal challenges from regulatory bodies. The distinction made by Judge Torres offers a more refined lens through which digital assets can be evaluated, suggesting that not all transactions involving these assets should be automatically subjected to securities laws. This perspective could encourage innovation and participation in the crypto market by alleviating some of the regulatory uncertainties that have previously deterred entities from engaging with digital assets.

Following this decision, there were two notable developments. First, Judge Torres denied the SEC's request for an interlocutory appeal, which aimed to challenge the court's findings regarding secondary market sales. This denial means that, at least in the near term, the decision will stand as a non-binding precedent against considering such transactions as securities. Secondly, the SEC voluntarily dismissed charges against individual defendants associated with Ripple, signaling a potential shift in how aggressively the regulatory body will pursue claims against crypto asset issuers and their executives in the future.

The Ripple case, particularly through the lens of the July 2023 decision, paints a complex picture of the evolving regulatory environment for digital assets. It illustrates the legal challenges and debates surrounding the classification and treatment of cryptocurrencies, highlighting the delicate balance regulators must strike between fostering innovation and protecting investors. As the digital asset space continues to grow and diversify, the insights gleaned from this case will undoubtedly play a critical role in shaping the future regulatory landscape, influencing how laws are interpreted and applied to similar cases moving forward.

3. Market Implications of Considering Crypto Assets Securities

One might wonder why the digital world hesitates to embrace the structured domain of securities classification. Indeed, *what's the fuss about being labeled a security?* After all, stepping into the realm of the registered seems like it could save a lot of sleepless nights, tossing and turning over the what-ifs of regulatory boogeymen lurking in the shadows.

Yet, it's not that simple. True, categorizing crypto assets as securities means enveloping them in a regulatory cocoon designed to safeguard investors and promote transparent, efficient markets. However, this move would fundamentally alter the lifecycle of these assets—from their issuance and trade to their governance. If crypto assets were indeed pigeonholed as securities, the implications would be profound, rendering them arguably the most constrained instruments in the market, shackled by regulations unfit for their digital essence. But, before diving deeper into the ramifications, let's unfold the obligations and transformations token issuers must face under the security tag.

3.1 Requirements for Tradable Securities

For crypto assets to be tradable as securities, issuers would need to comply with registration requirements, unless an exemption applies. This involves disclosing detailed information about the asset, the issuer's business, the risks involved, and the use of proceeds from the sale. Such disclosures are intended to provide investors with the information necessary to make informed investment decisions. Crypto market participants have recognized the importance of disclosure and, without clear guidelines, have routinely produced white papers to provide information to investors. However, the requirements to be compliant with securities law are much more extensive. Examples of such compliance challenges include the following:

- **Audited Financial Statements and Internal Controls:** Issuers of securities are required to prepare and provide audited financial statements to regulators and investors, along with implementing internal controls over financial reporting. For many blockchain projects, especially those in early stages or those operating in a decentralized manner, meeting these requirements can be cumbersome especially given the nature of decentralized finance, i.e. who should compile and files the statements?
- **CEO and CFO Certifications:** Securities regulations require that the CEO and CFO of the issuing company certify the accuracy of financial statements and compliance with reporting requirements. This requirement presupposes a centralized entity with identifiable leadership, which might not exist in decentralized projects.
- **Compliance with Regulation Fair Disclosure (FD):** Regulation FD aims to prevent selective disclosure by ensuring that all material information is made available to all investors at the same time. In the context of decentralized projects, where information might be disseminated in a variety of informal channels (e.g. social media, discord channels), ensuring compliance with Regulation FD can be challenging.
- **Quarterly and Annual Reporting:** Securities issuers are obligated to file comprehensive quarterly and annual reports, detailing their financial condition, risk factors, and other material information. For crypto projects, particularly those without clear revenue models or traditional business operations, these requirements may be burdensome and not particularly informative for investors used to evaluating digital asset projects on different criteria.
- **Proxy Statements and Annual Meetings:** Issuers must hold annual shareholder meetings and prepare proxy statements in advance. This presupposes a level of formal corporate structure and shareholder engagement that may not be present or necessary in a crypto project, especially those governed by decentralized autonomous organizations (DAOs) or similar structures.
- **Traditional Shareholder Rights:** Securities regulations grant certain rights to shareholders, including voting rights, dividends, and information rights. However, holders of crypto assets typically do not have rights commonly associated with traditional equity or debt instruments, especially in projects where governance and operational decisions are made through decentralized consensus mechanisms.

Asking a fresh blockchain project to meet all these regulatory requirements is like asking a newborn to run a marathon. Adorable, but wildly unrealistic. These examples also illustrate the dissonance between traditional securities regulations and the nature of crypto projects. Adapting these projects to fit within the existing regulatory framework designed for conventional securities imposes significant operational burdens, and risks stifling innovation, and ultimately not serving the regulatory objectives we discussed at the beginning of this chapter.

3.2 Trading Crypto Assets Recognized as Securities

These disclosure requirements are not the only hurdle. If anything, the key obstacles are dictated by how securities are traded, at least in the United States.

- **Securities Exchange Act Compliance for Trading:** If tokens are classified as securities, they can only be traded on registered national securities exchanges (NSE) or through exempt alternative trading systems (ATS), which are subject to strict regulatory requirements regarding market surveillance, anti-fraud measures, and investor protection. This limitation restricts the ability of digital assets to be traded freely on the multitude of exchanges and platforms currently available in the crypto ecosystem, i.e. they could not be traded on decentralized exchanges like Uniswap.
- **Listing Standards of National Securities Exchanges:** National Securities Exchanges have listing standards that include requirements for financial reporting, corporate governance, and market capitalization. Many crypto projects, particularly those that are open-source and decentralized, cannot meet these standards because they do not have traditional corporate governance structures or clear financial reporting mechanisms.
- **Broker-Dealer and Exchange Registration:** The operation of a platform as a broker-dealer or exchange requires registration and compliance with specific regulatory frameworks. Crypto exchanges and decentralized trading platforms operate under a different model, facilitating peer-to-peer transactions without taking custody of assets, which does not fit neatly into the existing regulatory definitions of exchanges or broker-dealers.
- **Custody Rules:** Securities regulations have strict custody rules to protect investors' assets, requiring registered custodians. The concept of custody differs significantly in the context of crypto assets, where individual control over private keys is a fundamental aspect of asset security and ownership.

Even the current market structure does not seem to be able to fit crypto assets into the security box. Coinbase, for instance, is not classified as a National Securities Exchange (NSE) but operates as a cryptocurrency exchange platform, allowing users to buy, sell, and trade cryptocurrencies. While it is one of the largest and most well-known platforms in the cryptocurrency space, it does not have the same regulatory status or function as a National Securities Exchange, which is specifically designated for trading securities under the regulatory oversight of bodies like the SEC. So, in the case that some digital assets were to be recognized as securities, those could not be traded on Coinbase.

But could crypto assets be traded on other NSE or ATS, then? Unfortunately, in the current state of regulations, no. Securities exchanges must comply with a range of rules concerning market fairness, transparency, and investor protection. This includes requirements related to reporting trades, maintaining an orderly market, and safeguarding against abusive trading practices such as manipulation and insider trading. Cryptocurrencies are often not recognized as securities by their issuers and thus do not conform to these listing and regulatory requirements. Additionally, the decentralized nature of cryptocurrencies and the lack of a centralized issuer pose compliance challenges with traditional securities regulations.

For instance, broker-dealers currently face significant regulatory hurdles when attempting to custody crypto assets, particularly when those assets are recognized as securities. The regulatory framework, primarily governed by the SEC's Customer Protection Rule (Rule 15c3-3), mandates broker-dealers to safeguard customer securities and cash, ensuring their readiness to be returned to customers should the firm fail. This rule, while designed to protect customers' traditional securities, imposes requirements that don't neatly apply to the custody of digital asset securities due to the unique nature of blockchain technology and digital assets.

Digital assets are held in digital wallets, with ownership and transactions verified and recorded on a decentralized ledger, without the need for centralized custodians. The custody of digital assets involves managing cryptographic keys that control access to these assets on the blockchain. Losing these keys can result in the irreversible loss of assets, and unauthorized access can lead to theft, which are concerns not typically associated with traditional securities custody.

Moreover, the decentralized nature of most blockchain-based assets means that there isn't a single entity (like a brokerage or bank) that can unilaterally control or recover assets. This contrasts sharply with traditional securities, where a broker-dealer can exert control over and accurately account for the securities it holds for customers.

Applying Rule 15c3-3 to digital asset securities, therefore, requires adaptation to accommodate the technological and operational differences between digital and traditional assets. Broker-dealers must implement systems and controls that ensure the secure custody of digital assets while still complying with the protective intent of the rule. This might involve technological solutions for key management, third-party custody services specialized in digital assets, or innovative approaches to comply with the rule's requirements while addressing the risks specific to blockchain technology.

To address these challenges and adapt to the evolving landscape of digital assets, the SEC introduced a new category known as "special purpose broker-dealers" (SPBDs). These entities are authorized to both custody and transact in crypto asset securities, a significant development given that traditional broker-dealers and alternative trading systems were previously barred from custodial activities involving crypto assets. However, the SPBD regime comes with its own stringent conditions. For instance, SPBDs are limited to dealing with digital assets also recognized as securities, excluding most crypto assets, including those with high liquidity and market capitalization, from their scope.

The approval of Prometheum Ember Capital LLC as the first SPBD marks a critical step toward creating a federally regulated ecosystem for digital asset securities. This move by the SEC and FINRA indicates a readiness to engage with and regulate the digital asset space more constructively. However, the stringent conditions imposed on SPBDs highlight the complexities and challenges of integrating traditional regulatory frameworks with the innovative nature of digital assets. The regulatory requirements focus on ensuring investor protection and market integrity but also underscore the need for technological adaptations and enhanced security measures unique to the custody and management of digital asset securities.

The introduction of SPBDs and the ongoing discussions around broker-dealer custody of digital assets reflect a broader effort to reconcile the rapid innovation in the crypto space with the established principles of financial regulation.

4. Is the Crypto Market a Wild West Then?

Not really. Even though crypto assets are not universally regulated as securities, there have been numerous enforcement actions by regulatory bodies that shed light on their stance toward the industry. These actions provide valuable insights into the regulatory priorities and interpretations concerning digital assets, helping market participants better understand the legal landscape and the types of activities that may draw regulatory scrutiny. Through these enforcement actions, regulators are signaling their areas of concern and how existing laws might apply to the evolving crypto space, guiding practitioners in navigating compliance while fostering innovation.

4.1 Insider Trading Case

One example is the insider trading case involving Ishan Wahi, a former product manager at Coinbase Global Inc, which marks a pivotal moment in the intersection of cryptocurrency and U.S. securities law. In May 2023, Wahi was sentenced to two years in prison, a decision that underscored the seriousness with which U.S. prosecutors and the legal system are addressing fraudulent activities within the rapidly evolving crypto market.

Ishan Wahi's case was notably recognized as the first insider trading case involving cryptocurrency by U.S. prosecutors. His sentencing by U.S. District Judge Loretta Preska in Manhattan federal court came after he pleaded guilty to two counts of conspiracy to commit wire fraud. The case shed light on a "massive abuse" of trust within Coinbase, one of the world's largest cryptocurrency exchanges, highlighting significant challenges in ensuring ethical conduct and legal compliance within the crypto industry.

The scheme orchestrated by Wahi involved sharing confidential information about upcoming listings of digital assets on Coinbase with his brother, Nikhil Wahi, and a friend, Sameer Ramani. Leveraging this insider information, the trio engaged in trading 55 digital assets before their listing announcements were made public, netting $1.5 million in illicit profits between June 2021 and April 2022. Nikhil Wahi, having pleaded guilty to a wire fraud conspiracy charge, was sentenced to 10 months in prison in January, while Ramani remains at large.

This case is significant for several reasons. First, it represents a direct action by U.S. legal authorities to apply traditional securities law principles, specifically those pertaining to insider trading, to the crypto market. The application of laws designed to protect market integrity and prevent fraud to the relatively new and technically complex field of cryptocurrency signals a willingness and capability of regulatory bodies to adapt existing legal frameworks to new financial technologies and markets.

Moreover, the case highlights the challenges cryptocurrency exchanges and other participants in the crypto ecosystem face in implementing and enforcing compliance and ethical standards. Unlike traditional securities exchanges, which have well-established protocols and systems for safeguarding against insider trading, the decentralized and digital nature of cryptocurrency markets presents unique vulnerabilities and enforcement difficulties.

The sentencing of Ishan Wahi also serves as a stark reminder to individuals and entities operating within the crypto space of the legal obligations and ethical standards they must adhere to. It underscores the fact that despite the innovative and transformative potential of cryptocurrencies and blockchain technology, participants in these markets are not beyond the reach of traditional law enforcement mechanisms.

4.2 Binance

Binance, one of the largest cryptocurrency exchanges globally, reached a significant settlement with the United States government, marking a pivotal moment in the ongoing dialogue around cryptocurrency regulation and enforcement. This settlement, which involved admitting to violations of United States laws around money laundering and terror financing, resulted in Binance agreeing to pay $4.3 billion in fines. This outcome was the culmination of months, sometimes years, of investigations by United States government agencies into Binance's operations, underscoring the intensifying scrutiny of cryptocurrency exchanges by regulatory bodies.

The U.S. Justice Department's probe into Binance began years before the indictment was unsealed, with other U.S. regulatory agencies, including the Commodity Futures Trading Commission (CFTC) and the SEC, launching their actions against the crypto exchange. This comprehensive legal challenge highlights the multifaceted nature of regulatory enforcement in the crypto space, encompassing issues of trading irregularities, market manipulation, unregistered securities sales, and violations of sanctions.

The timeline leading to the settlement was marked by significant events, starting with suspicions in 2018 and escalating with formal charges and lawsuits from the CFTC, which filed suit against Binance's founder, Changpeng "CZ" Zhao, and others for trading irregularities and market manipulation. The SEC also filed suit, bringing 13 charges against Binance, including allowing U.S. customers to use the exchange for transactions involving unregistered securities. These legal actions pointed to systemic issues within Binance's operations, related to compliance with U.S. laws governing financial transactions and securities.

Binance's response to these challenges included efforts to block the SEC's access to certain documents and to dismiss the suits filed against it, arguing against the SEC's interpretation of securities law and the CFTC's jurisdiction over its activities. Despite these defensive measures, the eventual settlement required significant concessions from Binance, including financial penalties and operational changes to comply with U.S. regulations.

This settlement is significant for several reasons:

- **Regulatory Precedent:** It establishes a precedent for how the U.S. government approaches enforcement actions against major players in the cryptocurrency market, signaling a no-tolerance policy for violations of money laundering and terror financing laws.
- **Global Operations:** The case highlights the challenges global crypto exchanges face when operating within the U.S. legal framework, underscoring the importance of compliance with a complex web of regulations that govern financial transactions and securities trading.
- **Market Impact:** The settlement may influence the operational practices of other cryptocurrency exchanges and financial services operating within or targeting U.S. customers, potentially leading to increased compliance measures and changes in business models to adhere to U.S. laws.
- **Legal Clarity:** This resolution may serve as a reference point for future legal actions and regulatory guidelines, contributing to the evolving legal landscape surrounding cryptocurrency operations, especially concerning AML/CFT compliance, securities regulations, and international sanctions.
- **Consumer Confidence:** By holding Binance accountable, the settlement may also play a role in restoring or enhancing consumer confidence in the regulatory system's ability to protect investors and maintain market integrity in the rapidly evolving cryptocurrency space.

Changpeng Zhao, also known as "CZ," the former CEO of Binance, was sentenced to four months in prison on April 30, 2024, after pleading guilty to violating U.S. money-laundering laws. U.S. District Judge Richard Jones issued the sentence in Seattle, rejecting the prosecution's request for a three-year term. The charges against Zhao involved Binance's inadequate anti-money-laundering protocols, which allowed transactions supporting illegal activities, including terrorism and drug trafficking.[5] In conclusion, the settlement between Binance and the U.S. government is a landmark development in cryptocurrency regulation, emphasizing the critical importance of legal compliance for crypto exchanges operating globally. It not only marks a significant enforcement action by U.S. regulators but also sets a critical precedent for the regulatory treatment of crypto assets, potentially shaping the future landscape of crypto regulation and enforcement worldwide.

4.3 Regulation by Enforcement

In a world where cryptocurrencies zigzag through the regulatory frameworks with the precision of a hyperactive toddler drawing with crayons, the SEC has taken a stance that might remind one of a stern librarian amidst a room of noisy children. Rather than laying

---

[5] See https://www.aljazeera.com/economy/2024/4/30/former-binance-ceo-cz-sentenced-to-four-months

down a comprehensive rulebook for digital assets, the SEC has opted for a "we'll know it when we see it" approach, making its presence felt through targeted enforcement actions. This strategy has sparked widespread discussion within the financial and legal communities.

This section delves into the SEC's method of "regulation by enforcement," a strategy that, in the absence of comprehensive legislative guidelines, utilizes enforcement actions to establish regulatory benchmarks within the crypto space. By examining key cases and decisions, we explore how this approach has shaped the regulatory landscape, providing de facto rules for market participants while also raising questions about clarity, fairness, and the future direction of crypto regulation.

BlockFi

For instance, the SEC's actions against BlockFi and Kraken represent pivotal moments in the evolving regulatory landscape of the cryptocurrency industry, highlighting the U.S. Securities and Exchange Commission's commitment to extending traditional financial regulations to crypto asset service providers.

BlockFi's legal entanglement with the SEC centered on its flagship offering, the BlockFi Interest Account (BIA), which allowed customers to deposit their cryptocurrencies in exchange for interest payments. This innovative financial product, blending traditional banking's interest-earning features with the burgeoning world of cryptocurrency, promised to be a game-changer for crypto holders seeking to generate returns on their investments. However, the SEC scrutinized this arrangement, arguing that BIAs constituted investment contracts and thus should be treated as securities under U.S. law.

The heart of the SEC's case against BlockFi lay in the assertion that the firm had not registered its BIA offerings, violating securities laws that mandate such registration to ensure investor protection through transparency and disclosure of material information. Moreover, by operating in a manner similar to that of a traditional investment company but without adhering to the stringent requirements of the Investment Company Act of 1940, BlockFi faced additional charges, underscoring the regulatory expectations for entities offering investment products.

The settlement reached between BlockFi and the SEC, involving a $50 million penalty and the cessation of BIAs, was groundbreaking for several reasons. First, it underscored the SEC's rigorous application of traditional securities laws to novel crypto-based financial products, signaling to other crypto lending platforms and similar entities that they too must align their operations with federal securities laws or face regulatory action. Second, the requirement for BlockFi to attempt compliance with the Investment Company Act highlighted the complexities and challenges crypto businesses face when integrating with the existing financial regulatory framework.

BlockFi's subsequent move to register its products with the SEC came amidst financial turmoil, culminating in the company filing for bankruptcy. This development serves as a cautionary tale for the crypto industry, illustrating the significant operational and financial burdens that can accompany efforts to achieve regulatory compliance post-enforcement action.

Kraken's Regulatory Charges Kraken (Payward Inc. and Payward Ventures Inc.) was charged by the SEC for operating its crypto trading platform without registering as a securities exchange, broker, dealer, and clearing agency. This operation was found to have unlawfully facilitated the buying and selling of crypto asset securities, intertwining services typically provided separately by regulated entities and thus, evading the investor protections afforded by registration, including SEC inspection and record-keeping requirements. The SEC's complaint underscored the substantial risks posed to investors due to Kraken's alleged failure to register, highlighting concerns over conflicts of interest and the safeguarding of customer assets. The complaint further alleged poor internal controls and record-keeping practices at Kraken, presenting significant risks of loss to its customers. This case was part of a broader regulatory effort to bring crypto asset trading platforms into compliance with securities laws, emphasizing the necessity of lawful operation to protect investors and maintain market integrity.

Coinbase and its Lend Program

The unfolding saga surrounding Coinbase's ultimately abandoned "Lend" program presents a critical case study in the complex regulatory landscape facing the crypto industry. In June 2023, the SEC raised concerns that Coinbase was operating as an unregistered national securities exchange, broker, and clearing agency. This scrutiny extended to Coinbase's staking-as-a-service offerings, which the SEC suggested amounted to an unregistered securities offering, thus potentially violating securities laws.

The situation started escalating in September 2021 when Coinbase, aiming to capitalize on the burgeoning interest in crypto assets, announced its "Lend" program. This initiative promised users the opportunity to stake their USDC stablecoin holdings in return for an annual percentage yield (APY) of 4%—an attractive offer in the low-interest-rate environment of traditional banking. However, before the program could launch, the SEC issued a Wells notice to Coinbase. A Wells notice is a formal declaration that the SEC staff intends to recommend enforcement action; it provides the recipient an opportunity to respond with arguments as to why such action should not be taken. It is noteworthy that receiving a Wells notice before the launch of a product is an unprecedented step, signaling the SEC's proactive stance in preempting potential regulatory violations.

Faced with the prospect of legal action, Coinbase publicly contested the SEC's position, arguing for clarity in the regulatory framework governing crypto assets. Despite this initial resistance, the practical realities and legal uncertainties led Coinbase to cancel the "Lend" program, illustrating the delicate balance between regulatory compliance and innovation in the crypto sector.

These enforcement actions against Coinbase and similar entities mark critical points of reference for understanding the legal parameters within which the crypto industry operates. As digital assets continue to evolve, the interplay between innovation and regulation remains a pivotal area of contention, shaping the trajectory of this dynamic sector.

4.4 (De)Banking Crypto

Another potential tactic to curb the growth of crypto companies is to exclude them from the traditional financial system. The phenomenon of "debanking" within the cryptocurrency industry adds a complex layer to the already intricate dance between regulatory entities and crypto enterprises. Traditional financial institutions have increasingly distanced themselves from businesses operating within the crypto space, a trend that has accelerated following the collapses of Silvergate and Signature Banks. Debanking crypto companies is like breaking up with someone using a Post-it note. Banks are saying, "It's not you, it's me. . .but also, it's definitely you."

Silvergate Bank, known for its crypto-friendly banking services, faced a downfall that can be attributed to a combination of market volatility, regulatory pressures, and the bank's heavy exposure to the cryptocurrency market. The bank's troubles became pronounced following the dramatic downturn in the crypto market in 2022, which was marked by declining asset prices and the collapse of major crypto entities.

The bank announced its voluntary liquidation and winding down of operations in early March 2023. This decision came after a tumultuous period where Silvergate faced significant liquidity issues. These were exacerbated by the rapid withdrawal of deposits by its crypto clients, who were reacting to the bank's financial instability and growing concerns over its sustainability amid a harsh regulatory environment and the bearish crypto market. The bank's failure was notable for its impact on the crypto industry, given Silvergate's role as a key financial bridge between traditional banking and cryptocurrency businesses.

Signature Bank, another prominent institution serving the crypto industry, was shut down by regulators in March 2023 as part of a broader effort to stabilize the banking sector following the bank runs that occurred in the wake of Silicon Valley Bank's and Silvergate's issues. The closure was also tied to concerns over liquidity and depositor confidence, which were critical in maintaining the bank's operations.

The closure of Signature Bank has sparked controversy, with some suggesting it was part of an effort to target the cryptocurrency industry. Former Congressman Barney Frank, who is also a board member of Signature Bank, claimed that regulators shut down the bank to send an "anti-crypto message" and to signal that cryptocurrencies are risky and problematic.[6]

However, the New York Department of Financial Services (NYDFS) has refuted these claims. NYDFS Superintendent Adrienne Harris stated that the decision to close Signature Bank was due to liquidity issues and a crisis of confidence in its leadership, not because of its involvement with the crypto sector. She described the notion that the bank's closure was part of a broader crackdown on crypto, referred to by some as "Operation Choke Point 2.0," as "ludicrous."[7]

---

[6] See https://decrypt.co/123346/signature-bank-shut-down-anti-crypto-barney-frank and https://decrypt.co/123494/why-signature-bank-really-shut-down.
[7] See https://cryptonews.com/news/new-york-finance-regulator-clarifies-signature-bank-shutdown-unrelated-crypto-activities-bullish-for-industry.htm

The bank's executives also maintained that Signature was in solid financial shape and that its closure was unwarranted, pointing to broader regulatory scrutiny and financial instability in the banking sector as contributing factors.[8] This divergence in perspectives highlights the ongoing tension between regulatory bodies and the cryptocurrency industry amidst a landscape of increasing regulatory actions and financial oversight.

The collapses of Silvergate and Signature Banks have had profound implications for the cryptocurrency industry, severing crucial financial lifelines and fostering a climate of uncertainty. These events have led to increased calls for clearer regulatory frameworks that can accommodate the unique aspects of digital assets while ensuring financial stability and depositor protection.

Observers have noted that the regulatory environment, particularly the cautious stance of financial watchdogs toward banks engaging with crypto businesses, may have indirectly contributed to these banks' downfalls. The situation has sparked a debate about the need for a balanced approach that supports innovation in the financial sector without compromising the safety of the banking system.

These events have not only amplified the banking sector's hesitance but have also spurred discussions about the broader implications for the accessibility of financial services to crypto-related businesses.

The downfall of Silvergate and Signature Banks left many crypto ventures in a precarious position, struggling to find traditional banking services that are essential for their operation, from managing cash flow to facilitating transactions with customers and partners.

Observers argue that the regulatory pressures contributing to the debanking phenomenon may reflect an indirect strategy by regulators to limit the crypto industry's growth by curtailing its access to essential financial services. This perspective suggests that by increasing the regulatory and compliance burdens on banks serving crypto clients, regulators indirectly exert control over the crypto industry's expansion. The rationale behind this view is that without the support of traditional financial institutions, crypto companies may face significant operational challenges, hindering their ability to compete and innovate within the financial sector.

The combined impact of debanking, alongside the SEC's proactive enforcement actions, places the crypto industry in a state of uncertainty. Only the most agile and well-prepared companies, often those with significant legal resources, can navigate this complex regulatory environment.

5. International Perspectives

As the digital currency landscape continues to evolve at a rapid pace, countries around the globe are taking varied approaches to regulate this burgeoning space. Each

---

[8] See https://decrypt.co/140354/signature-executives-crypto-friendly-bank-solvent-capitalized

jurisdiction is crafting its regulatory strategy based on its unique financial ecosystem, technological advancements, and consumer protection needs. This section explores these diverse international approaches to crypto regulation, shedding light on the global effort to balance innovation with investor safety and market integrity.

5.1 EU Approach

The European Union has positioned itself as a frontrunner in the global race to regulate the rapidly expanding crypto market by enacting the Markets in Crypto-Assets (MiCA) framework. This comprehensive regulatory package offers a clear set of rules for crypto assets, service providers, and issuers within the EU, providing much-needed legal clarity and investor protection that has been somewhat lacking in jurisdictions like the United States.

The MiCA regulation marks a significant step toward establishing a comprehensive regulatory framework for the crypto industry. Enacted following the definitive vote by the European Parliament on April 20, 2023, and ratified by the Economic and Financial Affairs Council of the EU on May 16, 2023, MiCA aims to introduce a unified regulatory environment across the EU, emphasizing transparency, security, and uniformity in the digital assets space.

MiCA delineates clear regulatory obligations for crypto-asset service providers (CASPs) and token issuers, thereby replacing fragmented national regulations with a cohesive set of rules applicable throughout the EU. This regulation covers a broad spectrum of activities and entities within the crypto domain, including exchanges, wallet providers, and platforms offering crypto to fiat transactions, as well as advising and portfolio management services related to crypto assets.

The regulation categorizes crypto assets into several types, notably asset-referenced tokens, e-money tokens, and utility tokens, each subject to specific regulatory provisions. Asset-referenced tokens and e-money tokens, which encompass stablecoins, are particularly emphasized due to their potential impact on financial stability and monetary policy. MiCA stipulates stringent requirements for these stablecoins, including the necessity for backing by liquid assets and adherence to operational standards that ensure consumer protection.

Moreover, MiCA addresses the issuance of crypto assets, mandating the publication of a whitepaper that meets specific transparency criteria for token offerings. This requirement aims to provide investors with essential information, thereby facilitating informed investment decisions. The regulation also implements provisions to combat market abuse, ensuring that CASPs operate with integrity and transparency.

Implications for Crypto Businesses For entrepreneurs and businesses in the crypto space, navigating MiCA entails understanding its broad scope and the specific obligations it imposes on different types of crypto assets and related activities. Compliance with MiCA means adhering to rigorous standards for operational conduct, marketing communications, and the handling of customer assets, among other aspects. Businesses must also navigate the requirements related to the issuance of tokens, ensuring that token offerings are conducted in a manner consistent with MiCA's provisions.

One of the notable changes introduced by MiCA is the ban on algorithmic stablecoins, reflecting the EU's cautious stance on these innovative but potentially volatile instruments. For stablecoin issuers, particularly those backing their tokens with fiat currencies or other assets, MiCA mandates the maintenance of a 1:1 reserve ratio and establishes guidelines for asset custody and management.

Adapting to MiCA means engaging with regulatory authorities, potentially seeking authorization or registration as a crypto-asset service providers (CASP), and maintaining ongoing compliance through transparent reporting and diligent operational conduct. For businesses operating across the EU, MiCA provides an opportunity to streamline regulatory compliance across member states, offering a clearer path to expansion and cross-border operations within the EU's single market.

MiCA introduces several specific processes and requirements that are pivotal for entities operating within the crypto space in the European Union. These elements are designed to ensure that the activities of CASPs and issuers are conducted in a manner that upholds the integrity of the market and protects investors. Here are some detailed aspects of MiCA that highlight its comprehensive approach to regulation:

- **Authorization and Registration:** One of the cornerstone requirements of MiCA is that CASPs must obtain authorization from competent national authorities within the EU to operate. This process involves demonstrating compliance with MiCA's operational and organizational standards, including those related to governance, risk management, and the handling of client assets.
- **Consumer Protection Measures:** MiCA places a strong emphasis on protecting consumers in the crypto market. CASPs are required to implement clear procedures for the resolution of complaints, safeguard client assets, and ensure transparent communication. This includes detailed disclosures about the risks associated with crypto-asset investments.
- **Operational Resilience:** Under MiCA, CASPs must establish robust frameworks to ensure operational resilience. This includes measures to prevent and mitigate cyberattacks, data breaches, and other operational risks. CASPs are also required to have contingency plans in place to address potential failures or disruptions in their services.
- **Market Abuse Regulations:** MiCA extends EU market abuse regulations to cover crypto-assets, prohibiting insider dealing, unlawful disclosure of inside information, and market manipulation. CASPs and participants in the crypto market are required to establish safeguards against these practices and report suspicious activities to relevant authorities.
- **Stablecoin Oversight:** For issuers of asset-referenced tokens and e-money tokens (stablecoins), MiCA mandates strict capital requirements, including the maintenance of adequate reserves. These reserves must be protected, segregated from other assets,

and subject to regular audits. Stablecoin issuers are also required to provide holders with a claim at any time at par value, ensuring the redeemability of tokens.

- **Whitepaper Disclosure for Token Issuance:** Entities seeking to issue crypto assets under MiCA must publish a whitepaper that complies with specific disclosure requirements. This document should provide detailed information about the issuer, the project, the rights of token holders, and the risks associated with the investment. The whitepaper must be filed with the competent authority before the public offering or admission of trading on a trading platform.

- **Cross-Border Services and Passporting:** MiCA introduces a passporting system that allows CASPs authorized in one EU member state to provide their services across the entire EU without needing further authorization. This facilitates the expansion of crypto businesses across borders within the EU's single market.

- **Supervision and Enforcement:** Competent authorities in EU member states are tasked with supervising CASPs and issuers to ensure compliance with MiCA. This includes conducting investigations and imposing sanctions for non-compliance. MiCA establishes a harmonized framework for administrative sanctions and remedial measures, enhancing the enforcement capabilities of regulators.

The MiCA regulation marks a significant development in the crypto asset regulatory landscape, providing a harmonized framework aimed at fostering innovation while ensuring market stability, transparency, and investor protection. In a nutshell, it shows that it can be done!

5.2 Singapore

Singapore's Payment Services Act (PSA), which came into force on January 28, 2020, represents a significant overhaul of the regulatory framework governing payment services within the country. It also marks a significant step in the regulatory landscape for crypto assets, offering a structured approach to oversight in the rapidly evolving digital payment space. Under the PSA, crypto assets, referred to as Digital Payment Tokens (DPTs), fall under a specific category of regulated payment services. This inclusion is pivotal as it subjects entities dealing with DPTs, including crypto exchanges and wallet services, to the scrutiny and regulatory requirements set forth by the Monetary Authority of Singapore (MAS).

The PSA requires these entities to obtain a license to operate, dividing the licenses into three categories: money-changing license, standard payment institution license, and major payment institution license. The classification depends on the volume of transactions handled and the range of services offered. For crypto service providers, this framework ensures that they adhere to legal standards concerning anti-money laundering (AML) and counter-financing of terrorism (CFT), consumer protection, and the stability of their operational framework.

In overseeing the crypto space, the MAS has been proactive in updating its guidelines to address emerging risks and market developments. One of the key efforts includes enhancing the AML/CFT framework in alignment with international standards set by the Financial Action Task Force (FATF). Crypto exchanges and wallet providers are required to implement robust measures to detect and prevent money laundering and terrorist financing activities. This involves conducting thorough customer due diligence, monitoring transactions for suspicious activities, and reporting any anomalies to the authorities.

Furthermore, the MAS has issued guidelines to discourage cryptocurrency trading among the general public, emphasizing the speculative and volatile nature of crypto assets. While not outright banning cryptocurrencies, the MAS aims to protect retail consumers from potential losses that could arise from cryptocurrency investments.

An example of the MAS's regulatory actions in the crypto space is its issuance of warnings and its enforcement actions against non-compliant operators. For instance, the MAS has ordered several digital payment token service providers to cease offering services to Singapore residents due to non-compliance with regulatory requirements. Additionally, the MAS closely monitors the activities of licensed operators to ensure continuous compliance with the PSA, including audits and compulsory reporting of financial activities.

The PSA's application to crypto assets and the MAS's diligent oversight exemplifies Singapore's balanced approach to fostering innovation in the fintech sector while ensuring the financial system's integrity and stability are maintained. This regulatory environment encourages responsible growth in the crypto market, making Singapore one of the leading global fintech hubs.

5.3 Japan

In Japan, the regulatory framework for cryptocurrencies and blockchain technology does not fall under a singular, omnibus regulation but rather is defined by the functionality and usage of tokens. The primary legislative acts governing these digital assets include the Payment Services Act (PSA) and the Financial Instruments and Exchange Act (FIEA), with each act catering to different facets of the crypto space based on the classification of tokens.

The PSA is pivotal in regulating cryptocurrencies (termed "Crypto Assets") and electronic payment instruments (EPIs), including stablecoins like USDC and USDT. Under the PSA, businesses engaged in buying, selling, or exchanging crypto assets or managing these assets for others must register as Crypto Asset Exchange Service Providers (CAESPs). Similarly, operations involving EPIs necessitate registration as Electronic Payment Instruments Exchange Service Providers (EPIESPs). The PSA distinguishes algorithmic stablecoins from EPIs, categorizing them as Crypto Assets due to their lack of fiat collateralization and algorithmic value linkage.

The FIEA also governs "security tokens," which represent digital forms of traditional securities like shares, bonds, or fund interests. Entities dealing in these tokens must register as Type I Financial Instruments Business Operators (Type I FIBOs). Non-fungible tokens (NFTs), given their unique characteristics and lack of payment functionality, generally fall outside the regulatory purview of the FIEA and PSA.

A notable legislative development is the introduction of the Amendment Act, which came into effect on June 1, 2023. This act specifically targets the regulation of stablecoins, requiring them to be issued by licensed entities like banks or trust companies and imposing strict anti-money laundering (AML) and counter-financing of terrorism (CFT) measures, including adherence to the "travel rule."

6. Regulatory Considerations for DeFi

Regulating Decentralized Finance (DeFi) presents a unique set of challenges that go beyond the already complex task of classifying crypto assets as securities. At the heart of DeFi is a paradigm shift toward financial systems that operate on decentralized networks, largely autonomous and without central authority. This decentralization, while offering innovation and inclusivity in finance, complicates regulatory oversight due to the absence of traditional intermediaries like banks and exchanges, which are typically regulated entities. Furthermore, the programmable nature of smart contracts, which execute transactions on DeFi platforms, introduces a layer of technical complexity that traditional financial regulations are not designed to address. These factors combined—lack of central oversight, reliance on code for compliance, and the global, borderless nature of blockchain networks—make the regulatory landscape for DeFi significantly more intricate, requiring novel approaches to ensure consumer protection, market integrity, and financial stability.

One of the primary challenges is the absence of a centralized entity to oversee and regulate. Traditional financial systems operate under well-established regulatory frameworks with clear oversight by designated authorities. DeFi's decentralized nature means there isn't a single entity responsible for the platform's operations, complicating the enforcement of compliance and regulatory standards.

Furthermore, DeFi platforms operate on blockchain networks that are inherently global and borderless. This global nature raises questions about jurisdiction since users from across the world can interact with these platforms without the platform necessarily having a physical presence in those users' locations. Determining which legal and regulatory standards apply becomes a complex issue for regulators.

Ensuring consumer protection and market integrity within DeFi ecosystems is also a significant challenge due to the pseudonymous nature of blockchain transactions and the absence of intermediaries to perform due diligence, manage risks, and ensure compliance with know-your-customer (KYC) and anti-money laundering (AML) regulations.

The unique challenges posed by DeFi are well represented by the case involving Tornado Cash. Tornado Cash, created by Roman Semenov and Roman Storm, emerged as a decentralized, non-custodial privacy solution built on the Ethereum blockchain. It leveraged cryptographic techniques, specifically zero-knowledge proofs, to allow users to obfuscate the origins and destinations of their cryptocurrency transactions. This process, known as "mixing," pooled funds from various users, thereby anonymizing individual transactions within the collective pool.

The U.S. government's intervention came on the heels of allegations that Tornado Cash was used to launder over $7 billion worth of virtual currency since its inception in 2019, including funds linked to cybercrimes and operations by the Lazarus Group, a North Korean state-sponsored hacking collective. In response, the U.S. Department of the Treasury's Office of Foreign Assets Control (OFAC) sanctioned Tornado Cash in August 2022, effectively blocking it and marking a bold step in applying sanctions to a decentralized entity. The founders of Tornado Cash faced charges from the U.S. Department of Justice (DOJ) for money laundering, operating an unlicensed money transmitting business, and violating sanctions.

From a technical standpoint, Tornado Cash's design as an immutable set of smart contracts on public blockchains like Ethereum means that despite sanctions, the protocol continues to operate. **Figure 5** depicts how it works. Its front-end remains accessible via decentralized web protocols such as the InterPlanetary File System (IPFS) and The

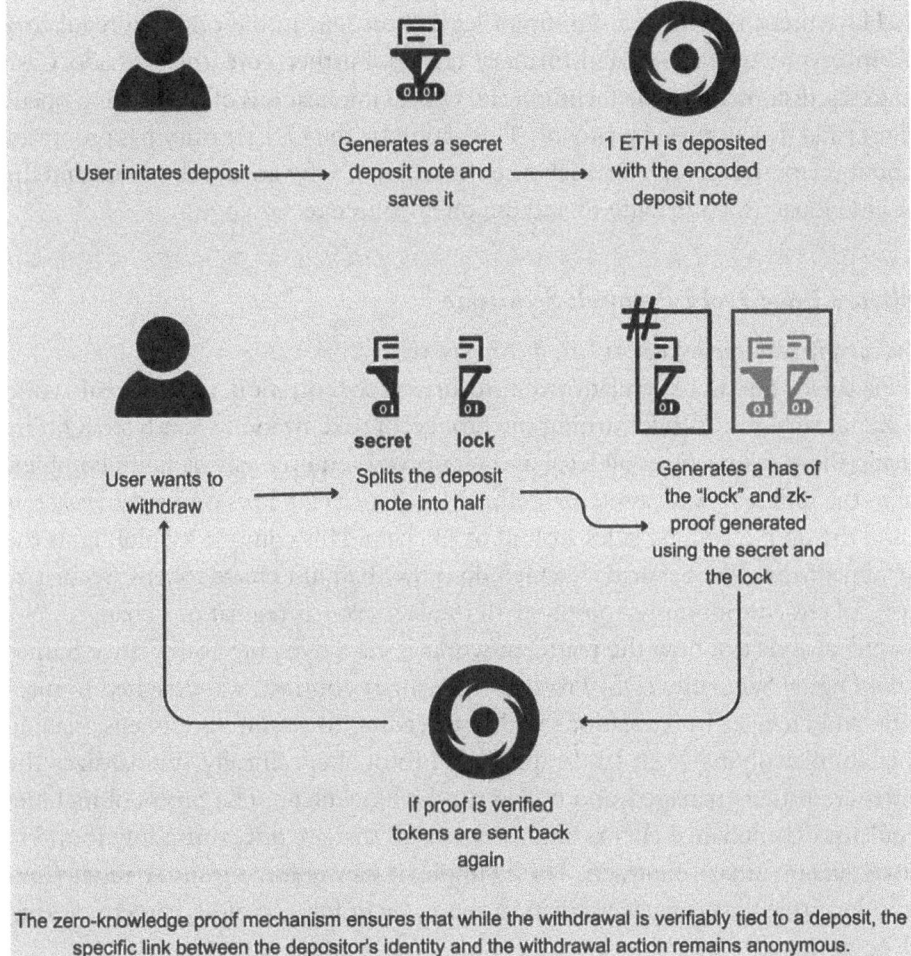

User initates deposit ⟶ Generates a secret deposit note and saves it ⟶ 1 ETH is deposited with the encoded deposit note

User wants to withdraw ⟶ secret lock Splits the deposit note into half ⟶ Generates a has of the "lock" and zk-proof generated using the secret and the lock

If proof is verified tokens are sent back again

The zero-knowledge proof mechanism ensures that while the withdrawal is verifiably tied to a deposit, the specific link between the depositor's identity and the withdrawal action remains anonymous.

Figure 5   How Tornado Cash works

Onion Router (Tor), demonstrating the challenges regulators face in curbing the use of decentralized technologies. The immutability of the blockchain means that the smart contracts are still operable, so users can still transact with it and call the necessary functions.

Sanctioning Tornado Cash kicked off more drama than a reality TV show reunion. Now everyone's arguing about privacy, money, and who's going to get voted off the blockchain. While Tornado Cash was purportedly used by bad actors to obscure illicit funds, it also served legitimate privacy needs for users looking to protect their financial data from public exposure on the blockchain. The case raises questions about the balance between privacy rights and the need for regulatory oversight to prevent financial crimes.

Alexey Pertsev, a developer for Tornado Cash, was sentenced to 64 months in prison on May 14, 2024, by a Dutch court. Pertsev was found guilty of facilitating the laundering of $1.2 billion through Tornado Cash. The court ruled that Pertsev's creation and operation of the service enabled criminals to launder illicit funds, including those tied to cybercrime and other illegal activities. The prosecution highlighted that Pertsev should have been aware of the illegal uses of Tornado Cash, which lacked sufficient barriers against money laundering. His sentencing marks a significant legal precedent in the ongoing regulatory crackdown on cryptocurrency-related financial crimes. Furthermore, the Tornado Cash case has led to discussions about the technical and ethical implications of sanctioning open-source software and decentralized protocols. This action by the U.S. Treasury has prompted concerns about the potential for overreach into the realm of software development and the freedom of individuals to contribute to and use open-source technology.

6.2 Compliance Proof DeFi Protocol: Securitize

Is all hope to comply with the regulators lost, then? Not yet.

Securitize stands out as a key platform in securities' tokenization, turning real-world assets into digital versions.[9] While turning the process of tokenization sounds straightforward, ensuring these tokens meet all legal and regulatory requirements is quite complex. This is due to the different ways assets are defined legally, varying laws on securities across countries, and the ever-changing rules around blockchain. This complexity highlights the crucial role of platforms like Securitize, which do more than just create tokens. Securitize ensures these tokens continuously comply with the law, even as regulations change.

The technical aspect of how the platform works is via a dynamic compliance framework and the Digital Securities (DS) Protocol. The smart contracts are designed to integrate updates and changes in regulations without needing to reissue the tokens, making them adaptable to evolving legal landscapes. DS Protocol specifically standardizes the way securities are issued, managed, and traded on the blockchain. The protocol includes built-in regulatory compliance checks and mechanisms that are not commonly found in standard tokenization smart contracts. For example, it can enforce transfer restrictions based on the investor's location, accreditation status, or holding periods directly within the token's operational rules.

---

[9] In Chapter 9, we looked in depth at how this process works and its growing importance in the blockchain field.

Also, they have a unique approach to investor validation. Its smart contracts work in conjunction with off-chain identity verification processes to ensure that all participants meet the necessary accreditation and KYC (Know Your Customer) standards. Once verified, investors receive digital credentials that allow them to transact within Securitize's ecosystem, ensuring that only qualified participants can engage in trading.

These processes attracted different financial services institutions that want to enter the blockchain space. In March 2024, BlackRock launched its first tokenized fund the "BlackRock USD Institutional Digital Liquidity Fund Ltd." (BUILD) in collaboration with Securitize on Ethereum. It attracted $245 million in deposits during its first week. This initiative underscores the potential of blockchain technology to revolutionize investment strategies when regulatory standards are met.

6.3 NFTs

As we have already discussed in Chapter 10, NFTs represent ownership or proof of authenticity of a unique item or asset on a blockchain. While initially focused on digital art, the use of NFTs has expanded into various sectors, including entertainment, real estate, and identity verification.

NFTs challenge existing regulatory frameworks that weren't designed to address the ownership, transfer, or sale of digital tokens representing unique assets. This raises questions about how NFTs should be classified (as securities, commodities, or otherwise) and regulated. However, an even bigger hurdle is ensuring that NFTs respect existing intellectual property rights and provide adequate protection for consumers against fraud, misrepresentation, and copyright infringement. The ease of replicating digital content creates challenges in verifying authenticity and ownership.

Copyright law, which protects original works of authorship such as literature, music, and art, is particularly relevant to NFTs. The act of minting an NFT, which involves creating a blockchain record for the digital asset, does not in itself infringe on copyright if the minter owns the copyright or has obtained permission from the copyright holder. However, selling or commercializing NFTs linked to copyrighted material without appropriate rights can lead to infringement claims. This complexity is exemplified in situations where digital art is tokenized and sold as NFTs without clear rights or licenses from the copyright owners.

6.3.1 The MetaBirkins Case
The MetaBirkins case represents a fascinating intersection between digital innovation, intellectual property rights, and the burgeoning market of non-fungible tokens (NFTs). The MetaBirkins case revolves around a series of NFTs created by artist Mason Rothschild. These NFTs depicted digital representations of the iconic Birkin bags, produced by the luxury fashion brand Hermès. Rothschild's MetaBirkins, while not physical objects, were sold as digital collectibles, leveraging the blockchain technology characteristic of NFTs to verify ownership and authenticity. The digital artwork aimed to comment on the concepts of luxury and value in the digital era, mirroring the real-world exclusivity and desirability of Birkin bags.

However, Hermès did not view Rothschild's project as a harmless or flattering tribute. Instead, the company initiated legal action against Rothschild, accusing him of infringing on its trademark rights. Hermès argued that the MetaBirkins NFTs could confuse consumers and dilute the prestigious Birkin brand, leveraging the trademark's reputation without authorization and potentially for commercial gain. MetaBirkins turned into the courtroom drama of the year, pitting high fashion against high tech. It's like "Legally Blonde" meets "The Matrix," with more lawyers and less leather.

The MetaBirkins case raises several crucial questions about the regulation of NFTs and digital assets at large. One of the primary issues is the application of traditional intellectual property laws to the digital and decentralized realm of blockchain technology. Trademark law traditionally protects against uses that cause consumer confusion or dilute a brand. However, determining infringement in the context of digital art and NFTs, where the line between commercial use and artistic expression can be blurred, poses a unique challenge.

A key aspect of trademark infringement is the likelihood of consumer confusion. The case prompts a reevaluation of what constitutes confusion in the digital marketplace, especially when digital assets like NFTs may be perceived differently by consumers than physical goods.

The MetaBirkins case also delves into the tension between an artist's freedom of expression and the commercial implications of that expression. The defense might argue that NFTs, as digital art, should be protected under free speech, while the plaintiff might emphasize the commercial nature of selling NFTs, which could infringe on trademark rights. In June 2023, Hermes won a permanent ban on MetaBirkins sale.

6.3.2 The OpenSea Inside Trading Case   Nathaniel Chastain, a former product manager at OpenSea, which operates as Ozone Networks, Inc., was sentenced to three months in prison for insider trading. This sentencing by the U.S. Attorney's Office for the Southern District of New York was announced on August 22, 2023, highlighting the case's importance as the first-ever digital asset insider trading scheme prosecuted. Chastain's role at OpenSea involved selecting NFTs to be featured on the platform's homepage, a position that granted him access to confidential information about which NFTs were scheduled for prominent display—an aspect directly influencing the market value of these assets.

During his tenure from approximately June to September 2021, Chastain exploited this insider information for personal financial gain, purchasing dozens of NFTs before they were featured on OpenSea's homepage and selling them at substantial profits following their feature. This illegal activity was facilitated through the use of anonymous digital wallets and accounts on OpenSea, enabling Chastain to obscure the connection between his insider knowledge and trading actions. The profits from these transactions were significant, with Chastain selling the NFTs at two to five times his initial purchase price, capitalizing on the increased market value driven by the homepage feature.

The sentencing of Chastain to prison, alongside additional penalties including three months of home confinement, three years of supervised release, a $50,000 fine, and the forfeiture of the Ethereum gained from his illicit trades, underscores the gravity with which the U.S. justice system views insider trading in the NFT marketplace.

7. Concluding Remarks

As we conclude this chapter on the regulation of digital assets, it becomes increasingly evident that a one-size-fits-all approach to regulation cannot adequately address the multifaceted challenges and opportunities presented by the digital asset space. Therefore, what should be the basic principles? A regulatory framework should be activity-based, risk-adjusted, and technology-neutral, to ensure that regulation is both effective and adaptive to innovation. This approach respects the principle that similar activities should incur similar regulatory responsibilities, irrespective of the technology used to execute them, and recognizes the varying levels of risk associated with different types of digital asset activities.

Activity-Based Regulation An activity-based regulatory approach focuses on the function and impact of a digital asset activity rather than its form or the technology it employs. For example, whether a platform facilitates the exchange of digital tokens through traditional order books or decentralized finance (DeFi) protocols, it should be subject to the same basic regulatory standards concerning anti-money laundering (AML), know your customer (KYC) policies, and market manipulation safeguards. This ensures that all entities performing similar roles in the financial system are held to comparable standards of accountability and consumer protection.

Risk-Adjusted Regulation Regulation should be proportionate to the risks that different activities pose to investors, consumers, and the broader financial system. For instance, a large-scale exchange trading a wide array of digital assets might pose significant systemic risk and should therefore, be subject to more stringent regulatory oversight compared to a small, community-driven project offering a niche digital collectible. By tailoring regulatory requirements to the size, scope, and risk profile of an activity, regulators can prevent undue burden on smaller players while concentrating resources on monitoring and mitigating systemic risks.

Technology-Neutral Regulation A technology-neutral framework ensures that regulation is based on the substance of an activity rather than the specific technology used to conduct it. This principle is crucial in fostering innovation while ensuring that regulatory objectives are met. For example, whether a financial product is issued on a blockchain as a token or through traditional means should not determine its regulatory treatment. Instead, the focus should be on the rights, obligations, and risks associated with the product. This approach ensures that regulation remains effective even as new technologies emerge and evolve.

Implementing this framework requires regulators to engage with a broad range of stakeholders, including legal experts, consumer advocates, and the digital asset industry, to understand the nuances of digital asset activities and the technologies that enable them. It also calls for a flexible regulatory approach that can adapt to new developments and risks in the digital asset space.

An example of this framework in action could involve the regulation of stablecoins. Rather than creating a new, bespoke regulatory regime based solely on the technology underlying stablecoins, regulation could be structured around the economic functions and risks of these assets, such as their use in payments, their potential to impact monetary policy, and the need for reserve transparency and stability.

In conclusion, as digital assets continue to blur the lines between technology and finance, a regulatory framework that is activity-based, risk-adjusted, and technology-neutral offers a balanced pathway forward. It allows for the protection of investors and consumers while providing the regulatory clarity and flexibility needed to support innovation and the responsible growth of the digital asset ecosystem. As we sail the stormy seas of the digital asset world, our regulatory compass is spinning. Here's to hoping we don't hit an iceberg named "Unintended Consequences."

End-of-Chapter Questions

Multiple-Choice Questions

1. **What does the SEC use to determine if a digital asset is a security?**
   (A) The Ripple Test.
   (B) The Howey Test.
   (C) The Bitcoin Criterion.
   (D) The Blockchain Protocol.

2. **Which act regulates Crypto Asset Service Providers (CASPs) in Singapore?**
   (A) Digital Currency Act.
   (B) Payment Services Act.
   (C) Crypto Securities Act.
   (D) Financial Institutions Act.

3. **What is the primary challenge in applying AML/CFT regulations to the crypto market?**
   (A) High transaction fees.
   (B) The pseudo-anonymous nature of transactions.
   (C) Blockchain's transparency.
   (D) High energy consumption of mining.

4. **What significant action did the SEC take against Coinbase regarding its "Lend" program?**
   (A) Encouraged its global expansion.
   (B) Issued a Wells notice.
   (C) Granted a special license.
   (D) Offered a regulatory exemption.

5. **What is a key legal challenge NFTs present?**
   (A) Defining blockchain protocol standards.
   (B) Interoperability with traditional finance.
   (C) Intellectual property rights infringement.
   (D) Ensuring transaction speed.

6. **Which regulatory framework in the EU focuses on crypto assets?**
   (A) GDPR for Crypto.
   (B) MiCA.
   (C) Crypto Consumer Act.
   (D) EU Digital Finance Package.

7. **What complicates the regulation of DeFi platforms?**
   (A) Centralized governance models.
   (B) Lack of traditional intermediaries.
   (C) Over-reliance on fiat currencies.
   (D) Transparency of blockchain technology.

8. **Which regulatory approach does Singapore use to oversee the crypto market?**
   (A) Strict prohibition of all crypto activities.
   (B) Payment Services Act.
   (C) Light-touch, market-driven regulation.
   (D) Full integration with traditional banking systems.
9. **In the context of the chapter, what broader regulatory issue does the Tornado Cash case highlight?**
   (A) The need for crypto-specific legal frameworks.
   (B) Challenges in regulating decentralized platforms.
   (C) The efficiency of blockchain technology.
   (D) The impact of crypto on traditional banking.

Open Questions

1. Explain how the Howey Test is applied to determine whether a digital asset is considered a security and discuss its relevance to Bitcoin.
2. Describe the concept of "debanking" and its impact on the crypto industry following the collapse of Silvergate and Signature Banks.
3. Discuss the significance of the SEC's action against BlockFi and its implications for the crypto lending industry.
4. Reflect on the role and challenges of multiple regulatory bodies in the United States, such as the SEC, CFTC, FinCEN, and IRS, in regulating the crypto market.
5. Analyze the implications of the MetaBirkins case on intellectual property rights within the NFT market.

Chapter 12

Beyond HODL

Mastering the Art and Science of Crypto Trading

Preface

In a world where "blockchain" is the buzziest of buzzwords and "crypto" could well be the answer to the ultimate question of life, the universe, and everything (move over, 42!),[1] there lies a vast, wild, and often weird landscape known as the crypto market. It's a place where fortunes are made and lost in the blink of an eye, where tokens featuring dogs can somehow become more newsworthy than most global currencies, and where the term "HODL" is not just a typo but a way of life.[2]

But strip away the memes, the hype, and the sometimes-religious zeal for decentralization, and what are you left with? Surprisingly, an old friend: traditional finance principles. Yes, that's right. Beneath the veneer of revolution, much of what's happening in crypto isn't newfangled chaos—it's good old-fashioned finance wearing a funky new hat.

---

[1] This is a nod to "The Hitchhiker's Guide to the Galaxy," a science fiction series by Douglas Adams. In the series, "42" is humorously presented as the "Answer to the Ultimate Question of Life, the Universe, and Everything," as calculated by a supercomputer over millions of years.

[2] The term "HODL" originated from a post on the BitcoinTalk forum in December 2013. The post, titled "I AM HODLING," was written by a user named GameKyuubi, who misspelled "HOLD" in the context of holding onto Bitcoin rather than selling it during a market downturn. The typo quickly caught on in the cryptocurrency community and has since become a widely used term to describe a strategy of holding onto cryptocurrency investments despite market volatility.

Take our friend Beta, a measure of a stock's volatility in relation to the overall market. In the traditional world, a high beta might mean a stock is prone to dramatic swoons and surges. In crypto land, high beta can mean that when Bitcoin sneezes, the entire market catches a cold—or throws a party.

Now, onto factor investing. It's like taking the "sorting hat" of finance and plopping it onto the head of each cryptocurrency to see where it fits. Size? Check. Value? Check. Momentum? Check, check, and check—if it's Tuesday and the Twitter sentiment is just right.

But how does one navigate this wild west of finance? How do you manage a portfolio when your assets could be as varied as a digital plot of virtual land and a stake in a decentralized autonomous organization (DAO) that's trying to buy the U.S. Constitution? It's like being a cowboy riding a bull, except the bull is made of code, and the rodeo is on the moon.

Of course, not everyone is ready to saddle up for this rodeo. The skeptics—let's call them the "crypto cautious"—will rightly point out the risks. They'll remind us that for every blockchain success story, there's a tale of rug pulls, scams, and projects that vanished into the digital ether, taking investors' hopes and dreams with them. They'll talk about the regulatory Wild West, where the sheriff often arrives just in time to tally up the losses.

And what do the traditional financial institutions make of all this? Some may view crypto as a youthful upstart, a rebel without a cause—or at least without a clear regulatory framework. Others, perhaps envisioning a digitally native future, are dipping their toes in the crypto waters, experimenting with blockchain as cautiously as one might test a hot bath.

In our crypto chapter, we'll ride through the landscape of digital asset pricing with the steadiness of a seasoned Wall Street trader and the excitement of a Silicon Valley visionary. We'll understand why, even here in the land of "to the moon" and "wen lambo," the principles of finance hold strong—they just drive a fancier car.

A bull rodeo on the moon

So, join us on this journey through peaks and valleys lined with smart contracts and white papers, as we apply the wisdom of yesteryear's finance to tomorrow's crypto markets. We'll discover that whether we're talking about dollars, Dogecoins, or digital art, the rules of the game might not be so different after all. Who knows, by the end of it, you might even convince your skeptical Aunt Marge to buy a Satoshi or two.

1. Introduction

One of the most common questions people ask when confronted with the exponential growth of the crypto industry is, "What accounts for the value of digital tokens?" Skeptics' typical responses—speculation, self-fulfilling prophecies, and Ponzi schemes—are wrong for a large set of digital tokens. This dogmatic belief results in many investors missing out on outsized returns. Yet even crypto native users have difficulty articulating why their preferred token will be the next big thing in this space. This chapter aims to demystify the valuation of cryptocurrencies, arguing that, much like their counterparts in the stock and bond markets, crypto assets can be appraised through a systematic and rational approach.

This chapter seeks to bridge the gap between traditional financial wisdom and the pioneering world of cryptocurrencies. By leveraging established financial frameworks and adapting them to the unique characteristics of crypto assets, you will have a pragmatic understanding of how to trade these new forms of digital assets. Far from being an arcane art, valuing crypto assets is a discipline that, while requiring adaptation, remains rooted in the fundamental principles of financial analysis.

Let's start with the basics.

1.1 Volatility, Correlations, and Betas

In the realm of finance theory, accurately assessing an asset's risk is crucial for investors aiming to make informed decisions. This assessment traditionally revolves around two key components: volatility and correlation with the overall market. When applied to cryptocurrencies, these concepts allow us to delve deeper into the inherent risks and behavior of these digital assets, particularly through the lens of crypto's beta—a metric that serves as a true measure of an asset's risk.

1.2 Volatility in Cryptocurrencies

Volatility represents the degree to which the price of an asset fluctuates over time. In the context of cryptocurrencies, volatility is notably high compared to traditional financial assets like stocks and bonds. This elevated volatility stems from several factors unique to the crypto market, including but not limited to market sentiment, regulatory news, technological advancements, and liquidity constraints. The high volatility of cryptocurrencies can lead to significant price swings, which, while presenting potential opportunities for substantial returns, also introduces a heightened risk level for investors.

Bitcoin, the flagship cryptocurrency, has been known for its high volatility since its inception. This characteristic is often attributed to several factors, including its relatively small market size (in comparison to traditional financial markets), the speculative nature of investors, regulatory news, and its nascent market infrastructure. Despite this, **Figure 1** shows that there's a discernible trend where Bitcoin's volatility has shown signs of decline as the market matures.

Over the past few years, as Bitcoin has gained more mainstream acceptance and the infrastructure surrounding cryptocurrencies has developed (with the advent of futures trading, more sophisticated exchange platforms, and institutional investment), its price volatility has seen a gradual decline. This maturation process reflects a growing liquidity pool (in the sense of volume and adoption) and a diversifying investor base, both of which tend to stabilize market fluctuations.

However, it's crucial to note that the "decline" in volatility is relative. Bitcoin and other cryptocurrencies can still experience price swings that would be considered

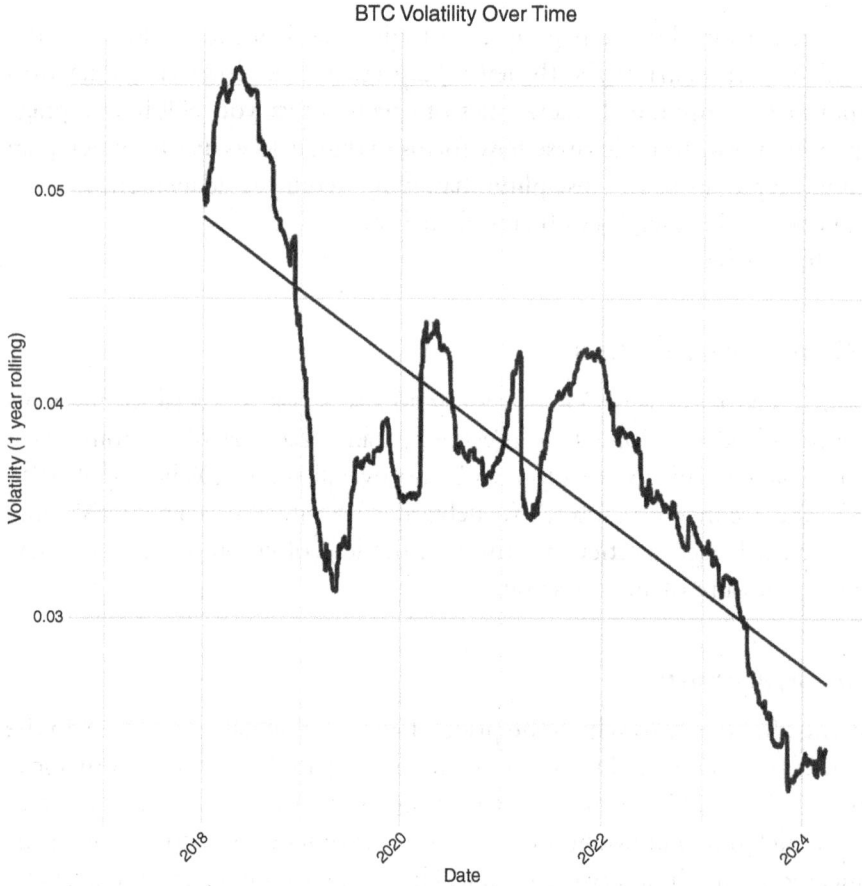

Figure 1   Bitcoin volatility

extreme in the traditional financial markets. For example, double-digit percentage moves within a single day are not uncommon in the crypto space, whereas such moves would be historic anomalies for indices like the S&P 500. **Figure 2** shows that BTC's volatility, as well as those of other major cryptocurrencies such as Ethereum, Solana, and BNB, remains significantly higher than that of traditional financial instruments such as the S&P 500 and the Nasdaq 100. The S&P 500, a stock market index tracking the performance of 500 large companies listed on stock exchanges in the United States, is known for its stability and is often used as a benchmark for the overall health of the U.S. stock market. Its volatility is markedly lower than that of Bitcoin for several reasons. Maybe it is not a fair comparison. The S&P 500 covers a wide range of sectors, diluting the impact of sector-specific stocks. Stock markets are heavily regulated and have been established for much longer, contributing to investor confidence and stability. Finally, the investor base of the S&P 500 is more diverse, including retail investors, institutional investors, and pensions funds, which generally have a longer investment horizon compared to the relatively speculative and retail-driven crypto market.

The comparison between Bitcoin's volatility and that of the Nasdaq 100 index offers another interesting perspective on the nature of risk and return in the cryptocurrency versus traditional equity markets. The Nasdaq 100, comprising 100 of the largest non-financial companies listed on the Nasdaq stock market, is known for its tech-heavy composition. This sector bias toward technology and innovation makes the Nasdaq 100 more volatile than broader market indices like the S&P 500 but typically less so than Bitcoin. Similarly to crypto assets, technology stocks are often subject to rapid growth

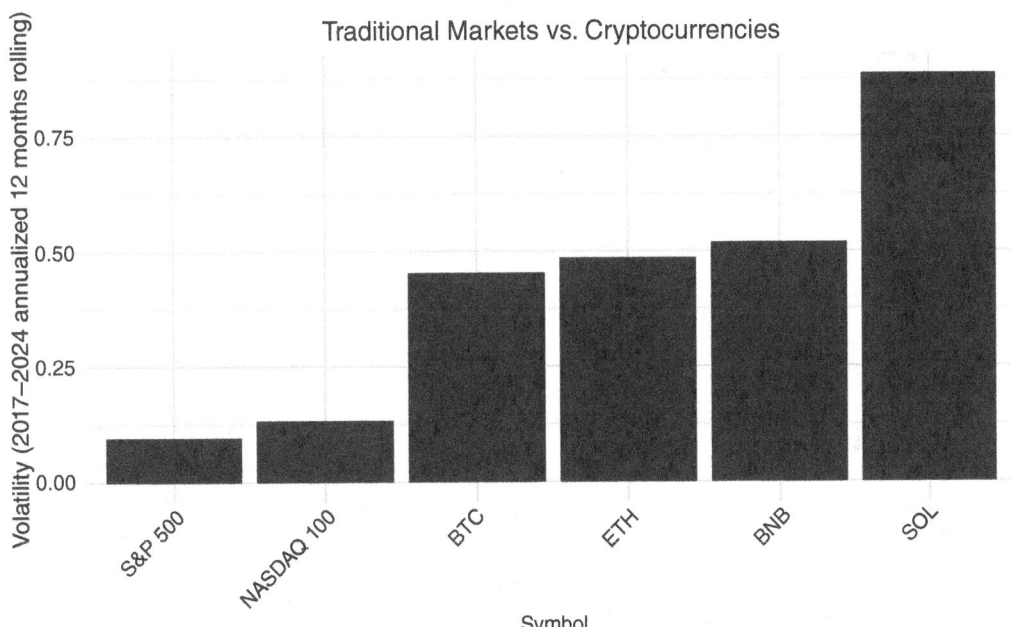

Figure 2   Cryptocurrencies and traditional markets

expectations and can be highly reactive to changes in market sentiment, technological advancements, and regulatory changes affecting the tech sector.

When comparing the volatility of major cryptocurrencies, like Bitcoin and Ethereum, with the constituents of the Nasdaq 100, an interesting observation emerges (**Figure 3**). While it's widely acknowledged that cryptocurrencies exhibit high volatility, a closer examination of the Nasdaq 100 constituents—particularly those in the tech and biotech sectors—reveals that the volatility of some of these stocks is not markedly far off from that of the leading digital assets. This observation nuances the conversation around risk and volatility in investment portfolios, especially for investors drawn to high-growth potential assets.

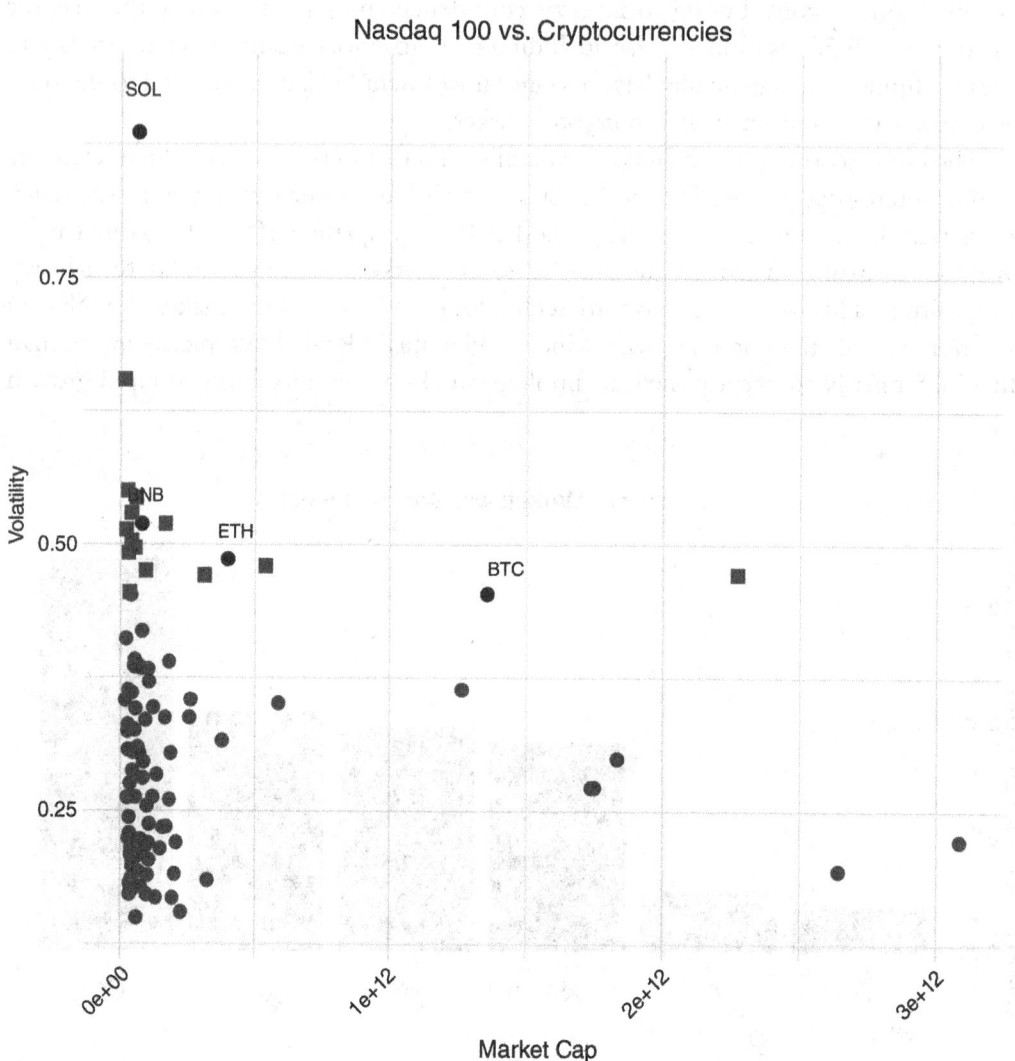

Figure 3   Nasdaq 100 constituents and Cryptocurrencies. Squares indicate the companies that have a higher annualized volatility than BTC

This similarity can partly be attributed to the shared characteristics of high growth potential and investor speculation on future value. Both high-growth stocks and major cryptocurrencies are driven by expectations of future returns rather than current earnings, making their prices more susceptible to investor sentiment and less anchored by traditional valuation metrics.

For investors, recognizing that the volatility of certain Nasdaq 100 stocks is comparable to that of major cryptocurrencies offers a more nuanced perspective on risk. It challenges the notion that cryptocurrencies are inherently more volatile or risky than all traditional financial assets. Instead, it suggests that high volatility is a characteristic of high-growth potential investments, regardless of whether they are digital assets or equity in pioneering companies. *The question about whether to buy or not BTC can then be reframed as: should I increase my exposure to tech by X percentage points?*

This understanding should inform portfolio construction and risk management strategies. Investors attracted to the growth potential of tech and biotech sectors within the Nasdaq 100, and those interested in cryptocurrencies, must account for similar levels of volatility and risk exposure. Diversification, both within asset classes and across them, becomes crucial in managing this risk.

In summary, while cryptocurrencies like Bitcoin and Ethereum are often highlighted for their volatility, a detailed examination of the constituents of the Nasdaq 100 reveals that some stocks exhibit comparable levels of fluctuation. This comparison not only sheds light on the nature of volatility in relation to growth potential but also emphasizes the importance of a balanced approach to risk management in the pursuit of high returns. Investors should therefore consider both traditional and digital assets within the broader context of their investment strategy and objectives, leveraging the growth opportunities each offers while mindful of the inherent risks.

1.3 Correlation with Traditional Markets

Volatility is only part of the picture. Measuring the correlation between cryptocurrencies and traditional financial markets is a critical exercise for investors aiming to construct a diversified portfolio. Diversification is a fundamental investment strategy that involves spreading investments across different assets or asset classes to reduce risk. The effectiveness of diversification hinges on the principle that asset prices do not move in perfect unison; some assets may perform well when others do not, thus smoothing out the overall returns and reducing the portfolio's volatility over time.

Correlation measures the degree to which two assets move in relation to each other. It is quantified by the correlation coefficient, which ranges from –1 to +1. A coefficient of +1 indicates that the assets move perfectly together, –1 signifies that they move in exactly opposite directions, and 0 implies no relationship in their movements. For diversification purposes, assets with low (near zero) or negative correlations are sought after, as they offer the best risk-reduction benefits when combined in a portfolio.

Thus, the rationale behind measuring this correlation is twofold:

1. **Diversification Benefits:** If cryptocurrencies exhibit low or negative correlation with traditional assets, they can be valuable tools for portfolio diversification. Adding cryptocurrencies to a portfolio that predominantly holds traditional assets could potentially lower overall portfolio risk and improve returns, as the non-correlated assets could buffer against market downturns in traditional markets.

2. **Risk Management:** Understanding the correlation dynamics helps in risk management. For instance, if cryptocurrencies start showing a higher correlation with traditional markets during periods of market stress, this behavior could influence how they are used in portfolio construction. Investors might need to reassess the role of cryptocurrencies in achieving diversification and adjust their investment strategy accordingly.

Cryptocurrencies, being a relatively new asset class, have been subject to scrutiny regarding their correlation with traditional markets such as stocks, bonds, and commodities. Initially, cryptocurrencies were believed to operate independently of traditional financial markets, offering an attractive diversification proposition. However, as shown in **Figure 4,** the correlation between cryptocurrencies and traditional assets can vary over time and across different market conditions. For example, during significant financial downturns or global uncertainties, all assets, including cryptocurrencies, may become more correlated as investors react similarly across the board, seeking liquidity or moving toward safe-haven assets, i.e. investors are prone to offload risky assets and purchase safer ones like Treasuries. Overall, the correlation between stock market and BTC (as a proxy for the overall crypto market) has increased since 2020.

Why? The observed increase in the correlation between Bitcoin (BTC) and the stock market can be attributed to a confluence of factors that reflect both the maturation of the cryptocurrency market and its growing integration with traditional financial systems. This trend toward higher correlation has important implications for investors, especially considering the potential impact of Bitcoin ETFs (Exchange-Traded Funds) on this dynamic.

Over recent years, there has been a significant increase in institutional interest and investment in Bitcoin and other cryptocurrencies. As institutional investors, such as hedge funds, mutual funds, and pension funds, begin to include BTC in their portfolios, the price movements of Bitcoin are increasingly influenced by factors that affect traditional financial markets. This includes macroeconomic indicators, interest rates, and liquidity conditions, leading to a more pronounced correlation with the stock market.

Bitcoin's growing mainstream acceptance as an investment asset has aligned its price movements more closely with investor sentiment, which also drives the stock market. In times of economic optimism or pessimism, we see similar investor behavior across both markets, leading to concurrent price movements.

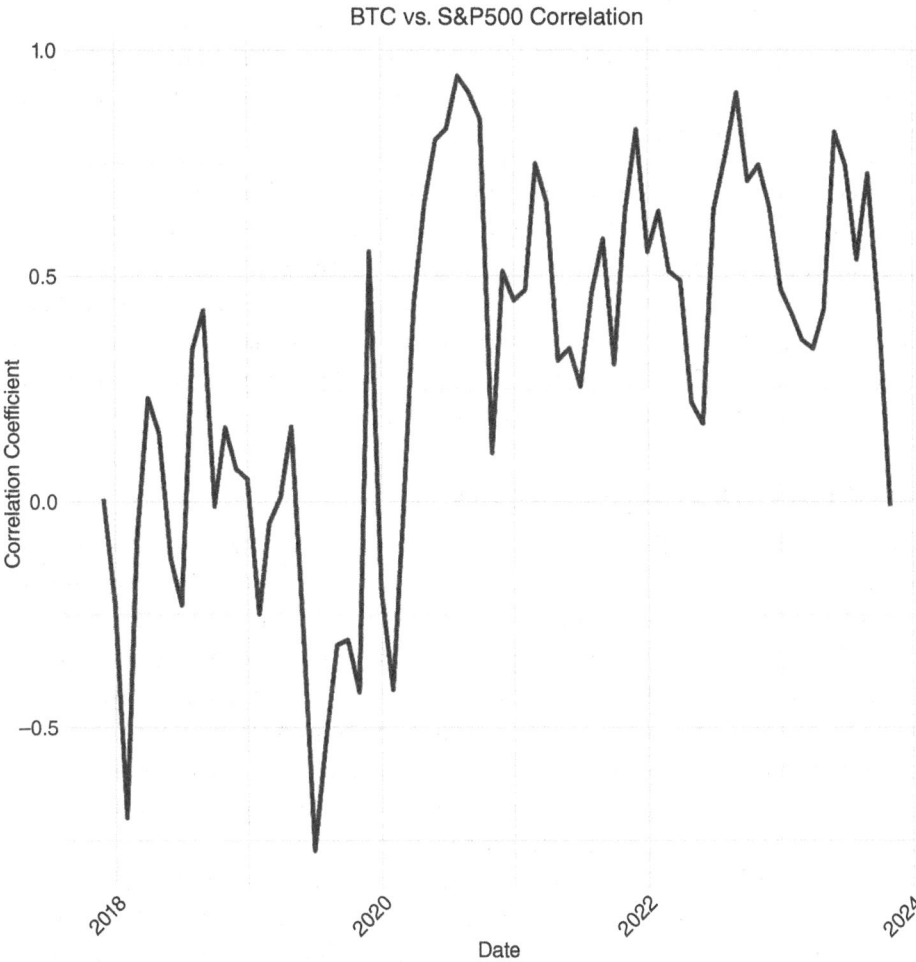

Figure 4   Correlation Between S&P500 and BTC

The introduction of Bitcoin ETFs is poised to further increase the correlation between Bitcoin and the stock market for several reasons:

1. **Enhanced Accessibility and Exposure:** Bitcoin ETFs make it easier for a broader range of investors, especially those who prefer traditional investment vehicles, to gain exposure to Bitcoin without the complexities of direct cryptocurrency ownership. This ease of access means that market sentiments and macroeconomic factors influencing traditional investors are more likely to impact Bitcoin in ways similar to stocks.

2. **Increased Institutional Involvement:** ETFs are a familiar and regulated investment product for institutional investors. The availability of Bitcoin ETFs could lead to increased participation by these investors in the cryptocurrency market, further aligning Bitcoin's price movements with those of traditional assets.

3. **Liquidity and Price Discovery:** Bitcoin ETFs contribute to improved liquidity and price discovery for Bitcoin. The mechanisms of creating and redeeming ETF

shares in response to market demand can lead to more efficient pricing that reflects both crypto-specific factors and broader market conditions. This could lead to tighter price correlations with the stock market, especially if the ETFs become a significant part of the trading volume.

As the integration between cryptocurrency markets and traditional financial systems deepens, the correlation between Bitcoin and the stock market is likely to evolve. While higher correlation might reduce Bitcoin's perceived benefit as a diversification tool, it also signifies the cryptocurrency's growing acceptance and maturation as an investable asset class. Investors will need to carefully consider these dynamics when assessing Bitcoin's role in their portfolios, especially as the landscape continues to change with new developments like the introduction of Bitcoin ETFs.

1.4 Modern Portfolio Theory and Cryptocurrencies

Modern Portfolio Theory (MPT), introduced by Harry Markowitz in 1952, provides a framework to construct portfolios that optimize or maximize expected return based on a given level of market risk, emphasizing that risk is an inherent part of higher reward.

In the high-octane world of cryptocurrency investment, risk-adjusted performance metrics serve as the instruments in the investor's toolkit, harmonizing the discordant notes of risk and reward into a symphony of strategic insight. Among these, the Sharpe ratio is definitely one of the most used ones. Originally conceptualized by William Sharpe to guide the allocation of traditional financial assets, this eponymous metric has found a new proving ground in the digital asset realm.

The Sharpe ratio, by its essence, quantifies the additional return an investor receives per unit of increase in risk. Defined as the difference between the portfolio's return and the risk-free rate divided by the portfolio's standard deviation, it offers a succinct assessment of performance by capturing the premium earned over a riskless endeavor. In traditional markets, treasury bills often embody this risk-free rate, but its analogue in crypto markets remains a subject of contention, given their nascence and inherent volatility.

Suppose an investor's portfolio, heavily laden with cryptocurrencies, yields an annual return of 20% in a landscape where the risk-free rate hovers at 2%. With a portfolio standard deviation, or volatility, of 10%, the Sharpe ratio would register at a robust 1.8—a siren calls to those seeking the allure of high returns for comparatively moderate volatility. Yet, as cryptocurrencies often dance to an erratic rhythm, the practicality of the Sharpe ratio in crypto markets must acknowledge the unpredictable crescendos and diminuendos of digital asset volatility.

As the cryptocurrency market continues to captivate and unsettle investors with its significant price fluctuations, the application of the Sortino ratio has gained prominence. This measure refines the Sharpe ratio by specifically focusing on downside volatility—the primary concern for investors. Distinctly, the Sortino ratio evaluates the risk of negative returns by considering only the standard deviation of these adverse movements.

For instance, a cryptocurrency exhibiting high volatility but with negative returns displaying a standard deviation of 8% might present a Sortino ratio of 2.25, given a 20% return and a 2% risk-free rate. This metric could appeal to investors more concerned with mitigating losses than capturing maximal gains.

However, neither the Sharpe nor the Sortino ratio fully encapsulates the complex risk landscape of the cryptocurrency markets. The Calmar ratio emerges as another critical metric, comparing the annualized return of an investment to its maximum drawdown over a specified timeframe. It focuses not on the frequency of investment declines but on the severity of its largest downturn. A cryptocurrency providing an annualized return of 15% facing a maximum drawdown of 30% would yield a Calmar ratio of 0.5. This value starkly reflects the inherent volatility of investing in cryptocurrencies, marked by potentially steep gains and losses.

The still growing maturity and diversification of the crypto market underscores the complexity of applying these metrics. Unlike traditional assets, which may benefit from extensive historical data, cryptocurrencies often have a shorter history, increasing the estimation risk for expected returns and volatilities crucial to these performance measures.

The importance of such metrics remains significant despite these challenges. For example, the application of the Sharpe ratio to cryptocurrencies necessitates a nuanced understanding of their atypical behavior. Traditional assets generally show Sharpe ratios below 1, reflecting returns per unit of risk below the risk-free rate. Conversely, cryptocurrencies have, at times, demonstrated Sharpe ratios substantially above 1, suggesting the potential for extraordinary returns relative to volatility. However, given the volatile nature of the crypto market, such periods may be transient, and the associated risks are not always evident.

The Sortino ratio, by ignoring positive volatility that benefits investors, provides a more accurate measure of risk in the tumultuous cryptocurrency market. Additionally, the Maximum Drawdown metric offers a direct insight into potential losses, not softened by average performance, highlighting the severe risk of significant value declines.

I will give you a couple more so that you cannot be easily impressed by those YouTubers playing as finance gurus.

Exploring further, the Omega ratio considers the complete distribution of returns, capturing skewness and kurtosis, which are particularly pronounced in cryptocurrency returns due to their asymmetric and heavy-tailed nature.

Opinions on these metrics vary widely. Advocates for cryptocurrency investment strategies might argue that the exceptional growth potential of digital assets justifies the high Sharpe ratios, even considering significant volatility. They assert that cryptocurrencies remain an appealing option for investors willing to accept downside risk for portfolio diversification.

Conversely, critics emphasize the risks underscored by these metrics, particularly the Maximum Drawdown, suggesting that cryptocurrencies' unpredictability makes them unreliable for sustained investment strategies. They caution against systemic risks and regulatory uncertainties that traditional metrics may not fully capture.

From the vantage point of traditional financial institutions, these metrics serve as a bridge to understanding the risk profile of crypto assets. These institutions are increasingly interested in the potential of crypto assets to offer uncorrelated returns and new opportunities for portfolio diversification. They recognize that while the risk may be higher, the fundamental principles of risk management and portfolio optimization still apply. Through careful application of these measures, they seek to cautiously navigate the promising yet uncertain waters of crypto investment.

1.5 Market Risk and Beta Coefficients

Diving into the dynamic world of cryptocurrencies through the lens of traditional financial analysis introduces us to the concept of beta coefficients, a measure historically rooted in the Capital Asset Pricing Model (CAPM). Beta, a statistical measure of an asset's volatility in relation to the broader market, illuminates the risk landscape of investing in cryptocurrencies when juxtaposed against traditional financial markets.

Beta measurement for cryptocurrencies operates on the same principle as it does for traditional assets: it quantifies the tendency of an asset's returns to respond to swings in the market. A beta of 1 implies that the asset moves in tandem with the market; a beta greater than 1 indicates higher volatility than the market; and a beta less than 1 suggests lower volatility. For instance, a cryptocurrency with a beta of 1.5 is more volatile than the broader market, suggesting that it might offer higher returns in bullish conditions but pose greater risks during downturns.

For cryptocurrencies, beta measurement follows a similar concept but with its own set of challenges and nuances:

- **Market Benchmark:** Determining an appropriate market benchmark is challenging because the crypto market lacks a universally accepted index that represents the entire market. Various crypto indices exist, but they might not fully capture the market dynamics as traditional indices do for stocks.
- **High Volatility:** Cryptocurrencies are inherently more volatile than most traditional assets. This can lead to higher beta values, indicating a strong reaction to market movements. However, the extreme price swings in crypto markets can make beta a less stable metric over time.
- **Data Availability:** Reliable historical price data is essential for calculating beta. While data for major cryptocurrencies is readily available, the relative youth of the market means there's less historical data compared to traditional assets.

High beta values in crypto investments carry significant implications. While they promise amplified returns during market upswings, they also expose investors to intensified losses during downturns. This double-edged sword embodies the speculative allure of cryptocurrencies but necessitates a sophisticated risk management strategy. High beta cryptos can supercharge a portfolio's performance, yet they demand resilience and a strategic approach to timing, diversification, and hedging.

Consider, for example, the volatile journey of Bitcoin. Its beta, when measured against traditional market indices like the S&P 500, has varied over time, reflecting periods of alignment with broader market movements as well as instances of divergent behavior. This variability underscores the importance of continuous monitoring and analysis for investors who include high beta cryptocurrencies in their portfolios.

Moreover, the implications of these high beta values extend beyond individual portfolio management to influence the broader narrative around cryptocurrencies. They challenge traditional notions of asset allocation, prompting a reevaluation of risk tolerance, investment horizons, and the very definition of diversification. For traditional financial institutions, the high beta nature of cryptocurrencies offers both an opportunity and a cautionary tale. It invites exploration of new frontiers in asset management and financial innovation but underscores the need for robust analytical frameworks capable of navigating the crypto market's unique volatility.

News from the Ivory Tower

The world of cryptocurrency can feel like a wild ride, but research is shedding light on the forces shaping its ups and downs. Studies by Liu, Tsyvinski, Wu (2019), Liebi (2022), and Liu, Tsyvinski (2020) paint a fascinating picture.

Imagine a compass guiding your crypto investments. The first key factor is the **crypto market itself**. Just like stocks, the overall market trend significantly impacts individual currencies. But there's more to the story. Think of smaller, scrappier cryptos with something to prove. The research suggests they tend to outperform established giants, a phenomenon captured by the **size factor**. Additionally, the **momentum factor** comes into play, where cryptos with a history of strong performance are more likely to keep going up.

Liebi (2022) took things a step further by adding a **value factor** to the mix. This factor considers how actively a cryptocurrency's network is used, potentially revealing undervalued gems.

Liu and Tsyvinski (2020) didn't stop there. They built a comprehensive "crypto compass" with several factors:

- **Network factors:** How busy is the cryptocurrency's highway? This reflects real-world usage and activity.
- **Momentum factor:** Still relevant, this factor helps identify cryptos riding a wave.
- **Investor Attention:** Whether it's positive buzz or panicked headlines, investor attention can significantly impact prices.

Interestingly, the study found that factors related to production costs and traditional valuation metrics didn't have a major influence.

2. Trading Strategies: Part 1

Having explored the fundamentals of applying financial tools to cryptocurrency assets, let's get our hands dirty with some trading strategies. This section will delve into various common trading strategies that have found their place within the cryptocurrency market, each demonstrating a different level of complexity and success. The execution of these strategies spans a broad spectrum; some necessitate merely the establishment of a single account on a cryptocurrency exchange, while others demand the orchestration of multiple accounts, the crafting of smart contracts, and the deployment of trading bots that operate round the clock. In the following discussions, we will not only describe these trading strategies but also enrich our exploration with practical code examples, offering a tangible glimpse into the mechanics and digital craftsmanship required to navigate the volatile waters of the cryptocurrency trading world.

This guide is more like a treasure map drawn by pirates. Intriguing? Absolutely. A guaranteed X marks the spot? Not so much. So, as you gear up to navigate these digital waters, remember, you're steering the ship at your own risk. This isn't financial advice; it's more like a compass handed to you by a friend who's just as lost at sea. Chart your course wisely, matey, and may your crypto adventures be thrilling (but don't blame the parrot if things go awry).

2.1 Buy and Hold

A common strategy that many crypto enthusiasts deploy is a buy and hold (or HODL) strategy, where the investor buys a particular cryptocurrency and holds it in their exchange account or wallet long-term. These investors share the view that cryptocurrency values will rise significantly in the next several years and hope to benefit from the increase in price. Implementing the strategy is quite simple as investors only need an account at a cryptocurrency exchange to trade these assets. But the KYC process can be cumbersome, user experiences on exchanges can be confusing and difficult to understand, and recent centralized exchange issues, such as the collapse of FTX, and Binance's legal troubles with the DOJ, may deter users from opening new accounts. The launch of Bitcoin ETFs, Grayscale's GBTC, and Fidelity's FBTC, make investing in Bitcoin significantly easier as users can purchase these ETFs to gain exposure to crypto on their brokerage accounts. However, the historical volatility of cryptocurrencies can increase the risk of the strategy as investors may see drawdowns of over 50% for several years at a time. Because most of these investors are true believers of cryptocurrency, they can often tolerate the volatility and drawdowns and continue to hold their portfolios with "diamond hands."

The importance of such a strategy is that it provides a valuable benchmark for other investment strategies due to its emphasis on long-term value appreciation and resilience against market volatility. Unlike active trading, which requires constant monitoring and quick decision-making, HODLing promotes patience and conviction in the underlying technology and potential of cryptocurrencies. This approach minimizes the emotional stress of market fluctuations and reduces transaction costs, providing a stable, straightforward framework against which the performance and complexity of other strategies can be measured. So when you hear about great returns from professional traders, always ask how that would have compared to hold the top cryptocurrencies over the same time period. It is similar to check the fund manager performance against the S&P500. Even Warren Buffett has mostly underperformed the S&P500 . . . .[3]

2.2 Momentum and Trend Following Strategy

Because cryptocurrencies often grow in value very quickly during consecutive days or weeks, or collapse very suddenly, many hedge funds employ a strategy that purchase cryptocurrencies when prices are on an uptrend or sell cryptocurrencies when prices are on a downtrend. This class of strategies is called momentum trading strategies or trend following strategies because they analyze the momentum and trend of price movements to decide the allocation of the portfolio. There are many types of indicators that traders use as signals for their trading decisions. For instance, investors look at the moving average of prices and compare it to the current price. To compute a moving average, the trader needs to know one parameter: the lookback window. A moving average with lookback window w days is computed by taking the average of the prices in the last w days. If the current price is above the moving average, then the strategy buys (longs) the underlying asset. If the price is below the moving average, then the strategy sells (shorts). Because the strategy buys and sells, we usually label it a long-short strategy.

Many cryptocurrency exchanges do not yet have the same shorting functionality as traditional brokerages where one can borrow the asset to sell. Instead, these exchanges offer a new product named perpetual swaps, which are futures contracts with no expiration date. The price of the contract is pegged to the price of the underlying cryptocurrency through a mechanism called funding rates. We will discuss the details of this new instrument in the basis trade strategy below. The most important thing to know now is that you can both long and short this instrument, allowing your trend following strategy to take advantage of both uptrends and downtrends.

The following Python code shows how one can compute the moving averages and generate a signal to buy or sell:

```
# start with a Pandas dataframe that contains daily price of a
cryptocurrency
# you can get this data from data providers or straight from the exchange
price_df

# compute the 30 day moving average
price_df['moving_average'] = price_df['price'].rolling(window=30).mean()

# to calculate the signal, we need to compare the current moving average
and the current price
current_ma = price_df.iloc[-1]['moving_average']
current_price = price_df.iloc[-1]['price']
if current_ma < current_price:
    signal = "buy"
```

[3] See https://www.linkedin.com/pulse/warren-buffett-has-underperformed-sp-500-last-20-years-jain-cfa.

```
else:
    signal = "sell"

# insert functionality to trade on the exchange with your signal here
```

In the code example, we use a 30-day moving average for our signal. First, we need daily pricing data, which you can get from cryptocurrency data providers or straight from the exchange API. Next, we compute the 30-day moving average and save it as a new column. Finally, we compare the current moving average with the current price to determine whether we should buy or sell.

There are many other iterations of the strategy, too. For example, we could have a long-only strategy where, instead of selling when the price is below the moving average, we simply hold cash until the signal buy returns. We could also use an exponential moving average instead of a simple moving average so that we make recent price movements more impactful to our signal generation. Another modification could have the strategy compare multiple moving averages to create a set of signals that together give you a more accurate signal.

The strategy does have risks and tends to only do well in periods where uptrends or downtrends are clear in the market. It is possible that the signal generates false positives or false negatives where trends do not last long enough for the strategy to take advantage of it. The choice of the moving average window is crucial. Too long and the moving average may not react quickly enough to changes in the trend, leading to late exits or late entries, and loss of funds. Too short and the strategy may have too many false positives, and the strategy will start accruing trading fees quickly, at the expense of your returns.

For example, let's examine Bitcoin's price from July 2020 to June 2021 for hints of trends (**Figure 5**). The figure shows the daily price level of BTC. From July to January, we see a clear uptrend in prices where buying Bitcoin is a great idea and highly profitable as the price jumps from $10,000 to $40,000. But, at the same time, we also see periods of downtrends, such as in January 2021, end of March 2021, and May 2021, where the portfolio can just hold cash or go short. In these situations, following the trend of price movements can be a very profitable strategy as you take advantage of moments where Bitcoin's price is increasing significantly.

2.3 Breakout Strategy

Another strategy examines situations where prices break out of a certain range; hence the name breakout strategy. There are situations where the price of a cryptocurrency is bound within a range and is not increasing or decreasing significantly, but when it finally breaks out of this range, the price can skyrocket or crash. The strategy can give investors the upper hand as it allows them to have exposure to the market in the early stages of an uptrend or downtrend, potentially adding more gains than a trend following strategy that needs to confirm the existence of the trend before entering the market. One way to generate a signal is to look at the maximum and minimum price in a moving window. For example, an investor can use the max and min price of the asset in the last 30 days,

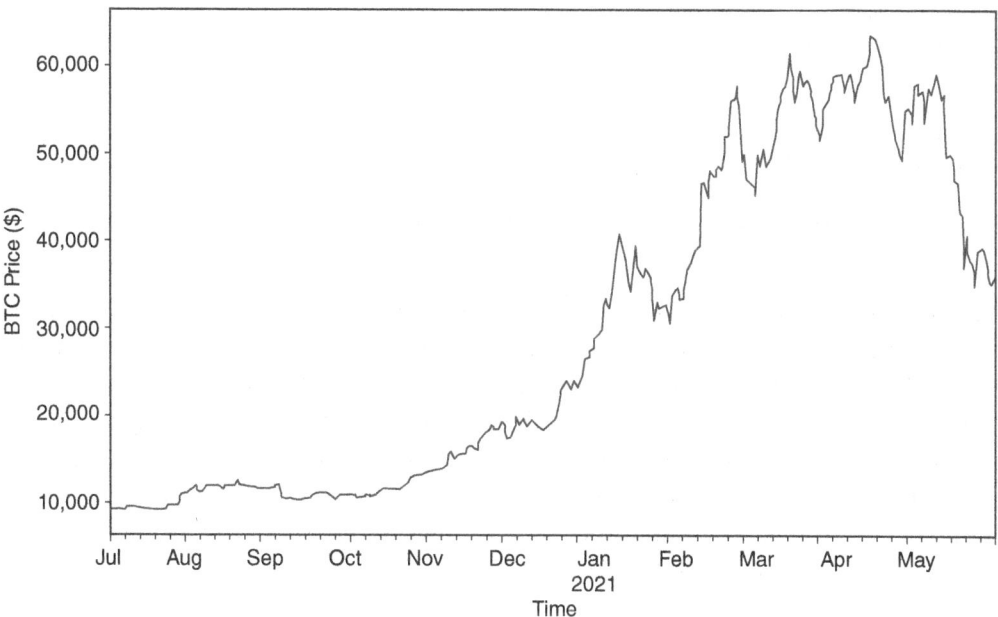

Figure 5   BTC price from July 2020 to June 2021

and then use the current price to calculate the price relative to the range. The relative price can then be used to generate the signal by simply determining if the price is out of range. If the price is out of range, then the investor can choose to go long or go short (or go to cash/stablecoins in a long-only strategy). If the price is still within the range, the investor should not trade and should hold cash/stablecoins until there is a breakout. The following Python code is an example of how an investor can calculate the relative price and use it as an indicator for a breakout:

```
# start with a Pandas dataframe that contains daily price of a
cryptocurrency
# you can get this data from data providers or straight from the exchange
price_df

# compute the 30 day max and min
price_df['max_price'] = price_df['price'].rolling(window=30).max()
price_df['min_price'] = price_df['price'].rolling(window=30).min()

# to calculate the signal, we need to examine the price relative to
the range
current_max = price_df.iloc[-1]['max_price']
current_min = price_df.iloc[-1]['min_price']
current_price = price_df.iloc[-1]['price']
relative_price = (current_price - current_min) / (current_max
- current_min)
if relative_price < 0:
    # the current price is breaking out below the min
    signal = "sell"
```

```
elif relative_price > 1:
    # the current price is breaking out above the max
    signal = "buy"
else:
    # the current price is still within the range
    signal = "cash"

# insert functionality to trade on the exchange with your signal here
```

Although the example simply examines if the relative price indicates a breakout, an investor could transform the relative price with a normalization calculation and combine it with other indicators to generate a more complex signal that might generate better returns. Like with trend following strategies, the choice of the moving average window is crucial to the profitability of the strategy. An additional challenge is that once the price hits the limits of your specified range, it may not continue increasing or decreasing. Instead, the price might revert into the range and toward the mean price over that window. In this situation, one could deploy a mean reversion strategy.

2.4 Mean Reversion Strategy

A mean reversion strategy takes advantage of a market regime where price movements are generally sideways and stuck within a range with no trends. The strategy assumes that, regardless of recent price movements, the price will revert to a specific level after some time. For example, suppose that BTC has been trading between \$30,000 and \$32,000 consistently over the last few weeks. Your mean reversion strategy could decide to buy when price is near \$30,000 and sell when it returns to the mean of \$31,000, or short when price is near \$32,000 and buy it back when it returns to the mean. If the price stays in the range and the mean reversion pattern continues, the strategy will be profitable as you buy low and sell when price increases back to the mean or sell high and buy it back when price decreases back to the mean.

---

[4] A Bollinger Band® is a technical analysis tool defined by a set of trendlines plotted two standard deviations (positively and negatively) away from a simple moving average (SMA) of a security's price, but which can be adjusted to user preferences for more or fewer standard deviations. This method was developed by John Bollinger in the 1980s. The Bollinger Bands consist of three lines:

1. **The Middle Band:** This is the simple moving average (SMA) of the security's price. It typically uses the 20-day moving average but can be adjusted to any period depending on the trader's strategy.
2. **The Upper Band:** This is calculated by adding (2 x standard deviation) to the middle band (SMA). This band adjusts to market volatility, widening during volatile periods and contracting during calmer periods.
3. **The Lower Band:** This is calculated by subtracting (2 x standard deviation) from the middle band (SMA).

The key concept behind Bollinger Bands is market volatility. The bands widen when volatility increases and narrow when volatility decreases. Traders and analysts use Bollinger Bands to identify potential overbought or oversold conditions, momentum, and possible price breakouts.

For instance, a price moving closer to the upper band is often seen as overbought, suggesting a potential selling opportunity, whereas a price near the lower band may be considered oversold, indicating a potential buying opportunity. A price breakout above the upper band or below the lower band may signal a continuation of the current trend.

Bollinger Bands are widely used in various markets including stocks, forex, and cryptocurrencies, offering a dynamic approach to understanding market behavior and potential price movements.

A simple mean reversion strategy uses an indicator called Bollinger Bands to find the range that the cryptocurrency is trading in.[4] The upper limit of the range is computed as a few standard deviations above the moving average of the cryptocurrency's price, and the lower limit of the range is computed as a few standard deviations below the moving average. The moving standard deviation is computed just like the moving average, where the investor examines prices in the last w days and computes the standard deviation of the price within that window. Then, when the price is above the range, we short the cryptocurrency, and when the price is below the range, we long the cryptocurrency to earn a profit as the price reverts to the mean. To exit the position, users can choose from a variety of conditions: exiting when the price returns to the mean or exiting when the price crosses the other limit and reverse the position. For example, the following Python code finds the range by computing 2 standard deviations above and below the moving average and determines if an investor should create a position or not:

```python
# start with a Pandas dataframe that contains daily price of a cryptocurrency
# you can get this data from data providers or straight from the exchange
price_df

# compute the 30 day moving average and the standard deviation
price_df['moving_average'] = price_df['price'].rolling(window=30).mean()
price_df['moving_std'] = price_df['price'].rolling(window=30).std()

# to calculate the signal, we need to first determine the range
current_avg = price_df['moving_average'].iloc[-1]
current_std = price_df['moving_std'].iloc[-1]
current_price = price_df['price'].iloc[-1]
upper_limit = current_avg + 2 * current_std # upper limit is 2 stds
above the mean
lower_limit = current_avg - 2 * current_std # lower limit is 2 stds
below the mean

# now we can generate the signal based on the range and decide if we
should create a position
if current_price < lower_limit:
    # price is below the range, so it will increase back to mean and
we will buy
    signal = 'buy'
elif current_price > upper_limit:
    # price is above the range, so it will decrease back to mean and
we will sell
    signal = 'sell'
else:
    # price is within the range, so we won't do anything
    signal = 'cash'

# insert functionality to trade on the exchange with your signal here
```

The code above first finds the moving average and standard deviation. Then, it computes the upper and lower limit of our Bollinger band using 2 standard deviations. Finally, when the price is below the range, the strategy will create a position and buy the cryptocurrency; when the price is above the range, the strategy will sell; and when the price is within the range, the strategy will stay in cash. The two parameters of lookback window and number of standard deviations are crucial as they can determine the timing and frequency of trading. As with the previous strategies, these parameters will affect your profitability significantly. As with the breakout strategy, a risk is that there is no mean reversion pattern, or the pattern changes away from mean reversion, and your position is now at a loss. For example, let's examine Bitcoin's price in 2023 in **Figure 6** below.

Overall, price grows from below $20,000 to near $45,000, but during the year, there are periods where a breakout strategy is appropriate and periods where a mean reversion pattern is evident. For instance, in the period from mid-March to mid-June or late June to early August, the price seems to be stuck within a range, so deploying a mean reversion strategy may be ideal (**Figure 6**). However, we also see periods where price no longer exhibits a mean reversion pattern and, instead, breaks out of the range, like in the middle of June, and the middle of August. In the right market conditions, these strategies can be highly profitable as they take advantage of patterns in recent price movements, but the key is in knowing what market regime is present.

2.5 Arbitrage

Arbitrage is a strategy that aims to exploit price differences across different markets and exchanges. Because there are many different cryptocurrency exchanges where investors can trade the same asset, prices may sometimes diverge. In traditional finance, many hedge funds already take advantage of the price differences, so these opportunities are fleeting. But the cryptocurrency market is relatively new with a low number of institutional

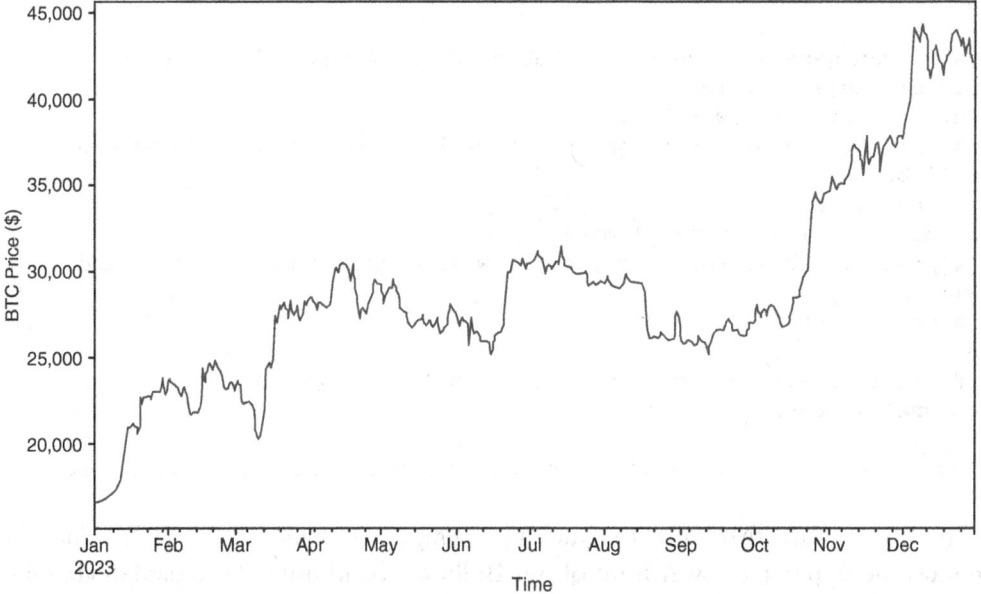

Figure 6   BTC price in 2023

investors involved, so there is greater market inefficiency, leading to longer lasting arbitrage opportunities. At its most basic level, arbitrage is a strategy where investors can exploit the price difference of a single asset on two different exchanges. For example, Bitcoin could be trading at $50,000 on exchange A and $50,500 on exchange B. The arbitrageur would then buy Bitcoin on exchange A, transfer it to exchange B, sell at the higher price, and profit from the difference. Exchange A and exchange B do not necessarily have to be centralized exchanges like Binance or Coinbase—a trader could also exploit price differences between centralized exchanges (CEXs) and decentralized exchanges (DEXs), or between DEXs. If a difference exists and is lasting, the particular exchange does not matter.

Let's view an example of how to complete a DEX-DEX arbitrage between Uniswap V2 and Sushiswap. User codeesura on Github has written a Solidity smart contract that arbitrages an asset's price relative to ETH on both exchanges. A simplified version of the code with some comments is in the following code snippet:

```
// SPDX-License-Identifier: MIT
pragma solidity ^0.8.0;

interface IUniswapV2Router {
    function swapExactTokensForTokens(
        uint amountIn,
        uint amountOutMin,
        address[] calldata path,
        address to,
        uint deadline
    ) external returns (uint[] memory amounts);
}

interface ISushiSwapRouter {
    function swapExactTokensForTokens(
        uint amountIn,
        uint amountOutMin,
        address[] calldata path,
        address to,
        uint deadline
    ) external returns (uint[] memory amounts);
}

interface IWETH9 {
    function approve(address guy, uint wad) external returns (bool);
    function transferFrom(address src, address dst, uint wad) external
    returns (bool);
}

contract ArbitrageBot {
    address private constant WETH_ADDRESS =
    0xB4FBF271143F4FBf7B91A5ded31805e42b2208d6;
    address private constant UNISWAP_ROUTER_ADDRESS =
    0x7a250d5630B4cF539739dF2C5dAcb4c659F2488D;
    address private constant SUSHISWAP_ROUTER_ADDRESS =
    0x1b02dA8Cb0d097eB8D57A175b88c7D8b47997506;
```

```
    IUniswapV2Router private uniswapRouter;
    ISushiSwapRouter private sushiswapRouter;
    IWETH9 private WETH;

    constructor() {
        uniswapRouter = IUniswapV2Router(UNISWAP_ROUTER_ADDRESS);
        sushiswapRouter = ISushiSwapRouter(SUSHISWAP_ROUTER_ADDRESS);
        WETH = IWETH9(WETH_ADDRESS);
    }

    function executeArbitrage(address tokenAddress, uint256 amountIn)
external {
        // Transfer WETH from the caller to this contract
        require(WETH.transferFrom(msg.sender, address(this), amountIn),
"WETH transfer failed");

        // Approve Uniswap Router to spend WETH
        require(WETH.approve(UNISWAP_ROUTER_ADDRESS, amountIn), "Uniswap
approval failed");

        // Execute swap on Uniswap
        address[] memory path = new address[](2);
        path[0] = WETH_ADDRESS;
        path[1] = tokenAddress;
        uint256[] memory amountsUniswap = uniswapRouter.swapExactTokens
ForTokens(amountIn, 0, path, address(this), block.timestamp);
        uint256 amountOutUniswap = amountsUniswap[1];

        // Approve Sushiswap Router to spend the token
        IWETH9(tokenAddress).approve(SUSHISWAP_ROUTER_ADDRESS,
amountOutUniswap);

        // Execute swap on Sushiswap
        path[0] = tokenAddress;
        path[1] = WETH_ADDRESS;
        uint256[] memory amountsSushi = sushiswapRouter.swapExactTokens
ForTokens(amountOutUniswap, 0, path, msg.sender, block.timestamp);
        uint256 amountOutSushi = amountsSushi[1];

        require(amountOutSushi > amountIn, "Arbitrage not profitable");
    }
}
```

The code example completes a specific trade where a user first buys a token using ETH on Uniswap V2, then sells it back to ETH on Sushiswap for a profit. To ensure that the transaction will be successful, the trader needs to check that the price of the asset is higher on Sushiswap relative to the price on Uniswap V2.

While the premise of the strategy is simple, there are still many risks that users must be aware of. An investor may not be the only one to identify an opportunity and might not even be the one to execute the transaction first. So they can end up in a loss if someone else exploits the opportunity first. On CEX-CEX or CEX-DEX arbitrage transactions, an investor may need to hold inventory of different cryptocurrencies or be willing to wait for transaction confirmations because transferring funds from one exchange to the other is not trivial and requires time.

2.6 Statistical Arbitrage

A statistical arbitrage strategy requires an investor to examine the statistical patterns of price movements across the cryptocurrency market. Examples include patterns in correlation, skew, kurtosis, or a combination of measures to create a statistical model that governs the rules of your trading strategy. The goal is to identify patterns and anomalies, and to take advantage of these anomalies. These strategies are generally computationally intensive and highly secretive as analysts find a niche in the patterns that has not yet been exploited. If these models are revealed, the anomaly may disappear as more traders take advantage of it, rendering the strategy unprofitable.

A very simple example is to look at the correlation between cryptocurrencies. Because BTC is the most popular cryptocurrency and is sometimes seen as a proxy for the entire ecosystem, market trends tend to follow the price trends of BTC. If BTC price increases, it is likely that the entire cryptocurrency market will also increase in value. An investor can take advantage of this correlation. For example, from 2020 to 2024, BTC and ETH daily returns had a Pearson correlation coefficient of 0.82, BTC and DOGE had a correlation of 0.32, and BTC and AVAX had a correlation of 0.55. If BTC prices are increasing, an investor can take advantage of BTC's leading role in determining market returns to buy another cryptocurrency early before it also increases. However, there are risks as this lead-lag relationship may only last a few minutes, or even seconds in highly liquid pairs, so the trader needs a strategy that can react quickly to changes in the market. Furthermore, if there is news regarding a specific token that does not apply to BTC, the correlation may disappear. Understanding the dynamics of the lead-lag relationship is crucial for this strategy.

2.7 Smart-Beta Strategies

The empirical research has shown how factors like market movement, size, momentum, and network activity influence cryptocurrency returns. This paves the way for an exciting concept: Smart Beta Strategies for crypto.

Imagine a bridge between passive and active investing in the crypto world. Smart beta takes a passive approach, following a set of rules, but uses alternative weighting schemes compared to traditional market capitalization-based indexes.

Here's how smart beta could be applied to crypto:

- Factor-Based Weighting: Instead of simply buying a basket of cryptos based on their market cap (like Bitcoin having the biggest weight), a smart beta strategy might overweight smaller, high-momentum cryptos (based on the size and momentum factors).
- Network-Centric Focus: A strategy could prioritize cryptos with a high network factor, indicating active usage and potentially more value.
- Investor Attention Filter: Imagine a smart beta strategy that downplays cryptos with excessive negative press (even if it affects the momentum factor) and focuses on those with a more balanced level of investor attention.

These are just a few examples. The beauty of smart beta is its customizability. It might allow investors to reach their targeted exposure, e.g., gain exposure to specific factors you believe will drive returns. Furthermore, diversification across factors can potentially mitigate risk compared to focusing on a single crypto.

One of the key challenges is that past performance isn't a guarantee of future results, and backtesting smart beta strategies in this new market might not be entirely reliable.

Having said all the caveats, let's now build one!

The strategy will:

1. Collect historical price data for a selection of cryptocurrencies.
2. Calculate momentum for each cryptocurrency over a specific period.
3. Rank cryptocurrencies based on their momentum.
4. Construct a portfolio by allocating more weight to cryptocurrencies with higher momentum.

This example will use Python with Pandas for data manipulation and Matplotlib for plotting. We'll simulate the strategy with historical price data, assuming this data is available in a CSV file format for simplicity.

```
import pandas as pd
import numpy as np
import matplotlib.pyplot as plt


# Load historical price data from CSV
# Assuming the CSV has columns: Date, Symbol, and Close
data = pd.read_csv('crypto_prices.csv')
data['Date'] = pd.to_datetime(data['Date'])
data.set_index('Date', inplace=True)


# Calculate momentum
# Here, we use a simple 90-day return as a proxy for momentum
lookback_period = 90  # days
momentum = data.groupby('Symbol')['Close'].pct_change(lookback_period).
shift(-lookback_period)


# Average momentum over the period for simplicity
avg_momentum = momentum.groupby('Symbol').mean()


# Rank cryptocurrencies based on momentum
ranked_symbols = avg_momentum.rank(ascending=False)


# Assume we want to invest in top 5 cryptocurrencies based on momentum
top_n = 5
portfolio_symbols = ranked_symbols[ranked_symbols <= top_n].
index.tolist()
```

```
# Assuming equal weight for simplicity
weights = np.ones(len(portfolio_symbols)) / len(portfolio_symbols)

# Portfolio construction
portfolio_data = data[data['Symbol'].isin(portfolio_symbols)]
portfolio_returns = portfolio_data.groupby('Date')['Close'].mean().
pct_change()

# Cumulative returns of the portfolio
cumulative_returns = (1 + portfolio_returns).cumprod() - 1

# Plotting the cumulative returns
cumulative_returns.plot()
plt.title('Smart Beta Strategy Performance')
plt.xlabel('Date')
plt.ylabel('Cumulative Returns')
plt.show()
```

This Python example provides a foundational approach to building a smart beta strategy based on momentum in the crypto market.

This example assumes you have a CSV file named crypto_prices.csv with historical price data for various cryptocurrencies. The file should contain at least three columns: Date, Symbol, and Close. You may need to adjust the data loading and processing based on your actual data structure.

- Momentum Calculation: This simple example uses a 90-day price return as a proxy for momentum. More sophisticated methods might consider volatility adjustment or different time frames.
- Portfolio Construction: The strategy selects the top 5 cryptocurrencies based on their average momentum over the period and assigns equal weight to each. This is a simplification for demonstration purposes.

This basic example does not account for transaction costs, slippage, or out-of-sample testing, which are important for a real-world trading strategy.

3. Step-Up the Game: Perpetuals

Diversity in trading instruments allows investors to harness market fluctuations to their advantage. The cryptocurrency market, in its relentless pursuit to bridge the gap with its traditional counterparts, has introduced perpetual contracts, which offer a distinct twist on traditional futures contracts. These innovative financial instruments enable traders to speculate on the future price movements of assets like cryptocurrencies, without needing to own or physically handle the underlying asset. This section delves deeper into the defining characteristics and mechanisms that underpin perpetual contracts, shedding light on their operation and appeal.

3.1 Characteristics of Perpetual Contracts

No Expiry Date: One of the hallmark features of perpetual contracts is the absence of an expiry or settlement date. This contrasts sharply with traditional futures contracts, which are bound by predetermined settlement dates. The indefinite nature of perpetual contracts affords traders the flexibility to hold positions for an extended duration, provided they continue to meet the necessary margin requirements. This feature caters to a broad range of trading strategies, from short-term speculation to long-term position holding, without the constraint of time.

Margin Trading: Perpetual contracts facilitate margin trading, where traders can significantly leverage their positions. Leverage allows traders to command a considerable stake in the underlying asset with a relatively modest capital outlay. While this mechanism can substantially magnify potential profits, it concurrently escalates the risk factor, potentially leading to substantial losses. Traders must navigate the leveraged trading landscape with caution, keeping a vigilant eye on market movements and margin calls.

Funding Mechanism: A critical aspect of perpetual contracts is the funding mechanism, designed to anchor the market price of the contract to the spot price of the underlying asset. This mechanism operates through periodic payments made between traders, based on the prevailing market conditions. If the price of the perpetual contract exceeds the spot price, suggesting a predominance of long positions, those in long positions compensate their short-position counterparts, and vice versa. This dynamic funding exchange plays a pivotal role in aligning the perpetual contract prices with underlying market values, ensuring a fair and balanced trading environment.

Mark Price: In an effort to curb market manipulation and guarantee equitable liquidations, perpetual contracts employ a mark price system. The mark price serves as a stable reference point for the asset's value, typically derived from a weighted average of spot prices across multiple exchanges. This system provides a safeguard against price manipulation, ensuring that liquidation processes are conducted fairly and reflect genuine market conditions.

By combining the speculative capabilities of futures contracts with the flexibility of indefinite holding periods, along with mechanisms for leverage, fair pricing, and equitable liquidations, perpetual contracts stand at the forefront of modern trading strategies.

3.2 How Perpetual Contracts Work

In the realm of perpetual contracts, traders embark on a speculative journey, predicting whether the price of an asset will ascend or descend. By opening a long position, a trader expresses confidence that the asset's price will increase. Conversely, initiating a short position signals a belief in the asset's impending decline. The outcome, whether profit or loss, hinges on the asset's price trajectory from the moment the position is established. This direct link between speculation and financial outcome underpins the essence of trading with perpetual contracts.

Perpetual contracts are distinguished by their provision of leverage, enabling traders to amplify their exposure to price fluctuations with a fraction of the asset's total value. This leverage magnifies both potential gains and the susceptibility to losses, introducing a significant risk of liquidation. Should the market veer unfavorably, diverging sharply from the trader's position, the exchange might liquidate the position to avert a negative balance in the trader's account. This mechanism safeguards the integrity of the market and the exchange, ensuring that losses do not exceed the trader's initial margin.

Comparison with Traditional Futures   While both perpetual contracts and traditional futures allow traders to speculate on price movements, several key differences distinguish the two:

- **Expiry Date:** Traditional futures contracts are defined by their expiry dates, upon which the contracts are settled either through physical delivery of the asset or cash settlement. Perpetual contracts, devoid of an expiry date, eschew this settlement process, allowing positions to remain open indefinitely.
- **Price Alignment:** Traditional futures prices may diverge significantly from the spot price of the underlying asset as they near expiration, influenced by factors such as time decay. Perpetual contracts employ a funding mechanism to consistently align the contract price with the spot price, mitigating prolonged discrepancies.
- **Trading Objectives:** While both instruments are used for hedging and speculation, the indefinite nature of perpetual contracts makes them particularly attractive for traders seeking long-term exposure without the need to rollover positions as futures contracts expire.
- **Market Participants:** Traditional futures markets often attract a broader range of participants, including institutional investors and corporations looking to hedge against price volatility in commodities, currencies, and other assets. Perpetual contracts, predominantly found in cryptocurrency markets, cater more to retail and speculative traders drawn to the crypto asset class.

In summary, perpetual contracts offer a dynamic and flexible alternative to traditional futures, tailored to the fast-paced and speculative nature of cryptocurrency markets. The ability to hold positions indefinitely, coupled with the mechanisms for leverage and price alignment, positions perpetual contracts as a pivotal tool for modern traders. However, the increased risk of liquidation underlines the need for prudent risk management and a deep understanding of market forces.

Let's delve into a numerical example that illustrates the mechanics and potential outcomes of trading with leveraged perpetual contracts in the cryptocurrency market, focusing on Bitcoin as the asset of interest.

Initial Conditions   A trader embarks on their trading journey with an initial balance of $1,000. Looking to amplify their market exposure, they decide to utilize a leverage of 10x.

This leverage allows them to open a position worth $10,000, despite only having $1,000 in their trading account. Given the current Bitcoin spot price of $50,000, their $10,000 position equates to 0.2 BTC. This is the starting point from which we'll explore two distinct scenarios: one where the price of Bitcoin increases, and another where it decreases.

Scenario A – Price Increase   Imagine the market moves in the trader's favor, and the price of Bitcoin rises to $55,000. To determine the profit from this price movement, we apply the formula:

$$\text{Profit} = (\text{New Price} - \text{Entry Price}) \times \text{Position Size}$$

Plugging in the numbers:

$$\text{Profit} = (\$55,000 - \$50,000) \times 0.2 \text{ BTC} = \$1,000$$

The trader achieves a $1,000 profit from this trade, effectively doubling their initial margin, thanks to the power of 10x leverage. This scenario highlights the upside potential of leveraged trading, where favorable market movements can significantly amplify returns.

Scenario B – Price Decrease   Conversely, let's examine the outcome if the Bitcoin price falls to $45,000. The calculation for the trader's loss is similar, albeit with the price difference reflecting a decrease:

$$\text{Loss} = (\text{Entry Price} - \text{New Price}) \times \text{Position Size}$$

Which calculates to:

$$\text{Loss} = (\$50,000 - \$45,000) \times 0.2 \text{ BTC} = \$1,000$$

In this scenario, the $1,000 loss wipes out the trader's initial margin. This starkly demonstrates the heightened risk associated with leveraged trading, where adverse price movements can lead to substantial losses, potentially equaling the entire margin.

Additionally, in perpetual contracts, traders are subject to funding fees, which ensure the perpetual contract price remains anchored to the spot price. Assuming a positive funding rate of 0.01% every 8 hours, and the trader holds their position for 24 hours (or three 8-hour intervals), the funding fee calculation would be:

$$\text{Funding Fee for 24 hours} = \$10,000 \times 0.01\% \times 3 = \$3$$

Hence, for holding a $10,000 position over 24 hours in this leveraged trade, the trader would incur a $3 funding fee. This fee is relatively small compared to the profit or loss from the trade but is an essential consideration for traders, especially in longer-term positions or during periods of high funding rates.

This example elucidates the double-edged sword of leveraged trading with perpetual contracts: while leverage can magnify gains, it equally amplifies risks, making it possible to lose one's initial investment from adverse price movements. Moreover, funding fees add an ongoing cost to maintaining a leveraged position, underscoring the importance of strategic trade management and risk assessment in the volatile cryptocurrency markets.

Contango

For traders of perpetual contracts, understanding contango is vital for strategy formulation. Contango is a market condition in which the future price of an asset is higher than its current spot price. This term is often discussed in the context of futures markets but is also highly relevant for perpetual contracts in the cryptocurrency market. The relevance of contango to perpetual contracts stems from the way these instruments are structured and the impact of market conditions on their pricing and trading strategies.

Perpetual contracts incorporate a funding rate mechanism to balance the discrepancy between the perpetual contract price and the spot price. When the market is in contango, traders holding long positions (betting on price increases) might have to pay funding to those holding short positions. This dynamic encourages the price of the perpetual contract to align more closely with the spot price, affecting traders' profitability and trading strategies.

Then, traders need to account for the impact of contango on their trading strategies, especially when holding positions over longer periods. In a contango market, the cost associated with maintaining a long position due to funding rate payments can erode profits or amplify losses. Traders might adjust their strategies based on their expectations of the contango condition persisting or reversing, impacting their decisions on opening, holding, or closing positions.

Contango also provides arbitrage opportunities for traders who can exploit the price difference between the perpetual contracts and the spot market. By simultaneously going long on the spot market and short on the perpetual contracts (or vice versa, depending on the specific market condition), traders can attempt to profit from the convergence of prices over time. However, executing such strategies requires a sophisticated understanding of market dynamics and careful risk management.

The presence of contango in the market can also serve as an indicator of prevailing market sentiment, suggesting that traders expect the future price of the asset to rise. This expectation can influence overall market behavior, with traders adjusting their positions based on their perceptions of future market movements.

What are the Factors Leading to Contango?

Expectation of Future Price Increases: One of the primary drivers of contango is the collective anticipation of traders regarding future price escalations of the underlying asset.

When traders forecast an upward trajectory in asset prices, the consequent surge in demand for long positions can propel the price of perpetual contracts above the prevailing spot price.

High Leverage Usage: Cryptocurrency markets are notorious for offering substantial leverage options to traders. This facility allows traders to exponentially increase their buying power, albeit at higher risk. In scenarios where a significant number of traders opt to go long with leveraged positions, this aggregated demand can skew the perpetual contract prices above the spot prices, particularly in markets characterized by pronounced volatility and liquidity.

Cost of Carry Adjustments through Funding Rates: Unlike traditional futures, which incorporate the cost of carry (the cost associated with maintaining an asset until the contract's expiry) into their pricing, perpetual contracts rely on the funding rate mechanism for a similar adjustment. This mechanism plays a pivotal role when traders exhibit a willingness to incur additional costs to sustain leveraged positions. Such behavior can elevate the perpetual contract's price over the spot price, mirroring a cost of carry effect but adapted to the perpetual market's mechanics.

Market Sentiment and Speculation: The overall mood and speculative outlook of the market can also foster contango conditions. Optimism about future price gains can trigger an influx in demand for perpetual contracts, driving their prices to exceed the spot price as traders clamor to capitalize on anticipated market movements.

Constraints in Spot Market Liquidity: At times, the spot market may face liquidity shortages, rendering the perpetual market a more viable or attractive platform for trading the asset. This shift in preference can augment demand within the perpetual market, pushing its prices above those in the constrained spot market.

3.3 Platform Example: GMX

Imagine you've just stumbled upon the trading strategy of the century, a brilliant plan that promises to navigate the turbulent seas of the crypto market with the grace of a seasoned captain. The catch? Your master plan hinges on the artful dance of trading perpetuals. So, where does one embark on such a daring financial voyage? The answer, my intrepid trader, lies with the illustrious GMX—the go-to arena for gladiators of the perpetual trading coliseum. Here, in the bustling metropolis of GMX, traders from all corners of the digital realm converge, seeking to wield their strategies in the perpetual markets with precision and flair. Welcome to the grand stage of GMX, where your trading aspirations meet execution!

GMX is a decentralized spot and perpetual exchange that supports low swap fees and zero price impact trades. It differentiates itself from traditional AMMs like Uniswap by offering a unique trading experience focused on derivatives and leverage, with features tailored to traders seeking perpetual futures contracts and leveraged positions. GMX combines an AMM model with a multi-asset pool that supports both spot trading and leveraged trading without the need for traditional order books.

GMX offers a comprehensive platform for both spot and leveraged trading without the constraints of traditional exchanges. At its core, GMX facilitates an innovative trading environment through several key mechanisms that cater to the needs of traders and liquidity providers alike. Let's delve into how GMX operates, highlighting its unique features and the benefits they offer to the DeFi community.

The Foundation of GMX: Multi-Asset Pool   Central to GMX's operation is its multi-asset pool, which typically encompasses a variety of assets such as ETH, USDC, among others. This pool serves a dual purpose, providing the necessary liquidity for both spot and leveraged trades. By aggregating multiple assets into a single liquidity pool, GMX ensures that traders can execute their strategies efficiently, benefiting from the depth and diversity of the available liquidity.

GLP Token: The Heart of Liquidity Provision   Liquidity providers (LPs) are the backbone of the GMX ecosystem, depositing assets into the multi-asset pool and receiving GLP tokens in return. These tokens are more than just a receipt; they represent the holder's stake in the pool, entitling them to a share of the trading fees generated across the platform. This system incentivizes the provision of liquidity and aligns the interests of LPs with the overall success and volume of trading activity on GMX.

Trading on GMX: Spot and Perpetual   GMX stands out by offering users the flexibility to engage in both spot trading and perpetual trading within a decentralized framework. Spot trading allows users to swap one asset for another directly, catering to those looking for immediate exchanges. Meanwhile, perpetual trading offers a way to speculate on the price movements of underlying assets through contracts that do not expire, broadening the scope of trading strategies that can be employed on the platform. GMX utilizes Chainlink's Decentralized Oracle Network to provide accurate and timely price feeds for both spot and perpetual contract trading, optimizing liquidation prices and minimizing irregular changes.

Dynamic Pricing Mechanism   A hallmark of GMX's design is its dynamic pricing mechanism, which leverages an oracle average to adjust prices. This approach is designed to mitigate the risk of price manipulation, ensuring that traders encounter fair and transparent trading conditions. Notably, this pricing mechanism enables zero price impact trades, distinguishing GMX from traditional automated market makers (AMMs) where significant trades can skew prices unfavorably.

Fee Structure and Rewards   GMX boasts a competitive fee structure, with trading fees set lower than many conventional exchanges. A portion of these fees is directly distributed to GLP token holders, rewarding them for their contribution to the platform's liquidity. Furthermore, GMX incentivizes active participation by offering rewards to traders who provide liquidity and engage in trading activities. This system creates a virtuous cycle, where increased trading volume enhances the rewards for liquidity providers, thereby attracting more liquidity to the platform.

In summary, GMX redefines the landscape of decentralized trading by blending the liquidity benefits of multi-asset pools with the flexibility of spot and perpetual trading. Its innovative GLP token system rewards liquidity provision, while the dynamic pricing mechanism and competitive fees foster a fair and advantageous trading environment. As DeFi continues to evolve, GMX's integrated approach to liquidity, trading, and rewards positions it as a compelling platform for traders and liquidity providers seeking to capitalize on the opportunities within the decentralized finance space.

Numerical example Alice, intrigued by the potential of leveraged trading on GMX, decides to capitalize on her prediction that the price of Ethereum (ETH) is poised for an upward trajectory. With an initial investment of $1,000 in USDC, Alice is drawn to the prospect of amplifying her market exposure through leverage—a powerful tool offered by GMX that allows traders to punch above their weight, so to speak.

Embarking on this financial voyage, Alice opts for a 5x leveraged long position in ETH. This strategic move effectively elevates her stake in the game to $5,000 worth of ETH, quintupling her buying power and her potential profit margin, all while starting with her original $1,000. It's a bold play, and one that hinges on the future price movement of ETH.

As fortune would have it, the markets sway in Alice's favor, with ETH's price climbing by an impressive 10%. In a conventional trading scenario, such as a spot market, a 10% increase on Alice's initial $1,000 investment would translate to a modest $100 profit—not a sum to scoff at, but hardly earth-shattering. However, the beauty of leverage unfolds in this very moment; Alice's foresight and the leverage magnify her profit to a striking $500, mirroring the 10% gain but applied to the leveraged position of $5,000.

Feeling content with the fruits of her strategic foresight, Alice decides it's time to cash in on her gains and close her position. Here, the reality of trading fees comes into play. GMX, known for its competitive fee structure, applies a nominal 0.1% fee for both entering and exiting trades. For Alice, this means a fee of $5 at the time of opening her position (0.1% of $5,000) and a slightly higher $5.05 upon exit (0.1% of $5,050, accounting for her profit). These fees, totaling $10.05, are a small price to pay for the leverage and liquidity provided by GMX.

After all is said and done, Alice walks away with a net profit of $489.95—a sum derived from her $500 profit adjusted for the trading fees. This example not only showcases the enticing potential of leveraged trading on GMX but also highlights the platform's appeal through low fees and the absence of direct price impact on trades. It's a testament to how GMX enables traders like Alice to navigate the volatile waters of cryptocurrency markets with confidence and strategic advantage.

Buoyed by Alice's successful gamble on Ethereum's price surge using the GMX platform, Marco, too, decides to venture into the realm of leveraged trading. Unlike Alice, whose prudent bet on Ethereum reaped a handsome reward, Marco sets his eyes on Ripple's XRP, a token known for its loyal community and wild price swings.

With a zeal that could rival that of any crypto evangelist, Marco takes his $1,000 savings and decides to go all-in on XRP, leveraging his position 5x to control $5,000 worth of the token. In Marco's mind, the principle of HODL (hold on for dear life) is not just a strategy but a sacred mantra, one that he believes will see him through to untold riches.

However, the cryptocurrency markets, much like the sea, are fickle and unforgiving. Shortly after Marco's investment, XRP's price takes an unexpected nosedive, dropping by 20%. In a spot trading scenario, such a downturn would mean a $200 loss on Marco's initial investment—a bitter pill to swallow, but not a fatal blow. But Marco's leveraged position magnifies this loss fivefold, resulting in a $1,000 decrease in the value of his position, effectively erasing his entire savings.

Yet, Marco, armed with a blend of overconfidence and a war cry of "HODL to the moon," is still convinced that XRP is on the brink of a massive rally. This unwavering belief blinds him to the perilous reality of his situation. As XRP's price continues to plummet, the specter of liquidation looms ever closer. Leveraged trading, especially with a highly volatile asset like XRP, is akin to dancing on a tightrope—without a safety net.

Finally, the inevitable happens. XRP's price decline triggers a forced liquidation of Marco's position by the exchange, a safety mechanism designed to prevent his account balance from going negative but one that also obliterates his investment. In the end, the trading fees become mere salt in his financial wounds.

Differences with Uniswap   While both platforms facilitate the trading of cryptocurrencies without the need for traditional intermediaries, GMX and Uniswap cater to distinct trading preferences and strategies through their operational differences.

As we have discussed, Uniswap operates as an Automated Market Maker (AMM) that allows for the exchange of ERC-20 tokens through liquidity pools. It's known for its simplicity, user-friendly interface, and open participation model, where anyone can become a liquidity provider by contributing to existing pools or creating new ones. Uniswap's model emphasizes equality and accessibility, making it an attractive option for casual traders and those new to DeFi. However, its design does not inherently support leveraged trading or derivative products, focusing instead on spot trading.

GMX, on the other hand, carves a niche for itself by specializing in decentralized spot and perpetual trading with leverage. Unlike Uniswap, GMX offers traders the ability to engage in leveraged positions on a variety of assets, not limited to ERC-20 tokens. The platform's multi-asset pool, which underpins its trading mechanism, allows for more complex trading strategies that are typically associated with traditional finance, such as long and short positions with up to 50x leverage. Furthermore, GMX employs a unique pricing mechanism that seeks to mitigate price manipulation and ensure fair trading conditions, an essential feature for traders engaging in leveraged trading.

Trader Preferences   The choice between GMX and Uniswap often comes down to the trader's risk appetite, preferred trading strategies, and familiarity with complex financial instruments. Casual traders and those seeking simplicity and minimal risk might gravitate toward Uniswap for its straightforward swap mechanism and the ability to provide liquidity in a variety of tokens. In contrast, experienced traders, drawn by the allure of higher potential returns through leveraged trading and sophisticated strategies, may find GMX more aligned with their trading goals. These traders are likely to be comfortable navigating the complexities and risks associated with leverage, including the potential for liquidation.

In conclusion, while Uniswap and GMX both play instrumental roles in democratizing access to financial markets, they cater to distinct segments of the DeFi community. Uniswap's egalitarian and accessible model appeals to a broad audience, encouraging participation in liquidity provision and spot trading. GMX, with its focus on leveraged and perpetual trading, attracts a more niche group of traders seeking to leverage sophisticated strategies that mirror those of traditional financial markets.

4. Trading Strategies: Part 2

Let's discuss additional trading strategies that make use of Perpetuals.

4.1 Basis Trade with Perpetual Swap Contracts

As we discussed, perpetual swap contracts (perps or perp swaps for short) are a new type of financial instrument created by the cryptocurrency exchange BitMEX, now widely adopted in the market, that is a futures contract with no expiration date. The prices of traditional futures contracts typically diverge from the price of the underlying, reflecting market sentiment toward the asset, but converge at expiration. Historically, the price difference between the contract and the underlying, called the basis, is small as the funding rates work exactly as intended. Many investors implement a strategy to take advantage of the funding rate to earn a low-risk yield with a fully hedged position. This strategy is the basis trade.

Most cryptocurrency investors are believers in the industry and believe that the price of cryptocurrencies will continue to increase over time, so the price of the perp swap is usually above the price of the underlying as people expect future prices to be above the current level. Because of this basis, longs will typically pay shorts a positive funding rate. **Figures 7 and 8** chart the BTC/USDT perp swap and the DOGE/USDT perp swap's funding rate on Binance from 2020 to 2024. When the rate is positive, longs are paying shorts, and when the rate is negative, shorts are paying longs. As you can see, rates can swing wildly but are consistently positive and can sometimes even reach 300% to 400% on an annualized basis. Because of these attractive rates, investors will short the perpetual to earn this rate, but purely shorting the contract also exposes the trader to a lot of risk in case BTC price increases significantly. The basis trade strategy involves a user buying BTC on the spot market and shorting the same amount of BTC on the perp swap

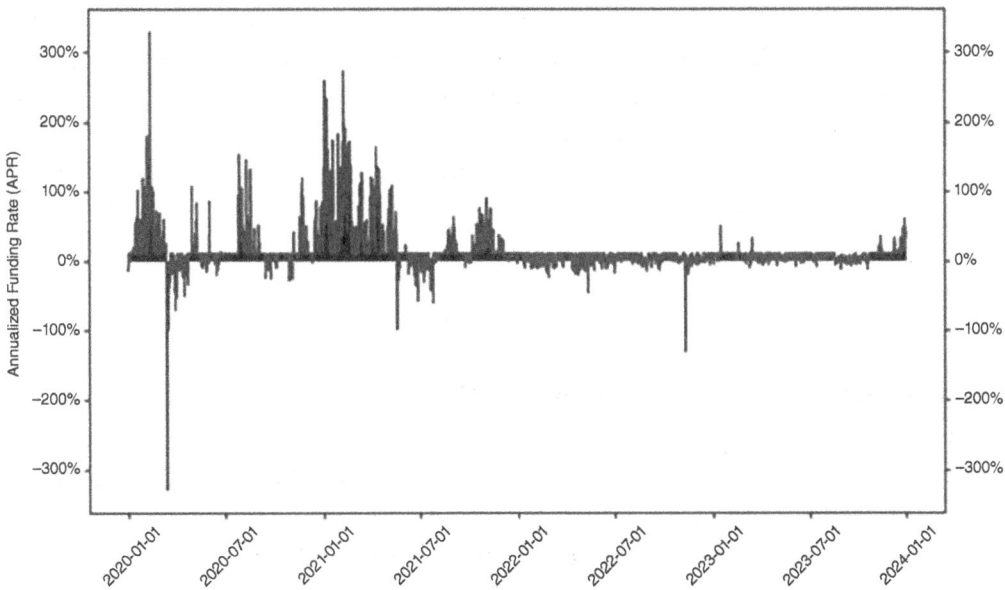

Figure 7 Annualized BTC funding rates on Binance from 2020 to 2024

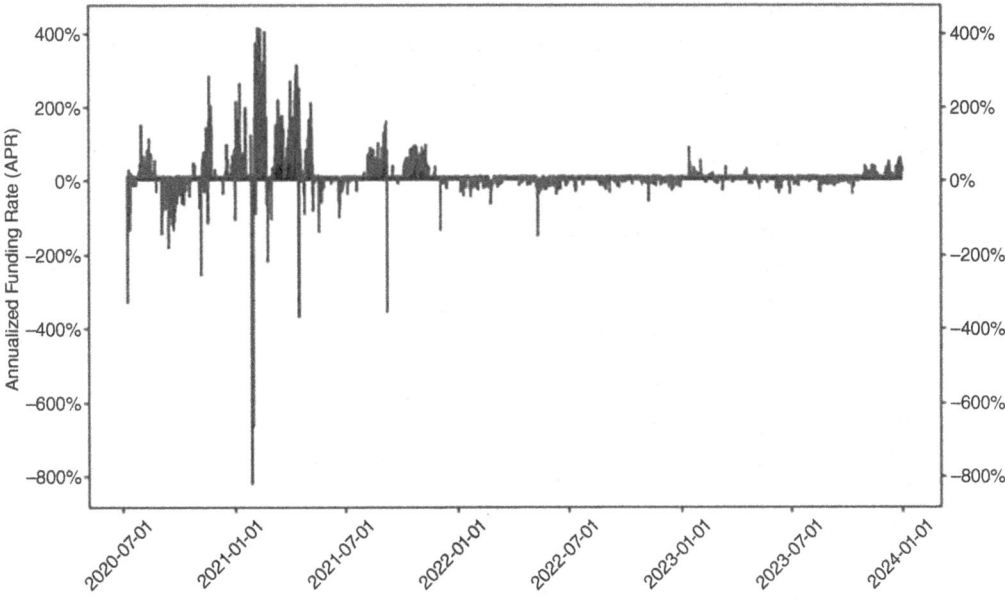

Figure 8 Annualized DOGE funding rates on Binance from 2020 to 2024

market to create a fully hedged position. The position can be fully hedged because the price of the perp swap closely mirrors the price of the underlying, so exposure to price swings is minimized. With these hedged positions, investors can receive the funding rate at regular intervals without having to worry about price swings. So, the net position does act like receiving an interest rate on the cryptocurrency.

With attractive rates of up to 400%, many investors piled into the strategy during the 2020–21 bull market. As prices increased exponentially, so did funding rates, making the strategy even more profitable and attractive. Many hedge funds across the world were created solely based on this strategy, attracting millions of dollars. But, as more traders exploited the strategy, the basis started to get smaller. After the bull market ended, rates stayed consistently low. The basis trade, as a strategy, went away. And so did those same hedge funds.

EXPLORING THE FRONTIER. ETHENA: THE DELTA-NEUTRAL STABLECOIN

A different use case for a basis trading strategy: a stablecoin. Unlike traditional stablecoins pegged to real-world assets like the U.S. dollar, Ethena utilizes a unique mechanism to maintain its peg: **delta-neutral hedging**. Here's a breakdown of how it works:

1. **Collateralized by Staked ETH (stETH):**
   Ethena doesn't rely on physical assets or even other cryptocurrencies. Instead, it uses staked ETH (stETH) as collateral. This means users deposit stETH, which represents locked Ethereum tokens earning staking rewards, into the Ethena protocol.
2. **Shorting ETH for Hedging:**
   To maintain its 1 U.S. dollar peg, Ethena employs a clever strategy. It takes the deposited stETH and simultaneously opens a short position of an equivalent value in ETH on a centralized exchange (CEX). This short position essentially acts as an insurance policy.
3. **The Delta-Neutral Magic:**
   Here's where the delta hedging comes in. "Delta" refers to the rate of change of an option's price relative to the underlying asset (ETH in this case). By taking a short position equal to the value of the deposited stETH, Ethena aims to achieve a delta-neutral portfolio. This means any price swings in ETH, up or down, are offset by the gains or losses in the short position.

Benefits of Ethena's Approach:

- **Stability:** The short position helps ensure the USDe stablecoin stays close to its $1 peg, even if the price of ETH fluctuates.
- **Yield Generation:** Users benefit from staking rewards on their deposited stETH, offering an additional source of return.

Potential Considerations:

- **Centralized Exchange Reliance:** Using CEXs for shorting introduces a degree of reliance on centralized entities.
- **Smart Contract Risk:** While Ethena utilizes off-exchange custody solutions to mitigate some risks, there's always inherent risk associated with smart contracts.
- **Newer Approach:** Compared to established stablecoin models, Ethena's approach is relatively new, and its long-term viability needs further observation.

In essence, Ethena is tokenizing the basis strategy that we described above and created a stablecoin out of it!

4.2 Liquidity Provision

Another strategy that can be implemented on decentralized finance (DeFi) platforms is liquidity provision. DEXs require users to deposit funds in a liquidity pool so that other traders can trade against the pool. These traders pay a transaction fee that is routed to the liquidity providers (LPs), providing an incentive for depositing into these pools. So, a simple strategy that a user can implement is to provide liquidity on these exchanges and earn the trading fees. For example, Uniswap has provided a guide to depositing and managing liquidity on their V3 platform using a Solidity smart contract. We highlight the function for creating a new position in the following code snippet:

```
// Credit for this code goes to the Uniswap foundation
/// @notice Calls the mint function defined in periphery, mints the same
amount of each token.
/// For this example we are providing 1000 DAI and 1000 USDC in liquidity
/// @return tokenId The id of the newly minted ERC721
/// @return liquidity The amount of liquidity for the position
/// @return amount0 The amount of token0
/// @return amount1 The amount of token1
function mintNewPosition()
    external
    returns (
        uint256 tokenId,
        uint128 liquidity,
        uint256 amount0,
        uint256 amount1
    )
{
```

```
// For this example, we will provide equal amounts of liquidity in
both assets.
// Providing liquidity in both assets means liquidity will be earning
fees and is considered in-range.
uint256 amount0ToMint = 1000;
uint256 amount1ToMint = 1000;

// transfer tokens to contract
TransferHelper.safeTransferFrom(DAI, msg.sender, address(this),
amount0ToMint);
TransferHelper.safeTransferFrom(USDC, msg.sender, address(this),
amount1ToMint);

// Approve the position manager
TransferHelper.safeApprove(DAI, address(nonfungiblePositionManager),
amount0ToMint);
TransferHelper.safeApprove(USDC, address(nonfungiblePositionManager),
amount1ToMint);

// The values for tickLower and tickUpper may not work for all
tick spacings.
// Setting amount0Min and amount1Min to 0 is unsafe.
INonfungiblePositionManager.MintParams memory params =
    INonfungiblePositionManager.MintParams({
        token0: DAI,
        token1: USDC,
        fee: poolFee,
        tickLower: TickMath.MIN_TICK,
        tickUpper: TickMath.MAX_TICK,
        amount0Desired: amount0ToMint,
        amount1Desired: amount1ToMint,
        amount0Min: 0,
        amount1Min: 0,
        recipient: address(this),
        deadline: block.timestamp
    });

// Note that the pool defined by DAI/USDC and fee tier 0.3% must
already be created and initialized in order to mint
(tokenId, liquidity, amount0, amount1) = nonfungiblePositionManager
.mint(params);

// Create a deposit
_createDeposit(msg.sender, tokenId);

// Remove allowance and refund in both assets.
if (amount0 < amount0ToMint) {
    TransferHelper.safeApprove(DAI, address(nonfungiblePosition
    Manager), 0);
    uint256 refund0 = amount0ToMint - amount0;
    TransferHelper.safeTransfer(DAI, msg.sender, refund0);
}
```

```
    if (amount1 < amount1ToMint) {
        TransferHelper.safeApprove(USDC, address(nonfungiblePosition
        Manager), 0);
        uint256 refund1 = amount1ToMint - amount1;
        TransferHelper.safeTransfer(USDC, msg.sender, refund1);
    }
}
```

The code shows an example of depositing 1,000 DAI and 1,000 USDC in liquidity on Uniswap V3 on the full range. Users can collect any trading fees that have been accrued using the function *collectAllFees*. They can also modify their positions using the functions *decreaseLiquidityInHalf,* and *increaseLiquidityCurrentRange.*

As we have discussed in Chapter 8, a significant risk that arises with being a liquidity provider is the risk of impermanent loss. In short, this loss refers to the difference in your portfolio value after being a liquidity provider and your portfolio if you simply held on to the tokens you originally deposited. The loss exists because the DEX will adjust your LP position mix based on the current price of the pool, so the number of tokens that you deposited may change throughout the lifetime of your position. In general, price movements of the tokens deposited in any direction lead to impermanent loss, meaning that pools that include volatile tokens are especially susceptible to impermanent loss. In some cases, the trading fees accrued can outweigh these losses, but the losses are often too large for the trading fees to cover it. Instead, many investors hedge their positions using futures or options so that the effect of price movements is minimized and investors can just earn the trading fees. For example, let's consider a Uniswap V3 LP that deposits ETH and USDT between the price ranges of $1,800 and $2,200. The value of the position at different price levels can be represented by the following **Figure 9**.

The diagram looks very similar to the payoff diagram of selling a put option with a strike price of $2,000, except for the curvature in the $1,800–$2,200 range. Because the payoff diagram is so similar, a potential investor could hedge the position by buying a put to offset the drop in value of the position when the price of ETH decreases and lowers the effects of impermanent loss. The payoff diagram, at expiration, of buying a put option with a strike price of $2,000 is shown in **Figure 10**.

Given that the shape of the payoff diagram of both positions seem to offset each other, investors could buy a put option to hedge their Uniswap V3 position. **Figure 11** plots the value of the position before and after the hedge.

The value of the hedged position is not affected by price movements as much as the value of the unhedged position, so the investor could limit their losses by hedging their position and simply collect trading fees. Hedging with a put option is not the only method, as others have used perpetual swaps or other option-based positions like covered calls. However, hedging does bring its own set of risks with additional trading fees, losses due to improper hedges, and expensive option premiums.

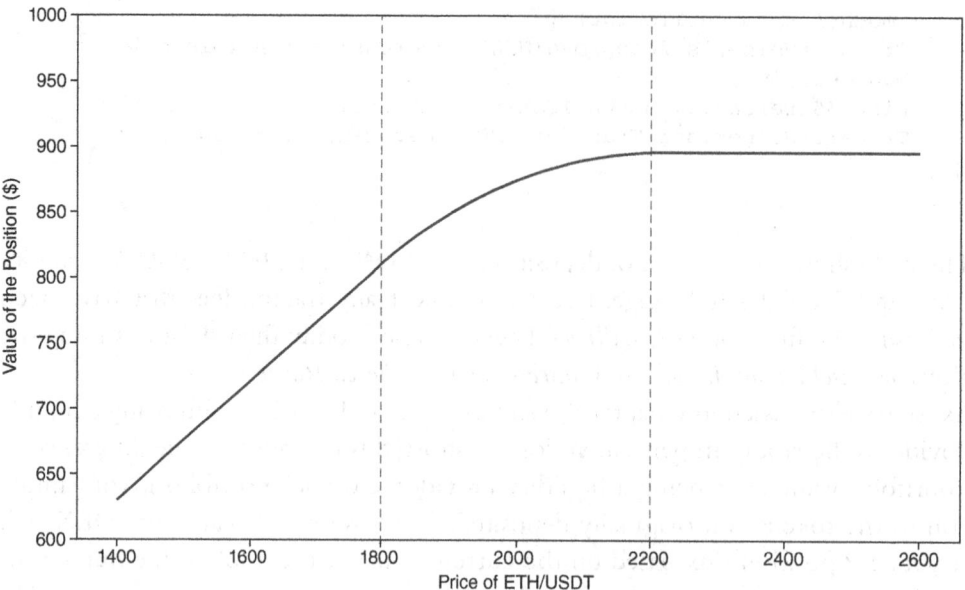

Figure 9　Payoff diagram of Uniswap V3 LP position for the ETH/USDT pair with lower bound of $1,800 and upper bound of $2,200

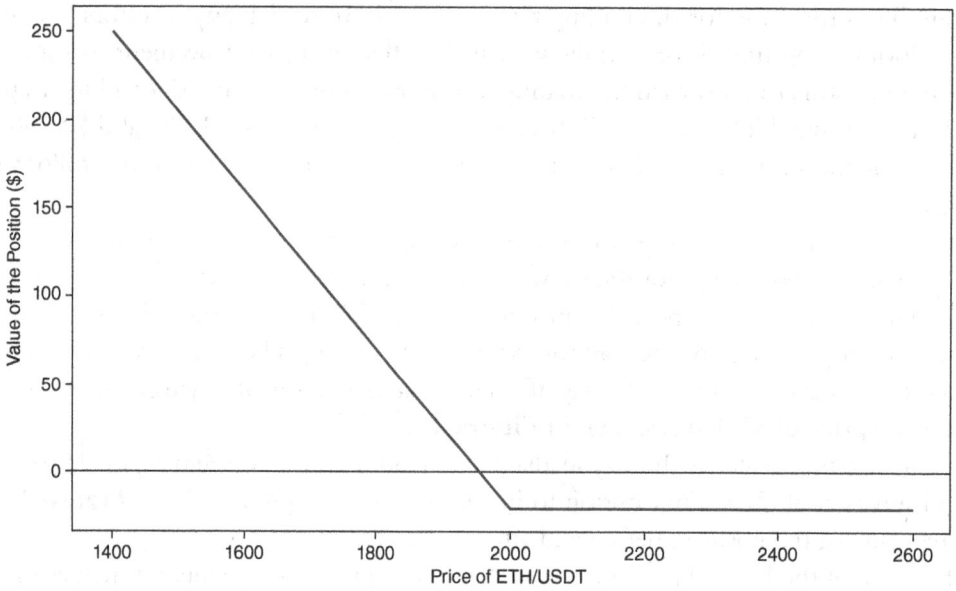

Figure 10　Payoff diagram of buying a put option with a strike price of $2,000

4.3 Options

Cryptocurrency options is a rising segment of the market with more CEXs and DEXs offering these contracts to investors. Options as a financial instrument give investors the ability to create complex positions to take advantage of volatility, price movements, and

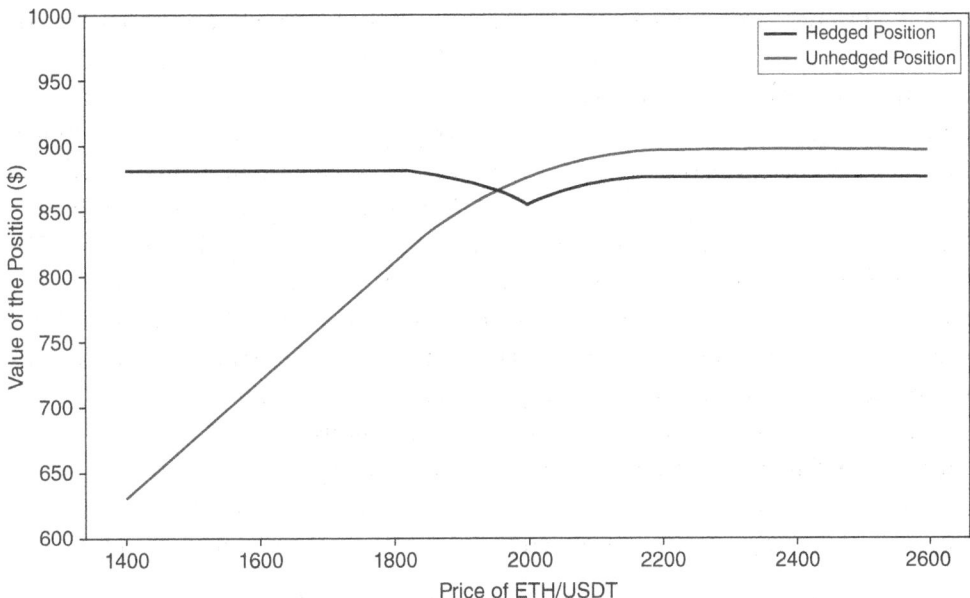

Figure 11   Payoff diagram of the unhedged and hedged Uniswap V3 LP position

other opportunities. For example, a simple strategy would be to buy an at the money straddle when you expect volatility to increase. Buying an at the money straddle involves buying an at the money call and an at the money put, both with the same strike price. If an investor expects volatility to increase and price movements to be significant but is unsure if the price will increase or decrease, they can use a straddle to generate a return regardless of the direction of the price movement and take advantage of the increasing volatility. Many other strategies are possible such as taking advantage of implied volatility skews in the volatility smile, and relative value across different maturities or strikes.

With its many innovations, the cryptocurrency market offers the opportunity to run distinct trading strategies. The above strategies are just examples of the possibilities that exist. The market is still relatively young and inefficient, meaning that many anomalies and opportunities may be available for investors to take advantage of. But remember, always do your own research and verification before deploying any particular strategy, as the high volatility in the market can lead to significant losses.

4.4 Tactical Asset Allocation Strategies Incorporating Crypto

Tactical Asset Allocation (TAA) is a dynamic investment strategy that actively adjusts the asset mix in a portfolio based on short-term market forecasts. Incorporating cryptocurrencies into TAA involves several unique considerations:

- **Correlation:** Cryptocurrencies have shown periods of low correlation with traditional assets like stocks and bonds, making them an attractive option for diversification. However, this correlation can change quickly, necessitating constant monitoring.

- **Market Signals:** Utilizing market signals such as momentum indicators, trading volumes, and news sentiment can be particularly effective in crypto markets for identifying tactical allocation opportunities.
- **Data:** TAA strategies often rely on a broad array of economic indicators, corporate earnings reports, and historical data. The availability of long-term data allows for the use of various models to predict market trends. Cryptocurrencies lack extensive historical data, making some traditional forecasting models less reliable. Instead, TAA strategies may lean more on technical analysis, sentiment analysis (e.g. social media trends), and blockchain-specific metrics like hash rates and wallet activity. Crypto markets operate 24/7, leading to a constant influx of market data and the need for around-the-clock monitoring. Liquidity can also vary significantly across different cryptocurrencies and exchanges, impacting TAA decisions.
- **Transaction Costs:** Transaction costs can be higher, especially with smaller or less liquid cryptocurrencies. Additionally, tax regulations for cryptocurrencies can be complex and vary by jurisdiction, affecting the net outcome of TAA strategies.

Let's get our hands dirty and start seeing how to code such a strategy.

Implementing a Tactical Asset Allocation (TAA) strategy in the crypto market using Python involves several steps, including data collection, signal generation, and portfolio adjustment based on those signals. For this example, we'll create a simplified version of a TAA strategy that uses moving averages as the basis for making investment decisions. The strategy will allocate between Bitcoin (BTC) and Ethereum (ETH) based on their 30-day and 90-day moving averages.

Step 1: Data Acquisition

The initial phase involves the procurement of historical price data for BTC and ETH. This step can be efficiently executed utilizing the **yfinance** library to extract data, coupled with the **pandas** library for data manipulation and analysis in Python.

```
import yfinance as yf
import pandas as pd

# Retrieve historical price data for BTC and ETH
btc_data = yf.download('BTC-USD', start='2020-01-01')
eth_data = yf.download('ETH-USD', start='2020-01-01')

# Calculate moving averages
btc_data['30d_ma'] = btc_data['Close'].rolling(window=30).mean()
btc_data['90d_ma'] = btc_data['Close'].rolling(window=90).mean()
eth_data['30d_ma'] = eth_data['Close'].rolling(window=30).mean()
eth_data['90d_ma'] = eth_data['Close'].rolling(window=90).mean()
# Generate signals for BTC
btc_data['Signal'] = 0
btc_data['Signal'][btc_data['30d_ma'] > btc_data['90d_ma']] = 1
```

```
# Generate signals for ETH
eth_data['Signal'] = 0
eth_data['Signal'][eth_data['30d_ma'] > eth_data['90d_ma']] = 1

# Example portfolio adjustment logic
if btc_data['Signal'].iloc[-1] == 1:
    # Increase allocation to BTC
    pass
if eth_data['Signal'].iloc[-1] == 1:
    # Increase allocation to ETH
    pass
```

This approach underscores a fundamental TAA strategy where allocation decisions are primarily influenced by trend-following indicators, such as moving averages. It's important to note that this example provides a foundational framework, and additional complexities, risk management practices, and optimization techniques should be considered for a comprehensive strategy deployment.

5. Concluding Remarks

At this point, it should be evident that the crypto markets are a dynamic extension of traditional financial wisdom adapted to the new age of digital assets. This chapter unwrapped the intricacies of crypto trading, leveraging established frameworks to demystify the valuation and trading of cryptocurrencies. It illustrates that, at its core, the crypto market does not defy but rather adheres to and evolves from foundational financial principles.

You should be familiar with the risk and return profiles unique to crypto assets, and the application of Modern Portfolio Theory to diversify and optimize portfolios that include cryptocurrencies. Traditional financial metrics like the Sharpe and Sortino ratios, albeit with certain adaptations, remain relevant in assessing the risk-adjusted performance of crypto investments. The similarities and distinctions between crypto assets and traditional financial markets extend into beta coefficients and factor investing.

We have discussed a variety of investment strategies, ranging from buy-and-hold to more complex approaches such as momentum trading, mean reversion, and statistical arbitrage, underpinning the diversity and adaptability of strategies from traditional markets to crypto trading. Special attention is given to the unique aspects of perpetual contracts, emphasizing their role in facilitating both speculative opportunities and hedging strategies without the constraints of expiry dates found in traditional futures contracts. Please take all of these strategies with a grain of salt; they should serve just as guidance for those of you who want to start investing in this space or at least be informed about how trading in these markets occurs.

In conclusion, this chapter elucidates that the principles guiding sound investment and trading strategies in traditional financial markets are applicable and being ingeniously adapted within the crypto market. It dispels the myth of an anarchic crypto space, revealing a structured and principled environment where risk management, strategic planning, and informed decision-making prevail. The evolution of trading instruments like perpetual contracts and the rise of platforms like GMX signify the crypto market's maturation, embodying the fusion of traditional finance's rigor with the innovative spirit of digital assets. This amalgamation underscores a future where finance principles continue to underpin the burgeoning world of cryptocurrency, offering a bridge for investors navigating between the old and the new, the traditional and the digital, the established and the emerging.

End of Chapters Question

Multiple Choice Questions

1. **What is the primary goal of a Smart Beta Strategy?**
   (A) To outperform the market index.
   (B) To fully automate the trading process.
   (C) To eliminate all risks associated with trading.
   (D) To replicate the market index exactly.

2. **What does a high beta in crypto signify?**
   (A) The asset is less volatile than the market.
   (B) The asset is as volatile as the market.
   (C) The asset is more volatile than the market.
   (D) The asset has no volatility.

3. **What does HODL stand for in the context of crypto trading?**
   (A) Hold On for Dear Life.
   (B) High Operational Demand Level.
   (C) Hold Only During Loss.
   (D) None of the above.

4. **Which factor might a Smart Beta Strategy overweight in its portfolio construction?**
   (A) Larger, well-established cryptocurrencies.
   (B) Smaller, high-momentum cryptocurrencies.
   (C) Cryptocurrencies with the best logos.
   (D) Cryptocurrencies mentioned in the news the most.

5. **What does a perpetual contract in crypto allow for?**
   (A) Trading with an expiry date.
   (B) Trading without an expiry date.
   (C) Trading only during daytime.
   (D) Trading exclusively on weekends.

6. **What mechanism helps perpetual contracts align with the spot market price?**
   (A) Voting by the community.
   (B) The funding rate mechanism.
   (C) A random number generator.
   (D) Expert predictions.

7. **What strategy might a trader use during a clear uptrend in the market?**
   (A) Buy and Hold.
   (B) Mean Reversion.
   (C) Trend Following.
   (D) None of the above.

8. **What does contango in the market indicate?**
   (A) The spot price is higher than the futures price.
   (B) The futures price is higher than the spot price.
   (C) Prices are expected to decrease.
   (D) Prices are stable.

9. **What might cause a cryptocurrency's price to break out of a range?**
   (A) A decrease in trading volume.
   (B) Regulatory approval.
   (C) Lack of investor interest.
   (D) Significant news or events.

10. **In a Smart Beta Strategy, what might an "Investor Attention" factor consider?**
    (A) How often a cryptocurrency is mentioned in academic papers.
    (B) The cryptocurrency's price volatility.
    (C) Media and news coverage of the cryptocurrency.
    (D) The age of the cryptocurrency.

Open Questions

1. Explain how the funding rate mechanism works in perpetual contracts and its purpose.
2. Describe the concept of "Contango" and how it affects traders using perpetual contracts.
3. How do Smart Beta Strategies differ from traditional market-cap-weighted index strategies in crypto?
4. What are the potential risks of employing a Mean Reversion Strategy in the crypto market?
5. Discuss how the introduction of Bitcoin ETFs might influence the correlation between Bitcoin and the stock market.

Coding Exercises

Exercise 1: Implementing a Simple Momentum Strategy

Objective: Write a Python script that calculates the 30-day momentum for a crypto-currency and signals whether to buy or sell based on whether the momentum is positive or negative.

Requirements:

1. Load historical price data from a CSV file into a Pandas DataFrame. Assume the CSV has columns for **Date** and **Close**.
2. Calculate the 30-day momentum (today's price minus the price 30 days ago).
3. Print a "Buy" signal if the momentum is positive, and a "Sell" signal if the momentum is negative.

Exercise 2: Calculating and Plotting Bollinger Bands for Mean Reversion Strategy

Objective: Develop a script to calculate and plot Bollinger Bands for a given crypto-currency's price data, and identify points where the price crosses the upper or lower band.

Requirements:

1. Load daily price data into a Pandas DataFrame.
2. Calculate the 20-day moving average and the 2 standard deviations above and below this moving average to create the Bollinger Bands.
3. Plot the closing prices and the Bollinger Bands on the same chart.
4. Highlight days where the closing price crosses above the upper band or below the lower band.

Exercise 3: Implementing a Breakout Strategy

Objective: Create a function that identifies breakout points for a cryptocurrency when the price exceeds the highest high or the lowest low of the previous N days.

Requirements:

1. Use a rolling window to find the highest high and lowest low of the last N days.
2. Compare today's price to these levels to identify a breakout.
3. The function should return "Buy" if the price is above the highest high, "Sell" if below the lowest low, and "Hold" otherwise.

Exercise 4: Arbitrage Between Two Exchanges

Objective: Write a script that identifies arbitrage opportunities for a cryptocurrency between two exchanges.

Requirements:

1. Simulate two datasets representing the price of a cryptocurrency on two different exchanges, each with columns for **Date** and **Close**.
2. Calculate the price difference between the exchanges for each day.
3. Identify opportunities where buying on one exchange and selling on the other would result in profit, after accounting for a simulated transaction fee of 0.1%.

Exercise 5: Smart Beta Portfolio Construction

Objective: Construct a simple Smart Beta portfolio based on the equal weighting of cryptocurrencies that have a momentum factor above a certain threshold.

Requirements:

1. From a dataset of multiple cryptocurrencies, calculate the 90-day momentum for each.
2. Select cryptocurrencies whose momentum is above the median momentum of the dataset.
3. Construct a portfolio by equally weighting the selected cryptocurrencies.
4. Calculate and plot the cumulative returns of this portfolio.

Chapter 13

Game Over for Bankers
The Unlikely Rise of Sofa-Surfing Capitalists

Preface

Welcome to the fantastical world of GameFi, where the only thing more volatile than the cryptocurrency market is the in-game drama of breeding digital pets. Picture this: a universe so enthralling that it can only be described as the lovechild of Wall Street and *World of Warcraft*, conceived in a blockchain. This isn't just any tale of virtual conquests and digital loot; no, my friends, this is the epic saga of Axie Infinity—a game that turned the traditional gaming model on its head, flipped the table, and then built a new table out of non-fungible tokens (NFTs).

But wait, there's a twist in the tale—a heist so grand it could make the *Ocean's Eleven* crew hang up their burglary gloves in shame. The Ronin Network hack, a caper that saw millions in cryptocurrency vanish into the digital ether, poses a question more profound than "To be or not to be?" Instead, we ponder, "To hack or not to hack?" And in the aftermath, like a phoenix rising from the ashes of cybersecurity despair, we witness the resilience of a community banding together, led by Sky Mavis and their merry band of validators, on a quest to rebuild trust and security in a world where the line between virtual and reality gets blurrier by the day.

Just when you thought our journey through the GameFi galaxy couldn't get any wilder, we stumble upon The Sandbox—not your childhood's sandbox where the biggest worry was a cat mistake, but a virtual metaverse where creativity meets cryptocurrency,

577

GameFi Adventureland: Where fun meets finance in pixel-perfect harmony

and your digital dreams can become a (virtual) reality. Imagine a digital world where every voxel (think of it as a 3D pixel, for the uninitiated) is a chance to build, own, and monetize your creations. The Sandbox is where gamers, artists, and would-be moguls buy, sell, and ply their digital trade on parcels of virtual land using the native SAND token as the currency of this new realm.

As we embark on this journey through the chapter, prepare for a ride through the highs of P2E earnings that could rival a small country's GDP, and the lows of existential dread as we ponder the sustainability of it all. Will the game economy crumble under its weight, or will it evolve, adapt, and thrive? Only time will tell.

So, dear readers, buckle up. You're about to dive headfirst into a tale of intrigue, innovation, and digital pets that are inexplicably worth more than your car. Welcome to the world of GameFi, where the future of gaming is not just about having fun—it's about staking your claim in the new digital frontier. Just remember, in GameFi, fortune favors the bold, the blockchain-savvy, and, occasionally, the utterly bewildered.

1. Introduction

The advent of GameFi signifies a shift in the digital landscape, merging the domains of gaming, blockchain technology, and decentralized finance (DeFi) into a cohesive and

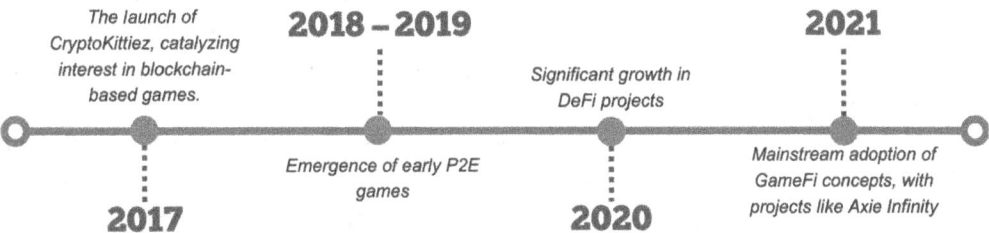

Figure 1 Milestones for GameFi

innovative ecosystem. This introductory section aims to delineate the concept, historical development, and core components of GameFi, elucidating its mechanisms and examining its capacity to revolutionize the gaming industry. We will then delve into several examples, which will be instrumental to look at GameFi through different lenses, later in the chapter.

GameFi, a contraction of "gaming" and "finance," embodies the integration of blockchain-based financial mechanisms within digital gaming platforms. This model diverges from conventional gaming paradigms by embedding intrinsic economic incentives into the gameplay, fostering a "play-to-earn" (P2E) ecosystem. Unlike traditional models where the economic flow is unidirectional—with players primarily spending to enhance their gaming experience—GameFi introduces a bidirectional flow, enabling players to accrue real-world cryptocurrency rewards through their engagement and contributions to the game.

The inception of GameFi can be traced back to notable experiments with blockchain in gaming, most prominently illustrated by the launch of CryptoKitties in 2017. As the first widely recognized application of NFTs within a gaming context, CryptoKitties allowed players to purchase, breed, and trade digital cats on the Ethereum blockchain, pioneering the notion of verifiable digital ownership and asset value within games. This marked a crucial milestone, demonstrating the viability of leveraging blockchain technology to create immersive, economically viable gaming experiences.

Following CryptoKitties, the GameFi ecosystem witnessed rapid expansion and diversification, propelled by advancements in blockchain technology and the growing sophistication of DeFi principles. The following were the key milestones in this evolution (**Figure 1**).

The GameFi model is underpinned by several key blockchain-based components, each playing a crucial role in creating a decentralized, secure, and financially incentivized gaming environment:

– **Blockchain:** At the heart of GameFi is the blockchain which records all transactions and interactions within the game. Blockchain technology ensures transparency, security, and immutability of in-game assets and financial transactions, fostering trust among players and developers.

- **NFTs:** NFTs are used to represent unique in-game assets such as characters, items, or parcels of virtual land. Unlike traditional digital assets, NFTs are stored on the blockchain, providing verifiable ownership and the ability to trade or sell assets in open marketplaces.
- **Cryptocurrencies:** Digital currencies serve as the medium of exchange within GameFi platforms, enabling players to buy NFTs, enter competitions, and receive rewards. Cryptocurrencies facilitate transactions among players and integrate the game's economy with the broader digital asset market.
- **Smart Contracts:** These self-executing contracts with the terms of the agreement directly written into code automate and enforce the rules of the game, transactions, and distribution of rewards. Smart contracts ensure the fairness and transparency in P2E mechanisms and DeFi activities within the game.

Modern GameFi platforms also incorporate a range of DeFi elements, such as yield farming, staking, and sophisticated tokenomics, into their infrastructures. These elements are instrumental in creating rich, interactive economies where players can engage in activities ranging from asset trading and investment to participating in governance through DAOs. By tokenizing in-game assets as NFTs, GameFi ensures the uniqueness, scarcity, and transferability of items, characters, and land, further embedding financial dynamics into the gaming experience.

Historical Context: From Twitch Streams to Blockchain Dreams The evolution of gaming, particularly with the advent of platforms like Twitch, has significantly altered the landscape of digital entertainment, paving the way for the integration of various forms of digital experiences, including the emergence of blockchain and GameFi ecosystems.

Twitch, launched in 2011, revolutionized the gaming industry by transforming it from a predominantly solitary activity into a communal and spectator-driven experience. This platform enabled gamers to live stream their gameplay, thereby creating communities around specific games, streamers, and genres. Twitch brought forth the concept of games as a spectator sport, giving rise to the esports industry and significantly influencing game development to cater to both players and viewers.

The interactive nature of Twitch, where viewers can chat with streamers and other viewers in real time, introduced new levels of engagement within the gaming community. This interaction fostered a deeper connection between streamers and their audiences, creating opportunities for content monetization through subscriptions, donations, and sponsorships. This model highlighted the potential for gamers not only to entertain but to earn from their gaming skills and personalities.

The success of Twitch underscored the demand for games that support community interaction and engagement. Developers began designing games with features conducive to streaming, such as spectator modes and interactive elements that viewers could influence during live streams. This shift in game development philosophy emphasized the importance of the gaming experience as a shared, interactive medium, extending beyond traditional gameplay.

The interactive, community-focused nature of platforms like Twitch set the stage for the adoption of blockchain technologies in gaming. Blockchain further amplifies the aspects of community engagement, ownership, and monetization introduced by streaming platforms. With blockchain, the concept of digital ownership through NFTs allows players to own, trade, and profit from in-game assets in ways previously unimagined, effectively blending gaming with financial investment.

GameFi, as an extension of this evolution, leverages the decentralized and community-driven aspects of blockchain to create games where financial mechanisms are integral to the gameplay. This progression toward GameFi represents a natural expansion of digital experiences in gaming, where the lines between playing, creating, and earning are increasingly blurred.

In summary, the evolution of gaming, catalyzed by platforms like Twitch, has not only transformed how games are played and experienced but also how they are monetized and owned. This trajectory, emphasizing community, interactivity, and economic participation, naturally led to the integration of blockchain technologies, culminating in the GameFi revolution. Here, the fusion of gaming with decentralized finance opens up new frontiers for digital experiences, marking the latest chapter in the ongoing evolution of the gaming industry.

2. The Mechanics of GameFi

Let's now look at the mechanics of GameFi and of its core elements, particularly the Play-to-Earn model, the role of NFTs, and the integration of DeFi principles. Each of these components contributes to the distinctive nature of GameFi, merging gaming with blockchain technology to create a new paradigm where gameplay is not just entertaining but also financially rewarding.

2.1 Play-to-Earn Model

The Play-to-Earn (P2E) model is central to the GameFi ecosystem, fundamentally altering the traditional gaming narrative by allowing players to earn real-world value through in-game activities. Unlike traditional games where in-game achievements or currency have no value outside the game, P2E games reward players with digital assets that have external economic value, typically in the form of cryptocurrencies or NFTs. These rewards can be earned through various means, including the following:

- **Completing Tasks and Challenges:** Players can earn rewards by completing specific in-game tasks, quests, or challenges set by the game developers.
- **Battling Other Players:** Competitive gameplay, such as player versus player (PvP) battles, often rewards winners with tokens or valuable NFTs.

- **Progressing Through Game Levels:** Advancing through the game or achieving certain milestones can unlock rewards.

This model not only incentivizes gameplay but also fosters a dynamic economy within the game, where players can generate income, contributing to financial inclusion and empowerment.

2.2 Why Is Having a Token Such a Big Deal?

Adding a token to a game fundamentally transforms the gaming experience by embedding *tradable* value within the game's ecosystem. This tradability is crucial for the P2E model, enabling the conversion of in-game achievements into real-world economic gains.

The introduction of tokens in P2E games creates a direct link between gaming activities and financial rewards. Unlike traditional in-game currencies that hold value only within the game's universe, tokens in P2E games are designed to be traded on external cryptocurrency exchanges or marketplaces. This tradability ensures that the time and effort players invest into the game can translate into tangible earnings, providing a significant incentive for both casual and dedicated gamers.

Tokens enhance the liquidity of digital assets obtained within games, allowing players to easily buy, sell, or trade their earnings. This liquidity is pivotal in establishing a vibrant, dynamic economy around the game, where assets can rapidly change hands based on supply-and-demand dynamics. Furthermore, the accessibility of tokens across global exchanges democratizes participation in the game's economy, enabling players from different geographical locations to engage in the ecosystem without the barriers often encountered in traditional financial systems.

By rewarding players with tokens for their in-game achievements, the P2E model fosters a sense of ownership and empowerment. Players are not merely consumers of content but active participants in the game's economy, with the autonomy to make strategic decisions regarding their assets. This empowerment extends beyond the game, as players can leverage their tokens for financial planning, investment, or conversion into fiat currencies, thereby integrating their virtual successes into their real-world financial landscape.

Tokens also serve as a catalyst for economic engagement within the game, encouraging players to explore various financial strategies, from direct trading to more complex interactions like staking or providing liquidity. This economic engagement fosters a deeper connection between players and the game, contributing to community building. Players share strategies, collaborate on economic goals, and contribute to the game's development, creating a feedback loop that enhances the game's value and appeal.

In sum, consider a P2E game that rewards players with its native token for completing quests, battling opponents, and achieving certain milestones. A player who earns tokens through various in-game activities can choose to do the following:

- Trade the tokens on a cryptocurrency exchange for other digital currencies or fiat money.

- Use the tokens within the game to purchase exclusive items, unlock new levels, or participate in special events.
- Stake the tokens in a liquidity pool to earn interest, further increasing their holdings without additional gameplay.

This example illustrates how tokens not only serve as a reward mechanism but also open up a spectrum of economic activities and strategic opportunities for players.

In summary, adding a token to a P2E game introduces a new dimension of tradable value, enhancing the gaming experience with financial incentives, liquidity, and player empowerment. This integration of tokens into gaming ecosystems marks a significant evolution in the digital entertainment industry, where economic and recreational activities converge, offering players unparalleled opportunities for engagement and reward.

2.3 NFTs in Gaming

NFTs have become a cornerstone in GameFi, changing the way digital ownership and the tradability of in-game assets are perceived and managed. As unique, blockchain-based tokens, NFTs represent various elements within a game—ranging from characters and equipment to expansive parcels of virtual land. This representation is not merely symbolic; it confers several critical properties on these digital assets, fundamentally altering their role within gaming ecosystems.

One of the most transformative aspects of NFTs in gaming is their capacity to provide unambiguous proof of ownership. Unlike traditional digital assets, which reside on centralized servers and are governed by the terms of service of gaming platforms, NFTs are recorded on the blockchain. This ensures that each asset is indelibly linked to its owner, offering a level of security and sovereignty previously unattainable in digital gaming. Furthermore, the blockchain records a transparent history of transactions for each NFT, including previous owners and sale prices. This provenance enhances trust among players and collectors, as the lineage of an asset can be easily verified, adding depth and narrative value to the digital item.

Another significant advantage offered by NFTs in the GameFi ecosystem is their potential for interoperability. This feature allows digital assets to traverse various gaming platforms and virtual worlds, a stark contrast to traditional gaming assets locked within a single game. Developers who embrace this interoperability design NFTs to conform to shared standards, enabling characters or items acquired in one game to be utilized in another. This not only increases the utility and lifespan of digital assets but also enriches the gaming experience, allowing players to weave their collections into a broader tapestry of digital experiences. The potential for interoperability underscores the transformative nature of NFTs, turning isolated gaming environments into a connected universe of virtual economies.

NFTs inherently possess marketability that extends beyond the confines of the game in which they were created. Through open marketplaces dedicated to the trade of NFTs, players have the unprecedented ability to monetize their in-game achievements and holdings. These marketplaces facilitate the buying, selling, and trading of NFTs, leveraging the principles of supply and demand to determine the value of digital assets. The scarcity of certain NFTs, whether due to limited edition releases, in-game achievements, or unique attributes, can drive significant demand and, consequently, substantial profits for players. This open economy model not only enables players to reap financial rewards from their gaming prowess and strategy but also fosters a dynamic and vibrant market for digital collectibles.

In conclusion, NFTs are redefining the landscape of digital gaming, introducing a new paradigm where ownership, interoperability, and marketability of in-game assets are enhanced by blockchain technology. As GameFi continues to evolve, the role of NFTs is set to expand, promising a future where gaming is not only a source of entertainment but also a platform for innovation, creativity, and economic opportunity.

2.4 Is This Really New?

Purchasing items within popular games like *Fortnite* and *League of Legends* is a multibillion-dollar business. Is doing it on a blockchain such a revolutionary thing? Yes, let's see why.

Traditional online games like *Fortnite* and *League of Legends* operate within centralized systems controlled by their respective developers, Epic Games and Riot Games. These games have revolutionized online gaming and esports, offering players vast universes of competition and play without direct economic benefit. Purchases within these games, such as *Fortnite*'s V-Bucks or *League of Legends*' Riot Points, facilitate the acquisition of cosmetic items, characters, and other in-game content. However, these transactions do not confer **ownership**; the assets remain within the control of the game's ecosystem, with no real-world value or the possibility for legal real-money trading outside the game. The economic models of these games are built on microtransactions and in-game purchases, offering a play-for-fun experience where financial investments enhance gameplay or aesthetics rather than offer a pathway to earning.

Moreover, *Fortnite* and *League of Legends* have established themselves as behemoths in the gaming and esports arenas, creating communities and competitive landscapes that have engaged millions worldwide. Their success is anchored in compelling gameplay, continuous updates, and community building rather than the financialization of in-game assets. While these games allow for the spending of money, the flow is generally one-way, with players purchasing items to enjoy a more enriched gaming experience without the expectation of financial return.

In contrast, the introduction of GameFi, underpinned by blockchain technology, has ushered in an era where digital assets carry real-world value, and players are stakeholders within the game's economy, a stark contrast to the model embraced by *Fortnite* and *League of Legends*.

In the heart of GameFi's innovation is the blockchain, which enables the tokenization of in-game assets as non-fungible tokens, granting players true ownership. This means that when a player acquires an item, character, or piece of land within a GameFi ecosystem, they possess a digital asset that can be traded, sold, or even leveraged across different platforms outside the game itself. Furthermore, the play-to-earn model intrinsic to GameFi transforms gaming from a leisure activity into a potential income source. Players can earn cryptocurrency through gameplay, achieving objectives, or contributing to the game's ecosystem, thereby intertwining entertainment with financial opportunity. **Figure 2** captures the key differences between traditional games and GameFi.

The distinctions between GameFi and traditional gaming models epitomized by *Fortnite* and *League of Legends* underscore a broader dialogue about the future of gaming. Where GameFi offers a new frontier where gaming meets finance, traditional online games continue to prioritize immersive experiences, community engagement, and competitive play. Each model appeals to different aspects of what gaming means to individuals, from entertainment and competition to investment and economic opportunity, reflecting the diverse ecosystem that the gaming world has become.

2.5 Integration of DeFi Elements

Let's now delve into how the tokens purchased within a game can be levered outside of it. By incorporating DeFi concepts such as yield farming, staking, and liquidity pools into gaming ecosystems, GameFi platforms can offer players not only entertainment but also opportunities for financial engagement and investment.

2.5.1 Yield Farming in GameFi   Players can engage in activities that mirror yield farming by completing quests, participating in events, or contributing to the game's ecosystem in ways that earn them in-game tokens. These tokens often have utility both within the

Figure 2   Traditional games versus GameFi

game—for purchasing items or unlocking features—and in the broader cryptocurrency market, where they can be traded or staked.

Example: *Alien Worlds* implements yield farming through its planetary governance and mining activities. Players mine for Trilium (TLM), the native token, which can then be staked on different planets to participate in governance and earn additional rewards, simulating yield farming dynamics within the game's universe.

2.5.2 Staking Mechanisms   Staking is another core DeFi mechanism that GameFi projects have adopted to incentivize player participation and investment. By locking up certain amounts of in-game or native tokens, players can earn rewards, gain voting rights within the game's ecosystem, or enhance their in-game characters or assets.

Example: *Splinterlands*, a collectible card game, allows players to stake the game's native token, DEC, to receive various benefits, including increased rewards from battles, participation in governance, and eligibility for special tournaments. This not only incentivizes longer-term engagement with the game but also aligns players' interests with the success of the game ecosystem.

2.5.3 Liquidity Pools and Trading   GameFi platforms often feature their own decentralized exchanges (DEXs) or integrate with existing DEXs to facilitate the trading of in-game assets and tokens. Players can contribute to liquidity pools, providing liquidity for token pairs related to the game, and earn transaction fees or other rewards in return. This not only enhances the liquidity of in-game assets but also allows players to engage directly with the financial mechanics of liquidity provision and exchange.

Example: *DeFi Kingdoms* is a notable instance where GameFi meets DeFi head-on. The game incorporates a DEX within its medieval-themed world, allowing players to trade in-game items and the native JEWEL token. Players can provide liquidity to various pools within the game's marketplace, earning rewards and influencing the game's economy.

The integration of DeFi elements into GameFi does more than merely add financial mechanisms to gaming. It transforms games into comprehensive ecosystems where entertainment, community participation, and economic investment converge. Players become stakeholders in the game's success, with the opportunity to influence its development, participate in its economy, and benefit from its growth. Furthermore, the incorporation of DeFi mechanisms democratizes access to financial systems, allowing players from various backgrounds to learn about and engage with complex financial concepts in an accessible and engaging manner.

Finally, the amalgamation of DeFi elements within GameFi represents a forward-looking approach to gaming, where the boundaries between play, community, and finance are increasingly blurred. Through yield farming, staking, and liquidity pools, GameFi projects offer an experience that promises both entertainment and economic opportunity, underscoring the revolutionary potential of blockchain technology in creating new paradigms for digital interaction and financial engagement.

3. Economic Implications of GameFi

We have seen that GameFi introduces player-driven economies where players have significant control over the supply and demand of in-game assets, essentially determining their value. This economic model is a departure from traditional gaming, where the game developers set fixed prices for items or services. In GameFi, the market dynamics within the game world are reflective of real-world economics, with the value of in-game assets fluctuating based on player activities, scarcity, and demand.

To better understand the GameFi tokenomics, let's try to answer the following key question: *why anybody would purchase gaming tokens in the real world?*

Users might be interested in purchasing tokens linked to games on an exchange for several reasons. Firstly, these tokens often have significant in-game utility. They can be used to buy items, unlock special features, or enhance gameplay experiences. For instance, players might need tokens to acquire rare items, skins, or characters that provide a competitive edge or enhance their enjoyment of the game. This is not that different from what already exists in traditional gaming.

Additionally, many see these tokens as an investment opportunity. If a game becomes popular, the demand for its tokens can rise, increasing their value. Early adopters can potentially profit from this appreciation, adding a financial incentive to participate in the game's ecosystem. This is definitely new. While it is interesting and potentially rewarding, it is one aspect that makes this tokenomics model more "ponzi like," and so inherently risky and unsustainable.

Some tokens also come with governance rights, allowing holders to participate in decision-making processes about the game's development and future updates. This decentralized approach gives players a sense of ownership and control over the game, encouraging them to invest in the token to have a say in its evolution.

Social recognition within the gaming community also plays a role. Owning tokens in popular games can signify a player's commitment and achievements, offering a form of social status. Additionally, developers often reward token holders with exclusive access to events, early releases, or special content, making purchasing tokens even more appealing.

Lastly, some game tokens are designed to be interoperable with other games or platforms, enhancing their utility and value. Players might buy tokens because they can use them across multiple games, increasing the tokens' versatility and worth.

For example, in games like Axie Infinity, players breed, battle, and trade digital pets called Axies. The rarity and desirability of certain Axie traits can drive up demand, leading to higher prices on the marketplace. This dynamic ecosystem allows players to engage in economic strategies, such as investing in rare assets or speculating on market trends, to earn profits.

One of the most heralded aspects of GameFi is its potential for financial inclusion, particularly in developing countries. Many players in these regions have turned to GameFi as a significant source of income, leveraging the play-to-earn model to

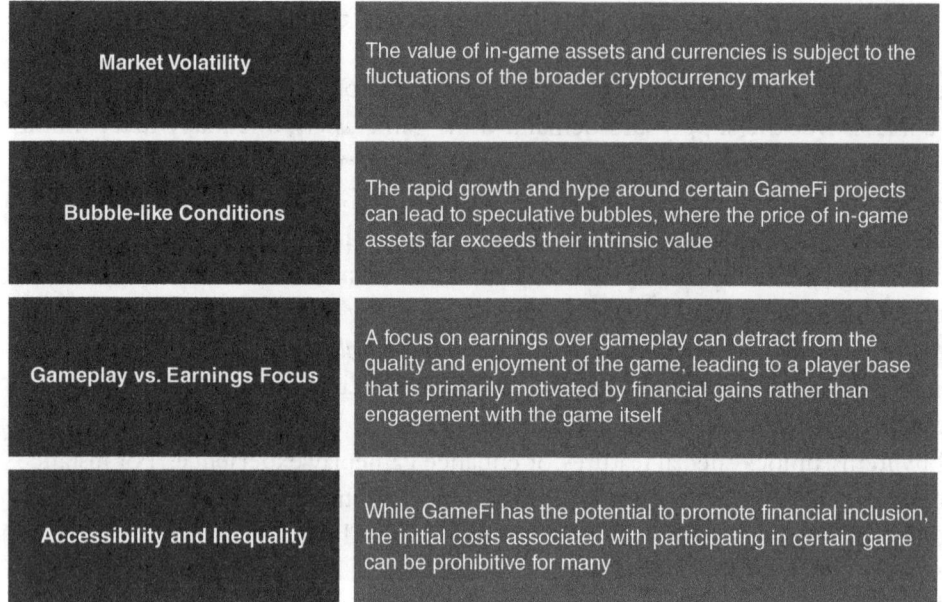

Figure 3   Challenges of GameFi

supplement or even replace traditional forms of employment. The accessibility of GameFi, requiring only a basic internet connection and sometimes even modest computing resources, opens up economic opportunities to individuals who might be excluded from traditional financial systems.

However, this reliance on GameFi for income also raises questions about long-term sustainability and the impact of market volatility on players' livelihoods. The stability of GameFi platforms and the currencies or assets earned is closely tied to broader cryptocurrency market trends, which can be highly volatile.

While GameFi presents exciting opportunities for players and investors, there are several challenges to its sustainability (**Figure 3**).

- **Market Volatility:** The value of in-game assets and currencies is subject to the fluctuations of the broader cryptocurrency market, which can introduce a significant risk for players relying on GameFi earnings as a stable source of income.
- **Bubble-like Conditions:** The rapid growth and hype around certain GameFi projects can lead to speculative bubbles, where the price of in-game assets far exceeds their intrinsic value. Even the basic question of how to compute the fundamental value of these tokens is difficult to answer. When these bubbles burst, they can lead to market crashes that harm players and undermine confidence in the GameFi model.
- **Gameplay vs. Earnings Focus:** A focus on earnings over gameplay can detract from the quality and enjoyment of the game, leading to a player base that is primarily motivated by financial gains rather than engagement with the game itself. This can affect the long-term viability of the game and its economy.

- **Accessibility and Inequality:** While GameFi has the potential to promote financial inclusion, the initial costs associated with participating in certain games (e.g. purchasing NFTs to start playing) can be prohibitive for many, exacerbating inequalities within and between communities.

Addressing these challenges requires careful consideration of the economic models underlying GameFi projects, as well as broader regulatory and community support to ensure fair play, stability, and sustainability. As the GameFi space continues to evolve, finding a balance between financial incentives and engaging gameplay will be crucial for its long-term success and acceptance.

Let's now look at some examples.

PROMINENT PROTOCOL: THE SANDBOX

Figure 4   The Sandbox

The Sandbox is a virtual world that leverages a voxel-based game maker, enabling players to create, share, and monetize gaming experiences (**Figure 4**). Its use of NFTs and the native cryptocurrency, SAND, exemplifies the potential of blockchain technology to empower creators and players alike.

A *voxel-based game world* refers to a type of digital environment constructed from voxels, which are the three-dimensional equivalents of pixels. The term *voxel* itself is a portmanteau of *volumetric* and *pixel*, indicating these are small, distinct cubes that make up the game's landscape and objects within a three-dimensional space. This approach allows for highly detailed and interactive environments, where every part of the game world can be modified, manipulated, or interacted with in a granular manner.

Characteristics of Voxel-Based Game Worlds

- **Granular Control and Customization:** Since voxel-based environments are made up of individual cubes, players and developers can achieve a high level of detail and customization. This includes creating complex structures, landscapes, and objects block by block, much like building with digital LEGO.
- **Destructible and Constructible Environments:** Voxel worlds often feature dynamic landscapes that players can alter in real time. This could involve digging tunnels, constructing buildings, or even reshaping the terrain itself, offering a tangible sense of impact on the game world.
- **Enhanced Spatial Dynamics:** The use of voxels adds depth to the gaming experience by introducing true three-dimensionality. This can influence gameplay mechanics, such as line-of-sight, movement, and strategy, making the spatial dynamics a crucial aspect of game design.
- **Resource Management and Crafting:** Many voxel-based games incorporate elements of resource gathering and crafting. Players can extract resources from the environment and use them to craft tools, structures, or other items, emphasizing survival and creativity.

The Sandbox is a prominent example of a voxel-based game world that leverages blockchain technology. It provides a decentralized platform for creating, sharing, and monetizing interactive experiences and games. In The Sandbox, everything from the terrain to the objects and characters is made from voxels, offering players unparalleled freedom to design and interact with the game environment.

Players can use VoxEdit, a dedicated tool, to create voxel-based assets—ranging from simple items to complex characters and animations (**Figure 5**). These assets can be tokenized as NFTs, ensuring their ownership and provenance.

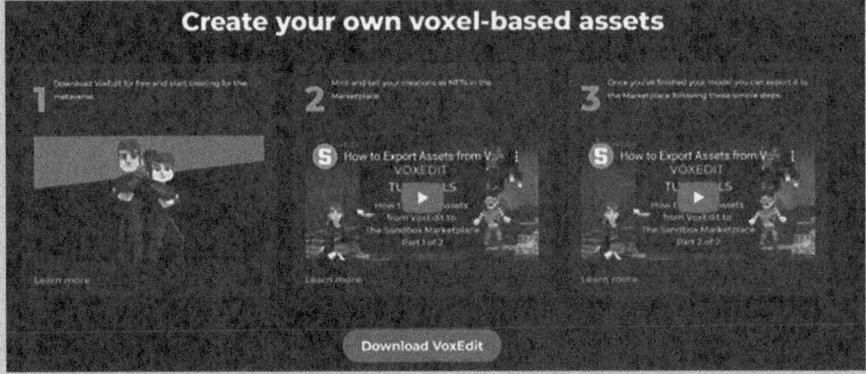

Figure 5   VoxEdit

The Sandbox integrates DeFi elements by allowing players to buy, sell, and trade their voxel creations on the marketplace. The use of SAND, an ERC-20 utility token, facilitates transactions within this virtual economy.

The game emphasizes user-generated content, empowering players to not only design their voxel creations but also develop entire games and experiences within their LAND parcels, which are sections of the game world owned by players.

The Sandbox utilizes the Ethereum blockchain to tokenize in-game assets, including voxel-based creations, experiences, and parcels of virtual land, as non-fungible tokens. This tokenization process is critical for several reasons.

- **Immutability and Provenance:** Blockchain technology ensures that once an asset is created and tokenized, its ownership history and authenticity are permanently recorded and easily verifiable. This mitigates issues of fraud and duplicates common in digital spaces.
- **Smart Contracts for Automated Transactions:** The Sandbox marketplace leverages smart contracts to automate the buying, selling, and trading of NFTs. These contracts execute predefined conditions without the need for intermediaries, reducing transaction costs and enhancing trust among participants.

By allowing creators to monetize their voxel assets and experiences directly, The Sandbox fosters an ecosystem where digital artists, game designers, and entrepreneurs can generate income. This model not only incentivizes high-quality content creation but also provides a new avenue for digital entrepreneurship. The integration of SAND, The Sandbox's native ERC-20 token, into the ecosystem facilitates liquidity and enables dynamic market conditions. Creators can price their assets in SAND, benefiting from the token's market movements and the broader economic activities within the platform. The sale and development of virtual land in The Sandbox introduces a novel form of digital investment. Landowners can develop their parcels with unique experiences or lease them to other creators, generating passive income. The finite nature of land within The Sandbox, coupled with its potential for development, creates scarcity and demand, driving up the value of these digital properties.

In sum, The Sandbox exemplifies the democratizing potential of GameFi by providing a technical and economic framework where ownership, creativity, and entrepreneurship converge. Through the strategic use of NFTs, smart contracts, and the SAND token, The Sandbox empowers creators and players, reshaping the traditional narratives of gaming and digital ownership.

The Sandbox provides several key features and tools to its users.

- **VoxEdit:** A powerful tool for creating and animating 3D objects (called ASSETS in The Sandbox universe) which can be exported as NFTs and used within games or sold in the marketplace.
- **Game Maker:** Allows users, even those without coding skills, to build interactive games in The Sandbox universe by placing ASSETS and designing gameplay mechanics around them (**Figure 6**).
- **Marketplace:** A decentralized platform for buying, selling, or trading user-generated ASSETS, LANDS (virtual real estate in The Sandbox universe), and experiences. The use of blockchain technology ensures that transactions are secure and transparent, and that creators retain ownership rights.

The SAND token transcends the conventional utility of digital currencies within gaming environments by embodying the roles of a medium of exchange, a tool for governance, and a means for staking, intricately weaving together the fabric of The Sandbox's virtual world.

As a medium of exchange, SAND enables a myriad of transactions within The Sandbox ecosystem. From acquiring virtual real estate, known as LAND, to trading various in-game items and creations, SAND facilitates a vibrant and dynamic market. This market not only underscores the value and liquidity of digital assets but also mirrors real-world economic principles, offering insights into asset valuation in digital spaces. Moreover, the use of SAND extends to the platform's marketplace, where players and creators exchange goods and services, thus propelling the economic vitality of The Sandbox.

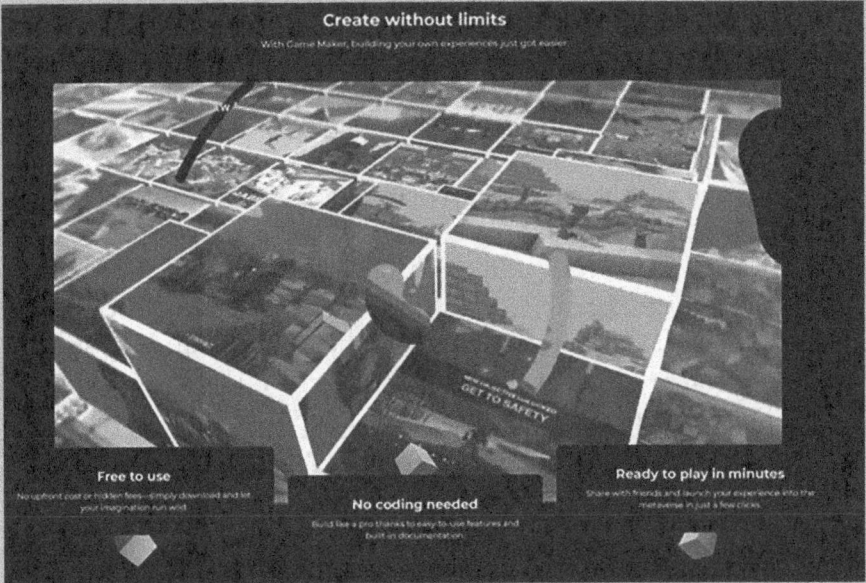

Figure 6   Game Maker in The Sandbox

Beyond its economic utility, SAND vests its holders with governance rights, allowing them to partake in the decentralized decision-making process of The Sandbox platform. Through a decentralized autonomous organization (DAO), SAND holders wield influence over the platform's development trajectory by voting on proposals ranging from feature updates to strategic partnerships. This governance mechanism embodies the decentralized ethos of blockchain, ensuring that The Sandbox evolves in alignment with its community's aspirations and feedback.

Staking SAND tokens serves multiple strategic functions within the ecosystem. Participants who stake their SAND can earn rewards, thereby incentivizing long-term engagement and investment in the platform. Additionally, staking plays a crucial role in the crafting of GEMs and CATALYSTs—items essential for defining the scarcity and attributes of ASSETS within the game. This linkage between economic participation and creative output aligns the interests of creators and investors, fostering a cohesive and collaborative community. Furthermore, staking SAND can afford users priority access to LAND sales, highlighting the token's role in facilitating engagement with and investment in the virtual landscape of The Sandbox.

4. Technological and Developmental Considerations

In the GameFi space, the integration of blockchain technology presents unique opportunities and challenges, particularly around the scalability of networks and the cost of transactions. These challenges stem from the inherent properties of blockchain networks, where decentralization and security often come at the expense of scalability (remember the *blockchain trilemma*). Traditional blockchains like Bitcoin and Ethereum face difficulties in handling increased demand from gaming activities due to network congestion and high transaction costs.[1]

To address these challenges, several scalability solutions have been developed:[2]

- **Layer 2 Protocols:** Solutions like the Lightning Network for Bitcoin and Raiden Network for Ethereum aim to alleviate the main blockchain's load by moving transactions off-chain. This allows for instantaneous transactions with minimal fees, significantly increasing the potential transactions per second (TPS).
- **Off-Chain Scaling Solutions:** Plasma for Ethereum uses "child chains" running parallel to the main chain to enhance speed and efficiency. This approach allows each

---

[1] https://koop360.com/blog/gamefi-in-2024-exploring-opportunities-challenges/
[2] https://masterthecrypto.com/blockchain-scalability-solutions-crypto-scaling-solutions/

child chain to operate independently, potentially handling a specific category of transactions while still leveraging the security of the main chain.

- **Consensus Mechanisms:** Altering the blockchain's consensus mechanism can also offer scalability benefits. Delegated proof-of-stake (DPOS) and Byzantine fault tolerance (BFT) variations, including practical Byzantine fault tolerance (PBFT) and federated Byzantine agreement (FBA), provide mechanisms through which blockchains can achieve higher transaction throughput while maintaining security and decentralization to varying degrees.

For instance, platforms like The Sandbox or Axie Infinity must efficiently process a vast number of transactions to facilitate gameplay, asset trading, and governance activities. By implementing layer 2 solutions or adopting novel consensus mechanisms, GameFi projects can enhance their scalability, ensuring a smooth and responsive gaming experience for users.[3]

Furthermore, even if transaction load could be handled, there is still the issue of **finality**. Fast finality is crucial for GameFi for several reasons, primarily revolving around user experience, security, and economic efficiency.

In gaming, especially in real-time or interactive environments, users expect immediate feedback and results from their actions. Fast finality ensures that transactions (such as purchases, trades, or rewards) are confirmed almost instantly, maintaining a seamless and engaging user experience. Delays can lead to frustration and disrupt the flow of the game, which can be detrimental in a highly competitive and immersive environment.

In GameFi, players often engage in numerous microtransactions, such as buying in-game items, earning rewards, or trading assets. Fast finality ensures that these transactions are processed quickly, reducing the waiting time and enabling players to continue their activities without interruption. This is particularly important for games that involve economic strategies, where delays in transactions could lead to missed opportunities and losses.

Fast finality also reduces the window of vulnerability where a transaction can be altered or reversed. By ensuring quick and irreversible transactions, fast finality enhances the overall security and trustworthiness of the game's economic system.

In GameFi, players often own unique digital assets, such as NFTs (non-fungible tokens), which can represent characters, items, or other in-game elements. Fast finality ensures that the ownership and transfer of these assets are recorded promptly, which is essential for maintaining accurate and reliable records of ownership. This is critical for preventing disputes and ensuring that players can confidently trade and use their assets.

Finally, many GameFi projects aim to create interconnected ecosystems where assets and tokens can move freely between different games and platforms. Fast finality facilitates this interoperability by ensuring that transactions are quickly and reliably confirmed across different systems. This seamless integration is vital for the growth and success of the broader GameFi ecosystem.

---

[3] https://koop360.com/blog/gamefi-in-2024-exploring-opportunities-challenges/

Avalanche's Subnets and the Ronin network present innovative solutions. These platforms tackle the scalability issue head-on, enabling GameFi projects to offer users a seamless and cost-efficient gaming experience.

4.1 Avalanche Subnets

As we have seen in Chapter 3, Avalanche's approach to scalability through Subnets allows for the creation of app-specific blockchains, which operate alongside the main Avalanche network but with distinct consensus rules and validator sets. This design facilitates infinite scalability by enabling multiple AppChains to run in parallel, each tailored to the specific needs of a GameFi project. Subnets can significantly reduce congestion on the main network by diverting traffic to these dedicated channels, effectively lowering transaction costs and enhancing performance. The Subnet structure also permits custom virtual machines and independent tokenomics, allowing GameFi projects to optimize their operations and reduce expenses for end users. Moreover, Subnets support regulatory compliance and privacy measures, catering to a wide range of project requirements.

Real-world examples of Avalanche Subnets include the DFK Chain, developed for DeFi Kingdoms, and the Swimmer Network, designed for Crabada. These Subnets have demonstrated the potential to process transactions faster and more cost-effectively than on the main Avalanche C-Chain, underscoring the utility of this solution in supporting high-volume GameFi projects.[4]

This design allows for parallel processing of transactions across multiple Subnets, significantly increasing the network's overall capacity.

- **Custom Virtual Machines (VMs):** Subnets allow developers to implement custom VMs, such as the Ethereum VM (EVM) for Ethereum compatibility or entirely new VMs optimized for specific types of games or applications. This flexibility enables GameFi developers to design their blockchain environment to support complex game mechanics and large player bases without being constrained by the performance limitations of a general-purpose blockchain.
- **Dedicated Validators:** By using a dedicated set of validators for each Subnet, Avalanche ensures that game transactions are processed swiftly and securely. Validators in a Subnet are incentivized through transaction fees in $AVAX or the Subnet's native token, ensuring their commitment to maintaining the network's integrity and performance.
- **Independent Tokenomics:** Subnets empower GameFi projects to establish their token economies, customizing aspects such as gas fees and token distribution to suit their game's economics. This autonomy allows for the creation of sustainable and player-friendly economic models.

---

[4] https://www.covalenthq.com/blog/avalanche-subnets/

4.2 Solana: Speed Demon in the GameFi Arena

Solana has emerged as a compelling alternative to Ethereum in the GameFi landscape. It boasts several key advantages that make it well-suited for fast-paced, high-transaction volume games.

- **Blazing-Fast Transactions:** Solana leverages a unique proof-of-history (PoH) consensus mechanism alongside proof-of-stake (PoS) to achieve significantly faster transaction speeds compared to Ethereum. This translates to near-instantaneous in-game actions and a smoother user experience, especially crucial for real-time games.
- **Lower Transaction Fees:** Solana's efficient architecture minimizes the computational resources required for processing transactions, resulting in significantly lower fees compared to Ethereum, particularly during periods of high network congestion. This makes it more cost-effective for players to engage in frequent in-game transactions like buying/selling items or participating in rapid gameplay activities.

While Solana shines in terms of speed and fees, it's important to acknowledge its evolving ecosystem compared to Ethereum.

- **Limited Decentralization:** Solana utilizes a validator set considered less decentralized than Ethereum's. This raises concerns about potential centralization risks and the network's vulnerability to attacks if a small group of validators collude.
- **Newer Developer Tools:** Ethereum boasts a more mature developer ecosystem with a wider range of established tools and libraries for building complex blockchain applications. While Solana is rapidly catching up, developers may find a steeper learning curve when working on the platform.
- **Interoperability Challenges:** While some cross-chain bridges exist, interoperability between Solana and other blockchains is still under development. This can limit the potential for in-game assets to be seamlessly used across different GameFi ecosystems built on other blockchains.

The decision between Ethereum and Solana for a GameFi project depends on specific priorities:

- For fast-paced games with a high volume of in-game transactions and a focus on affordability, Solana's speed and lower fees might be more attractive.
- However, if a project prioritizes a highly decentralized network, a wider range of existing developer tools, and the potential for future interoperability with other blockchain ecosystems, Ethereum may still be the preferred choice.

As both Ethereum and Solana continue to evolve, it's possible that the future of GameFi doesn't favor a single dominant platform. We might see a multichain landscape where different protocols cater to the specific needs of various GameFi projects. Ultimately, the choice of platform will depend on the specific game's design, target audience, and desired user experience.

Case Study: Axie Infinity: Video Game Meets Blockchain[5]

Axie Infinity is a blockchain-driven game that epitomizes the convergence of gaming with the concepts of P2E mechanics and NFTs (**Figure 7**). Axie Infinity leverages blockchain technology to create a digital ecosystem where players can earn real-world value through gaming activities. At its core, players breed, raise, and battle creatures known as Axies, with these activities and victories in battles contributing to the player's ability to earn cryptocurrencies, primarily in the form of Small Love Potion (SLP) tokens and Axie Infinity Shards (AXS). These tokens can be traded on various cryptocurrency exchanges, converted into fiat currency, or used within the ecosystem for further breeding or purchasing Axies. The crucial aspect of Axie Infinity's model is the tokenization of game assets as NFTs, providing verifiable ownership and the ability to sell or trade these assets outside the game's platform.

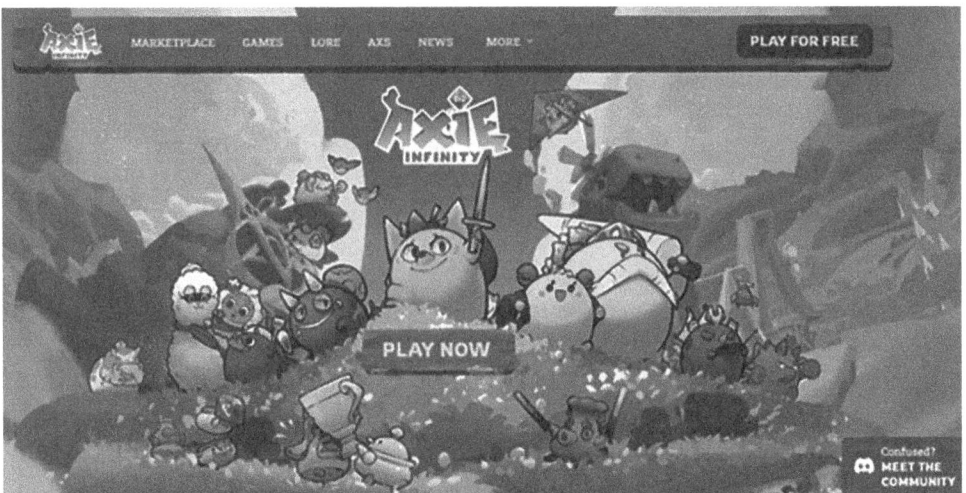

Figure 7   Axie Infinity

Why did I pick Axie as a case study in GameFi? A detailed exploration of its evolution, economic model, and the hurdles it encountered provides a lens to examine broader implications for the gaming industry and blockchain technology at large. **Figure 8** reports Axie players count over time, showing a pick up at the end of 2021. The narrative encapsulates the game's innovative approach to monetization and community engagement, juxtaposed with its challenges such as economic sustainability and the notorious Ronin network hack. Axie is helpful to achieve the following objectives:

---

[5] For a more detailed case study and teaching material about Axie Infinity, including a guide for in-class discussion, see the Harvard Business School case I co-wrote with Wenyao Sha called "Axie Infinity: Video Game Meets Blockchain" available at https://hbsp.harvard.edu/product/224021-PDF-ENG?Ntt=marco%20di%20maggio& itemFindingMethod=search.

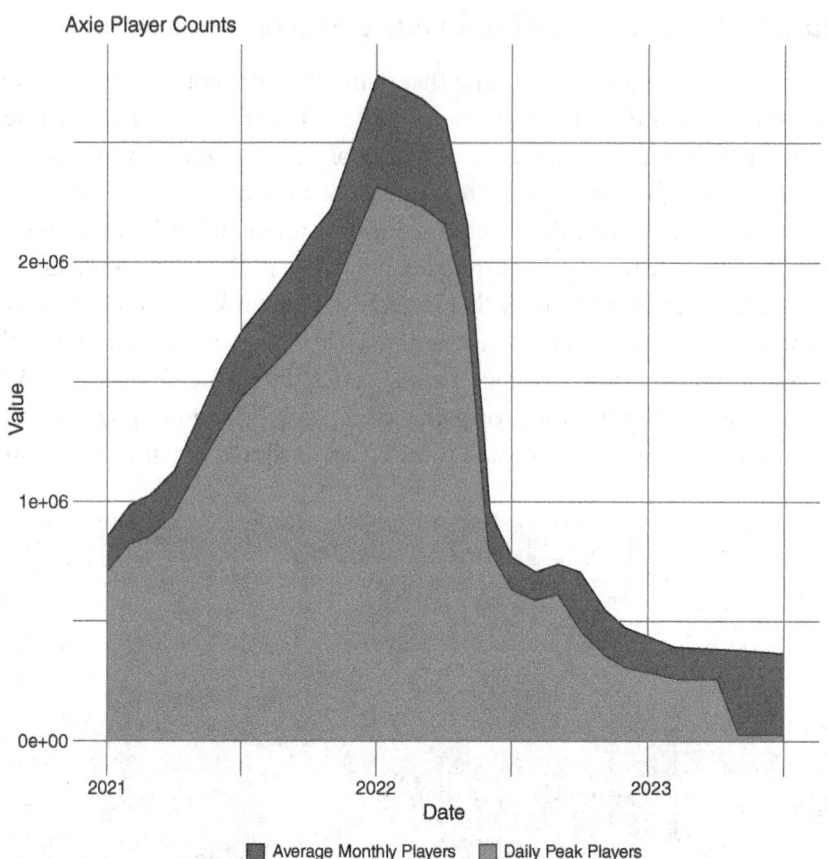

Figure 8   Axie player counts (Priori Data, 2024)

- **In-Depth Understanding of Play-to-Earn Model:** Beyond grasping the basics of the P2E model, discussing Axie is instrumental to dissect its revolutionary impact on gaming monetization, player engagement, and the broader economic implications for participants across varied socio-economic backgrounds.
- **Blockchain Technology and NFT Integration in Gaming:** This objective aims to foster a nuanced comprehension of how blockchain technology underpins the functionality of NFTs in gaming, enhancing digital ownership and creating new avenues for gamers to derive real-world value from virtual assets.
- **Economic and Social Impacts:** It also offers an example of the dual-edged sword of blockchain-based games, exploring how they offer economic opportunities, especially in developing countries, while also examining potential pitfalls including market volatility and the risk of unsustainable economies.
- **Sustainability and Scalability Challenges:** The case will encourage critical discussions on the viability of blockchain gaming economies, focusing on the inherent scalability issues, the balancing act between player rewards and economic health, and strategies for fostering long-term sustainability.

Traditional gaming monetization strategies, such as those seen in *World of Warcraft*, typically revolve around game sales, subscriptions, in-game purchases, and microtransactions. In these models, any in-game earnings or assets, such as gear or currency, remain within the game's ecosystem and do not possess real-world value. Players spend money to enhance their gaming experience but cannot earn real money through their in-game activities. The value generated within these games benefits the developers and publishers exclusively.

Axie Infinity's P2E model represents a significant departure from traditional gaming monetization strategies, introducing a novel blend of gaming and financial investment powered by blockchain technology. Blockchain technology's application in Axie Infinity serves several critical functions that enhance transparency, security, and ownership, yet it brings along challenges related to complexity and scalability.

The following are the advantages of blockchain in Axie Infinity:

- **Transparency and Security:** Blockchain's immutable ledger ensures that all transactions within Axie Infinity are transparent and tamper-proof. This enhances the game's security (not guaranteed as we will see soon), allowing players to trust in the fairness of the game's economy and the authenticity of their digital assets.
- **Ownership of Digital Assets:** Through NFTs, blockchain technology enables true ownership of in-game assets. Players can buy, sell, or trade their Axies with the assurance that their ownership is verifiable and recognized across the blockchain network. This level of ownership over digital assets is a stark contrast to traditional games, where in-game items typically remain under the control of game developers.
- **Decentralized Economy:** Axie Infinity leverages blockchain to facilitate a player-driven economy where users can earn cryptocurrencies (AXS and SLP) through gameplay. This decentralized approach allows players to influence the game's economy directly, unlike traditional gaming models where the economy is centrally managed by the game's developers.

Comparison with Other (Earlier) Blockchain Games CryptoKitties, one of the first blockchain games to gain mainstream attention, serves as an early example of how NFTs can be used to represent unique digital assets in a game. Like Axie Infinity, CryptoKitties allows players to collect, breed, and trade digital cats as NFTs. However, Axie Infinity expands on this concept by incorporating a more complex economy, strategic gameplay elements, and a broader range of activities that can generate earnings for players. While CryptoKitties primarily highlighted the potential of NFTs in gaming, Axie Infinity demonstrates the possibilities of a fully-fledged blockchain-based game economy, setting a precedent for future GameFi projects.

In summary, blockchain technology's role in Axie Infinity exemplifies the innovative potential of integrating gaming with decentralized finance and digital ownership.

The integration of blockchain, while offering numerous benefits, introduces a layer of complexity, especially for players unfamiliar with cryptocurrency and NFTs. Setting up digital wallets, understanding gas fees, and managing blockchain transactions can be daunting for new users, potentially hindering broader adoption. Being built on the Ethereum blockchain, Axie Infinity faces challenges related to scalability and high transaction costs, especially during periods of network congestion.

For this reason, Sky Mavis (owner of Axie Infinity) developed the Ronin network for Axie Infinity, which serves as a sidechain to Ethereum, offering a targeted solution to the scalability challenges faced by the game on the Ethereum mainnet. By processing transactions on Ronin before finalizing them on Ethereum, Axie Infinity benefits from the following:

- **Reduced Transaction Costs:** Ronin minimizes the gas fees associated with in-game transactions, making it economically viable for players to perform frequent in-game actions such as breeding Axies or buying and selling in-game items.
- **Faster Transaction Speeds:** The dedicated infrastructure of the Ronin network allows for faster processing times compared to the congested Ethereum mainnet. This speed is critical for maintaining a seamless gaming experience.
- **Security and Interoperability:** While operating independently, Ronin maintains a high level of security and benefits from interoperability with Ethereum, allowing players to move assets between the Ronin sidechain and the Ethereum mainnet.

Let's look at a basic example illustrating the interaction between the Ronin network and Ethereum, which involves simulating a simplified bridge mechanism. This bridge facilitates the transfer of assets (e.g. Axies as NFTs) between Ethereum and Ronin. In a practical scenario, such a bridge involves complex security measures, validations, and interoperability features to ensure seamless and secure asset transfers. Here, I'll provide an illustrative example focusing on the conceptual process rather than a fully operational code due to the inherent complexities and security considerations of bridging two blockchains.

Conceptual Overview

1. **Locking on Ethereum:** Users lock their Axie NFTs into a smart contract on Ethereum as a precursor to transferring them to Ronin.
2. **Minting on Ronin:** Equivalent NFTs are minted on Ronin, representing the locked Axies from Ethereum.
3. **Burning on Ronin for Return:** To transfer back to Ethereum, the NFTs on Ronin are burned.
4. **Unlocking on Ethereum:** The original Axie NFTs are unlocked on Ethereum, completing the round-trip.

```
// SPDX-License-Identifier: MIT
pragma solidity ^0.8.0;
import "@openzeppelin/contracts/token/ERC721/IERC721.sol";

contract EthereumAxieBridge {
    address public admin;
    IERC721 public axieContract;

    // Mapping to track the locked Axies
    mapping(uint256 => bool) public lockedAxies;

    event AxieLocked(uint256 indexed axieId);
    event AxieUnlocked(uint256 indexed axieId);

    constructor(address _axieContract) {
        admin = msg.sender;
        axieContract = IERC721(_axieContract);
    }

    function lockAxie(uint256 axieId) external {
        require(axieContract.ownerOf(axieId) == msg.sender, "Not
the owner");
        axieContract.transferFrom(msg.sender,
address(this), axieId);
        lockedAxies[axieId] = true;

        emit AxieLocked(axieId);
    }

    function unlockAxie(uint256 axieId) external {
        require(msg.sender == admin, "Only admin can unlock");
        require(lockedAxies[axieId], "Axie not locked");

        lockedAxies[axieId] = false;
        axieContract.transferFrom(address(this),
msg.sender, axieId);

        emit AxieUnlocked(axieId);
    }
}
```

For the Ronin side, you would need a corresponding contract that can mint and burn Axie NFTs based on the operations performed on Ethereum. Given Ronin's specialized nature for Axie Infinity and its distinct environment, the actual implementation details would depend on Ronin's specific NFT standards and bridge protocols, which are proprietary and beyond standard ERC-721 operations shown here.

The following are additional considerations:

- **Security and Validation:** In practice, transferring assets between blockchains requires rigorous security checks, including validation of asset locking and minting through cryptographic proofs or a network of trusted validators to prevent fraudulent activities.

- **Admin Roles:** The *admin* in these contracts is a placeholder for more complex governance mechanisms, potentially involving multisig wallets or DAOs for decentralized decision-making.
- **Cross-Chain Communication:** The examples don't cover the cross-chain communication layer required to synchronize operations between Ethereum and Ronin securely. Real implementations use oracles or specific bridging protocols to relay information securely between chains.

One of the key questions raised by the popularity of Axie Infinity is the following:

- What are the economic and social implications of Axie Infinity's model for players and the wider community? In other words, can these games have any impact on the real economy?

Quite surprisingly, yes. Axie Infinity's model has melded entertainment with tangible economic opportunities through its P2E framework. This model has far-reaching economic and social implications, not only for individual players but also for communities at large, particularly in developing countries where the potential for income generation has had a profound impact.

The game has created avenues for income generation that were previously unimaginable in the context of traditional gaming. In regions where economic opportunities may be limited, Axie Infinity has become a viable source of income for many, enabling players to earn through engaging in the game's ecosystem. This dynamic has particularly resonated in countries like the Philippines, where the game gained immense popularity amid the economic downturn caused by the COVID-19 pandemic. Stories have emerged of individuals and families who have been able to sustain themselves, pay for education, or even build houses through earnings from the game.[6] This phenomenon underscores the potential of GameFi projects to contribute to financial inclusion and economic empowerment on a global scale.

Beyond the economic opportunities, Axie Infinity fosters a strong sense of community and shared purpose among its players. The game's emphasis on cooperative play, trading, and governance creates a collaborative environment where players can connect, share strategies, and support one another. This community aspect is further enhanced by the decentralized governance model, which encourages players to participate in decision-making processes regarding the game's development and future direction. Such engagement fosters a sense of ownership and belonging among community members, enhancing the social fabric of the Axie Infinity ecosystem.

---

[6] For some examples, see the CoinDesk article on Axie Infinity's effect in the Philippines: https://www.coindesk.com/business/2021/05/11/for-filipinos-axie-infinity-is-more-than-a-crypto-game/.

However, the game's economic model also presents challenges and risks, notably speculative behavior and concerns regarding sustainability. The initial surge in the game's popularity was accompanied by significant speculation on Axie NFTs and the game's native tokens, leading to volatile market conditions. Such speculative dynamics can create barriers to entry for new players (as the tokens become more expensive) and raise questions about the game's long-term viability. The sustainability of Axie Infinity's economy hinges on a delicate balance between incentivizing player engagement, managing token supply and demand, and continually refreshing the game's content to maintain player interest.

Furthermore, evaluating the long-term social and economic impacts of Axie Infinity's model is complex. While the game has undoubtedly provided financial benefits for many, there is ongoing debate about the implications of spending extensive hours in virtual economies, the risk of dependency on volatile cryptocurrency markets, and the need for regulatory oversight to protect players.

In essence, Axie Infinity exemplifies the transformative potential of blockchain-based gaming to create new economic realities and foster vibrant online communities. Yet, it also highlights the need for sustainable economic models that can support long-term growth and stability, ensuring that the fusion of gaming and finance remains beneficial for all participants. As the GameFi space continues to evolve, the lessons learned from Axie Infinity's pioneering model will undoubtedly shape the future of digital economies and their integration into our social fabric.

How to Survive a Hack?   One of the most fascinating chapters in Axie Infinity's evolution centers around its response to the Ronin Network hack. This incident not only tested the resilience and security frameworks of one of the leading GameFi platforms but also spotlighted the strength and adaptability inherent in the Axie Infinity community and its developers, Sky Mavis.

The Ronin Network hack, which affected Axie Infinity, stands as one of the most significant security breaches in the DeFi realm, marking a pivotal moment for the Ronin Network and the broader crypto community. The incident unfolded in March 2022 when attackers stole approximately 173,600 ETH and 25.5 million USDC, totaling around $624 million. The breach wasn't detected until a user reported an inability to withdraw 5,000 ETH from the project's bridge, highlighting a critical lapse in monitoring for unauthorized transactions.[7]

The attack exploited vulnerabilities within the Ronin Network's security framework, specifically targeting its proof-of-authority (PoA) model. The Ronin Network utilizes a set of nine validator nodes for transaction approvals on its bridge,

[7] https://www.halborn.com/blog/post/explained-the-ronin-hack-march-2022

requiring a majority of five for authorization. Attackers managed to control four validators directly associated with Sky Mavis, the developer behind Axie Infinity, and a fifth validator through a social engineering attack and subsequent exploitation of an outdated permission granted to Sky Mavis for facilitating transactions on behalf of Axie DAO.[8]

The Ronin Network hack unfolded in a series of calculated steps that exploited human vulnerabilities and technical oversights. Initially, the attackers employed a spear-phishing strategy, targeting an employee of Sky Mavis. This insidious approach led to the compromise of the employee's credentials, a critical first breach that underscored the often-underestimated power of social engineering in cyberattacks.

With the stolen credentials in hand, the attackers infiltrated Sky Mavis's internal systems, penetrating the defenses to access crucial components connected to the Ronin Network. This breach was not just a testament to the attackers' cunning but also highlighted the interconnected risks within digital ecosystems, where a single point of vulnerability can lead to widespread compromise.

The intrusion's primary objective became apparent as the hackers managed to seize control over five of the nine validator nodes within the Ronin Network. In a PoA system, where transactions and network decisions are endorsed by a select group of validators, control over the majority translates directly into control over the entire network. This pivotal moment in the hack demonstrated the critical importance of securing validator nodes in PoA systems, underscoring a fundamental security principle: the concentration of control creates a concentration of risk.

Armed with control over these nodes, the attackers executed their final maneuver: authorizing unauthorized withdrawals from the Ronin bridge. This bridge, serving as a conduit for asset transfers between Ronin and other blockchains such as Ethereum, became the point of exfiltration for the attackers. By commandeering the majority of validator nodes, they were able to forge transactions that siphoned off assets, culminating in a staggering theft that reverberated through the crypto community.

This orchestrated attack on the Ronin Network serves as a stark reminder of the multifaceted threats facing blockchain ecosystems today. From the initial social engineering to the final unauthorized transactions, each step reveals vulnerabilities at both the human and technical levels, highlighting the imperative for comprehensive security measures that address both aspects to safeguard the future of GameFi and decentralized finance.

This incident not only highlighted the security vulnerabilities facing these innovative platforms but also brought to the forefront a critical question that many in the blockchain space must grapple with: **How can a protocol rebound from a significant security breach?** The actions taken by the development team in

[8] https://cryptopotato.com/the-biggest-ever-crypto-hack-what-happened-in-the-ronin-bridge-attack/

the aftermath are crucial. They are faced with the daunting task of not only securing the network against future threats but also preserving the trust and cohesion of their community to prevent the unraveling of their digital ecosystem.

Sky Mavis, the developer behind Axie Infinity, undertook significant steps to navigate the aftermath and restore trust within its community.

Sky Mavis managed to secure $150 million in funding led by crypto exchange Binance, alongside contributions from Animoca Brands, a16z, Dialectic, Paradigm, and Accel. This funding was instrumental in reimbursing users who lost funds during the hack. The quick mobilization of support from major players within the crypto space underscored the collaborative effort to stabilize the Ronin network and Axie Infinity ecosystem after the breach. Sky Mavis also committed to reopening the Ronin bridge after implementing the necessary security upgrades and conducting thorough audits, which were essential steps to ensure such a breach would not reoccur.[9]

Moreover, Sky Mavis acknowledged the hack was facilitated by a social engineering attack that compromised a small validator set of the Ronin Network. In response, the company announced plans to increase the number of validators from 9 to 21 within three months. This move was aimed at enhancing the network's security framework by diversifying the validator set, making it more resilient against future attacks. The expansion of validators is a critical step in decentralizing the network's control and mitigating risks associated with having a concentrated validator set.

These measures reflect Sky Mavis's dedication to safeguarding its ecosystem and maintaining the integrity of its GameFi platform. By raising substantial funds for reimbursement, committing to significant security improvements, and enhancing the network's decentralization, Sky Mavis demonstrated resilience and a proactive approach to overcoming one of the crypto space's most significant security challenges. These actions set a precedent for how blockchain-based platforms can respond to and recover from security breaches, ensuring the continued growth and sustainability of the GameFi sector.

5. GameFi Tokenomics

In the realm of GameFi, tokenomics play a critical role in defining the internal economies of games, creating sustainable business models that benefit gamers, investors, and developers alike. The evolution of GameFi from its initial P2E model, exemplified by early successes like Axie Infinity, to more refined approaches aims to address sustainability concerns and foster long-term value creation.

---

[9] See https://techcrunch.com/2022/04/06/axie-infinity-creator-raises-150m-round-to-compensate-victims-of-625m-ronin-hack/ and https://www.cryptopolitan.com/sky-mavis-raises-150m-to-refund-ronin-network-hack-victims/.

GameFi 1.0, characterized by the P2E model, demonstrated the potential of integrating digital assets and cryptocurrencies within gaming ecosystems. Axie Infinity's model, for example, created a significant market cap by attracting a large player base engaged in earning AXIE tokens. However, this model faced challenges regarding sustainability, as the continual need to sell tokens to realize earnings introduced selling pressure, impacting token value during market downturns. This highlighted the need for GameFi projects to develop mechanisms that balance token supply and demand, ensuring economic stability while providing earning opportunities for players.[10]

The concept of sustainable tokenomics in GameFi seeks to address these challenges by considering the entire economic lifecycle within games. Sustainable models propose that not all participants in the game economy should earn equally; instead, rewards should be distributed based on value creation, skill, and contribution to the ecosystem. This approach mirrors traditional economies where value creation and distribution are key to sustainability. For instance, a game might use sales proceeds to mint an initial balance of tokens for new users, balancing token supply with demand while also ensuring that players have the resources needed to engage with the game's economy from the start. Successful players could see their balances increase as a reward for skillful play, with mechanisms in place to prevent inflation and ensure the long-term viability of the game's economy.

Furthermore, GameFi 2.0 envisions models where financial incentives are aligned with skill development and retention, fostering a competitive environment where improvement and strategic play are rewarded. This evolution toward more balanced and sustainable economic models not only enhances the player experience but also attracts investment by creating more predictable and stable in-game economies.

In summary, the shift toward sustainable tokenomics in GameFi represents a critical evolution in the intersection of gaming and finance. By addressing the challenges faced by early GameFi models, developers can create more engaging, economically viable, and sustainable gaming experiences that attract a broad spectrum of participants, from casual players to serious investors.

In the GameFi space, various mechanisms are employed to prevent inflation and sustain the economic model, ensuring the long-term viability and player engagement within these virtual economies. By examining different approaches taken by GameFi projects, we can understand how these mechanisms contribute to a more sustainable economic model.

One common approach is the implementation of **issuance and burning mechanisms**. A controlled issuance size prevents token inflation by limiting the number of tokens that can enter circulation, thereby maintaining the token's value. Concurrently, active burning mechanisms, where tokens are removed from circulation through various in-game activities, help to counterbalance any inflationary pressures. For instance, Axie Infinity made significant adjustments to its SLP token issuance, reducing rewards in

---

certain game modes and introducing more avenues for token burning, such as special cosmetics and upgraded features, which contributed to stabilizing the token's price after a period of decline.[11]

Another important aspect is the **distribution** of tokens, where a fair and community-centric distribution model is crucial. This involves allocating a significant portion of the total token supply toward player rewards, staking, and community governance, encouraging participation and investment in the game's ecosystem. Axie Infinity, for example, allocates 20% to Play to Earn and nearly 50% to users, promoting community engagement and ownership.

The **utility** of tokens within the game and beyond also plays a pivotal role. Broadening the use cases for a game's tokens—beyond just in-game transactions to include staking for additional rewards, participation in governance, and trading on external markets—enhances their value and appeal. Extending token utility outside the game, for example, through partnerships with other projects or platforms, can further increase the token's attractiveness and utility.

Locking periods are another mechanism employed to prevent speculation and stabilize the token economy. By establishing periods during which tokens cannot be sold, games can dampen price volatility and speculative trading, ensuring a more stable economic environment that favors long-term players and investors over short-term speculators. This approach aligns the interests of the game's developers and its community by incentivizing sustained engagement and investment.

GameFi projects like *Legends of Mitra* and *Sipher* illustrate the diversity of tokenomics models in play, from single-token economies, which simplify transactions but may present challenges in balancing utility with value retention, to multitoken systems, which separate platform governance from in-game currencies, potentially offering greater stability and flexibility in economic design.[12]

DeFi applications like staking, yield farming, and token swapping are increasingly integrated into GameFi projects, providing additional avenues for token utility and player earnings. For example, *League of Ancients* and *Bad Days* allocate portions of their tokens to yield farming and staking pools, enriching the economic interaction within the game.

By adopting these strategies, GameFi projects strive to create balanced, engaging, and sustainable economies that support a diverse ecosystem of players, developers, and investors, ultimately contributing to the longevity and success of the platform.

In the GameFi sector, the balance between engaging gameplay and economic incentives is pivotal for fostering long-term player engagement. A well-designed game should not only captivate players with its mechanics and storyline but also integrate a solid economic system that rewards active and engaged players without solely prioritizing return on investment. This balance is essential in preventing the game from becoming overly monetized to the point where gameplay feels secondary to financial gains, which can detract from the overall gaming experience.

---

[11] https://www.cryptoglobe.com/latest/2022/03/complete-guide-to-crypto-gaming-tokens/
[12] https://coincentral.com/gamefi-guide/

Creating exclusivity through in-game assets and achievements is one approach to maintaining game interest and value over time. For instance, games like CSGO with their highly sought-after Counter-Strike skins and MIR4's manual achievements showcase how limited availability and player-driven achievements can enhance player retention by making certain items or accomplishments challenging to obtain. This not only maintains the game's excitement but also curbs power creep, ensuring that new and existing players remain engaged and that the game's economy stays balanced.

Effective tokenomics and NFT design also play a crucial role in GameFi, where the balance of power among NFTs and players must be carefully managed. In both player-versus-player (PVP) and player-versus-environment (PVE) settings, the power attributed to NFTs should be significant yet balanced to prevent a pay-to-win dynamic. Strategies to maintain this equilibrium include providing high-quality content for heavy investors (whales) while allowing new or less invested players opportunities to progress and potentially challenge these whales. Such a balanced approach encourages a diverse player base and fosters a thriving game community.

Moreover, periodically changing a game's meta can keep the gameplay fresh and appealing to various player types. This involves adjusting game mechanics to promote different play styles or introducing new content that encourages players to adapt their strategies. However, it's crucial to manage these changes carefully to prevent alienating existing players. Drawing inspiration from games like *Honor of Kings* and *Clash Royale*, developers can attract and retain players by ensuring the gameplay remains dynamic and inclusive, catering to diverse preferences and play styles.[13]

Ultimately, the success of a GameFi project hinges on its ability to merge captivating gameplay with a balanced and sustainable economic model. By focusing on the player experience and ensuring the intrinsic value of participation beyond financial rewards, GameFi developers can create engaging and lasting gaming ecosystems.

In the GameFi sector, achieving a balance between engaging gameplay and economic incentives is crucial for crafting games that captivate players in the long term. This balance ensures that while players are drawn to the game for its potential earnings, they stay for the gameplay, narrative, and community. Two mechanisms widely used to mitigate inflation in GameFi and ensure economic sustainability are the multitoken economy and the implementation of fixed versus oracle (variable) pricing systems.

Multitoken Economy: The multitoken approach allows GameFi projects to segregate different economic activities and values within the game. For instance, one token can be designated for governance, allowing players to vote on game developments, while another token serves as the in-game currency for transactions and rewards. This structure supports diverse in-game interactions such as token conversions or mixing tokens for character progress or crafting, ultimately contributing to a sustainable tokenomics model. The key to success with either multitoken or single-token economies lies in the thoughtful distribution of tokens and their utility within the game ecosystem.

---

[13] https://www.coingecko.com/learn/effective-tokenomics-player-retention-blockchain-gaming

Fixed vs. Oracle (Variable) Pricing System: The use of blockchain oracles in GameFi can adjust in-game transaction costs in line with the fiat price of the token, maintaining low and fixed-entry costs. However, this model introduces volatility in reward payouts, as the value of in-game tokens paid out is also pegged to fiat currency, potentially affecting gameplay during market fluctuations. Conversely, a fixed pricing system simplifies reward estimations but could deter new players if token prices surge. Notably, several high-profile GameFi projects that relied on oracle pricing have faced challenges, highlighting the importance of choosing a pricing system that aligns with the game's long-term vision and market stability.

Examples of tokenomics in action within the GameFi space include **Axie Infinity**, **The Sandbox**, **Blast Royale**, and **Plutonians**, each adopting unique approaches to token utility, distribution, and economic models to foster engaging and sustainable gaming environments. Axie Infinity, for example, utilizes its AXS token for staking rewards, NFT purchases, and governance, demonstrating a comprehensive integration of the token within the gaming experience. Similarly, The Sandbox leverages its SAND token for asset purchases, governance, and staking, closely mirroring the utility found in AXIE.

Blast Royale introduces an innovative twist by planning a dual-token economy, with Blast token ($BLST) serving multiple purposes within the game, from governance votes to crafting and exclusive access to NFT airdrops. This multifaceted utility is designed to deepen player engagement and ensure a balanced economic model.

Plutonians and Silks offer additional perspectives on token utility and economic design, from Plutonians' intricate use of tokens for space travel and game expansion to Silks' real-world mirroring approach where digital representations of thoroughbred racehorses compete, showcasing the diversity and creativity within GameFi tokenomics.[14]

These examples illustrate the evolving landscape of GameFi, where innovative tokenomics models are continually being developed to ensure both the economic sustainability of the game and an engaging, rewarding experience for players.

6. Community and Governance

DAOs have significantly transformed the GameFi ecosystem by empowering players with governance rights and democratizing decision-making processes. This innovative approach allows community members to directly influence game development, asset management, and even the economic models within games. DAOs operate based on collective decision-making facilitated by blockchain technology, ensuring transparency, inclusivity, and a level of engagement previously unseen in traditional gaming models.

In the world of blockchain gaming, DAOs serve multiple pivotal roles.

---

[14] For a discussion of these topics, see https://www.cryptowisser.com/gamefi-tokenomics-basics/; https://www.bnbchain.org/en/blog/sustainable-gamefi-to-play-or-to-earn; and https://www.coinfantasy.io/blog/best-tokenomics-for-crypto/.

- **Game Development:** By leveraging DAO structures, GameFi projects can incorporate player feedback and suggestions directly into the game development process. This crowdsourced approach to game design can lead to more innovative and player-centric outcomes. For instance, DAO members can propose and vote on various aspects of game design, such as characters, storylines, mechanics, and artwork, fostering a collaborative development environment.
- **Platform and In-Game Governance:** DAOs are instrumental in governing both the gaming platforms themselves and specific in-game elements. Players and token holders can participate in crucial decision-making processes regarding platform upgrades, policy changes, and in-game economic policies. This level of involvement ensures that the game evolves in a direction that reflects the community's preferences and values.
- **Economic Incentives and Asset Ownership:** Blockchain gaming often features tokenized in-game assets and currencies that players can truly own, trade, and monetize. DAOs facilitate the collective management of these assets, allowing players to have a say in distribution, monetization strategies, and even dispute resolution. The transparent and decentralized nature of DAOs ensures fair and unbiased processes, enhancing trust within the gaming community.

Real-world examples of DAOs in action within the GameFi space include Alien Worlds and Yield Guild Games (YGG). Alien Worlds, for example, operates with multiple DAOs representing different planets within its game universe, allowing players to govern aspects of their respective planets collectively. On the other hand, YGG operates as a decentralized guild, pooling resources and assets to create value across various play-to-earn games, demonstrating the versatility and potential of DAOs in enriching the GameFi experience.

In conclusion, DAOs are reshaping the governance and development of GameFi projects, providing a framework for more democratic, transparent, and player-driven gaming ecosystems. As the gaming industry continues to evolve, DAOs stand to play a crucial role in fostering innovation, community engagement, and the democratization of game development and governance.

7. Concluding Remarks

GameFi, where gaming meets finance, has rapidly gained traction by introducing DeFi elements into digital gaming platforms. This chapter delved into the multidimensional nature of GameFi, exploring its historical context, core mechanics, and economic implications, while also highlighting future directions and open questions in this burgeoning sector.

There are a few things to highlight as the key takeaways.

First, I'd consider the play-to-earn model as a real revolution in this space and a notable application of blockchain. The P2E model allows players to earn real-world value through gaming activities, challenging traditional gaming's unidirectional economic flow.

On the technical side, the role of NFTs in GameFi representing unique in-game assets and providing verifiable ownership and the ability to trade or sell in open market-places shows that the power of NFTs is about ownership, not pretty pictures. This is what allows players to engage in a more immersive and financially rewarding gaming experience. Relatedly, the integration with several DeFi elements shows the power of interoperability of blockchain. Specifically, GameFi incorporates DeFi mechanisms such as staking, yield farming, and liquidity pools, transforming games into comprehensive ecosystems where players can engage in financial strategies, participate in governance, and benefit from the game's growth. The possibility to create such a comprehensive eco-system also highlights the power of having a token that can be represented on a chain, something that would not be possible to achieve with fiat money.

However, one aspect that should also be kept present is that the development of GameFi has escalated the scalability challenges of existing blockchain networks, with layer 2 solutions and off-chain scaling trying to address network congestion and high transaction costs.

Several open questions remain. For instance, a critical issue for GameFi is how to balance engaging gameplay with non-ponzi financial incentives to ensure players remain motivated by the game's narrative and community rather than just financial gains. Also, the long-term sustainability of GameFi depends on addressing issues like market volatil-ity and economic stability. The governance of these ecosystems is still an open question. DAOs are becoming central to GameFi, allowing players to influence game development and governance. How effectively these structures can maintain engagement and decen-tralized decision-making is a significant question. Finally, it remains to be seen whether the quality of the games on the blockchain, in terms of graphics and user engagement, can reach the level of traditional games.

Coding Example

Let's now walk through an example of how you can create a simulation-based game that rewards players with tokens when they succeed. Our hypothetical game is called *Monster Hunt*. Players will hunt monsters, and if they succeed, they will receive Monster Tokens. For the sake of the example, the player successfully hunts the monster based on a random number generator with a 50% chance of success. The following is the full code:

```solidity
// SPDX-License-Identifier: MIT
pragma solidity ^0.8.0;

contract MonsterHunt {

  // Define the in-game currency (simple ERC20 implementation)
  mapping(address => uint256) public monsterTokenBalance;

  // Store player information (replace with a mapping if needed for
  scalability)
```

```
address payable public player1 = payable(msg.sender); // Replace with
desired player address
address payable public player2 = payable(tx.origin); // Replace with
desired player address

// Event to signal a successful monster hunt
event MonsterHunted(address hunter, uint256 reward);

// Function to mint monster tokens (for testing purposes)
function mintMonsterTokens(address recipient, uint256 amount) public {
  monsterTokenBalance[recipient] += amount;
}

// Function to simulate a monster hunt
function huntMonster(address payable hunter) public {
  require(hunter == player1 || hunter == player2, "Only registered
  players can hunt");
  // Simulate random monster hunt outcome (modify for actual
  game logic)
  uint256 randomNumber = uint256(keccak256(abi.encodePacked(blockhash
  (block.number - 1), msg.sender)));
  uint256 reward = randomNumber % 100 > 50 ? 10 : 0; // 50% chance of
  getting a reward (10 tokens)

  if (reward > 0) {
    // Increase monster tokens for the hunter
    monsterTokenBalance[hunter] += reward;
    emit MonsterHunted(hunter, reward);
  }
 }
}
```

We first define the contract named **MonsterHunt**. For the in-game MonsterToken currency, we define a simple **monsterTokenBalance** mapping to track player balances within the contract itself, rather than relying on an external ERC-20 token. Each player's address acts as a key, and the corresponding value represents their MonsterToken balance. We next define the two players that will be involved in our hypothetical game: **player1** and **player2**. These variables are declared as address payable to allow sending ETH rewards to the players' accounts. It is **important** to replace these addresses with the actual addresses of your test accounts, either from Ganache or from another development environment, prior to deployment.

The **MonsterHunted** event is emitted when a player successfully hunts a monster so that users tracking the contract can see which player succeeded and what the resulting reward was.

The **mintMonsterTokens** function is used simply for testing purposes and allows you to mint an arbitrary number of MonsterTokens. The function takes a **recipient** address and the **amount** of Monster Tokens as arguments and subsequently increases the **recipient**'s balance by the specified amount. It's important to note that this function would not be used in a real game; it's for providing initial tokens to players during testing.

The **huntMonster** function is where our monster hunt simulation takes place. The function takes the address of the **hunter**, or the player participating, and must be one of the registered players (**player1** or **player2**). It simulates a random monster hunt outcome by using keccak256 and blockhash to generate a random number. With a 50% chance of success, the contract assigns a reward of 10 MonsterTokens to the hunter. In this case, it would increase the hunter's **monsterTokenBalance** and emit a **MonsterHunted** event. However, in a real game, the actual game logic should be coded in here so that the hunter can realistically attempt to hunt the monster and reap the benefits of their gameplay.

To test the contract, you will need to complete a few steps. First, set up a local blockchain environment such as through Ganache or a similar tool to run a local Ethereum node.[15] Next, you'll need to compile the contract using a Solidity compiler such as on the Remix IDE (https://remix.ethereum.org/). Now you can deploy your compiled contract to the local testing blockchain that you set up. Finally, interact with the contract's functions—use the **mintMonsterTokens** function to provide initial tokens to your players and use the **huntMonster** function with the player addresses to simulate hunting. You can always view the state of the hunt by reviewing the token balances of your players in the **monsterTokenBalance** mapping.

The example, although simple, conveys the mechanics of how one could develop a gaming dApp that allows users to earn rewards in the form of the platform's native tokens (in our case, MonsterTokens). Once you complete the testing steps, you can simulate a monster hunt and see if you succeed. Happy hunting!

---

[15] Note that Ganache and Truffle are no longer being maintained: https://www.binance.com/en/square/post/2023-09-22-consensys-to-phase-out-truffle-and-ganache-focus-on-metamask-tools-1188501.

End-of-Chapter Questions

Multiple-Choice Questions

1. **Which game is recognized as the first widely recognized application of NFTs within a gaming context?**
   (A) Axie Infinity
   (B) The Sandbox
   (C) *Fortnite*
   (D) CryptoKitties

2. **What key advantage does Solana offer over Ethereum for GameFi applications?**
   (A) Higher transaction fees
   (B) Slower transaction speeds
   (C) Lower transaction fees and faster speeds
   (D) More centralized validation process

3. **What does a multitoken economy in GameFi help prevent?**
   (A) Player engagement
   (B) Inflation
   (C) Fun gameplay
   (D) Financial inclusion

4. **What is the primary purpose of DAOs in GameFi?**
   (A) Decrease transparency
   (B) Centralize decision-making
   (C) Govern game development and platform governance
   (D) Limit community engagement

5. **Which of the following is not a method used by GameFi projects to address scalability?**
   (A) Layer-2 protocols
   (B) Centralized databases
   (C) Off-chain scaling solutions
   (D) Consensus mechanism alterations

6. **How does The Sandbox use SAND token within its ecosystem?**
   (A) Only for buying virtual land
   (B) Only for governance
   (C) For transactions, governance, and staking
   (D) None of the above

7. **Which is a key difference between GameFi and traditional online games like *Fortnite*?**
   (A) Traditional games offer financial incentives
   (B) GameFi games do not use blockchain technology
   (C) GameFi allows players to earn real-world value
   (D) Traditional games utilize NFTs

8. **What is the primary challenge of blockchain technology in gaming as highlighted by the chapter?**
   (A) High speed of transactions
   (B) Scalability and transaction costs
   (C) Lack of security measures
   (D) Too much decentralization

9. **Which GameFi project is noted for its use of a voxel-based game world?**
   (A) CryptoKitties
   (B) Axie Infinity
   (C) The Sandbox
   (D) *Fortnite*

10. **Which approach is NOT used by GameFi projects to create sustainable economies?**
    (A) Issuance and burning mechanisms
    (B) Fixed pricing systems
    (C) Locking periods for tokens
    (D) Unlimited token supply

Open Questions

1. How does the emergence of GameFi challenge the business models of traditional gaming industries, and what implications does this have for future game development and player engagement?

2. Discuss the mechanisms GameFi projects can employ to ensure the long-term economic sustainability of their ecosystems. What challenges do these mechanisms face, and how can they be overcome?

3. Analyze how GameFi contributes to the concept of digital ownership and the interoperability of assets across different gaming platforms and ecosystems. What benefits and challenges does this present to players and developers?

Coding Exercises

Exercise 1: Crafting Your First GameFi NFT

Objective: Create a simple NFT representing a digital asset in a game. This NFT should have unique attributes and be tradable.

1. **Setup:** Use OpenZeppelin's ERC-721 implementation for NFT creation.
2. **Task:** Define an NFT for a game character with attributes such as **name**, **level**, and **strength**. Ensure each NFT minted has a unique identifier and can store these attributes.
3. **Challenge:** Implement a function that allows the NFT owner to **level up** their character by increasing its level and strength, simulating character growth within the game.

Exercise 2: Implementing a Simple Play-to-Earn Mechanism

Objective: Create a smart contract that rewards players with tokens for achieving certain milestones within your game.

1. **Setup:** Utilize an ERC-20 token as the in-game currency.
2. **Task:** Develop a smart contract function **recordAchievement** that updates player achievements and rewards them with tokens based on the milestone reached.
3. **Challenge:** Include a mechanism to prevent abuse (e.g. cooldown periods for earning rewards from the same achievement or validating achievements through multiple validator signatures).

Exercise 3: Integrating DeFi Elements into Your GameFi Project

Objective: Enhance your GameFi project with DeFi functionalities by creating a liquidity pool for your game's currency and enabling staking.

1. **Setup:** Assume you have an ERC-20 token being used as your game's currency.
2. **Task:** Design a smart contract that acts as a liquidity pool for your game's currency against ETH. Players should be able to add liquidity to the pool and receive liquidity provider (LP) tokens in return.
3. **Challenge:** Implement a staking mechanism where players can stake your game's LP tokens to earn rewards over time. This involves calculating reward amounts based on the duration and amount of LP tokens staked.

General Guidelines for Exercises:

- Start with the OpenZeppelin library for secure, standardized implementations of ERC-20 and ERC-721 tokens.
- Ensure functions modifying state variables are properly secured, using modifiers to restrict access where necessary.
- Test your contracts thoroughly on a development network like Ganache or use Remix for a more interactive approach before deploying to a public testnet.
- Consider the user experience in your game design, ensuring that interactions with smart contracts are intuitive and add value to the gameplay.

Chapter 14

Branding on the Block
How Blockchain Is Redefining Connections in the Web3 Era

Preface

Welcome to the enthralling world of Web3,[1] where blockchain is not just a tech buzzword but the new frontier for branding, luxury, and digital engagement. If you've ever wondered what happens when traditional luxury brands crash into the futuristic techno-sphere of blockchain, you're in for a treat.

Imagine a world where your favorite high-fashion brand not only offers you clothes but also throws in a digital identity, a sprinkle of cryptocurrency, and exclusive access to virtual worlds—all wrapped up in a smart contract. This isn't your grandma's shopping spree; this is shopping on steroids in the metaverse, with a blockchain receipt.

Now, as for the new generations, they're swapping baseball cards (or soccer cards in my case) for non-fungible tokens (NFTs), and you can bet it's not just for the love of the game. Forget about dusty cards stashed in shoeboxes; today's youth are trading digital art like high-rollers in an art gallery. The stakes are high, the games are digital, and the players are as likely to be wearing virtual reality (VR) headsets as they are to be sporting the

---

[1] The term "Web3" was coined by Ethereum co-founder Gavin Wood in 2014. It represents his vision for a more decentralized and user-centric internet, leveraging blockchain technology to build a more equitable online ecosystem.

latest streetwear. It's a brave new world where your digital wallet's weight determines your clout, not the brand of your shoes.

In this chapter, we delve into how storied brands like Gucci are turning the digital world into their runway. They're not just dipping their toes into Web3; they're diving headfirst. From NFTs that are more than just JPEGs (think digital art meets haute couture) to decentralized autonomous organizations (DAOs) where your vote actually decides the next big fashion trend, the fusion of tech and luxury is redefining what it means to be chic.

But it's not all catwalks in cyberspace. In this dazzling era of digital collectibles, traditional luxury brands face a conundrum. How do they maintain an aura of exclusivity when their latest must-have isn't a limited-run scarf but a piece of digital art that can be endlessly replicated? The answer lies in the magic of the blockchain—creating digital scarcity in a world of abundance. Just as Hermes might limit a bag to a few hundred pieces, their digital counterparts limit the NFTs, ensuring that even in the virtual world, not all that glitters is available. So, as we navigate this new digital frontier, remember, exclusivity isn't going anywhere; it's just getting a blockchain makeover. Whether it's a digital Hermes Birkin or a Gucci NFT, the game of luxury exclusivity continues—it's just now there's a new way to keep score.

Web3 Fashion Week: Where catwalk meets cryptowalk and pixels are the new couture

So, buckle up, dear reader. You're about to explore how luxury brands are knitting their heritage with bytes and blockchain to stitch together the future of fashion. By the end of this chapter, you'll either be ready to buy your next designer dress with Bitcoin or seriously contemplate how a digital twin might upstage your real-life wardrobe. Let's decode the enigma of luxury in the age of Web3.

1. Introduction

Blockchain technology has recently emerged not just as a financial tool but as a revolutionary framework for brands aiming to redefine their interaction with consumers. Web3, the next generation of the internet, leverages blockchain technology and decentralization to create a more user-centric and equitable digital ecosystem. It takes the principles of blockchain and cryptocurrencies and applies them to a wider array of traditional domains, involving product companies in this transformation. These companies are now using Web3 technologies (the ones we talked about in the previous chapters) to innovate and enhance their offerings in significant ways. For instance, in supply chain management, companies like IBM are implementing blockchain to enable transparent, real-time tracking of goods, ensuring authenticity and reducing fraud. In the entertainment sector, firms such as Spotify are exploring decentralized streaming platforms that give artists greater control over their royalties and content distribution. In the realm of digital identity, companies like Microsoft are developing decentralized identity solutions that empower users to own and control their personal data. By adopting Web3 technologies, these companies are enhancing the efficiency, security, and transparency of their operations, pioneering new business models, and driving the evolution of traditional industries towards more decentralized and user-focused systems.

This chapter delves into the multifaceted ways blockchain can empower brands, from ensuring product authenticity and enhancing customer loyalty to streamlining operations and fostering transparent communities.

If you have ever been interested in marketing and how the field is evolving, this is the chapter for you!

The key point is that this new wave of the internet, characterized by decentralized networks and powered by blockchain technology, is not just a technical marvel; it is a transformative business opportunity. As we delve into the realm of Web3, it becomes evident that its influence extends far beyond tech-savvy circles, touching the core strategies of some of the world's most renowned brands.

A telling sign of Web3's growing importance in the corporate sector is the surge in patent filings related to blockchain technology and not just about NFTs.[2] This trend underscores a significant shift in corporate strategy, with brands across various industries recognizing the potential of Web3 to revolutionize business models, customer engagement,

---

[2] For more about the patent filings, see the work by Marc Baumann available at https://www.dematerialzd .xyz/p/exclusive-key-insights-from-3200.

and value creation. The increasing investment in these technologies is not just a pursuit of innovation but a strategic move to stay ahead in a rapidly changing digital landscape. By securing patents in Web3-related technologies, brands are not only protecting their innovations but also laying the groundwork for future developments in this dynamic and potentially lucrative field.

Web3 technologies offer brands unprecedented opportunities to foster deeper connections and engagements with their communities. Blockchain's inherent transparency and security features allow brands to create trusted, decentralized platforms where consumers can interact directly with the creators and each other, potentially bypassing traditional intermediaries. This direct interaction not only enhances consumer trust but also allows brands to build vibrant communities around their products and services.

In the Web3 space, communities are not just passive recipients of brand messages but active participants in the brand narrative. They engage in shaping product development, marketing, and even in governance through mechanisms like DAOs, where community members have a say in brand decisions.

As this chapter unfolds, we will explore several case studies of global brands that have successfully integrated Web3 technologies into their business strategies. These examples will not only illustrate the practical applications of blockchain but also highlight the challenges and considerations that come with adopting this technology. We will delve into how brands are navigating the complex regulatory, technical, and social landscapes of Web3 to unlock new value for their businesses and their communities.

The use cases are quite broad and different brands have focused on different areas. Just to give you an idea, Web3 introduces true digital ownership through NFTs, allowing consumers to own, trade, or sell digital items like art, music, and virtual goods. This not only opens up new revenue streams for brands but also deepens customer engagement by offering unique digital products and experiences. In addition, blockchain facilitates decentralized marketplaces that eliminate intermediaries, reduce costs, and increase efficiency, enabling brands, particularly smaller ones, to directly access global markets. The technology's immutable nature also provides undeniable proof of authenticity and provenance, crucial for luxury brands to verify their products' authenticity and combat counterfeiting.

Moreover, blockchain enhances data security and privacy, allowing consumers to control their data and decide who gets access, thus building trust, especially in sectors like finance and healthcare. Additionally, smart contracts on the blockchain automate transactions and agreements without intermediaries, and programmable money can trigger automatic payments based on predefined conditions, ideal for loyalty rewards programs that issue tokens based on consumer purchases.

Furthermore, through DAOs, Web3 allows token holders to participate in governance decisions, increasing customer loyalty and engagement by letting them influence product development or community funding. Lastly, tokenization involves creating digital tokens that represent real-world assets on the blockchain, offering brands a new mechanism for simplifying capital raising by accessing global funding directly.

These capabilities enable brands to not only innovate and differentiate themselves in the marketplace but also build deeper, more trusting relationships with consumers. By harnessing Web3 technologies, brands can significantly enhance their offerings and interactions, reshaping how they connect with the digital world.

2. Strategic Web3 Applications for Brand Growth and Engagement

In this section, we will analyze the strategic applications of Web3 technologies through six distinct categories, captured in **Figure 1**, each offering unique concepts and benefits. Web3 is characterized by its decentralized architecture, blockchain backbone, and user ownership of data. This architecture empowers consumers to control their personal information securely and transparently while enabling companies to interact directly with their audiences through trust-based digital economies. The use of blockchain provides immutable verification and tamper-proof records, which are crucial for safeguarding product authenticity, provenance, and digital asset ownership. Furthermore, the

Category	Strategic Concepts	Examples	Value Proposition
A Identity and Data Management	• Digital Identities and Consumer Interaction • Decentralized Data Management	• IBM's Digital Health Pass • Civic • uPort	• Enhanced consumer trust and data privacy • Compliance with GDPR and CCPA • Personalized marketing aligned with consumer preferences
B Exclusive Content and Token-Gated Access	• NFTs for Exclusive Collectibles • Token-Gated Content and Memberships	• Nike's RTFKT • IWC Schaffhausen's Diamond Hand Club • Ticketmaster NFT Ticketing	• Drive fan loyalty through exclusivity • New revenue streams via digital collectibles • Deeper brand interaction
C Community Engagement	• NFT-Based Community Engagement	• Adidas "Into the Metaverse" • Lacoste's UNDW3 Project • NBA TopShot	• Strengthen customer relationships and brand loyalty • Data-driven insights on customer behavior and engagement
D Product Development and Co-Creation	• Digital Twins Linking Physical Goods • Co-create Digital Goods that are "Owned" by Users	• Dior B33 Sneakers • Nike's .SWOOSH Studio	• Extend product lifecycle via continuous updates • Elevate customer loyalty through personalization • Foster creativity and differentiation
E Verification and Authenticity	• Blockchain-Based Product Provenance	• Vacheron Constantin Blockchain Certificates • Dior's NFC-enabled Sneakers • Prada	• Safeguard brand reputation with verifiable authenticity • Combat counterfeiting • Create long-term value for high-value products
F Digital Revenue Streams and Intellectual Property Monetization	• Monetize Intellectual Property via NFTs • Web3-Driven Loyalty Programs	• Porsche Digital Cars • Gucci • Starbucks Odyssey Program • Shake-Shack and Venmo Cashback	• Tap new revenue streams through virtual goods • Extend brand presence in virtual worlds • Transform loyalty programs into immersive experiences

Figure 1 Strategic Web3 applications

development of NFTs introduces a new paradigm for digital ownership, enabling the creation of exclusive content, token-gated experiences, and community ecosystems that boost loyalty and foster deeper brand interaction.

Identity and data management enable brands to ensure compliance and foster consumer trust by implementing self-sovereign digital identities and decentralized data control. This allows consumers to own and manage their data directly, granting brands access to accurate information while adhering to privacy regulations like GDPR. Web3 applications in this realm include blockchain-based identity verification systems, offering greater transparency and secure, tamper-proof data storage.

Exclusive content and token-gated access create deeper fan loyalty and innovative revenue streams through NFTs and membership-based communities. Brands can offer exclusive digital collectibles, virtual goods, or gated experiences that are accessible only to holders of specific tokens. This strategy generates value by enhancing the sense of exclusivity and belonging among dedicated customers.

Community building and engagement leverage tokenized ecosystems to strengthen customer relationships and gain actionable insights into consumer preferences. By using NFTs and token-based rewards, brands can cultivate engaged communities that participate directly in brand-related activities, providing valuable feedback and increasing brand loyalty.

Product development and co-creation extend product lifecycles and boost personalization via digital twins and user-generated goods. Digital twins, linked to physical goods through NFTs, provide continuous updates, special access, and seasonal releases that keep customers engaged over time. Co-creation platforms empower customers to design or customize their own digital products, aligning brands more closely with consumer preferences.

Verification and authenticity safeguard brand reputation by leveraging blockchain for verifiable provenance and tamper-proof certificates. By recording the entire product journey, blockchain ensures that high-value products can be authenticated, preventing counterfeiting and enhancing resale value.

Finally, digital revenue streams and intellectual property monetization open new opportunities through NFTs and Web3 loyalty programs. Brands can extend their presence into virtual worlds and generate new revenue from digital assets like virtual fashion or artwork, all while transforming loyalty programs into immersive experiences that strengthen consumer relationships.

Together, these strategies equip brands to harness Web3's full potential for innovative growth and differentiation. Let's explore each of these strategies in more detail.

A. Identity and Data Management

1. Digital Identities and Consumer Interaction

Web3 enables the creation and use of digital identities, which consumers can use to interact securely and privately across various platforms. These identities are controlled by the consumers themselves, not by corporations, which shifts the dynamics of consumer data usage. Brands that respect and incorporate these self-sovereign identities into their ecosystems can build deeper trust and loyalty. For example, a digital identity could allow users to seamlessly verify their age or membership status without revealing any additional personal information, simplifying access to age-restricted products or loyalty rewards.

These identities are decentralized and controlled by the individual, rather than any central authority. This method leverages cryptographic techniques, ensuring that the individual's identity and transactions are secure and private.

For brands, digital identities can enhance customer interactions and operational efficiency in several ways.

- **Age Verification:** A brand selling age-restricted products (like alcohol or certain media content) may need to verify the age of online purchasers. Customers can use their verifiable credentials to prove they are of legal age without revealing their exact birthdate or other personal details. This simplifies the purchase process, enhances privacy, and reduces liability for brands.
- **Membership and Loyalty Programs:** Brands often offer exclusive content or discounts to members or loyal customers, requiring verification of membership status or purchase history. Customers can use digital identities to authenticate their membership status securely and privately whenever they interact online or in physical stores. This process can be automated and integrated into digital wallets or brand apps, enhancing user experience and engagement.
- **Personalized Marketing:** Effective marketing increasingly relies on personalization, which traditionally has required collecting extensive customer data, raising privacy concerns. Digital identities allow customers to control what information they share with brands. Brands can then use this selectively shared data to tailor marketing strategies without compromising consumer privacy, aligning with GDPR and other privacy regulations.

Examples   There are several companies that utilize Web3 in their identity verification processes. IBM's Digital Health Pass leverages blockchain technology to manage verifiable health credentials, which not only cater to the immediate needs of health data management but can also be extended to customer verification for businesses that require health data for access to services. Similarly, uPort offers an open identity system built on Ethereum, enabling users to register and control their own identities, manage credentials, and sign transactions, facilitating a secure and decentralized way to handle personal identity. Additionally, Civic utilizes blockchain to provide users with the means to create and manage their identity verification securely. Once established, this identity can be used to access a range of services, while offering robust privacy controls, thus enhancing user autonomy over personal data and how it is shared across platforms.

These implementations show how digital identities in Web3 can simplify transactions, enhance customer privacy, and provide a new level of interaction between brands and consumers. Brands that adopt this technology not only prepare for a future of enhanced digital interaction but also build trust and loyalty by respecting consumer privacy and data sovereignty.

2. Decentralized Data Management With Web3, brands can shift toward more decentralized data management systems, which provide consumers with greater control over their personal data. This transparency can alter consumer relations by positioning the brand as more consumer-friendly and privacy-conscious. For example, a brand could implement a decentralized system where consumer data from loyalty programs is stored on a blockchain, giving consumers visibility and control over who accesses their information and for what purpose. Decentralized data management would impact brands in several ways.

- **Enhanced Consumer Trust and Brand Reputation:** By using a decentralized approach, brands can significantly enhance consumers' trust, as they provide a platform where data privacy and control are prioritized. Brands that adopt decentralized data management are seen as pioneers in privacy and consumer rights, which can be a significant differentiator in markets increasingly concerned with data abuse.
- **Compliance and Transparency:** With increasing regulations like GDPR in Europe and CCPA in California, decentralized data management can help brands achieve compliance more efficiently by providing inherent data protection and audit capabilities. Brands can demonstrate to consumers and regulators that they are using data ethically, enhancing transparency and accountability.
- **Targeted Marketing and Personalization:** Decentralized systems can lead to more accurate and verifiable consumer data since consumers are incentivized to share accurate data directly in exchange for rewards or services. With reliable data, brands can tailor their marketing efforts more effectively, enhancing customer satisfaction and engagement.

Examples IBM has developed blockchain solutions that facilitate transparent consumer data management, allowing companies to give consumers control over who accesses their data and for what purpose. In practical applications such as supply chain management, this technology is instrumental in tracking and verifying product origins, ensuring authenticity and compliance with safety standards. Similarly, uPort (now Veramo) offers self-sovereign identity management solutions on the Ethereum blockchain, enabling users to create and manage their own identities and associated data. Brands collaborating with uPort can offer users a secure way to share their identity data, enhancing trust and streamlining identity verification processes. By adopting these decentralized data management systems, brands not only align with modern data protection regulations but also prioritize consumer privacy, a strategic approach that is essential for building long-term customer relationships and establishing the brand as a leader in responsible data practices.

B. Exclusive Content and Token-Gated Access

1. NFTs for Exclusive Content and Collectibles

NFTs offer a unique way for brands to engage with consumers by creating exclusive or limited edition digital content. These can range from digital collectibles and virtual goods to exclusive access passes for events or experiences. NFTs can also be used to gamify consumer interactions, offering rewards that have both real-world and digital world value.

Some specific applications and how they can benefit the specific brands can be summarized as follows:

- **Exclusive Content and Collectibles:** A fashion brand could release a limited series of digital wearables as NFTs that can be used in virtual worlds or augmented reality (AR) environments. These digital goods could be linked to physical items, enhancing their value. This not only creates an exclusive product line that can increase brand visibility and prestige but also taps into new revenue streams from digital natives and tech-savvy consumers.
- **Access to Events and Experiences:** A music label could issue NFTs that serve as access passes to virtual concerts or exclusive backstage content. These NFTs could also include special features, like a meet-and-greet with artists or limited edition digital merchandise. This approach enhances fan engagement and creates a more memorable and personalized experience that builds lasting loyalty.
- **Gamification and Loyalty Programs:** A brand could gamify its customer engagement by offering NFTs as rewards for certain consumer behaviors, such as making purchases or participating in community events. These NFTs could then be used to unlock special perks or experiences. Gamification can significantly increase customer interaction and time spent engaged with the brand, leading to higher sales and deeper loyalty.

Examples   Several large firms have used this technology. Nike's strategic acquisition of RTFKT capitalizes on the studio's expertise in creating digital footwear and apparel, which has been instrumental in designing NFTs tailored for the gaming and virtual reality communities. This initiative allows consumers to use and showcase Nike products within digital realms such as games or VR platforms, effectively extending Nike's brand presence into burgeoning virtual markets (**Figure 2**).

Meanwhile, Clinique has embraced the potential of NFTs through their MetaOptimist campaign, which not only celebrates customer stories but also provides NFT holders with exclusive access to special skincare products and events (**Figure 3**). This innovative approach has enabled Clinique to enhance brand engagement and connect with a younger, digitally savvy audience, illustrating the transformative impact of NFTs in traditional business sectors.

Figure 2   Nike Dunk Genesis NFT on RTFKT (RTFKT Inc./RTFKT.com/last accessed May 22, 2024)

By leveraging NFTs for customer engagement, brands can create novel, exciting interactions and deepen their relationships with consumers, all while exploring new business models and revenue opportunities in the evolving digital landscape.

2. Token-Gate Content, Products, or Experiences   Token-gating is an innovative Web3 strategy where access to certain content, products, or experiences is restricted and can be unlocked only through the ownership of a specific digital token, typically an NFT. This approach leverages blockchain technology to verify ownership automatically, ensuring that only token holders can access certain benefits. This method is particularly valuable for brands as it enhances customer loyalty and engagement by creating exclusivity and a sense of prestige around their offerings. It also facilitates deeper interactions with the

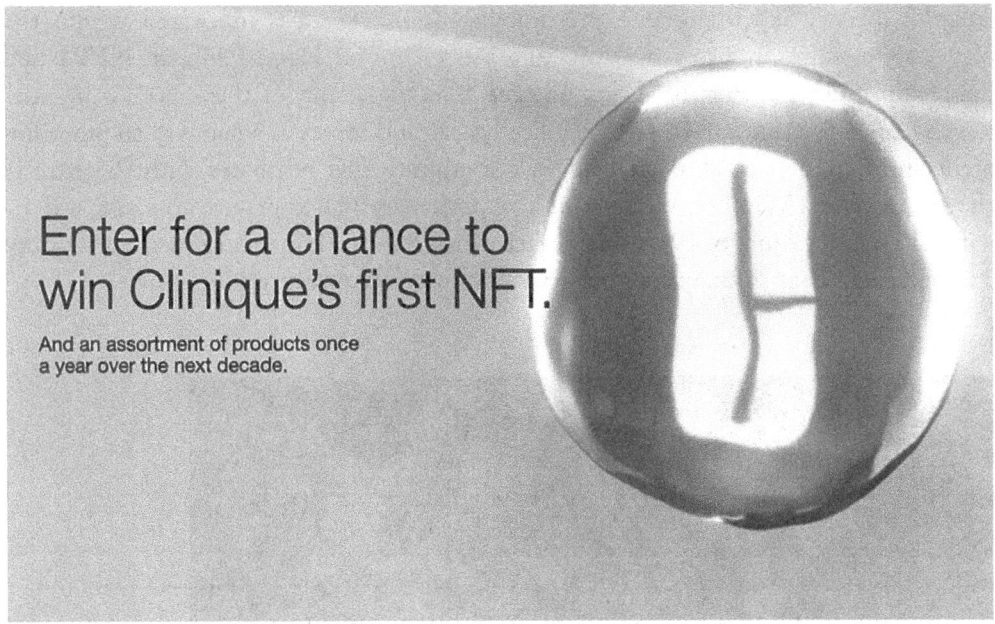

Figure 3   Clinique's NFT (Clinique Laboratories, llc./Clinique.com/last accessed May 22, 2024)

brand's ecosystem by incentivizing purchases and participation in community events or experiences.

By integrating token-gated access into their strategies, brands can leverage several compelling benefits that significantly enhance their market positioning and customer relations.

- **Enhanced Customer Loyalty:** Token-gating inherently creates an exclusive environment by offering access to specialized products and experiences. This exclusivity fosters a VIP feeling among customers, strengthening their emotional and psychological investment in the brand. Customers feel valued and unique, which deepens their loyalty and often translates into repeated engagement and advocacy for the brand.
- **Increased Brand Value:** The use of NFTs for token-gated access not only adds a layer of exclusivity but also imbues the brand with a sense of novelty and innovation. This modern approach can elevate a brand's prestige, making it more attractive not only to current customers but also to potential new customers who value cutting-edge digital experiences. This strategy effectively positions the brand as a leader in leveraging new technologies, enhancing its reputation in both the digital and physical marketplaces.
- **Innovative Marketing:** Token-gating is a powerful tool for crafting unique marketing campaigns that stand out in a crowded digital landscape. By requiring ownership of NFTs for access to certain content, brands can create more targeted and appealing marketing initiatives that resonate with tech-savvy demographics. This approach not only taps into new customer segments but also creates buzz around the brand as it aligns itself with the latest digital trends, from blockchain to immersive virtual experiences.

Examples   IWC Schaffhausen, a prestigious watchmaker, has innovated within the luxury watchmaking industry by launching the Diamond Hand Club, an NFT-based membership program (**Figure 4** and **Figure 5**). Ownership of these NFTs provides access to exclusive events, both virtual and physical, and serves as a gateway to premium content and experiences, thus fostering a community that resonates with the brand's heritage and values. Members enjoy unique experiences such as private concerts, watch-making classes, and tours of IWC's manufacturing facilities, enhancing customer loyalty and integrating clients into a more engaged and interactive community.

Figure 4   IWC Diamond Hand Club (IWC/nft.iwc.com/last accessed May 22, 2024)

Figure 5   IWC Diamond Hand Club (IWC/nft.iwc.com/last accessed May 22, 2024)

Similarly, Ticketmaster has adopted NFTs to revolutionize ticketing for events. These NFTs serve dual purposes: they are proof of purchase that helps combat ticket fraud and act as collectible items that may increase in value over time. This strategy enhances the event experience by providing attendees with unique digital memorabilia that commemorates their participation, adding an additional layer of value to the event experience.

In summary, token-gating not only secures content in a novel and engaging way but also enhances customer engagement through exclusivity and personalized experiences, paving the way for deeper brand loyalty and innovative marketing strategies. This approach is exemplified by brands like IWC Schaffhausen with their forward-thinking in the luxury watch industry and Ticketmaster's use of NFTs to enhance the event-going experience.

C. Community Engagement

NFTs can be used strategically to cultivate a dedicated community by offering exclusive access and unique interactions around a brand's products or experiences. This approach leverages the inherent capabilities of blockchain, such as secure, transparent transactions and tokenized ownership, to foster a sense of belonging and active participation among community members. For brands, this translates into an engaged audience that not only supports but also actively contributes to the brand ecosystem, enhancing both customer loyalty and brand value.

Engaging directly with consumers through tokenized experiences or products helps brands achieve a deeper connection with their audience, enhancing customer retention and increasing the lifetime value of each customer. This strategy allows brands to bypass traditional advertising, reaching consumers in a more personal and engaging way. Moreover, the data generated from blockchain transactions provides invaluable insights into consumer behavior, enabling brands to tailor their offerings more effectively.

Examples Adidas ventured into the Web3 space with its "Into the Metaverse" NFT drop, created in collaboration with Bored Ape Yacht Club and other notable entities in the NFT space (**Figure 6**). This initiative allowed NFT holders to access exclusive Adidas products and experiences, effectively bridging digital and physical offerings. The collaboration was not just about launching a product but creating an ecosystem where NFT ownership unlocks a new level of engagement with the brand. This move helped Adidas tap into a new market segment passionate about digital collectibles and the metaverse, thereby expanding its community and reinforcing its position as an innovator in the digital fashion space.

Similarly, Lacoste launched the UNDW3 project, which involved a series of NFTs that provided owners with access to exclusive physical and digital products (**Figure 7**). This initiative was aimed at creating a community around a shared lifestyle and aesthetic, highlighted by both digital innovation and exclusive fashion pieces. By owning an NFT, members could access special releases, events, and more, enhancing their engagement and loyalty to the Lacoste brand.

Figure 6   Adidas NFT Drop ((Adidas/adidas.co.uk/metaverse/last accessed May 22, 2024)

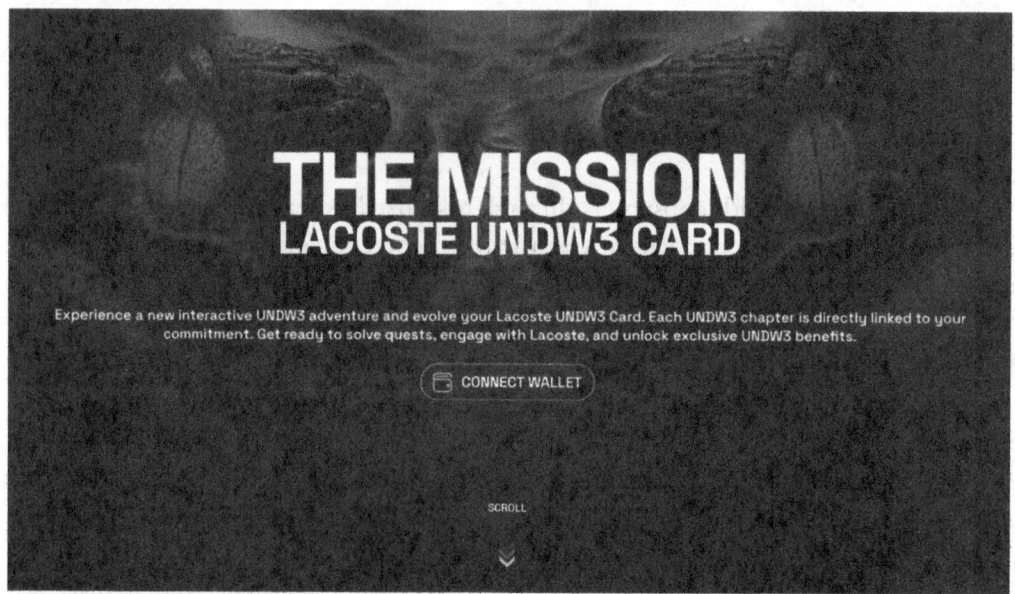

Figure 7   Lacoste UNDW3 (Lacoste/undw3.lacoste.com/last accessed May 22, 2024)

As discussed in Chapter 10, NBA Top Shot offers officially NBA Top Shot, a blockchain-based platform, offers officially licensed NBA collectible highlights as NFTs (**Figure 8**). For the NBA, this creates a new avenue to engage with fans, offering them a way to own a piece of their favorite moments in basketball history.

These examples illustrate how integrating Web3 technologies into a brand's strategy can significantly enhance community engagement. Adidas and Lacoste, by embracing NFTs and the broader capabilities of blockchain, have not only fostered stronger connections with their communities but also set themselves apart in competitive markets.

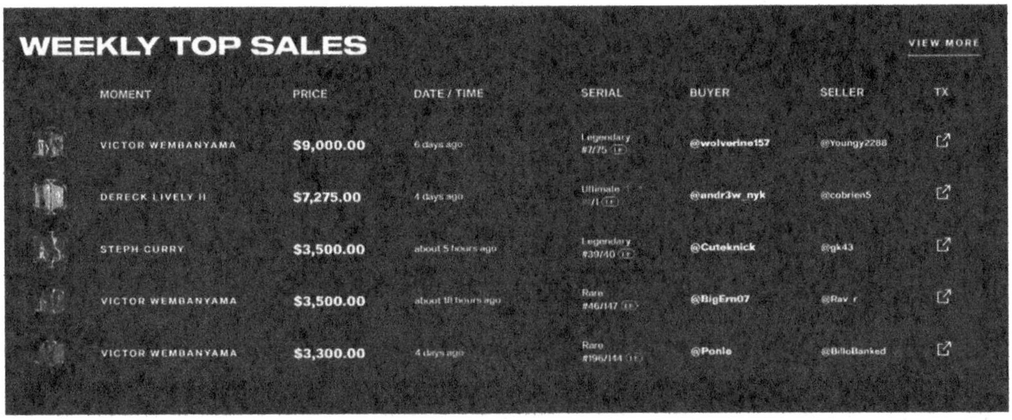

Figure 8 NBA TopShot (NBA Properties, Inc./nbatopshot.com/last accessed May 22, 2024)

They have effectively utilized NFTs as more than just digital assets; they have turned them into keys that unlock unique brand experiences and cultivate a sense of exclusivity and community belonging. This strategic move helps maintain customer interest and loyalty, which is crucial in the fast-paced world of fashion and lifestyle brands.

D. Product Development and Customization

1. Digital Twins Linking Physical Goods
The concept of linking physical goods with virtual counterparts involves creating digital versions or representations of physical products, often in the form of NFTs. These digital twins serve as both a proof of ownership and a bridge to additional digital content, enhancing the overall value of the physical purchase. For brands, this blending of physical and digital realms offers a unique way to engage with tech-savant consumers who appreciate the added value and exclusivity that digital enhancements can provide. This approach not only elevates the consumer's experience but also integrates cutting-edge technology into traditional retail models, making products more appealing and interactive.

Incorporating digital twins with physical products allows brands to do the following:

- **Extend Product Lifecycles:** Digital twins can dramatically extend the lifecycle of a product beyond the physical ownership or initial use phase. By linking a physical item to a digital counterpart, brands can continuously update the digital content, keeping the consumer engaged over a longer period. For example, a brand could release seasonal updates, new digital features, or exclusive virtual events linked to the physical product. This ongoing engagement helps maintain the product's relevance and keeps customers connected to the brand, potentially leading to repeat purchases or sustained usage.
- **Enhance Customer Engagement:** Digital twins often provide customers with unique digital content or interactive experiences that are not possible with purely physical items. This could include access to virtual reality experiences, augmented reality enhancements, or membership in exclusive online communities. For instance, a fashion brand might offer virtual fittings or style simulations via an app linked to the

purchase of a physical garment. These engaging digital experiences can significantly enhance customer satisfaction and loyalty, turning a single purchase into a gateway for ongoing brand interaction.

- **Increase Perceived Value:** The integration of digital twins with physical products also enhances the perceived value of the purchase. Consumers today are looking for more than just physical goods; they value unique experiences and digital enhancements that elevate the ownership experience. The exclusivity and novelty of having a digital version of a product can make it significantly more appealing, especially to younger, tech-savvy consumers who appreciate the fusion of digital and physical realms. This increased perceived value can justify higher price points and differentiate a product in a crowded market.

- **Drive Innovation:** Adopting digital twins encourages brands to continuously innovate, not just in product development but across their operations, including marketing, customer service, and consumer engagement strategies. This push for innovation helps brands stay ahead in a market that is increasingly shifting toward digital solutions. It fosters a culture of creativity and technological advancement within the company, encouraging the exploration of new tools and platforms that could open up additional revenue streams. For example, a brand could leverage blockchain technology not only to authenticate the ownership of a physical product but also to create a secure, transparent supply chain that adds further value to the customer's purchase experience.

Examples   Dior introduced the B33 Sneakers, which come with a digital twin in the form of an NFT. These sneakers are not just physical products but also include NFC chips that link to a digital certificate of authenticity. Owners can unlock exclusive digital content and early access to future product releases, enhancing the value of their purchase. This initiative positions Dior at the forefront of luxury fashion innovation, blending traditional craftsmanship with modern technology to create a unique consumer experience that spans both physical and virtual worlds.

In a similar vein, Adidas' collaboration with BAPE (A Bathing Ape) involves the release of limited-edition sneakers that are paired with digital assets (**Figure 9**). These digital assets might include exclusive online content or integration into digital environments like video games or virtual worlds. Such collaborations not only generate buzz but also create a community of users who are engaged both online and offline, further cementing the brand's presence in both realms.

The integration of physical products with digital twins is revolutionizing the retail and fashion industries. It offers consumers a new way to experience products, while also providing brands with a platform for continuous engagement. This dual approach not only satisfies the demand for innovative and exclusive content but also sets a new standard in the luxury and lifestyle sectors, encouraging other brands to explore the potential of such technologies. As seen with Dior and Adidas, this strategy effectively merges the tactile and digital, offering a comprehensive experience that enhances consumer satisfaction and loyalty.

Figure 9   Adidas x BAPE Collaboration ((Adidas/adidas.com/last accessed May 22, 2024)

2. Co-create Digital Goods That Are "Owned" by Users   Co-creating digital goods is a transformative approach where brands enable consumers to design or customize their products, typically through digital platforms. This model has gained momentum with the rise of Web3 technologies, allowing for deeper integration of consumer inputs into the product development process.

This interaction isn't just about choosing colors or patterns; it extends to significant aspects of the shoe design, making consumers feel like true creators. The benefits for brands adopting this model include the following:

- **Enhanced Customer Engagement:** By allowing consumers to participate in the creation process, brands can increase the time and emotional investment a consumer spends with their product. This engagement often translates into a stronger brand connection and higher satisfaction rates.
- **Increased Consumer Loyalty:** When consumers put personal effort into designing a product, their emotional stake in the brand and the end product increases. This personal investment can lead to higher loyalty and repeat purchases, as consumers develop a personal attachment to the brand.
- **Valuable Consumer Insights:** Consumer choices during the design process provide brands with direct feedback on consumer preferences without traditional market research. This data can inform future product designs and marketing strategies, making them more aligned with consumer desires.

- **Market Differentiation:** Offering a co-creation experience can distinguish a brand from its competitors. It positions the brand as innovative and customer-centric, appealing to modern consumers who value personalized experiences and products.

Examples   Nike's .SWOOSH Studio merges creativity with commerce. Participants can design shoes that are not only visually appealing but also technically sound, as they use the same design principles employed by Nike's own designers. These digital designs potentially have a path to becoming actual products, adding a thrilling possibility for users that their creations might be worn by millions.

Nike's use of the .SWOOSH Studio also taps into trends like the growing interest in NFTs and digital ownership, pushing the boundaries of how traditional fashion and footwear brands interact with the evolving digital landscape (**Figure 10**). This approach not only secures Nike's position as a leader in innovation but also as a brand deeply connected to its consumer base through technology and creativity.

In conclusion, co-creating digital goods presents a forward-thinking strategy that leverages digital platforms to enhance consumer interaction, offering a unique blend of creativity, personalization, and technology to foster deeper brand connections and market innovation.

E. Verification and Authenticity

Product provenance involves leveraging Web3 and blockchain technology to authenticate the legitimacy of high-value products, particularly in the luxury sector. This approach is particularly beneficial for brands because it addresses critical issues such as counterfeiting and unauthorized resales, which can significantly undermine brand reputation and customer trust.

Figure 10   Nike .SWOOSH Studio (NIKE, INC./swoosh.nike/last accessed May 22, 2024)

Verification and provenance via blockchain technology involve creating an immutable digital ledger for each product. This ledger records every transaction associated with the product—from its creation to each point of sale—ensuring a transparent trail of ownership and history. A way of doing this could be creating and issuing limited edition digital assets or NFTs that are directly linked to physical items. This approach is particularly advantageous for luxury brands and artists who seek to capitalize on the unique attributes of blockchain—immutability, transparency, and security—to authenticate the rarity and exclusivity of their products.

Verifiable rarity through blockchain technology allows brands to issue digital certificates or tokens that prove the authenticity and limited nature of a product.

This method improves brand strategy in several ways.

- **Enhanced Consumer Trust:** Providing a secure and transparent record of a product's history reassures customers about the authenticity of their purchases, thereby enhancing trust in the brand.
- **Increased Resale Value:** Products with verifiable authenticity and clear provenance often retain or increase their value over time, which is particularly significant in the luxury market.
- **Protection Against Counterfeiting:** Blockchain's immutable nature makes it nearly impossible to forge or alter the history of registered products, thus protecting against counterfeiting.
- **Regulatory Compliance and Transparency:** As industries face increasing regulation around authenticity and origin, blockchain provides a way to meet these requirements transparently and efficiently.

Examples   Vacheron Constantin, one of the oldest luxury watchmakers, has adopted blockchain technology to issue digital certificates of authenticity for their watches. Each piece is accompanied by a unique, tamper-proof digital certificate that details the watch's provenance and ownership history. This not only assures the buyer of the watch's authenticity but also significantly enhances the ease of resale, as the digital certificate can be easily and securely transferred to new owners.

For its B33 sneakers, Dior incorporates Near Field Communication (NFC) technology to connect each physical sneaker to a digital passport. This passport holds detailed information about the sneaker's manufacturing process, materials, and journey through the supply chain. By scanning an NFC chip embedded in the sneaker, customers can access this data, ensuring the product's authenticity and providing a rich history that adds to the item's value and customer experience.

Prada has launched the "Crypted" initiative, which features limited edition NFTs paired with special edition physical items. These NFTs serve as digital proofs of authenticity and ownership, and they are designed to enhance the desirability of the physical items by ensuring their rarity and exclusivity. For instance, owning a Prada Crypted NFT might grant the holder ownership of a limited edition handbag, with the NFT acting as a digital certificate that confirms the item's authenticity and limited issuance (**Figure 11**).

Prada's approach not only leverages the unique capabilities of blockchain to enhance product value but also taps into the growing market of digital collectibles, which appeals to a new generation of luxury consumers who are comfortable with digital technology and value exclusivity. This strategy helps Prada maintain its reputation as a forward-thinking luxury brand, while also creating a new revenue stream and connecting with a broader audience.

By integrating the issuance of limited edition NFTs with their high-value physical products, brands like Prada can effectively use blockchain to create a new type of luxury good that meets modern consumers' demand for products that are both exclusive and technologically innovative. This strategy not only enhances the brand's appeal but also establishes a new model for luxury retail in the digital age.

In summary, the use of blockchain for verification and provenance is a powerful application in the luxury goods industry, allowing brands to secure their products' authenticity, enhance customer trust, and preserve or even increase the value of their goods over time. This strategy not only supports direct consumer benefits but also upholds the brand's reputation in a market where authenticity is paramount.

F. Digital Revenue Streams and Intellectual Property Monetization

1. Monetize Intellectual Property via NFTs

The concept of "Monetize IP" within the realm of Web3 involves leveraging blockchain technology to create and market digital assets based on a brand's intellectual property. This approach enables brands to tap into new revenue streams by digitizing and selling their unique content, designs, or trademarks as digital assets, such as NFTs. These assets can be anything from digital artwork and virtual fashion to digital renditions of physical products like cars or watches.

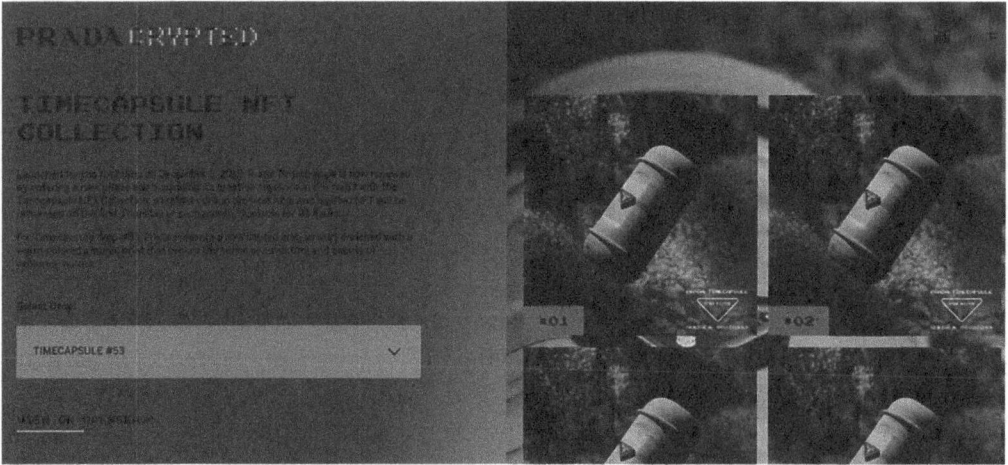

Figure 11   Prada Crypted (Prada/prada.com/last accessed May 22, 2024)

Monetizing intellectual property through digital assets offers several advantages for brands.

- **New Revenue Streams:** By creating digital versions of their products or brand elements, companies can generate additional income from existing assets, reaching new markets and consumer segments.
- **Brand Extension into Digital Spaces:** This strategy allows brands to establish a presence in emerging digital environments, such as virtual worlds and online platforms, extending their brand's reach and influence.
- **Enhanced Consumer Engagement:** Digital assets can offer interactive and exclusive experiences that enhance consumer engagement with the brand. For example, owning a digital asset may grant access to private events, special promotions, or virtual environments.
- **Innovation Leadership:** Adopting this strategy positions a brand as a leader in digital innovation, appealing to tech-savvy and younger demographics increasingly spending time in digital and virtual spaces.

Examples As we are going to see in more details in our case study, Gucci has actively engaged in creating digital goods, particularly in the fashion sector. One notable project was the sale of virtual sneakers that can be "worn" in augmented reality (AR) or used within virtual worlds and games. These digital products allow users to interact with the Gucci brand in completely new ways, enhancing the customer's digital experience and aligning Gucci with cutting-edge digital trends.

Porsche has ventured into Web3 by offering digitally tokenized versions of its iconic cars (**Figure 12**). These digital representations are not only collectibles but can also be used in virtual environments, such as racing games or virtual reality experiences. By monetizing its car designs in the digital realm, Porsche taps into a market of enthusiasts and collectors who might not purchase a physical Porsche but are eager to engage with the brand in a virtual format.

These initiatives by Gucci and Porsche showcase how effectively digital assets can be used to monetize a brand's intellectual property. Gucci's digital sneakers and Porsche's virtual cars serve as both marketing tools and revenue-generating assets. They provide fans and customers with new ways to interact with and experience their favorite brands, thereby broadening the brands' appeal and accessibility.

In summary, the strategy to monetize IP through Web3 technologies not only opens new avenues for revenue but also enhances brand engagement and presence in digital spaces. This approach allows brands to stay relevant and competitive in an increasingly digital world, where traditional physical interactions are continually complemented by virtual experiences.

2. Web3-Driven Loyalty Programs In the evolving digital landscape, brands are increasingly leveraging Web3 technologies to transform traditional loyalty programs into dynamic,

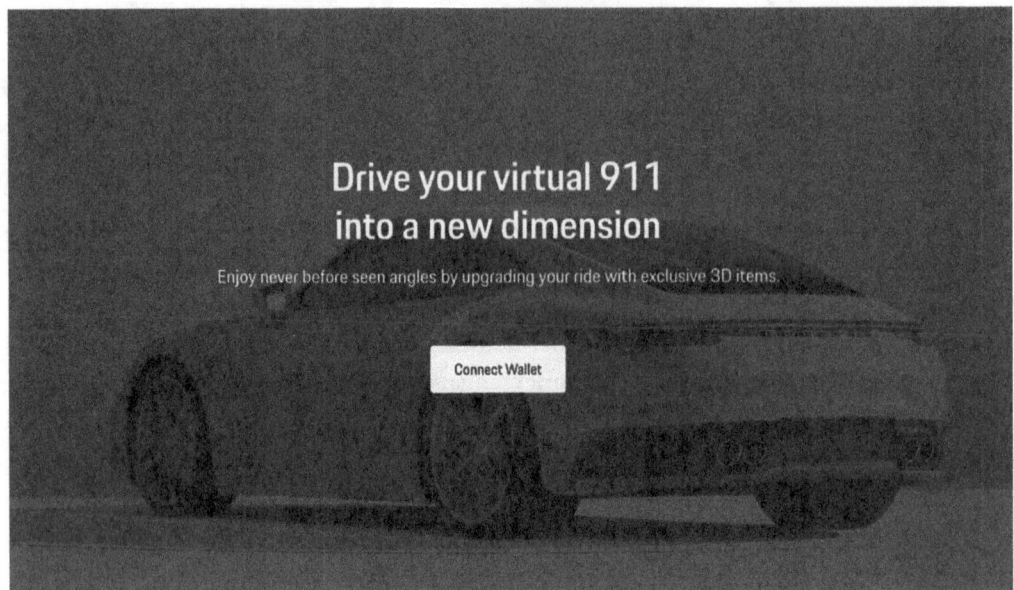

Figure 12   Porsche on Web3 (porsche.com)

interactive platforms. These loyalty applications utilize blockchain and NFTs to offer unique rewards and experiences that foster deeper customer engagement and loyalty. This approach is particularly beneficial for brands because it not only enhances the value proposition for customers but also provides a more secure and engaging way to manage loyalty interactions.

Beyond NFTs, companies can directly integrate blockchain technology and cryptocurrencies into their loyalty programs to enhance customer engagement and provide real-time rewards. For example, a business could create its own cryptocurrency as a loyalty currency, which customers earn through purchases or engagement activities. These digital currencies can then be used for further purchases, exchanged for other cryptocurrencies, or even traded on decentralized exchanges, giving them tangible market value.

This approach not only incentivizes frequent purchases but also fosters a deeper connection with the brand, as customers become more invested in a loyalty program that offers real-world value and flexibility in how rewards can be utilized.

Blockchain based loyalty applications may impact companies in terms of the following:

- **Enhanced Customer Engagement:** By integrating NFTs into loyalty programs, brands can create more engaging and interactive experiences that resonate with a digital-savvy audience.
- **Increased Brand Loyalty:** Exclusive rewards and experiences available through NFTs can increase customer retention and turn regular customers into brand advocates.
- **Innovative Brand Perception:** Using cutting-edge technology like blockchain enhances the brand's image as innovative and forward-thinking, attracting a younger, tech-savant demographic.

- **Secure Transactions:** Blockchain's inherent security features ensure that all transactions and ownership records are secure and immutable, reducing fraud and enhancing trust.

Examples   Starbucks Odyssey represented a significant evolution of the company's existing loyalty program, integrating blockchain technology to offer a Web3 experience.[3] This platform allows customers to earn digital collectibles in the form of NFTs by engaging in various brand-related activities and challenges, known as *journeys*. These digital tokens not only act as loyalty points but also unlock access to unique experiences and rewards that are not available through traditional loyalty programs. For example, participants could unlock invitations to special events, discounts, or unique coffee-related experiences, enhancing the overall customer journey with Starbucks and encouraging continual engagement with the brand.

Shake Shack and Venmo have each incorporated blockchain technology into their operations to enhance their loyalty and rewards programs. Shake Shack has launched a promotional campaign where customers who make purchases using the Cash App's debit Cash Card receive a 15% cashback in Bitcoin. This initiative not only incentivizes spending but also introduces customers to cryptocurrency rewards, aligning with the increasing interest in digital currencies. Similarly, Venmo has introduced a feature called Cash Back to Crypto, allowing credit card users to convert their cashback rewards directly into cryptocurrencies like Bitcoin, Ethereum, Litecoin, and Bitcoin Cash. This feature is integrated within the Venmo app, facilitating easy access to cryptocurrencies and promoting its use among its customer base.

These programs are reshaping how brands think about customer loyalty. The use of blockchain and NFTs adds a layer of excitement and exclusivity, which is particularly appealing in competitive markets where brands are vying for customer attention and loyalty. This shift not only meets current consumer expectations for digital and personalized experiences but also sets a new standard for how loyalty programs can operate in the digital age, potentially leading to greater customer satisfaction and brand loyalty.

Real Case Study: Beyond the Runway: Gucci's Leap into the Web3 Era[4]

Case Summary

We have explored many different examples of ways in which traditional brands have used blockchain technologies to engage with their audiences. However,

---

[3] Starbucks decided to shut down its Odyssey program on March 31, 2024, after running it for about 15 months.
[4] For additional details about the case and the teaching materials, see the Harvard Business School case I wrote, together with Marc Baumann, available at https://hbsp.harvard.edu/product/224054-PDF-ENG?Ntt=marco%20di%20maggio&itemFindingMethod=search.

because of the novelty of these initiatives, it is challenging to determine whether any of these initiatives have actually been a success. To understand how to define success in a Web3 endeavor, we are going to examine the real case of Gucci.

Gucci's venture into the Web3 domain under the creative guidance of Alessandro Michele first and then Sabato De Sarno represents a bold fusion of its rich historical legacy with the frontier of digital innovation. This initiative not only extends the brand's influence into the digital realm but also redefines the essence of luxury for a digitally native audience.

Gucci embraced various aspects of Web3, delving into NFTs, virtual fashion, and cryptocurrency. This transition is highlighted by the launch of the "Gucci Cosmos" in The Sandbox (as we talked about in previous chapters), a virtual environment where users can interact with the brand in innovative ways. This platform allows visitors to explore a digital universe designed to reflect Gucci's heritage through interactive quests and experiences set in a virtual London.

Gucci entered the NFTs space through notable collaborations and launches, such as the Aria collection, which blends digital art with fashion. This venture, along with subsequent projects like 10KTF x Gucci Grail and SUPERGUCCI, highlights Gucci's commitment to integrating its brand ethos into the realm of digital ownership and collectability.

In terms of virtual fashion, Gucci has established its presence on platforms like Roblox, where it offers the Gucci Town experience, and Zepeto, providing interactive spaces for users to engage with the brand. These platforms serve as a bridge between gaming, art, and fashion, furthering the brand's strategy to reach a broader, tech-savvy audience.

Additionally, the adoption of cryptocurrencies as a payment method in select Gucci stores showcases the brand's progressive approach to new financial technologies, catering to the preferences of crypto-enthusiasts and aligning with its innovative spirit.

Overall, these strategic initiatives within Web3 not only extend Gucci's brand into new domains but also challenge the luxury fashion industry to rethink how brands can maintain their heritage while pioneering the digital future of fashion and luxury.

What Can We Learn from Gucci's Case?   Gucci's strategic pivot into the Web3 space is a fascinating case study on how traditional luxury brands can adapt to and shape the digital future. Gucci's integration into Web3 is reshaping how luxury is perceived and experienced by a new generation that interacts with fashion in fundamentally different ways.

REDEFINING LUXURY FOR THE DIGITAL GENERATION   Gucci's transition into Web3 through initiatives such as unique NFT collaborations and virtual fashion experiences signals a shift in how luxury brands can maintain relevance in a digital-first market. This evolution from physical to digital luxury items challenges conventional notions of value and exclusivity. For example, Gucci's Aria collection in the form of NFTs or their virtual environments in platforms like Roblox and The Sandbox illustrate how digital exclusivity can attract the attention of younger, tech-savvy consumers who value digital ownership as much as physical luxury.

IMPLICATIONS FOR THE LUXURY FASHION INDUSTRY   Gucci's foray into Web3 provides a blueprint for other luxury brands considering similar pathways. This digital transition not only opens up new revenue streams but also broadens the brand's appeal and accessibility. The luxury industry, traditionally rooted in exclusivity, now faces the challenge of balancing this exclusivity with the inclusivity that digital platforms offer. This shift might redefine competitive dynamics in the luxury sector, prompting brands to innovate continually to stay relevant.

EVALUATING SUCCESS IN WEB3 INITIATIVES   Measuring the success of Web3 initiatives poses unique challenges, especially in luxury fashion. Metrics might include digital sales figures, engagement rates on virtual platforms, and the resale value of digital assets on secondary markets. However, brands must also consider qualitative measures such as brand perception in digital communities and the effectiveness of digital initiatives in enhancing customer engagement and loyalty.

STRATEGIC MOTIVATIONS AND CHALLENGES   The strategic motivations behind Gucci's entry into Web3 likely include reaching a new audience base, enhancing brand innovation, and staying ahead in the competitive luxury market. As Gucci navigates these new waters, it encounters both opportunities, such as tapping into a burgeoning market of digital collectors and gamers, and challenges, such as ensuring brand prestige and exclusivity in a more accessible digital marketplace.

DEVELOPING FRAMEWORKS FOR WEB3 IN LUXURY FASHION   To navigate the complexities of Web3, luxury brands like Gucci can develop frameworks that help in strategically integrating digital technologies. This includes conducting market research to understand the digital consumer psyche, investing in technology to create immersive and exclusive digital experiences, and fostering partnerships with technology providers to ensure seamless integration of blockchain and NFT technologies.

This comprehensive approach not only illustrates how traditional luxury brands can maintain their heritage but also how they can pioneer the future of digital fashion and luxury, setting a standard for the industry's evolution. As more brands follow suit, the luxury fashion industry may witness a significant transformation in how products are created, marketed, and sold.

How do Gucci's Web3 projects showcase its dedication to both tradition and innovation, and how does the brand balance the adoption of new technologies with its established luxury ethos?

Gucci's strategic leap into Web3 not only showcases its commitment to innovation but also aligns with its heritage, reflecting a blend of traditional luxury ethos and cutting-edge digital engagement. This pioneering move is evident through Gucci's various Web3 initiatives that cater to a new generation of consumers who value both the tangibility of luxury goods and the virtual experiences offered by digital platforms.

Comparatively, Gucci's approach to integrating Web3 technologies sets it apart from other luxury brands that have either hesitated or adopted a more conservative stance toward digital transformation. For instance, while brands like Burberry and Louis Vuitton have also ventured into digital spaces through gaming and NFTs, Gucci has been particularly forward-thinking in creating interactive, immersive experiences that bridge the gap between traditional luxury and digital innovation. Burberry's engagement in the gaming world and Louis Vuitton's creative NFT ventures highlight a similar trajectory, underscoring a broad industry shift toward digital inclusivity without compromising on brand exclusivity.[5]

In terms of challenges, translating a luxury brand's traditional ethos into the digital domain involves careful navigation to ensure that exclusivity and brand prestige are not diluted. Gucci addresses this by ensuring that its digital assets, such as NFTs, not only reflect the brand's aesthetic and historical significance but also offer tangible value to consumers in the virtual world.

This shift heralds significant implications for the luxury industry, encouraging brands to reassess their strategies to engage with digitally savvy consumers. By analyzing Gucci's methods and comparing them with those of its competitors, it becomes evident that the luxury sector is at a pivotal juncture where embracing digital innovation can significantly enhance customer engagement and brand loyalty in the digital age.

What criteria should be considered when assessing Gucci's Web3 initiatives?

To evaluate Gucci's efforts in Web3 effectively, a multifaceted framework should be considered that encompasses several key dimensions.

- **Brand Engagement:** This involves measuring how effective Gucci's Web3 initiatives are at engaging existing customers and attracting new ones. Metrics could include the number of interactions on digital platforms, the frequency of digital

---

[5] https://www.salesforce.com/blog/luxury-retail-trends-web3/; https://jingdaily.com/posts/top-nft-triumphs-and-flops-how-luxury-brands-navigated-web3-in-2023

asset transactions, and social media engagement related to their Web3 activities. Focusing on the utility and personalized experiences enabled by Web3 technologies is vital. For Gucci, this includes exploring how tokenization and open ecosystems enhance customer engagement and loyalty through unique, empowered experiences. Ensuring the selection of appropriate technology partners is essential to augment Gucci's loyalty capabilities within Web3, aiming for initiatives that are innovative and deliver tangible value to consumers.

- **Digital Innovation:** Assess the novelty and technological sophistication of Gucci's Web3 projects. This could be evaluated based on the complexity and uniqueness of the NFTs, the features of the virtual environments they create, and how these initiatives push the boundaries of what's currently possible in Web3.

- **Consumer Interaction in Virtual Spaces:** Focus on how Gucci facilitates consumer interaction within these digital spaces. Consider factors such as user experience design, interactivity of the digital assets, and the overall user engagement within these platforms. Surveys and feedback from users interacting with Gucci's virtual spaces could provide insights into how these experiences strengthen consumer relationships with the brand. Metrics could include engagement rates on digital platforms, sales figures for digital assets, and feedback on consumer satisfaction and brand perception in the digital realm.

- **Alignment with Brand Heritage:** It's crucial to consider how these digital ventures reflect Gucci's traditional values and luxury ethos. Evaluate whether the Web3 initiatives enhance or dilute the brand's image of exclusivity and high-quality craftsmanship.

- **Market Impact:** Analyze the impact of Gucci's Web3 initiatives on its market position relative to competitors. This could involve looking at market share within the digital luxury market, perceptions of innovation in the industry, and how these initiatives are perceived compared to similar efforts by other luxury brands.

- **Sustainability and Relevance:** Critically evaluate the sustainability and relevance of luxury fashion in Web3 environments. Question whether Gucci's digital goods and experiences will endure as consumer preferences evolve, and how the brand ensures that its Web3 initiatives resonate with both traditional clientele and digital natives without diluting its luxury ethos.

By using this framework, stakeholders can gain a comprehensive understanding of the effectiveness and impact of Gucci's Web3 strategies, ensuring that they not only innovate but also maintain the core attributes that define their luxury brand identity.

CAN WE PUT SOME NUMBERS TO IT? WE CAN TRY. Quantitative metrics should play a crucial role in assessing the effectiveness and impact of a brand's initiatives, particularly in the evolving domain of Web3. These metrics provide a solid, data-driven foundation that sheds light on a brand's performance across various dimensions. By quantifying aspects such as brand awareness, sentiment, and consumer engagement, businesses can gain objective insights into how well their digital strategies resonate with their audience and align with their brand objectives. This structured approach enables brands like Gucci to navigate the complex digital landscape effectively, ensuring that their innovative efforts yield measurable and meaningful outcomes. Here are a few examples of how to quantitatively measure the company's performance along a number of dimensions:

- **Brand awareness** explores how well consumers recognize Gucci within the Web3 landscape. This awareness is gauged through surveys that query consumers on their recognition of Gucci's NFT collections or virtual fashion efforts, complemented by analyzing the frequency of Gucci's mentions across social media and Web3-related online discussions.
- **Brand sentiment** measures the public's perceptions and attitudes toward Gucci's Web3 initiatives. Utilizing sentiment analysis tools, we can sift through social media, online reviews, and forum discussions to gauge positive, negative, or neutral feelings. A predominance of positive sentiments indicates that Gucci's Web3 activities resonate well with the audience, whereas negative sentiments may highlight areas needing enhancement.
- **Brand equity** in the Web3 context reflects the added value Gucci accrues from its digital reputation, which influences consumers' engagement and purchasing behaviors. Metrics such as the price premium consumers pay for Gucci's NFTs compared to similar items, the resale value of these digital assets, and loyalty metrics in digital environments help quantify this equity.
- **Consumer engagement** looks at interactions within Gucci's Web3 realms, including transaction frequency with Gucci's digital assets and participation in virtual events. High levels of engagement suggest a robust consumer interest and active involvement in Gucci's digital offerings.
- **Conversion rates** assess the effectiveness of Gucci's Web3 strategies in prompting consumer actions like purchases of NFTs, participation in digital worlds, or cryptocurrency transactions. High conversion rates would indicate that Gucci's digital offerings are compelling and successfully driving consumer activity.
- **Return on investment (ROI)** for Web3 initiatives calculates the financial efficacy by comparing the revenues these digital ventures generate against the costs of their development and promotion. A positive ROI denotes that Gucci's investments into Web3 are producing tangible financial benefits for the brand.

A follow-up question anybody who is engaging with these initiatives should be able to answer is how should success be defined in this new digital era for luxury brands?

Defining success in Web3 for luxury brands like Gucci requires a nuanced approach that incorporates both the tangible impacts on the brand and the intangible benefits that emerge from digital innovation. This definition of success should blend traditional markers of brand performance with new metrics that capture the essence of Web3's contribution to the brand's evolution.

In the Web3 domain, the measure of success for luxury brands like Gucci goes beyond the straightforward metrics of financial returns. It involves a richer, more complex set of goals including the enhancement of the brand narrative, the cultivation of a vibrant community, and the innovation of digital luxury experiences. For Gucci, this translates into not merely launching NFTs or virtual environments but leveraging these platforms to forge deeper consumer connections, uphold and broadcast its storied heritage, and establish new benchmarks within the luxury digital ecosystem.

- **Enhancing Brand Narrative and Heritage:** The success of Gucci's Web3 initiatives can be qualitatively evaluated by how well these digital projects resonate with and reinforce Gucci's established brand story and values. It is crucial that these digital ventures not only echo but also amplify Gucci's legacy of craftsmanship and luxury, making these revered qualities palpable in the digital realm. This involves crafting digital experiences that are coherent with the luxurious and artisanal identity that Gucci has cultivated over decades.
- **Cultivating Community Engagement and Loyalty:** The strength and vitality of the community that Gucci constructs around its Web3 projects are fundamental to their success. This goes beyond mere numbers; it looks at how engaged the community is with Gucci's digital offerings. Successful community engagement would be evident in active participation in digital events, positive feedback and robust interactions within these digital spaces, and a general sentiment that favors Gucci's innovative approach.
- **Leading Digital Innovation in Luxury:** Another crucial qualitative metric is Gucci's ability to position itself as a leader and pioneer within the digital luxury space. Success in this area can be seen in how Gucci sets trends, influences the broader luxury market, and brings novel ideas to life that push the boundaries of what is possible in digital luxury. Gucci's role in driving innovation can solidify its status as a trailblazer, shaping the future of luxury in a digital-first world.

Overall, these qualitative measures offer a comprehensive view of how Gucci's Web3 initiatives not only align with but also enhance its brand strategy. This holistic approach ensures that Gucci's foray into digital spaces contributes meaningfully to its long-term brand equity and leadership in the luxury sector.

3. Concluding Remarks

What I would love for you to take away from this chapter is the pivotal role of blockchain in redefining consumer interactions through decentralized mechanisms, immutability, and the facilitation of true digital ownership, which are becoming so crucial in today's digital economy.

The low hanging fruit is how blockchain technology ensures the authenticity and traceability of luxury products. However, the really interesting part is how customer loyalty programs are revolutionized through smart contracts and NFTs. This enables brands to offer more personalized and engaging consumer experiences that extend beyond traditional rewards systems. Additionally, the use of decentralized autonomous organizations illustrates a shift toward more inclusive and participatory brand governance, where community members can influence decisions, thereby fostering a stronger connection and loyalty to the brand.

The integration of blockchain into marketing strategies allows for a secure and direct connection between brands and consumers, bypassing intermediaries and enhancing the efficiency and efficacy of transactions and interactions. This capability demonstrates how brands can leverage it to build communities and form a competitive advantage.

Even if the hype around NFTs has evaporated since 2022, the future of blockchain in branding is poised for substantial growth, with continuous innovations likely to further disrupt traditional business models and consumer interactions, the advancements in tokenization and digital asset management, are likely to significantly influence future marketing strategies and brand engagements, making this an exciting area!

Coding Examples

Token-Gate Content, Products, or Experiences

Let's develop a contract that manages access to multiple types of digital content and services based on ownership of specific tokens. This example will include features such as multiple access tiers, time-limited access, and event-based token checks, adding realism and practical utility for a wide range of applications such as media platforms, exclusive event access, or subscription services.

Example Code Concept

```solidity
// SPDX-License-Identifier: MIT
pragma solidity ^0.8.4;

import "@openzeppelin/contracts/token/ERC721/IERC721.sol";
import "@openzeppelin/contracts/access/Ownable.sol";
import "@openzeppelin/contracts/security/ReentrancyGuard.sol";

contract TokenGatedAccess is Ownable, ReentrancyGuard {
    IERC721 public nft;
```

```
    mapping(uint256 => uint256) public accessExpiry; // tokenId to
timestamp mapping
    mapping(address => bool) public premiumAccess;

    event AccessGranted(uint256 tokenId, address user, uint256 duration);
    event PremiumAccessGranted(address user);
    event PremiumAccessRevoked(address user);

    constructor(address nftAddress) Ownable() {
        nft = IERC721(nftAddress);
    }

    function grantAccess(uint256 tokenId, uint256 durationInDays)
public onlyOwner {
        require(nft.ownerOf(tokenId) != address(0), "Token does not
exist");
        require(durationInDays > 0, "Duration must be positive");
        accessExpiry[tokenId] = block.timestamp + (durationInDays *
1 days);
        emit AccessGranted(tokenId, nft.ownerOf(tokenId),
durationInDays);

    }

    function checkAccess(uint256 tokenId) public view returns (bool) {
        return accessExpiry[tokenId] > block.timestamp;
    }

    function grantPremiumAccess(address user) public onlyOwner {
        require(user != address(0), "Cannot grant access to zero
address");
        premiumAccess[user] = true;
        emit PremiumAccessGranted(user);
    }

    function checkPremiumAccess(address user) public view returns (bool)
{
        return premiumAccess[user];
    }

    function revokePremiumAccess(address user) public onlyOwner {
        require(premiumAccess[user], "User does not have premium
access");
        premiumAccess[user] = false;
        emit PremiumAccessRevoked(user);
    }
}
```

Key Features Explained:

- **NFT-Based Access Control:** The contract integrates with an NFT contract to check ownership of a specific token. Access is then granted based on token ownership, with an expiry date set for each token's access period.

- **Time-Limited Access:** It uses a mapping to track the expiry of access rights for each token, allowing for time-limited access to content or experiences. This is useful for subscriptions or temporary passes.
- **Premium Access:** The contract includes a separate mechanism for "premium" access, which can be granted at the owner's discretion to specific users regardless of NFT ownership. This feature can be used to provide lifetime access, special privileges, or complimentary premium services.
- **Event Emissions:** It emits events when access is granted, providing transparency and enabling external applications or services to react to changes in access rights.

Augment and Incentivize Community Building

Let's design a smart contract that not only issues tokens for community participation but also incorporates features such as role-based rewards, special achievements, and community voting mechanisms.

Example Code Concept

```
// SPDX-License-Identifier: MIT
pragma solidity ^0.8.4;

import "@openzeppelin/contracts/token/ERC20/ERC20.sol";
import "@openzeppelin/contracts/access/AccessControl.sol";

contract CommunityToken is ERC20, AccessControl {
    bytes32 public constant REWARDER_ROLE = keccak256("REWARDER_ROLE");
    mapping(address => uint256) public contributions;

    event ContributionAdded(address indexed contributor, uint256 amount,
uint256 totalContributions);

    constructor() ERC20("CommunityToken", "COMT") {
        _setupRole(DEFAULT_ADMIN_ROLE, msg.sender);
        _setupRole(REWARDER_ROLE, msg.sender);
    }

    function addContribution(address contributor, uint256 amount) public
onlyRole(REWARDER_ROLE) {
        contributions[contributor] += amount;
        _mint(contributor, amount);
        emit ContributionAdded(contributor, amount, contributions
[contributor]);
    }
```

```
    function setRewarder(address rewarder) public onlyRole
(DEFAULT_ADMIN_ROLE) {
        _setupRole(REWARDER_ROLE, rewarder);
    }

    function revokeRewarder(address rewarder) public onlyRole
(DEFAULT_ADMIN_ROLE) {
        revokeRole(REWARDER_ROLE, rewarder);
    }

    function rewardForSpecialAchievement(address contributor,
uint256 bonusAmount) public onlyRole(REWARDER_ROLE) {
        _mint(contributor, bonusAmount);
    }

    function redeemTokensForRewards(uint256 amount) public {
        require(balanceOf(msg.sender) >= amount, "Insufficient tokens");
        _burn(msg.sender, amount);
        // Logic to grant access to rewards or benefits
    }
}
```

Key Features Explained:

- **ERC20 Token:** This contract uses an ERC20 token, which is a standard for fungible tokens. Community members earn these tokens by participating in various activities or making contributions.
- **Role-Based Access Control:** Implements role-based permissions using OpenZeppelin's **AccessControl** to manage who can distribute rewards. This allows for decentralized administration where multiple parties can have the authority to issue tokens based on contributions.
- **Contribution Tracking:** Contributions of each member are tracked, and tokens are minted as rewards for these contributions. This not only incentivizes participation but also provides a transparent record of individual contributions.
- **Special Achievements:** The contract includes functionality to reward members for special achievements, which could be anything from recruiting new members to leading a project. This adds an additional layer of engagement and rewards.
- **Reward Redemption:** Members can redeem their tokens for various rewards. This could include exclusive access to content, merchandise, discounts, or even voting power in community decisions.

Connect Physical Goods to Virtual Counterparts

Let's consider a scenario where each physical product has an embedded NFC chip or QR code that links to a corresponding NFT. This NFT can then serve as a digital certificate of authenticity and ownership, as well as a gateway to digital experiences or content.

Example Code Concept

```solidity
// SPDX-License-Identifier: MIT
pragma solidity ^0.8.4;

import "@openzeppelin/contracts/token/ERC721/extensions/
ERC721URIStorage.sol";
import "@openzeppelin/contracts/access/Ownable.sol";

contract DigitalTwinRegistry is ERC721URIStorage, Ownable {
    // Mapping from physical item serial number to NFT tokenId
    mapping(string => uint256) public serialNumberToTokenId;
    // Mapping from tokenId to physical item's serial number
    mapping(uint256 => string) public tokenIdToSerialNumber;

    event DigitalTwinLinked(string serialNumber, uint256 tokenId);

    constructor() ERC721("DigitalTwin", "DTWIN") {}

    function registerItem(string memory serialNumber, string memory
 metadataURI) public onlyOwner {
        require(serialNumberToTokenId[serialNumber] == 0, "Item already
registered");

        uint256 tokenId = totalSupply() + 1; // Incremental tokenId,
could also use a counter
        _mint(msg.sender, tokenId);
        _setTokenURI(tokenId, metadataURI);

        serialNumberToTokenId[serialNumber] = tokenId;
        tokenIdToSerialNumber[tokenId] = serialNumber;

        emit DigitalTwinLinked(serialNumber, tokenId);
    }

    function verifyOwnership(string memory serialNumber) public view
returns (bool) {
        uint256 tokenId = serialNumberToTokenId[serialNumber];
        return tokenId != 0 && ownerOf(tokenId) == msg.sender;
    }

    function getTokenIdForSerialNumber(string memory serialNumber)
public view returns (uint256) {
        return serialNumberToTokenId[serialNumber];
    }

    function getSerialNumberForTokenId(uint256 tokenId) public view
returns (string memory) {
        require(_exists(tokenId), "Token does not exist.");
        return tokenIdToSerialNumber[tokenId];
    }
}
```

Key Features Explained:

- **Serial Number to Token Mapping:** The contract maintains a mapping from physical item serial numbers to NFT token IDs, ensuring each physical item can be uniquely linked to a digital counterpart.
- **NFT Minting:** The **registerItem** function allows the contract owner (likely the manufacturer or authorized distributor) to create a new NFT for each physical item by providing its serial number and metadata URI. This metadata can include details like the item's production date, specifications, and any other relevant data.
- **Ownership Verification:** The **verifyOwnership** function allows users to verify if they are the rightful owners of the digital twin by checking against the serial number linked to the NFT they own.
- **Event Emission:** The contract emits an event when a new digital twin is linked, which could be used by external systems to track the registration of new items.
- **Bidirectional Lookup:** Functions to retrieve the token ID using a serial number and vice versa are provided, enhancing the utility and accessibility of the data within the contract.

Co-create Digital Goods That Are "Owned" by Users

Let's design a contract that enables users to combine attributes from existing digital assets to create new, unique assets. This example will include user interactions, attribute inheritance, and even breeding or merging mechanisms similar to those seen in digital collectibles like CryptoKitties.

Example Code Concept

```
// SPDX-License-Identifier: MIT
pragma solidity ^0.8.4;

import "@openzeppelin/contracts/token/ERC721/extensions/
ERC721Enumerable.sol";
import "@openzeppelin/contracts/access/Ownable.sol";
import "@openzeppelin/contracts/utils/Counters.sol";

contract DigitalCreator is ERC721Enumerable, Ownable {
    using Counters for Counters.Counter;
    Counters.Counter private _tokenIdCounter;

    struct Asset {
        uint256 geneA;
        uint256 geneB;
        string category;
    }
```

```
mapping(uint256 => Asset) public assets;

event AssetCreated(uint256 indexed tokenId, uint256 geneA, uint256
geneB, string category);

constructor(address initialOwner) ERC721("DigitalCreator", "DCR")
Ownable() {
    transferOwnership(initialOwner); // Set the owner explicitly
}

function createAsset(uint256 geneA, uint256 geneB, string memory
category) public onlyOwner {
    uint256 tokenId = _tokenIdCounter.current();
    _tokenIdCounter.increment();
    assets[tokenId] = Asset(geneA, geneB, category);
    _mint(msg.sender, tokenId);
    emit AssetCreated(tokenId, geneA, geneB, category);
}

function breedAssets(uint256 parent1Id, uint256 parent2Id) public
returns (uint256) {
    require(ownerOf(parent1Id) == msg.sender && ownerOf(parent2Id) ==
msg.sender, "You must own the assets to breed them.");

    Asset storage parent1 = assets[parent1Id];
    Asset storage parent2 = assets[parent2Id];

    uint256 newGeneA = (parent1.geneA + parent2.geneA) / 2;
    uint256 newGeneB = (parent1.geneB + parent2.geneB) / 2;
    string memory category = parent1.category; // Assume same
category for simplicity

    uint256 newTokenId = _tokenIdCounter.current();
    _tokenIdCounter.increment();
    assets[newTokenId] = Asset(newGeneA, newGeneB, category);
    _mint(msg.sender, newTokenId);
    emit AssetCreated(newTokenId, newGeneA, newGeneB, category);

    return newTokenId;
}
}
```

Key Features Explained:

- **Asset Struct:** Defines the structure for digital assets, which includes genetic components (**geneA, geneB**) that determine characteristics of the asset, and a **category** that might relate to different classes of assets (e.g. types of digital art, characters, etc.).
- **Asset Creation and Minting:** The contract allows the contract owner to create new assets with specific genes and categories. It uses a counter to assign unique token IDs to each new asset.

- **Breeding Mechanism:** Similar to genetic algorithms, the breeding function takes two asset tokens, combines their attributes (genes), and creates a new asset. This simulates the process of combining features from two parent assets to create offspring with potentially unique attributes.
- **Ownership Checks:** The contract ensures that only the owner of both parent assets can breed them, enhancing security and integrity.
- **Event Emission:** The contract emits events when new assets are created, which can be useful for applications that track asset creation and transfers on the blockchain.

Verifiable Rarity/Limited Collections

```solidity
// SPDX-License-Identifier: MIT
pragma solidity ^0.8.4;

import "@openzeppelin/contracts/token/ERC721/extensions/
ERC721Enumerable.sol";
import "@openzeppelin/contracts/access/Ownable.sol";
import "@openzeppelin/contracts/security/ReentrancyGuard.sol";

contract LimitedEditionCollection is ERC721Enumerable, Ownable,
ReentrancyGuard {
    uint256 public maxSupply;
    uint256 public tokenPrice;
    bool public saleIsActive = false;
    mapping(address => bool) public whitelistedAddresses;
    mapping(uint256 => string) public tokenProvenance;

    event TokenPurchased(address buyer, uint256 tokenId, uint256 price);

    constructor(string memory name, string memory symbol, uint256
_maxSupply, uint256 _tokenPrice) ERC721(name, symbol) {
        maxSupply = _maxSupply;
        tokenPrice = _tokenPrice;
    }

    function flipSaleState() public onlyOwner {
        saleIsActive = !saleIsActive;
    }

    function setTokenPrice(uint256 newPrice) public onlyOwner {
        tokenPrice = newPrice;
    }

    function whitelistUser(address user) public onlyOwner {
        whitelistedAddresses[user] = true;
    }
```

```
    function removeWhitelistUser(address user) public onlyOwner {
        whitelistedAddresses[user] = false;
    }

    function buyToken(uint256 tokenId) public payable nonReentrant {
        require(saleIsActive, "Sale must be active to mint Tokens");
        require(whitelistedAddresses[msg.sender], "Caller is not
whitelisted");
        require(totalSupply() < maxSupply, "Purchase would exceed max
supply of Tokens");
        require(tokenId < maxSupply, "Invalid token ID");
        require(msg.value >= tokenPrice, "Ether value sent is not
correct");

        _safeMint(msg.sender, tokenId);
        tokenProvenance[tokenId] = string(abi.encodePacked("Minted by ",
msg.sender, " at block ", block.number));
        emit TokenPurchased(msg.sender, tokenId, msg.value);
    }

    function withdraw() public onlyOwner {
        uint256 balance = address(this).balance;
        require(payable(msg.sender).send(balance));
    }

    // Optional: Function to adjust provenance data if necessary
    function setProvenance(uint256 tokenId, string memory provenance)
public onlyOwner {
        require(_exists(tokenId), "ERC721Metadata: Provenance set of
nonexistent token");
        tokenProvenance[tokenId] = provenance;
    }
}
```

Objective: Managing a collection of limited-edition tokens, adding features like whitelisting, dynamic pricing, and provenance tracking. This will make the contract more suitable for managing verifiable rarity and exclusivity of limited edition NFTs.

Key Features Explained:

- **Whitelisting:** Users must be whitelisted to participate in the purchase of limited edition NFTs. This ensures that only pre-approved collectors can access these rare items, enhancing their exclusivity.
- **Sale Activation:** The owner can toggle the active state of the sale, allowing for controlled release periods.
- **Dynamic Pricing:** The contract allows the owner to change the price of the tokens, which can be used to adjust pricing based on demand or other factors.
- **Provenance Tracking:** Each token has a provenance record that is set at the time of minting. This feature adds an additional layer of verification for the item's history and authenticity.

- **Non-reentrant Purchases:** This security feature prevents re-entrancy attacks during the purchase process, protecting both the buyer and the contract from potential vulnerabilities.

This enhanced smart contract framework provides a robust system for managing limited edition collections, offering features that help maintain rarity and ensure the integrity of each transaction.

Loyalty Applications

Objective: This contract will incorporate features like tiered rewards, token-based rewards, redeemable points for services or products, and event triggers that award points based on specific customer actions.

Solidity Example:

```
// SPDX-License-Identifier: MIT
pragma solidity ^0.8.4;

import "@openzeppelin/contracts/token/ERC20/IERC20.sol";
import "@openzeppelin/contracts/access/Ownable.sol";
import "@openzeppelin/contracts/security/ReentrancyGuard.sol";

contract LoyaltyRewards is Ownable, ReentrancyGuard {
    IERC20 public rewardsToken;
    uint256 public rewardRate; // Points earned per dollar spent
    mapping(address => uint256) public pointsBalance;
    mapping(address => uint256) public tierLevel;

    event PointsEarned(address indexed user, uint256 points);
    event RewardRedeemed(address indexed user, uint256 points, string
reward);

    // Pass an initialOwner parameter to the constructor
    constructor(IERC20 _rewardsToken, uint256 _rewardRate, address
initialOwner) Ownable(initialOwner) {
    rewardsToken = _rewardsToken;
    rewardRate = _rewardRate;
    }

    function updateRewardRate(uint256 newRate) public onlyOwner {
        rewardRate = newRate;
    }

    function earnPoints(address user, uint256 amountSpent) public {
        uint256 points = calculateRewardPoints(amountSpent);
        pointsBalance[user] += points;
        updateTier(user);
```

```
            emit PointsEarned(user, points);
    }

    function redeemPoints(address user, uint256 points, string memory
reward) public {
            require(pointsBalance[user] >= points, "Not enough points to
redeem");
            pointsBalance[user] -= points;
            // Reward logic or call to an external system to handle the
reward
            emit RewardRedeemed(user, points, reward);
    }

    function calculateRewardPoints(uint256 amountSpent) private view
returns (uint256) {
            return amountSpent * rewardRate;
    }

    function updateTier(address user) private {
            uint256 currentPoints = pointsBalance[user];
            if (currentPoints >= 10000) {
                tierLevel[user] = 3; // Gold tier
            } else if (currentPoints >= 5000) {
                tierLevel[user] = 2; // Silver tier
            } else if (currentPoints >= 1000) {
                tierLevel[user] = 1; // Bronze tier
            } else {
                tierLevel[user] = 0; // No tier
            }
    }

    function getTierLevel(address user) public view returns (uint256) {
            return tierLevel[user];
    }

    function transferPoints(address from, address to, uint256 points)
public {
            require(pointsBalance[from] >= points, "Insufficient points");
            require(from != to, "Cannot transfer points to yourself");

            pointsBalance[from] -= points;
            pointsBalance[to] += points;
            updateTier(to);
            updateTier(from);
    }
}
```

Key Features Explained:

- **Tiered System:** The smart contract includes a tiered system where users can achieve
  different levels (e.g. Bronze, Silver, Gold) based on the points they accumulate. Each
  tier can potentially offer different benefits or rewards.

- **Dynamic Reward Rate:** The contract allows the owner (likely the business running the loyalty program) to update the rate at which customers earn points based on their spending.
- **Redemption of Points:** Users can redeem points for rewards. The function **redeem-Points** could interface with external systems to provide real-world utility like discounts, products, or services.
- **Event Emissions:** Events are emitted for earned points and rewards redeemed, which can be useful for tracking activities off-chain or in a user interface.
- **Point Transfers:** This allows transfer of points between users, adding a community aspect or enabling gifting, which can further enhance the engagement in the loyalty program.

End-of-Chapter Questions

Multiple Choice Questions

1. **What is the primary benefit of blockchain technology in enhancing brand engagement?**
   (A) It reduces the time needed for product development.
   (B) It increases the cost of marketing campaigns.
   (C) It enables secure, transparent interactions between brands and consumers.
   (D) It simplifies regulatory compliance without transparency.

2. **How do NFTs fundamentally change consumer-brand interactions?**
   (A) By increasing physical product sales.
   (B) By enabling true digital ownership and unique consumer experiences.
   (C) By eliminating digital marketing.
   (D) By reducing brand loyalty.

3. **Which Web3 feature directly contributes to improved data security and privacy for consumers?**
   (A) Decentralized autonomous organizations.
   (B) Increased use of centralized databases.
   (C) Blockchain's immutable nature.
   (D) Reduction in digital transactions.

4. **In the context of Web3, how is 'tokenization' beneficial for brands?**
   (A) It restricts the types of digital assets brands can create.
   (B) It allows brands to raise capital by issuing digital tokens representing real-world assets.
   (C) It limits brand interactions to nondigital environments.
   (D) It increases dependency on intermediaries.

5. **What does the "immutable provenance tracking" feature of blockchain offer luxury brands?**
   (A) Increased risk of counterfeiting.
   (B) Verification of product authenticity to combat counterfeiting.
   (C) Decreased consumer trust.
   (D) Simplified product returns.

6. **How do smart contracts facilitate operations within Web3 for brands?**
   (A) By requiring more intermediaries in transactions.
   (B) By automatically executing transactions based on predefined rules.
   (C) By complicating the transaction process.
   (D) By increasing transaction costs.

7. **What advantage do decentralized marketplaces offer smaller or independent brands?**
   (A) They increase operational costs.
   (B) They allow direct global market access without intermediaries.
   (C) They reduce brand visibility.
   (D) They limit consumer choice.

8. **What impact does the introduction of exclusive content and token-gated access have on consumer behavior?**
   (A) Decreases brand loyalty due to lack of exclusivity.
   (B) Increases consumer engagement through exclusivity and novelty.
   (C) Reduces interaction between the brand and consumers.
   (D) Simplifies access to products and services.

9. **How does integrating digital twins with physical products benefit brands?**
   (A) Reduces product lifecycle.
   (B) Disconnects the product from digital enhancements.
   (C) Enhances customer engagement by linking to unique digital content.
   (D) Decreases the perceived value of products.

10. **What challenge does "verification and authenticity" address for high-value products?**
    (A) Increases the likelihood of counterfeiting.
    (B) Decreases consumer trust in product authenticity.
    (C) Helps combat counterfeiting and unauthorized resales.
    (D) Simplifies product replication.

11. **How do digital revenue streams enhance brand presence in Web3?**
    (A) By limiting digital asset creation.
    (B) Through monetization of intellectual property via NFTs and digital products.
    (C) By decreasing brand engagement in digital spaces.
    (D) Reducing the brand's innovative capacity.

Open Questions

1. Discuss the implications of blockchain technology on traditional brand-consumer relationships. How does the shift toward decentralized networks and transparent transactions challenge or enhance these relationships?
2. Analyze the potential risks and rewards for a luxury brand venturing into Web3. Consider aspects such as brand reputation, consumer trust, and the balance between exclusivity and accessibility.
3. Evaluate the role of NFTs in transforming consumer engagement strategies for brands. What are the innovative uses of NFTs you have observed, and how do they contribute to a brand's growth and consumer loyalty?
4. Examine the impact of decentralized data management on consumer privacy and brand transparency. How can brands leverage this aspect of Web3 to align themselves with increasing global concerns about data privacy?
5. Reflect on the sustainability of digital luxury markets as they pertain to Web3 technologies. What challenges might brands face in maintaining value and exclusivity in rapidly evolving digital markets?

Coding Exercise

Coding Question: Your Very Own Collectible

Suppose that, after reading this book, you start dabbling with crypto, DeFi, and NFTs and start amassing a group of followers. You'd like to reward your followers with an NFT linked to an item that uniquely represents you and gives out rewards.

Objective: Implement an NFT contract that links to a physical good and provides rewards based on a variety of conditions, such as attending events.

Detailed Instructions:
1. **Contract Setup:** Choose an item that uniquely represents you that will be linked to your NFT. Begin with an ERC-721 or ERC-1155 contract, as appropriate.
2. **Item Metadata:** Embed metadata about your item into your contract.
3. **Ownership Management:** Include methods that allow holders to authenticate their ownership, and transfer their ownership to someone else.
4. **Set Up a Points System that Allows Holders to Earn Rewards:** Choose a reward system such as a tiered system or a linear system with milestones.
5. **Points Management:** Include methods that update the number of points based on real-world achievements and experiences, allow users to redeem points for rewards, and allow users to transfer points to others.
6. **Additional Mechanisms:** Feel free to add additional features that can help with community building, retention, and engagement. You can personalize the NFT so that it can represent who you are!

Chapter 15

When HAL Meets Satoshi

Merging Minds and Money on the Blockchain

Preface

Imagine a world where your computer not only talks back but also trades Bitcoin while brewing your morning coffee. That's right, we're diving headfirst into the enchanting chaos where artificial intelligence meets blockchain—the peanut butter and jelly of the tech world, if peanut butter could analyze vast datasets and jelly could decentralize finance.

In this whirlwind tour, we'll explore how AI is not just about robots dreaming of electric sheep but about machines dreaming up ways to manage your digital wallet.

Ah, OpenAI and its prodigious offspring, ChatGPT—where to begin? Over the last few months, these clever creations have been adopted faster than kittens in a viral internet video. ChatGPT, in particular, has spread through tech circles and beyond with the zeal of a Silicon Valley startup guru preaching the blockchain gospel at a TED Talk. ChatGPT has been hailed as the next big thing—so much so that you might expect it to start its own podcast any day now.

Yet, for all its prowess, ChatGPT has also shown a quirky side, occasionally producing responses that are as bewildering as finding a Wi-Fi signal in the middle of a desert. As we chuckle over its faux pas and marvel at its insights, it's clear that ChatGPT isn't just a tool; it's become a cultural phenomenon, teaching us as much about the quirks of artificial intelligence as about our own expectations of technology.

AI and Bitcoin: Because why let humans make financial mistakes when robots can do it faster and with more processing power?

We'll also see how AI and blockchain are like the odd couple of the digital era. On one hand, AI, with its brainy antics, is learning to write poetry, drive cars, and, yes, even trade stocks (move over, Wall Street). On the other, blockchain stands stoically, ensuring everything is on the ledger, never missing a beat, like the world's most meticulous bookkeeper.

We'll unravel how AI can help blockchain leap over technical hurdles and, in return, how blockchain promises a future where AI's power is not just held by the tech titans but is spread far and wide, like a well-executed blockchain transaction.

But it's not all rainbows and decentralized roses. The fusion of AI and blockchain does conjure some thorny questions. Who holds the digital keys to the kingdom when the kingdom is run by algorithms? What happens when smart contracts are a little too smart? And, importantly, can a machine invent a tastier snack than peanut butter and jelly?

1. Introduction to Generative AI

Artificial intelligence (AI) has been one of the most transformative fields in the modern era, influencing industries from healthcare to finance and driving significant advancements in technology. Its journey from theoretical concepts to practical applications has reshaped how we interact with machines and data, making what once seemed like science fiction a tangible reality. It has attracted significant investments totaling $25 billion in 2023.[1]

AI's roots can be traced back to the mid-20th century when the idea of a machine capable of mimicking human intelligence first began to take shape. The term *artificial intelligence* was coined by John McCarthy in 1956, during the Dartmouth Conference, which is often considered the birth of AI as a field. Early AI research in the 1950s and 60s focused on problem-solving and symbolic methods. By the 1980s and 90s, the advent of machine learning algorithms and the increase in computational power led to significant breakthroughs, especially in pattern recognition and logical operations.

Over the decades, several figures have made landmark contributions to the field. Alan Turing, often called the father of theoretical computer science and artificial intelligence, proposed the Turing test in 1950 as a practical yet profound criterion for determining whether a machine is capable of thinking. This test is based on the machine's ability to exhibit intelligent behavior indistinguishable from that of a human. In the Turing test, an interrogator engages in a natural language conversation with both a human and a machine without knowing which is which. If the interrogator is unable to consistently distinguish the machine from the human, the machine is considered to have passed the test, demonstrating artificial intelligence.

The significance of the Turing test lies in its focus on a machine's ability to simulate human-like responses rather than the accuracy of its answers. This test has inspired decades of debate and research in the philosophy of mind, cognitive science, and AI communities about what it means to "think" and the possibilities for machines to emulate human mental faculties.

Marvin Minsky and Geoffrey Hinton are other key figures in the evolution of artificial intelligence, particularly in the development of neural networks. Minsky, a pioneer from MIT, made vast contributions across various aspects of AI and cognitive psychology. He co-founded MIT's Artificial Intelligence Laboratory and developed several theories regarding how the human mind operates from a computational perspective. His work laid foundational insights into the ways machines might simulate human cognitive processes.

Geoffrey Hinton, often referred to as one of the "godfathers of deep learning," has been instrumental in the advancement of neural networks (something we will cover in detail below), which are algorithms modeled loosely after the human brain, designed to recognize patterns and solve common problems in the fields of AI, machine learning, and robotics. Hinton's research over several decades focused on the development of neural networks that utilize layers of mathematical functions called *neurons*. This structure enables the models to learn complex patterns in large amounts of data, which is a critical mechanism behind many modern AI applications—from speech recognition to image processing.

---

[1] https://www.chicagobooth.edu/review/ai-is-going-disrupt-labor-market-it-doesnt-have-destroy-it

Hinton's work particularly in the mid-1980s and 2000s, including his collaborative efforts on backpropagation and deep learning algorithms, revolutionized the ways that neural networks are understood and implemented. These contributions have not only enhanced the performance and capabilities of neural networks but have also allowed for more effective training of these systems on vast datasets, pushing forward the boundaries of what machines can learn and achieve.

Through their research, both Minsky and Hinton have significantly shaped the field of artificial intelligence, influencing both theoretical approaches and practical applications of AI technologies. Their work continues to impact new developments in AI, driving forward innovations that inch ever closer to replicating aspects of human intelligence in machines.

If the key advancements were made over 20 years ago, why are we seeing such significant growth and interest in AI now?

The 21st century has witnessed an unprecedented acceleration in the field of artificial intelligence, fueled largely by three pivotal developments: big data, enhanced computational power, and deep learning:

- **The Role of Big Data:** The exponential growth in data creation in recent decades has provided the raw material that feeds AI systems. Every digital process and social media exchange produces it, and AI algorithms require vast amounts of this big data to learn and make informed decisions.
- **Computational Power:** Advancements in hardware, particularly graphics processing units (GPUs) and more recently tensor processing units (TPUs), have dramatically increased the speed and capabilities of computational processes. These enhancements allow for the rapid processing of complex algorithms and large datasets, which are essential for training deep learning models.
- **Deep Learning and AI:** Deep learning, a subset of machine learning, employs layered (or "deep") neural networks that simulate the human brain's ability to learn from large amounts of data. This method has drastically improved the ability of machines to recognize patterns and make decisions.

These elements have synergistically transformed AI from a largely theoretical pursuit into a dynamic, practical tool capable of performing complex tasks that once required human intelligence. See **Figure 1** for how much more interest AI has attracted recently.

Major tech companies have been at the forefront of these advancements. Google, IBM, and Microsoft, among others, have dedicated substantial resources to developing AI technologies that push the boundaries of what machines can do. Google's DeepMind, for example, developed AlphaGo, an AI program that defeated the world champion in Go, a game known for its deep strategic complexity. IBM's Watson has shown capabilities ranging from defeating human champions in Jeopardy to aiding in medical diagnoses and treatment plans. Microsoft has integrated AI into its products to enhance customer experiences through more intuitive interfaces and predictive technologies.

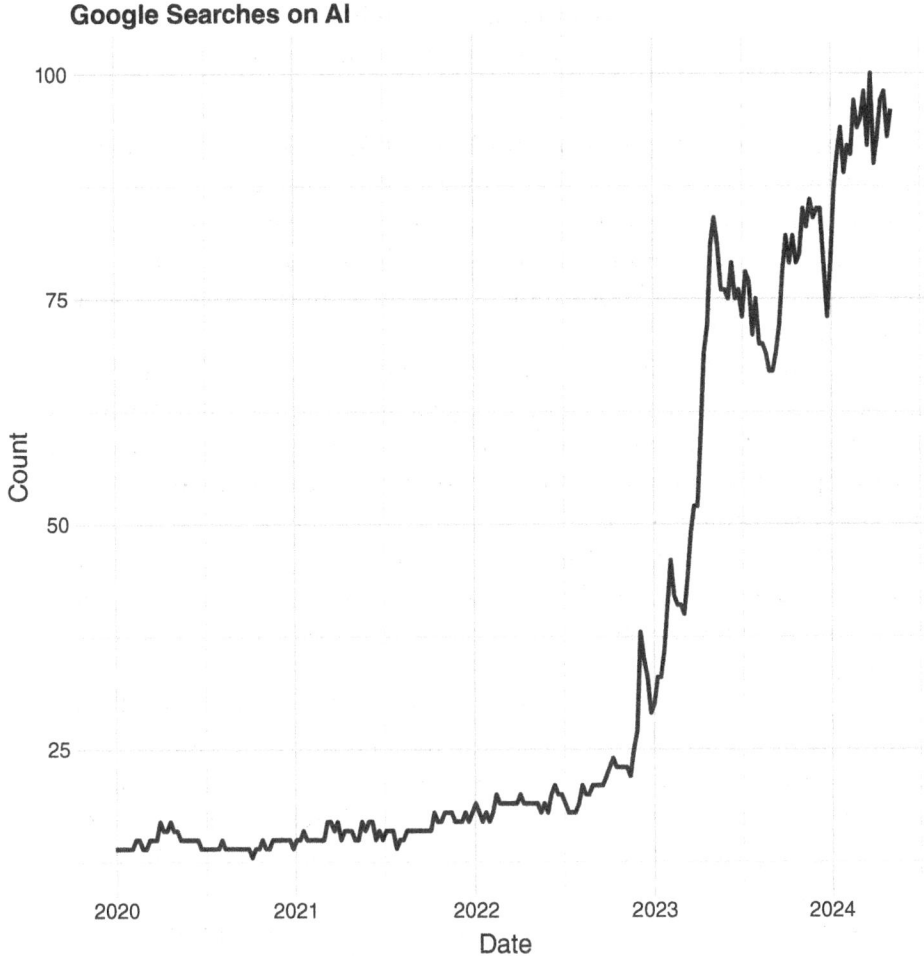

Figure 1 Number of Google searches for "AI"

The practical applications of AI are broad and impactful. In image recognition, AI systems can now identify and categorize images with greater accuracy than humans in some cases. In natural language processing, AI helps power conversational agents and real-time translation services that are becoming increasingly indistinguishable from human interaction. These technologies are not only enhancing consumer products and services but are also being leveraged to address complex societal challenges such as health care, climate change, and education.

The convergence of deep learning, big data, and computational advancements has thus not only accelerated the development of AI but has also expanded its applicability across different sectors, suggesting a future where AI could become as ubiquitous and essential as electricity is today. This backdrop sets the stage for exploring how generative

AI and blockchain technologies could further revolutionize industries by enhancing security, transparency, and efficiency in ways previously unimagined.

What Sets Generative AI Apart from Traditional AI?   Generative AI represents a fascinating and rapidly evolving branch of artificial intelligence that distinguishes itself by its ability to create new content, from realistic images and music to sophisticated written text and beyond. This type of AI moves beyond the traditional AI's capacity for understanding and categorizing information to actively producing original outputs that can mimic human creativity.

Traditional AI generally focuses on analyzing and learning from data to perform specific tasks such as recognizing speech, classifying images based on pre-defined categories, or making predictions based on historical data. It operates within a framework of responding to inputs (like answering questions or recommending products) based on patterns it has learned from datasets.

Generative AI, on the other hand, uses advanced machine learning techniques, such as generative adversarial networks (GANs), to go a step further. These technologies enable it not just to interpret data but to generate new data that it hasn't specifically seen during training.

Let's look at a practical example. Imagine you have an AI system designed to organize your photo library. This AI uses traditional machine learning models to analyze images and categorize them into predefined groups such as landscapes, portraits, and urban scenes. It can recognize objects, faces, and settings based on characteristics it has learned from a training dataset. The goal here is for the AI to understand and sort images based on existing data.

Now, consider a generative AI scenario where you want to create a brand-new image for a marketing campaign. You give the AI a brief, such as "generate a futuristic cityscape at sunset." Using a technique like a GAN, the AI would then generate a completely new image that did not previously exist, drawing from learned elements of futuristic buildings, sunset hues, and city layouts. This AI doesn't just categorize or modify existing images but creates new, unique visual content based on a mix of input parameters and its learned understanding of those elements.

Key Differences   These are the key differences:

- **Function:** Traditional AI is focused on understanding and categorizing data (reactive), whereas generative AI creates new data and content (proactive).
- **Output:** Traditional AI classifies and sorts based on learned patterns, while generative AI uses learned patterns to produce new, original works.
- **Complexity:** Generative AI typically involves more complex algorithms that not only understand data but also how to effectively mimic and innovate on that data to generate believable outputs that are coherent and contextually appropriate.

These examples highlight how traditional AI helps in understanding and managing information, whereas generative AI pushes boundaries into creating and simulating new forms of expression and data.

Generative AI and Crypto   The introduction of generative AI into the blockchain and cryptocurrency sectors marks a new chapter in the application of AI. Generative models like Generative Pre-trained Transformer (GPT) and others have the potential to automate and optimize various blockchain processes, enhance security protocols, and innovate in the creation of digital assets, including non-fungible tokens (NFTs). This intersection of generative AI and cryptocurrency not only fosters increased efficiency but also opens up novel avenues for creating and managing digital content and assets in ways previously unimagined.

This chapter will delve into how generative AI is being integrated into the crypto space, examining both the technological innovations and the broader implications for privacy, security, and regulatory compliance.

2. The Basics

Diving deep into the complexities of artificial intelligence could fill volumes, and while it's a fascinating subject, exploring it in exhaustive detail is beyond the scope of this book. Perhaps that's a journey we'll embark on in the next one. However, within these pages, I will provide enough foundational knowledge and insights to help you appreciate the powerful synergy between AI and blockchain technologies. By understanding the essentials of AI, you'll gain a clearer perspective on why combining AI with the cryptographic security and decentralized nature of blockchain can be a game-changer, potentially revolutionizing industries from finance to cybersecurity.

Still, to truly appreciate how generative AI works, I need to present a few fundamental concepts that underpin most modern AI systems, especially those involved in generating new content. I will start with some definitions, then discuss some examples and potentially also some code snippets.

- **Neural Networks:** Understand what neural networks are—computational models inspired by the human brain's structure and function. They consist of layers of nodes (neurons) that process input data, learn to recognize patterns, and make decisions. Knowing how these networks are structured and function is crucial for grasping how AI systems learn and operate.
- **Deep Learning:** This is a subset of machine learning that utilizes deep neural networks— neural networks with multiple hidden layers that allow for the processing of complex data with high levels of abstraction. Deep learning is at the heart of most generative AI models, enabling them to handle and generate intricate data like images, sound, and text.
- **Generative Adversarial Networks:** Learn about GANs, which consist of two neural networks—the generator and the discriminator—competing against each other.

The generator creates data, and the discriminator evaluates it. Through their interaction, the generator learns to produce more and more realistic data, making GANs powerful tools for generating high-quality synthetic data.

- **Backpropagation and Gradient Descent:** These are methods used to train neural networks, where backpropagation calculates the gradient of the loss function of a neural net (a measure of error), and gradient descent is a way to update the weights to minimize the loss. Understanding these techniques is key to appreciating how AI learns from data.

- **Loss Functions:** In the context of generative AI, knowing about different types of loss functions and how they influence the training process is important. Loss functions measure how well the AI model is performing a given task, such as how closely generated images match real images in GANs.

- **Overfitting and Underfitting:** These concepts describe potential pitfalls in training AI models. Overfitting occurs when a model learns the details and noise in the training data to the extent that it negatively impacts the performance of the model on new data. Underfitting occurs when a model is too simple to learn the underlying pattern of the data. Balancing the two is crucial for building effective AI models.

By understanding these fundamental concepts, we can gain a deeper insight into how generative AI operates and evolves, setting the stage for exploring its applications in various fields, including its integration with blockchain technologies.

Let's expand on these foundational elements. Feel free to skip if this is not your cup of tea and you are more interested in the intersection with crypto.

2.1 Statistical Learning to Generative AI

From a technical perspective, linear regressions and deep learning models essentially are built as optimizers. The general formula across of all can be encapsulated as an optimization problem where the goal is to minimize a loss function.

Minimize: $L(\theta) = L(y, \hat{y}(\theta, X))$

- $\hat{y}$ is the model's prediction given inputs X and parameters θ.

- L is the loss function measuring the error between predictions $(y, \hat{y})$.

Therefore, the distinction of the four, statistical learning, machine learning, deep learning, and generative AI is mostly due to the differences in computational requirements and the complexities of the overall loss function.

Statistical Learning: Statistical learning focuses on understanding data through models that infer relationships and predict outcomes based on historical data. Techniques such as regression analysis, classification, and clustering form the bedrock of this approach, facilitating the exploration of data patterns and decision-making based on statistical evidence.

The widely known model of ordinary least squares, or linear regression, can be shown as follows:

$$\hat{y} = \theta_0 + \theta_1 x$$

where the loss function is the mean squared error.

$$L(\theta) = (1/n) \star \Sigma(y_i - \hat{y}_i)^2$$

2.2 Transition to Machine Learning

Building on statistical foundations, machine learning introduces algorithms that can learn from and make predictions on data by building models from sample inputs. This phase expands on traditional statistics by using non-linear and complex models to tackle problems beyond the reach of standard statistical methods.

A simple example is LASSO regression, which is a penalized form of linear regression that is useful when there is a high number of predictors.

$$\hat{y} = \theta^T x$$

The Lasso loss function adds an L1 penalty to the standard mean squared error (MSE) term, which helps in feature selection by shrinking less important feature coefficients to zero. The L1 penalty term is proportional to the absolute value of the magnitude of the coefficients.

$$L(\theta) = (1/n) \star \Sigma(y_i - \theta^T x_i)^2 + \lambda \star \Sigma |\theta_j|$$

Let's consider a practical example. Imagine you are trying to predict the price of a house based on a variety of features (predictors) such as size, age, location, number of bedrooms, etc.

In traditional linear regression, you might predict the house price ($\hat{y}$) as a linear combination of these features: $y^\wedge = \theta^T x$ where θ represents the coefficients or weights assigned to each feature, and x represents the feature values.

Least absolute shrinkage and selection operator (LASSO) regression builds on this by introducing a penalty for the magnitude of the coefficients, which helps in handling scenarios with many features. This is particularly useful when some features might be irrelevant or less important for predicting the target variable (in this case, house prices).

The LASSO loss function modifies the traditional mean squared error (MSE) by adding an L1 penalty. This penalty is proportional to the absolute value of the coefficients: $Loss = MSE + \lambda \sum |\theta_i|$ where λ is a tuning parameter that controls the strength of the penalty. By adjusting λ, you can influence how much the coefficients are shrunk toward zero.

The key feature of the L1 penalty is its ability to shrink less important feature coefficients exactly to zero, effectively performing feature selection. This means that LASSO can simplify the model by eliminating some features entirely. For example, if the number of bedrooms has little impact on the house price in a specific market, LASSO might reduce its coefficient to zero, thereby ignoring this feature in the final model.

By reducing the complexity of the model (using fewer features), LASSO helps to prevent overfitting, which is a common problem where a model performs well on training data but poorly on unseen data. This makes the model more generalizable and robust to new, unseen data.

In summary, machine learning methods like LASSO regression allow for more complex and nuanced modeling compared to traditional statistics by incorporating techniques that manage large datasets with many variables, helping to identify the most relevant features and build more predictive models. This conceptual framework underlies many of the sophisticated machine learning models used in various predictive analytics today.

The following is a simple example of how you might implement LASSO regression in Python using the scikit-learn library. This example assumes you have a dataset with features and a target variable you want to predict—in this case, let's say the price of a house.

```
import numpy as np
import pandas as pd
from sklearn.linear_model import Lasso
from sklearn.model_selection import train_test_split
from sklearn.metrics import mean_squared_error

# Sample data: Let's assume you have a DataFrame 'df' with 'price' as the
target variable and other columns as features
# Example DataFrame creation (normally you would load this from a
data source)
data = {
    'size': [1500, 1800, 2400, 3000, 3500],
    'age': [10, 15, 20, 5, 1],
    'bedrooms': [3, 4, 3, 5, 4],
    'location': [5, 3, 2, 8, 10],  # Assume higher numbers are better
    'price': [400000, 500000, 600000, 650000, 700000]
}
df = pd.DataFrame(data)

# Splitting the data into features and target variable
X = df.drop('price', axis=1)  # Features
y = df['price']  # Target variable

# Split data into training and testing sets
X_train, X_test, y_train, y_test = train_test_split(X, y, test_size=0.2,
random_state=42)

# Creating and training the Lasso Regression model
lasso = Lasso(alpha=0.1)  # alpha is the regularization parameter
lasso.fit(X_train, y_train)
```

```
# Predicting and calculating the mean squared error
y_pred = lasso.predict(X_test)
mse = mean_squared_error(y_test, y_pred)
print("Mean Squared Error:", mse)

# Coefficients of the model
print("Coefficients:", lasso.coef_)
```

Explanation:

1. **Data Setup:** This example begins by creating a pandas DataFrame from a dictionary. In practice, you would likely load this data from a CSV file or another data source.
2. **Feature and Target Separation:** The features (X) and target (y, house prices) are separated.
3. **Data Splitting:** The dataset is split into training and testing sets to evaluate the model's performance on unseen data.
4. **Model Training:** A Lasso model is initialized with an alpha value that controls the strength of the regularization (penalty). The model is then trained on the training data.
5. **Prediction and Evaluation:** The trained model is used to make predictions on the test data, and the mean squared error is calculated to assess performance.
6. **Output Coefficients:** Finally, the coefficients of the predictors are printed out, showing the impact of each feature on the house price, with some possibly shrunk to zero due to the L1 penalty.

This code gives a straightforward implementation of LASSO regression that you can expand upon or integrate into larger projects, especially if you are looking to feature selection and regularization to improve model generalizability.

3. Neural Networks

Traditional machine learning models are effective for a wide range of predictive tasks but often struggle with data that contains complex patterns and high dimensionality. Neural networks, inspired by the structure and function of the human brain, overcome these limitations by using layers of interconnected nodes or neurons that can learn intricate structures in large datasets.

The architecture of neural networks is composed of several layers of interconnected nodes, also known as *neurons*, arranged in a system that closely mirrors the layered structure of the brain. Each layer serves a distinct purpose.

- **Input Layer:** This initial layer receives the raw input data. Just as our senses pick up stimuli and send this information to the brain, the input layer takes in raw data from the external environment.

- **Hidden Layers:** Situated between the input and output layers, one or more hidden layers transform the inputs into meaningful representations. These layers are where most of the computations take place, applying weights to inputs and passing them through functions to generate outputs that are fed to subsequent layers. Each neuron in these layers can be seen as a processing unit that makes independent decisions based on the data and the outcomes of previous layers.
- **Output Layer:** The final layer in a neural network, the output layer delivers the end results of the computations, such as a classification or prediction. This layer translates the complex representations learned by the network into understandable and usable outputs.

In neural networks, each neuron in a layer connects to numerous neurons in the following layer, creating a dense web of interconnections. These connections are not static; they carry weights that adjust dynamically as the network learns, a process driven by algorithms like backpropagation. During training, the network adjusts these weights based on the error of its output compared to the intended results, continually refining its predictions or classifications.

The connections' weights determine the influence of one neuron on another, acting as the gatekeepers of information flow within the network. By adjusting these weights, the network fine-tunes its internal parameters to minimize errors, enhancing its ability to make accurate predictions even in the face of complex, high-dimensional data (**Figure 2**).

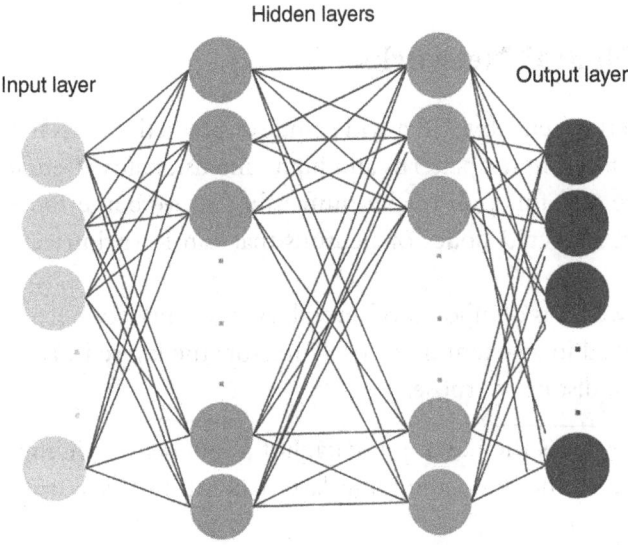

Figure 2   Example visualization of a neural network

How Neural Networks Function This is an explanation of how neural networks function.

1. **Forward Pass:**
   - **Linear Transformation:** In this step, each neuron in a layer receives input from the neurons in the preceding layer. These inputs are multiplied by the weights assigned to each connection linking neurons from one layer to the next. The result is a weighted sum of the inputs.
   - **Activation Function:** Once the linear transformation is done, the resulting weighted sum is passed through an activation function. This function introduces non-linearity to the model, allowing the network to learn and represent more complex patterns. Common activation functions include the following:
     - **Rectified Linear Unit (ReLU):** Used primarily to add non-linearity without affecting the scales of weight and inputs significantly. It outputs the input directly if it is positive; otherwise, it outputs zero.
     - **Sigmoid:** Useful for models where we need to predict the probability as an output since the probability of anything exists only between the range of 0 and 1. Sigmoid transforms values into the range between 0 and 1.
     - **Tanh (Hyperbolic Tangent):** Similar to the sigmoid, but it transforms values to range between –1 and 1, which can be more useful depending on the context.

2. **Backpropagation:**

   - **Error Calculation:** After the forward pass, the output of the network is compared to the actual expected output, and the difference between them is calculated using a loss function. This difference is commonly known as the error or loss, and it measures how well the network is performing.
   - **Weight Update via Gradient Descent:** To minimize the error, the network adjusts its weights. This adjustment is done through a process called backpropagation. Here, the gradient (partial derivatives) of the error with respect to each weight is computed to understand the direction and magnitude of change needed to minimize the error. The weights are then updated using an optimization technique such as gradient descent, which iteratively adjusts the weights in the opposite direction of the gradient to reduce loss.

Example 1: Recognize Handwritten Digits Imagine you have a neural network designed to recognize handwritten digits from 0 to 9, like the ones you see on mail envelopes.

1. **Input Layer:** The first layer, known as the input layer, receives the raw data. In this case, each handwritten digit image is converted into a grid of pixels. Each pixel's brightness level (from 0 for black to 255 for white) is fed into the network as a number. So, if the image is 28x28 pixels, you have 784 input neurons.
2. **Hidden Layers:** The data then passes through several hidden layers. Think of these

layers as a series of detectives, each specializing in recognizing more complex patterns than the previous one.

- **First hidden layer:** This layer might identify simple shapes like lines or curves.
- **Second hidden layer:** It might combine these lines and curves to recognize more complex shapes, like loops or corners.
- **Subsequent layers:** They continue this process, recognizing even more complex patterns, such as the overall structure of a digit (e.g. the roundness of a '0' or the angles of a '7').

3. **Weights and Learning:** As the image data moves through these layers, the connections (weights) between neurons adjust. Initially, the network might not recognize digits accurately, but as it processes more images and receives feedback (correct/incorrect identifications), it adjusts these weights to improve accuracy. This adjustment process, called backpropagation, minimizes the difference between the network's predictions and the actual labels (the correct digit).

4. **Output Layer:** Finally, the data reaches the output layer, which has ten neurons, each representing one digit (0-9). The neuron with the highest value indicates the network's prediction. For example, if the highest value is in the neuron representing '3', the network predicts that the input image is the digit '3'.

Why Multiple Layers Help: Each layer builds on the previous one's findings. By breaking down the problem into simpler, manageable parts and progressively combining these parts, the network can handle the complexity of recognizing handwritten digits, which vary widely in style and appearance. In other words, the network transforms the raw pixel data into more abstract and useful representations at each step, making it capable of handling the complex task of digit recognition accurately.

Example 2: Predicting House Prices   Imagine we have a neural network that aims to predict house prices based on features like size (sq ft), number of bedrooms, and age of the house. Here's a simplified look at how it might process this information:

- **Forward Pass:**
  - **Input Layer:** Receives raw data (e.g. [1200 sq ft, 3 bedrooms, 10 years]).
  - **Hidden Layer:** Applies weights to these inputs and sums them (e.g. weight1*1200 + weight2*3 + weight3*10). It then applies an activation function like ReLU to each summed input to introduce non-linearity.
  - **Output Layer:** Summarizes the outputs from the hidden layer into a single value, the predicted price.
- **Backpropagation:**
  - Suppose the actual price of the house is $300,000, but our network predicts $280,000. The loss function (say, mean squared error) calculates the squared difference between the predicted and actual prices.

- The network computes the gradient of this error and updates the weights accordingly to reduce the error. This might involve increasing the weight on the "sq ft" feature if the model finds it underestimates the impact of size on house price.

Through iterations of this process, with many examples, the neural network fine-tunes its weights to make increasingly accurate predictions. This illustrates the dynamic learning capability of neural networks, allowing them to adapt to complex patterns in data like housing prices, which depend non-linearly on various features.

Let's look at the corresponding Python example, which uses a neural network model to predict house prices based on features like size (sq ft), number of bedrooms, and age of the house. This example will utilize the scikit-learn library's MLPRegressor, a type of neural network designed for regression tasks.

```python
import numpy as np
from sklearn.neural_network import MLPRegressor
from sklearn.model_selection import train_test_split
from sklearn.metrics import mean_squared_error

# Example dataset: [square footage, number of bedrooms, age of the house]
X = np.array([
    [1500, 3, 10],
    [1800, 4, 5],
    [2400, 3, 20],
    [3000, 4, 15],
    [3500, 5, 10]
])

# Target variable: house prices
y = np.array([400000, 500000, 600000, 650000, 700000])

# Splitting the dataset into training and testing sets
X_train, X_test, y_train, y_test = train_test_split(X, y, test_size=0.2,
random_state=1)

# Creating the neural network model
model = MLPRegressor(hidden_layer_sizes=(100,), max_iter=1000,
activation='relu', random_state=1)

# Training the model
model.fit(X_train, y_train)

# Making predictions
y_pred = model.predict(X_test)

# Calculating Mean Squared Error to evaluate the model
mse = mean_squared_error(y_test, y_pred)
print("Mean Squared Error:", mse)

# Display predicted and actual values
print("Predicted House Prices:", y_pred)
print("Actual House Prices:", y_test)
```

1. **Data Setup:** We define a simple dataset (X) containing features for each house: square footage, number of bedrooms, and house age. The target variable (y) is the house price.

2. **Data Splitting:** The dataset is split into training and testing sets using train_test_split, with 80% of the data used for training and 20% for testing.

3. **Model Configuration:** We initialize an MLPRegressor. This is a type of neural network provided by scikit-learn that's suitable for regression tasks. We specify one hidden layer with 100 neurons (specified by hidden_layer_sizes=(100,)) and use the "ReLU" activation function.

4. **Training:** The fit method is used to train the model on the training data.

5. **Prediction:** After training, we use the predict method to estimate house prices on the testing set.

6. **Evaluation:** We evaluate the model's performance by calculating the mean squared error between the predicted and actual house prices on the testing set.

7. **Output:** Finally, the script prints the mean squared error, the predicted house prices, and the actual house prices for the test set to compare.

This example provides a basic introduction to using neural networks for regression in Python. The parameters of the neural network (like the number of hidden layers and the number of iterations) can be adjusted to improve the model's accuracy and to experiment with its performance on larger or more complex datasets.

What is the cost of adding hidden layers and number of iterations? If they improve accuracy, why not always pick a very large number of those?

Adding more hidden layers and increasing the number of iterations in a neural network model can potentially improve its accuracy by enabling it to learn more complex patterns and relationships in the data. However, there are significant costs and trade-offs associated with these adjustments:

- **Overfitting:** One of the biggest risks of adding too many hidden layers or having too many training iterations is overfitting. Overfitting occurs when a model learns the training data too well, including the noise and errors in the data. This can make the model perform very well on training data but poorly on unseen data (i.e. it has low generalization ability).

- **Computational Cost:** More hidden layers and a higher number of iterations require more computational resources. This can mean longer training times and higher costs, especially with very large datasets or complex models. Training deep neural networks can be particularly demanding, requiring powerful hardware such as GPUs or even clusters of GPUs to process efficiently.

- **Diminishing Returns:** As the complexity of the model increases, the improvements in performance can diminish. After a certain point, adding more layers or iterations may result in minimal gains in accuracy, which might not justify the additional computational costs and complexity.

- **Difficulty in Training:** Deeper networks are often harder to train effectively. This is partly because of the problem of vanishing gradients, where gradients used in backpropagation can become very small, effectively preventing weights from changing their values, which stalls the learning process. Techniques like using ReLU activation functions, batch normalization, and proper initialization help mitigate this issue but do not eliminate it.

- **Parameter Tuning:** A more complex model with many layers and parameters requires careful tuning of numerous hyperparameters, including the learning rate, layer sizes, types of layers, and regularization methods. This process can be time-consuming and requires a lot of experimentation and expertise.

Due to these reasons, while it may be tempting to just increase the number of hidden layers or iterations to boost performance, it's essential to balance the model's complexity with its effectiveness and efficiency. Effective model training involves finding the right architecture and training regime that offers the best trade-off between accuracy and generalization on unseen data, while also considering computational costs and training time.

3.1 Deep Learning: A Layered Approach to Complexity

Deep learning, a branch of machine learning focusing on neural networks with multiple hidden layers, continues to be a major driver of technological innovation. These "deep" networks are especially adept at processing layers of complexity in data. Here is an exploration into deep learning capabilities:

- **Hierarchical Feature Learning:** Deep learning networks are structured to recognize data at multiple levels of abstraction. For instance, in image processing, initial layers might identify edges and basic textures, while deeper layers may recognize more complex features such as faces or objects. This detailed layering allows deep neural networks to handle tasks from facial recognition in security systems to anomaly detection in medical imaging.
- **Sequential Data Processing:** Deep learning excels in handling data that comes in sequences, such as language or time series data. Recurrent neural networks (RNNs) and their more advanced variants like long short-term memory (LSTM) networks can maintain information in "memory" for a long time. This is crucial for tasks like language translation or stock market prediction, where the order and context significantly influence outcomes.
- **Reinforcement Learning Integration:** Combining deep learning with reinforcement learning has given rise to systems that can learn to optimize behaviors based on complex environments. This integration is at the heart of systems that learn to play and master games like Chess and Go or manage efficient energy use in large-scale systems like data centers.
- **Scalability and Flexibility:** Deep neural networks are inherently scalable. They can start with basic tasks and gradually take on more complexity as more data becomes available or as the network architecture becomes more sophisticated. This scalability is complemented by their flexibility, where the same underlying models can be adjusted with minor tweaks to address drastically different problems across fields.
- **Real-Time Processing:** Once trained, deep learning models can execute tasks in real time, a crucial advantage in applications like autonomous driving or real-time

language translation. These models can process live data streams, making split-second decisions that are as accurate as those made based on batch-processed data.

Challenges and Future Directions: Despite their impressive capabilities, deep learning models are not without challenges. They require large amounts of data and computational power, they pose risks of bias if not properly managed, and their complex nature makes them difficult to interpret, which can be a barrier in critical applications like healthcare.

In response to these challenges, future research in deep learning is focusing on making these models more efficient, ethical, and understandable. Techniques such as federated learning are being explored to train models on decentralized data, protecting privacy while still reaping the benefits of deep data insights. Meanwhile, advances in AI explainability seek to make neural networks more transparent and their decisions easier to understand.

In summary, while deep learning presents some challenges, its benefits and the vast potential it holds continue to drive forward its adoption and development, heralding new levels of AI integration in everyday technology and industrial applications.

Here is a basic example in Python, using the TensorFlow library:

```
import tensorflow as tf

# Create a simple neural network with one hidden layer
model = tf.keras.Sequential([
    tf.keras.layers.Dense(10, activation='relu', input_shape=(10,)),
# Hidden layer with 10 neurons
    tf.keras.layers.Dense(1, activation='sigmoid')  # Output layer
])

model.compile(optimizer='adam',
            loss='binary_crossentropy',
            metrics=['accuracy'])

# Generate some random data for demonstration
import numpy as np
x_train = np.random.random((100, 10))
y_train = np.random.randint(2, size=(100, 1))

# Train the model
model.fit(x_train, y_train, epochs=10)
```

The neural network we define here as the model has the following formula:
Input Layer to Hidden Layer:

$$z[1] = W[1] \star x + b[1]$$

$$a[1] = g[1](z[1])$$

Hidden Layer to Output Layer:

$$z[2] = W[2] \star a[1] + b[2]$$

$$\hat{y} = a[2] = g[2]\big(z[2]\big)$$

where:

- x is the input vector.
- W[1] and W[2] are the weights for the first and second layers, respectively.
- b[1] and b[2] are the biases for the first and second layers, respectively.
- g[1] and g[2] are activation functions (e.g. ReLU for g[1] and sigmoid for g[2]).
- $\hat{y}$ is the predicted output.

3.2 Generative AI

Having explored the foundational technologies of machine learning, such as LASSO regression models and neural networks, and delved deeper into the intricacies of deep learning, we can now transition to one of the most exciting frontiers in artificial intelligence: generative AI. While traditional models have been instrumental in predicting outcomes and classifying data, generative AI shifts the focus from interpretation to creation. This evolution represents a significant leap, moving AI from a tool that understands and analyzes the world as it is, to one that can imagine and create things that never existed before. From synthesizing realistic human voices to designing new proteins, generative AI opens up a realm of possibilities that challenge the very limits of machine capability and creativity. Let's explore how these generative models build on the sophisticated architectures and learning processes we've discussed and how they're used to generate new data and content with astonishing variety and fidelity.

At the heart of generative AI are machine learning models that understand and replicate the complex patterns and distributions of their training datasets. These models include generative adversarial networks and autoregressive models like Transformer-based architectures. Each model has a unique approach to generating data:

- **Generative adversarial networks** involve a dual-system of networks: a generator that creates data and a discriminator that evaluates it. This setup allows the generator to progressively improve its output to fool the discriminator, enhancing the quality and realism of the generated content.
- **Transformers** have revolutionized text generation in recent years. These models use mechanisms like attention and self-attention to process sequences of data, making them particularly effective for tasks that require understanding context over long sequences, such as in natural language processing.

To understand how generative AI works, it's essential to delve deeper into the mechanisms of the most common models used. Each of these has a unique approach to data generation.

Generative Adversarial Networks   GANs were first introduced by Ian Goodfellow and his colleagues in 2014. The seminal paper titled "Generative Adversarial Nets" was presented at the International Conference on Neural Information Processing Systems (NeurIPS). Goodfellow, then a PhD student at the University of Montreal, devised the GAN framework as a method to generate new data instances that are indistinguishable from the real data. The concept of having two neural networks, a generator and a discriminator, competing against each other was revolutionary and provided new avenues in unsupervised learning and beyond. The idea quickly caught on because of its powerful implications and the visually compelling way it could generate new content, such as images, videos, and music.

Let me provide some more details. We said that GANs consist of two neural networks, the generator and the discriminator, which are trained simultaneously in a zero-sum game framework. The generator's role is to produce data that is indistinguishable from real data, while the discriminator's role is to distinguish between the generator's output and actual data.

1. **Training Process:** During training, the generator receives random noise as input and transforms it into a data instance. The discriminator then evaluates this output alongside real data and tries to determine if it is real or synthetic. The generator's goal is to fool the discriminator by improving its output based on the feedback received.

2. **Backpropagation:** Both networks learn through backpropagation. The discriminator adjusts its parameters to get better at identifying real versus generated data. Simultaneously, the generator adjusts its parameters based on the discriminator's feedback to produce increasingly realistic data.

3. **Equilibrium:** Training continues until an equilibrium is reached where the generator produces data so close to real data that the discriminator cannot distinguish between the two, effectively guessing at a 50/50 rate.

The following is a simplified Python of creating a GAN that generates images resembling the MNIST dataset, which consists of handwritten digits:

```python
import numpy as np
import tensorflow as tf
from tensorflow.keras.datasets import mnist
from tensorflow.keras.layers import Dense, Flatten, Reshape
from tensorflow.keras.models import Sequential
from tensorflow.keras.optimizers import Adam

# Define the generator model
def build_generator():
    model = Sequential([
        Dense(128, activation='relu', input_dim=100),
        Dense(784, activation='sigmoid'),  # Output is 28*28=784
        Reshape((28, 28, 1))
    ])
    return model
```

```python
# Define the discriminator model
def build_discriminator():
    model = Sequential([
        Flatten(input_shape=(28, 28, 1)),
        Dense(128, activation='relu'),
        Dense(1, activation='sigmoid')
    ])
    return model

# Load MNIST data
(x_train, _), (_, _) = mnist.load_data()
x_train = x_train / 255.0
x_train = np.expand_dims(x_train, axis=-1)  # Reshape to (28, 28, 1)

# Instantiate the models
generator = build_generator()
discriminator = build_discriminator()
discriminator.compile(loss='binary_crossentropy', optimizer=Adam(0.0002,
0.5), metrics=['accuracy'])

# Create GAN model
discriminator.trainable = False
gan = Sequential([generator, discriminator])
gan.compile(loss='binary_crossentropy', optimizer=Adam(0.0002, 0.5))

# Training function
def train(epochs, batch_size=128):
    valid = np.ones((batch_size, 1))
    fake = np.zeros((batch_size, 1))

    for epoch in range(epochs):
        # Train discriminator
        idx = np.random.randint(0, x_train.shape[0], batch_size)
        real_imgs = x_train[idx]
        noise = np.random.normal(0, 1, (batch_size, 100))
        generated_images = generator.predict(noise)

        d_loss_real = discriminator.train_on_batch(real_imgs, valid)
        d_loss_fake = discriminator.train_on_batch
(generated_images, fake)
        d_loss = 0.5 * np.add(d_loss_real, d_loss_fake)

        # Train Generator
        noise = np.random.normal(0, 1, (batch_size, 100))
        g_loss = gan.train_on_batch(noise, valid)

        print(f"Epoch: {epoch+1}/{epochs}, D Loss: {d_loss}, G Loss:
{g_loss}")

# Train the GAN
train(epochs=30, batch_size=128)
```

Generator Model

- **Generator Function:** Constructs a generator model that transforms a 100-dimensional noise vector into a 28x28 pixel image.
- **Dense Layers:** Fully connected neural network layers. The first dense layer has 128 units and uses the ReLU activation function. It takes a 100-dimensional input (noise) and the second dense layer outputs 784 units (28x28 pixels), activated by a sigmoid function to ensure the output values are between 0 and 1 (representing pixel intensity).
- **Reshape Layer:** Changes the shape of the output to match that of MNIST images (28x28 pixels, single channel).

Discriminator Model

- **Discriminator Function:** Constructs a discriminator model that takes an image (28x28 pixels) and outputs a single scalar value representing the probability that the image is real (not generated).
- **Flatten Layer:** Converts the 28x28 pixel image into a flat vector of 784 elements.
- **Dense Layers:** The first dense layer has 128 units with ReLU activation. The second dense layer is a single unit with a sigmoid activation, outputting a probability (0 to 1)

Then, we load and preprocess the MNIST data by normalizing the images by dividing by 255 (making all pixel values between 0 and 1) and adding an extra dimension to indicate the channel (since MNIST is grayscale).

Training Function

In the training function we orchestrate the training of the discriminator and generator.

- **Real Images:** The discriminator is trained with real images labeled as valid (1).
- **Generated Images:** The generator creates images from noise, which the discriminator is trained to recognize as fake (0).
- **Generator Training:** Trains the generator to fool the discriminator, using the adversarial loss to improve its image generation.

Overall, this script alternates between training the discriminator to distinguish real from fake images and training the generator to create images that the discriminator classifies as real. This adversarial training continues for the specified number of epochs, ideally leading to a generator that can produce realistic MNIST-like digits.

Transformer-Based Models   The Transformer model was introduced by Vaswani et al. in the landmark paper "Attention is All You Need" in 2017. This model was revolutionary for its use of self-attention mechanisms, which allow it to weigh the significance of different words in a sentence, regardless of their distance from each other. This architecture was primarily developed at Google and marked a significant shift away from previous sequence-to-sequence models that relied on recurrent neural networks or convolutional neural networks (CNNs). Transformers have since become the foundation of many state-of-the-art natural language processing systems, including OpenAI's GPT series and Google's Bidirectional Encoder Representations from Transformers (BERT).

Let me provide a quick overview here, and offer a more detailed explanation in the appendix for the nerds like me. The key innovation of transformers is the use of self-attention mechanisms to weigh the importance of different words in a sentence, regardless of their distance from each other in the input.

- **Attention Mechanism:** This model assigns more weight to important parts of the input data and less weight to others, enabling it to maintain long-range dependencies and understand context better than traditional models.
- **Sequence Generation:** In generative tasks, transformers predict the next element in a sequence, such as the next word in a sentence, based on the elements that preceded it. This is done by training the model on a vast corpus of text and asking it to predict parts of the text during training, conditioning the model to generate coherent and contextually relevant text.
- **Scaling:** The effectiveness of transformers often scales with the size of the model and the dataset, leading to models like GPT, which can generate highly coherent and diverse text based on the training it received.

Thus, generative AI models like GANs and transformers work by understanding and replicating the complex distributions of their training data. Through their respective mechanisms, they can generate new data instances that are not only diverse but also strikingly similar to authentic data. This ability has vast applications across various fields, pushing the boundaries of what AI can achieve in creative and analytical tasks.

The following example is a transformer model trying to predict sentiment using the built-in IMDB dataset in TensorFlow:

```
import tensorflow as tf
from tensorflow.keras.datasets import imdb
from tensorflow.keras.layers import TextVectorization, Embedding,
Transformer, Dense
from tensorflow.keras.models import Sequential
from tensorflow.keras.preprocessing import sequence

# Load IMDB dataset
vocab_size = 10000
(x_train, y_train), (x_test, y_test) = imdb.load_
data(num_words=vocab_size)
x_train = sequence.pad_sequences(x_train, maxlen=200)
x_test = sequence.pad_sequences(x_test, maxlen=200)

# Build a simple transformer model
model = Sequential([
    Embedding(input_dim=vocab_size, output_dim=32, input_length=200),
```

```
    Transformer(block_size=32, num_heads=2, feed_forward_dim=32,
dropout_rate=0.1),
    Dense(1, activation='sigmoid')
])

model.compile(optimizer='adam', loss='binary_crossentropy',
metrics=['accuracy'])

# Train the model
model.fit(x_train, y_train, validation_data=(x_test, y_test), epochs=2,
batch_size=32)
```

The script begins by loading the IMDB dataset, which contains 50,000 movie reviews labeled as positive or negative. The data is preprocessed by limiting the vocabulary to the top 10,000 most frequent words and padding the sequences to a uniform length of 200 words to ensure consistency in input size, which is crucial for effective training and inference in neural networks.

The model itself is structured using TensorFlow's Keras API and comprises three main layers configured in a sequential model. First, an Embedding layer transforms the integer-encoded vocabulary into dense vector representations, providing a richer and more expressive input feature set. Then, a Transformer layer is applied, which utilizes mechanisms like multihead attention to better capture dependencies and nuances in the text data across different positions within the sequences. This layer is specifically designed to enhance the model's ability to focus on relevant parts of the input sequences for making predictions.

Finally, a Dense layer with a sigmoid activation function computes the probability that each review is positive, culminating in a binary classification model. The model is compiled with the Adam optimizer and binary crossentropy loss and then trained and validated using the preprocessed IMDB data over two epochs to demonstrate basic functionality and performance.

Another Example of Transformer-Based Model   One of the most well-known implementations of transformers is the GPT series developed by OpenAI. We'll look at how a transformer like GPT-3 generates text, such as composing an email.

Example: Composing an Email with GPT-3

Step 1: Input Preparation

- **Tokenization:** The first step is to convert the input text into a format that the model can understand. In the case of GPT-3, the input text (e.g. "Write an email to John about") is tokenized into smaller pieces, often words or subwords. These tokens are then converted into numerical values (token IDs) that represent each token uniquely.

Step 2: Adding Positional Encodings

- **Positional Information:** Since transformers do not inherently process sequential data as sequential, positional encodings are added to each token. These encodings provide the model with information about the relative or absolute position of the tokens in the sequence. This way, the model knows the order of the tokens and can maintain the context of words based on their positions.

Step 3: Passing Tokens Through the Transformer Blocks

- **Self-Attention Mechanism:** Each token (now with positional encodings) is passed through multiple layers of the transformer. In each layer, a self-attention mechanism allows the model to weigh the importance of all other tokens for each token in the sequence. For instance, in the email to John, the model determines how much attention to pay to "John," "email," and other contextual words when generating the next word.
- **Attention Scores:** The self-attention mechanism computes scores to establish how much focus to place on other parts of the input sentence when encoding a specific part of it.

Step 4: Generating Output

- **Output Prediction:** After processing the tokens through several layers of attention and feed-forward neural networks within the transformer, the model predicts the next token in the sequence. The prediction is based on the probability distribution of possible tokens and is influenced by the learned weights of the model, which have been adjusted during the training phase on a large corpus of text.
- **Iterative Generation:** This process is repeated for each new token generated, with each new token fed back into the model as part of the input sequence for the next prediction. This loop continues until the model generates a stopping token or reaches a predefined maximum length.

Step 5: Decoding the Output

- **Readable Text:** The sequence of output tokens is converted back into human-readable text. This text represents the composed email, which might read something like: "Dear John, I hope this message finds you well. I wanted to discuss our upcoming project...."

In this example, the transformer-based model, GPT-3, uses its layers of self-attention and feed-forward networks to understand and generate human-like text based on the input and its vast training data. The model effectively considers both the meaning of each word and its context within the sentence to produce coherent and contextually appropriate language. This ability makes transformers particularly powerful for tasks involving understanding and generating human language, setting a new standard in the field of natural language processing.

4. Blockchain and AI

Now that you have, I hope, a good understanding of AI, let's turn to the intersection of AI and blockchain technology which is emerging as a particularly fertile ground for transformative developments. AI's capabilities in data analysis, pattern recognition, and autonomous decision-making complement the inherent strengths of blockchain, such as security, transparency, and decentralization. This synergy promises to redefine the landscapes of both technologies, pushing the envelope on what can be achieved when human-like intelligence meets immutable ledger systems. There are several areas that are developing at the intersection of these two fields. Let's explore some together.

4.1 Decentralized Compute

The relentless advancement in AI technology over the past decade has seen a corresponding explosion in computational demands. OpenAI's research highlights an accelerating trend where compute requirements for training models, which initially doubled every two years from 2012, began doubling every three and a half months by 2018. This surge in demand has notably impacted the GPU market, pushing entities like crypto miners to repurpose their GPUs for cloud computing services—a strategy that underscores the intensifying scramble for powerful computational resources.

Amidst this backdrop, the acquisition of GPUs has become increasingly competitive. In a notable instance, Tether acquired a significant stake in Northern Data, securing 10,000 H100 GPUs from Nvidia, some of the most advanced units available for AI training, at a reported cost of $420 million. The scarcity of state-of-the-art hardware like the H100 GPU has led to prolonged wait times, often extending six months or more. Companies frequently find themselves bound by long-term contracts for computational power that may exceed their actual usage, contributing to inefficiencies in the compute market.

Decentralized compute networks offer a promising solution to these challenges. By leveraging blockchain technology, these networks facilitate a secondary market for computing power, where unused compute capacity can be leased out on-demand. This not only enhances market efficiency by unlocking new supply but also provides competitive pricing, making it feasible for more teams to train and run sophisticated AI models affordably.

Moreover, the decentralized nature of these systems introduces a critical layer of censorship resistance. As AI development becomes increasingly centralized among large tech corporations, there are growing concerns about these entities' disproportionate influence over the norms and values embedded within AI models. This centralization is accentuated by the fact that these corporations are often at the forefront of regulatory initiatives that may restrict AI development to within their ecosystems. Decentralized computing architectures disrupt this dynamic, democratizing access to necessary resources and fostering a more equitable environment for AI innovation across various sectors, from academia to independent developers.

In summary, decentralized compute platforms not only mitigate existing market inefficiencies by providing a fluid marketplace for computational resources but also play a crucial role in ensuring that the future landscape of AI development remains open and accessible to a diverse range of contributors.

Example: Akash Network Akash Network represents a significant innovation in decentralized cloud computing, offering an alternative to traditional cloud services dominated by large corporations. The platform is built on the Cosmos blockchain using the Cosmos SDK, which enables it to operate as a decentralized network where anyone can lease computing resources or provide them. This approach democratically opens up the cloud industry, allowing both individuals and companies to participate directly in cloud resource markets.

Technical Architecture: Akash employs a decentralized model where resources are offered by a variety of providers who compete in an open marketplace setting. This marketplace is facilitated through the use of Akash's native token, AKT, which is utilized for transactions within the network, including leasing computing power and settling payments. Users can define their computing needs using the Stack Definition Language (SDL), a YAML-compatible format that allows for detailed specification of deployment requirements and configurations.

The network leverages Kubernetes, a standard in container orchestration, to manage and scale containerized applications seamlessly across its decentralized framework. This setup allows users to deploy applications from simple web services to complex, scalable microservices landscapes without the overhead of managing physical servers or direct cloud service relationships.

Security and Governance: Security on the Akash Network is maintained through a delegated proof-of-stake (DPoS) consensus mechanism, where validators are responsible for maintaining the integrity of the blockchain and are chosen based on the amount of AKT staked to them by the community. This model not only secures the network but also ensures that the community plays an active role in governance through token staking and voting on proposals.

Economic and Accessibility Advantages: One of the key advantages of Akash Network is cost-efficiency, offering up to 85% lower prices compared to traditional cloud services. This price efficiency is achieved through its unique reverse auction system, where users can specify their price for services and choose from competing offers, optimizing their cloud spending according to budget and needs.

Overall, Akash Network's innovative approach to decentralized cloud computing addresses the issues of cost, accessibility, and centralization that are prevalent in traditional cloud services, making it a potential solution in the movement towards a more open and decentralized digital infrastructure. This platform also exemplifies how blockchain technology can disrupt established industries and pave the way for more decentralized and transparent systems.

4.2 Decentralized Machine Learning

Decentralized ML training represents a shift from traditional centralized computing models, where computation and data processing are typically performed on a single server or within a data center to a distributed model that leverages a network of multiple nodes.

This innovative method involves distributing data across multiple nodes within a network, ensuring that no single node holds the entirety of the data. Such a distribution enhances privacy and security, as it minimizes the risk of large-scale data breaches which are more probable in centralized systems.

One of the core features of decentralized ML is collaborative learning, often implemented through federated learning techniques. In this setup, various nodes across the network collaboratively train a shared predictive model while maintaining all training data locally. This approach effectively eliminates the need to centralize sensitive data, safeguarding individual privacy and compliance with data protection regulations.

Blockchain technology plays a crucial role in this decentralized framework, serving as the backbone for coordination among different nodes. It manages critical tasks such as the aggregation of model updates, validation of contributions, and even the distribution of incentives in the form of cryptocurrencies or tokens. These incentive mechanisms encourage participants to contribute their computing resources to the network, rewarding them for processing data, refining models, or validating transactions.

Moreover, decentralized ML reduces reliance on costly centralized infrastructure and cloud services, potentially lowering barriers to entry and operational costs. This aspect not only democratizes access to advanced ML capabilities but also enhances the system's resilience and scalability. The distributed nature of the network ensures that even if one node fails, the system remains operational, thereby increasing robustness against attacks or failures. Additionally, the network can scale more flexibly and efficiently; adding more nodes enhances computational power without the bottleneck of centralized processing.

In essence, decentralized ML harnesses the strengths of distributed computing and blockchain technology to create a more secure, efficient, and accessible framework for machine learning, opening up new possibilities for data privacy and collaborative model training across the globe.

Decentralized ML is particularly suitable for scenarios where data privacy is crucial, or where the data itself is naturally distributed across many users or locations, such as in healthcare, finance, and mobile applications. Despite its benefits, challenges such as ensuring data quality, managing network latency, and maintaining efficient and secure aggregation protocols remain active areas of research and development.

I am going to mention three examples of recent projects working in this area: Gensyn, Bittensor, and Ocean Protocol each approaching the integration of blockchain technology and decentralized machine learning (ML) from different angles, with unique frameworks and objectives.

Gensyn is a decentralized compute network designed to tackle the high costs and accessibility barriers associated with AI model training. By connecting various computing resources across the globe—from data centers to personal laptops—Gensyn forms a single virtual cluster that can be used for intensive machine learning tasks. This network is designed to be cost-effective and scalable, providing lower barriers to entry for ML developers and reducing dependency on expensive centralized compute resources. Gensyn's protocol also emphasizes a trustless system that uses advanced verification mechanisms to ensure that computations are performed correctly and efficiently.[2]

Bittensor focuses on creating a decentralized network where AI and machine learning models are not only developed but actively traded and monetized. It operates on a system where developers, validators, and users interact in a marketplace that rewards contributions with its native token, BTT. This setup aims to decentralize AI development, reducing reliance on central authorities and promoting innovation through collaborative efforts across the network.[3]

Ocean Protocol, meanwhile, concentrates on unlocking the value of data. It allows data providers to monetize their data while preserving privacy and control, fostering a secure environment for data sharing. The protocol uses blockchain technology to ensure transparency and security, facilitating data exchanges in a compliant manner. Ocean's primary focus is on creating a scalable and secure platform for data sharing and AI services, which is crucial for industries requiring vast data exchanges without compromising on security or compliance.[4]

Each of these platforms brings a distinct approach to integrating AI and blockchain, highlighting the diverse applications and benefits of decentralized technologies in advancing AI research and deployment. Whether focusing on data liquidity, computational power, or the creation of a new marketplace for AI services, all aim to enhance the capabilities and accessibility of AI technologies through decentralized solutions.

Example: Gensyn   Gensyn is at the forefront of integrating blockchain technology with AI to enable decentralized machine learning training. Utilizing a layer 1 proof-of-stake protocol built on the Substrate framework, Gensyn facilitates peer-to-peer interactions across its network. This architecture allows it to connect diverse computing devices globally, from consumer GPUs to custom ASICs and SoC devices found in smartphones and tablets, into a unified computing cluster. This approach aims to democratize access to computational resources, reducing dependencies on major cloud service providers like AWS and enhancing the scalability and affordability of AI model training.

The primary technical challenge Gensyn addresses is the perceived inefficiency of using blockchain for AI tasks, which typically require high data throughput and frequent updates. However, Gensyn's design minimizes computational overhead and ensures that machine learning tasks can be executed with minimal latency, which is critical for training neural networks effectively. The network leverages unused global computing

---

[2] https://protocol.ai/blog/meet-gensyn-the-machine-learning-compute-network
[3] https://phemex.com/academy/cryptocurrency-glossary/bittensor-tao
[4] https://www.coingecko.com/learn/the-intersection-of-ai-and-crypto

hardware to increase supply and reduce the costs associated with machine learning computations, positioning itself as a decentralized trust layer for AI development.

By providing a distributed cloud computing model on a pay-as-you-go basis, Gensyn not only makes machine learning more accessible but also adds a layer of trust and verification to AI development that is not reliant on centralized control. This model encourages a more equitable distribution of computational resources and fosters innovation in AI development across various sectors.

Gensyn operates on a peer-to-peer (P2P) network that utilizes the processing capabilities of various devices across the globe, including GPUs and SoCs, integrating them into a single computational cluster. This decentralized network reduces the dependency on centralized data centers and allows for more efficient use of the available hardware.

1. **Efficient Resource Utilization:** By harnessing underutilized resources from numerous devices, Gensyn can spread the computational load, effectively reducing the overhead that any single device would face. This broad distribution of tasks ensures that no single system is overwhelmed, which is often a limitation in centralized setups.
2. **Custom ASICs and SoCs:** The use of specialized hardware, such as application-specific integrated circuits (ASICs) and system-on-a-chip (SoC) devices, provides optimized performance for specific AI tasks. These devices are integrated within Gensyn's network to provide efficient processing power for machine learning tasks, thereby reducing overhead and enhancing performance.

For machine learning, especially in training neural networks, low latency is crucial to achieving quick and accurate results. Gensyn's network architecture is designed to keep latency to a minimum through several key strategies.

- **Localized Computation:** By distributing tasks across numerous nodes geographically and allowing data to be processed closer to where it is stored, Gensyn reduces the need for long-distance data transfers, which can introduce latency. Local processing ensures faster response times and quicker model updates.
- **Optimized Data Flow:** Gensyn's use of blockchain technology is tailored to support high data throughput and frequent updates necessary for machine learning workflows. The blockchain protocol is designed to handle large volumes of data efficiently, ensuring that the network can manage continuous streams of input and feedback necessary for training models without significant delays.
- **Scalable Infrastructure:** The Substrate-based blockchain framework allows Gensyn's network to scale dynamically according to demand. This scalability ensures that the network can accommodate increases in load without a corresponding increase in latency, maintaining performance regardless of the number of active users or the complexity of the tasks being processed.

By addressing these key areas, Gensyn's design not only supports the practical requirements of machine learning but also leverages the inherent benefits of decentralized systems, such as enhanced security and reduced costs, to provide a robust platform for AI development. This innovative approach positions Gensyn as a critical player in the future of decentralized machine learning, offering a scalable and efficient solution that could potentially transform how AI is developed and deployed globally.

> **Example: Bittensor** Bittensor is an innovative project that seeks to create a decentralized open-source ecosystem for AI development. This platform addresses significant bottlenecks caused by the centralized control of AI technologies by major corporations like Google, Microsoft, and IBM, which often limits innovation and accessibility.
>
> At the core of Bittensor's architecture is its unique approach to decentralizing AI applications through a network of subnets, each designed for specific AI tasks such as language translation or image recognition. This structure allows for the collaborative development and training of machine learning models across a distributed network, leveraging the combined computational power of numerous nodes (participants). This model aims to democratize access to AI development, making cutting-edge technology available to a broader range of developers and companies, thereby reducing costs and increasing the efficiency of training complex AI models.
>
> Bittensor utilizes its native cryptocurrency, TAO, as a means of payment within the network. TAO tokens are used to incentivize miners (those who provide computational power) and validators (those who ensure the integrity of the network and transactions). Furthermore, TAO also serves as a governance token, allowing token holders to vote on proposals and influence future changes within the network.
>
> The Bittensor network uses a consensus mechanism called the Yuma Consensus, which combines elements of proof of work (PoW) and proof of stake (PoS) to ensure decentralized governance and to reward participants based on their contributions. This setup not only secures the network but also ensures that contributions are fairly rewarded, promoting continuous improvement and participation.
>
> Overall, Bittensor stands out as a compelling project at the intersection of blockchain and AI, aiming to disrupt the centralized AI industry and offer a more accessible, transparent, and collaborative environment for AI development.

Technical Architecture and Decentralization This section provides an overview of the technical architecture (**Figure 3**):

- **Subtensor Network:** At the heart of Bittensor's architecture is the "subtensor" network, a blockchain specifically designed to support decentralized AI operations. This blockchain connects multiple platforms, known as *subnets*, each specialized for

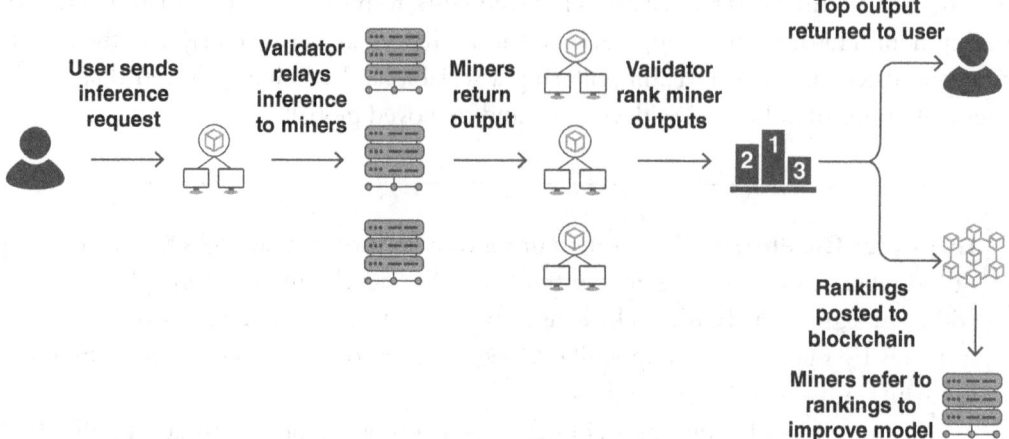

Figure 3   Bittensor

different AI tasks. For example, some subnets may focus on natural language processing, while others might handle image recognition or data analytics.

- **Decentralized Nodes (Neurons):** The network is comprised of nodes, referred to as *neurons*, that provide computational power and data storage. Each neuron contributes to the network by performing specific AI tasks, processing data, or validating transactions. This decentralized setup ensures that no single entity controls the network, enhancing security and resilience.
- **Mixture of Experts (MoE):** Bittensor uses a Mixture of Experts model to integrate the outputs from various subnets. This method allows the network to leverage specialized knowledge from different nodes, combining their expertise to solve complex problems more efficiently than any single AI model could.

Innovative Consensus and Operation Model   Bittensor introduces a unique "Proof of Intelligence" mechanism, where instead of traditional PoW used in cryptocurrencies like Bitcoin, it requires miners (servers in the Bittensor network) to run models that produce outputs in response to inference requests. This paradigm shift is central to Bittensor's operation, making it distinctively suited for decentralized machine learning processes.

Mixture of Experts   Bittensor utilizes a Mixture of Experts model to handle inference requests. This approach doesn't depend on a single generalized model but instead directs queries to the most suitable models for specific input types. This methodology can be likened to assembling a team of specialists for a project, where each specialist handles tasks they are best suited for, enhancing the overall efficiency and accuracy of responses.

Roles of Validators and Miners   In the Bittensor ecosystem, there are two primary roles: validators and miners. Validators send inference requests to miners and rank the quality of their outputs. The trustworthiness of validators is measured by "vtrust" scores, which reflect the accuracy of their rankings compared to other validators. High vtrust scores lead to higher TAO emissions for validators, incentivizing them to accurately assess and rank outputs.

Miners, on the other hand, are responsible for running the actual machine learning models and compete to provide the most accurate outputs for given queries. Successful miners earn TAO emissions based on the accuracy and usefulness of their contributions.

Yuma Consensus The interaction between validators and miners is governed by what's called the Yuma Consensus. This system encourages miners to produce high-quality outputs to earn TAO, while validators must accurately rank these outputs to maximize their own rewards. This setup not only incentivizes the production of quality intelligence but also ensures that the consensus mechanism aligns with the network's goal of fostering a reliable and effective decentralized machine learning platform.

Subnets and Applications As the Bittensor network matures, it introduces subnets— specialized networks within the larger Bittensor ecosystem, each incentivizing specific behaviors such as text prompting, data scraping, or image generation. These subnets can be thought of as niche communities within the broader Bittensor network, each contributing uniquely to the ecosystem's diversity and functionality. Subnets earn TAO based on their performance, evaluated by the root network, which is managed by the top validators.

By integrating blockchain technology with AI operations, Bittensor effectively decentralizes the development and deployment of AI models. This architecture not only mitigates the risks associated with centralized data storage (such as data breaches and privacy issues) but also democratizes access to AI technology. It allows individuals and smaller entities to participate in AI development without needing the extensive resources typically required in traditional settings.

The decentralized nature of the network also helps in mitigating biases and monopolistic control often seen in AI development controlled by major corporations. Then, with an open-source approach and a decentralized infrastructure, Bittensor facilitates a more equitable distribution of technology and knowledge.

Example: Ocean Ocean Protocol is a decentralized data marketplace designed to facilitate the secure and efficient exchange of data. It leverages blockchain technology to enable data owners to monetize their data while ensuring control and privacy. Here's an overview of how Ocean Protocol works and its implications for decentralized machine learning (ML) training:

- **Technical Infrastructure and Data NFTs:** Ocean Protocol utilizes blockchain technology to create a transparent, secure environment where data can be safely bought and sold. It introduces the concept of data NFTs, which represent ownership or usage rights over datasets. These NFTs are tied to data tokens that function as access control mechanisms, allowing data consumers to use the data in a controlled environment without exposing the actual data.

- **Decentralized Data Exchange:** At the core of Ocean Protocol is the decentralized data exchange platform that allows data providers to publish their datasets and offer them for sale. This marketplace is built on top of the Ocean Protocol blockchain, providing tools for data providers to mint data tokens that control access to the data. Data consumers can purchase these tokens to gain the right to use the data, typically for training AI models.
- **Compute-to-Data:** One of the innovative features of Ocean Protocol is Compute-to-Data. This technology allows data to be processed where it resides, without requiring the data to be moved or copied. This approach helps preserve privacy and reduces the risk of data breaches. In the context of machine learning, it means that AI developers can train models on private datasets without the datasets ever leaving their secure environments.
- **Monetization and Incentivization:** Ocean Protocol empowers data owners to monetize their data assets more effectively. By providing a marketplace for data, it opens up new revenue streams for data providers and gives AI developers access to a wide range of datasets that were previously inaccessible or too sensitive to share. The use of blockchain ensures that transactions are transparent and that participants are compensated fairly.
- **Governance and Sustainability:** The governance of Ocean Protocol is designed to be democratic and decentralized. Data providers and consumers govern the protocol through a decentralized autonomous organization (DAO), ensuring that no single party can control the network. This setup promotes a sustainable and equitable data economy where incentives are aligned among all stakeholders.

In summary, Ocean Protocol revolutionizes how data is shared, consumed, and monetized, providing a decentralized solution that addresses many of the privacy and security concerns associated with data sharing. For machine learning, this means access to diverse datasets on-demand, enabling more robust and innovative AI applications while maintaining compliance with data protection regulations.

5. Concluding Remarks

In my opinion, it's clear that the AI landscape, although incredibly promising, is going to face incredible challenges that will shape how these technologies are used in everybody's life in the future.

First, access to AI technology also remains a substantial barrier. For instance, training a single AI model like OpenAI's GPT-3 is estimated to cost several million dollars, not just in direct computational expenses but also in the energy required to power such computations. The training of GPT-3, one of the most advanced language models to date, reportedly consumed 1,287 kWh of energy per day over weeks, which equates to the monthly energy consumption of roughly three average U.S. homes.

This substantial financial and energy cost means that only well-funded organizations, typically large corporations or well-endowed research institutions, can afford to engage in developing cutting-edge AI technologies. As a result, this exclusivity restricts the democratization of AI technologies, concentrating the power and potential benefits of AI in the hands of a few. For example, major tech companies like Google, Amazon, and Microsoft dominate cloud AI services and hold significant influence over the advancements and applications of AI technologies.

Such a concentration not only stifles innovation by limiting participation from smaller entities and researchers but also raises concerns about privacy, bias, and ethical use of AI. Without broader access and collaborative opportunities, the development of AI risks being shaped by a narrow set of interests, potentially overlooking broader societal needs and ethical considerations.

At present, the operation of AI models in isolated environments severely restricts their potential for growth and innovation. Typically, AI models are developed for specific tasks or datasets, and due to the lack of standardization and interoperability between different AI systems, they cannot easily share insights or improve collectively through shared learning experiences. For instance, an AI model trained to recognize speech patterns in English cannot easily adapt its learnings to enhance another model designed to understand sentiment in text-based customer reviews. This inability to cross-utilize learnings not only duplicates efforts but also prevents the leveraging of synergies that could occur from multi-disciplinary insights.

Moreover, the integration of AI models with other applications or datasets often involves complex bureaucratic and technical hurdles. For example, an AI model developed in a healthcare setting to predict patient outcomes based on electronic health records may hold potential benefits for research in personalized medicine. However, attempting to integrate this model with genetic databases or other hospitals' systems for broader application would likely face significant challenges. These include navigating data governance and privacy laws, such as the General Data Protection Regulation (GDPR) in Europe or Health Insurance Portability and Accountability Act (HIPAA) in the United States, which impose strict conditions on data sharing and user consent. Additionally, technical barriers, such as differing data formats or incompatible APIs, further complicate this integration.

These issues add substantial complexity to the deployment and scaling of AI technologies, hampering their ability to innovate and evolve effectively. Without addressing these siloed operations and integration challenges, AI's impact remains limited to narrow, predefined scopes, thus missing out on broader, more transformative applications that could arise from more freely shared knowledge and capabilities.

The centralization of resources and data within large corporations not only constrains the democratization of artificial intelligence technologies but also raises substantial privacy concerns for users. When vast amounts of sensitive data are accumulated in the hands of a few powerful entities, the potential for misuse or breach becomes a significant risk.

For example, major tech companies that provide personalized services such as search engines, social media platforms, and e-commerce sites collect enormous volumes of personal data from their users. This data includes search histories, location data, personal interests, and purchasing behaviors, which are used to train AI models to predict user preferences and behavior. While this can enhance user experience and service personalization, it also creates a large target for cyberattacks. A breach in one of these centralized databases can expose the private data of millions of users.

Furthermore, the concentration of data in the hands of a few corporations gives them unprecedented control over the information narrative and user privacy. This control can lead to issues such as data exploitation without adequate user consent, where companies may use personal information for purposes beyond those originally agreed upon, such as targeted advertising or even political manipulation, as seen in incidents like the Cambridge Analytica scandal.

Additionally, there is the issue of surveillance and monitoring. Large corporations with access to continuous data streams can monitor user activities without clear checks and balances. This capability, especially when combined with advanced AI tools, can lead to a form of surveillance that is more intrusive than anything seen before, potentially violating personal freedoms and rights.

These privacy concerns highlight the need for stronger regulatory frameworks, enhanced transparency measures, and more robust data protection policies to ensure that as AI continues to evolve, it does so in a manner that respects and protects individual privacy. Furthermore, decentralizing AI data and processing can help mitigate some of these risks by distributing the power and control away from central entities, thus promoting a more secure and privacy-focused approach to AI development.

By harnessing the decentralized and secure framework offered by blockchain, there is a hopeful prospect for overcoming the current limitations of AI. Such advancements could not only democratize access to AI by reducing dependency on massive, centralized pools of resources but also enhance the collaborative potential of diverse AI systems. This could lead to a more integrated, accessible, and innovative AI landscape, where technology serves a broader range of purposes and is accessible to a wider array of users and developers.

This integration of blockchain technology with AI might really lead to a world where AI is *really* open and secure for everybody. This blend could very well be the key to unlocking the full potential of AI technologies, making them more versatile, inclusive, and effective in addressing complex problems across various domains.

Appendix: Transformers and Self-Attention Mechanism

We have seen that transformers improve language processing by using self-attention mechanisms. This technique helps the model focus on different parts of a sentence, weighing the importance of each word relative to others, regardless of their position in the sequence. *However, how can a model decide if something deserves more or less attention?*

Here's how it works:

1. Input Representation

Each word in a sentence carries context about the sentence's meaning. For instance, in the sentence "this book is the best blockchain book ever," the word "book" gains meaning from words like "best" and "blockchain." The model needs to understand this context to make accurate predictions.

Each word in a sentence is first converted into a numerical vector through a process called embedding. These vectors capture various properties of the words, including their meanings in context.

For the sentence "this book is the best blockchain book ever":

- "this" becomes a vector like [0.2, 0.1, 0.3],
- "book" becomes a vector like [0.5, 0.4, 0.1],
- and so on for each word in the sentence.

2. Query, Key, and Value Vectors

For each word in the input sentence, the model generates three types of vectors:

- **Query (Q):** Represents the word we're focusing on. This vector represents what we're looking for. Think of it as a question or a search query.
- **Key (K):** Represents the words we're comparing the query against. This vector represents what we have. Think of it as an answer or a search result.
- **Value (V):** Represents the information content of the words. This vector represents the actual content or information.

  For example, for the word "book":

- Q("book") What is "book" looking for? (Relevance to other words). It helps determine what other words "book" should pay attention to.
- K("this"), K("book"), etc., represent other words. What do these words offer in terms of relevance to "book"?
- V("this"), V("book"), etc., hold the actual information from those words.

3. Calculating Attention Scores

The model calculates attention scores by comparing the Query vector of the word we're focusing on (e.g. "book") with the Key vectors of all the words in the sentence. This tells us how relevant each word is to "book." In other words, to determine how relevant each word is to "book," the model calculates the similarity between Q("book") and all the K vectors (K("this"), K("book"), K("is"), etc.). This is done using a mathematical operation called the **dot product**.

- If the dot product is high, it means the word is relevant to "book."
- If the dot product is low, it means the word is less relevant.

For instance, if "book" needs to focus on "best" and "blockchain" more, the attention scores for these words will be higher.

4. Applying Softmax

These raw attention scores are then passed through a Softmax function to convert them into probabilities. This step ensures that the attention scores are normalized and add up to 1, making it easier to interpret them as weights. Higher probabilities mean the word is more relevant and should be focused on more. Lower probabilities mean the word is less relevant and should be focused on less.

So, after softmax, we might see that "best" and "blockchain" have higher probabilities, indicating that "book" should focus more on these words.

5. Weighted Sum of Value Vectors

Next, each Value vector is multiplied by its corresponding attention weight (the probabilities from the softmax step). The results are then summed to produce a weighted average. This process emphasizes important words and de-emphasizes less important ones.

For "book," the final representation is a mix of the information from "best," "blockchain," and other words, weighted by their importance.

6. Self-Attention Mechanism

The final step is to sum these weighted vectors to get a new, context-aware representation of "book." This representation captures not only the meaning of "book" but also the influence of important words like "best" and "blockchain." The self-attention mechanism means each word in the sentence attends to every other word (including itself) to gather contextual information.

Why This Works

1. **Dynamic Relevance:** Instead of treating all words equally, the model dynamically decides which words are important based on the context.
2. **Contextual Understanding:** By focusing more on relevant words, the model builds a better understanding of the sentence's overall meaning.

3. Handling Long-Range Dependencies: The attention mechanism allows the model to consider the entire sentence when determining relevance, even if the important words are far apart.

Example   Consider the sentence: "this book is the best blockchain book ever."

- **Q("book")** is generated to see what "book" is interested in.
- **K("best")**, **K("blockchain")**, etc., are generated to see what other words offer in terms of relevance.
- The model calculates how relevant "best" and "blockchain" are to "book" by comparing Q("book") with K("best") and K("blockchain").
    - If K("best") is highly relevant, the score is high.
    - If K("blockchain") is also highly relevant, its score is high too.
- Softmax normalizes these scores into probabilities.
    - Suppose "best" gets 0.3, "blockchain" gets 0.4, and other words get lower probabilities.
- The final representation of "book" is a weighted combination of V("best"), V("blockchain"), and others.
    - This means "book" now incorporates context from both "best" and "blockchain," understanding it as part of "the best blockchain book."

The final output is a vector that captures the essence of "book" while incorporating relevant context from "best," "blockchain," and other words. This context-aware representation is then used for further processing, such as predicting the next word or classifying the sentence.

By allowing each word to focus on all other words in the sentence, the attention mechanism ensures that the model can understand the context and relationships effectively, leading to better performance in language tasks.

End-of-Chapter Questions

Multiple-Choice Questions

1. **What is the primary function of the Turing test in AI?**
   (A) To measure the processing speed of a machine.
   (B) To determine if a machine can exhibit human-like intelligence.
   (C) To evaluate the machine's ability to improve its own algorithms.
   (D) To test the machine's ability in solving mathematical problems.

2. **Which model is known for using layers of mathematical functions called 'neurons'?**
   (A) Linear regression.
   (B) Generative adversarial networks (GANs).
   (C) Neural networks.
   (D) Decision trees.

3. **What role does Geoffrey Hinton have in the field of AI?**
   (A) Development of the Turing test.
   (B) Pioneering work in the use of generative adversarial networks.
   (C) Advancements in neural networks and deep learning.
   (D) Establishing the first AI lab at MIT.

4. **Which of the following is not a characteristic of decentralized machine learning?**
   (A) Data is stored on a single central server.
   (B) Enhances privacy by distributing data across nodes.
   (C) Uses blockchain for coordination between nodes.
   (D) Can operate independently of centralized infrastructure.

5. **What is the significance of GPUs in AI development?**
   (A) They are primarily used to enhance graphics quality.
   (B) They reduce the computational time for AI model training.
   (C) They are cheaper than other forms of processors.
   (D) They increase the data storage capacity for large AI models.

6. **Which AI model focuses on generating new data instances?**
   (A) Logistic regression.
   (B) Support vector machine (SVM).
   (C) Generative adversarial network (GAN).
   (D) Bayesian networks.

7. **What does the discriminator do in a GAN setup?**
   (A) Generates new data instances.
   (B) Distinguishes between real and generated data.
   (C) Calculates the loss function.
   (D) Optimizes the generative model.

8. **Which of the following is a use case for neural networks?**
   (A) Creating new pharmaceutical formulas.
   (B) Data entry automation.
   (C) Financial auditing.
   (D) Speech recognition.

9. **What mechanism do transformers use to manage data sequences?**
   (A) Recurrent loops.
   (B) Self-attention mechanisms.
   (C) Convolutional layers.
   (D) Activation functions.

10. **Why might increasing the number of hidden layers in a neural network not always be beneficial?**
    (A) It can lead to underfitting.
    (B) It simplifies the model too much.
    (C) It may cause overfitting and increase computational cost.
    (D) It reduces the accuracy of the model.

11. **Which concept describes the AI's ability to generalize from training data to new, unseen scenarios?**
    (A) Overfitting.
    (B) Underfitting.
    (C) Regularization.
    (D) Generalization.

12. **What does ReLU stand for in the context of neural networks?**
    (A) Regular expression logic unit.
    (B) Rectified linear unit.
    (C) Recursive linear utility.
    (D) Randomized logical unit.

13. **Which is a primary advantage of using deep learning in AI?**
    (A) It requires smaller datasets.
    (B) It processes simple models faster.
    (C) It captures complex patterns in data.
    (D) It uses less computational power.

14. **What is a major challenge associated with deep learning models?**
    (A) They require minimal computational resources.
    (B) They cannot handle large amounts of data.
    (C) They might not be interpretable and could be biased.
    (D) They are too fast for most modern hardware.

15. **Which algorithm is often used for training neural networks?**
    (A) Gradient descent.
    (B) K-means clustering.
    (C) A$\star$ search algorithm.
    (D) Euclidean algorithm.

Open Questions

1. Discuss how the architecture of GANs contributes to their ability to generate realistic data. What challenges might arise with their use?
2. Explain the impact of advancements in computational power on the development of AI from the 1980s to the present.
3. Describe how the Transformer architecture has changed the landscape of natural language processing. What makes it effective?
4. Assess the potential benefits and risks of decentralized machine learning networks. How could they change the AI development landscape?
5. Reflect on the ethical implications of AI and blockchain integration. What considerations should be made to ensure responsible use?

About the Author

Meet Professor Marco Di Maggio, a trailblazer at the intersection of fintech and traditional finance. With a PhD from MIT and a professorship at Harvard Business School, where he founded the Fintech, Crypto, and Web3 Lab, Professor Di Maggio now trains future tech billionaires and Web3 wizards at Imperial College.

Professor Di Maggio's expertise covers both the technical and economic aspects of Web3, blending academic rigor with real-world experience. He has authored numerous Harvard Business School cases on industry leaders like Uniswap, Avalanche, and Coinbase, many of which are featured in this book. His research has been highlighted by major media outlets, including the *New York Times* and the *Wall Street Journal*.

However, Professor Di Maggio isn't your typical Ivy League professor. He's not just a bystander in the crypto world. He has served on the advisory board of the Coinbase Institute, as a board member of the Mina Foundation, and as a consultant for top companies like Ripple. He also cofounded a cutting-edge company at the intersection of AI and crypto, named among Binance's Most Valuable Builders in 2024.

With deep roots in traditional finance, collaborating with asset managers and major banks, Professor Di Maggio offers a unique perspective. He understands what traditional sectors might lack and what Web3 can learn from them. This blend of old-school finance wisdom and cutting-edge tech knowledge makes his insights invaluable.

This book isn't a typical "Web3 will solve world hunger" manifesto though. Professor Di Maggio provides a balanced view, showcasing where blockchain shines and where it faceplants. From finance to fine art, real estate to insurance, he leaves no stone unturned and no industry unexplored.

Whether you're a blockchain student, finance veteran, tech enthusiast, or just curious why your nephew won't stop talking about "diamond hands," this book is your ticket to the next tech revolution.

About the Companion Website

If you are an instructor, you have access to the Instructor Companion Site for *Blockchain, Crypto, and DeFi: Bridging Finance and Technology* by Marco Di Maggio.

Please visit www.wiley.com/go/dimaggio/instructor to access ready-to-use slides for each chapter, perfect for classroom presentations and lectures, ensuring you can deliver comprehensive and engaging lessons.

Note that you will receive a prompt to register for the Instructor Companion Site the first time you attempt to access this material. If you have a Wiley instructor account, then you will merely need to sign in using this account. If you do not have a Wiley instructor account, you will receive a prompt to sign up for one.

As a purchaser of this book, you have access to the book's companion website. Please visit www.wiley.com/go/dimaggio and enter the password *dimaggio123*.

You can also scan the following QR code to be directed to the book's companion website:

The book's companion website is an online resource hub designed to enhance your learning and teaching experience by providing a wealth of additional materials.

What You'll Find:

- **Exhibits:** All exhibits from the book in full color.
- **Coding Exercises:** Practical exercises designed to enhance your coding skills and give you hands-on experience with blockchain technology.

Our goal is to provide you with all the tools you need to succeed, whether you're an instructor planning your next lesson or a student eager to deepen your understanding of blockchain, cryptocurrency, and decentralized finance (DeFi).

Stay Updated: The book's companion website is continuously updated with new resources to keep your knowledge current and comprehensive.

Visit today and take advantage of these invaluable resources to elevate your learning journey.

Happy learning!

Index